Cuba

a Lonely Planet travel survival kit

David Stanley

Cuba

1st edition

Published by
Lonely Planet Publications
Head Office: PO Box 617, Hawthorn, Vic 3122, Australia
Branches: 155 Filbert St, Suite 251, Oakland, CA 94607, USA
                      10 Barley Mow Passage, Chiswick, London W4 4PH, UK
                      71 bis rue du Cardinal Lemoine, 75005 Paris, France

Printed by
Colorcraft Ltd, Hong Kong

Photographs by
Rick Gerharter   David Stanley

Front cover: Guido A Rossi (Image Bank)
Title page: Raúl Martínez, courtesy Cuba Poster Project

Published
January 1997

National Library of Australia Cataloguing in Publication Data

Stanley, David.
    Cuba.

    1st ed.
    Includes index.
    ISBN 0 86442 403 5.

    1. Cuba – Guidebooks.
    I. Title. (Series: Lonely Planet travel survival kit).

917.2910464

text & maps © Lonely Planet 1997
photos © photographers as indicated 1997
all posters © Cuba Poster Project 1997 - no unauthorized reproduction please
climate charts compiled from information supplied by Patrick J Tyson, © Patrick J Tyson, 1997

David Stanley

David Stanley studied Spanish literature at schools in Canada, Mexico, and Spain, ending up with an honors degree from the University of Guelph, Canada. Stanley has spent much of the past three decades on the road with visits to 168 of the planet's 247 countries and territories. He has crossed six continents overland.

Between 1975 and 1979 David worked at hotels in Havana, Jibacoa Playa, Varadero, and Isla de la Juventud as the representative of a Canadian tour company. During the 1980s he wrote pioneering travel guidebooks to Alaska-Yukon and the Pacific Islands. His *South Pacific Handbook*, now in its 6th edition, has become the classic guide to the South Seas. Just prior to the fall of the Berlin Wall, he led Lonely Planet into Europe with the first three editions of *Eastern Europe on a Shoestring*, which he researched and wrote single-handedly. Many other writers have followed in his footsteps.

Stanley's long-standing attention to environmental and social issues has encouraged other authors to follow suit. By looking at things through local eyes he has long promoted responsible tourism and given readers a perspective different from the self-serving clichés of mainstream journalism. His conviction is that tourism should benefit the host country as much as it entertains the guests. Visitors have a right to demand fair value for their money but not at the expense of local residents or whatever it is they are trying to see. In *Cuba – a travel survival kit*, at least, the familiar fast-food chains and transnational consumer culture have not had to be consciously omitted.

From the Author

In this book I've tried to be honest and say what I really think without covering up for anyone. The field research was done

incognito and this book certainly isn't an 'official' view; in fact, I admit I'm often politically incorrect. It's hard to write about Cuba without being considered controversial by somebody, and the negative approach usually taken in the American mass media certainly doesn't foster understanding. If my book fires you up and makes you want to discover what's really going on, I will have achieved my goal.

This book is dedicated to the Cuban people themselves. May they overcome their present difficulties and have a happy and prosperous future.

The nationalities of those mentioned below are indicated by the following symbols: AUS (Australia), C (Canada), D (Germany), E (Spain), M (Mexico), NA (Netherlands Antilles), NL (Netherlands), P (Portugal), and USA (United States of America).

Thanks to ACG de Vos (NL) for providing a safe haven during the writing of this book and allowing unhampered use of his large personal library; to Bill Wouters (NL) for help in selecting the color photos; to Gustavo Pasos (NL) for supplying input for the Cuban music section; to James King McIntyre (USA) for investigating phantom flights between Miami and Havana; to Greg Mills (USA) for amusing insights into the American economic embargo; to Rick Gerharter (USA) for insights into the Havana social scene; and to Shelley Preston (AUS) and Peter Townshend (AUS) for checking addresses in Australia. My wife Ria drove our Daihatsu jeep for 6485 km up, down, and around Cuba between Baracoa and María la Gorda. Her assistance was indispensable.

Giorgio Grazzini of Arezzo, Italy, was the first to send Lonely Planet a reader's letter about Cuba after noticing an announcement of the book in the LP newsletter, *Planet Talk*. May Giorgio's nine pages of notes be the harbinger of an unending stream of feedback from all you readers out there!

Thanks also to the following tourism or solidarity-campaign workers who sent information to the author: Christoph C Floren (D), Solanges Hamelin (C), FAM Hernandez (NA), Hildegard Mehnert (M), Elio H Mora Despaigne (M), Pierre de la Motte (D), Udo Schwark (D), Deborah Shnookal (AUS), David Wald (USA), and Klaus-Peter Winter (E).

The book was actually written in Amsterdam and Apeldoorn, Netherlands; Cabanas, Portugal; and Toronto, Canada.

From the Publisher

Many folks contributed to a very smooth editing and layout process. Kate Hoffman edited the text and maps and oversaw the book through layout. Leigh Anne Jones proofread the text with verve. Cyndy Johnsen drew maps, researched illustrations, and laid out the book. Chris Salcedo provided assistance with the maps. Alex Guilbert drew the country map, assisted on others, and supervised overall map production. Hugh D'Andrade designed the cover and drew illustrations. Hayden Foell, Suzanne Bennett, and Mark Butler also contributed illustrations. Scott Summers checked over page design.

A special thanks goes out to the Cuba Poster Project and Lincoln Cushing for providing striking examples of this vibrant and sophisticated art form. The CPP is dedicated to the documentation and dissemination of Cuba's postrevolutionary poster art. Its codirectors have a specific license from the US Treasury Department to travel to Cuba for this purpose. The CPP (2827 7th St, Berkeley, CA 94710, (510) 845-7111, lcushing@igc.apc.org) is a project of the Oppositional Poster Conservation Initiative.

Warning & Request

Things change – prices go up, schedules change, good places go bad and bad places go bankrupt – nothing stays the same. If you find things better or worse, recently opened or long since closed, please tell us and help make the next edition even more accurate and useful.

We value all of the feedback we receive from travelers. Julie Young coordinates a small team that reads and acknowledges every letter, postcard, and email, and ensures that every morsel of information finds its way to the appropriate authors, editors, and publishers. Everyone who writes to us will find their name in the next edition of the appropriate guide and will also receive a free subscription to our quarterly newsletter, *Planet Talk*. The very best contributions will be rewarded with a free Lonely Planet guide.

Excerpts from your correspondence may appear in updates (which we add to the end pages of reprints); in new editions of this guide; in our newsletter, *Planet Talk*; or in the Postcards section of our Web site. Please let us know if you don't want your letter published or your name acknowledged.

Contents

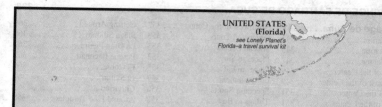

UNITED STATES
(Florida)
*see Lonely Planet's
Florida–a travel survival kit*

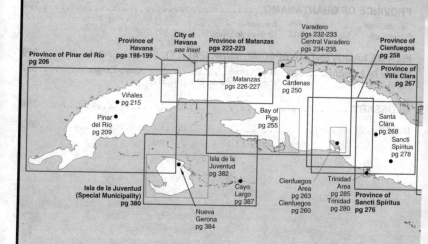

Province of Pinar del Río
pg 206

Province of Havana
pgs 198-199

City of Havana
see inset

Province of Matanzas
pgs 222-223

Varadero
pgs 232-233
Central Varadero
pgs 234-235

Province of Cienfuegos
pg 258

Province of Villa Clara
pg 267

Viñales
pg 215

Pinar del Río
pg 209

Matanzas
pgs 226-227

Cárdenas
pg 250

Bay of Pigs
pg 255

Santa Clara
pg 268

Sancti Spíritus
pg 278

Isla de la Juventud
pg 382

Cayo Largo
pg 387

Cienfuegos Area
pg 263
Cienfuegos
pg 260

Trinidad Area
pg 285
Trinidad
pg 280

Province of Sancti Spíritus
pg 276

Isla de la Juventud (Special Municipality)
pg 380

Nueva Gerona
pg 384

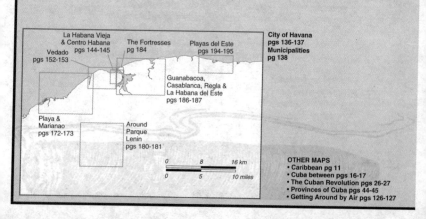

La Habana Vieja & Centro Habana
pgs 144-145

The Fortresses
pg 184

Playas del Este
pgs 194-195

City of Havana
pgs 136-137
Municipalities
pg 138

Vedado
pgs 152-153

Guanabacoa, Casablanca, Regla & La Habana del Este
pgs 186-187

Playa & Marianao
pgs 172-173

Around Parque Lenin
pgs 180-181

0   8   16 km

0   5   10 miles

OTHER MAPS
• Caribbean pg 11
• Cuba between pgs 16-17
• The Cuban Revolution pgs 26-27
• Provinces of Cuba pgs 44-45
• Getting Around by Air pgs 126-127

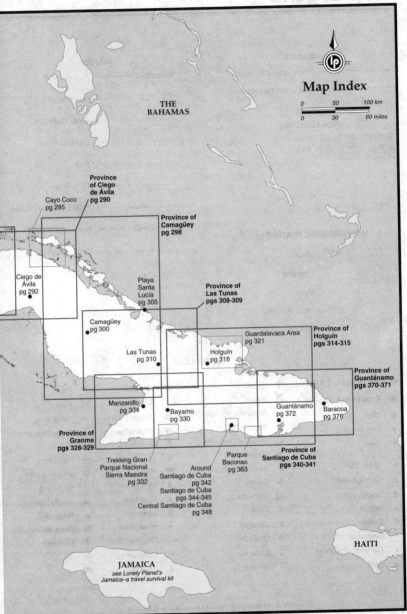

Map Index

THE
BAHAMAS

0   50   100 km
0   30   60 miles

Province
of Ciego
de Ávila
pg 290

Cayo Coco
pg 295

Province of
Camagüey
pg 298

Ciego de
Ávila
pg 292

Playa
Santa
Lucía
pg 305

Province of
Las Tunas
pgs 308-309

Camagüey
pg 300

Guardalavaca Area
pg 321

Province of
Holguín
pgs 314-315

Las Tunas
pg 310

Holguín
pg 318

Province of
Guantánamo
pgs 370-371

Manzanillo
pg 334

Bayamo
pg 330

Guantánamo
pg 372

Baracoa
pg 376

Province of
Granma
pgs 328-329

Trekking Gran
Parque Nacional
Sierra Maestra
pg 332

Around
Santiago de Cuba
pg 342
Santiago de Cuba
pgs 344-345
Central Santiago de Cuba
pg 348

Parque
Baconao
pg 363

Province of
Santiago de Cuba
pgs 340-341

HAITI

JAMAICA
see Lonely Planet's
Jamaica–a travel survival kit

Map Legend

BOUNDARIES

–··–··–··–··– International Boundary

–··–··–··–··– Provincial Boundary

AREA FEATURES

Park

HYDROGRAPHIC FEATURES

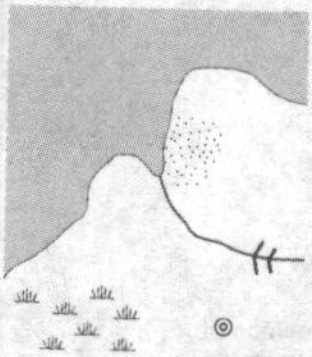

Water

Coastline

Beach

River, Waterfall

Swamp, Spring

ROUTES

Freeway

Major Road

Minor Road

Unpaved Road

Trail

Ferry Route

Railway, Railway Station

Metro, Metro Station

Walking Tour

SYMBOLS

NATIONAL CAPITAL
Provincial Capital
City
City, Small
Town

Hotel, B&B
Campground
Chalet, Hut
Hostel
Shelter
Restaurant
Bar (Place to Drink)
Café

Airfield
Airport
Archaeological Site, Ruins
Bank, ATM
Baseball Diamond
Beach
Bus Depot, Bus Stop
Castle
Cathedral
Cave
Church
Dive Site
Embassy
Garden

Gas Station
Golf Course
Hospital, Clinic
Information
Lighthouse
Lookout
Mine
Monument
Mountain
Museum
Music, Live
One-Way Street
Observatory
Parking

Park
Pass
Picnic Area
Police Station
Pool
Post Office
Shopping Mall
Snorkeling
Stately Home
Telephone
Tomb, Mausoleum
Trailhead
Winery
Zoo

Note: Not all symbols displayed above appear in this book.

Introduction

Cuba, the 'Pearl of the Antilles,' is the largest and least commercialized Caribbean country. Political factors have prevented Cuba from being sullied by mass consumer tourism, and it beckons the jaded traveler with its picturesque colonial towns, intriguing Afro-Cuban culture, rousing revolutionary monuments, almost 300 unblemished beaches, enchanting countryside, and potent rum – even the beer is excellent. Activities such as scuba diving, yachting, fishing, hiking, horseback riding, and bird watching are easily arranged. The Cuban people are sincerely friendly, and US citizens receive the same warm welcome that Cubans extend to all their guests: There's absolutely no ill will toward individual Americans.

For nearly four centuries Cuba was the main gateway to Spain's vast American empire and cities such as Havana, Matanzas, Trinidad, Sancti Spíritus, Camagüey, Bayamo, Baracoa, and Santiago de Cuba stand as sentinels to bygone glory. With 2,100,000 inhabitants, Havana is the largest city in the Caribbean. Founded on its present site in 1519, it's one of the oldest cities in the Americas. The Spanish built a chain of solid Spanish fortresses to keep out pirates, and these outposts still surround the picturesque old town, a designated UNESCO World Heritage Site.

The richness of Cuba's culture is well reflected in its many museums, several dozen of which are in Havana. The capital is a world-class artistic center with numerous galleries, theaters, and literary shrines gracing the quaint colonial streets and squares, and the country is a musical maverick where the rumba, mambo, chachachá, son, and salsa all originated. Its unspoiled landscape extends well beyond the magnificent coastline to verdant valleys, rugged mountains, and pristine reefs.

For the individual traveler Cuba is a fascinating smorgasbord of nonstop discovery and experience. It's a surprisingly easy country to visit: one can rent a car or

board a train and go anywhere. No special rules or regulations hamper tourists. This is one of the last truly unspoiled countries in the world, free of the surly locals and drug trade present on some other Caribbean islands. The hotels are numerous and inexpensive, and visitors can also stay in private homes. For the tourist who wants only a week or two in the sun, Cuba provides various smart resorts, plus glimpses of history in the making.

Despite the adverse political situation, Cuba is remarkably accessible to blockade runners from the US: Regular scheduled flights are available from Nassau, Montreal, Toronto, Mexico City, and Cancún. The trick is that you must book through a travel agency outside the US, and this guide provides the names, addresses, and telephone and fax numbers you'll need.

The agency or airline will arrange your Cuban tourist card and the officials in Havana don't stamp your passport, so Uncle Sam is none the wiser. You may not even need to change money, since cash US dollars are legal tender in Cuba.

Cuba offers the kind of adventure other destinations promise but seldom deliver. During the 1960s Cuba underwent the greatest social upheaval the Western Hemisphere had seen since the Spanish conquest, and against all odds the experiment continues today. Many memorable experiences await you. Slightly under a million tourists vacation in Cuba each year, compared to the 10 million that flock to the Bahamas. Only a few thousand US citizens visit Cuba each year. No doubt millions will come when the flights from Miami resume. Clearly, the time to go is now.

Should US Citizens Visit Cuba?

In conjunction with the US embargo against Cuba, the US government has prohibited its people from spending money in Cuba. This restriction has effectively prevented US citizens from visiting their neighbor for over three decades, although the enforcement of this law has fluctuated with the political climate.

The 1996 Helms-Burton Bill, which was signed into law by President Clinton on March 12, 1996, imposes without judicial review fines of up to US$50,000 on US citizens who visit Cuba at their own expense without US government permission. It also allows for confiscation of their property. In addition, under the Trading with the Enemy Act, they may also face up to US$250,000 in fines and up to 10 years in prison. At press time, it is unclear how this legislation will be implemented. We haven't heard of anyone who has actually been fined or imprisoned for visiting Cuba, although we have heard of travelers who have been notified that they may be. The author and publisher accept no responsibility for repercussions suffered by US citizens who decide to circumvent these restrictions. You may wish to contact the groups listed under Useful Organizations in the Facts for the Visitor chapter to inquire about current US policy and enforcement.

Those who support the US embargo argue that tourism to Cuba lends support to a 'repressive Communist dictatorship.' Lonely Planet believes the decision to visit Cuba should be a personal matter and that a visit to Cuba does not imply support for, or necessarily prop up, the current Cuban government. Travelers can play a positive role by keeping lines of communication open and spending their money wisely. Ironically, freedom of movement is one of the foundations of democracy, and it is no coincidence that, historically, totalitarian regimes have strictly limited the ability of their citizens to travel. Many Cubans depend on the tourist trade to survive, and by using the information in this book travelers will be able to spend their money in ways that most benefit ordinary Cubans. ■

Facts about Cuba

HISTORY

The first humans probably reached Cuba from South America around 3500 BC, although habitation proven by carbon dating stretches back only to 2000 BC. The Guanahatabey settled in the west and the Siboney throughout much of the rest of the island, including the coral cays (or keys) off the south coast. These fishers, hunters, and gatherers were later joined by agriculturalists known as the Taino, a branch of the Arawak Indians who inhabited most of the Caribbean islands and northern South America.

A century or two before the arrival of Columbus, the Taino fled westward from Hispaniola and Puerto Rico under pressure from the fierce Carib tribe (whose name was eventually corrupted into the English 'cannibal'). As the Taino arrived in Cuba they pushed the Siboney westward, and by the time the Spanish arrived in the late 15th century, three-quarters of Cuba's 100,000 native Indians were Taino-speaking Arawaks.

The Cuban Indians lived peacefully in villages, grew *boniatos* (sweet potatoes), *yuca* (manioc or cassava), yams, corn, pumpkins, peanuts, peppers, avocados, and tobacco. They had pottery, baskets, and stone implements. Idols of wood, stone, or bone represented *zenus* (spirits). The Tainos slept in cotton *hamacas* (hammocks) hung in thatched *bohíos* (huts) that were arranged around an open space in front of the dwelling of the *cacique* (chief) known as a *batey*. The greatest concentration of Indians was in the eastern part of the island, especially around the Bahía de Nipe, where agriculture was well developed.

The Colonial Period

On October 27, 1492, 15 days after 'discovering' San Salvador (or Watling's Island) in the Bahamas, Christopher Columbus (Cristóbal Colón in Spanish) sighted a large land mass that he named 'Juana' in honor of an heir to the Spanish throne. Columbus described Cuba as 'the most beautiful land human eyes have ever seen.' However, the island offered little gold, so the Spanish at first ignored it, establishing their initial base in the New World at Santo Domingo on the island of Hispaniola. Columbus thought Cuba was part of the coast of Asia, and only in 1508 did Sebastián de Ocampo complete the first circumnavigation, proving it was an island.

In 1512 a 300-member expedition from Hispaniola led by Diego Velázquez de Cuéllar landed at Baracoa near the easternmost tip of Cuba to begin a planned conquest on behalf of the Spanish Crown, and by the end of 1514 he had established seven settlements: Baracoa, Santiago de Cuba, Bayamo, Puerto Príncipe (Camagüey), Sancti Spíritus, Trinidad, and the first Havana. These towns were laid out on rectangular grids with a central square watched over by the main church, and each was run by a local authority called a *cabildo*. In 1515 Velázquez shifted his headquarters from Baracoa to Santiago de Cuba.

Velázquez was reasonably enlightened for his time and he tried to protect the Indians from the excesses of the other Spaniards, but his efforts were largely in vain and the Spanish slaughtered thousands of aborigines or forced them to flee west. Hatuey, a *cacique* who attempted to mount a resistance, was eventually captured and condemned to be burned at the stake. As a Franciscan monk moved to baptize Hatuey so that his soul at least would be saved, the Indian objected, declaring that he never wanted to see another Spaniard, not even in heaven.

Velázquez was not entirely satisfied with his gold-poor Cuban colony, and after 1516 he sponsored four expeditions to Mexico,

Indian leader Hatuey organized resistance to the invading Spaniards.

one of which resulted in Hernán Cortés' brutal conquest of 1519 to 1521. The Mexican adventures drew considerable manpower away from Cuba, but the first years of Spanish colonialism in Cuba still saw a flurry of activity as some gold was extracted from local mines and large estates were set up under an *encomienda* system under which the Indians were forced to labor on the pretext of receiving instruction in Christianity. Fray Bartolomé de las Casas, the 'Apostle of the Indies,' attempted to defend Cuba's Indians through appeals to the Spanish Crown for more humane treatment, and in 1542 the *encomienda* system was abolished in Cuba. During this callous exploitation, the Spanish introduced diseases such as smallpox that soon decimated the Indian populations, and by 1550 only about 5000 scattered survivors remained. (The Spanish returned to Europe infected with syphilis.)

As the number of native Indians decreased, the Spanish turned to African slaves as an alternate source of labor. The first were brought in as early as 1522, and unlike slavery in North America, Cuba's African slaves were kept together in tribal groups and were thus able to retain certain elements of their African cultures.

Cattle ranching, producing leather and dried beef, was the main industry until the early 18th century when tobacco (made into cigars and snuff) became the most important cash crop. Tobacco was grown commercially from 1580 onwards, and in 1717 the Spanish Crown granted itself a monopoly to buy and sell tobacco, generating much local resentment. Only in 1817 was this regulation repealed. Sugar cane had arrived with Diego Velázquez in 1512, but the expansion of sugar cultivation was limited by a lack of slaves.

During and after the conquest of Mexico, Cuba served as a transit point for Spanish treasure fleets carrying the wealth of the New World to Spain. Each summer galleons from Cartagena and Veracruz assembled in Havana harbor and sailed northeast to Spain as an annual *flota* (fleet). These riches attracted the attention of pirates such as the Frenchman Jacques de Sores, who plundered Havana in 1555. After this disaster Havana and Santiago de Cuba were properly garrisoned, and beginning in 1589 the mouths of their harbors were fortified with strong castles. Nevertheless, in 1628 the Dutch Admiral Piet Heyn captured the entire Mexican treasure fleet in Matanzas Bay, displaying Spanish naval weakness to the world, and Spain's Caribbean hegemony soon began to be seriously challenged by other European powers. The British took neighboring Jamaica in 1655, and by 1665 Cuba's towns were under almost continuous threat of attack. Haiti fell to the French in 1697.

In January 1762 Spain became involved in the Seven Years' War between Britain and France that had already cost France its colonies in Canada. In March the British dispatched a fleet to capture Havana and sever Spain's communications with the rest of Spanish America. British troops landed at Cojímar on June 6, captured Morro Castle from behind on July 30

A Cuban Chronology

3500 BC – first humans arrive in Cuba
1250 AD – Taino Indians arrive from the east
1492 – Columbus sights Cuba
1508 – Sebastián de Ocampo circum navigates Cuba
1512 – Diego Velázquez lands at Baracoa
1514 – first seven settlements established
1515 – Santiago de Cuba becomes capital
1518 – Hernán Cortés leaves for Mexico
1519 – Havana established at present site
1522 – first African slaves brought to Cuba
1542 – *encomienda* system abolished
1555 – French pirates sack Havana
1556 – Spanish captains-general move to Havana
1564 – first treasure fleet departs from Havana
1589 – Havana and Santiago de Cuba fortified
1607 – Havana declared capital of Cuba
1628 – Piet Heyn captures the *flota*
1674 – construction of Havana city walls begins
1700 – tobacco becomes the main export
1728 – University of Havana founded
1762 – the British capture Havana
1763 – the British trade Cuba for Florida
1765 – commerce with Spain liberalized
1790 – mass importation of African slaves
1800 – sugar becomes the main export
1818 – trade with all countries allowed
1820 – slave trade ineffectively abolished
1825 – most of Latin America has gained independence
1837 – first railway line built
1848 – US attempts to buy Cuba from Spain
1850 – Narciso López raises Cuban flag
1854 – US tries again to buy Cuba
1865 – importation of African slaves ends
1868 to 1878 – First War of Independence
1879 – slavery converted to 'apprenticeship'
1886 – 'apprenticeship' system ends
1895 to 1898 – Second War of Independence

1898 – Americans land at Santiago de Cuba, Spanish rule ends
1898 to 1902 – US military government controls Cuba
1901 – Platt Amendment imposed on Cuba
1902 – Cuba achieves independence
1903 – US takes Guantánamo naval base
1906 – US military intervention
1917 – US military intervention
1925 – first Communist Party founded
1933 – Machado dictatorship overthrown
1934 – Platt Amendment abrogated
1940 – second constitution proclaimed
1952 – Batista military coup
1953 – attack on the Moncada barracks by rebels
1956 – *Granma* lands rebels in Oriente
1956 to 1958 – Castro hides out in the Sierra Maestra
1958 – Che Guevara captures Santa Clara
1959 – Batista flees, rebels take control, first agrarian reform
1960 – large companies nationalized, US economic embargo begins
1961 – abortive Bay of Pigs invasion
1962 – Cuban Missile Crisis
1963 – second agrarian reform
1965 – refounding of the Communist Party
1966 – Tricontinental Conference in Havana
1967 – Che Guevara killed in Bolivia
1968 – small businesses nationalized
1972 – Cuba joins Comecon trading block
1975 – first Cuban Communist Party congress, number of provinces increased to 14, Cuban troops sent to Angola
1976 – third constitution comes into force
1979 – Non-Aligned Movement summit in Havana
1980 – 120,000 Cubans depart through Mariel
1988 – Cuban troops withdrawn from Angola
1990 – tourism surpasses sugar in importance, Castro declares five-year austerity program
1991 – Soviet Union collapses
1993 – Cubans allowed to hold US dollars
1995 – direct foreign investment approved
1996 – US tightens blockade of Cuba

and accepted the Spanish surrender on August 13. The British occupied Havana for 11 months, and during their stay they profited from importing 4000 African slaves. The 1763 Peace of Paris returned Cuba to Spain in exchange for Florida, and as compensation Spain was given the Louisiana Territory by France. (Spain held Louisiana from 1763 to 1803 when it fell into the hands of Napoleon, who promptly sold it to the USA.)

After this debacle the French Bourbon kings who occupied the Spanish throne attempted to reform public institutions in an effort to strengthen their administration. Prior to 1762 the Real Compañía de Comercio in Cádiz had a monopoly on Cuban trade, and the Council of the Indies in Seville controlled Cuba's government. The governors-general of Cuba merely followed instructions sent to them from Spain, and the influence of the incompetent, corrupt Spanish officials didn't extend far beyond the main towns: Pirates, smugglers, and escaped slaves dominated the countryside. Prior to the British occupation, only 15 North American ships visited Havana each year. The British threw open trade with the British colonies in North America, and 700 trading ships visited Havana during those 11 months. The returning Spanish captain-general allowed the liberalized trade to continue, and after 1765 Cuba was allowed to trade freely with seven Spanish ports instead of only with Cádiz. A chain of new fortresses was built around Havana.

After US independence in 1783 Cuba gradually replaced the British colony of Jamaica as the main supplier of sugar to the US market, and many Cuban planters desired union with the US to guarantee the continuation of slavery and free trade. In 1791 a slave uprising in nearby Haiti eliminated the main competitor to Cuba's sugar industry, and production sharply increased due to the labor of tens of thousands of newly imported African slaves. French planters fleeing Haiti set up coffee plantations and modernized the Cuban sugar industry. After 1818 Cuba was allowed to trade directly with any foreign port. By the 1820s Cuba was the world's largest producer of sugar.

Between 1810 and 1825 Mexico and all of mainland South America won their independence from Spain, leaving Cuba and Puerto Rico the only remaining Spanish colonies in the Western Hemisphere. The great liberator Simón Bolívar had wanted to free Cuba as well, but the US declared that it preferred continued Spanish rule and warned him to desist. In Cuba the Spanish authorities were reinforced by loyalists fleeing the former Spanish colonies and fresh immigrants from Spain. Both *peninsulares* (Spaniards born in Spain) and *criollos* or Creoles (Spaniards born in the New World) feared that independence might lead to a slave revolt similar to Haiti's, so they tended to support Spain. In 1820 diplomatic pressure from Britain forced Spain to agree to halt the slave trade although the import of African slaves continued unabated and by the 1840s some 400,000 were present.

Between 1838 and 1880 the Spanish continued to modernize Cuba's sugar industry until it accounted for a third of world production. Narrow-gauge railway lines were laid down to bring the cane to steam-powered *ingenios* (mills). The ruthless slave-owning planters expelled small farmers from their lands and cleared the island's cedar, ebony, and mahogany forests. Over half of the sugar was sold to the US, which had become Cuba's largest trading partner. In 1848 the US attempted to buy Cuba from Spain for US$100 million but was turned down. In 1854 the US increased the offer to US$120 million, but Spain also refused this.

In 1850 a 600-soldier force led by Narciso López, a former Spanish general who favored annexation to the US as a means of preserving slavery, set out from New Orleans, Louisiana, and captured Cárdenas, at that time the center of Matanzas' richest sugar-growing area. When the local Cubans refused to support what appeared to be a US filibuster, López quickly withdrew to Florida, with the Spaniards in close

Out for a stroll in Havana

Manuel Mendive, Cuba's
foremost living painter

Surveying the goods at the
cathedral craft market

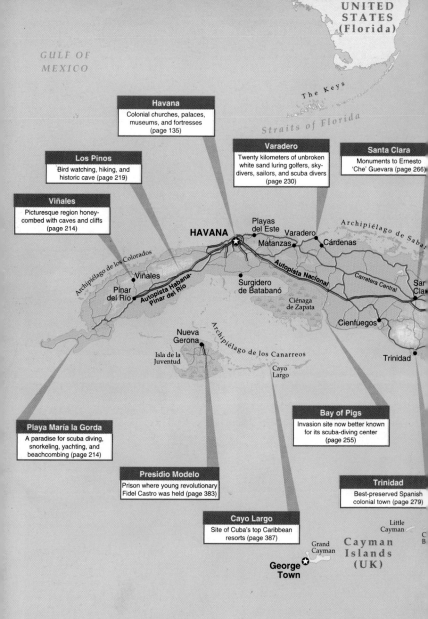

UNITED STATES (Florida)

GULF OF MEXICO

The Keys

Straits of Florida

Havana
Colonial churches, palaces, museums, and fortresses (page 135)

Varadero
Twenty kilometers of unbroken white sand luring golfers, sky-divers, sailors, and scuba divers (page 230)

Santa Clara
Monuments to Ernesto 'Che' Guevara (page 266)

Los Pinos
Bird watching, hiking, and historic cave (page 219)

Viñales
Picturesque region honeycombed with caves and cliffs (page 214)

Playas del Este

HAVANA

Varadero

Matanzas

Cárdenas

Archipiélago de Sabar

Viñales

Pinar del Río

Autopista Habana-Pinar del Río

Archipiélago de los Colorados

Surgidero de Batabanó

Autopista Nacional

Carretera Central

Sar Cla

Ciénaga de Zapata

Cienfuegos

Nueva Gerona

Archipiélago de los Canarreos

Isla de la Juventud

Cayo Largo

Trinidad

Playa María la Gorda
A paradise for scuba diving, snorkeling, yachting, and beachcombing (page 214)

Bay of Pigs
Invasion site now better known for its scuba-diving center (page 255)

Presidio Modelo
Prison where young revolutionary Fidel Castro was held (page 383)

Trinidad
Best-preserved Spanish colonial town (page 279)

Little Cayman

Cayo Largo
Site of Cuba's top Caribbean resorts (page 387)

Grand Cayman

Cayman Islands (UK)

C B

George Town

CARIBBEAN SEA

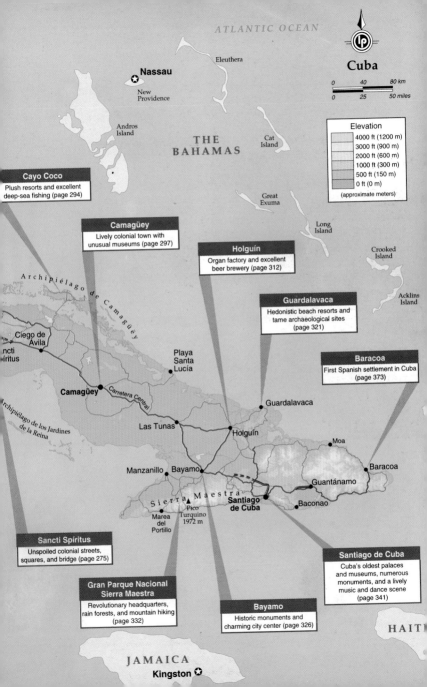

ATLANTIC OCEAN

Cuba

Eleuthera

Nassau

New
Providence

Andros
Island

THE
BAHAMAS

Cat
Island

Elevation

4000 ft (1200 m)
3000 ft (900 m)
2000 ft (600 m)
1000 ft (300 m)
500 ft (150 m)
0 ft (0 m)
(approximate meters)

Great
Exuma

Long
Island

Crooked
Island

Acklins
Island

Cayo Coco
Plush resorts and excellent
deep-sea fishing (page 294)

Camagüey
Lively colonial town with
unusual museums (page 297)

Holguín
Organ factory and excellent
beer brewery (page 312)

Guardalavaca
Hedonistic beach resorts and
tame archaeological sites
(page 321)

Baracoa
First Spanish settlement in Cuba
(page 373)

Archipiélago de Camagüey

Ciego de
Ávila

ncti
íritus

Playa
Santa
Lucía

Camagüey

Carretera Central

Archipiélago de los Jardines
de la Reina

Las Tunas

Guardalavaca

Holguín

Moa

Baracoa

Guantánamo

Manzanillo   Bayamo

Sierra Maestra

Marea
del
Portillo

Pico
Turquino
1972 m

**Santiago
de Cuba**

Baconao

Sancti Spíritus
Unspoiled colonial streets,
squares, and bridge (page 275)

**Gran Parque Nacional
Sierra Maestra**
Revolutionary headquarters,
rain forests, and mountain hiking
(page 332)

Bayamo
Historic monuments and
charming city center (page 326)

Santiago de Cuba
Cuba's oldest palaces
and museums, numerous
monuments, and a lively
music and dance scene
(page 341)

HAITI

JAMAICA
Kingston

Market vendors

Matanzas farm worker

Havana school kids say '¡Queso!'

pursuit. A few months later he landed in Pinar del Río with a mixed company of Cubans and Americans, and was captured and executed by the Spaniards. These efforts received little support from either the US government or the Cuban planters who feared they might trigger a slave rebellion. An enduring legacy of the affair is the present Cuban flag designed by López. Its single white star (like that of slaveholding Texas) appears on a red Masonic triangle against horizontal white and blue stripes, ironic symbols of the annexation effort.

In 1862 the British finally began enforcing the ban on slave trading enacted in 1820. Most of the slaves had arrived on US ships, and only the distraction of the US Civil War allowed the British to act without fear of major repercussions. After the importation of African slaves was effectively stopped in 1865, indentured Chinese laborers and Mexican Indians were brought in to serve as *macheteros*, who cut sugar cane. In 1867 an attempt to reform Cuba from within failed in the face of Spanish duplicity. A commission elected by the wealthy landowners was allowed to voice their position, which included gradually phasing out of slavery with compensation; however, Spain did nothing to implement their proposals.

The Wars of Independence

In 1868 Spain's reactionary policies in Cuba, especially its refusal to consider internal autonomy, finally sparked the declaration of a Cuban republic by rebels in Oriente Province. At this time eastern Cuba was an economic backwater with most of its small sugar mills powered by oxen rather than steam. The Creole planters around Bayamo had been plotting a rebellion for some time, and when the wife of one betrayed the conspirators through her confessor, the captain-general in Havana ordered their arrest, forcing them to act.

On October 10, 1868, Carlos Manuel de Céspedes launched the uprising at his plantation, La Demajagua. Céspedes called for the abolition of slavery, but only after independence had been achieved and then with compensation. To avoid alienating the wealthy planters in the west, he did not declare the immediate emancipation of the slaves, although he did free his own.

At first the rebels captured much of the eastern part of the island, but the Spanish placed the cities under martial law and built a fortified ditch across the island from Júcaro to Morón to isolate the rebel-held east. The rebels fought indecisively and made no bold move to emancipate the slaves (despite the example set by US President Lincoln, who on January 1, 1863, emancipated US slaves, a strategy that contributed greatly to the north's military victory in the Civil War). When a reactionary militia was formed in the west to support continued Spanish rule, the rebels met at Guáimaro in April 1869 and passed

General Máximo Gómez organized rebel forces against Spanish rule in 1895.

a constitution that declared the slaves free, though they were to continue working for their former masters for wages.

The cautious rebel council rejected General Máximo Gómez' proposal to invade western Cuba, and Céspedes was removed from office (to die in a Spanish ambush soon after). In 1874 and 1875 rebels under Gómez did manage several brief forays west, but this First War of Independence dragged on into a Ten Years' War. In February 1878 a pact was finally signed at El Zanjón in which the rebels were granted an amnesty. General Antonio Maceo and several others rejected this in the 'Protest of Baraguá,' and after an additional three months of fighting Maceo went into exile. Some 200,000 people had died and much property was destroyed. Essentially, the war was lost because the liberal planter leadership in the east was unwilling to destroy the country's economy through harsh measures and the slaveholding landlords in the west supported Spain.

The 17-year interval between the end of Cuba's First War of Independence and the beginning of the second failed to produce the internal autonomy the Creole community desired, although the government in Madrid did enact a few reforms. In 1879 Spain announced the abolition of slavery with no compensation beginning in 1888, before which the ex-slaves were required to continue working for their masters as 'apprentices.' Many employers found it cheaper to pay laborers to cut their cane from January to July rather than feed and house 'apprentices' all year long, and the system was terminated two years early in 1886. Most positions in the civil service continued to be filled by peninsular Spaniards.

During the 1880s there was a boom in railway construction as both sugar mills and plantations grew larger. US investors snapped up bankrupt Spanish plantations and other segments of the economy for a song. Some Cuban planters and businessmen continued to call for annexation to the US as a solution to their problems, a position supported by several US presidents beginning with Thomas Jefferson. In 1890

tariffs on most trade between the US and Cuba were removed. While fostering prosperity, this arrangement made Cuba totally dependent on sugar, as other industries could not compete with US mass production. Throughout the 19th century, Cuba's trade with the US had been larger than that with Spain, and by the end of the century US trade with Cuba was larger than US trade with the rest of Latin America combined. Cuba was the United States' third largest trading partner after Britain and Germany.

Meanwhile a circle of émigrés in the US plotted a return to Cuba. Their most effective spokesman was a writer named José Martí, who had earned an international reputation as a poet, playwright, and essayist. Martí spent 14 years in exile in Mexico and later in the US, and although impressed by American industriousness, he was repelled by its materialism. Acutely aware of how the US had seized half of Mexico's national territory in 1848, he denounced the exploitation of the poor by US banking and industrial monopolies in his writings. Just prior to his death in the early days of the Second War of Independence, Martí wrote to a Mexican friend:

I am every day now in danger of giving my life for my country and for my duty as I understand it and have the courage to realize it, which is to prevent in good time that, with the independence of Cuba, the US should extend its power over the Antilles and fall with that much more weight on our lands of America. What I have done up to today, and will do, is for this. I lived inside the monster, and I know its entrails; and my sling is the sling of David.

By 1890 the autonomist movement in Cuba had been discredited by Spanish political incompetence and inflexibility, so with interest in independence again on the increase, Martí dedicated himself almost exclusively to the movement as a writer, speaker, and organizer. By 1892 the movement was strong enough for Martí to travel to Santo Domingo to engage General Máximo Gómez as military commander of the revolution. Antonio Maceo was recruited in Costa Rica, where he had set up a banana plantation.

José Martí

Cuba's national hero, José Martí, was born to Spanish immigrant parents in Havana on January 28, 1853. While still at high school Martí became involved in anticolonial activities, and in 1869 he published a political tract and the first issue of a newspaper called *La Patria Libre*. A war of independence had broken out in Oriente the previous year and the Spanish colonial authorities were in no mood to allow criticism, so in October 1869 Martí was arrested on treason charges and in April 1870 he was sentenced to six years at hard labor.

After several months at a Havana stone quarry the young prisoner was exiled to the Isla de Pinos (today Isla de la Juventud) in October 1870. There he spent nine weeks before his deportation to Spain, where he was allowed to enroll in a university. In 1874 Martí graduated from law school, but both the war and his critical writings had continued and official permission to return to Cuba was denied. Martí went to Mexico City and got a job with a newspaper in 1875. In 1877 he married a Cuban woman and obtained a teaching post in Guatemala.

The First War of Independence ended in 1878 and Martí was able to return to Cuba under a general amnesty. In Havana the authorities prevented Martí from practicing law, and in 1879 his conspiratorial activities and anticolonial statements at public debates led to his arrest and a second sentence of exile to Spain. After traveling to France, the US, and Venezuela, Martí finally settled in New York City, where he was to remain until just three and a half months prior to his death.

In New York Martí served as a correspondent for the Buenos Aires newspaper *La Nación* and the Caracas paper *La Opinión Nacional*. His columns describing the North American scene made him well known throughout Latin America, and he was appointed consul of Uruguay in New York. In 1892 Martí's relentless advocacy of Cuban independence and his organizational work in New York and Florida led to his election as chief delegate of the newly formed Partido Revolucionario Cubano.

On April 11, 1895, Martí, the Dominican general Máximo Gómez, and four others landed near Baracoa in eastern Cuba to launch the Second War of Independence. They soon made contact with rebels led by Antonio Maceo, but on May 19, 1895, Martí was killed during a brief skirmish with the Spanish at Dos Ríos on the Cauto River in present Granma Province. Deprived of their political leader, the Cubans fought on under the military leadership of Maceo and Gómez only to have imminent victory snatched from them by a US intervention three years later.

In his own time Martí was best known for essays that set out his vision of a secular republic and warned of the threat to Cuba from sporadic US imperialism (the US had annexed half of Mexico less than four decades earlier). Although history was to confirm his worst fears in this regard, it's Martí's poetry that is most appreciated today. In literary circles Martí is regarded as one of the initiators of the school of modernism in Latin American poetry. Decades after his death, lines from Martí's *Versos Sencillos* (1891) were incorporated into the best known Cuban song of all time, *Guajira guantanamera*:

Yo soy un hombre sincero	I'm a sincere man
de donde crece la palma,	from the land of the palm tree,
y antes de morirme quiero echar	and before I die I wish to sing
mis versos del alma.	these heart-felt verses.
Con los pobres de la tierra quiero yo mi	With the poor of the land I want
suerte echar,	to share a fate,
y el arroyo de la sierra me complace	and the mountain stream pleases me
más que el mar.	more than the sea.

In 1894 the US upped the stakes by declaring an abrupt increase in tariffs, shattering Cuba's sugar-based economy and destabilizing Spain's shaky colonial system. Martí and the others landed in eastern Cuba in April 1895, and on May 19, Martí, conspicuous on his white horse, was shot and killed in a brief encounter. Had he lived he would certainly have become Cuba's first president; instead, he became his country's national hero whose life and vast literary legacy have inspired Cubans ever since. Martí was a firm advocate of racial equality and independence from both Spain and the US. Always the idealist, in death he became a martyr.

Unwilling to repeat the mistakes of the first war of independence, Gómez and Maceo drove west in October 1895, reaching Las Villas in November and Matanzas Province by Christmas. Everything in their path, including sugar fields, plantations, and towns, was set on fire. By January 1896 Maceo had reached Pinar del Río, and Gómez was fighting in the vicinity of Havana. In panic the Spaniards sent an equally ruthless captain-general, Valeriano Weyler, to Cuba. Weyler reorganized the Spanish army and built north-south lines across the country to restrict the rebel's movements. The *guajiros* (country people) were forced into fortified camps in a process known as *reconcentración*, and anyone found supporting the rebellion was liable for execution. (These highly effective counterinsurgency tactics were later copied by the British during the Boer War.) In Pinar del Río Weyler exerted heavy pressure on the rebels in this way, and in December 1896 Antonio Maceo was killed south of Havana trying to break out to the east.

Weyler's methods brought Cuba's agricultural economy to a standstill with thousands killed, estates burned, and towns sacked. In June 1897 Spanish Prime Minister Antonio Cánovas, a hard-line opponent of Cuban independence, was assassinated in Spain by an anarchist with Cuban connections. The new Spanish government favored resolving the conflict by granting

autonomy, and in October Weyler resigned. The Spaniards adopted a conciliatory tone, attempting to persuade the Cubans to accept the home rule under the Spanish flag that they had initially wanted, although by now the rebels would be satisfied with nothing short of full independence.

US Intervention
As Martí had feared, the US government had been biding its time, and it now seemed that the moment to seize Cuba had come. Largely to increase their circulation, the US tabloid press stoked war fever throughout 1897, printing sensational and often inaccurate articles on Spanish atrocities. When William Randolph Hearst's illustrator Frederick Remington asked permission to return from Havana as all was quiet, the eminent publisher replied, 'Please remain. You furnish the pictures and I'll furnish the war.' Hearst's ally in this campaign was the assistant secretary of the navy, Theodore Roosevelt, who viewed Cuba as an opportunity to cover himself in glory.

In January 1898 the US battleship *Maine* was sent to Havana 'to protect US citizens.' The *Maine* lay at anchor off the city just west of the harbor mouth for three weeks before it mysteriously blew up on February 15, 1898, killing 266 US sailors. The Spanish claimed the explosion had been caused by an accident in the ship's ammunition store, while the Americans blamed a Spanish mine. Some Cuban writers have asserted that the Americans blew up the *Maine* themselves to provide the pretext for intervening in Cuba, a theory not entirely beyond the realm of possibility. It may or may not have been a coincidence that the captain of the *Maine* and most of his officers were safely ashore when the bomb went off. In 1911 the *Maine* was raised and sunk in deep water to remove a navigational hazard from the harbor mouth, so the real cause will never be known.

After the explosion on the *Maine*, pandemonium broke loose in the US and President William McKinley offered to resolve the problem peacefully by purchasing Cuba from Spain for US$300 million, a proposition rejected by the Spaniards. The Spanish tried desperately to avoid a conflict with the Americans. On April 9 Spain declared a ceasefire in the civil war with the Cubans, and withdrew the *reconcentración* orders for the rural populace. These measures failed to impress the Americans, who demanded a full Spanish withdrawal, and on April 25 the US declared war on Spain. From the onset the Spanish knew they were doomed to lose the war, and they only wanted a quick military defeat that would allow them to surrender with honor to a superior force. Any move to capitulate without such a face-saving gesture might have led to an uprising in Spain itself and the overthrow of the monarchy.

By May 28 the US had blockaded the Spanish fleet at Santiago de Cuba Bay. The only important land battle of the war took place on July 1 when the US Army attacked Spanish positions on San Juan Hill just east of Santiago de Cuba. The 700 Spanish defenders held up 6000 US troops all day, inflicting casualties on them of 223 dead, 1243 wounded, and 79 missing (compared to Spanish losses of 102 dead and 552 wounded). Future US President Theodore Roosevelt personally led the celebrated charge of the 'Rough Riders' up San Juan Hill and claimed a great victory! Historian Hugh Thomas (author of *Cuba, or The Pursuit of Freedom*) argues that had the Spanish counterattacked instead of withdrawing, the Americans would have suffered a humiliating defeat.

On July 3 the outgunned Spanish fleet tried to break out of Santiago de Cuba Bay. Although they managed to evade the chaotic US fleet, the wooden Spanish ships caught fire in a strong tail wind and ran aground. Of 2225 Spanish sailors, 1670 managed to get to shore and surrendered. US losses in this non-battle were one dead and two wounded.

Meanwhile the US tightened its siege of Santiago de Cuba and the Spaniards took the opportunity to surrender on July 17, 1898. The US military leaders foolishly refused to allow the rebel commander in Oriente, General Calixto García, or his troops to enter Santiago de Cuba for the surrender ceremony, largely because they became alarmed when they learned that García and many of his followers were black. Instead, the Americans decided to let the Spanish municipal authorities remain in their positions. As a result, the disgusted Cubans in Santiago de Cuba made little effort to help their American conquerors when they began dying of yellow fever, malaria, and dysentery at the rate of 200 a day. On August 7 the enfeebled US forces began withdrawing to the US, as Calixto García's army moved northwest to obtain the surrender of Spanish forces in Holguín and elsewhere.

On December 12, 1898, a peace treaty ending the 'Spanish-American' War was signed in Paris by the Spanish and the Americans. The Cubans were not invited. An amendment known as the Teller Resolution (after Senator Henry M Teller of the US state of Colorado), passed simultaneously with the declaration of war on Spain, had committed the US to respect Cuban self-determination, and only this prevented the US from adding Cuba when they annexed Puerto Rico, Guam, and the Philippines. Cuba was placed under US military occupation instead.

The first US governor of Cuba, General John R Brooke, disbanded the mostly black Cuban army but left the white former Spanish officials in their posts. The Americans considered the Cuban rebels disorderly and corrupt, and had them demobilized and turned out onto the streets. Brooke was soon replaced by General Leonard Wood, an ambitious medical doctor who worked to improve public health, built US-style schools, and conducted public works, all with the overt intention of tying Cuba to the US. Throughout its history Cuba had been wracked by yellow fever epidemics, and although a Cuban doctor name Carlos Juan Finlay (1833 – 1915) had discovered in 1881 that a certain type of mosquito was the carrier, the Spanish authorities had done nothing to implement Finlay's suggestions. Wood launched a campaign that soon eradicated yellow fever.

In November 1900 Wood convened an assembly of elected Cuban delegates who drew up a constitution similar to that of the US. Then, at the instigation of US Secretary of War Elihu Root, Connecticut Senator Orville Platt attached a rider to the US Army Appropriations Bill of 1901 giving the US the right, among other things, to intervene militarily in Cuba's internal affairs whenever the US decided such intervention was warranted. This was approved by President McKinley and the Cubans were given the choice of accepting the Platt Amendment or remaining under US military occupation indefinitely. In the end, they accepted this humiliating amendment as the lesser of two evils, and in 1903 the US used it to obtain a naval base at the mouth of Guantánamo Bay, a shameful legacy that persists to this day.

After Independence

The US intervention endowed Cuba with a series of weak, corrupt, dependent governments. Cuba became an independent republic on May 20, 1902, after Tomás Estrada Palma was elected president. However, a revolt broke out when Estrada Palma's Liberal opponents accused him of employing fraud to obtain a second term. This led to a US military intervention in September 1906. A US governor named Charles Magoon held power until January 1909 when a deal was worked out specifying that the Liberals and Conservatives would alternate in power under the threat of Platt Amendment intervention. Elections were carefully managed to ensure that the results came out right.

The first Liberal president, José Miguel Gómez, initiated corruption, incompetence, and discrimination against blacks which persisted until 1959. When Afro-Cubans in Oriente demonstrated against this discrimination in 1912, some 3000 were slaughtered by government troops. The same year the US intervened militarily to put down a revolt by former slaves in Pinar del Río, and in 1917 US soldiers were back again to ensure a steady flow of sugar during WWI.

By the 1920s US companies owned two-thirds of Cuba's farmland and most of its mines. The US saw Cuba as a source of raw materials and a market for finished US products. Manufacturing in Cuba itself was crippled by high US tariffs on most Cuban goods other than raw sugar, tobacco leaves, and unprocessed minerals. Yet Cuba's sugar industry boomed during the 1920s, and with prohibition in force in the US from 1919 to 1933, tourism based on gambling and prostitution flourished. Only a few benefited, however, and when commodity prices collapsed in the wake of the Great Depression, Liberal President Gerardo Machado y Morales used terror to quell the resulting unrest.

In August 1933 Machado was toppled during a spontaneous general strike. Chaos followed and on September 4 an army sergeant named Fulgencio Batista (who took no part in the overthrow of Machado) seized power in a noncommissioned officers' coup. In November 1933 Franklin D Roosevelt was elected president of the US, and as part of his 'good neighbor' policy toward Latin America he arranged for the abrogation of the Platt Amendment on May 29, 1934. The lease on the Guantánamo naval base was extended for 99 years.

Batista served as the army's chief of staff from 1934 to 1940, and in 1940 he had a democratic constitution drafted guaranteeing many rights. He was duly elected president that year and during WWII he won US favor by supporting the Allied war effort. In 1944 Batista allowed free elections, but his preferred candidate lost. The next two governments led by presidents Grau and Prío of the Partido Auténtico were corrupt and inefficient. Public services hardly existed and millions were unemployed. In 1947 Eduardo Chibás formed the Partido Ortodoxo to fight corruption, and in 1948 Batista set up the Partido de Acción Unitaria in an attempt to make a comeback.

On March 10, 1952, just three months before the scheduled election date, Batista taged a second military coup that Washington recognized two weeks later. Batista's coup was motivated mostly by his impending defeat in the presidential election, but it invalidated the 1940 constitution and prevented the almost certain election to the House of Representatives of a young Ortodoxo candidate named Fidel Castro. Opposition politicians were unable to unite against the dictator, who sought legitimacy through rigged elections in 1955 and 1958. By this time over half of Cuba's land, industry, and essential services were in foreign hands, and Batista's cronies enriched themselves with bribes.

The Cuban Revolution

After the Batista coup a revolutionary circle formed in Havana, including Abel Santamaría (later tortured to death by Batista's troops), his sister Haydée Santamaría, Melba Hernández, Fidel Castro, and others. They decided on a dramatic gesture that would signal a general uprising throughout the country. On July 26, 1953, Castro led 119 rebels in an attack on the Moncada army barracks in Santiago de Cuba, the second most important military base in Cuba at that time. It had been assumed that the soldiers would be drunk due to a carnival then in progress, but the assault failed when a patrol jeep encountered Castro's motorcade by chance, costing the attackers the essential element of surprise.

After the abortive assault 55 of the men detained by the army were cruelly tortured and murdered. Castro managed to escape into the nearby foothills from where he intended to launch a guerrilla campaign, and it was only through extraordinary luck that he was captured a week later by an army lieutenant named Sarría, who took him to Santiago de Cuba's main jail instead of immediately shooting him as the army chiefs had secretly ordered. Castro's capture soon became known and the Batista regime had no choice other than to put him on trial. Castro was a lawyer by profession and his defense summation at the trial was later edited and released as a political

manifesto entitled *History Will Absolve Me*. In the end he was sentenced to 15 years imprisonment on the Isla de Pinos (now called Isla de la Juventud).

In February 1955 Batista got himself elected president in a fraudulent election, and in an effort to win legitimacy and popular support he freed all political prisoners in May 1955. Castro departed for Mexico in July 1955, but he left behind in Santiago de Cuba a Baptist schoolteacher named Frank País to organize the underground resistance of the 26th of July Movement, or 'M-26-7' as it was commonly called. In December 1955 students at Havana University formed the Directorio Revolucionario (DR), which was led by José Antonio Echeverría. When the Partido Ortodoxo entered into compromise negotiations with Batista in February 1956, Castro severed all ties between the M-26-7 and that party.

In Mexico the M-26-7 trained and equipped a revolutionary force, and on December 2, 1956, Castro and 82 companions landed from the motor vessel *Granma* at Playa Las Coloradas near Niquero in Oriente. Three days later the group was decimated in an initial clash with Batista's army at Alegría de Pío, but Castro and 22 others (including an Argentine doctor named Ernesto 'Che' Guevara, Fidel's brother Raúl, and future *comandantes* Camilo Cienfuegos and Juan Almeida) escaped into the Sierra Maestra where the M-26-7 underground leader in Manzanillo, Celia Sánchez, managed to send them supplies.

On January 17, 1957, the guerrillas scored their first success by overrunning a small army outpost on the south coast. Herbert L Matthews of the *New York Times* interviewed Castro in the Sierra Maestra on February 17, 1957, bringing his group to the attention of the American public for the first time. Matthews portrayed Castro as a romantic hero, winning him a degree of popularity in the US and limiting the amount of overt military support US officials could provide to Batista. In March 1957 Frank País sent 52 new recruits from

Santiago de Cuba and the rebel army's strength grew.

On March 13, 1957, university students belonging to the Directorio Revolucionario attacked the Presidential Palace in Havana in an unsuccessful attempt to assassinate Batista. Batista had learned of the attack beforehand and concentrated his defenses on the palace's top floor which could only be reached by an elevator. The attackers fought their way into the building and reached Batista's office on the second floor but were unable to proceed as the elevator had been blocked. Batista's troops soon surrounded the building and many of the attackers were shot trying to escape down the marble stairway. Of the 35 students

A young Fidel Castro organized revolutionary activities from headquarters in the Sierra Maestra.

who attacked the palace, 32 were killed. In a simultaneous assault, members of the Directorio captured Radio Reloj and broadcast news of the dictator's overthrow, but they were also killed as they came out of the building. After this episode Batista's men rounded up and murdered anyone vaguely connected with the incident, as well as many other political opponents. Echeverría was killed and Batista's reprisals pushed most opponents of the dictatorship toward Castro's M-26-7.

On May 28, 1957, the M-26-7 overwhelmed 53 Batista soldiers at the army post in El Uvero and captured badly needed supplies. On July 30, Frank País was trapped in Santiago de Cuba and shot. Yet reinforcements from the cities continued to trickle in and by the end of 1957 Castro was able to establish a fixed headquarters at La Plata, high up in the Sierra Maestra. Radio Rebelde began broadcasting from La Plata in February 1958, and in March Raúl Castro led a party of rebels into the Sierra de Cristal on the north coast of Oriente, where they set up a second front.

In April 1958 a general strike failed to bring Batista down, largely because the Cuban Communist Party (PSP) refused to cooperate. In fact, the Communist Party provided no support to the rebels until mid-1958, when they seemed to be winning. In May Batista sent an army of 10,000 into the Sierra Maestra to liquidate Castro's 300 armed guerrillas. By August this advance had been defeated and a great quantity of arms captured by the rebels, a crucial turning point of the revolution. After Batista's offensive fizzled, Castro sent columns led by Che Guevara and Camilo Cienfuegos to set up additional fronts in Las Villas Province, which they reached in October and November after marches of incredible endurance. They planned for Guevara to capture Santa Clara and cut Cuba in two, while Cienfuegos pushed west into Pinar del Río, and Fidel and Raúl Castro encircled Santiago de Cuba. Ever conscious of Cuban history, Castro was merely repeating the westward drive of Máximo Gómez and Antonio Maceo in 1895.

In the Sierra del Escambray of central Cuba, Guevara and Cienfuegos formed a united front with guerrillas from the Directorio Revolucionario. Road and rail links across the country were cut, and when Batista's troops tried to turn back these rebels in November, his soldiers were defeated. The army's weakness was becoming evident and on November 30, 1958, Castro's column took the town of Guisa near Bayamo after a pitched battle. On December 28 Guevara's men advanced on Santa Clara and the next day they captured an armored train Batista had sent to reinforce the city. Two days later the city fell to the rebels despite the 3000 Batista troops stationed there.

At 9 pm on December 31 Batista's general in Santiago de Cuba warned the dictator that the city was about to fall, so at 2 am on January 1, 1959, Batista fled to the Dominican Republic, which was then ruled by fellow dictator Rafael Trujillo. (Batista took with him US$40 million in government funds and died in comfortable exile in Spain in 1973.) To prevent opportunists from stepping into the vacuum, Guevara and Cienfuegos immediately set out for Havana, which they reached on January 2. Castro's column had entered Santiago de Cuba the night before, as workers all across Cuba responded to his call for a general strike. Right up until the end, US Ambassador Earl T Smith had maintained close ties with Batista.

The Socialist Revolution

On January 5, 1959, the Cuban presidency was assumed by Manuel Urrutia, a judge who had defended the M-26-7 prisoners during the 1953 Moncada trials. Castro entered Havana on January 8 and on February 16 he was named prime minister. Among the first acts of the revolutionary government were cuts in rents and electricity rates, and racial discrimination was abolished.

In April 1959 Castro made a private visit to Washington to address a gathering of the National Press Club. So as not to have to meet the Cuban leader, President Eisenhower (whose knowledge of Latin American affairs was negligible) made a point of leaving on a golfing holiday and Vice President Richard Nixon received Castro at the White House. Nixon accused Castro of being a Communist or under the influence of Communists, something Castro had always denied. Castro later observed that the Americans were far more concerned about possible Communist infiltration into his administration than in finding out what he planned to do to reform Cuba. After their one-hour meeting Nixon set in motion a process of anti-Castro subversion that eventually led to the Bay of Pigs.

Back in Cuba, most of 1959 was devoted to the promised agrarian reform. In May all estates over 400 hectares were nationalized during the First Agrarian Reform with the holdings of large US companies such as the United Fruit Company directly affected. The first half of 1959 also saw revolutionary groups supported by Cuba launch unsuccessful campaigns against undemocratic regimes in Panama, Nicaragua, and the Dominican Republic. In July 1959 President Urrutia resigned after criticizing the agrarian reforms, and he was replaced by Osvaldo Dorticós, an M-26-7 leader from Cienfuegos.

In October 1959 Huber Matos, the government's military chief of Camagüey, attempted a counterrevolutionary coup, and Cuban émigrés from Miami provoked Castro by flying a B-25 bomber over Havana. In response to these events, Castro formed a popular militia to defend the revolution. Soon after there was a purge of the judicial system, and many judges and lawyers left the country. CIA-backed guerrillas began operating in the Sierra de Escambray in central Cuba around this time.

Meanwhile Cuba's economic problems mounted as thousands of professionals, managers, and technicians who didn't share Castro's vision of a new society left the country for exile in Miami. As relations with the US deteriorated due to the land

MARCH 13, 1957
University students attack Presidential Palace and attempt to assassinate Batista

JANUARY 1, 1959
Batista flees Havana for the Dominican Republic

JANUARY 2, 1959
Che Guevara and Camilo Cienfuegos enter Havana

JANUARY 8, 1959
Castro enters Havana

OCTOBER TO DECEMBER 19[?]
Che Guevara marches from Sierra Maestra to Santa Clar[a] captures Santa Clara

HAVANA

Havana

Matanzas

Matanzas

Las Villas

Santa Clara

GULF OF MEXICO

Pinar del Río

Pinar del Río

Playa Larga

Cienfuegos

Sierra del Escambray

Bay of Pigs

APRIL 17, 1961
Invasion by US-backed Cuban émigrés

Isla de la Juventud

1953 to 1955
Castro and other Moncada rebels held at Presidio Modelo

SEPTEMBER 5, 1957
Abortive naval revolt against Batista

1960 to 1965
Counterrevolutionary gangs operate in Sierra del Escambra[y]

CARIBBEAN SEA

seizures, Cuba made overtures to the Soviet Union to provide a balance. In February 1960 Soviet Vice Premier Anastas Mikoyan visited Cuba at the head of a trade delegation. Important contracts were signed and the USSR agreed to send technicians to replace some of those who had left for the US.

On March 4, 1960, the French ship *Coubre,* bearing a cargo of Belgian arms, blew up mysteriously in Havana harbor killing 81 people and wounding 200 more. CIA-backed émigrés were accused of being behind the sabotage and relations with the US declined further. Two weeks later President Eisenhower authorized the CIA to train and arm a counterrevolutionary force to overthrow the Castro government. These provocations led Cuba to resume diplomatic relations with the Soviet Union in May 1960.

A new crisis erupted in June 1960 when refineries in Cuba owned by Texaco, Standard Oil, and Shell bowed to US pressure and refused to refine Soviet petroleum rather than the Venezuelan crude they

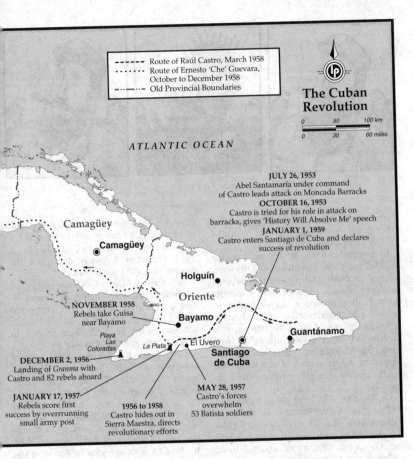

Route of Raúl Castro, March 1958
Route of Ernesto 'Che' Guevara, October to December 1958
Old Provincial Boundaries

The Cuban Revolution

0   50   100 km
0   30   60 miles

ATLANTIC OCEAN

JULY 26, 1953
Abel Santamaría under command of Castro leads attack on Moncada Barracks

OCTOBER 16, 1953
Castro is tried for his role in attack on barracks, gives 'History Will Absolve Me' speech

JANUARY 1, 1959
Castro enters Santiago de Cuba and declares success of revolution

Camagüey
● Camagüey

Holguín ●

Oriente

NOVEMBER 1958
Rebels take Guisa near Bayamo

Bayamo ●

Guantánamo ●

Playa Las Coloradas

La Plata   El Uvero

Santiago de Cuba

DECEMBER 2, 1956
Landing of *Granma* with Castro and 82 rebels aboard

JANUARY 17, 1957
Rebels score first success by overrunning small army post

1956 to 1958
Castro hides out in Sierra Maestra, directs revolutionary efforts

MAY 28, 1957
Castro's forces overwhelm 53 Batista soldiers

had been purchasing from their own subsidiaries at inflated prices. Two weeks later these companies were nationalized. After this, Cuba was dependent on the USSR for its fuel and the degree of economic leverage the US could apply diminished sharply.

On July 6 President Eisenhower cut 700,000 tons from the Cuban sugar quota, but a few days later the USSR offered to buy any sugar the US rejected. This clumsy US bullying greatly strengthened Castro's position, as he could now present himself as a defender of Cuban sovereignty against US aggression.

In August 1960 the Cuban government nationalized the American-owned telephone and electricity companies and 36 sugar mills, including US$800 million in US assets. The outraged Americans quickly pushed through a resolution by the Organization of American States (OAS) condemning 'extra-continental' (Soviet) intervention in the Western Hemisphere, to which Cuba responded in September 1960 by establishing diplomatic relations with

Mission: Assassinate Fidel   Method: Exploding cigar   Result: ¿¡Viva Fidel?!

Communist China and issuing a call for other Latin American countries to throw off US neocolonial control.

In September 1960 the Committees for the Defense of the Revolution (CDR) were formed to consolidate grassroots support for the revolution, and later these neighborhood bodies played a decisive role in health, education, social, and voluntary labor campaigns. Also in September, at a meeting of the United Nations in New York, Soviet Premier Nikita Khrushchev agreed to supply arms to Cuba to defend itself against émigré groups based in the US.

On October 13, 1960, most banks and 382 major Cuban-owned firms were nationalized, and the next day an Urban Reform Law nationalized rental housing. On October 19, 1960, a partial trade embargo was imposed on Cuba by Washington, to which Cuba responded five days later by nationalizing all remaining US businesses in the country. In effect, the Cold War politicians in Washington, DC, had driven Castro and the revolution straight into the arms of the Soviet Union.

Conflict with the USA

By January 1961 the US embassy in Havana had become the crux of destabilization attempts against Cuba, so Castro ordered the embassy to reduce its staff from 300 to the same number then serving at the Cuban embassy in Washington (11 persons). The US broke off diplomatic relations with Cuba and promptly banned US citizens from traveling to Cuba. In March 1961 President Kennedy abolished the remaining Cuban sugar quota.

Since the middle of 1960 several CIA operations had been attempting to assassinate and/or overthrow Castro, supported by a budget of US$13 million. Fantastic schemes were hatched, such as one to make Castro's beard fall out by using a powder planted in his shoes and another involving an exploding cigar. The US mafia was offered US$150,000 plus expenses to 'eliminate' Castro, but even the mafia bosses were unable to find anyone willing to take the risk. Antidemocratic elements were at work in Washington, and it's significant that E Howard Hunt Jr, the CIA operator who helped plan the catastrophic Bay of Pigs invasion, was later a key player in the equally disastrous Watergate burglary that brought down Richard Nixon.

The most famous US aggression against Cuba began on April 14, 1961, when some 1400 Cuban émigrés trained by the CIA in Florida and Guatemala set sail in six ships from Puerto Cabeza, Nicaragua. Nicaraguan dictator Luis Somoza saw them off and requested that they bring back a few hairs from Fidel's beard. The next day planes from Nicaragua bombed Cuban airfields, but they failed to eliminate the Cuban Air Force. On April 16, during a speech honoring the seven Cuban airmen killed in the raids, Castro proclaimed the socialist nature of the Cuban revolution for the first time.

The next day the invaders landed at Playa Girón and Playa Larga in the Bay of Pigs (Bahía de Cochinos in Spanish). Cuban planes immediately attacked their supply ships, sinking two and forcing the rest to withdraw, leaving the troops stranded on the beaches without most of their equipment. A total of 11 counterrevolutionary aircraft were shot down, including all of the B-26 bombers flown from Nicaragua that day. Castro took personal charge of the revolutionary forces moving against the 'mercenaries,' and within 72 hours the counterrevolutionaries at the beachheads surrendered after about 200 of them had been killed. President Kennedy had allowed the US Navy to escort the invading ships to Cuba, but direct US military involvement in Cuba was further than he was willing to go and he canceled US air cover during the landings. (This crucial decision may have cost him his life. Observers such as filmmaker Oliver Stone suspect that right-wing Cuban exiles embittered by Kennedy's 'betrayal' and fearful that he was preparing to make peace with Castro could have been involved in the 1963 assassination. A book titled *ZR Rifle* by Claudia Furiati, published by Australia's Ocean Press, provides disturbing evidence of CIA involvement in the plot to kill the president.) Eventually 1197 of the men captured at the Bay of Pigs were 'ransomed' by the US for US$53 million in food and medicine.

During his 1961 May Day speech, Fidel Castro reaffirmed that the Cuban Revolution was socialist, and on December 1, 1961, he declared that he had been a Marxist-Leninist since his university days. He claimed that he had concealed his Communist beliefs to avoid damaging the chances of success of the revolution. In his book *Castro*, American biographer Peter Bourne argues that this was mostly an attempt to outflank members of the old Communist Party who were occupying increasingly important positions in the administration and a ploy to ensure Soviet support in Cuba's confrontation with the US. Bourne and others such as British historian Hugh Thomas say that Castro was forced into his Marxist-Leninist position by the pressure of events. Bourne sees Castro as a Cuban nationalist of the school of José Martí whose first concerns were Cuban independence and social justice. If he had to become a Communist to survive, so be it. As a bonus Castro received the full support of thousands of disciplined Communist Party militants in carrying out his reforms.

Playing the superpowers off against one another certainly did keep Cuba afloat in a hostile environment for three decades, and the experience in Chile from 1970 to 1973 seems to indicate that it's impossible to carry out a genuine social revolution in Latin America with an intact military and parliamentary opposition subject to outside manipulation. Had Castro allowed free elections, a free press, an independent judiciary, and all the other checks and balances of modern democracy to continue after 1961, his social revolution would probably have failed.

After their stinging defeat at the Bay of Pigs, the Americans tried to put Cuba in quarantine. They declared a full trade embargo in June 1961 and in January 1962 managed to have Cuba expelled from the Organization of American States, followed by OAS economic sanctions. However, many moderate Latin American leaders felt uncomfortable joining the US crusade against Cuba, given the long history of US interventions south of the border. America's closest neighbors, Mexico and Canada, who understood the idiosyncrasies of US foreign policy better than anyone else, refused to bow to American pressure to sever diplomatic relations with Cuba, as did many others.

By the middle of 1961, inventories in Cuba had been exhausted and the country was facing shortages of almost everything. Rationing began in March 1962. That month, when the Soviets failed to respond promptly to Cuba's bid to join the Socialist bloc (with the assurance of full military and economic aid such status would imply), Castro launched a purge of old Communist Party officials to convince Moscow that he was in charge and that socialism had been achieved through his revolution and not through the working class led by the Party, as envisioned in classical Marxism. All revolutionary groups in Cuba were merged into a single National Directorate of the Integrated Revolutionary Organizations.

In April 1962 Khrushchev decided to install missiles in Cuba to use as bargaining chips in the Soviet Union's ongoing rivalry with the US. The Berlin Wall had been erected in August 1961 and US attempts to destabilize East Germany through Berlin were as much a bone in the Soviet throat as Cuba had become for the Americans. Castro only wanted short-range missiles capable of hitting Miami, a sufficient deterrent against invasion in his eyes, but Khrushchev sent medium-range missiles capable of striking anywhere in the US. Even though the US had surrounded the Soviet Union with far more powerful and numerous missiles soon after WWII, Washington objected strongly to receiving the same treatment.

On October 22, 1962, President Kennedy ordered the US Navy to stop Cuba-bound Soviet ships in international waters and to carry out searches for missiles. This led to the Cuban Missile Crisis, which brought the world closer to the brink of nuclear war than it has ever been. Only after receiving a secret assurance from Kennedy that Cuba would not be invaded did Khrushchev defuse the crisis on October 28 by ordering the missiles dismantled. The crisis had a sobering effect on superpower relations, and a year later the US and the USSR signed a treaty banning nuclear testing in the atmosphere. Khrushchev's decision to withdraw the missiles without consulting or even informing Castro infuriated him, and in Moscow Khrushchev's climb down was interpreted as a sign of weakness, which would lead to his fall from power two years later.

Shortly after the missile crisis the US focused on new military adventures in Vietnam, and largely forgot Cuba. In April 1963 Kennedy ordered the CIA to stop financing the attacks of exile groups on Cuba.

Building Socialism

During the first decade of the revolution Cuba's economy was run on a trial-and-error basis marked by inconsistency, disorganization, falls in production, declining quality, and growing bureaucracy. As president of the National Bank and later as minister of industries, Che Guevara had pushed for centralization and moral rather than material incentives for workers, but these proved ineffective. Inexperience and the departure of so many trained people took their toll.

In August 1963 some 10,000 medium-size farms were taken over in the Second Agrarian Reform which fixed maximum private holdings at 65 hectares. Over two-thirds of Cuban farmland was now held by the state.

In 1968 Cuba underwent a mini Cultural Revolution or 'Great Revolutionary Offensive,' in which some 55,000 surviving small businesses and holdings were nationalized, and self-employment and private trading were banned. Bureaucrats were assigned to agricultural work in the countryside, while military officers filled posts in government and the economy. Self-defense brigades of workers were formed in the factories and on state farms. Of course, production sagged and the shortages became worse than ever.

Despite massive Soviet aid the Cuban economy languished during the late 1960s, and the effort to produce 10 million tons of sugar in 1970 almost led to economic breakdown as the many consumer scarcities were multiplied by the overemphasis on sugar. After this failure more attention was placed on careful economic planning and the sugar harvest was increasingly mechanized.

Conditions improved slowly during the 1970s as a new generation of technicians and managers dedicated to the revolution graduated from school to replace those who had left for the US. Half of Cuba's 6000 doctors left the country during the early '60s, but by 1974 the number was back up to 9000 doctors.

After 1970 the personal style gave way to the planned style both in economics and in the political sphere with closer ties to the Soviet Union. In 1972 Castro visited every country in Eastern Europe and soon after Cuba was admitted to the CMEA or Comecon, the Soviet-led Council for Mutual Economic Assistance, resulting in debt relief and increased prices for Cuban exports. An unprecedented Soviet aid package was announced in early 1973. However, the economic planning was done in a centralized and arbitrary way. Trade with the Soviet bloc gradually increased from 65% of the total in the early 1970s to 87% in 1988, a degree of dependence which is costing the country dearly today.

In 1975 the first congress of the Communist Party of Cuba approved a process known as institutionalization. A third Cuban constitution was drawn up to replace the Ley Fundamental (Fundamental Law) enacted in February 1959. This was approved by referendum in February 1976 and Fidel Castro replaced Osvaldo Dorticós as president. To decentralize decision-making on local issues, the government increased the number of provinces from six (Pinar del Río, La Habana, Matanzas, Las Villas, Camagüey, and Oriente) to the present 14 in 1975. An actual Soviet system was installed in Cuba.

In 1975 the OAS sanctions against Cuba were lifted and about the same time the first Canadian tour groups began arriving in Cuba (many of them led by the author of this book).

Cuban Internationalism

After the US defeat at the Bay of Pigs, the Kennedy administration launched an 'Alliance for Progress' that channeled economic aid to Latin American countries to counter Cuban attempts to export revolution. Unfortunately, this coincided with a period when many democratic Latin American governments were being overthrown by military coups, and by 1964 the time looked ripe for a continentwide revolution. Both Castro and the legendary Ernesto 'Che' Guevara began actively supporting guerrilla movements in both Latin America and Africa.

In 1965 Guevara participated in guerrilla actions in Zaire, and some 1000 Cuban troops were sent to the Congolese Republic to support a socialist regime. By 1966 Cuban advisors were in Guinea and assistance was being given to rebels fighting Portuguese colonialism in Angola and Mozambique. The Tricontinental Conference in Havana in January 1966 firmly established Cuba as a leader of revolution throughout the Third World.

In November 1966 Guevara personally launched a guerrilla campaign in southeast Bolivia, but the local Communist Party failed to support it. Guevara had hoped Bolivia would be the first step in the liberation of the entire continent, as Simón Bolívar had liberated South America from Spain in the 1820s. In panic, the US sharply increased military aid to the South American dictators, and on October 9, 1967, Guevara was captured by Bolivian troops and murdered in the presence of US advisors. After Guevara's death Cuban interest in Latin American revolution subsided. Cuban support for 'terrorism' had dampened the country's relations with the rest of Latin America and contributed to its isolation.

Cuban involvement in Africa ran deeper. Angola was due to become independent from Portugal on November 11, 1975, but just a month before that date, South Africa sent 10,000 troops into the country with US support to install a client regime. In response, Cuba dispatched 18,000 soldiers to Angola to defend the Marxist MPLA of Agostinho Neto (an old friend of Castro's). The South Africans had not expected much opposition and were only lightly armed, and the Cubans drove them back, the first important military setback ever suffered by the apartheid regime.

This Cuban victory was applauded throughout the Third World, and when the Non-Aligned Movement met in Sri Lanka a year later, they decided that their 1979 meeting would be in Havana, which meant that Castro would be the movement's president for three years. Since the 1960s Cuba had been attempting to balance its reliance on the Soviet Union by participating in the Non-Aligned Movement, and the invitation to host the 1979 summit and chair the movement from 1979 to 1982 was a great victory.

In late 1977 Cuba sent 17,000 troops to Ethiopia to fight an invasion of the Ogaden region by US-backed forces from Somalia. This ill-considered move undertaken at Soviet behest soured relations with the Carter administration, and beginning in 1980 the Cuban troops were pulled out of Ethiopia. After an agreement between Cuba, South Africa, and Angola in December 1988, the 50,000 Cuban troops then present in Angola were also withdrawn, and in 1990 Namibia became independent of South Africa (a stipulation of the agreement). Over 2000 Cubans died in Angola and in July 1991 Nelson Mandela visited Cuba to demonstrate his gratitude for the pivotal role this small country had played in the defeat of apartheid.

In February 1973 Cuba and the US signed a reciprocal agreement on the return of hijackers in which both countries promised to punish anyone attempting to launch attacks on the territory of the other. On September 1, 1977, the US established an interests section in Havana and Cuba opened one in Washington. A restoration of diplomatic relations seemed to be in the offing when anti-Communist hard-liner Zbigniew Brzezinski, President Carter's national security advisor, scuttled the talks.

After the US intervention in Grenada in October 1983 large quantities of arms were distributed to Cuban factories, collective farms, schools, and neighborhood committees for use in the event of a US invasion, reducing Cuba's reliance on the professional army. No other country in Latin America would have dared do such a thing.

Communism in Crisis

By the mid-1980s the inefficiencies of Cuba's Soviet-style economy had become obvious, as quality was sacrificed to meet production quotas set by central planners, and ordinary citizens were alienated from government by the vertical command structure. In 1986 a process known as the 'rectification of errors' began which attempted to reduce bureaucracy and allow more decision-making at local levels. In 1989 an anticorruption campaign led to the highest levels as General Arnaldo Ochoa Sánchez, a hero of the war in Angola, was tried for complicity in drug trafficking and sentenced to death.

In the middle of the rectification process came the collapse of Eastern European communism in 1989. As trade and credits dried up, President Castro declared a five-year *período especial* austerity program in August 1990. For almost three decades Cuba had adhered closely to Soviet foreign policy, to the extent of endorsing the invasion of Czechoslovakia in 1968 and tilting toward the USSR in its conflict with China. Soviet economic subsidies in the form of above-market prices for Cuban exports totaled around US$5 billion a year, and the loss of this support was a disaster to which Cuba is still trying to adjust.

In late 1991 Russia announced that their 11,000 military advisors and technicians in Cuba would be withdrawn. The US refused to do likewise and thousands of US troops remain at the Guantánamo naval base in eastern Cuba. The US tightened the noose around Cuba with the 1992 Torricelli Act, which forbids foreign subsidiaries of US companies from trading with Cuba and bans ships that have called at Cuban ports from US ports for six months. Ninety percent of the trade banned by this malicious law consisted of food, medicine, and medical equipment. (Despite the withdrawal of its military personnel, Russia continues to operate a powerful tracking station in Cuba capable of monitoring most radio transmissions from the US. In exchange for use of this facility Russia provides

A charismatic speaker, President Castro has extolled the virtues of Communism but conceded greater individual economic freedom.

spare parts for Cuba's large arsenal of Soviet-era military equipment.)

In October 1991 at the Fourth Congress of the Cuban Communist Party in Santiago de Cuba, President Castro declared that he would remain loyal to Communism and that ideological concessions could endanger the revolution. Economic reforms, however, were not ruled out. In December 1991 the National Assembly removed references to Marxism-Leninism from the Cuban Constitution, and although state socialism has not been renounced, the ideals of José Martí and economic survival now take precedence over the dogma of the founding fathers of Soviet Communism. Also in 1991 Rapid Response Brigades were organized to give ordinary Cubans a chance to actively oppose the sort of counterrevolutionary demonstrations that had led to the overthrow of Communist regimes in East Germany, Czechoslovakia, Romania, and the Soviet Union.

However, the strain of the 'special period' was bringing Cuba to the breaking point, and in a 1993 speech to mark the 40th anniversary of the attack on Moncada, President Castro announced that henceforth individual Cubans would be allowed to possess US dollars. In August 1993 the constitution was amended to allow Cubans to hold foreign currency, to open dollar bank accounts, and to spend cash dollars at hard currency shops. In September 1993 self-employment in over 100 trades was legalized. Taxes on dollar incomes and profits were announced in August 1994, and in October farmers markets were opened. In September 1995 a law was approved allowing foreign companies to run wholly owned businesses and possess real estate in Cuba, even though the Cuban state was to continue to control the workforce. Previously only joint ventures with state-owned companies had been permitted.

These reforms have inevitably led to the reemergence of class differences in Cuba as those with dollars gain access to goods and services out of reach to other Cubans. Many Cubans are desperate for dollars and prostitutes known as *jineteras* (jockeys) have reappeared on Havana's Malecón. Cuban émigrés returning for visits from the US find themselves treated like royalty for the dollars in their wallets. Many of the nouveau riche are black marketeers or the relatives of those who abandoned their country, and this has fostered much resentment. People who have loyally supported the revolution over the years have been impoverished. Yet the changes have relieved some of the pressure for even greater change and have given Cuba's socialist system a chance of survival. And unlike many far wealthier countries facing financial crises, not a single school, hospital, senior home, or kindergarten has been closed and Cuba's undeniable achievements in health, education, and sport have not been sacrificed.

Cuba was extremely fortunate to have built a merchant marine of its own in the '60s and '70s; during the two decades after 1959 the total tonnage of Cuban ships was multiplied nine times. Without these ships the collapse of the Soviet Union and the withdrawal of Soviet shipping would have been catastrophic for Cuba.

Recent US Policy

The prickly question of Cuban-American relations continues to hang over both countries like a dark cloud. The USA and Cuba are natural trading partners, and the anachronistic US embargo has deprived US companies of numerous opportunities to do business in Cuba. Washington's travel restrictions alone cost US tour companies, travel agencies, airlines, and hotel and catering chains billions of dollars a year in lost tourism revenues. By giving firms from other western countries an early start in investing in Cuba, the current US embargo will probably be a key factor limiting US economic domination of post-Castro Cuba.

It's hard to think of a foreign policy area where US politicians have gotten it wrong so consistently for so long.

There's little doubt that US government policy has greatly strengthened the Castro regime, both by accepting most of the opposition as political refugees and by making it easy for Castro to present himself as a Cuban nationalist struggling against a hostile neighbor. Of course, the 5911 outstanding claims against Cuba by US investors totaling US$1.8 billion (or US$5.6 billion with interest) will have to be considered in any settlement, but Cuba also has legitimate damage claims against the US stemming from Washington's illegal interference in Cuba's trade with third countries.

Immediately after the collapse of the Soviet Union in 1991 US policy toward Cuba was based on the assumption that without Soviet support the Castro government would soon topple and that all that was required was a tightening of the economic screws and a little patience. Yet by 1993 the effects of the Soviet withdrawal had bottomed out and a year later the Cuban economy again began to grow. The economic reforms provided an outlet for those who felt oppressed by state ownership and the number of joint ventures with Canadian, European, and Latin American companies increased.

The prospect of Castro's 'Communist' government actually managing to survive and of economic relations with the US eventually being renewed filled the embittered Miami exiles and their right-wing political allies with horror. Thus the hawkish chairman of the Senate Foreign Relations Committee, Jesse Helms, and Congressmember Dan Burton drafted legislation to allow US investors to take legal action in the American courts against foreign companies utilizing their confiscated property in Cuba. The executives of such companies are refused entry to the US. The bill also prevents any US president from lifting the embargo until a transitional government is in place in Havana

'Hey Imperialists, we have absolutely no fear of you!'

and requires US representatives to international financial organizations to oppose loans to Cuba.

The Helms-Burton Bill was rejected by most moderate American politicians, including President Clinton, as prejudicial to US interests. They recognized that overt US interference in the trade and investment practices of friendly countries could have serious repercussions and that US voters were more concerned with issues such as illegal immigration of the kind likely to be unleashed by a political upheaval in Cuba. Clinton indicated that he would veto Helms-Burton unless it were softened.

With their political influence in Washington dwindling, extremist elements in the Cuban exile community adopted desperate measures, and one outfit called 'Brothers to the Rescue' began provocative incursions into Cuban territory. Brothers' original mission had been to rescue Cuban refugees at sea, but after the flow of rafters was effectively stopped in May 1995, Brothers turned to more direct action. On July 13, 1995, the Cuban coast guard stopped a flotilla of 12 boats, six planes, and two helicopters from entering Cuban waters, but one plane managed to slip through and buzzed Havana's Malecón. In September a second flotilla fizzled after one of the boats sank off Key West. On January 9 and 13, 1996, planes sent from Florida by Brothers dropped thousands of anti-government leaflets on Havana. The Cuban government issued public and private warnings that unless the flights ceased those responsible would face serious consequences. Events came to a head on February 24, 1996, when two Cessna aircraft were rashly shot down by Cuban jets. Brothers claimed the planes were over international waters at the time, but Cuba insisted that they had entered a forbidden zone in spite of prior radio warnings.

In the hysteria that followed, the Helms-Burton Bill was swiftly passed by the US Congress and signed into law on March 12, 1996, by a wobbly President Clinton. American presidents have always looked upon Cuba as a domestic political issue, and Clinton couldn't afford to appear 'weak' in an election year. By hastily signing legislation he knew to be flawed, Clinton was merely continuing the American tradition of reacting to events in Cuba instead of trying to find accommodation with its southern neighbor.

The conditions attached to Helms-Burton make it highly unlikely that Cuban-American relations will improve for a very long time, or at least as long as Fidel Castro or any immediate successor is in power. A majority of Cubans will probably be willing to put up with the present hardships rather than face an uncertain future under renewed US control. In Eastern Europe the disillusionment with primitive capitalism and shock-treatment economics has been reflected in a return to power through the ballot box of former Communists, a lesson not lost on Cubans.

Internationally these US attempts to legislate for the world have been widely condemned, and by employing big-stick

Human Rights in Cuba

The Cuban government has been criticized over its human rights record, and it's a fact that many individuals who would be considered 'prisoners of conscience' in the western context are presently being held in Cuban jails simply for voicing opinions critical of Cuba's present leadership or for attempting to organize a political opposition. Stiff prison sentences are handed out at summary trials. While this situation has to be condemned, it must also be viewed in the context of a small country perpetually threatened with destabilization by a powerful neighbor.

Unlike many other Latin American countries, there are no 'death squads' in Cuba carrying out extrajudicial murders, and lethal 'disappearances' off the streets are unknown. Cases of torture during detention or sexual abuse of women by the security forces are also extremely rare, if they have ever happened at all. Police violence or official corruption would likely be severely punished if they came to light. Compared to countries like Colombia, Peru, Brazil, Guatemala, and Venezuela, Cuba's human rights record is good.

When questioned about human rights, Cuban officials usually point to the many social rights enjoyed by Cubans and question the sincerity of agencies, such as the International Monetary Fund, which impoverish millions through crippling austerity programs while firing human-rights bullets at selected Third World governments they do not control. Despite all its problems, Cuba's health and educational facilities are more accessible to the average citizen than those of many rich countries including the US. Basic human rights such as these are often overlooked by human-rights activists. ■

Canadian government has introduced legislation allowing Canadian companies to claim damages from anyone filing suit against them in an American court under Helms-Burton. Many Latin American leaders view Cuba as a bulwark against unimpeded US hegemony in the Western Hemisphere, which is why some of them have been quietly backing Fidel Castro.

Emigration Yesterday & Today

After the nationalization of all industries and businesses, much of the top managerial and technical staff of the affected companies left for exile in the US. From 1959 until mid-1962 Cubans could leave by simply boarding the regular twice-daily flight to Miami, and some 250,000 did exactly that. From 1965 to 1970 another 250,000 left for the US on special chartered flights. The Cuban Adjustment Act of 1966 declared that any Cuban reaching US territory by any means was eligible for a residence permit.

In April 1980 a third wave of 120,000 refugees reached Miami via the Cuban port of Mariel. These migrants were generally poorer than those who had fled to Florida immediately after the revolution, and the Cuban government even took advantage of the chaotic exodus to send prison inmates and the mentally retarded north. The criminals have done well and they now control the lucrative south Florida drug trade.

In December 1984 Cuba and the US signed an agreement whereby up to 20,000 ordinary Cubans and 3000 former political prisoners and their families a year would be allowed to immigrate legally to the US. In practice, only about 1000 ordinary Cubans received visas each year while the political-prisoner quota was fully used, a deliberate policy of encouraging dissent by rewarding dissidents with admission to the US.

In early August 1994 a new crisis erupted after several boats were hijacked to Florida in separate incidents that cost two Cuban soldiers their lives. Miami radio stations beamed inflammatory messages at Cuba, leading to rioting in Havana and a surge in illegal immigration to the US.

tactics out of fashion since the 1930s, the US government has won much sympathy for Cuba. In November 1995 the United Nations General Assembly voted 117 to three to condemn the US economic embargo against Cuba, the fourth consecutive vote of this kind in four years. The

On August 12, after being accused of using excessive force to block Cubans from departing, President Castro ordered the Cuban coast guard not to stop anyone from leaving Cuba. When this became known some 35,000 Cubans took to the sea on rafts and small boats, and on August 19 President Clinton was forced to rescind the US open-door policy toward illegal Cuban immigration and order that the *balseros* (boat people) be taken to the Guantánamo naval base. Eventually most were admitted to the US.

At present some 1,500,000 Cuban immigrants live in the US, 700,000 of them in southern Florida (about 11 million Cubans remain in Cuba). After 1965 most Cuban Americans realized that they wouldn't be returning home anytime soon and they built new lives for themselves in the US. In large part these population movements, particularly those after 1970, must be viewed as part of a general pattern of migration from Latin America to the US that began during WWII and continues today. Like the Puerto Ricans in New York and the Mexicans in California, most of the Cubans who have traveled north in recent years have done so for economic reasons and not as a result of any personal political persecution (by 1970 about 35% of Puerto Ricans were residents of the mainland USA).

In May 1995 the US government was forced to concede that most of the 1994 arrivals – over half of whom were young men between the ages of 18 and 21 – were in fact economic migrants, and an agreement was signed with Cuba whereby future illegal immigrants intercepted by the US authorities would be returned to Cuba. The US also promised to grant a minimum of 20,000 visas a year to Cubans wishing to immigrate.

GEOGRAPHY

Caught like a cigar between the fingers of Florida and Yucatán, Cuba lies just south of the Tropic of Cancer at the mouth of the Gulf of Mexico. The Atlantic Ocean is to the north and the Caribbean Sea to the south. Havana is 170 km southwest of Key West, Florida, while Pinar del Río Province is 210 km northeast of the Yucatán, Mexico, and Santiago de Cuba is 270 km northeast of Montego Bay, Jamaica. The 77-km-wide Windward Passage separates Cuba from Haiti.

At 110,860 sq km Cuba is almost exactly the same size as Bulgaria and just a bit smaller than the US state of Louisiana or the North Island of New Zealand. You could easily fit Scotland, Northern Ireland, and Wales into this major Caribbean country. Largest and westernmost of the West Indies, Cuba forms part of the Greater Antilles along with Jamaica, Hispaniola (Haiti and the Dominican Republic), and Puerto Rico; the Lesser Antilles consists of the Leeward and Windward Islands to the east. Cuba is three times bigger than the Dominican Republic and nine times larger than Jamaica; in fact, it's almost as big as all the other Caribbean islands combined.

Cuba's 104,945-sq-km main island is the 15th largest island in the world – 1250 km long and between 31 and 191 km wide. The distance from Cabo de San Antonio in the west to Punta de Quemado in the east is about the same as from Paris to Budapest or Miami to Nashville.

Aside from the crocodile-shaped main island, there's also Isla de la Juventud (2200 sq km) and over 4195 low-lying, mostly uninhabited coral cays and islets which together total another 3715 sq km. Offshore island groups include the Archipiélago de los Colorados off northern Pinar del Río, the Archipiélago de Sabana off northern Villa Clara, the Archipiélago de Camagüey off northern Ciego de Ávila, the Archipiélago de los Jardines de la Reina off southern Ciego de Ávila, and the Archipiélago de los Canarreos around Isla de la Juventud. The main island's 5746 km of coastline include many white-sand beaches and the offshore islands have even more.

Forested mountains make up a quarter of Cuba's territory, and fertile plains used for grazing cattle or growing sugar cane account for much of the rest. In Pinar del Río are the eroded *alturas* of the 175-km-long Cordillera de Guaniguanico, which includes the Sierra de los Órganos and the Sierra del Rosario, neither higher than 699 meters. In the center of the country is the medium-height Sierra del Escambray (also known as the Sierra de Guamuhaya), which reaches 1140 meters. To the southeast the generally flat, rolling countryside of Camagüey grows into the rugged mountains of Oriente with Pico Turquino (1972 meters) the highest peak in the Sierra Maestra. Folded upwards in the relatively recent geological past by the clash of tectonic plates, the Sierra Maestra stretches 250 km from Guantánamo Bay west to Cabo Cruz.

The 7200-meter-deep Cayman Trench between Cuba and Jamaica forms the boundary of the North American and Caribbean plates, the collision of which occasionally generates earthquakes affecting Cuba. In comparison, the Great Bahama Bank between Cuba and the Bahamas is relatively shallow. Tectonic movements have tilted the island leading to uplifted limestone cliffs along parts of the north coast and low mangrove swamps on the south. Submerged valleys or *bolsas* (pockets) have created excellent harbors such as those of Cienfuegos, Santiago de Cuba, and Guantánamo.

For geographical purposes, Cuba can be divided into five regions. The Occidental Region from Pinar del Río to Matanzas Province consists of low hills or uplifted coral formations along the north, plains in the middle, and swamps along the south. The Central Region between Santa Clara and Ciego de Ávila centers on a knot of medium-level hills surrounded by plains and swamps. The Camagüey Region is a vast savanna. The Oriental Region, or 'Oriente,' at the eastern end of the island is Cuba's most scenic region with its finest mountains, rivers, and bays. Rich deposits of nickel, iron, and other metals are found in northeastern Holguín Province. Isla de la Juventud, Cuba's fifth region, has been extensively planted with grapefruit trees since the revolution.

Large lakes and rivers do not exist in Cuba, but a number of great reservoirs have been built for irrigation, supplementing the almost unlimited groundwater held in Cuba's limestone bedrock. Some reservoirs such as the Embalse Zaza near Sancti Spíritus and the Embalse Hanabanilla in Villa Clara have been stocked with largemouth bass. Cuba's longest river is the 343-km Cauto north of Bayamo, although it's not navigable by anything bigger than small boats. All the other rivers of this long,

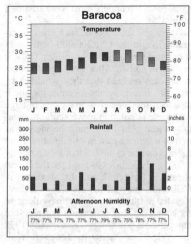

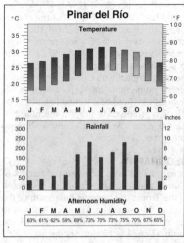

narrow country are minor. Many rivers go underground and some even empty into the ocean below sea level.

CLIMATE

Cuba's pleasant subtropical climate is strongly influenced by the gentle Northeast Tradewinds that shift slightly to the east in summer. Due to the island's long, tapered shape, few places are far from these moderating sea breezes and there are no pronounced seasonal variations in temperature. The only seasons are the rainy summer season (May to October) and the drier winter season (November to April). The mean average temperature in the warmest months (July and August) is 27.4°C, while in the coolest month (February) it's 22.2°C. Except in mountain areas, eastern Cuba is slightly warmer than

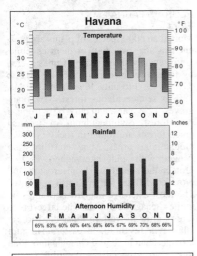

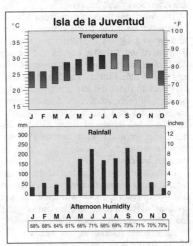

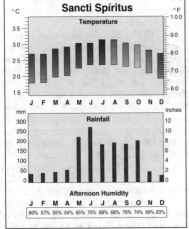

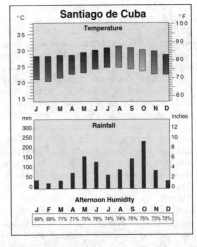

the west. The mean annual temperature is 25.5°C. Humidity ranges from 81% in summer to 79% in winter.

The mean annual rainfall is 1375 mm; in the rainy season, the island receives 1059 mm and in the dry season 316 mm. The rainiest months are September and October. The heaviest rainfall occurs in the east where the mountains catch the prevailing winds off the Atlantic. The rainstorms are often short and heavy.

The hurricane season runs from June to November with the worst storms in September and October. Hurricanes usually form over the Atlantic east of the Lesser Antilles, then move northwest toward Cuba and north into Florida and the Bahamas. Havana and Pinar del Río are generally hit harder and more frequently than the provinces to the east. Such storms are characterized by winds of over 250 km an hour and torrential rain, but they're not life-threatening to persons sheltering in modern buildings.

Though south of Florida and the Bahamas, Cuba is the northernmost of the main Caribbean resorts and in winter it can get cool at night. Frosts are unknown (the lowest temperature ever recorded was 1°C at Alacranes, Matanzas, on January 21, 1971). In the west, most winter rainfall is caused by cold fronts moving southeast from North America and these can create prolonged periods of bad weather. The waters off the Caribbean coast are a few degrees warmer than those on the Atlantic side.

Although there are almost no tides, Cuba's shores are washed by several currents. Driven by the Northeast Tradewinds, the Caribbean Current flows northwest along the island's south coast and into the Gulf of Mexico. Here the waters build up and flow east between Cuba and Florida as the relatively fast Gulf Stream, which continues north along the coast of North America. The Bahamas Current off the Atlantic is squeezed into the narrow channel between the Bahamas and Cuba's north coast to create a strong westbound current that eventually merges with the northbound Gulf Stream. Some of the Bahamas water continues southwest toward Cabo de San Antonio.

Considering these currents and the prevailing winds, it's not hard to understand why sailors find it easier to circumnavigate Cuba counterclockwise. To go clockwise would involve a hard fight against adverse currents and winds all along the north coast east of Havana.

FLORA & FAUNA
Flora
More than 6000 species of plants are present in Cuba, over half of them endemic. Unfortunately, the portion of Cuba covered by forests declined from 90% in 1812 to 54% in 1900 to only 19% today. Of this, 43% is semideciduous forest, 31% mangroves, 12% pines, and only 1.5% tropical rain forest. Semideciduous or tropical green forests are found in rocky or lower mountainous areas. Many coastlines are fringed with spiderlike mangroves that protect the shorelines from erosion and provide a habitat for small fish and birds. The most extensive mangrove swamps lie in the Ciénaga de Zapata. The largest pine forests grow in western Pinar del Río, on Isla de la Juventud, in eastern Holguín Province, and in central Guantánamo. Pine forests are especially susceptible to fire damage and much pine reforestation has been necessary.

The 1000-meter elevation level divides Cuba's vegetation between the low-lying *tierra caliente* (hot zone) and the higher *tierra templada* (temperate zone). Rain forests exist at higher altitudes in the Escambray, Sierra Maestra, and Macizo de Sagua-Baracoa between 500 and 1500 meters. The number of species decreases with the elevation and the trees are spaced farther apart. Since growth continues year-round the grain of the timber does not show annual rings. Original rain-forest species include ebony and mahogany, but today most reforestation is in eucalyptus. Citrus trees have been planted in large numbers in flat areas, and the fast-growing Caribbean pine also does well in Cuba's sandy soil.

Cuba's most characteristic tree is the stately royal palm *(Reistonea regia)* depicted on the country's coat of arms. It's easily distinguished by the green stalk at the top, and there are said to be 20 million royal palms in Cuba reaching up to 40 meters tall. The cork palm *(Microcycas calocoma)* is a living link with the Cretaceous Period (between 65 and 135 million years ago). It's very rare and found mostly in the west. The *palma barrigona* (big belly palm, *Colpothrinax wrightii*) is easily distinguished by its shape.

The *jagüey* is a huge fig tree with aerial roots. The royal poinciana, or flamboyant tree, an exotic import from the Far East, has bright orange and red flowers that bloom around Christmas. The *uva caleta* (sea grape, *Coccoloba uvifera*) is a tree with grapelike fruit found along much of the coast. The *yagruma* tree is easily recognizable for its large leaves, which are green on top and white on the bottom. The agave, or century plant, is found in drier areas. Its long pointed stalks contain a strong fiber called sisal, or heniquen.

All three primary cultures of Cuba – Indian, African, and European – have considered the *ceiba* or *kapok* (silk-cotton tree) sacred silk-cotton tree. It's notable for its wide trunk and billowing top. Buoyant brown fibers obtained from the fruit pods of this tree can be used as stuffing in life preservers, although the fiber's flammability has led to replacement by synthetic fibers.

There are hundreds of species of orchids in Cuba. The national flower is the white *mariposa* (butterfly jasmine).

Fauna

The areas where the endemic fauna is least disturbed are the swamps of southern Matanzas, the mountainous areas, and the offshore islands of the five main archipelagos.

The ubiquitous royal palm

Reptiles & Mammals Apart from the sea creatures, the most abundant representatives of Cuba's fauna are reptiles such as crocodiles, iguanas, lizards, salamanders, sea turtles, and 15 species of nonpoisonous snakes. The crocodiles are restricted to the Ciénaga de Zapata. A survivor of the distant past is the *manjuarí* (alligator gar, *Atractosteus tristoechus)*, a combination of fish and reptile considered a living fossil.

The *majá* is Cuba's largest snake. A relative of the larger anaconda of South America, this boa can grow up to four meters long. It kills its prey by strangulation and is able to swallow objects five times bigger than its mouth. Like other pythons, the majá is an agile tree climber and its excellent eyesight makes up for poor senses of smell and hearing. This primarily nocturnal snake avoids humans.

The largest indigenous land mammal is the *jutía* (tree rat, *Capromys)*, an inoffensive rodent about 60 cm long that lives on tree leaves. Like the iguanas, it survives mostly on offshore islands. Bats are more common throughout the country. The most

The world's smallest bird, the zunzuncito, is about as long as a grasshopper.

notable marine mammal is the manatee, a large seal-like creature that inspired mermaid legends among early sailors.

Several species of scorpions are present in Cuba. Unique to Cuba is the *polimita*, a land snail with delicately colored bands found in Guantánamo and Santiago de Cuba Provinces.

Birds Among the 350 species of birds found in Cuba are the crane, flamingo, fly-catcher, hawk, hummingbird, kingbird, mockingbird, nightingale, owl, parakeet, parrot, pelican, royal thrush, sparrow, warbler, wren, and woodpecker. Prime bird-watching areas include the Península de Guanahacabibes in Pinar del Río, the Ciénaga de Zapata near the Bay of Pigs, the Sierra Maestra, the mountains behind Baracoa, and Isla de la Juventud.

The *tocororo* (Cuban trogon, *Priotelus temnuros*) was selected as the national bird for its red, white, and blue feathers, the colors of the Cuban flag. This forest bird, a member of the quetzal family, has short wings and a long tail, and it can climb trees by using its feet.

Cuba hosts the world's smallest bird, the bee hummingbird (*Mellisuga helenae*), called the *zunzuncito* or *pájaro mosca* (fly bird) by the Cubans. The male weighs only two grams and is just a bit bigger than a grasshopper. In May or June the slightly larger female lays two jellybean-size eggs in a four-cm-wide nest. As the zunzuncito hovers before a flower, extracting nectar with its long bill, its wings beat so fast they're invisible to the human eye. Habitat

destruction has restricted these birds to remote areas such as the Ciénaga de Zapata. The June 1990 issue of *National Geographic* contains several rare photos of the zunzuncito.

The Zapata wren (*Ferminia cerverai*) and Gallinuela de Santo Tomás (*Cyanolimnas cerverai*) are also found only in the swamps of Matanzas' Zapata Peninsula. A much more common Cuban bird is the white cattle egret, which often hitches rides on the backs of cows enjoying the abundant supply of insects found there. *Tiñosas* (turkey vultures) are often visible circling overhead in search of carrion. The green parrot moves into the nests of woodpeckers in trunks of the big belly palm.

National Parks

There's a lot of confusion in Cuba over what constitutes a national park, and you'll often see amusement parks or resort areas such as Parque Baconao near Santiago de Cuba granted that lofty title in Cuban travel brochures. Few if any of the so-called national parks have facilities such as visitor centers, interpretative displays, park maps, camping areas, and marked hiking trails, and no definitive list of Cuban national parks seems to exist.

No doubt this situation will change as Cubans recognize the commercial value of ecotourism. Meanwhile, only the Parque Nacional Ciénaga de Zapata in Matanzas Province, the Gran Parque Nacional Sierra Maestra in Granma, and Parque Nacional Turquino in Santiago de Cuba have some of the characteristics of national parks in other parts of the world.

Four UNESCO-approved biosphere reserves do exist in Cuba: the Reserva Sierra del Rosario and the Reserva Península de Guanahacabibes, both in Pinar del Río Province; Parque Baconao in Santiago de Cuba Province; and the Reserva Cuchillas de Toa in Guantánamo Province. Once again, no uniform management practices or standards apply in these reserves, and as yet what scant development has occurred caters to the needs of organized bus tours. Of course, this lack of services won't hinder fully self-sufficient travelers who like exploring areas untouched by mass tourism. Occasionally you will be charged a stiff entry fee or forced to take along an expensive official guide. (We mention some instances of this and would appreciate having readers bring other cases to our attention.)

GOVERNMENT & POLITICS

The Constitution of February 1976 provides for a 589-member Asamblea Nacional del Poder Popular (National Assembly of People's Power) elected every five years. In July 1992 the constitution was amended to allow direct elections by universal suffrage and secret ballot (previously the National Assembly was elected indirectly by the municipalities). Half of the candidates are nominated by mass organizations, while the other half are chosen by elected municipal delegates from among their ranks (previously all were nominated by Communist Party committees). There's only one candidate for each assembly seat and a negative vote of at least 50% is required to reject a candidate, which makes elections something of a referendum on candidates previously selected.

The National Assembly elects the 31-member Consejo de Estado (Council of State), which has a president, first vice president, five additional vice presidents, and a secretary. This body represents the National Assembly between its twice annual meetings and the Council's president is the head of government and state. The president nominates a 44-member Consejo de Ministros (Council of Ministers), which must be confirmed by the National Assembly.

The only political party is the Partido Comunista de Cuba (PCC), which was formed in October 1965 by merging cadres from the Partido Socialista Popular (the pre-1959 Communist Party founded by Julio Antonio Mella in 1925) and veterans of the guerrilla campaign, including members of Castro's M-26-7 and the Directorio Revolucionario 13 de Marzo. The present party is led by First Secretary Fidel Castro. Every five years, party congresses elect a 225-member Central Committee, which in turn chooses the 26 members of the Political Bureau. The Communist Party of Cuba doesn't run the country, however – the members of the Council of State do that. Consensus is sought in most decision-making, and contrary to popular belief outside Cuba, Castro doesn't decide everything.

The most important mass organizations are the Confederación de Trabajadores Cubanos (CTC), a trade union confederation; the Asociación Nacional de Agricultores Pequeños (ANAP), an association of small private farmers; the Federación de Mujeres Cubanas (FMC), a women's federation founded in 1960; the Unión de Jóvenes Comunistas (UJC), a student group; and the Comités de Defensa de la Revolución (CDR), a neighborhood-watch organization with over seven million members. Frank and open discussions of the economic problems facing the country take place regularly at assemblies of these organizations, and union members have a say in decisions on production targets and investment.

Prior to the provincial and national elections of February 1993 the Miami radio stations broadcast urgent messages to Cuba calling on voters to spoil their ballots as a sign of protest, while Fidel Castro toured the country urging Cubans to approve the entire slate. In the end, 98.8% of Cubans went to the polls and only 7.2% of ballots were blank or spoiled nationwide (14.3% in Havana). Another 10.4% crossed out some of those named, but the rest approved the entire list, an impressive vote of confidence in the present leadership in

difficult times. About a third of those elected were not Communist Party members, and 22.7% of those chosen for the National Assembly were women, a level exceeded only in Scandinavia.

Castro has held the post of President since its inception in 1976, and in 1993 he was reelected for a five-year term. He's also commander-in-chief of the National Defense Council. Raúl Castro serves as first vice-president and minister of the Revolutionary Armed Forces. Despite the economic difficulties, Castro continues to enjoy broad popular support, as demonstrated at a 200,000-strong Havana rally he addressed in August 1994 after disorder provoked by inflammatory radio broadcasts from Miami. You won't find any Cuban streets, schools, or factories named after Castro or any statues of him in public places because living revolutionaries cannot be honored in this way in Cuba.

Cuba is divided into 169 municipalities, including the Special Municipality of Isla de la Juventud (2398 sq km), and 14 provinces: the City of Havana (727 sq km), the Province of Havana (5731 sq km), Pinar del Río (10,925 sq km), Matanzas (11,978 sq km), Villa Clara (8662 sq km), Cienfuegos (4178 sq km), Sancti Spíritus (6744 sq km), Ciego de Ávila (6910 sq km), Camagüey (15,990 sq km), Las Tunas (6589 sq km), Holguín (9301 sq km), Granma (8372 sq km), Santiago de Cuba (6170 sq km), and Guantánamo (6186 sq km). The municipal assemblies are elected by universal suffrage every 2½ years, and these in turn elect their own executive committees. Isla de la Juventud is administered by the central government.

ECONOMY

Until recently Cuba had a centrally planned economy controlled by the government according to policy guidelines laid down by the Communist Party of Cuba. All economic activities except small farming were government operated and all

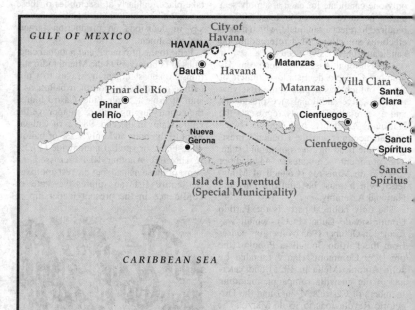

employees worked for the state. There was no direct taxation because resources could be assigned any way the state planners saw fit. State enterprises were not required to make a profit and prices were arbitrary. Full employment was guaranteed and labor productivity was low.

Things began changing in July 1992 when direct foreign investment in joint ventures and other forms of economic association with state enterprises became easier (joint ventures had been possible since 1982, and the first such agreement was signed in 1988). Enterprises created in this way operate on a for-profit basis and are independent of government control, except that state enterprises have the first option to supply raw materials and purchase the products. Joint ventures may also export their own products, and the repatriation of profits and capital is guaranteed. Profits are taxed at 30% and the local payroll is subject to a 25% tax, paid in hard currency. Latin American and Caribbean companies receive preferential treatment in these matters in the name of regional cooperation. The countries with companies most active in joint ventures are Canada, Spain, Panama, Italy, and Mexico, and by the end of 1995 foreign investment in Cuba totaled US$2.1 billion in some 212 joint ventures (compared to only 20 joint ventures operating in 1991). Another 300 new projects are presently under negotiation.

In 1995 the reforms were carried further and it became possible for foreign companies to operate in their own right without creating any joint venture. The biggest investments are in tourism, mining, energy, communications, and agriculture, and the only sectors where investment is not allowed are national defense, health, and education.

Since September 1993 Cuban nationals have been allowed to set up personal or family businesses and private trading by individual Cubans has had a major

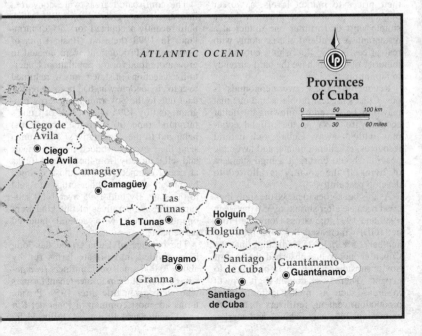

impact in the retail and catering fields. Cuban entrepreneurs are still not allowed to employ other Cubans for wages, although partnerships are permitted. In fact, the government had no choice but to allow self-employment since the joint ventures were authorized to lay off excess workers, bringing unemployment back to Cuba. On January 1, 1996, personal income taxes of between 10% and 50% came into force on all hard-currency earnings (gifts from abroad and pensions are exempt). Given the delicate balance in Cuba today, these reforms are probably irreversible.

Visitors to Cuba often comment on the bare shelves in state-operated stores where Cubans are able to spend pesos and the long queues whenever something is available. This is a result of the artificially low prices these establishments must charge, which are in line with the actual peso wages most state employees still receive (200 pesos a month and up). If state retail outlets and restaurants were to increase their prices to market levels, a worker might have to labor one month to buy a simple shirt or to order one dinner at a restaurant. A parallel dollar economy with real prices is now flourishing but only a minority of Cubans have the hard currency to tap into it.

Reconciling these two economies is now Cuba's biggest problem, and one that may only be solved by allowing the dollar economy to grow as the official economy withers away. Cuba's rich natural resources, excellent climate, and favorable position should ensure it a high standard of living if the country is allowed to develop peacefully.

As this book goes to press, the signs look good because after shrinking 35% between 1989 and 1993, the Gross Domestic Product (GDP) increased 0.7% in 1994 and another 2.5% in 1995, indicating that the Cuban economy has absorbed the loss of Soviet subsidies and is again beginning to expand. There was double-digit growth in areas such as nickel mining, steel production, cement, fertilizers, petroleum extraction, tobacco, fishing, and market gardening; if the troubled sugar industry is excluded from the calculation, Cuba grew 7% in 1995. The peso has been stabilized by tightening the money supply, and the government's budget deficit has been reduced (from 33% of GDP in 1993 to 7.4% in 1994 and only 5% in 1995) by cutting subsidies to loss-making industries and downsizing the bureaucracy.

Agriculture

Prior to the revolution 47% of arable or grazing land was held by only 1% of landowners and 8% of farms occupied 70% of the land. On October 10, 1958, while still fighting in the Sierra Maestra, the rebel army declared that small holdings worked by tenant farmers, sharecroppers, and squatters would become their property. The First Agrarian Reform Law of May 1959 nationalized landed estates *(latifundios)* over 400 hectares, and the Second Agrarian Reform Law of August 1963 expropriated all holdings larger than 65 hectares.

The confiscated areas were converted into state farms *(granjas estatales),* which until recently accounted for 75% of farmland. In 1993 the first 'Basic Units of Cooperative Production' were created to grow more food for the population. Underutilized sections of state farms were turned over to city people who had become redundant due to the government austerity program, and by 1995 almost half of Cuba's farmland (and 90% of its cane fields) belonged to the cooperatives. These units send their excess produce into the towns and sell it directly from the backs of trucks at prices competitive with those charged by private farmers. Other crops are sold to the state. By mid-1995 over 1400 self-supporting cooperatives of this kind were operating, each with several hundred participants.

The balance of Cuba's land has long been divided into private farms run by about 70,000 small-scale farmers *(campesinos)*, many of them former tenant farmers who were given title after 1959. Private farms are most common in Pinar del Río and Guantánamo Provinces, followed by

Sugar Cane

Sugar cane originated on the island of New Guinea in the South Pacific and was widely used in ancient India. The Arabs brought the plant to medieval Spain and the first Spanish explorers carried it to the New World. Sugar cane is initially propagated from cuttings and three crops can be harvested from one planting. After the third harvest the stumps are removed and the field is replanted. The soil must be well drained to avoid root rot and chemical fertilizers are used. The fields are weeded by hand until the cane is high enough to form a canopy (mature cane is over three meters high). About 2000 mm of rainfall is required during the growing season, and cane is harvested in the dry season (January to May). Sugar cane is susceptible to various diseases and pests, and much effort is expended breeding resistant hybrid varieties with ever higher sugar contents. ∎

Sancti Spíritus, Holguín, and Granma. Since October 1994, private farmers can sell their surplus crops (above official production quotas) in public markets for personal profit. A high percentage of state and cooperative land is devoted to sugar production, while small private farmers often specialize in tobacco, coffee, and food production.

The main agricultural product is sugar, and until the early 1990s Cuba produced about seven million metric tons per annum, a level surpassed only by Brazil. Since 1970 mechanization has been widely used in the *zafra* (sugar harvest), and today most cane is cut by mechanical harvesters. Fuel shortages in the early 1990s led to a partial return to manual harvesting, and by 1995 production had fallen to 3.3 million tons, the lowest level in 50 years. In an attempt to reverse this trend, the government obtained US$300 million in foreign financing for its sugar industry in 1996, resulting in a harvest of 4.5 million tons that year. Sugar accounts for about 70% of Cuba's export revenue; it's shipped mostly to Russia and China either crude, refined, or as molasses. The molasses can be made into rum, the cane-juice froth into fertilizer, and the crushed fibers into paper or construction material. Most mills are now fueled by spent fibers, which are burned. The harvesting season for cane is January to May. The government will have to spend millions of dollars modernizing Cuba's dilapidated sugar mills over the next few years.

Other crops include tobacco, coffee, rice, corn, sweet potatoes, beans, and tropical fruit such as oranges, grapefruit, bananas, mangoes, and pineapples. Cattle and pigs account for most livestock. The Zebu (Brahman) breed of cow, resistant to heat but a low milk producer, has been crossed with Holstein bulls imported from Canada to produce an acclimatized breed that is also a good milk producer. Since 1990 curtailed fodder imports from Eastern Europe have downsized the Cuban dairy herd by 50% and slashed milk production by 75%. Due to fuel shortages oxen have partially replaced tractors in the fields.

Unreliable rainfall has long been a problem for Cuban agriculture, but since the revolution numerous dams have been constructed and large areas are irrigated.

Mining

Cuba is rich in mineral ores, especially nickel, cobalt, chrome, copper, tungsten, manganese, and iron. Salt is obtained through the solar evaporation of sea water. About 37% of the world's nickel reserves lie along the coast of northeastern Holguín Province between Mayarí and Moa. The large nickel processing plants at Nicaro and Moa were built by US companies during WWII, but in 1960 these were nationalized and later expanded using inefficient Soviet technology. Since 1990 Canadian mining companies such as Sherritt International have become involved in joint ventures to develop Cuba's mining potential. Much of the nickel is shipped to Sherritt's smelter near Edmonton, Canada, for further refining, and eventually sold in Western Europe by a Bahamas-based marketing company. By 1995 Cuban nickel production had again reached the 1989 level of 40,000 metric tons after sharp drops resulting from the disruption of trade with the former Soviet Union.

Fishing

Fishing is Cuba's third most important primary industry (after sugar and nickel). During the first two decades of the revolution the Cuban fishing fleet increased six times. Havana is the most important fishing port, followed by Surgidero de Batabanó, Santa Cruz del Sur, and Manzanillo. Tuna and hake *(merluza)* are the most important species taken in international waters, while around Cuba there are important shrimp, lobster, and red snapper fisheries.

Industry

Cuba's main industrial products are processed sugar, tobacco (including cigarettes and cigars), nickel, petroleum, chemicals, cement, timber (mahogany), paper, medicines, processed food and drink, textiles, shoes, and other consumer goods. In the construction industry the emphasis has been on new construction rather then renovating older properties.

Cuba's textile industry relies on large quantities of imported cotton, resulting in a clothing shortage reflected in the absence of style. Most Cubans dress any way they can without any nod to fashion and you'll seldom see such a potpourri of styles, often on the same individual. Few women wear bras, and the men often sport the wrong size pants and shirts that are too small.

Biotechnology & Pharmaceuticals

Since 1981 Cuba has plowed tremendous resources into medical high technology, especially in the biotechnology, pharmaceutical, and medical equipment fields, all of which have been given top priority as a means of diversifying the economy. The relative value of raw materials like sugar

and nickel is declining on world markets, and during the next century only countries with some form of high technology will be able to achieve a decent standard of living.

Already the country's advanced pharmaceutical industry earns US$100 million a year selling over 200 products, such as vaccines against meningitis, hepatitis B, and other diseases, on Third World markets not effectively controlled by the western drug cartels. Biotechnology is used in agriculture for mass planting and to produce efficient, disease-resistant varieties. As yet foreign investment in these 'strategic' industries has not been allowed, and this is a prioritized area not subject to the cutbacks of the período especial. The high quality and low production costs indicate that the Cuban pharmaceutical industry could boom if acceptable foreign partners were found.

Tourism

Tourism is Cuba's largest source of foreign exchange. Prior to the revolution Cuba was the leading tourist destination in the Caribbean, and only after Cuban tourism virtually stopped in 1961 did destinations such as Jamaica become popular. International tourism returned to Cuba in 1975, when Canadians on package tours started arriving in large numbers, and since 1990 tourism has become a top priority. The beach resorts of Playas del Este, Varadero, Cayo Largo, Cayo Coco, Playa Santa Lucía, Guardalavaca, Marea del Portillo, and Baconao are already well developed. In fact, Varadero is the largest tourist resort in the Caribbean.

Yet with under a million foreign tourists a year, Cuba is far from inundated. Much smaller countries such as the Bahamas and Puerto Rico receive 10 times as many visitors, and Jamaica and the Dominican Republic each get four times as many. To look at it another way, Bahamas gets 14 tourists a year for every local resident, while Cuba gets one tourist a year for every 14 Cubans. This is partly why the Cubans are still so sincerely friendly.

In 1995 Cuba earned US$1 billion from tourism. Canada sends the most tourists to Cuba, followed by Italy, Germany, Spain, Mexico, and Argentina. Of the 750,000 foreign visitors Cuba receives each year, almost a quarter are Canadians (Cuba is the top Caribbean destination for Canadian tourists). Between 1991 and 1993 tourism increased at an annual average rate of 17.2% and Cuban planners project over 2.5 million annual visitors bringing in US$3 billion annually by the year 2000, even without taking into account the possible return of mass American tourism. During the first quarter of 1996 visitor levels increased 45% over the same period in 1995.

At the moment Cuban resorts are a hot investment: The number of beds in Cuban resort hotels is doubling every decade. On July 1, 1996, Canada's independence day, the Vancouver company Wilton Properties Ltd signed a US$544 million deal to build 11 hotels in Cuba, including one in Havana, five at Playa Jibacoa, three on Cayo Largo, and two on Isla de la Juventud. This huge investment provides some indication of the response of Canadian firms confronted with the American Helms-Burton law, which attempts to dictate the trade and investment policies of other countries conducting business in Cuba. Wilton is putting up 50% of the money to build the 4200 rooms over the next decade. (Previously the Cuban government had owned all hotels and foreign companies only held management contracts.)

Trade

In 1959 some 70% of Cuba's trade was with the US, but Cuba's expropriation of millions of dollars in US-owned assets brought this to an end. By 1961 only 4% of trade was with the US, and in 1962 Washington pressured other countries to implement a hemisphere-wide ban on trade with Cuba, but this was only partly successful. Cuba signed its first trade agreement with the Soviet Union in February 1960, and by 1990 the USSR bought 81% of Cuba's exports and supplied 66% of its imports. Canada, Mexico, Argentina, Japan, Spain,

Italy, and other Western European countries also greatly increased their trade with Cuba after 1959, snapping up contracts US companies were no longer allowed to accept.

In 1995 Cuba's total foreign trade was less than a third what it had been in 1989, and the sharp reduction in trade with the Soviet Union has led to prolonged economic hardship, exacerbated by the continuing US blockade. Already in 1990 the Soviets had cut their oil shipments to Cuba by 50% and reduced other deliveries, and after 1991 the premium prices the Soviet Union had once paid for Cuban products were sharply reduced. Due to shortages of hard currency in both countries, a barter system has been adopted. The collapse of the Russian ruble did have the beneficial effect (for Cuba) of slashing the country's 21 billion ruble debt to the former Soviet Union.

As the flow of Soviet petroleum slowed, Cuba imported tens of thousands of bicycles from China to replace gasoline-powered transportation, and by 1995 Cuba was getting by on half the energy it had used before 1991. Ironically, Cuba may one day become a major petroleum exporting country if current exploration efforts by Canadian, British, French, and Swedish companies on a potential oilfield off the north coasts of Havana and Matanzas Provinces bear fruit. The country already pumps up over a million tons of heavy crude oil a year from the Boca de Jaruco and Varadero fields, most of it with a high sulfur content and useful only for electricity generation and cement production.

Cuba's biggest export items are sugar, nickel, tobacco, citrus fruit, fish, shellfish, coffee, and cement. The main imports are machinery, petroleum, and food (mostly grain). Cuba continues to barter about half its sugar crop to Russia for fuel and fertilizer. In October 1995 Cuba and Russia signed a three-year trade agreement guaranteeing Cuba about half its petroleum requirements in exchange for sugar. About 30% of Cuba's trade is still with Russia, although in dollar terms it's only a fraction of previous levels (US$400 million in 1995 compared to US$8753 million in 1989). Canada is Cuba's largest trading partner with over CDN$500 million in bilateral trade in 1995. Spain and Mexico currently hold third and fourth place.

Since 1986 Cuba has been unable to properly service its US$9 billion hard currency debt, damaging its commercial relations with countries such as Japan (which holds a quarter of the debt). In 1994 Cuba's debt to Mexico was cleared when a Mexican company, Domos International, bought a 36.5% share in Cuba's telephone system in a US$1.5 billion debt-for-equity swap. The Italian telecommunications firm Stet bought another 12.5% in 1995. The old compensation claims of US companies against Cuba could easily be cleared up in the same way, but Washington has a much broader agenda as regards Cuba.

POPULATION & PEOPLE

Cuba has approximately 11 million inhabitants. The largest cities are Havana (2,100,000), Santiago de Cuba (420,000), Camagüey (300,000), Holguín (230,000), Guantánamo (205,000), and Santa Clara (200,000). Others, in descending order, include Bayamo, Cienfuegos, Pinar del Río, Las Tunas, Matanzas, Manzanillo, Ciego de Ávila, and Sancti Spíritus. The most heavily populated regions of the country are around Havana, between Cienfuegos and Santa Clara, and Oriente.

Cuba's native Indians were almost entirely wiped out during the first half century of Spanish rule. To replace them as laborers, the Spanish imported African slaves, over 800,000 of whom were brought to Cuba from West Africa during Spanish rule. Most belonged to the Yoruba and Bantu tribes, and some of their original traditions survive today in the various Afro-Cuban religions. The African population was strengthened between 1919 and 1926 when a quarter million black laborers were recruited from Jamaica and Haiti to work on the plantations.

Prior to the revolution there was much discrimination against blacks both socially and in employment, but this was banned after the revolution. Mixed marriages have become commonplace, and the proportion of blacks and mulattos is increasing gradually due to improved health services and a higher percentage of white emigrants. Officially the present population is 66% white, 12% black, and 22% mulatto, although other sources estimate the proportion of mixed blood to be as high as 50%. The percentage of blacks in the population is noticeably higher in eastern Cuba.

Almost all Cuban whites are of Spanish origin, and their numbers were increased by an influx of a million immigrants from Spain and the Canary Islands between 1900 and 1929.

Some 125,000 Cantonese men were brought to Cuba as laborers between 1853 and 1874, but after their eight-year contracts expired most left due to poor conditions. Another 30,000 Cantonese men arrived during the 1920s. Most of those who stayed married Cuban women and the Chinese element is now highly diffused although a small Chinatown does exist in Havana.

SOCIAL RIGHTS
Housing

Soon after the revolution rents on housing were reduced 50% and since 1962 rent payments have been limited to 10% of family income. The Urban Reform Law of October 1960 converted rent payments into mortgage payments on a five to 20 year basis, making owners out of renters, and almost half a million Cuban families acquired title to their homes or lands in this way. The sale of such housing is prohibited, but units can be traded among owners. Prefabricated apartment blocks have been built throughout the country, often in rural areas or in modern housing developments outside the cities. By chance, this process has saved the historic centers of cities such as Havana from being knocked down by developers, although much prerevolution housing is poorly maintained.

Since the revolution the Third World trend of concentrating development in the main cities has been reversed, and the government has worked to improve conditions in the countryside. Thus there has been very little new construction in Havana since 1959. Soon after the revolution the miserable slums that had once encircled the city were demolished, and a series of new satellite cities of modern apartment buildings was erected, the most notable of which are Habana del Este and Alamar, on the coast just east of Havana. Since 1970 much of the construction of new homes has been carried out by 'microbrigades,' teams of around 30 volunteer workers who assemble highrise buildings from prefabricated parts under expert guidance. Participants get first priority on apartments in these complexes. The formation of microbrigades permitted a five-fold increase in the value of construction between 1970 and 1975. Today such work is severely limited by a shortage of materials.

Education

The greatest successes of the revolution have been in the fields of education and public health. Prior to the revolution a quarter of adult Cubans were illiterate and another million were semiliterate. Ten thousand teachers were unemployed and 70% of the rural population had no schools. After 1959 all private schools were nationalized and education became free and universal. Former military garrisons were turned into schools.

In 1961 all schools were closed for eight months and some 250,000 students and teachers were sent to rural areas to teach reading and writing, resulting in Cuba's present literacy rate of 94.5%. This campaign brought tens of thousands of city youth into contact with the country people, breaking down racial barriers and instilling revolutionary spirit. The early literacy campaigns were followed up with continuing education programs to ensure that nearly every adult attained a sixth-grade level. Today education up to the ninth grade is compulsory.

A special effort has been made to build schools in rural areas that previously had been totally neglected. Since 1970 many

'secondary schools in the countryside' have been constructed, especially on Isla de la Juventud. At these schools, agricultural work is combined with study, making it financially possible for this developing country to offer a high school education to every child. At the hundreds of such schools students divide their time between classes and work in the fields, allowing the facilities to be utilized in two shifts. Room and board is free.

In fact, education is free from kindergarten through university and schools are accessible to virtually all children. Schoolbooks are provided at no charge and scholarships are available to those studying away from home. No country in the world

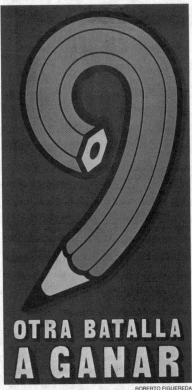

OTRA BATALLA
A GANAR

ROBERTO FIGUEREDA
COURTESY CUBA POSTER PROJECT

offers more than that. Since 1959 the focus of education has shifted from the liberal arts to technical and professional training, with the intention of reducing class differentiation and promoting manual labor. There are 47 institutes of higher education including universities in Havana, Matanzas, Santa Clara, Camagüey, and Santiago de Cuba. In all, some 300,000 teachers instruct three million students.

Yet while the educational system has taught Cubans many practical skills, it has been less successful in teaching people to make individual decisions, and this is reflected in the low efficiency of some sectors of the state economy. And just as an American family's wealth often determines the type of education the children receive, so too a Cuban family's political background could influence whether the children will be able to go to university (the offspring of anyone convicted of antistate activities would be at a serious disadvantage).

The Federación de Mujeres Cubanas runs free day-care centers *(círculos infantiles* or *jardines de la infancia)* that accept children under seven years of age, a boon for working women. In 1991 some 170,000 children were enrolled at 1136 nursery schools.

Public Health

Cuba's public health system is easily the best in Latin America. Before the revolution the infant mortality rate stood at 60 per 1000 live births, but in 1995 it was 9.4 deaths for every 1000 live babies, among the lowest in the world. About 97% of births take place at maternity hospitals. Life expectancy has increased from 55 years to 76. This and a declining birthrate, the free availability of contraception and abortion, and continuing outward migration have led to a progressive aging of the population. It's estimated that by the year 2025 a quarter of Cubans will be over 60 years of age as those born during the baby boom of the 1960s reach retirement age.

Since 1959 hundreds of hospitals, polyclinics (half hospital/half clinic), and clinics have been built, and tens of thousands of doctors and nurses have been trained to replace those who left for the US. In 1960 a rural health system was created and medical graduates are required to do a two-year internship in the countryside after graduation. In 1958 there was only one rural hospital, but by 1975 the number had increased to 58, and between 1958 and 1975 Cuba's public health budget increased by 20 times. In 1996 21.5% of Cuba's budget was devoted to public health and education. At present Cuba has a doctor for every 270 inhabitants, one of the highest ratios in the world, and 421 clinics and 267 hospitals are spread throughout the land.

Cuban medicine excels in quality as well as quantity. Many foreigners come to Cuba for specialized treatment, and drugs such as the cholesterol-reducing PPG or Ateromixco created at Cuban research institutes are exported around the world. Over the years Cuba has expended huge resources on biotechnology and pharmaceutical research, and Cuban medicines may one day become widely available on world markets. All medical attention at state polyclinics including dentistry and hospitalization is free for Cubans. Clinics specialized in treating foreigners charge reasonable fees in dollars

ARTS

Since the revolution there has been a conscious effort to promote Cuban culture, which had previously been suffocated by foreign commercial culture. Dozens of art schools were created, museums opened, and theater groups formed. Musicians were guaranteed a salary, and a national film industry was established. To balance the influence of North American mass culture, Cuba's unique African culture was revalued and Afro-Cuban folklore ensembles were granted subsidies. The National Ballet of Cuba has received international acclaim. The Consejo Nacional de Cultura (National Cultural Council) coordinates activities in the fields of music, art, drama, and dance.

Dance

The rumba is a dance style of Afro-Cuban origin in which the rhythm is provided by drums, *maracas* (rattles), and a singer. Never a specific genre in its original setting, the term 'rumba' originally referred to any of the lively and often erotic dances of former slaves. Underscoring it all are the Afro-Cuban rituals of *santería*, in which African deities *(orishas)* have merged with Catholic saints. Rhythms played on *batá* drums evoke ghosts who take possession of the dancers in certain rituals. Varieties of Cuban rumba include the slower *yambú*, the faster *guaguancó*, and the acrobatic *columbia*. The latter originated as a devil dance of the Náñigo rite, and today it's performed only by solo males.

During the late 1920s rumba spread to New York, where the original percussion/vocal form was corrupted by placing greater emphasis on the tune through the addition of horns and strings to the lineup. The three-step ballroom rumba subsequently propagated by Hollywood has little to do with the original Cuban dance. Within two decades this big-band rumba had developed into mambo under the influence of Afro-Cuban jazz. In mambo, the two fast side steps and one slower forward step of ballroom rumba are replaced by a step back, a step forward, and a close. The chachachá was invented in the early '50s specifically to appeal to white dancers: not too fast, easy to learn, and with simple lyrics to the songs.

Unlike the rumba, the *habanera* developed among Cuba's Spanish population and spread to Europe during the late 19th century. The habanera is a slow to moderate dance for couples in which the feet barely leave the floor and provocative gestures of the eyes, head, hips, and limbs mirror the music. The high-pitched singing is reminiscent of flamenco. Around 1910 the habanera was developed into the tango in Argentina; the slow, romantic Cuban *bolero* also emerged from this milieu.

Danzón also has upper-class roots compared to the more popular rumba. It's an urban orchestral dance that began as an offshoot of Spanish *contradanzas* picked up by domestic servants during the colonial era. On a signal the dancers suddenly stop and wait a few beats before starting again. Danzón was in style from 1880 until 1940 and it had a lasting influence on Cuban popular music.

In the *danza tajona*, often performed for tourists, the dancers weave ribbons around a pole and then unwind the ribbons at great speed. Shows at Cuban hotels invariably feature a conga as the band comes down and leads a snake of dancing bodies around the floor. The conga originated as a dance for African slaves who could only take short steps due to the shackles on their feet. Today its one-two-three-kick is an irresistible icebreaker.

Music

Cuban music is a happy combination of forceful African rhythms and Spanish poetic melody which ethnomusicologist Fernando Ortíz termed 'a love affair between the African drum and the Spanish guitar.' Cuba is a living model of cross-cultural fertilization and during the '60s and '70s the process came full circle as Cuban arrangements inspired new trends in West African pop music. Similarities in sound between the dance bands of Cuba and Francophone Africa are no coincidence. In fact, musicians on four continents have long drawn energy and inspiration from Cuban rhythms, and salsa artists from New York to Puerto Rico continue to play predominantly Cuban music. The drumming and strumming you hear on Cuban streets and country lanes has deep cultural roots, and Cuba's rumba revolution continues to shake the world.

Most contemporary popular music in Cuba is based on *son,* the Cuban equivalent of American country music. Son lyrics consist of rhyming eight-syllable *décima* verses. The form originated in the hills of Oriente in the late 19th century and was popularized with the advent of radio in the 1920s. At that time son was played by a *sexteto* of guitar, *tres* (a Cuban guitar with three sets of double strings), double bass,

Cuban Musical Instruments

During slavery in the US, drumming was prohibited, but in Cuba the opposite was true. When Cuban popular music began to diversify and spread in the early 20th century, Cuban musicians had a whole range of instruments at their disposal.

The strong rhythms in Cuban music are usually provided by the *tumbadora* (conga), a tall barrel-like drum held together by metal hoops. The *bongó* is a pair of small round drums joined by a piece of wood. The *batá* is a conical drum of varying size used in Afro-Cuban religious rituals. Folk dances are often accompanied by a single-skinned drum of Congolese origin called a *joca*.

The gourd-shaped rattle called the *maraca* is one of the only Cuban musical instruments of pre-Hispanic origin. *Chequeré* rattles (a gourd covered with beads) are used in Afro-Cuban religious rituals. The *maruga* is a metal shaker. The *güiro* is an elongated gourd rasped with a stick, although there are also tin güiros. The *cata* or *guagua* is a wooden tube beaten with sticks. No band would be complete without *claves,* two wooden sticks tapped together to set the beat.

The *tres* is a small folk guitar with three sets of double steel strings. The similar *quatro* has four sets of double strings. Cuban folk groups often include a West-African hand piano or *marímbula,* a wooden box with five metal keys. The only wind instrument in Cuban folk music is the *botija,* a clay jug with a short narrow neck bearing an opening on the side for blowing. Musicians vary the pitch of the tones by moving a hand along the neck of the jug. During carnival a small five-note horn called a *corneta china* produces a sharp sound like the bagpipe. Modern instruments commonly used in Cuba include the bass, clarinet, guitar, saxophone, trombone, and trumpet.

Cuba is the only country outside Europe with a tradition of street organs. During the 19th century refugees from Haiti brought the French mechanical organ to Oriente where Hispano-Cuban sones, boleros, and danzones soon replaced waltzes and azurkas in the repertoire. The Cubans made the European organ dynamic by adding a second crank that the operator uses to vary the speed at which the boards pass through the machine. Five or six percussionists joined an organ grinder to form an orchestra playing popular Cuban dance music under the control of the organ grinder, who can innovate stops or breaks. ■

and bongó, plus two singers who played the *claves* (two sticks tapped together to set the beat) and maracas. A decade later a cornet was added to form a *septeto* or *sonora*. During the '40s and '50s horn and drum sections were added to the son ensembles to create big bands that played rumba, mambo, and chachachá. *Charanga* is the

same but with flutes and fiddles added to the mix.

In the '60s and '70s Cuban son and other Latin rhythms stirring in New York combined to create a loosely defined style related to jazz called salsa. Cuban exiles such as Celia Cruz embraced salsa as a substitute for their lost roots, and catchy salsa tunes were soon blaring from radios and jukeboxes all across Latin America. The phenomenal commercial success of New York salsa has displaced more authentic Cuban sounds in the glitzy American music marketplace, but the real thing awaits rediscovery in Cuba.

Visitors to Cuba will find a Casa de la Trova in most large towns where guitar-toting *trovadores* (troubadours) sing *trovas* (ballads) in traditional *décima* verse. It's a genre comparable to the protest songs of American folk singers such as Joan Baez and the *nueva canción* of Latin American artists like Mercedes Sosa of Argentina. *La nueva trova* emerged in Cuba in the early '70s, yet the tradition of singing romantic son ballads has a long history in Cuba. Ñico Saquito from Santiago de Cuba wrote over five hundred such ballads.

The most famous Cuban song is *Guajira guantanamera*, composed in 1929 by Joseíto Fernández (1908 – 1979). In the late 1950s Cuban musician Hector Angulo added lyrics from the *Versos Sencillos* of José Martí, and this version was popularized by American folk singer Pete Seeger at a 1963 Carnegie Hall concert in solidarity with Cuba. Also during the '60s, Carlos Puebla sang songs in praise of the revolution. Current leading lights of the *nueva trova* movement are acoustic guitar players Pablo Milanés and Silvio Rodríguez. Carlos Varela is an up-and-coming rock artist. These singers are allowed some latitude in their social criticism, and the lyrics are a type of social poetry favoring equality and a better life for the people.

Classical Music In the realm of classical music, pianist Ignacio Cervantes (1847 – 1905) composed a series of romantic *Danzas Cubanas* based on Afro-Cuban and Creole traditions. Later the ethnomusicological research of Fernando Ortíz (1881 – 1969) allowed composers Amadeo Roldán (1900 – 1939) and Alejandro García Caturla (1906 – 1940) to write orchestral works based on Afro-Cuban themes. Caturla also set the poems of Alejo Carpentier and Nicolás Guillén (see

Literature below) to music. Eliseo Grenet (1893 – 1950) and Ernesto Lecuona (1896 – 1963) made liberal use of Afro-Cuban rhythms in *zarzuelas* (operettas) such as Lecuona's *María la O* (1930), based on the classic Cuban theme of the mulata betrayed by a white man (available in Cuba on compact disc).

Popular Music During the 1920s groups such as the Sexteto Nacional de Ignacio Piñeiro, Sexteto Boloña, and Sexteto Matancero popularized son in the US. The first big Cuban hit of those years was *El Manicero* (The Peanut Vendor), played by Don Azpiazu and his Havana Casino Orchestra in New York in 1930. Antonio Arcaño y sus Maravillas adapted the danzón to mambo rhythms after 1938. The same period was the heyday of the Septeto Anacaona, comprised of seven sisters, one of the few women's bands of the time.

From 1927 the famous trumpeter Félix Chappottín played with the Sexteto Habanero, which had formed in 1920. The blind tres player Arsenio Rodríguez took over the band in 1940 and expanded the horn section under influence of the American big-band sound. The three or four trumpets extended the expressive possibilities while a piano reinforced the melody and a *tumbadora* (tall drum) kept the beat. A prolific composer, Rodríguez reinforced the African element in Cuban music through his lyrics and rhythms. In 1950 he moved to New York and formed another group, while Chappottín and Miguelito Cuní took over the band in Cuba. Harry Belafonte has referred to Rodríguez as the father of salsa.

Born in Spain but raised in Cuba, Xavier Cugat (1900 – 1990) was the first Cuban musician to achieve mass popularity in the US. Xavier Cugat and His Gigolos were already providing music for Hollywood before Cugat became bandleader of New York's Waldorf Astoria Orchestra in 1933. Although his smooth arrangements of Latin American dance music were a great mainstream success, Cugat's rumbas were not really Cuban.

During the '40s Frank 'Machito' Grillo (1912 – 1984) made his mark in New York by mixing jazz with Afro-Cuban music. During a long career Machito passed effortlessly from mambo to chachachá and salsa as tastes evolved. It was Enrique Jorrín (1926 – 1987) and his Orquestra América who really popularized chachachá in New York with *La Engañadora* recorded in 1953. Drummer and singer Chano Pozo (1915 – 1948) brought Cuban jazz to the fore with numbers such as *Manteca*. He was murdered by another Cuban in Harlem.

During the '50s piano player Pérez Prado (1916 – 1989) was known as the 'King of the Mambo.' As early as 1942 Prado was preparing mambo arrangements for the Orquestra Casino de la Playa in Cuba, and by 1949 he was leader of his own band in Mexico City. Although highly commercialized, Prado's torrid trumpets, swinging organs, and pervasive beat in hits like *Cherry Pink and Apple Blossom White* (1955) and *Patricia* (1958) anticipated American rock and roll.

A more bona fide mambo band leader and singer was Benny Moré (1919 – 1963), 'El Bárbaro del Ritmo' (The Barbarian of Rhythm). Throughout the '40s Moré sang with various groups in Havana, Mexico City, and Panama, including those of Miguel Matamoros (1894 – 1971), author of *Son de la Loma*, and Pérez Prado. Back in Cuba in 1953, Moré formed a Banda Gigante comprised of 21 black musicians like himself. Benny's band and velvet voice were without rivals in their time, though his bohemian lifestyle and heavy drinking led to an early death from liver disease.

The year 1950 saw the introduction of television and long-playing records to Cuba, and by this time radios and cinemas were widespread. The large dance orchestras mentioned above were sustained by this media, while groups like Cuarteto D'Aida and Los Zafiros, and female singers such as Paulina Álvarez (the 'empress of danzonete'), María de los Ángeles Santana, Esther Borja, Celeste Mendoza, Rita Montaner, and María Teresa Vera (also a guitarist and band leader) became popular nightclub performers as tourism from the US boomed.

After the 1959 revolution Afro-Cuban music was revalued and during the '60s Pello el Afrocán popularized a fast drum dance called the *mozambique*. The Ballet Folklórico Cutumba, founded at Santiago de Cuba in 1961, and the Havana-based Conjunto Folklórico Nacional continue to perform Afro-Cuban dances.

Charanga bands still active in Cuba today include the Septeto Nacional de Ignacio Piñeiro (first formed in 1927 and reestablished in 1985), the Orquestra Aragón (founded in 1939), and the Orquestra Ritmo Oriental (formed in the '50s). In 1970 Juan Formell, a veteran of Elio Revé's Orquestra Revé, founded Orquestra Los Van Van and transformed the traditional charanga lineup by adding modern instruments such as the electric guitar, electric bass, and drum battery. The repertoires of the Orquestra Original de Manzanillo and Conjunto Rumbavana are also excellent examples of the ability of musicians to adapt son to changing conditions.

Cuba's top jazz band is Irakere, founded in Havana in 1973 by pianist Jesús 'Chucho' Valdés. Irakere's Afro-Cuban drumming doesn't obscure the group's deep son roots. NG La Banda, a band of the *nueva generación* formed in 1988, mixes Cuban tradition with jazz and rap. Riding on the same wave are Charanga Habanera, Moncada, Manolín the Salsa Doctor, and Paulito y Su Elite. Other notables include jazz pianist Gonzalo Rubalcaba, Pachito Alonso y sus Kini Kini, Juan Carlos Alfonso y el Dan Den, Isaac Delgado, and Adalberto Álvarez y Su Son.

One of the best contemporary son bands is Grupo Sierra Maestra, founded in 1980. Their lineup comprises a lead singer, three guitar-type instruments, trumpet, bass, bongó, percussion, piano, and various acoustical instruments. The Familia Valera Miranda plays son dance music around Oriente at weddings, birthday parties, and receptions. Cuarteto Patria, formed in Santiago de Cuba in 1940, continues to play traditional son and bolero under the leadership of Eliades Ochoa. Also from 1940, Cañambú performs son with singer Arístides Ruiz Boza. Síntesis is a Yoruba rock group.

Los Muñequitos de Matanzas play authentic contemporary rumba employing only percussion and voice. Folkloyuma is a traditional rumba cabildo formed in Santiago de Cuba in 1964. The Conjunto Clave y Guaguancó and Afrocuba de Matanzas also play real rumba, as does singer Lázaro Ros.

Celina González (born 1928) lives in Havana and sings with the band Campo Alegre led by her son Reutilio Domínguez. Her *música guajira* combines the music of Cuban country folk of Spanish descent or *guajiros* with the Afro-Cuban tradition (Celina herself is a devotee of the Yoruba goddess Changó, or Santa Bárbara). Abelardo Barroso fits his *guajiras* (country-music songs) into the charanga format. Merceditas Valdez sings traditional Yoruba songs to the batá drumming of Jesús Pérez.

While in Cuba, you'd be foolish to miss a performance by any of the artists or groups mentioned above, and quality recordings of their music are readily available on CDs produced by the state record company Egrem (Empresa de Grabaciones y Ediciones Musicales) for Artex (Promociones Artísticas y Literarias). A good introduction to Cuban music is provided on the Egrem-Artex series *Antología de la Música Cubana* (especially volumes 1 and 2) and *Joyas de la Música Cubana* (particularly volume 3), sold at most hotel shops. The sampler *Fiesta Cubana Guajiras* is also outstanding. (All Egrem-Artex CDs are marked 'Made in Canada,' so you should have no problem taking them home if you're from the US.)

Literature

The real lives of Cuban writers have often mirrored their country's long struggle for freedom, independence, and social justice. The lyric poet José María de Heredia y Heredia (1803 – 1839) from Santiago de Cuba was forced into exile by the Spanish colonial authorities soon after graduating from law school. In Mexico he wrote *En el Teocali de Cholula,* followed a few years later by the *Ode to Niagara,* among the earliest examples of Spanish romanticism.

The self-educated mulatto poet Gabriel de la Concepción Valdés (1809 – 1844), better known as 'Plácido,' wrote romantic verses that were popularized as songs. Plácido is best remembered for his involvement in an abortive slave uprising at Matanzas that led to his death before a Spanish firing squad.

Cuba's greatest 19th-century novelist, Cirilo Villaverde y de la Paz (1812 – 1894), also struggled against Spanish colonial rule and was imprisoned in 1848. Later he fought alongside General Narciso López (see the Colonial Period section under History above) and spent many years in exile in the US. His most celebrated work is *Cecilia Valdés*, the story of a slave trader's son who falls in love with a beautiful mulata who eventually turns out to be his illegitimate sister. No book has ever come closer to capturing the emotions of slavery in Cuba and the class differences stifling colonial society, and the novel's violent ending foreshadowed the actual fate of colonialism itself. Years later composer Gonzalo Roig used the story in a zarzuela of the same name.

Cuba's most famous and influential writer is José Martí (1853 – 1895), the revolutionary leader who died in one of the initial clashes of the Second War of Independence. Martí's collected works comprise 25 volumes of poems, plays, and essays written in an uncomplicated style accessible to most readers. In 1871 Martí was deported to Spain for his revolutionary writings, and he spent most of his life in exile, including long stays in New York where he served as correspondent for several leading South American newspapers. His last book of poetry, *Versos Sencillos,* is considered his best, while *Los Estados Unidos* is a collection of essays reflecting his ambivalent feelings about the US.

During the 1930s the mulatto poet Nicolás Guillén (1902 – 1989) played a leading role in the Afro-Cuban movement then transforming Cuban literature, music, and dance, and some of the onomatopoetic verses in Guillén's *Sóngoro Cosongo* (1931) can be recited to the beat of a drum. His works championed social and racial equality, and as a journalist covering the Spanish Civil War he supported the Republican side and became a Communist. He spent the Batista years in exile, and *La Paloma de Vuelo Popular* and *Elegías* (both published in 1958) protest the repression and US domination of the time. After 1959 Guillén returned to Cuba and in 1961 he helped found the Unión Nacional de Escritores y Artistas Cubanos (National Union of Cuban Writers and Artists). His prolific writings made him the poet laureate and cultural ambassador of the revolution.

The career of historical novelist Alejo Carpentier (1904 – 1980) partly parallels that of Guillén. In 1927 Carpentier was imprisoned by the Machado regime and he subsequently spent most of the years until 1959 in exile in France and Venezuela. After his return to Cuba he served as head of the national publishing company, professor of literature at the University of Havana, and Cuban cultural attaché to France. Carpentier's first novel, *Ecué-Yamba-O* (1933), deals with Afro-Cuban culture. In the surrealistic novel *El Reino de Este Mundo* (1949) Carpentier explores Haiti's African roots through the life of the tyrannical Henri Christophe. *El Siglo de las Luces* (1962) is set in the Caribbean during the French revolution, while *El Recurso del Método* (1974) is a caricature of the Machado dictatorship. *Concierto Barroco* (1974) is considered Carpentier's masterpiece, a 93-page novel in which a wealthy Mexican and his black servant travel to Europe for the carnival season and through a Vivaldi opera they rediscover their common Latin American identity.

Other contemporary Cuban writers of note include: José Lezama Lima (1910 – 1976), whose controversial novel *Paradiso* (1966) explores homosexual relationships; Guillermo Cabrera Infante (born 1929), author of the innovative novel *Tres Tristes*

Tigres (1967) about cultural decadence during the Batista era; Edmundo Desnoes (born 1930), best known for *Memorias del Subdesarrollo* (1965), an existential novel about failure; and Miguel Barnet (born 1940), master of the testimonial novel.

Apart from the influence of the writers just mentioned, Cuba has had an important impact on Latin American literature through competitions organized by the Casa de las Américas. Among others, Colombia's Nobel Prize winner Gabriel García Márquez has had a long and cordial relationship with revolutionary Cuba.

Architecture

Nothing remains of the architecture of Cuba's Indian population, although a reconstructed Arawak village called Villa Guamá exists as a tourist resort near the Bay of Pigs. The traditional thatched farmhouse of Cuba, the *bohío*, is derived from an indigenous dwelling.

Many architectural styles adopted in Cuba – including renaissance, baroque, and neoclassical – originated in Europe. Only a handful of 16th-century renaissance structures survive in Cuba. These include the Casa de Diego Velázquez in Santiago de Cuba and the Parroquia de San Juan Bautista in Remedios. The Spanish colony left behind mostly baroque buildings, and among the many superb 18th-century churches are the Catedral de San Cristóbal de La Habana; the Iglesia de Nuestra Señora del Rosario near Havana; the Iglesia de Nuestra Señora de la Soledad and the Iglesia de Nuestra Señora de la Merced, both at Camagüey; and the Iglesia Parroquial Mayor de San Salvador at Bayamo. There are many impressive 18th-century baroque palaces in Havana, including the Palacio de los Capitanes Generales, the Palacio del Segundo Cabo, and the Casa de la Obra Pía. Trinidad, in the Province of Sancti Spíritus, also has numerous baroque buildings, such as the Palacio Brunet. A fine example of 18th-century baroque military architecture is the Fortaleza de San Carlos de la Cabaña in Havana.

The 19th century was mostly an era of neoclassical construction, the earliest and finest representatives of which are El Templete in Havana and a few palaces such as Casa Cantero in Trinidad. Also built in this style were churches such as the Catedral de San Carlos Borromeo in Matanzas and the Catedral de la Purísima Concepción in Cienfuegos, and grand theaters like the Teatro Sauto in Matanzas, the Teatro Tomás Terry in Cienfuegos, and the Teatro Principal in Camagüey. Neoclassical construction continued into the 20th century with the Universidad de La Habana and neoclassical colonnades along streets and squares throughout the country.

There are few neo-Gothic buildings in Cuba, the Iglesia del Santo Angel Custodio in Havana being a notable exception. The early 20th century produced a number of distinguished neobaroque buildings such as the Centro Gallego and the Ministerio de Relaciones Exteriores, both in Havana. The Moorish-style Palacio de Valle in Cienfuegos also dates from this time.

Contemporary architecture in Cuba is both functional and striking. An early example of a large modern building intended to impress is the Palacio de las Convenciones (1979) in Havana's Cubanacán District. The Estadio Panamericano near Havana and Antonio Maceo International Airport at Santiago de Cuba (both from 1991) are additional examples along these lines. In recent years the most noteworthy new buildings have been hotels such as the star-shaped Hotel Meliá Varadero and the horseshoe-shaped Hotel Sol Palmeras, both at Varadero, and the pyramid-shaped Sierra Mar Resort near Santiago de Cuba. One of the finest examples of a modern building that incorporates the remains of an earlier construction is Restaurante Las Ruinas at Parque Lenin near Havana.

Film

After the revolution the government created a film industry from scratch, placing special emphasis on the documentary. Cuba's national movie company is the Instituto Cubano del Arte e Industria Cinematográfica (Cuban Institute of Cinematographic Art and Industry).

Cuba's most acclaimed director of recent years has been Tomás Gutiérrez Alea (1928 – 1996), whose *Fresa y Chocolate* won the jury's special prize at the 1994 Berlin Film Festival. This humorous film about an uncomfortable liaison between a straight young Cuban and a homosexual that eventually develops into friendship is a poignant plea for human tolerance and understanding. Earlier films by Gutiérrez Alea include *La Muerte de un Burócrata* (1966), a critique of bureaucratic muddling; *Memorias del Subdesarrollo* (1969), based on the novel by Edmundo Desnoes; and *Cartas del Parque* (1988), the touching tale of two lovers who correspond through an intermediary.

Another important Cuban director is Humberto Solás (born 1941) whose 1968 film *Lucía* is the story of three women of the same name who lived in different eras. In 1976 Solás' *Cantata a Chile* won the main prize at the Karlovy Vary Film Festival.

Painting

Little is known about Cuban painting before José Nicolás de la Escalera (1734 – 1804), who worked in the second half of the 18th century. The early 19th-century painter Vicente Escobar (1762 – 1834) can already be considered part of the *costumbrista* movement that produced realistic images of everyday life.

In 1818 the French painter Jean Baptiste Vermay (1786 – 1833), decorator of El Templete on Havana's Plaza de Armas, became the first director of the Academy of San Alejandro, which was destined to decisively influence Cuban art right into the 1920s. In 1878 the Cuban painter Miguel Melero (1836 – 1907) took over direction of the academy.

Two trends are evident in 19th-century academic landscape painting: romanticism as exemplified by Esteban Chartrand (1840 – 1883) and José Joaquín Tejada (1867 – 1943); and realism as represented by Valentín Sanz Carta (1849 – 1898) and Guillermo Collazo (1850 – 1896).

In the early years of this century many Cuban painters visited Europe where they learned techniques and were exposed to trends. By 1925 many were back in Cuba, abandoning academic art and producing the type of avant-garde paintings that had sensationalized Europe several decades earlier. Artists like Eduardo Abela (1889 – 1965), Víctor Manuel García (1897 – 1969), Marcelo Pogolotti (1902 – 1988), and Roberto Diago (1920 – 1957) saw Cuba through fresh eyes and produced paintings reminiscent of Picasso and Gauguin.

During the '40s and '50s Cuban painting became ever more individualistic as artists sought to express their Cuban identity in their own way. By this time the European forms of expression had been fully absorbed, and although the paintings and stained-glass windows of René Portocarrero (1912 – 1985) bear a resemblance to those of Marc Chagall, they are original works of great expressive power. Amelia Peláez (1896 – 1968) adorned Havana buildings with colorful ceramic murals. Other outstanding figures from this period include Wilfredo Lam (1902 – 1982) and Marianao Rodríguez (1912 – 1990). Cuba's leading contemporary artist, Manuel Mendive (born 1944), incorporates Afro-Cuban mythology into his work.

With the revolution Cuban artists gained a new social role as articulators of a rediscovered national identity. Historical subjects taken from Cuba's 19th-century wars of independence became popular, and there was a return to realism, but Cuban artists continued to experiment freely with new means of expression. Posters and billboard art were adopted as a means of directly communicating with common people in a simple and often compelling way. The political art one sees along Cuban roads and highways has a value quite apart from its messages. In the '60s Raúl Martínez (born 1927) elevated poster painting to a high art form with a series of political paintings of Castro, Guevara, Martí, and others.

SOCIETY & CONDUCT

Like Spaniards, most Cubans are quite courteous and polite toward guests, and will try to please you if at all possible. Because of this, their statements sometimes gloss over reality, their promises may be wishful thinking, and their appointments are often not kept. This characteristic can be extremely annoying to those unaccustomed to Latin ways.

A first line of defense is to avoid suggesting the answer in your question. If things don't work out exactly as you expected or desired, have an alternative plan ready and avoid getting angry. It's far better to display a sense of humor than to make a fool of yourself by showing your temper. If a situation is really intolerable, just try to get around it or avoid it. Attempting to correct a problem inherent in the system or culture, or telling the Cubans how they should correct it, is an utter waste of time. Generally, the more people working on a problem the longer it will take to get anything done.

Always remember that the Cubans understand their political situation far better than you do. Rather than say what you think, ask the Cubans what they think is good or bad about their system. Just don't try to generate political discussions in hotel lobbies, bars, or other public places where those nearby may only understand a small part of what is being said and you could end up seriously embarrassing someone without even realizing it. Bystanders may only hear 'Fidel Castro' or 'Communism' – words Cubans themselves do not utter casually. An equivalent situation in a US context might be having a stranger quiz you about abortion in a public place. Self-proclaimed dissidents should be avoided.

Generally, the Cubans will pick up on your attitude instantly, and if you come across as friendly, you'll always get a friendly response. If you look the other way and avoid eye contact, they'll do exactly the same. It's rare for a Cuban to be indifferent toward travelers, as happens all the time in North America and Europe.

RELIGION

Prior to the revolution 85% of Cubans were nominal Roman Catholics, although only about 10% attended church regularly (compared to about 5% today). The largest Protestant denomination was Baptist. Cuban Catholicism had always been the religion of the affluent, and Cuban Protestants were usually poorer. Protestant churches were granted fewer privileges before the revolution, so they had less to lose after.

Afro-Cuban Religions

Slaves brought from West Africa between the 16th and 19th centuries carried with them a system of animistic beliefs that they managed to hide behind a Catholic veneer. The slave owners were poor missionaries and they kept tribes together in order to pit one group against another. Some speculate that in Cuba today there are more followers of the Afro-Cuban religions than practicing Roman Catholics. Tribes such as Arará, Lucumí, and Congo are organized in *cabildos* (associations). Abakuá is a secret society made up of male members known as *ñáñigos*. Initiates address each other as *ambia, asere,* and *monina*, and say *qué volá?* instead of the usual *qué tal?* or *como está?* Such phrases are common in contemporary Havana slang.

The largest Afro-Cuban religion is an amalgam of Catholic and Yoruba beliefs known as santería or *Regla de Ocha*. In santería, Catholic saints and apparitions of the Virgin are associated with Yoruba deities or *orishas*. Unlike the Catholic saints, however, the orishas do not represent perfection and they have many human frailties. The concepts of original sin and a final judgment are unknown. Instead, ancestral spirits are worshipped.

Among the most important orishas is the androgynous creator god Obatalá, who is always dressed in white and associated with Christ or Nuestra Señora de la Merced. Obatalá's wife, Odudúa, goddess of the underworld, is also associated with the Virgin. Obatalá's son, Elegguá (St Anthony), is the god of destiny. Yemayá, the goddess of the ocean and mother of all orishas, is identified by the color blue and associated with Nuestra Señora de Regla. Changó, the Yoruba god of fire and war, lives in the tops of the royal palm trees and controls the lightning. His color is red and he's associated with Santa Bárbara. His son Aggayú Solá, god of land and protector of travelers, is associated with San Cristóbal (St Christopher). Ochún, wife of Changó and companion of Yemayá, is the goddess of love and the rivers. As might be expected, she's a very powerful orisha and is associated with Cuba's patroness, the Virgin de la Caridad del Cobre (whose color is yellow). Ogún is associated with John the Baptist. Babalú Ayé (St Lazarus) is the orisha of disease.

The rites of santería are controlled by a male priest called a *babalawo* or *babalao* who is often consulted for advice, to cure sicknesses, or to grant protection. Offerings are placed before a small shrine in the babalawo's home. Although the figures of Catholic saints mounted on the shrines represent a variety of orishas, the real power resides in stones draped with colored bead necklaces. The stones are believed to harbor the spirits of the orishas and they must be fed with food, herbs, and blood. Animals such as chickens, doves, and goats are sacrificed during rituals, and the babalawo sprays rum onto the altar from his mouth.

Cubans are surprisingly open about santería, and travelers are welcome to inspect household shrines and attend ceremonies. It's unlikely anyone will be offended if you ask them about santería; in fact, they'll probably be pleased that you're interested in Cuban culture. Many hotels stage special santería shows for visitors and cult objects are often sold in hotel shops. If you attend a santería ceremony at a private residence, you'll probably be expected to leave a few dollars for the saint (and babalawo) on the altar. ■

In 1959 there were about 700 Catholic priests in Cuba, a majority of them from Spain. Some 140 of the Spaniards were expelled for reactionary political activities, and another 400 left voluntarily. The rest were allowed to continue their work unhindered. The Nationalization of Education Law of June 1961 transferred control of Catholic and other private schools to the government. In 1966 some foreign priests were allowed to return to Cuba and church services were never prohibited.

Government policy toward the church remains basically live and let live. There is no religious persecution, although the separation of church and state is complete. A July 1992 constitutional amendment guarantees freedom of religion in Cuba, but restrictions do limit proselytizing beyond church walls. Visitors are welcome to attend religious services.

The religious beliefs of former African slaves have merged with Catholic iconography and doctrines in a number of Afro-Cuban cults called santerías, which combine African deities with Catholic saints. Adherents of the Afro-Cuban religions regard Catholicism as the form of santería followed by the descendants of the Spanish tribe from Europe. The Afro-Cuban religions have been tolerated since 1959, and there are probably more followers of santería than pure Catholicism.

LANGUAGE

Spanish is the only language spoken by all Cubans and a knowledge of it is a great help in traveling around the country on your own. Away from the hotels and tourist centers, few people speak English and then only very poorly. Almost all museum captions in Cuba are in Spanish only. Luckily Spanish is a phonetic language that is easy to pick up.

In this book we list the things to see in Spanish. If you speak no Spanish at all, you can always ask directions simply by pointing to the name in this guide. But almost without effort, speakers of English and Romance languages will soon learn the meaning of key words like *iglesia*

(church) and *museo* (museum). The most important Spanish word for the traveler is *hay*, which is pronounced exactly the same as the ocular 'eye' and means 'there is' (some). *No hay* means 'there isn't' (any). Never hesitate to try out your broken Spanish on Cubans!

Words of Arawak Indian origin that have passed into Spanish and other European languages are *barbacoa* (barbecue), *canoa* (canoe), *cigarro* (cigar), *hamaca* (hammock), *huracán* (hurricane), *maíz* (maize), *patata* (potato), and *tabaco* (tobacco). The only words of African origin are associated with the Afro-Cuban religions, but Afro-Cuban speakers have given Cuban Spanish its rhythmical intonation and soft accent.

Phrasebooks & Dictionaries

Lonely Planet's *Latin American Spanish* phrasebook by Anna Cody is a worthwhile introduction to the language. Another useful resource is a paperback Spanish-English/English-Spanish dictionary. It will also make a nice gift for some friendly Cuban when you're about to leave the country.

Pronunciation

Spanish pronunciation is, in general, consistently phonetic with almost every letter pronounced. Once you're aware of the basic rules, they should cause little difficulty. Speak slowly to avoid getting tongue-tied until you become confident of your ability. To familiarize yourself with the sound of the language, check out a set of Spanish language-learning cassettes from your local library as you're preparing for the trip.

Pronunciation of the letters f, k, l, n, p, q, s, and t is virtually identical to English.

Vowels Spanish vowels are very consistent and have easy English equivalents.

a is like 'a' in 'father.'
e is like 'e' in 'bet.'
i is like 'i' in 'machine.'
o is like 'o' in 'note.'
u is like 'oo' in 'food.' When the vowel

sound is modified by an umlaut, as in 'Camagüey,' it is pronounced 'w.'

y is considered a vowel when it stands alone or appears at the end of a word, in which case its pronunciation is identical to Spanish 'i.' When next to a vowel it's a consonant pronounced like the 'y' in 'yes.'

Consonants Spanish consonants generally resemble their English equivalents, but there are some major exceptions.

b resembles its English equivalent but is undistinguished from 'v.' For clarification, refer to the former as 'b larga,' the latter as 'b corta.' The word for the letter itself is pronounced like English 'bay.'

c is like the 's' in 'see' before e and i, otherwise like English 'k.'

d closely resembles 'h' in 'feather.'

g is like a guttural English 'h' before Spanish 'e' and 'i,' otherwise like 'g' in 'go.'

h is invariably silent.

j most closely resembles English 'h' but is slightly more guttural.

ll is like the 'y' is 'yes.'

ñ is like 'ni' in 'onion.'

r is nearly identical to English except at the beginning of a word, when it is often rolled.

rr is very strongly rolled.

v resembles English, but see 'b,' above.

x is like 'x' in 'taxi' except for very few words for which it follows Spanish or Mexican usage as 'j.'

z is like 's' in 'sun.'

Diphthongs Spanish is an easy language to pronounce, as each vowel is pronounced separately except when they occasionally create a diphthong – a combination of two vowels forming a single syllable. In Spanish, the formation of a diphthong depends on combinations of 'weak' vowels ('i' and 'u') or strong ones ('a,' 'e,' and 'o'). Two weak vowels or a strong and a weak vowel make a diphthong, but two strong ones are separate syllables.

A good example of two weak vowels forming a diphthong is the word *diurno* (during the day). The final syllable of

obligatorio (obligatory) is a combination of weak and strong vowels.

Stress Stress, often indicated by visible accents, is very important, since it can change the meaning of words. The second-to-last syllable is stressed if the word ends in 's,' 'n,' or a vowel; otherwise, the last syllable is stressed. Spanish accents are used only to indicate deviations from this rule, in which case the accented syllable is stressed. Thus *sótano* (basement), *América*, and *porción* (portion) all have the stress on different syllables.

An accent also appears on adverbs such as *cuánto?* (how much?) and *cuándo?* (when?) even when according to the rule they shouldn't need one, but this technicality needn't concern beginners. When words appear in capitals, the written accent is sometimes omitted but is still pronounced.

Greetings & Civilities

In their public behavior, the Cubans are very informal, but when approaching a stranger for information, you should always preface your question with a greeting like *buenos días* or *buenas tardes*. Cubans routinely address one another as *compañero* or *compañera* (comrade), but the traditional *señor* and *señora* are always used with foreigners.

yes	*sí*
no	*no*
thank you	*gracias*
you're welcome	*de nada*
hello	*hola*
good morning	*buenos días*
good afternoon	*buenas tardes*
good evening/night	*buenas noches*
goodbye	*adiós, chau*
I don't speak much Spanish.	*Hablo poco español.*
I understand.	*Entiendo.*
I don't understand.	*No entiendo.*

Useful Words & Phrases

and	*y*
to/at	*a*

for	por, para
of/from	de, desde
in	en
with	con
without	sin
before	antes
after	después
soon	pronto
already	ya
now	ahora
right away	en seguida
here	aquí
there	allá
Where?	¿Dónde?
Where is . . . ?	¿Dónde está . . . ?
Where are . . . ?	¿Dónde están . . . ?
here	aquí
When?	¿Cuándo?
How?	¿Cómo?
How much?	¿Cuánto?
How many?	¿Cuántos?
How much does it cost?	¿Cuánto cuesta?
I would like . . .	Me gustaría . . .

Getting Around

airplane	avión
bicycle	bicicleta
bus	guagua, autobús, ómnibus
car	auto
hitchhike	hacer botella
motorcycle	motocicleta, moto
ship	barco, buque
taxi	taxi
train	tren
truck	camión

I would like a ticket to . . .
  Quiero un boleto/pasaje a . . .
What's the fare to . . . ?
  ¿Cuánto cuesta hasta . . . ?
When does the next plane/train/bus leave for . . . ?
  ¿Cuándo sale el próximo avión/ tren/ómnibus para . . . ?
first/last/next
  primero/último/próximo
single/return (round-trip)
  ida/ida y vuelta

Around Town

airport	aeropuerto
train station	estación de ferrocarril
bus terminal	terminal de ómnibus
bathing resort	balneario
toilet	baño
post office	correo
letter	carta
postcard	postal
airmail	correo aéreo
registered mail	certificado
stamps	sellos

Geographical Expressions

The expressions below are among the most common you will encounter in this book and in Spanish language maps and guides.

archipelago	archipiélago
bay	bahía
beach	playa
bridge	puente
cape	cabo
cove	ensenada
highway	carretera, vía
hill	cerro
lagoon	laguna
lake	lago
marsh	estero
mount	cerro
mountain range	cordillera
national park	parque nacional
pass	paso
point	punta
reef	arrecife
reservoir	embalse
river	río
swamp	ciénaga
waterfall	cascada, salto

Accommodations

hotel	hotel, villa
reception	carpeta
single room	habitación para una persona
double room	habitación doble
What does it cost?	Cuánto cuesta?
per night	por noche

all inclusive	*todo incluído*
shared bath	*baño compartido*
private bath	*baño privado*
too expensive	*demasiado caro*
cheaper	*mas económico*
May I see it?	*¿Puedo verla?*
I don't like it.	*No me gusta.*
the bill	*la cuenta*

Food

The words below are alphabetized in Spanish for easy reference when deciphering Cuban restaurant menus, most of which will be in Spanish only.

agua	water
aguacate	avocado
aguja	swordfish
ahumado	smoked
ajiaco	meat stew
ajo	garlic
albóndiga	meatball
almíbar	sweet syrup or juice
apio	celery
arroz	rice
asado	roasted
atún	tuna
azúcar	sugar
bacalao	cod
batido	milkshake
bebida	drink
bistec	beefsteak
bocadillo	sandwich
boniato	sweet potato
bonito	striped tuna
café	coffee
camarones	shrimp
cangrejo	crab
carne	meat
cebolla	onion
cerdo	pork
cereza	cherry
cerveza	beer
chatinos	banana chips
cherna	sea-bass
chicharrón	pork rind
chorizo	sausage
chuletas	chops
ciruela	plum

cocina	kitchen
col	cabbage
coliflor	cauliflower
conejo	rabbit
congrí	rice and red beans
cordero	lamb
enchilado	shellfish stew
ensalada	salad
espinacas	spinach
flan	caramel pudding
fresa	strawberry
frijoles	beans
frito	fried
fruta	fruit
fruta bomba	papaya
garbanzos	chickpeas
guanábana	soursop
guayaba	guava
guisantes	peas
hamburgesa	hamburger
helado	ice cream
hervido	boiled
hielo	ice
huevo	egg
jamón	ham
jugo	juice
langosta	lobster
leche	milk
lechón	suckling pig
lechuga	lettuce
legumbres	vegetables
limón	lemon
maíz	corn
malanga	taro
mantequilla	butter
manzana	apple
mariscos	seafood
merluza	hake
mermelada	jam
moros y cristianos	rice and beans
ñame	yam
naranja	orange
natilla	caramel pudding
oca	goose
ostiones	oysters
paella	seafood and rice casserole
pan	bread
papas	potatoes

pargo	red snapper
pepino	cucumber
pera	pear
pescado	fish
picadillo	mincemeat
pimienta	pepper
piña	pineapple
plátano	banana
pollo	chicken
puerco	pork
puré	mashed potatoes
queso	cheese
res	beef
revoltillo	scrambled eggs
revuelto	scrambled
ron	rum
rosbif	roast beef
sal	salt
salchicha	sausage
salsa	sauce
sopa	soup
tasajo	jerked beef
té	tea
ternera	veal
tiburón	shark
tocino	bacon
tomates	tomatos
toronja	grapefruit
tortilla	omelette
tortuga	turtle
tostada	toasted
tostones	banana chips
vegetariano	vegetarian
vino	wine
yuca	manioc, cassava
zanahoria	carrot

Days of the Week

Monday	*lunes*
Tuesday	*martes*
Wednesday	*miércoles*
Thursday	*jueves*
Friday	*viernes*
Saturday	*sábado*
Sunday	*domingo*

Time

Telling time is fairly straightforward. Eight o'clock is *las ocho*, while 8:30 is *las ocho y treinta* (literally, eight and thirty) or *las ocho y media* (eight and a half). However, 7:45 is *las ocho menos quince* (literally, eight minus fifteen) or *las ocho menos cuarto* (eight minus one quarter). Times are modified by morning *(de la mañana)* or afternoon *(de la tarde)* instead of am or pm. It's also common to use the 24-hour clock, especially with transportation schedules.

Numbers

1	*uno*	101	*ciento uno*
2	*dos*	102	*ciento dos*
3	*tres*	110	*ciento diez*
4	*cuatro*	120	*ciento veinte*
5	*cinco*	130	*ciento treinta*
6	*seis*	200	*doscientos*
7	*siete*	300	*trescientos*
8	*ocho*	400	*cuatrocientos*
9	*nueve*	500	*quinientos*
10	*diez*	600	*seiscientos*
11	*once*	700	*setecientos*
12	*doce*	800	*ochocientos*
13	*trece*	900	*novecientos*
14	*catorce*	1000	
15	*quince*		*mil*
16	*dieciseis*	1100	
17	*diecisiete*		*mil cien*
18	*dieciocho*	1200	
19	*diecinueve*		*mil doscientos*
20	*veinte*	2000	
21	*veintiuno*		*dos mil*
22	*veintidós*	5000	
30	*treinta*		*cinco mil*
31	*treinta y uno*	10,000	
40	*cuarenta*		*diez mil*
50	*cincuenta*	50,000	
60	*sesenta*		*cincuenta mil*
70	*setenta*	100,000	
80	*ochenta*		*cien mil*
90	*noventa*	1,000,000	
100	*cien*		*un millón*

Facts for the Visitor

PLANNING

When to Go

Winter (December to April) is Cuba's peak tourist season, a time when plane-loads of Canadians and Europeans arrive in pursuit of the southern sun. Cubans take their holidays in July and August, when the local beaches are at their most crowded. These seasons are reflected in hotel prices, which run about 25% higher in those periods. The prime seasons for participating in the various sporting activities appear in the Activities section below. For the approximate dates of some of the main festivals, turn to Public Holidays & Special Events. The hot, rainy season runs from May to October, although the seasonal variations are less than those in North America and Europe. In short, there isn't a really bad time to visit Cuba, but the facilities do become overcrowded at Christmas, Easter, and around July 26, times to avoid if possible.

What Kind of Trip?

The type of plane ticket you buy will depend on whether you want to spend most of your time at the beach or you'd rather see the cities and perhaps drive around the countryside. If your main aim is a week or two of holidays between the sun and surf, you'll find it much cheaper and easier to book a package tour that includes flights, airport transfers, accommodations, and breakfast and dinner. Those bound for the towns, however, will do better to make as few advance reservations as possible to allow maximum flexibility.

Because of fuel shortages the number of public buses available for getting around on your own has declined sharply in the past few years, although train travel is still readily available. It's no problem at all to strap on a backpack and tour much of Cuba by rail, staying at budget hotels or in private rooms along the way. As yet, very few people are doing this, so you'll be something of a pioneer.

Those willing to spend a bit more money can see Cuba in relative comfort from behind the wheel of a rental jeep. Obtaining fuel for cash dollars is easy enough and you can go almost anywhere you like. Lots of hotels are available around the country and they'll usually scramble to find you a room. Your biggest problem will be food; the hotel and other state-run restaurants are slow and overpriced, and what's available at street stalls is basic. Both low- and high-budget travelers on their own will do better to eat at private restaurants *(paladares)*, which are growing in number around Cuba.

Maps

The best all-purpose map is the *Automapa Nacional* available at hotel shops and car rental offices in Cuba. The highway information is reliable, there's a complete index, and road rules are outlined in English. It's a must for motorists.

Also excellent is the *Mapa Turística Cuba* published by the Instituto Cubano de Geodesia y Cartografía (which also uses the name Ediciones GEO). In addition to the island map, it contains an indexed map of Havana, nine other city or regional maps, a highway distance chart, and a bit of general information.

Geodesia y Cartografía also publishes Guía Turística map books for La Habana Vieja, Varadero, and Santiago de Cuba, and individual Mapa Turística city plans of most Cuban towns. It's worth picking these up at hotel shops if you want to explore an area in depth.

The best map published outside Cuba is the Freytag & Berndt 1:1,250,000 Cuba map, originally published in Hungary. The island map is good and indexed town plans of Havana, Playas del Este, Varadero, Cienfuegos, Camagüey, and Santiago de Cuba are thrown in for free. The *Bartholomew*

Cuba Holiday Map is exactly the same as the Freytag & Berndt map, but it is more expensive.

Also available is Hildebrandt's Cuba map at 1:1,100,000. It has a table of distances and some superficial tourist information in three languages but only a small map of Havana. Hildebrandt would do well to replace the useless tourist information with town and regional plans.

What to Bring

Special items to bring include a hat, sunglasses, sunscreen, a small folding umbrella, a flashlight, batteries, matches, a candle, a bottle opener, a canteen, pens, paper, reading material, a Spanish-English dictionary, insect repellent, tampons, and all personal toilet articles and cosmetics. Those traveling with babies should also bring disposable diapers. Don't bother bringing a sleeping bag or sheet unless you're planning to pitch your own tent.

Locally produced medicines are cheap in Cuba, but most foreign medications are unavailable. It's always wise to carry basic supplies such as adhesive bandages, antidiarrhea pills, aspirin and other pain killers, and disinfectant.

Only standard color print film is available and even then it's better to bring your own (up to five rolls per person maximum). Pack your film in a lead bag to protect it from airport X-ray machines.

The temperature seldom drops below 15°C, so only light cotton clothing is required. However, a lightweight sweater may be useful as many hotel restaurants and most hotel rooms are air-conditioned. Avoid bringing synthetic garments; these quickly become uncomfortable in hot weather. Thin clothing that can be added in layers is much better than a heavy coat you'll probably never use. In January and February a windbreaker may be necessary. Shorts are fine for both men and women at the tourist resorts, but men are usually required to wear long trousers to dinner at hotels. Occasionally a museum or church will turn away tourists if they're wearing shorts or transparent clothing.

Away from the beach hotels, it's unwise to wear flashy clothes in Cuba as these only mark you as a foreign tourist, to the delight of panhandlers and assorted hustlers. Wearing shorts when visiting towns is equivalent to carrying a large sign marked 'tourist.' You'll be more accepted if you dress simply and modestly.

Food is scarce in Cuba and most hotel shops sell only cookies, candies, soft drinks, and alcohol. You'll be less dependent on the inefficient hotel restaurants if you take along a plug-in water heater of the kind for sale at stores stocking small electrical gadgets (such as Radio Shack in North America). With this you can heat water in a metal or glass cup (plastic might melt) to make tea, powdered soup, instant noodles, and so on, all of which you must bring with you. The heater must take 110 to 125 volts (as in North America), as few hotel rooms have 220-volt outlets (see the Electricity section below for a warning about voltages). Also consider packing a few bags of nuts since you won't be able to buy much nutritious snack food in Cuba.

For an idea of the sort of things you'll be able to pick up in Cuba itself, see the Things to Buy section at the end of this chapter. If you think you might need something not mentioned there, plan to bring it.

Gifts Reader Giorgio Grazzini of Arezzo, Italy, sent us this:

To help balance the effect of the unfair commercial blockade, two friends and I decided to bring something for a Cuban school. Before leaving Italy we bought 100 cheap ball-point pens for about US$16 and when I was in Santa Clara I donated them to a primary school. The headmistress, teachers, and the children were all quite moved and happy, and I was so impressed that my friends and I are now preparing a parcel of pens, pencils, erasers, and solar calculators to mail to Cuba.

If you decide to follow Giorgio's example, we suggest giving the items to a responsible person at the school and not directly to the children or to people on the street. Try to pick a school in an area off the tourist track and don't disturb the school's routine.

Other things to take to Cuba are medicines, calculators, and computers to donate to neighborhood polyclinics, and used clothing for Cuban friends. Be prepared, however, to have your gifts rejected at times. The Cubans are a proud people and the last thing they want is charity from condescending foreigners. It might be better to inquire first and only produce the goods after you're told they'd be welcome.

Organizations sending humanitarian aid to Cuba include the following groups, all of which are deserving of your support:

Center for Cuban Studies
   124 W 23rd St, New York, NY 10011, USA
   (☎ 212-242-0559, fax 212-242-1937)
Cuba-Infomed
   PO Box 450, Santa Clara, CA 95052, USA
   (☎ 408-243-4359, fax 408-243-1229)
Cuba Solidarity Campaign
   129 Seven Sisters Rd, London N7 7QG, UK
   (☎ 0171-263-6452, fax 0171-561-0191)
US/Cuba Medical Project
   198 Broadway, Suite 800, New York, NY
   10038, USA
   (☎ 212-227-5270, fax 212-227-4859)

SUGGESTED ITINERARIES

Independent travelers with only a week to see Cuba should concentrate on a small area, such as either Havana-Matanzas-Varadero or Holguín-Bayamo-Santiago de Cuba. Two weeks would be enough for Havana visitors to extend their trips to one or more of Pinar del Río, the Bay of Pigs, and Isla de la Juventud. Santiago de Cuba-bound visitors with two weeks could throw in Baracoa, Marea del Portillo, and perhaps Guardalavaca.

Visitors willing to rent a car for a month could see most of Cuba in that time. Budget travelers with a month to see Cuba by train and bus could go Havana-Santa Clara-Cienfuegos-Trinidad-Sancti Spíritus-Ciego de Ávila-Camagüey-Bayamo-Santiago de Cuba-Holguín-Havana. A good alternative to flying into Havana would be booking your international flight in and out of Holguín or Santiago de Cuba, which are less crowded places for beginning a trip.

THE BEST & THE WORST

In the personal opinion of the author, the following are the best and worst attractions of Cuba:

Top 10

- *Alto del Naranjo*
  The unparalleled combination of natural beauty, hiking possibilities, and revolutionary sites make this unique place well worth the drive or trek.

- *Baracoa*
  Sitting on a picturesque bay at the east end of the island, Cuba's oldest colonial town offers intriguing historical sites, stimulating excursions, a laid-back atmosphere, and agreeable accommodations.

- *Camagüey*
  This seldom-visited city harbors a wealth of historical monuments and museums. There are also good facilities and a lively street life.

- *Isla de la Juventud*
  The pace slows noticeably on this untouristed agricultural island, and it's a pleasure to explore the small riverside town and surrounding sites on foot. Some of Cuba's best scuba diving is off the south coast.

- *La Habana Vieja and Its Fortifications*
  No one will want to miss this wonderful city, and the nightlife rivals that of New York.

- *Parque Céspedes in Bayamo*
  Off the beaten tourist track, Bayamo's place in Cuban history is best absorbed on one of the shady benches around its central square.

- *Parroquia de San Juan Bautista in Remedios*
  The architectural and artistic wealth of this little-known colonial church will dazzle you.

- *Trinidad*
  Cobbled streets, cool colonial courtyards, ramshackle mansions, colorful handicrafts, lush tropical vegetation, and a wealth of museums – Trinidad has it all, and some of Cuba's finest beach and mountain resorts are just a short drive away.

- *Villa Turística Los Pinos, Pinar del Río Province*
  Hikers, bird watchers, and romantics will love

this unpublicized mountain resort created in the 1960s by Fidel's secretary Celia Sánchez.

• *Mayabe Beer*
If you thought good beer could only be brewed in cold countries like Canada or Germany, think again. There's no better way to end a day than with a bottle of chilled Mayabe, available everywhere.

Bottom 10

• *American Naval Base, Guantánamo*
This humiliating relic of early 20th-century American imperialism is a sterile expatriate camp soaking up American tax dollars in the name of US political hegemony in Latin America.

• *Ciego de Ávila*
Skip this dreary provincial town on your trip across the island.

• *Ernesto Guevara Nickel Smelter, Moa*
If environmentalism is your interest, the grit, smoke, and wastes of Moa will set your teeth on edge.

• *Hustlers on Plaza de Dolores, Santiago de Cuba*
This city's persistent panhandlers and confidence men make you grateful the police don't allow them to operate in Havana.

• *Juraguá Nuclear Power Plant, near Cienfuegos*
Juraguá's sinister round dome looming on the city's horizon is another potential nuclear threat.

• *Oil Refinery, near Havana Harbor*
The chimneys of this facility drop black soot over the city 24 hours a day.

• *Playa Santa Lucía*
The beach is OK and the scuba diving fine, but Santa Lucía is separated from the rest of Cuba by endless stretches of flatlands and swamp. Even if you're after only a glimpse of the sea, you'll find more memorable resorts elsewhere in Cuba.

• *Valle de la Prehistoria in Baconao*
The cement dinosaurs here are Disneyland without the rides and crowds. It's so tacky it's almost funny.

• *Varadero Oil Field*
When the winds are blowing the wrong way, suffocating sulfuric fumes from the wells drift across the peninsula's resorts in the dead of night.

• *Villa Maspotón, Pinar del Río*
The only draw of this desolate place is a chance to boost your ego by killing local birds.

TOURIST OFFICES
Tourist Offices Abroad

Cuba has an extensive network of tourism promotion offices overseas that are excellent sources of free brochures and information. We provide a complete list of these below, and it's well worth dropping in or giving them a call. Other Cuban travel companies with offices around the world include the government hotel corporation Grupo Cubanacán and Cubana Airlines, both potential sources of useful information (addresses below).

Argentina
Cuban Tourist Board, Paraguay No 631, 2do piso A, Buenos Aires
(☎ 54-1-311-4198)

Canada
Bureau de Tourisme de Cuba, 440 Boulevard René Lévesque Ouest, Bureau 1402, Montreal, Quebec H2Z 1V7
(☎ 514-857-8004, fax 514-875-8006)
Cuban Tourist Board, 55 Queen St East, Suite 705, Toronto, Ontario M5C 1R6
(☎ 416-362-0700, fax 416-362-6799)

France
Office de Tourisme de Cuba, 280 Boulevard Raspael, Paris 75014
(☎ 33-01-4538-9010, fax 33-01-4538-9930)

Germany
Cuban Tourist Board, An der Hauptwache 7, 60313 Frankfurt/Main
(☎ 49-69-288-322, fax 49-69-296-664)

Italy
Ufficio di Promozione ed Informazione Turistica di Cuba, Via General Fara 30, terzo piano, Milano 20124
(☎ 39-2-6698-1463, fax 39-2-669-0042)

Mexico
  Cuban Tourist Board, Insurgentes Sur
  No 421, Complejo Aristos, Edificio B,
  Local 310, Mexico City 06100, DF
  (☎ 52-5-574-9454)

Netherlands
  Cuban Tourist Board, Jan van Gentstraat 130,
  1171 GN Badhoevedorp
  (☎ 31-20-659-9271, fax 31-20-659-9218)

Spain
  Oficina de Promoción e Información
  Turística de Cuba, Paseo de La Habana 27,
  Madrid 28036
  (☎ 34-1-411-3097, fax 34-1-564-5804)

Cubanacán Offices The hotel corporation Grupo Cubanacán has offices worldwide that provide information about their hotels and sell Cuban travel videos, but they don't book tours or reserve rooms.

Brazil
  Cubanacán, Avenida Bandera Paulista
  600-1A, Itaim-Bibi CEP 04532-00
  (☎ 55-11-822-6625, fax 55-11-822-4926)

Canada
  Cubanacán, 372 Bay St, Suite 1902,
  Toronto, Ontario M5H 2W9
  (☎ 416-601-0343, fax 416-601-0346)

France
  Cubanacán Tour Maine, Montparnasse,
  BP 15883, Avenue du Maine, 75755 Paris
  Cedex 15
  (☎ 33-01-4538-8966, fax 33-01-4538-8968)

Italy
  Cubanacán, Via Fablo Filzi 33,
  20124 Milano
  (☎ 39-2-6671-1219, fax 39-2-6671-0839)

Mexico
  Cubanacán, Sonora No 149–301, Colonia
  Hipódromo Condesa, DF 06140
  (☎ 52-5-256-4714)

Netherlands
  Cubanacán, Visseringlaan 24,
  2288 ER Rijswijk
  (☎ 31-70-390-5152, fax 31-70-319-3452)

Spain
  Cubanacán, Pedro Mugurusa No 3, 1A,
  Madrid 28036
  (☎ 34-1-350-8813, fax 34-1-359-8637)

UK
  Cubanacán Skylines, Unit 49, Limeharbor,
  Docklands, London E14 9TS
  (☎ 44-171-537-7909, fax 44-171-537-7747)

Local Tourist Offices

To date most tourism to Cuba has been of the packaged variety, and there are almost no general tourist information offices for individual travelers. You can always try the state-run travel agencies such as Havanatur and Rumbos, although their function is to book accommodations, rental vehicles, sightseeing tours, flights, and so on, and they have little or no information on alternative moneysaving possibilities. Outside of the main centers of Havana, Varadero, and Santiago de Cuba, you'll be lucky to find even them, much less a tourist office.

Cubana Offices Cuba's national airline, Cubana de Aviación, has offices in many of the world's large cities. In addition to those listed below, there are offices in Bogotá, Buenos Aires, Cologne, Guayaquil, Moscow, Panama City, Rio de Janeiro, Santiago de Chile, and Sao Paulo. These are often good sources of brochures and information.

Belgium
  Rue des Ménapiens 9–11, 1040 Bruxelles
  (☎ 32-2-734-8008, fax 32-2-734-8022)

Canada
  4 Place Ville Marie, Suite 405, Montreal,
  Quebec H3B 2E7
  (☎ 514-871-1222, fax 415-871-1227)

Dominican Republic
  Calle San Francisco de Macorís No 58,
  Sector Don Bosco, Santo Domingo
  (☎ 809-687-7114, fax 809-686-0275)

France
  Tour Maine Montparnasse, 33 Avenue
  du Maine, BP 171, 75755 Paris
  Cedex 15
  (☎ 33-01-4538-3114, fax 33-01-4538-3110)

Germany
  Frankfurter Tor 8A, 1034 Berlin
  (☎ 49-30-589-3409)

Jamaica
  Cubana Airlines, 22 Trafalgar Rd 2, ND
  Floor Suite 11, Kingston 10
  (☎ 1-809-927-7355)

Mexico
  Temístocles 246, Colonia Polanco, C.P.
  11550 México, DF
  (☎ 52-5-255-3776, fax 52-5-255-0835)
  Avenida Yazchilán No 23 SM-24 M-22,
  Cancún, Quintana Roo
  (☎ 52-98-877333)

Spain
  Princesa 25, Edificio Exágono, Madrid
  (☎ 34-1-542-2923, fax 34-1-541-6642)
UK
  49 Conduit St, London W1R 9FB
  (☎ 44-171-734-1165, fax 44-171-437-0681)

VISAS & DOCUMENTS
Passports & Tourist Cards
Everyone needs a passport valid at least six
months ahead and a tourist card (tarjeta de
turista). Those booking a package tour will
receive the card together with their other
travel documents. Those traveling independently can obtain the card through the
travel agency or airline office that sells
them their plane ticket or at a Cuban consulate (call ahead and ask if you have to
make an appointment to apply). If necessary, you can also buy the card upon arrival
at Havana's José Martí International
Airport (but not at other airports). Everyone – including babies – must have a
card. Theoretically, nationals of Denmark,
Italy, Norway, Sweden, Switzerland, and
Yugoslavia don't require visas or tourist
cards, but check this with your air carrier.

The cards cost CDN$14 in Canada or 25
Dutch guilders in Holland when obtained
through a travel agency or airline, or about
twice that when purchased at a consulate or
airport. It's always better to obtain the card
beforehand rather than hope to pick one
up at Havana airport as airline personnel
at many airports deny boarding to those
without a card. The passport number
entered on the tourist card must correspond
to the number of the passport you'll use to
travel (if you get a new passport, you'll
also need a new card). Don't enter journalist in the occupation column as that would
indicate that you require a visa.

The tourist card allows a stay of four
weeks and this can be extended for another
four weeks without difficulty upon payment of a US$25 fee. Incidentally, the
tourist card is only a means of collecting money for the Cuban government, and
once inside Cuba itself you'll never have to
show it unless you try to extend your stay at
an immigration office. The card can be
safely stowed away with your air ticket in
your money belt (don't leave it in your
passport as it could fall out and get lost).
Replacing a lost tourist card in Cuba costs
US$25 and you won't be allowed to leave
the country until you've paid.

Visas
Anyone wishing to prearrange a stay of
longer than four weeks must apply for a
regular visa (US$25) at a consulate, but
rather than enter into such a process it's
much easier simply to extend your stay
after arrival. Visas are required of business
travelers and journalists on assignment,
and application should be made through a
consulate at least three weeks in advance
(longer if you apply through a consulate in
a country other than your own). Visitors
with visas must apply for an exit permit
from an immigration office after arriving
in Cuba. Those planning to stay in Cuba
over three months must have an HIV test.

Visa Extensions Visa extensions up to
180 days are possible, one month at a time,
at the discretion of the Cuban immigration
authorities. The correct procedure is to go
to an immigration office and show the officials your tourist card and passport. If
they're willing to give you an extension,
you must then go to a hotel tour desk and
pay the US$25 fee. Upon receiving the
receipt, immigration will give you an
extension. If they think you're a legitimate
tourist, you'll have no problem getting an
extension. Anyone staying longer than 90
days requires an exit permit to leave Cuba.

Entry Permits for Cubans
& Naturalized Citizens
Naturalized citizens of other countries who
were born in Cuba require an entry permit
(autorización de entrada) issued by a
Cuban embassy or consulate. In November 1995 a new travel document called
a Vigencia de Viaje was announced for
Cubans resident abroad. It would allow
the holder to visit Cuba as many times
as he or she liked over a two-year period.
Persons hostile to the revolution or with a

criminal record would not be eligible. Current information is available at all Cuban diplomatic offices.

The Cuban government does not recognize dual citizenship. All persons born in Cuba are considered Cuban citizens unless they have formally renounced their Cuban citizenship at a Cuban diplomatic mission and the renunciation has been accepted. Cuban Americans with questions about dual nationality can contact the Office of Overseas Citizens Services, Department of State, Washington, DC 20520.

Mexican Tourist Cards

Travelers (other than Mexicans) making a return trip to Cuba from Mexico or continuing to Mexico from Cuba must have a Mexican tourist card or visa; otherwise, they could be refused entry to Cuba. Mexican tourist cards are issued free of charge by Mexican consulates and tourist offices around the world, and those making a roundtrip to Cuba via Mexico should obtain two cards, one for each journey through Mexico. Your travel agent or airline will be able to provide advice.

Licenses for US Visitors

In 1961 the US government imposed an order limiting the ability of its own citizens to visit Cuba. Airline offices and travel agencies in the US are forbidden to book tourist travel to Cuba via third countries. However, the Cuban government has never banned Americans from visiting Cuba and continues to receive US passport holders under exactly the same terms as any other visitor. In addition, there is absolutely no popular animosity against individual Americans in Cuba, and those who approach the country with respect will receive the same warm welcome Cubans extend to all their visitors.

Americans can easily go to Cuba via Canada, Mexico, or the Bahamas. American travel agents are prohibited from handling tourism arrangements, so most Americans must work though a foreign travel agency. Travel agents in those countries routinely arrange Cuban tourist cards,

flight reservations, and accommodations packages. We list a number of agents in the Getting There & Away chapter.

The immigration officials in Cuba know very well that a Cuban stamp in a US passport can create problems. When you hand over your passport to the Cuban immigration officer, request that he not stamp it. The officer will instead stamp your tourist card or a separate visa form that is collected as you leave Cuba. Be aware that if you will be transiting Jamaica on your way to Cuba, Jamaican immigration may stamp 'Departure for Cuba' in your passport if you alert them of your plans.

The US government has an 'Interests Section' in Havana, but American visitors are advised to avoid all contact with this heavily guarded office unless they have official US government permission to be in Cuba. Unofficial US visitors should be especially careful not to lose their passport while in Cuba as this would put them in a very difficult position.

The US government does issue special 'licenses' to visit Cuba to journalists, academics engaged in research, foreign officials based in the US, and occasionally on humanitarian grounds. In October 1995 the list of categories was expanded to include: students enrolled in a course in Cuba sponsored by a US college or university; teachers involved in educational exchanges; anyone with an established interest in the subject matter attending a meeting or conference organized by an international institution or association that regularly sponsors meetings and conferences in other countries; professionals attending a Cuban-sponsored conference or seminar; persons collecting information for an organization with an established interest in international relations; freelance journalists willing to provide a detailed description of their proposed research; religious missionaries; and fully hosted individuals who travel on non-Cuban flights. Cuban-Americans may visit relatives in Cuba once a year without a license 'in cases of extreme humanitarian need.' Such permits are never issued for the purpose of business travel or tourism.

For more information contact the Licensing Division (☎ 202-622-2480, fax 202-622-1657), Office of Foreign Assets Control, US Department of the Treasury, 1500 Pennsylvania Ave NW, Annex Building, 2nd Floor, Washington, DC 20220. Travel arrangements for those eligible for a license can be made by US companies such as Marazul Tours in New Jersey (listed in the Getting There & Away chapter). License holders are only allowed to spend US$100 per person per day for land arrangements.

Under the 'Trading with the Enemy Act,' goods originating in Cuba are prohibited from entering the US. Cuban cigars, rum, books, and so on will be confiscated by US customs, and the officials can create additional problems if they feel so inclined. Possession of Cuban goods inside the US is also banned. Theoretically one can receive a US$50,000 fine and 10 years in prison for attempting to smuggle Cuban goods into the US, but we've never heard of anyone actually being prosecuted for this crime.

Technically, the US government doesn't prohibit its own citizens from going to Cuba, only from spending money there. The 1996 Helms-Burton Bill, which was signed into law by President Clinton on March 12, 1996, imposes without judicial review fines of up to US$50,000 and confiscation of property on US citizens who visit Cuba at their own expense without US government permission. In addition, under the Trading with the Enemy Act, they may also face up to US$250,000 in fines and up to 10 years in prison. It remains to be seen how this legislation will be implemented. However, we haven't heard of anyone who has actually been fined or imprisoned for visiting Cuba, although we have heard of travelers who have been notified that they may be. The author and publisher accept no responsibility for anyone affected. We believe the decision to visit Cuba should be a personal matter.

. If you do choose to go and wish to avoid unnecessary hassles with the US border guards, American travelers should get rid of anything related to their trip to Cuba, including used air tickets, baggage tags, travel documents, receipts, and souvenirs, before returning to the US. Most US customs officers have better things to do than trying to catch Americans who have been to Cuba, but you could always come up against an overzealous officer.

Onward Tickets

Everyone entering Cuba must have a return or onward plane ticket, and individuals not on a package tour could be asked to show US$50 for every day they plan to spend in Cuba (in practice, this almost never happens). Those not on a tour may be told by the travel agent or airline clerk that they need a hotel voucher for at least three nights accommodations (not necessarily consecutive nights). The agent should be able to arrange this; otherwise, you can purchase the voucher from a tour desk at the airport in Cuba itself. The immigration officials in Cuba usually don't ask to see any vouchers, and if you can avoid prepaying for accommodations, do so as urban hotels are usually cheaper when paid for on the spot. If you enter the name of a likely hotel in the respective space on your tourist card, the question probably won't come up (don't leave that space blank).

Passengers in transit to third countries may stay 72 hours without a visa or tourist card as long as they arrange hotel accommodations at the airport tour desk and have confirmed flight reservations. Cruise ship passengers may also disembark for up to 72 hours without a tourist card or visa.

Photocopies

About the best travel insurance available is a photocopy of the information pages of your passport, visas, birth certificate, credit cards, airline tickets, driver's license, and other documents, and a list of all your traveler's check numbers with the phone number you'd need to call should they be lost (the same number will usually freeze lost credit cards upon request). If possible, cárry a spare US$50 bill somewhere on your person so you won't suddenly be destitute if everything else is stolen.

Travel Insurance

Travel insurance won't be of much use here unless you have a very serious accident. Emergency medical care is free in Cuba and outpatient treatment at special clinics designed for foreigners is reasonable, so travel health insurance will only pay off if you require prolonged hospitalization or an emergency medical evacuation to your home country (make sure that's covered). Most plans only reimburse expenses above those already covered by your regular group insurance and are invalid if you don't have another policy. Some policies specifically exclude 'dangerous activities' such as scuba diving, water-skiing, trekking, or simply riding a motor scooter. If such activities are on your agenda, you don't want that sort of policy.

In Cuba you'll probably have to pay your medical bills up front in cash or by credit card and wait until you get home to be reimbursed by the insurance company. Make sure you keep all documentation. Some policies ask you to call back to a center in your home country where an immediate assessment of your problem is made.

Cancellation insurance is only valid if you have a health or family reason for not making the trip – being refused a visa or canceling the trip because you've changed your mind are not covered. Even if the tour operator or airline cancels the trip for their own reasons, the insurance fee itself is non-refundable. So buying cancellation insurance is the same as buying a lottery ticket: There's always a chance you'll win, but it's usually money down the drain.

Baggage insurance is similar. If you routinely purchase baggage insurance for all your trips, you'll probably do so for this trip. Otherwise, there's no reason to make a special case of Cuba. If you're really concerned, ask your airline about the maximum baggage claims allowed by the insurance included in the price of your air ticket. Always carry valuable or irreplaceable items in your hand luggage.

These insurance policies have many other complicated restrictions listed in the fine print, and they're usually only valid for residents of the country in which they are issued. If you're offered travel insurance issued by a US company (including foreign subsidiaries), be sure to ask if it covers you in Cuba. Your travel agent will invariably push travel insurance at you just to earn another commission, so be prepared.

Driver's License & Permits

Either your regular driver's license or an international driving permit is sufficient to rent a car in Cuba.

Hostel Card

There are no youth hostels in Cuba, so a Hosteling International card won't prove useful.

Student, Youth & Senior Cards

We're not aware of any discounts or special privileges accruing from these cards in Cuba. We would be grateful if readers brought anything of this kind to our attention. You might be allowed free or reduced entry to a museum by showing a student card, but such treatment is usually as a personal favor granted by the museum staff rather than any official policy (before 1990 all museums were free to everyone).

International Health Card

A yellow-fever vaccination is required if you're arriving directly from a South American country where the disease is endemic (check with your airline not less than two weeks in advance). Yellow fever vaccinations are valid for 10 years.

Otherwise, no vaccinations are required, although a tetanus vaccination may be a good idea if you'll be heading far off the beaten track (if you're on a package tour, forget it). See the Health section below for more detailed information.

Special Entry Procedures

Yacht No prior visas or reservations are required of those traveling by yacht, but you will have to purchase tourist cards upon arrival if you plan to stay longer than

72 hours. In light of ongoing provocations by Florida-based Cuban exiles, it's important that private yachts bound for Cuba try to make radio contact with the Cuban port authorities over channel 16 (VHF) or the National Coastal Network over 2790 or 7462 HF (SSB) before crossing the 12-mile limit. Say *llamando seguridad marítima* (calling marine security) and quote the name of the port. If you're approaching Havana, call the Marina Hemingway over channel 72 and they'll arrange everything. At Varadero it's the Marina Acua on channel 68.

If you receive no answer, continue sailing toward your port of entry with your yellow quarantine flag flying below the Cuban courtesy flag. Repeat the message at regular intervals, and eventually a Cuban official will answer and ask for information about your boat. All you need to do from then on is to follow the instructions. Head for the Guarda Frontera wharf if entering through a small port.

The best way to facilitate clearance formalities is to send a telex to 511-336 or 511-243 TURCU or a fax to 53-7-33-3104 at least 72 hours in advance. List the names, dates and places of birth, occupations, and passport numbers of all passengers and crew, and state the name, color, type, size, and registration number of the vessel, the last port cleared, the expected port of entry, and the estimated arrival time. It's not compulsory, however, so don't worry if you can't manage to do this.

Official ports of entry on the north coast are Santa Lucía in Pinar del Río province, the Marina Hemingway at Havana, any of the three marinas at Varadero, Playa Santa Lucía, Bahía de Naranjo near Guardalavaca, and Baracoa. On the south coast you have a choice of Santiago de Cuba, Manzanillo, Casilda, Jagua, Cayo Largo, and the Hotel Colony on Isla de la Juventud. Required documents include the passports of everyone on board; the ownership papers, title, and registration certificate of the vessel; and the clearance document *(zarpe)* from your last port with Cuba listed as your destination. For maximum

flexibility ask for 30 days even if you only expect to be in Cuban waters for a week.

Much more information about all these matters is contained in *The Cruising Guide to Cuba* by Simon Charles, mentioned in the Books section below.

Private Plane The pilots of private planes must contact the Instituto de Aeronáutica Civil de Cuba (telex 511-737 CIVCU), Calle 23 No 64, Vedado, La Habana, not less than 10 days prior to landing at a Cuban airport or 48 hours before a flight over Cuban territory. The communication should mention whether it will be a commercial or private flight and list the type, color, and registration number of the aircraft, the departure point, expected place of arrival, and flight times. Prepayment of the reply is required. Failure to follow this procedure could have serious consequences.

EMBASSIES
Cuban Embassies Abroad
Australia
    Cuban Consulate-General, 16 Manwaring Ave, Maroubra, NSW 2035
    (☎ 61-2-311-4611, fax 61-2-311-1255)
Belgium
    Cuban Embassy, Robert Jonesstraat 77, 1180 Brussels
    (☎ 32-2-343-0020, fax 32-2-344-9691)
Canada
    Cuban Embassy, 388 Main St, Ottawa, Ontario K1S 1E3, Canada
    (☎ 613-563-0141, fax 613-563-0068)
    Cuban Consulate-General, 5353 Dundas St West, Suite 401, Etobicoke, Ontario M9B 6H8, Canada
    (☎ 416-234-8181, fax 416-234-2754)
    Cuban Consulate-General and Trade Commission, 1415 Pine Ave West, Montreal, Quebec H3B 1B2
    (☎ 514-843-8897, fax 514-982-9034)
France
    Cuban Embassy, 16 Rue de Presles, 75015 Paris
    (☎ 33-01-4567-5535, fax 33-01-4566-8092)
Germany
    Cuban Embassy, Kennedy Allee 22, 53175 Bonn (☎ 49-228-3090, fax 49-309-244)
Mexico
    Cuban Embassy, Presidente Masarik 554,

Colonia Polanco, 11560 México, DF
(☎ 52-5-280-8039, fax 52-5-280-0839)
Netherlands
Cuban Embassy, Prins Mauritslaan 6, 2582
LR Den Haag
(☎ 31-70-354-1417, fax 31-70-352-0159)
Cuban Consulate, Stationsplein 45, 3013
AK Rotterdam (☎ /fax 31-10-412-8970)
UK
Cuban Embassy, 167 High Holburn, London
WC1V 6PA, England
(☎ 44-171-240-2488, fax 44-171-836-2602)
USA
Cuban Interests Office, 2639 16th St NW,
Washington, DC 20009 (☎ 202-797-8609)

Foreign Embassies in Cuba

Austrian Embassy, Calle 4 No 101 at Avenida 1,
in Miramar (☎ 33-2394; weekdays 9 am to
noon)
Belgian Embassy, Avenida 5 No 7408 at
Avenida 76 in Miramar-Playa (☎ 33-2410;
weekdays 9 am to 2 pm)
British Embassy, Calle 34 No 708 at Avenida 7
in Miramar (☎ 33-1771; weekdays 8:30 am
to noon)
Canadian Embassy, Calle 30 No 518 at
Avenida 7 in Miramar (☎ 33-2516; Monday,
Tuesday, Thursday, and Friday 8 am to
4:30 pm, Wednesday 8 am to 1:30 pm)
French Embassy, Calle 14 No 312 between 3
and 5 in Miramar (☎ 33-2132; weekdays
10 am to noon)
Italian Embassy, Paseo No 606 between 25 and
27 in Vedado (☎ 33-3334; weekdays 10 am
to 1 pm)
Japanese Embassy, Calle N No 62 at Calle 15
behind Servi-Cupet in Vedado (☎ 33-3454;
weekdays 8 am to 3 pm)
Mexican Embassy, Calle 12 No 518 at 7 in
Miramar (☎ 33-2383; weekdays 9 am to
noon)
Netherlands Embassy, Calle 8 No 307 between
3 and 5 in Miramar (☎ 33-2512; weekdays
8:30 to 11:30 am)
Spanish Embassy, Capdevila No 51 at
Agramonte in Centro Havana (☎ 33-8029;
weekdays 9 am to 1 pm)
Swedish Embassy, Avenida 31 No 1411
between 14 and 18 in Miramar (☎ 33-2563;
weekdays 9 am to noon)
Swiss Embassy, Avenida 5 No 2005 between 20
and 22 in Miramar (☎ 33-2611; weekdays
9:15 am to 1 pm)
US Interests Section, Calzada between L and M
in Vedado (☎ 33-3550)

CUSTOMS

Cuban customs regulations allow visitors to bring along their personal belongings (including clothes, shoes, toilet articles, photographic equipment, binoculars, musical instrument, tape recorder, radio, personal computer, tent, fishing rod, tennis racket, nonmotorized bicycle, canoe or kayak under five meters long, surfboard, and other sporting gear), gifts up to a value of US$100, and 10 kilograms of medicine (excluding veterinary or blood-based medicines). In addition, those over the age of 18 may import three liters of wine or other alcoholic beverages, plus a choice of either 200 cigarettes, 50 cigars, or 250 grams of cut tobacco.

Unused items that do not fit into the categories mentioned above are subject to a 100% customs duty to a maximum of US$1000. For information on importing consumer goods worth over US$1000 and not for personal use, contact a Cuban consulate.

It's prohibited to export over US$5000 per person in cash from Cuba. Those carrying larger amounts of cash should fill out a customs declaration (declaración de valor) upon arrival in which case they will be allowed to export up to the amount imported and declared.

Items one cannot bring into Cuba include narcotics, explosives, motorized vehicles, obscene publications, and prerecorded video cassettes. The import of firearms, ammunition, weapons, telecommunications equipment, flora and fauna specimens, live animals, biological or pharmaceutical goods of animal origin, and unprocessed food (including all fresh fruit, meat, or vegetables) is restricted, so check beforehand. Canned, processed, and dried food is usually no problem. Even if you could manage to get a pet onto the plane, it would be put into quarantine upon arrival in Cuba and wouldn't be allowed into your hotel in any case.

MONEY

Three currencies circulate in Cuba. The Cuban peso or moneda nacional, divided into 100 centavos, is officially linked to the US dollar at the rate of one to one. On the street, one dollar is worth about 20 pesos. Although this seems like a bargain, it doesn't mean much since there's little to buy with pesos. A more powerful currency is the US dollar or *divisas*, which will buy almost anything. In December 1994 the *peso convertible* was introduced, and it really does have exactly the same value as the dollar.

As a foreign tourist you'll pay for virtually everything purchased from state entities in cash dollars or convertible pesos. This includes hotel rooms and activities; meals and drinks at state-owned restaurants and bars; souvenirs, alcohol, and cigars from hotel or hard currency shops; museum admissions; sightseeing excursions; rental cars; gasoline; taxi rides; and train or airline tickets. Things that can be paid for in Cuban pesos include snacks and drinks at self-service cafeterias; street stalls; some private restaurants; city bus fares; most cinema tickets; haircuts (except at hotels); postage stamps at local post offices (not hotel post offices); some books; and purchases in local stores where goods are freely available *(venta libre)* instead of rationed *(por libreta)*.

Since 1993 a parallel economy has emerged in which scarce goods and services are sold to Cubans for dollars, and getting to know which currency to use in which situations is an important part of learning how to survive in Cuba. Begin by assuming that everything paid for at a hotel or resort will be priced in dollars. Well-stocked supermarkets, snack bars selling canned drinks, and shops that carry compact discs invariably charge in dollars. You'll soon learn to recognize the hard-currency shops; otherwise, try paying in Cuban pesos and you'll soon be corrected if you're wrong. A basic rule of thumb is that if something desirable is available and there's no crowd of Cubans pushing for access, it's probably a hard-currency product.

Things are complicated at many state-owned restaurants, cafes, and bars where Cubans are allowed to pay in pesos, but foreigners must pay exactly the same amount in dollars. The best policy here is to assume that you'll be charged dollars and only sit down if you think it's worth the money. Also be aware that Cubans often say 'pesos' to foreigners when they really mean dollars, although *moneda nacional* has only one meaning – Cuban pesos.

Considering all of this, the best type of money to bring with you to Cuba is US cash dollars (in fact, visitors aren't allowed to bring Cuban pesos into the country). American bank notes are all the same color and size, so you must be careful when using them. Many Cuban cashiers are paranoid about getting stuck with counterfeit American currency, and you'll often be asked to show your passport when you spend a US$50 or US$100 bill. Your passport number and the serial number of the bank note will then be entered in a ledger – counterfeiters beware! Thus it's slightly better to have cash dollars in small bills, but you'll usually have no problem making change at major hotels and gas stations.

Costs

For a Caribbean destination, Cuba is reasonably affordable. A double room at a medium-priced beach resort in the high season will cost US$50 for the room only or US$100 including all meals and local drinks. A tourist hotel in a city will cost around US$30 double or US$20 double at a budget sports or university hotel. A room in a private home will be US$10 to US$15 double. A buffet lunch or dinner at an international resort will cost US$15 per person, while a filling meal at a private restaurant can be had for around US$5. Expect to pay US$1 for a can of beer at a city bar or US$2 at a resort. One hundred kilometers by train will cost US$4.

On the other hand, a beach holiday at an international resort in Cuba is only cheap if you book an all-inclusive package tour. Staying in private rooms, eating in private restaurants, and traveling in private taxis or by public transport is also inexpensive, but as soon as you start paying in dollars for official accommodations, meals, and transportation on a day-to-day basis, costs rise fast. Don't expect the black market to reduce your expenses since the Cuban peso doesn't buy much these days. Cuba isn't cheap the way Guatemala and Indonesia are cheap.

Traveler's Checks & Credit Cards

Credit cards and traveler's checks issued by US companies such as American Express, Citibank, and Diners Club or traveler's checks that clear through New York are not negotiable in Cuba. Eurocheques are also not accepted. Banamex, Carnet, Eurocard, JCB, MasterCard, and Visa credit cards issued by non-US banks are quite acceptable, as are Thomas Cook and Visa traveler's checks expressed in US dollars provided they are not issued by a US bank. Take along several cards if you plan large expenditures as maximum credit limits could apply. Cash advances are usually possible only on Visa and MasterCard (the best cards to take to Cuba). Avoid paying small amounts by credit card as the procedure is slow and your passport will be required. Most businesses in Cuba add a surcharge of 2% to 5% to your bill if you pay by credit card.

Expect a 2% commission to be charged when you change traveler's checks into cash US dollars at the state-owned Banco Nacional de Cuba or 3% at the privately owned Banco Financiero Internacional. Hotel receptions deduct 4% commission. There's often no commission to change foreign cash into cash US dollars, but the rate of exchange may be lower (ask). Don't write in the place, date, or payee when signing a traveler's check as it will probably be refused. Getting a refund for checks lost in Cuba is extremely difficult, and all you can do is report the loss and wait till you reach another country.

International Transfers

It's difficult to have money transferred telegraphically to Cuba and as a tourist you should avoid bothering with it. In emergencies, relatives, friends, or business associates abroad should be able to send money to you through Antillas Express (☎ 514-385-9449 or 514-385-9221), 9632 Charton Ave, Montreal, PQ H2B 2C5, Canada. Antillas promises delivery in under five days to Havana or 15 days elsewhere in Cuba for a commission of US$20 to US$85 depending on the amount. You can use the same system to send cash to Cuban relatives or friends.

Currency

The Cuban peso comes in notes of one, three, five, 10, 20, 50, and 100 pesos, and coins of one, two, five, 20, and 40 centavos, and one and three pesos. Each note is a distinct color. The seldom-seen one-centavo coin is called a *kilo*, the five-centavo coin a *medio*, and the 20-centavo coin a *peseta*. The three-peso coin bearing the likeness of Che Guevara makes a nice souvenir. It's even possible to buy peso bank notes in mint condition at airport departure lounges.

The convertible peso comes in multicolored notes of one, three, five, 10, 20, 50, and 100 pesos, and there are also special coins marked 'Intur' of the same size and value as US coins (five, 10, 25, and 50 cents and one peso). The purpose of the convertible peso is to reduce the 'float' of US currency in circulation, and it's worth exactly the same as the US dollar. Of course, they're only negotiable in Cuba, but excess convertible pesos can be changed into real dollars at the airport without question. The government hopes eventually to merge the convertible and nonconvertible pesos, but that isn't likely to happen soon. Although the export of Cuban currency is officially prohibited, Cuban customs won't bother with a few coins.

Changing Money

Dollar traveler's checks and most other hard currencies can be changed into cash dollars at hotel exchange desks and banks for 2% to 4% commission. If you're staying at a tourist resort, you'll hardly ever have the chance to spend Cuban pesos, so it's probably not worth changing any money at all. Otherwise, change only a small amount such as US$10 maximum. Excess non-convertible pesos can be reconverted into dollars at the airport to a maximum of 10 pesos per person, verified by an original exchange receipt.

Black Market

The Cuban peso is not convertible on world markets and the import/export of the currency is prohibited. To obtain dollars to purchase goods at hard-currency shops, Cubans must change their pesos on the black market and the number of pesos they must pay to buy a dollar fluctuates a great deal. In August 1994 the Cuban peso was trading at 120 to the dollar, but by early 1996 it had been brought down to 20 to the dollar by a government financial austerity program. Prices on the free market came down with the exchange rate (which was good for ordinary Cubans). Which way the peso will go in the future is anyone's guess, but any Cuban will be able to tell you the current rate. For some reason the dollar seems to be worth slightly more in the eastern part of the country.

Changing money on the black market is fairly straightforward and doesn't usually involve the risk of being cheated or arrested. However, it's still illegal and some caution should be observed. Since you can't do much with the pesos anyway, US$10 should buy you an ample supply. Watch for hefty, comparatively well dressed men hanging around near hard-currency department stores or anywhere Cubans need dollars to buy goods or services. They'll certainly see you first. To get your attention, they may mutter *divisas* or display a wad of bills.

Keep the bank note you're willing to change in another pocket, separate from your main stash, and don't even show it until you've carefully counted the pesos and put them away. If any irregularity occurs, such as the trader becoming excited and telling you to hurry up or unknown third parties moving in, hand back all the pesos and walk away quickly. If for any reason the trader takes the pesos

back from you after you've counted them, break off contact immediately as a sleight-of-hand trick is sure to follow. When the deal is done, move on immediately. Keep in mind that the pesos won't be of much use to you anyway, so don't put yourself in a dangerous position by being too eager to get them.

The Cuban government carefully protects its tourist industry, and you'll almost never be asked to change money at beach resorts or in places where package tourists congregate. Some cities are more lax about controlling the black market than others and the situation changes all the time. You'll certainly arouse resentment if you make jokes about the black market or brag about how cheap something is. Interestingly, you can always tell whether a Cuban has access to dollars by looking at his or her shoes. It's a sure thing that anyone wearing flashy sneakers didn't buy them with pesos.

In October 1995 the government took a first step toward legalizing the black market by opening a chain of exchange offices called Casas de Cambio or Cadeca that change dollars and pesos back and forth at the free-market rate. The newspaper *Granma* announced that this was being done on an experimental basis to control speculation. By mid-1996 several Cadeca offices were operating in Havana and Varadero, but they were less common elsewhere. Cadeca will give you the same rate or better than the guys on the street and trading with them involves no risk at all, although not all Cadeca offices deal in moneda nacional.

Tipping & Bribes

Tips and service charges are never included in the bill at restaurants, and until 1993 tipping was discouraged. It's still not essential, but if you feel you were well attended at a restaurant, a dollar to the staff will be welcome. If you have to eat more than once in a restaurant where table service (instead of a buffet) is the norm, a tip on the first occasion could save you a lot of waiting time later. Give the money directly to the waiter by rounding up as you're paying rather than leaving it on the table; just don't overtip or give Cuban pesos. At hotels leave tips for the housekeeper on the pillow (if you leave your pajamas or something else on your pillow it could be taken for a tip).

Other people who deserve a US$1 tip are museum personnel who give you a complete tour, hotel guards who watch your rental car all night, or anyone in the service industry who does you a special favor beyond the call of duty. Refrain from handing out money, soap, pens, candies, chewing gum, or anything else to children or panhandlers on the street as this only creates a nuisance.

Don't even consider offering money to persons in official positions as a way of obtaining preferential treatment because – unlike the rest of Latin America – governmental corruption is extremely rare in Cuba, and you'll only make matters much worse. If the police are interested in you, it isn't because they want to be paid off.

Taxes

No additional taxes or service charges will be added to your bills in Cuba, although this could change as the Cuban government rushes to copy practices all too familiar in North America and Europe.

POST & COMMUNICATIONS
Postal Rates

Postcards take $0.40 to the Americas, $0.45 to Europe, and $0.50 to other countries. Letters are $0.65 to the Americas, $0.75 to Europe, and $0.85 to other countries. Post stamps (sellos) are sold for pesos at town post offices or for dollars at the hotels.

Sending & Receiving Mail

Mailboxes are blue. The mail service is no worse than in any other Latin American country and even the US Postal Service delivers postcards mailed from Cuba! Be prepared, however: One postcard sent by the author to a friend in Europe took three months to arrive. For important business

mail, DHL Express offers a courier service from Cuba that utilizes the regular daily flights to Mexico.

If you'll be spending a long time in Cuba and need to receive mail, a DHL office may be able to help.

Telephone

To call Cuba from abroad, dial your international access code (which varies from country to country), Cuba's country code 53, the city or area code, and the local number. Only local numbers beginning with 22, 33, or 66 can be dialed directly from abroad. City codes include:

Batabanó	62
Bayamo	23
Camagüey	32
Ciego de Ávila	33
Cienfuegos	432
Guantánamo	21
Havana	7
Holguín	24
Las Tunas	31
Matanzas	52
Morón	335
Nueva Gerona	61
Pinar del Río	82
Playa Girón	59
Playa Santa Lucía	32
Playas del Este	687
San Antonio de los Baños	650
Sancti Spíritus	41
Santa Clara	422
Santa Cruz del Norte	692
Santiago de Cuba	226
Trinidad	419
Varadero	5
Viñales	8

Throughout Cuba, the information number is 113 during business hours. To get the operator, dial 110. The telephone company's repair service is at 114. Emergency numbers include 115 to call the fire department, 116 to call the police, and 118 to call an ambulance. Remember, however, they'll only speak Spanish.

Within Cuba it's highly unlikely you'll ever dial a call yourself. Most public telephones are out of order. The ones that do work usually have long lines of people waiting to place calls. Improvements to the system are supposedly on the way, but the network is still antiquated and inefficient, so don't count on being able to make much use of it. All towns have a telephone center where you can place long-distance calls, but the best service is available at the post offices of large hotels. You usually tell the number to a hotel receptionist or telephone center attendant, and they dial it for you.

If you do find an operable public phone and wish to place a long-distance call within Cuba, dial 0, the city or area code (see above), and the local number. To get a line out of the country, Cuba's international access code is 88 from hotel rooms or 119 from card phones (check the code with your hotel receptionist or the attendant at the telephone center). Wait for the high-pitched dialing tone before entering the country and local codes of your destination. To place a call through the operator, dial 09.

International telephone calls are expensive, costing US$2.50 a minute to Canada or US$5.50 a minute to Europe with a six-minute minimum. Six seconds into the next minute you're charged for a full minute. Collect and calling-card calls are not possible from Cuba, but magnetic telephone cards are being introduced at Varadero and elsewhere. Card phones work out cheaper because there's no minimum and your call can't cost more than the prepaid value of the card.

Service to the USA is especially bad because the US government doesn't allow US telephone companies to pay toll charges owing to Cuba. In March 1996 a Brazilian company installed 30 card telephones around Havana, and these are certainly worth checking out. The first new telephone directories in 20 years were published around the same time.

Fax & Telex

Faxes and telexes can be sent from international post offices in large cities and at major hotels.

BOOKS

Lonely Planet

If you'll be combining your trip to Cuba with visits to other Caribbean islands, check out our guide to the Eastern Caribbean by Glenda Bendure and Ned Friary, which is a practical guide to the Windward and Leeward Islands. Our guide to Jamaica, by Christopher Baker, is a colorful whirl through the coastal and interior regions.

If you'll be heading to Miami, our city guide by Nick Selby will prove indispensable. If you're planning to explore the beaches and swamps beyond Miami, consider our guide to Florida by Nick Selby and Corinna Selby.

Guidebooks

A guidebook intended for the independent budget traveler is *Travellers Survival Kit Cuba* by Simon Calder and Emily Hatchwell. Although the upmarket resorts are mentioned only in passing, the other listings are comprehensive and the coverage is completely different from your Lonely Planet guide, which makes it a good bet if you want a second opinion on everything.

Cuba Official Guide by British writer AG Gravett, offers some good background information on Cuba's flora and fauna, the tobacco industry, and historical sights around Havana. The best guide in German is *Cuba Ein Reisehandbuch* by Ewald M Söller. There's also an *Insight Guide to Cuba.*

Yachties will want to order *The Cruising Guide to Cuba* by Simon Charles. First published in 1994, this handy little volume includes sketch maps of all the main anchorages and lots of practical tips for both yacht owners and charterers. Only a very foolish mariner would sail into Cuban waters without one.

For an overall guide to the region check out *Caribbean Islands Handbook* published annually by Passport Books.

Travel

A Continent of Islands: Searching for the Caribbean Destiny by Mark Kurlansky places Cuban culture in its contemporary

Caribbean setting. Although Kurlansky deals with the entire region, references to Cuba are sprinkled throughout the book.

In *Driving through Cuba: An East-West Journey*, Carlo Gébler mixes impressions obtained on a three-month drive around Cuba in 1987 with brief essays on Cuban history. Gébler's dour view of the 1959 revolution is balanced by his unflattering account of how the US stole the 1898 revolution.

In *Six Days in Havana* James A Michener and John Kings tell of a Cuba very different from the country that informants in Miami had led them to expect. Pico Iyer includes some amusing impressions of Cuba in his travelogue *Falling Off the Map: Some Lonely Places of the World*. Iyer's first novel, *Cuba and the Night*, is also set there.

Although a bit out of date and rather slow moving at times, Tom Miller's *Trading with the Enemy* (subtitled 'A Yankee Travels Through Cuba') is an interesting and reasonably even-handed account of life in Cuba. There's lots about the difficulties of life behind the blockade and an amusing account of the less than luxurious life with a Cuban baseball team. The author's travels around Cuba includes a visit to Guantanamo Bay, one of those crazy situations where to step from one side of a border to another involves a long and roundabout trip.

History & Politics

Cuba, or The Pursuit of Freedom by Hugh Thomas is a monumental 1696-page history of Cuba from 1762 to 1962. Though hostile to the revolution, it's a valuable reference source on almost everything that happened during that period. Leslie Bethell's *Cuba: A Short History* is a readable summary of events between 1750 and 1992.

Herbert L Matthews, the *New York Times* editorial writer who interviewed Fidel Castro in the Sierra Maestra in 1957, sympathetically evaluates personalities, motivations, and achievements in *Revolution in Cuba*. Matthews writes that 'the coverage of the Castro Revolution in the American news media has been one of the greatest failures in the history of American journalism.' Matthews' own writings were truly a candle in the darkness.

Castro: A Biography of Fidel Castro by Peter Bourne is a primary source for understanding the Castro era. *Face to Face with Fidel Castro*, the transcript of an interview Castro granted Nicaraguan writer Tomás Borge, presents Castro's opinions on a wide range of topics. *Can Cuba Survive? An Interview with Fidel Castro* by Mexican journalist Beatriz Pagés also enhances our understanding of this exceptional individual. In *Fidel and Religion* Castro tells Brazilian liberation theologist Frei Betto about his childhood and education at Jesuit schools.

Che Guevara and the Cuban Revolution: Writings and Speeches of Ernesto Che Guevara, edited by David Deutschmann, includes a selection of articles, speeches, and letters by this colorful revolutionary hero of the '60s. Guevara's most important books are *Guerrilla Warfare* (1960), *Reminiscences of the Cuban Revolutionary War* (1963), and *Man and Socialism in Cuba* (1965). Deutschmann is also editor of *Che – A Memoir by Fidel Castro* in which Castro describes his relationship with Guevara.

Thomas G Paterson's *Contesting Castro* is a detailed examination of American-Cuban relations during the 1950s with important clues to what went wrong. Paterson shows how the 1962 Cuban Missile Crisis was a direct result of the misguided policies of the Eisenhower and Kennedy administrations. For a view of the American economic embargo, see *Cruel and Unusual Punishment: The US Blockade of Cuba* by Mary Murray. For a day-by-day record of developments between 1959 and 1990, see *The Cuban Revolution and the United States: A Chronological History* by Jane Franklin.

Cuba: Talking about Revolution is a highly provocative discussion of the Cuban situation between Cuban intellectual Juan Antonio Blanco and American aid worker

Resources for Reading
One of the best sources of books in English about Cuba is Ocean Press (☎ 61-3-9372-2683, fax 61-3-9372-1765), GPO Box 3279, Melbourne, Victoria 3001, Australia. Their 30 Cuba-related titles can be ordered through the Talman Company (☎ 212-431-7175, fax 212-431-7215), 131 Spring St, New York, NY 10012, USA, and Central Books (☎ 0181-986-4854, fax 0181-533-5821), 99 Wallis Rd, London E9 5LN, UK.

Another excellent resource is Pathfinder (☎ 212-741-0690, fax 212-727-0150), 410 West St, New York, NY 10014, USA. It publishes numerous autobiographical books by Ernesto 'Che' Guevara and Fidel Castro, including a new edition of Guevara's *Episodes of the Cuban Revolutionary War, 1956–58*.

Guidebooks
Adventure Guides Series to Jamaica, the Dominican Republic, Puerto Rico, the Virgin Islands, and Barbados, Harry S Pariser (New Jersey: Hunter Publishing)
Caribbean Islands Handbook (Trade & Travel Publications, 6 Riverside Court, Lower Bristol Rd, Bath BA2 3DZ, UK)
The Cruising Guide to Cuba, Simon Charles (Cruising Guide Publications, Box 1017, Dunedin, FL 34697-1017, USA; ☎ 813-733-5322 or 800-330-9542, fax 813-734-8179)
Cuba Ein Reisehandbuch, Ewald M Söller (Kobo Verlag, Hauptstrasse 116, D-53454 Remagen, Germany)
Cuba Official Guide, AG Gravette (London: Macmillan Press)
Guide to Cuba, Stephen Fallon (Bradt Publications)
Insight Guide to Cuba (Boston: Houghton Mifflin, 1995)
Travellers Survival Kit Cuba, Simon Calder & Emily Hatchwell (Oxford: Vacation Work)

Travel
A Continent of Islands: Searching for the Caribbean Destiny, Mark Kurlansky (New York: Addison-Wesley Publishing, 1992)
Cuba and the Night, Pico Iyer (New York: Alfred A Knopf, 1995)
Driving through Cuba: An East-West Journey, Carlo Gébler (London: Hamish Hamilton, 1988)
Falling Off the Map: Some Lonely Places of the World, Pico Iyer (New York: Alfred A Knopf, 1993)
Six Days in Havana, James A Michener & John Kings (Austin: University of Texas Press, 1989)

Medea Benjamin. Blanco sees the American obsession with Cuba as an inevitable result of Cuba's continuing defiance of American authority, which must be punished as a warning to others.

General
Dreaming in Cuban by Cristina García is an intriguing novel about the real and imaginary worlds affecting relationships in a Cuban family. The characters are torn between differing outlooks in a compelling tale strongly influenced by Afro-Cuban religious beliefs.

Graham Greene's *Our Man in Havana*, first published in 1958, is an entertaining story about a British vacuum cleaner salesman who enlists in the British secret service to earn money to support his daughter's expensive tastes. To justify his stipend, he pretends to recruit subagents and sends in bogus reports, which mysteriously begin to come true.

Cuba: Five Hundred Years of Images by Jorge Guillermo is a *National Geographic*-style assessment of Cuba's colonial history. The color photography by Brynn Bruyn conveys the flavor of the period. *National Geographic* magazine itself published remarkably equitable feature articles

History & Politics
Can Cuba Survive? An Interview with Fidel Castro, Beatriz Pagés (Melbourne, Australia: Ocean Press)
Castro: A Biography of Fidel Castro, Peter Bourne (New York: Dodd, Mead & Company, Inc., 1986)
Che – A Memoir by Fidel Castro, David Deutschmann, ed. (Melbourne, Australia: Ocean Press)
Che Guevara and the Cuban Revolution: Writings and Speeches of Ernesto Che Guevara, David Deutschmann, ed. (Sydney, Australia: Pathfinder/Pacific and Asia, 1987)
Contesting Castro, Thomas G Paterson (New York: Oxford University Press, 1994)
Cruel and Unusual Punishment: The US Blockade of Cuba, Mary Murray (Melbourne, Australia: Ocean Press, 1993)
Cuba, or The Pursuit of Freedom, Hugh Thomas (London: Eyre & Spottiswoode, 1971)
Cuba: A Short History, Leslie Bethell (Cambridge University Press, 1993)
Cuba: Talking about Revolution, Juan Antonio Blanco & Medea Benjamin (Melbourne, Australia: Ocean Press, 1994)
The Cuban Revolution and the United States: A Chronological History, Jane Franklin (available from the Center for Cuban Studies, 124 W 23rd St, New York, NY 10011, USA)
Face to Face with Fidel Castro, Tomás Borge (Melbourne, Australia: Ocean Press, 1993)
Fidel and Religion, Frei Betto (Melbourne, Australia: Ocean Press)
Guerrilla Warfare, Ernesto Che Guevara (1960)
Man and Socialism in Cuba, Ernesto Che Guevara (1965)
Reminiscences of the Cuban Revolutionary War, Ernesto Che Guevara (1963)
Revolution in Cuba, Herbert L Matthews (New York: Charles Scribner's Sons, 1975)

General
Dreaming in Cuban, Cristina García (New York: Alfred A Knopf, 1992)
Our Man in Havana, Graham Greene (1958)
Cuba: Five Hundred Years of Images, Jorge Guillermo (New York: Abaris Books, 1992)
National Geographic magazine, January 1977, August 1989, and August 1991
Cuba in Focus, Simon Calder & Emily Hatchwell (Latin America Bureau, 1 Amwell St, London EC1R 1UL, England, 1995; ☎ 44-171-278-2829, fax 44-171-278-0165)
Cuban Women Confront the Future, Vilma Espín (Melbourne, Australia: Ocean Press, 1992)
Cuba: World Bibliographical Series, Volume 75, Jean Stubbs (ABC-CLIO Ltd., 35A Great Clarendon St, Oxford, OX2 6AT, England, 1999) ■

on Cuba in their January 1977, August 1989, and August 1991 issues.

Cuba in Focus (1995), a useful 75-page introduction to Cuba's people, politics, and culture by Simon Calder and Emily Hatchwell, is available from the Latin America Bureau.

Cuban Women Confront the Future by Vilma Espín examines how women's roles have changed in 30 years of revolution.

Cuba: World Bibliographical Series, Volume 75, by Jean Stubbs, contains critical reviews of 900 important books about Cuba. Published in 1996, it's right up to date.

ONLINE SERVICES
In January 1996 the Cuban government opened an official Web site at http://www.cubaweb.cu in cooperation with a Canadian Internet service provider. Cubaweb features news reports from the Cuban press plus information on investment, tourism, trade, science, medicine, culture, and many other subjects.

Visit http://www.netpoint/~cubanet for the view from Miami. This exile-operated site provides quite different information about Cuba and offers links to additional Cuba-related sites.

For general background information, try

Cuba Internet Resources (http://ix.urz.uni heidelberg.de/~pklee/Cuba/). You'll find links to all Cuba information that the developer considers interesting. The site also provides links to all possible services and search engines.

NEWSPAPERS & MAGAZINES
Government Publications
All media is operated by the government. The national daily newspaper is *Granma,* the official organ of the Communist Party of Cuba. The paper was founded in 1963 through the merger of two former papers, *Revolución* and *Hoy,* and is named for the motor vessel *Granma* that carried Fidel Castro's band from Mexico to Cuba in 1956 (the name of the boat itself means 'Grandmother'). Many other former daily newspapers are now published only weekly due to paper shortages. Even *Granma* itself sells out fast, so quickly get in line whenever you see it being sold. Even if you can't read Spanish, it makes a good souvenir and the cultural listings are easy to decipher.

Granma Internacional, a weekly summary of the Cuban press, is published in Spanish, English, French, Portuguese, and German. It's possible to subscribe by sending a check or money order for US$40 to Granma Internacional, Apartado 6260 CP, La Habana 6, 10699 Cuba (fax 53-7-33-5176), or pay cash at their office at General Suárez and Territorial near the Plaza de la Revolución in Havana. In the UK you can subscribe by sending £30 to CSC (Granma), 928 Bourges Blvd, Peterborough PE1 2AN.

Other Havana newspapers include *Trabajadores,* the organ of the Central de Trabajadores de Cuba (published Monday to Saturday), *Juventud Rebelde* (every Sunday), *Tribuna de La Habana,* and *Habanero.* Among the many provincial newspapers are *Guerrillero* (Pinar del Río), *Girón* (Matanzas), *5 de Septiembre* (Cienfuegos), *Vanguardia* (Santa Clara), *Adelante* (Camagüey), *Ahora* (Holguín), *Sierra Maestra* (Santiago de Cuba), and *Victoria* (Isla de la Juventud).

Bohemia (☎ 81-2353 or 81-1464, fax 33-5511), Avenida de la Independencia and San Pedro, Plaza de la Revolución, La Habana, is a Cuban newsmagazine published weekly in Spanish.

Cuba's monthly business magazine is *Business Tips on Cuba* (☎ 53-7-33-1797, fax 53-7-33-1799), Calle 30 No 302 at 3, Miramar, La Habana. It's packed with useful information on investment opportunities in Cuba and there are simultaneous editions in English, French, Spanish, Italian, German, Portuguese, and Russian.

The tourism magazine *Prisma* is published every other month in English and Spanish by Prensa Latina (☎ 3-5886, fax 33-3476), Calle 21 No 406, Vedado, La Habana. Copies of this and other Cuban magazines such as *Cuba Internacional* are available at airport kiosks and the main hotels.

Foreign Publications
A welcome alternative to the biased and often misleading information about Cuba appearing in the US mainstream media is the *CUBA Update* published every other month by the Center for Cuban Studies (☎ 212-242-0559, fax 212-242-1937), 124 W 23rd St, New York, NY 10011, USA. It costs US$35 a year to US addresses (or US$50 with membership included). The center's stated goal is 'contributing to a normalization of relations between Cuba and the US.'

The Miami Herald Publishing Company (☎ 305-376-3324 or 800-376-3324, fax 305-995-8026), One Herald Plaza, Suite 671, Miami, FL 33132, USA, issues a surprisingly evenhanded and comprehensive monthly report on the Cuban economy called *Cuba News.* As the US$350 annual subscription rate indicates, it's aimed mostly at top executives who need reliable information on which to base critical business judgments. A detailed index of previous issues is sent to subscribers twice a year.

Another excellent source of political and economic news about Cuba is the monthly *Cuban Review* (☎ 31-20-684-9876, fax

31-20-688-0366), Buyskade 39d, 1051 HT Amsterdam, the Netherlands. Subscriptions for individuals are US$40 a year. This publication is highly recommended for investors who want to keep up on current trends.

RADIO & TV

Broadcasting is the domain of the Instituto Cubano de Radiodifusión, which operates Cuba's radio stations. Radio Havana broadcasts around the world on shortwave. A station called Radio Taíno has programs in English and Spanish 24 hours a day on AM frequency 1180 in Havana and 1100 at Varadero. Radio Reloj is a 24-hour news station.

Television was introduced into Cuba in 1950 and today there are two Havana-based national channels, Tele Rebelde (on the air weekdays from 7 to 11 pm, Saturday from 5 to 11 pm, and Sunday from 10 am to 11 pm) and CubaVision (weekdays from 6:30 to 11 pm, Saturday from 5 pm to 1:30 am, and Sunday from noon to 11 pm). Local TV stations such as Tele Cubanacán in Santa Clara, Tele Cristal in Holguín, and Tele Turquino in Santiago de Cuba are given time on the same channels before the national programs come on the air. They also substitute local programs for some of the Havana programs relayed over regional transmitters.

Tele Rebelde specializes in news and sports, and sometimes carries programs produced by CNN or other foreign networks. CubaVision features movies, soap operas, and documentaries. Both channels broadcast a 30-minute news report at 12:30 and 8 pm weekdays and 1 and 8 pm weekends, although foreigners will find it boring due to the emphasis on industrial and agricultural production reports. At least there isn't any advertising.

Many hotels provide a tourist channel called Canal del Sol that carries a mix of tourist advertising, sports, and movies. It's on the air from 7 to 9 am and 2 pm to 2 am. Cable television sets in the top hotels also receive a variety of foreign stations via satellite.

PHOTOGRAPHY
Film & Equipment

Only color print film is readily available in Cuba, costing about US$7.25 for a roll of 24 or US$8.75 for a roll of 36. You can buy it at most hotel and tourist shops. A chain of Photo Service shops with branches in most Cuban towns develops color print film, sells the most common camera batteries, and has a small selection of other materials. Rather than hoping to find film, batteries, and lens-cleaning tissue in Cuba, however, it's better to bring your own supplies with you from home.

Restrictions

Taking photos of military facilities, soldiers, or factories is not permitted. Photography inside museums used to be prohibited, but now that museums charge admission, many allow it. It's always best to ask first – some museums charge extra if you take pictures and it's better to know beforehand.

Photographing People

Cubans love to have their pictures taken and will happily pose if you ask 'Puedo tomar una foto?' (Can I take a photo?) Be prepared to have your subjects quickly write out their names and addresses on a piece of paper with the request that you mail them prints, which is fun to do. If you enjoy photographing people, Cuba is paradise.

TIME

Cuba is five hours behind GMT/UTC, the equivalent of Eastern Standard Time in the US and Canada. If it's noon in Havana it will be 6 pm in continental Western Europe, 5 pm in Britain, 11 am in Mexico City, 9 am in California, 5 am in New Zealand, and 2 am in Melbourne, Australia.

Cuba is on daylight-saving time from April to September, during which Cuba is only four hours behind GMT/UTC. In other words, clocks are turned an hour back at the beginning of October and an hour forward in late March.

ELECTRICITY
Voltage & Cycles
The most common electrical voltage in Cuba is 110 volts, 60 cycles, the same as in North America. Confusingly, however, some of the newer hotels operate on 220 volts, and in some hotel rooms one outlet will supply 220 volts while another is 110 volts! It's usually the outlet supplying the air conditioner that is 220 volts, but always check carefully before plugging in any electrical appliance, especially if your device takes 110 volts, as it will quickly burn out in 220 volts. If you can't live without your hair drier or electric shaver, bring along a transformer to convert to the other voltage, just in case.

Plugs & Sockets
North American-style plugs and outlets are the norm. If your plug has anything other than two flat parallel prongs, you'll need to bring a plug adapter too as none are available in Cuba. A few new hotels have European-style outlets with two round plugs.

WEIGHTS & MEASURES
Cuba uses the metric system. Occasionally one hears references to old American and Spanish measurements, such as an American gallon (3.785 liters), an *arroba* (25 Spanish pounds or 11.5 kg), a *caballería* (13.4 hectares), a *quintal* (100 Spanish pounds or 46 kg), and a *vara* (36 inches).

LAUNDRY
There are no coin laundries in Cuba, although most hotels offer a laundry service that charges on a per piece basis. It's easier to bring clothes that don't require much cleaning and to use the sink in your room to wash small items. If you decide to do that, it's handy to have a small sink plug that fits a variety of drains, washing powder wrapped in two layers of plastic bags, and about five meters of string with which to erect a clothes line in your room.

HEALTH
Cuba is a healthy country. Yellow fever was eliminated in 1901, polio in 1963, malaria in 1968, and diphtheria in 1971. Gastritis, tuberculosis, tetanus, and most infectious diseases are greatly reduced. Thanks to a successful vaccination campaign, less than a dozen cases of meningitis occur each year. As in developed countries, the main causes of death are heart disease, strokes, and malignant tumors. Compared to the rest of Latin America, the medical facilities available to both travelers and local residents here are excellent, and compared to Canada and the US, the cost of medical treatment for foreigners is extremely low. Hospital emergency departments are open around the clock, and first visits to the doctor at both hotel infirmaries and public hospitals are free of charge.

Fees in dollars must be paid at 'international clinics' for foreigners at Havana, Varadero, Cienfuegos, Trinidad, Playa Santa Lucía, Guardalavaca, and Santiago de Cuba. These specialized clinics operated by Servimed, a branch of the Cubanacán Corporation, offer immediate attention by English-speaking doctors at US$20 for an ordinary consultation or US$25 for a specialist consultation. They also arrange dental treatment and this might be an interesting place to have a checkup. If you have lots of time and speak a bit of Spanish, it's possible to queue up for service at any of the numerous polyclinics intended to serve the Cuban population. The care at these is also good.

A branch of Servimed specializes in 'health tourism' for foreigners interested in taking advantage of Cuba's advanced medical facilities. Specialties include dentistry, plastic surgery, hypertension, diet, skin diseases, drug addiction, 'night blindness,' Parkinson's disease, heart disease, bone deformities, paralysis, and rheumatism. Information is available through any of the Cubanacán offices listed under Tourist Offices above.

As always, travel health depends on your predeparture preparations, your day-to-day health care while traveling, and how you handle any medical problem or emergency that does develop. While the list of potential dangers that follows can seem quite frightening, few travelers to Cuba experience more than upset stomachs and sunburn. We provide this information for reference in case of need, although for most visitors it will only constitute amusing poolside reading.

Predeparture Preparations

Medical Kit A small, straightforward medical kit is a wise thing to carry if you'll be traveling around on your own. A kit could include:

- Aspirin or a similar drug, for pain or fever.
- Antihistamine, useful as a decongestant for colds and allergies, to ease the itch from insect bites or stings, and to help prevent motion sickness.
- Antibiotics, useful if you're traveling well off the beaten track, but they must be prescribed and you should carry the prescription with you. (See the paragraph below about using antibiotics.)
- Kaolin preparation (Pepto-Bismol), Imodium or Lomotil, for stomach upsets.
- Rehydration mixture, for treatment of severe diarrhea. This is particularly important if traveling with children, but it is recommended for everyone.
- Antiseptic such as Betadine that comes as impregnated swabs or ointment, and an antibiotic powder or similar 'dry' spray, for cuts and grazes.
- Calamine lotion, to ease irritation from bites or stings.
- Bandages, for minor injuries.
- Scissors, tweezers, and a thermometer (note that mercury thermometers are prohibited by airlines).
- Insect repellent, sunscreen, suntan lotion, lip balm, and water purification tablets.
- A couple of syringes, in case you need injections. Ask your doctor for a note explaining why they have been prescribed.
- Motion-sickness medication.
- Throat lozenges.
- Condoms.
- First-aid booklet.

Ideally antibiotics should be administered only under medical supervision and never be taken indiscriminately. Take only the recommended dose at the prescribed intervals, and continue using the antibiotic for the prescribed period, even if the illness seems to be cured earlier. Antibiotics are quite specific to the infections they can treat. Stop immediately if there are any serious reactions and don't use the antibiotic at all if you are unsure that you have the correct one.

If a medicine is available in Cuba, it will generally be available over the counter and the price will be much cheaper than in northern countries. In practice, all medicines are in short supply or unavailable, and you should consider leaving surplus medicines with a local clinic rather than carrying them home.

Health Preparations Make sure you're healthy before you start traveling. Dental treatment is good and inexpensive in Cuba, so you needn't worry there. If you wear glasses, take a spare pair and your prescription as losing your glasses can be a real problem. If you require a specific medication, take an adequate supply, as it probably won't be available locally.

Immunizations Vaccinations provide protection against diseases you might meet along the way. The only immunization currently necessary to enter Cuba is for yellow fever and then only if one is arriving directly from South America. However, some other vaccines may be worth considering if you plan to travel far off the beaten track. Plan ahead for getting your vaccinations: Some of them require an initial shot followed by a booster, while some vaccinations should not be given together. It's recommended that you begin at least six weeks prior to travel.

Most travelers from developed countries will have been immunized against various diseases during childhood, but your doctor may still recommend booster shots against tetanus and measles. The period of protection offered by vaccinations differs widely and some are contraindicated if you are pregnant. Vaccinations include:

Infectious Hepatitis The most common travel-acquired illness can be prevented by vaccination. Protection can be provided in two ways:

with the antibody gamma globulin or a new vaccine called Havrix. In the US it is called Hepatitis A vaccine. Havrix is the more expensive of the two, and you must take it at least three weeks before departure, but it is recommended because it provides up to 10 years of immunity. Gamma globulin lasts only six months and may interfere with the development of immunity to other diseases, so careful timing is important with its use.

Tetanus & Diphtheria Boosters are necessary every 10 years. Although there's no diphtheria in Cuba, you may as well be protected against tetanus.

Typhoid Available either as an injection or oral capsules, the typhoid vaccination provides protection from one to three years and is useful if you are traveling for long in rural areas.

Yellow Fever Travelers planning a trip involving a visit to the Amazon region should get this vaccination, and it's a requirement for anyone arriving in Cuba directly from South America. Protection lasts 10 years. You usually have to go to a special yellow-fever vaccination center, and vaccination is contraindicated during pregnancy.

Basic Rules

Care in what you eat and drink is the most important health rule; stomach upsets are the most likely travel health problem, but the majority of these upsets will be relatively minor. Don't become paranoid; after all, trying the local food is part of the experience of travel.

Water When in doubt, the number one rule is don't drink the water and that includes ice. If you don't know for certain that the water is safe, always assume the worst. Bottled water or soft drinks are safe and are readily available at hotel shops. Take care with fruit juice, particularly if water may have been added. Tea or coffee should be OK, since the water should have been boiled.

Food Thoroughly cooked food is safest but not if it has been left to cool or if it has been reheated. Shellfish such as mussels, oysters, and clams should be avoided unless they're served in a high-class restaurant, as

should undercooked meat, particularly in the form of mince or ground beef. Steaming does not make bad shellfish safe for eating.

Nutrition If your food is poor or limited in availability, if you're traveling hard and fast and therefore missing meals, or if you simply lose your appetite, you can soon start to lose weight and place your health at risk.

Make sure your diet is well balanced. Eggs, beans, lentils, and nuts are all safe ways to get protein. Fruits you can peel (bananas, oranges, or grapefruits, for example) are always safe and a good source of vitamins. Try to eat plenty of grains (rice) and bread. Remember that although food is generally safer if it is cooked well, overcooked food loses much of its nutritional value. If your diet isn't well balanced or if your food intake is insufficient, it's a good idea to take vitamin and iron pills on a long trip.

When you're sweating, make sure you drink enough – don't rely on feeling thirsty to indicate when you should drink. Not needing to urinate or very dark yellow urine is a danger sign. Always carry a water bottle with you on long trips. Excessive sweating can lead to loss of salt and therefore muscle cramping. Salt tablets are not a good idea as a preventative, but in places where salt is not already used adding some to your food can help.

Climatic & Geographical Considerations

Sunburn A sunburn could be the biggest annoyance you'll encounter on a Cuban holiday, and with increasingly dangerous solar radiation reaching us due to environmental degradation it's important to apply sunscreen regularly. In Cuba you can get sunburned surprisingly quickly, even through clouds. Use a sunscreen (SPF 15 minimum) and take extra care to cover areas that don't normally see sun – for example, your feet. A hat provides added protection, and you should also use zinc cream or some other barrier cream for your nose and lips. Calamine lotion or aloe gel is good for mild sunburn.

Prickly Heat Prickly heat is an itchy rash caused by excessive perspiration trapped under the skin. It usually strikes people who have just arrived in Cuba from a cooler country and whose pores have not yet opened sufficiently to cope with greater sweating. Keeping cool by bathing often, using a mild talcum powder, and even resorting to air-conditioning may help until you acclimatize.

Heat Exhaustion Dehydration or salt deficiency can cause heat exhaustion. Take time to acclimatize to high temperatures and make sure you drink sufficient liquids. Wear loose clothing and a broad-brimmed hat. Do not do anything too physically demanding.

Salt deficiency is characterized by fatigue, lethargy, headaches, giddiness, and muscle cramps, and in this case salt tablets may help. Vomiting or diarrhea can deplete your liquid and salt levels.

Motion Sickness Eating lightly before and during a trip will reduce the chances of motion sickness. If you are prone to motion sickness, try to find a place that minimizes disturbance – near the wing on aircraft, close to midships on boats, near the center on buses. Fresh air usually helps; reading and cigarette smoke don't. Commercial motion-sickness preparations, which can cause drowsiness, have to be taken before the trip commences; when you're feeling sick it's too late. Ginger is a natural preventative and is available in capsule form.

Diseases of Poor Sanitation

Diarrhea A change of water, food, or climate can all cause the runs; diarrhea caused by contaminated food or water is more serious. Despite all your precautions you may still have a mild bout of traveler's diarrhea, but a few rushed toilet trips with no other symptoms is not indicative of a serious problem. Moderate diarrhea,

involving half a dozen loose bowel movements in a day, is more of a nuisance.

Dehydration is the main danger with any diarrhea – children dehydrate particularly quickly. Fluid replacement remains the mainstay of management. Weak black tea with a little sugar, soda water, or soft drinks allowed to go flat and diluted 50% with bottled water are all good. With severe diarrhea a rehydrating solution is necessary to replace minerals and salts, but in an emergency you can drink a solution of eight teaspoons of sugar to a liter of bottled water and eat salted crackers at the same time. You should stick to a bland diet as you recover.

Lomotil or Imodium can be used to bring relief from the symptoms, although they do not actually cure the problem. Use these drugs only when absolutely necessary – that is, if you *must* travel. For children Imodium is preferable, but under all circumstances fluid replacement is the most important thing to remember. Do not use these drugs if you have a high fever or are severely dehydrated.

Antibiotics may be needed for diarrhea that lasts for more than five days, or that is severe, or for watery diarrhea with fever and lethargy or with blood and mucus (gut-paralyzing drugs like Imodium or Lomotil should be avoided in this situation). Alcohol must be avoided during treatment and for 48 hours afterwards.

Hepatitis Hepatitis A is a common problem among travelers to areas with poor sanitation. With good water and adequate sewage disposal in most industrialized countries since the 1940s, very few young adults now have any natural immunity and must be protected. Protection is through the new vaccine Havrix (Hepatitis A vaccine) or the antibody gamma globulin.

The disease is spread by contaminated food or water. The symptoms are fever, chills, headache, fatigue, feelings of weakness and aches and pains, followed by loss of appetite, nausea, vomiting, abdominal pain, dark urine, light colored feces, jaundiced skin, and the whites of the eyes possibly turning yellow. In some cases you may feel unwell, tired, have no appetite, experience aches and pains, and be jaundiced. You should seek medical advice, but in general there is not much you can do apart from resting, drinking lots of fluids, eating lightly, and avoiding fatty foods. People who have had hepatitis must forgo alcohol for six months after the illness, as hepatitis attacks the liver and it needs that amount of time to recover.

Hepatitis B, which used to be called serum hepatitis, is spread through contact with infected blood, blood products, or bodily fluids – especially through sexual contact, unsterilized needles, and blood transfusions. Other risk situations include having a shave in a local shop or having your ears pierced.

The symptoms of type B are much the same as type A except that they are more severe and may lead to irreparable liver damage or even liver cancer. Although there is no treatment for hepatitis B, an effective prophylactic vaccine is readily available in most countries. The immunization schedule requires two injections at least a month apart followed by a third dose five months after the second. Persons who should receive a hepatitis B vaccination include anyone who anticipates contact with blood or other bodily secretions, either as a health care worker or through sexual contact with the local population. Travelers who intend to stay in the country for a long period of time should definitely be immunized.

Typhoid Typhoid fever is another gut infection that travels the fecal-oral route – contaminated water and food are responsible. In its early stages typhoid resembles many other illnesses: Sufferers may feel like they have a bad cold or the initial stages of a flu, as early symptoms are a headache, a sore throat, and a fever that rises a little each day until it is around 40°C or more. The victim's pulse rate is often slow relative to the degree of fever present and gets slower as the fever rises – unlike a normal fever where the pulse rate

increases. There may also be vomiting, diarrhea, or constipation.

In the second week the high fever and slow pulse continue and a few pink spots may appear on the body; trembling, delirium, weakness, weight loss, and dehydration are other symptoms. If there are no further complications, the fever and other symptoms will slowly diminish during the third week. Still, you must get medical help since pneumonia (acute infection of the lungs) or peritonitis (perforated bowel) are common complications, and typhoid is very infectious. Keep the victim cool and hydrated.

Worms These parasites are most common in rural areas and a stool test when you return home is not a bad idea. Worms can be present on unwashed vegetables or in undercooked meat, and you can pick them up through your skin by walking in bare feet. Infestations may not show up for some time, and although they are generally not serious, if left untreated they can cause severe health problems. A stool test is necessary to pinpoint the problem and medication is often available over the counter.

Diseases Spread by Animals & People

Tetanus This potentially fatal disease is found in most tropical areas, but it is rare in Cuba. It's difficult to treat but is preventable with immunization. Tetanus occurs when a wound becomes infected by a germ that lives in the feces of animals or people, so clean all cuts, punctures, or animal bites. Tetanus is also known as lockjaw, and the first symptom may be discomfort in swallowing, or stiffening of the jaw and neck; this is followed by painful convulsions of the jaw and whole body.

Tuberculosis (TB) This disease is also rare in Cuba and does not pose a serious risk to travelers. Young children are more susceptible than adults and routine vaccination is a sensible precaution for children under 12. TB is commonly spread by coughing or by unpasteurized dairy products from infected cows.

Sexually Transmitted Diseases STDs are spread through sexual contact with an infected partner. Abstinence is the only 100% preventative, but using condoms is also effective. Gonorrhea and syphilis are common STDs; sores, blisters, or rashes around the genitals, discharges, or pain when urinating are common symptoms. Symptoms may be less marked or not observed at all in women. Syphilis symptoms eventually disappear completely, but the disease continues and can cause severe problems in later years. The treatment of gonorrhea and syphilis is by antibiotics. There is no cure for herpes (which causes blisters but is not normally very dangerous) or for AIDS.

HIV/AIDS HIV, the human immunodeficiency virus, may develop into AIDS, acquired immune deficiency syndrome (SIDA in Spanish), and any exposure to blood, blood products, or bodily fluids may put an individual at risk. Since all blood transfusions are screened in Cuba and the sharing of dirty needles between intravenous drug abusers is negligible, most cases are a result of sexual contact with foreigners (although Cuban soldiers returning from Africa could also have been infected). HIV testing is compulsory for all Cubans, and foreign visitors may also be tested (often without being informed of the test) if they are admitted to a Cuban hospital.

Cuba's policy of isolating HIV carriers in special sanitariums is an extreme step that the government has taken in light of the AIDS epidemics in neighboring Haiti, Bahamas, and Florida. While limiting the freedom of HIV-positive persons, this policy has undoubtedly prevented others from becoming infected and helped avoid a public health disaster. By 1995, 234 Cubans had died of AIDS and another 900 were HIV positive (71.2% of them male). In recent years sexually responsible patients have been allowed to leave the sanitariums to work or spend time with their families, and patients from the Santiago de las Vegas sanitarium outside Havana have

formed a rock group called VIH to participate in AIDS education programs among the young. AIDS treatment is free and infected persons continue to receive their full salaries whether they work or not.

Apart from abstinence, the most effective preventative is to practice safe sex using condoms. Condoms (*preservativos*) are available in some pharmacies, though they are low quality (I'm told it's worth wearing two). It's impossible to detect the HIV-positive status of an otherwise healthy-looking person without a blood test, so the golden rule should be 'safe sex or no sex.' Cuba has invested millions of dollars in AIDS research and a Cuban HIV preventative vaccine is presently under development.

Insect-Borne Diseases
Dengue Fever There is no prophylactic available for this mosquito-spread disease; the main prevention is avoiding mosquito bites. A sudden onset of fever, headaches, and severe joint and muscle pains are the first signs before a rash starts on the trunk of the body and spreads to the limbs and face. After a further few days, the fever will subside and recovery will begin. Serious complications are not common, but full recovery can take up to a month or more.

Typhus Typhus is spread by ticks, mites, or lice. It begins as a bad cold, followed by a fever, chills, headache, muscle pains, and a body rash. There is often a large painful sore at the site of the bite and nearby lymph nodes are swollen and painful.

Tick typhus is spread by ticks. Seek local advice on areas where ticks pose a danger and always check your skin carefully for ticks after walking in a high-risk area such as a tropical forest. A strong insect repellent can help prevent bites.

Cuts, Bites & Stings
Cuts & Scratches Skin punctures can easily become infected in hot climates and may not heal for long periods. Treat any cut with an antiseptic. Where possible avoid bandages and Band-aids, which can keep wounds moist.

Bites & Stings Bee and wasp stings are usually painful rather than dangerous. Calamine lotion will give relief and ice packs will reduce the pain and swelling. There are some spiders with dangerous bites, but these are not usually fatal and antivenins are usually available. Scorpion stings are notoriously painful but very rarely fatal. If you're bitten, suck the poison out and make a little cut with a sterile knife so the poison will come out with bleeding. If possible, kill the creature so the doctor will know which serum to administer.

Scorpions, spiders, ants, and other biting creatures often shelter in shoes or clothing. If you're staying in primitive accommodations, develop the habit of shaking out your clothing before putting it on. Check your bedding before going to sleep. Don't walk barefoot, and when reaching for a shoe or branch, always check for critters first. Luckily, poisonous spiders and scorpions aren't common.

Jellyfish Local advice is the best way of avoiding contact with these sea creatures which have stinging tentacles. The stings from most jellyfish are rather painful but not lethal. Dousing in vinegar will de-activate any stingers that have not 'fired.' Calamine lotion, antihistamines, and analgesics may reduce the reaction and relieve the pain.

Sea Urchins Before you run or jump into the sea, check whether there are any sea urchins lying in wait on the bottom. These miniature pin cushions have quills that penetrate your body if you step or fall on them. Once in, they break off and have to be cut out with a knife. (The quills are made of calcium and if left untreated will eventually decompose into your body.)

Women's Health
Gynecological Problems Poor diet, lowered resistance due to the use of antibiotics for stomach upsets, and even contraceptive pills can lead to vaginal infections when traveling in hot climates.

Wearing skirts or loose-fitting trousers and cotton underwear will help to prevent infections.

Yeast infections, characterized by a rash, itch, and discharge, can be treated with a diluted vinegar or lemon-juice douche, or with yogurt. Trichomoniasis is a more serious infection; symptoms are a discharge and a burning sensation when urinating. Male sexual partners must also be treated, and if a vinegar-water douche is not effective, seek medical attention.

TOILETS
All large hotels have public toilets somewhere between the front desk and the restaurant. In most towns there are also public toilets in some central location, often with a 10-centavo entry fee. Some restaurants, however, do not have toilets for public use.

Since public toilets are not that common, you should use them when you see them. The men's section has a sign that says *hombres* or *señores*, the women's side *mujeres* or *señoras*. Toilet paper probably won't be supplied.

WOMEN TRAVELERS
As in many other resort areas where northerners come in search of the southern sun, unaccompanied female travelers are often considered fair game for a certain type of local man (be prepared for open stares). Although force is seldom used, it's wise to quickly repulse unwelcome approaches of this kind by making it clear you're not interested or inventing a husband. Otherwise, it could be hard to get rid of the character later. You're definitely safer in Cuba than in any other Caribbean country, but it's always good to stay within earshot of other people. Virtually any Cuban will run to your assistance at the first scream.

Almost any foreign woman without a man at her side should be prepared for instant proposals of marriage. A lot of Cubans would like to get out of Cuba and a foreign spouse is seen as the easiest way to go. (Foreign men are also targeted by

Cuban women.) Of course, such unions seldom endure long after the main goal is achieved.

Despite the emphasis on female breasts and buttocks in Cuban cabaret entertainment, topless or nude sunbathing is not acceptable, even at the beach resorts. This probably has more to due with typical macho attitudes than any socialistic moral prudery (under Marshall Tito Yugoslavia was the naturist capital of the world), and it's quite likely that as tourism develops some of the tops will come off, though probably only at the main hotels where the Cuban public isn't allowed. Meanwhile, unless you're very daring, it's best to take your cues from other sunbathers.

GAY & LESBIAN TRAVELERS

Cuba has come a long way since the early 1960s when some gays were forced into labor camps for 'rehabilitation,' and homosexuality is now more or less accepted. The film *Fresa y Chocolate* led to a national discussion about tolerance, and although homophobia still exists there are no laws against homosexuality. However, there have been reports of gays being subjected to unofficial police harassment.

A San Francisco reader sent us this:

As anywhere else, the response to gays depends very much on the individual's attitudes and the particular situation. Street violence and physical assaults are not common in Cuba, so I felt no fear walking on the streets with gays or having physical contact with other men on the street.

In Havana the block where the Cine Yara is located is a well-known gathering spot for gays and lesbians. Gays also gather at a beach on a tiny island in Laguna Itabo in Playas del Este.

DISABLED TRAVELERS

Unfortunately most Cuban hotels don't provide any special facilities for disabled persons. If you require these, ask your travel agent to verify that the tour company can address such needs before you book your trip.

TRAVEL WITH CHILDREN

Cuba is a safe place to bring children. The traffic on the roads is limited and security is good. Most tour companies offer reduced prices for children under the age of 12 provided they share the accommodations of their parents. Only a token amount is charged for children under the age of two. Some hotels such as the Sierra Mar Resort southwest of Santiago de Cuba and Las Brisas Club Resort at Guardalavaca offer special day programs for young guests that give parents some time to themselves. Almost any hotel reception will be able to arrange a babysitter for a nominal amount. For families staying in the towns there are many puppet shows and other performances for children in the main theaters, usually on Saturday and Sunday at 10 am and 5 pm.

USEFUL ORGANIZATIONS

The following nonpolitical support groups work to foster better relations between Cuba and their respective countries. Most publish newsletters, hold social or cultural evenings, and organize educational tours to Cuba. They're well worth contacting if your interests go beyond a beach holiday.

Australia
  Australia-Cuba Friendship Society,
  PO Box 1, 52 Victoria St, Carlton South,
  Victoria 3053 (☎ 61-3-9857-9249)
Canada
  Canadian Cuban Friendship Association,
  PO Box 743, Station F, Toronto, Ontario
  M4Y 2N6 (☎ 416-654-5585)
UK
  Cuba Solidarity Campaign, c/o Red Rose
  Club, 129 Seven Sisters Rd,
  London N7 7QG (☎ 0171-263-6452,
  fax 0171-561-0191)
USA
  Center for Cuban Studies, 124 W 23rd St,
  New York, NY 10011
  (☎ 212-242-0559, fax 212-242-1937)
  Global Exchange, 2017 Mission St, Room
  303, San Francisco, CA 94110
  (☎ 415-255-7296, fax 415-255-7498)
  USA/Cuba-Infomed, PO Box 450, Santa
  Clara, CA 95052
  (☎ 408-243-4359, fax 408-243-1229)

DANGERS & ANNOYANCES

In terms of crime Cuba is the safest country in Latin America, although things like shoes and towels left unguarded at the beach could disappear, especially from public beaches. It's unwise to take your passport or a lot of money to a nightclub or disco. Purse-snatching and pickpocketing are not unknown in Havana. If you rent a car, always park in a well-lit place and lock the doors. However, violent crime against tourists is almost unheard of.

Your biggest human problem will be the various panhandlers and hustlers who will hassle you for one thing or another in the city centers. The beggars are a direct side effect of tourism caused by the foolishness of previous visitors who amused themselves by handing out money, soap, pens, candies, chewing gum, and other things to people on the street. The mendicants will usually go away if you say '*Por favor, no moleste*.' (The police do attempt to keep beggars away from the tourist sights, but silly tourists often undermine their efforts.)

The hustlers are called *jineteros* (jockeys) in Spanish, and they've learned that the easiest way to get dollars is to latch onto a foreign tourist. In order to size you up, they'll often begin by asking where you're from and at which hotel you're staying. To avoid bad feelings, be polite with them – at first. If you need a guide to show you around town or to help you find a private room or restaurant, they'll oblige, and you'll pay for their help either through a direct tip or in the form of a commission added onto your room or meal. If you don't want a paid guide, let the person know it by saying '*No, gracias*.' If that doesn't work and he becomes a nuisance, switch over to '*No moleste*.' Every so often you'll run into a crazy (but generally harmless) person.

BUSINESS HOURS

Some offices are open Monday to Saturday from 8:30 am to 5:30 pm with a lunch break from 12:30 to 1:30, although many stay open continuously from 9 am to 5 pm. Offices remain closed every other Saturday. Post offices are generally open Monday to Saturday from 8 am to 6 pm with some main post offices open as late as 10 pm. Banks and exchange offices are only open weekdays from 8:30 am to noon and 1:30 to 3 pm, and Saturdays from 8 to 10 am, but hotel receptions will change money almost anytime. Hotel tourist bureaus are usually open from 8 am to 8 pm, although they may stop making reservations at 7 pm.

Shopping hours are generally Monday to Saturday from 9:30 am to 12:30 pm and 2 to 5 pm. In Havana many shops open from 12:30 to 7:30 pm. Every second Saturday is a day off. Pharmacies are generally open from 8 am to 8 pm, but those marked *turno permanente* or called *pilotos* are open 24 hours, offering late-night service through a small window. Museums usually open Tuesday to Saturday from 9 am to 5 pm and Sunday from 8 am to noon. Most churches open only for mass, although you'll sometimes be let in the back door if you ask around. Daylight hours in Cuba are from 6 am to 6 pm year-round with only 15 minutes of twilight in the evening.

PUBLIC HOLIDAYS & SPECIAL EVENTS
Public Holidays

Cuba's public holidays include January 1 (Liberation Day), May 1 (Labor Day), July 25, 26 and 27 (Celebration of the National Rebellion), and October 10 (Day of Cuban Culture).

Liberation day recalls January 1, 1959, when Cuba was liberated from the Batista dictatorship. The national rebellion celebrated in July honors the July 26, 1953, attack on army barracks in Santiago de Cuba and Bayamo. The Day of Cuban Culture marks the beginning of the First War of Independence on October 10, 1868. On those days most shops, offices, and museums are closed. Christmas was abolished as a public holiday in 1969 because it coincided with the beginning of the sugar harvest and caused economic disruption.

Other important dates not marked by public holidays but still commemorated include:

Royal poinciana (or flamboyant)

The strange banana blossom

Cuba's national flower, the mariposa

Coconuts

Cuba's national tree, the royal palm

Banana farm in Matanzas

Carving out a niche at the cathedral craft market

Palm fashions

Producing handmade books at
Ediciones Vigía in Matanzas

A painting by Raúl Martínez
in Havana's Palacio de Bellas Artes

The wheel goes 'round at
Trinidad's pottery factory.

January 2 (victory of the 1959 revolution)
January 28 (birthday of José Martí)
February 24 (beginning of the 1895 War of Independence)
March 8 (International Women's Day)
March 13 (anniversary of the 1957 attack on Batista's palace)
April 4 (Children's Day)
April 19 (commemoration of the 1961 victory at the Bay of Pigs)
Second Sunday in May (Mother's Day)
Third Sunday in June (Father's Day)
July 30 (day of the martyrs of the revolution)
September 28 (anniversary of the founding of the Committees for the Defense of the Revolution in 1960)
October 8 (the day in 1967 on which Che Guevara was murdered)
October 28 (the day in 1959 on which Camilo Cienfuegos was killed in a plane crash)
November 27 (commemoration of eight medical students killed by the Spaniards in 1871)
December 2 (landing of the *Granma* in Oriente in 1956)
December 7 (anniversary of the death of Antonio Maceo)
December 25 (Christmas)

Some care should be taken in planning your activities on those days as schedules could be disrupted slightly.

Special Events

Until 1990 carnival was celebrated in Havana and Santiago de Cuba during the last two weeks of July and the first week of August to coincide with the holidays around July 26. Carnival marked the end of the sugar harvest and it originated as a period in which the slaves were allowed to celebrate. For those 10 days the drum was king. The economic austerity of recent years has led to the suspension of carnival and even the more touristy carnival at Varadero formerly held in late January and early February no longer takes place. In 1996, however, an attempt was made to revive the Havana carnival with performances in front of the Capitolio on Friday, Saturday, and Sunday evenings throughout the month of February.

Other dates of special events that are on the books but may not necessarily be taking place include:

February
First two weeks, Jornadas de la Cultura Camagüeyana
Every other year, Havana International Jazz Festival
April
First week, Semana de la Cultura at Baracoa
Electroacoustic Music Festival in Varadero
May
First week, Romería de Mayo in Holguín
Every other year, International Guitar Festival in Havana
June
End of the month, Fiestas Sanjuaneras in Trinidad
June or July
Festival of Caribbean Culture in Santiago de Cuba
Cucalambé Folklore Festival in Las Tunas
August
Bolero de Oro in Santiago de Cuba
Benny Moré International Festival of Popular Music in Cienfuegos

Late August and early September
    Every other year, Havana International Theater Festival
October
    Havana Festival of Contemporary Music
    Beginning October 10, 10 'days of culture' throughout the country with many musical events
    Mid-October, Festival del Bailador Rumbero in Matanzas
    Late October, International Ballet Festival in Havana
    End of October, Fiesta Iberoamericana de la Cultura in Holguín
October or November
    Festival de la Toronja at Isla de la Juventud
November
    Second half of November, Semana de la Cultura Trinitaria in Trinidad
    Late November, International Festival of Caribbean Music in Varadero
December
    International Choir Festival in Santiago de Cuba
    International Festival of Latin American Film in Havana

Be aware that during the current *período especial* some or all of the events mentioned above could be suspended. You may be able to obtain advance information by phoning the main hotel in the city where the festival is scheduled to take place.

ACTIVITIES
Cuba's top outdoor activities organization is Marinas Puertosol (fax 53-7-33-3156), which operates a chain of marinas and yacht clubs all around Cuba. Its specialties are yachting, scuba diving, underwater photography, deep-sea fishing, freshwater fishing, and boat rentals. It also owns the exclusive Hotel Colony on Isla de la Juventud.

Cycling
Cuba offers many good roads for cycling. Most large resort hotels rent bicycles by the hour or day, and it's possible to buy used bicycles in Havana. For information on touring Cuba by bicycle, turn to Bicycle in the Getting Around chapter.

Hiking & Trekking
Resort areas with good hiking possibilities in the vicinity include Guane (Campismo El Salto), Viñales, Soroa, Las Terrazas (Hotel Moka), Sierra de Güira (Villa Turística Los Pinos), San Antonio de los Baños (Hotel Las Yagrumas), Playa Jibacoa (Campismo El Abra), Hanabanilla, Topes de Collantes, Marea del Portillo, El Saltón (Santiago de Cuba Province), and Baracoa. Unfortunately, marked trails are rare in Cuba, and hiking maps and guides nonexistent, though it's usually possible to hire a local resident as a guide for a nominal dollar fee. In places where officialdom has recognized the moneymaking potential of hiking, attempts are sometimes made to force foreigners to hire official guides at inflated rates. An example of this is the bird-watching walks in the Playa Larga (Bay of Pigs) area.

Cuba's premier mountain hike is the three-day trek over the Sierra Maestra from Alto del Naranjo, south of Bartolomé Maso in Granma Province, to Las Cuevas on the south coast (or vice versa). En route one crosses Pico Turquino (1972 meters), Cuba's highest mountain. For more information turn to the Gran Parque Nacional Sierra Maestra section in the Granma Province chapter.

Horseback Riding
Horses can be hired by the hour at beach resorts such as Varadero (Hotel Oasis), Playa Santa Lucía, Guardalavaca, Sierra Mar, and Cayo Largo. The two resorts at Marea del Portillo operate equestrian excursions to local waterfalls on a regular basis. Ecotourism hotels in the interior such as Cabañas Aguas Claras (Pinar del Río), Hotel La Ermita (Viñales), Hotel Moka (Las Terrazas), Hotel Valle del Yumurí (near Matanzas), Villa Santo Domingo (Granma Province), Villa El Saltón (Santiago de Cuba), and Hotel Hanabanilla (Villa Clara) also offer horseback riding. In Havana, horses are kept at Parque Lenin.

Special tourist ranches have been set up at El Oasis (Baconao) and the Casa del Campesino (Trinidad). Perhaps the finest such facility is the Hacienda Los Molinos, a working cattle ranch between Trinidad and Sancti Spíritus. Rustic accommodations are available at Los Molinos and there are unlimited riding possibilities in the surrounding countryside.

Surfing & Windsurfing

The top surfing season is December to April when the Northeast Tradewinds are at their strongest and the best breaks are on Atlantic shores facing north or east. From August to September tropical storms can drive huge waves into the south coast. Surfers will have to bring their own boards, as they'll find none for rent.

Conditions for windsurfing are often good at Varadero, Guardalavaca, Marea del Portillo, and Cayo Largo. Many beach resorts rent equipment.

Yachting

Bareboat and crewed yacht charters in Cuba can be arranged through KP Winter, SA (☎ 34-971-490900, fax 34-971-491605), Club Marítimo, E-07610 Ca'n Pastilla, Mallorca, Spain, which operates Cubanáutica yacht charter bases at Varadero and Cayo Largo. At Varadero, check with Cubanáutica/KP Winter (☎ /fax 66-7403), Calle 3 near the Kawama Hotel In Havana it's Cubanáutica/KP Winter (☎ 33-4546, fax 33-4545), Paseo No 309 between 13 and 15. For more information turn to the Chartered Yacht section in the Getting Around chapter and also see Yachting under Activities in the Varadero and Havana sections.

The main cruising season for yachts is winter (December to April) when the weather is mild, the winds are reliable, and hurricanes are unknown. Favorite anchorages along the north coast include Santa Lucía in Pinar del Río Province, Cayo Levisa, Cayo Paraíso, the Marina Hemingway at Havana, the three marinas of Varadero, Cayo Libertad in the Bahía de Cárdenas, Cayo Guillermo, Cayo Coco, Playa Santa Lucía, Bahía de Naranjo near Guardalavaca, Cayo Saetía, and Baracoa. On the south coast there's Santiago de Cuba, Chivirico, Marea del Portillo, Manzanillo, Júcaro, Ancón Peninsula, Cienfuegos, Cayo Largo, Isla de la Juventud, and María la Gorda.

In Cuba you won't encounter the overcrowding, commercialization, crime, and unfriendliness that characterize some other much-publicized yachting destinations not far from these shores. As Simon Charles writes in his excellent *Cruising Guide to Cuba* (see the Books section earlier in this chapter), 'There is nowhere between Canada and the Antarctic South Pole where you will find any equivalent cruising ground, still unspoiled, and so conveniently located.'

Scuba Diving

Over 30 diving centers around Cuba offer scuba diving, including Marlin Dive Centers at the Marina Hemingway (Havana), Varadero, Cayo Coco, Playa Santa Lucía, Guardalavaca, Baconao (Santiago de Cuba), Sierra Mar (Chivirico), Marea del Portillo, and Rancho Luna (Cienfuegos). Other scuba facilities are found at María La Gorda (Pinar del Río), Cayo Levisa, Villa El Salado (Mariel), Marina Tarará (Playas del Este), Cayo Guillermo, Jardines de la Reina, Ancón (Trinidad), Playa Girón, Cayo Largo, and the Hotel Colony (Isla de la Juventud). Expect to pay around US$30 per dive with an extra charge if you need to rent equipment.

When choosing a resort, you would be wise to consider the weather. The south and west coasts of Cuba are calm all winter (November to April), and the north coast is quieter in summer (May to September). You'll have the best chance of finding optimum conditions if you pick the right coast in the right season. Cave diving is possible at Playa Girón and Varadero. You needn't worry about sharks in Cuban waters as attacks are extremely rare. There are decompression chambers at Cárdenas, at the Naval Hospital at Habana del Este, and at the Hotel Colony on Isla de la Juventud.

If you've never dived before, consider taking an open-water scuba certification course offered by most dive centers for around US$365, plus US$90 for books and registration with the Confederación Mundial de Actividades Subacuáticas. If you're planning to do this, book a two-week tour package as one week would be rushed. Otherwise, a brief 'resort course' will give you a taste of scuba diving for under US$100. Certified divers will want to bring along their own mask, snorkel, fins, regulator, buoyancy compensator, certification card, logbook and other gear, although it's also possible to rent equipment.

President Castro himself is an enthusiastic participant in this environmentally friendly sport, and it's possible to dive off his former protocol ship, the 45-meter *Coral Negro*, which can be chartered during the winter season. The 19-member crew includes two diving instructors and scuba equipment is aboard (maximum 12 passengers). The *Coral Negro* is variously based. Ask around at local marinas.

Golf

As yet, Cuba has only two golf courses, the nine-hole Havana Golf Club and the 18-hole Club de Golf Las Américas at Varadero. Golfing enthusiasts should book a tour to one of the resorts near the Varadero course (the Meliá Las Américas is the closest).

Fishing

Cuba's finest deep-sea fishing for sailfish, swordfish, tuna, mackerel, barracuda, and shark is along the northwest coast where the fast-moving Gulf Stream has created a prime game fishing area. Well-developed facilities for sport anglers exist at Cayo Levisa, Havana, Playas del Este, Varadero, Cayo Guillermo, Bahía de Naranjo (Guardalavaca), Isla de la Juventud, and Cayo Largo. Shore casting for bonefish and tarpon is practiced off the south coast at Jardines de la Reina and Cayo Largo.

There's freshwater lake fishing for largemouth bass *(trucha)* at Pinar del Río (Laguna Grande), Guamá (Lago del Tesoro), and Morón (Laguna La Redonda), and in the great reservoirs of central Cuba at Hanabanilla and Zaza. The main season is November to May.

The enthusiastic angler in search of a combination of sea and lake fishing should consider Cayo Guillermo, as there's good ocean fishing right off the resort and several freshwater lakes with fishing camps are within commuting distance.

In May the Ernest Hemingway International Marlin Fishing Tournament is held at Havana's Marina Hemingway (☎ 53-7-33-1150, fax 53-7-33-1149). In 1950 Hemingway himself donated the cup and helped draft the original rules and regulations of

HERIBERTO ECHEVERRIA
COURTESY CUBA POSTER PROJECT

this contest, which has been held annually ever since. Registration costs US$450/550 for teams of three/four anglers with four days of fishing using 30-pound line. Fully equipped boats can be hired at US$200 to US$450 a day with two weeks prior notice. Visas and prior reservations are not required of competitors arriving on their own boats. To take home the Ernest Hemingway Cup, an angler must have won three times, not necessarily in consecutive years.

Many people look upon deep-sea fishing as frivolous cruelty to noble fish. Having noted their concerns, we limit ourselves to providing factual information about the sport and leave it up to individual readers to decide whether they care to participate.

COURSES

An excellent way to justify an extended stay in Cuba while acquiring skills and learning Spanish is to take a course, and the largest organization offering study visits for foreigners is Mercadu SA (☎ 33-3893, fax 53-7-33-3028), Calle 13 No 951 at the corner of Avenida 8, Vedado, Havana 23, Cuba 12300. It can arrange regular study and working holidays at all five of Cuba's universities or virtually any of the many higher education or research institutes around Cuba. The catalog lists numerous programs, including study tours, research visits, participation at scientific events, regular academic study, extended research trips, and organized encounters with professionals in selected fields. Since 1991 Mercadu has operated a summer school in July and August that in 1996 included 151 courses at the universities of Havana, Matanzas, and Pinar del Río and various institutes in the fields of agriculture, communications, economics, education, medicine, science, sociology, sports, and technology. Mercadu also arranges registration at specialized symposiums, conferences, seminars, and workshops throughout the year.

Of special interest are Mercadu's intensive courses in the Spanish language and Cuban culture at Havana University, varying from two weeks to four months with three levels of participation. A placement text is given at the university at 9 am on the first Monday of every month. Classes of three to 10 students receive four or five hours of instruction daily from Monday to Friday. A two-week package costs US$320 for double-occupancy accommodations with breakfast and dinner at a university residence plus US$160 tuition; four weeks is US$470 lodging plus US$200 tuition; four months is US$1600 lodging plus US$700 tuition (US$10 a day extra for a single room). A participation certificate is issued.

Similar services are offered by the Grupo de Turismo Científico Educacional (☎ /fax 53-7-33-1697), Avenida 3 No 402, Miramar, Havana. It operates the Centro de Idiomas para Extranjeros José Martí (José Martí Languages Center for Foreigners), Calle 16 No 109 in Miramar, and can arrange accommodations for students at the Hostal Icemar across the street from the school as part of a package.

The Promotor Cultural at the Casa del Caribe (☎ 4-2285, fax 4-2387), Calle 13 No 154, Vista Alegre, Santiago de Cuba, organizes courses on Cuban culture, Afro-Cuban religions, history, music, and dance lasting anywhere from two weeks to one month. If you don't wish to book ahead, the group will probably be able to set you up with a private tutor on the spot and their prices are negotiable. During the Festival of Caribbean Culture in early July (of which they are the organizing body), there are workshops on Caribbean culture costing anywhere from US$20 to US$80 tuition for the week, and throughout the year they can arrange ecotourism programs for small groups including accommodations, food, and transportation.

Courses for foreigners can be arranged throughout the year by the Oficina de Relaciones Internacionales of the Instituto Superior de Arte (☎ 21-6075, fax 53-7-33-6633, email isa@reduniv.edu.cu), Calle 120 No 1110, Cubanacán, Playa, Havana 12100. Courses in percussion and dance are available almost anytime, but other subjects such as the visual arts, music, theater, and aesthetics are possible when professors are available. Prospective students should give notice at least 15 days in advance (and preferably two months). The school is closed for holidays in August, but courses for groups are still possible at that time with advance notice. Anyone bringing a group of at least 15 students to Cuba for such a course is eligible for free tuition and board. The institute also accepts graduate students for its regular winter courses and an entire year of study here (beginning in September) will cost US$2000 for amateur students or US$3500 for professionals. Successful students will be granted a diploma or certificate. Accommodations in student dormitories can be arranged at US$15 a day including breakfast and dinner for the first 30 days and US$9 a day for subsequent days. The institute's brochure declares that 'our courses are a pretext for dialogue, debate, and confrontation between specialists, teachers, and artists from around the world.'

The Centro Nacional de Conservación, Restauración y Museología (☎ 61-5043), Calle Cuba No 610, Havana, offers courses in the fields of artistic and architectural restoration.

The Escuela Internacional de Cine, Televisión y Video (☎ 0650-3152, fax 33-5341), Apartado Aereo 4041, San Antonio de los Baños, Provincia de La Habana, is a nongovernment organization that trains broadcasting professionals. The campus is at Finca San Tranquilino, Carretera de Vereda Nueva, five km northwest of San Antonio de los Baños. Prospective filmmaking students should contact them directly.

WORK

Each year teams of between 50 and 200 workers arrive at the Campamento Julio Antonio Mella near Caimito, 40 km southwest of Havana, from around the world to perform voluntary labor in solidarity with Cuba. The brigades bear romantic names, such as the Venceremos Brigade from the US, the Juan Rius Rivera Brigade (Puerto Rico), the José Martí Brigade (Western

Europe), the Nordic Brigade (Scandinavia), and the Southern Cross Brigade (Australia and New Zealand).

Members of the brigades or *(brigadistas)* spend about three weeks doing agricultural or construction work alongside Cuban workers. There's also a full program of activities including educational and political events and visits to factories, hospitals, trade unions, and schools. Entertainment is provided at the camp and excursions to the beach and places of interest are organized.

Participants pay their own airfare to Cuba, plus food, accommodations, and excursion fares. For more information contact:

Cuban Youth Tour, Canada
   (☎ 416-536-8901 or 416-651-7615)
International Work Brigade, Cuba Solidarity
   Campaign c/o The Red Rose Club, 129
   Seven Sisters Rd, London N7 7QG, UK
   (☎ 0171-263-6452, fax 0171-561-0191,
   email cubasi@gn.apc.org)
National Venceremos Brigade, PO Box 7071,
   Oakland, CA 94601, USA
   (☎ 510-267-0606)
US/Cuba Labor Exchange, PO Box 39188,
   Redford, MI 48239, USA
   (☎ 313-836-3752, fax 313-836-3752)

ACCOMMODATIONS
Tourist Hotels

Cuba has over 25,000 hotel rooms with 3000 new rooms being added every year. You have a choice of basic, relatively cheap lodgings intended for Cubans, and medium-priced hotels and expensive resorts especially designed for foreigners. The accommodations for foreigners invariably include such features as air conditioning, private toilet and shower, a radio or television (via satellite in the best places), a telephone, and often a refrigerator. Only the most upmarket hotels provide a bath tub as well as a shower. Many hotel rooms contain an empty Thermos that the hotel bar will fill with cold water upon request (otherwise it will remain empty throughout your stay).

Depending on the category, tourist hotels have a restaurant, cafeteria, bar, room service, cabaret, nightclub, disco, swimming pool, infirmary, barber shop, beauty salon, post office, souvenir shop, exchange office, excursions desk, car, moped, and bicycle rentals, and a taxi stand. (We note the shape of the swimming pools to suggest the overall quality of an establishment – many of the nicer hotels have nonrectangular pools.) In addition, the large beach resorts have a range of sporting facilities. The hotels for Cubans offer far fewer facilities (if any), and you may have to share a grubby communal toilet and shower down the hall. Short beds and undersized blankets and sheets are other hallmarks of the lower category hotels.

Tourist accommodations usually consist of either a room in a main hotel building, a hotel-style apartment, or a freestanding or duplex *cabaña* (bungalow). In the larger bungalows and villas you might get one room with private bath and share the sitting room, fridge, and kitchenette with other guests. It's rare to have to share a bathroom and shower in accommodations intended for foreign tourists, though it does happen at places originally intended to accommodate Cubans (including some budget hotels at Varadero and Playas del Este).

Even establishments called apartments often lack private cooking facilities for guests. Unfortunately, being able to cook your own meals is unusual, and you should assume that accommodations called *cabañas* are without cooking facilities unless these are specifically advertised. Apartments and bungalows that do have functioning kitchens (including some at Varadero and Playas del Este) are intended mostly for stays of several weeks. If you bring your own stove or other cooking gear, don't let the hotel staff know you're using it as unwelcome objections could arise. Pack it away before you leave the room.

Tourist hotels are classed from one to five stars, though it's often necessary to subtract one or two stars from the published category to arrive at something approximating international standards. The newer hotels under foreign management are the most likely to come closest

to providing Western European or North American-style service.

As yet, all hotels in Cuba are owned by state enterprises such as Cubanacán, Gaviota, Gran Caribe, Horizontes, and Islazul. Cubanacán operates a chain of 30 mostly new, large, and upmarket tourist hotels around the country. Many of Gaviota's properties are small and exclusive, some of them 'protocol' accommodations used at times by top government officials and foreign dignitaries (an indication of Gaviota's links to the Cuban armed forces). Gran Caribe owns some of Cuba's finest hotels, from the historic hostelries of Havana to top resorts at Varadero and Cayo Largo. Horizontes runs many of the big medium-priced establishments in Havana, Playas del Este, Varadero, and Oriente. Islazul's properties are a bit less expensive and also open to peso-paying Cubans who manage to obtain reservations.

Since 1988 these chains have signed management agreements with a dozen foreign hotel chains, including Accor (France), Amorim (Portugal), Club Venta (Italy), Commonwealth (Canada), Delta (Canada), Golden Tulip (Netherlands), Iberostar (Spain), LTI (Germany), Paradores de Tourismo (Spain), Riu (Spain), Sol Meliá (Spain), SuperClub (Jamaica), and Tryp (Spain), which have upgraded about 30 properties to international standards. If you're fussy about where you sleep, you ought to book a hotel under foreign management. Of course, Canadian and European hotel companies aren't interested in providing budget accommodations, but if efficient service comes first, you should definitely head their way. Specific foreign-operated beach hotels we can recommend include the Las Morlas, Tuxpán, and Sol Palmeras hotels at Varadero; Hotel Ancón near Trinidad; Las Brisas Club and the Río de Mares Resort at Guardalavaca; Farallón del Caribe and Marea del Portillo near Pilón; and the Bucanero Beach Resort and Balneario del Sol at Baconao near Santiago de Cuba.

Room prices are higher during the two high seasons, mid-December to April (especially Christmas and Easter) and in July and August. All other months are low season. Cubans tend to take their vacations during the school holidays in July and August, so the cheaper facilities can be especially crowded at that time. With the exception of package deals for the main beach hotels, it's less expensive to pay on the spot than to prepay rooms, and except at Varadero and Havana the hotels are seldom fully booked. In the odd case that a hotel is full and you don't have a rental car, ask the receptionist to call the next place to see if they have rooms. Otherwise, ask if they know of anyone renting private rooms in their own home.

Hotel reservations made at travel agencies inside Cuba are often not forwarded, and you may arrive to find the hotel full with no record of your booking. After a lot of hassle you could be sent to another hotel of lower category or to one in a worse location. Refunds in such cases are hard to obtain and the way everyone avoids accepting responsibility can be infuriating. Rather than trust a local agent it's usually better to call the hotel personally a day or two before to check prices and availability, and get the name of the employee who confirms your reservation. All such phone numbers are provided in this book.

The checkout time at most hotels is 2 pm and check-in is 4 pm. If the receptionist does you a favor by allowing you to occupy the room before 4 pm and the room hasn't yet been made up, politely ask when they're going to get around to it. If the shower, air conditioner, or something else in the room is out of order, request another room.

Upon checking into a hotel you'll be given a 'guest card' that can be used to charge meals and drinks. Hotel bookings made from abroad usually include continental breakfast, but in the city hotels the hotel restaurants have inconvenient schedules and the service is slow, preventing an early start. Unless you're staying at a beach hotel, it's better to avoid prepaying any meals. At the beach resorts, on the other hand, it's preferable to take a

'modified American plan' (MAP) with breakfast and dinner included as hotel meals bought individually get expensive. Lunch is less of a problem.

Some hotels are noisy until late at night due to loud music from the entertainment area or swimming pool, which is something to consider when selecting your room. Hopefully your travel agent won't have booked you into a hotel next to a construction site where workers are busy putting up yet another hotel. Early in the morning the maids may wake you by knocking on your door unless you put the 'please do not disturb' sign out. Be aware that foreign guests are usually not allowed to bring Cubans back to their hotel rooms.

Peso Hotels

A cheap, invariably old hotel intended for Cubans is called a 'peso hotel' because Cubans are allowed to pay for a room there using *moneda nacional*. In the past, some foreigners have also managed to pay in pesos, but this has largely ended and you'll usually have to pay in dollars. The Cubans are not stupid and it's unlikely they'll allow you to get your room at a 95% discount by paying in pesos you bought on the black market. If you want to know for sure, ask '*¿Puedo pagar en divisas aquí?*' (Can I pay in dollars here?) If the answer is no, they're not authorized to accept dollars, but if they'll still give you a room, you should say no more and pay in advance in pesos. If they answer yes, they'll gladly give you a room if one is available and you'll be expected to pay the bill in dollars.

Because foreigners seldom stay at the peso hotels – and many will not accept foreigners – prices are in flux. If you have to pay the exact dollar equivalent of the peso price at the official one to one rate, you'll find them overpriced. Some peso hotels have already recognized the demand for low-budget accommodations from foreign backpackers and have come up with special prices in dollars, usually around US$10 double. This is less than half what you'd pay at the cheapest tourist hotel, but many peso hotels are in bad repair, dirty, and noisy. On the positive side they're usually safe enough and very conveniently located.

In this book we list all of the peso hotels in the areas covered, including those that do not presently accept foreigners, as conditions can change fast. There's no harm in giving them a try, but you might ask to see the room before filling out the registration card. If you're willing to rough it, some peso hotels are really colorful and full of atmosphere.

Holiday Camps

There are no regular camping grounds in Cuba and it's very unlikely you'll ever see anyone sleeping in a tent or mobile home (caravan). What the Cubans call camping is actually a small resort consisting of simple cabins with shared bath. Most of these are at the beach, but some are in mountain areas. None are in towns or cities.

Holiday camps such as these are intended for Cubans, and they're often closed outside of Cuban holiday periods. In July and August they'll all be open and every cabin will be taken. Advance bookings are usually controlled by a central office called Campismo Popular in the main towns. If you want to stay at one of these resorts, it's a good idea to first visit the Campismo Popular office and try to make a reservation, in which case your arrival will be expected. Otherwise, you could go far out of your way only to find the place full, closed, or out of bounds to foreigners.

As yet very few foreign travelers have stayed in these places even though they're a viable option, costing around US$10 double. Once you have a reservation, your next problem will be getting there as public transport to such places is difficult (see the Getting Around chapter). If you brought your own bicycle to Cuba or have rented a car, you can always go directly to the camping resorts and ask if they have an available cabin. Your arrival will be rather extraordinary, so you'll probably be allowed to pitch your own tent on the premises even if the place is officially closed. You could easily be the first non-Cuban to inquire.

Cubamar (☎ 53-7-30-5536), Paseo No 306 at 15, Vedado, Havana 4, is Cuba's youth tourism organization. It operates large bungalow camps at Playa Jibacoa between Havana and Matanzas, and at Aguas Claras near Pinar del Río.

University & Sports Hotels

University dormitories are usually restricted to persons enrolled in courses, although two hostels in the Miramar district of Havana and one in Santiago de Cuba will accept anyone willing to pay around US$20 for a double room with shared bath. The sports hotels (hoteles deportivas) in Sancti Spíritus and Santiago de Cuba are slightly cheaper (they're used to house visiting teams). Although this category of accommodations is rare, listings for those that do exist are provided in the respective chapters.

Homestays

By law, Cubans are allowed to rent up to two rooms in their own homes, and since 1993 when it became legal for Cubans to have dollars a booming market in private tourist accommodations has emerged. The price for a room, single or double, varies between US$8 to US$15, depending on whether you found the place on your own or were brought there by a tout who will expect a commission. The bathroom will be shared and your hosts will probably be happy to prepare your dinner for around US$5 per person. All prices should be clarified upon arrival.

Unfortunately, there are still no travel agencies specializing in assigning private rooms, so you'll either have to let a hustler take you to one (which will add about US$5 per night to the price) or ask another traveler for a recommendation. In a few places such as Siboney (near Santiago de Cuba) and Trinidad, the hustlers will pounce on you the minute you arrive in town, but don't allow them to lead you to an address you already have.

Staying in a private home is a good way to meet a Cuban family, and the accommodations are usually better than those at a peso hotel for about the same price. For backpackers, it's an easy, inexpensive way to see Cuba and one that will probably become more common in the future. One of the biggest problems is noise, as Cuban homes don't usually have glass windows, only wooden shutters, and sound enters unhindered from other parts of the house and the street.

FOOD
Eating Out
Unless meals are included in your tour package, you'll find eating a daily problem in Cuba, a reflection of the general food shortages in the country. There's often little to buy for Cuban pesos at street stalls and most regular restaurants are overpriced. The service can be incredibly slow at both hotel dining rooms and state-run city restaurants, with long waits to order, to be served, and to pay, so bring along company or a good book. The waiters at some restaurants intended for Cubans are more accustomed to ordering their customers around than in providing service. The way they look at it, being allowed in at all is a privilege.

Restaurant menus are generally in Spanish only (see Food under Language in the Facts about Cuba chapter). What you get depends on the supplies delivered to the chef that day. Some days the selection's good, others it's pitiful. Always check the printed menu for prices before ordering and be wary if beer prices aren't listed, as these could be 50% higher than usual. Establishments without proper menus are best avoided.

Foreigners must pay in dollars at all state-run restaurants with table service even when Cubans can pay in pesos. The peso price on the menu is simply converted into dollars at the one to one rate, which results in the food costing more than it's worth. Portions are generally small and you don't get any better food or service than the Cubans at the next table who are paying 20

times less than you. The dollars you pay go straight into state coffers, and the only extra incentive for the serving staff (who collect their wages in pesos) is whatever tip you may care to leave.

It's unfortunate, but this situation makes most Cuban hotel restaurants and state-run city restaurants – including many of the restaurants mentioned in this book – quite uninteresting to independent travelers and we hesitate to recommend any of them. All is not lost, however: In recent years, largely due to competition from private restaurants, a new breed of state-run restaurant has appeared that insists on payment in dollars from all customers. The food and service at these tends to be better, and the prices are certainly lower because they're based on dollars instead of pesos. Many are operated by the Cuban tourism company Rumbos, a name to watch for.

Buffets In response to criticism of the service from previous guests, most of the large resort hotels now serve all of their meals as a smorgasbord or *mesa sueca*, and some of the buffets are excellent. The hotels under foreign management mount spreads as good as any in the world, and many of the state-run beach hotels try to do the same with varying degrees of success. Some days the staff is right there filling the bowls and trays as they empty, quickly calling for fresh supplies from the kitchen, while other times the dishes are laid out cold on the table with little selection. Often common drinking water is not available simply to force you buy a bottled drink. If this trick grates, help yourself to a couple of extra bowls of soup to wash the main course down or just walk out if you haven't already paid. The buffets do shield you from being held hostage by a surly waiter and you see what you're getting. If you're going on a beach holiday and don't want to have to fuss over food, you should make a point of buying a package that includes a buffet breakfast and dinner.

Cafeterias In the towns state-run lunch counters *(merenderos)* and self-service cafeterias selling food for pesos often indicate what's available by narrow removable strips inserted on a large signboard. As a particular item runs out, its strip is removed from the display. If nothing is posted on the board, it means nothing is available other than perhaps cigarettes, as is often the case.

Many peso snack bars and ice-cream parlors may appear not to have any customers waiting in line, but they're often out of view around the corner or across the street. If most tables are full but no one seems to be waiting at the door, look for the queue. As places become available the waiter goes to the door and waves over a number of people from the head of the line. As a foreigner you can often walk in without lining up, but you'll be expected to pay in dollars and won't be popular with the common folks waiting outside.

There are plenty of pizzerias around Cuba, but most serve a type of ready-made pizza patty that is warmed up (if you're lucky) just before being served. Real oven-baked or deep-pan pizza is usually not available. Cuban pizza from takeout windows is cheap and it fills your stomach, but that's all. Some of the best pizza is sold at private street stalls by the successful restaurateurs of the future. Quite a few people sell drinks and snacks out of the doors and windows of their family homes, and the price of these is always in pesos.

Private Restaurants The big news on the Cuban restaurant scene is the emergence of privately operated *paladares*, which have only been tolerated since 1995. To limit competition with the state-run restaurants, a paladar isn't allowed to have over 12 seats and officially they can only offer pork dishes and sometimes chicken. In practice, they usually have many other items (such as shrimp and lobster) that aren't listed on the menu, in which case you may be ushered into a back room to consume the forbidden foods.

Some paladares have written menus, while others don't; some take pesos, and others want dollars. If there's a menu, check how much beer costs and if it's over $10 you can assume the menu is in pesos. If you've changed money on the black market, it always works out cheaper to pay in pesos. In dollar terms, expect a filling and occasionally wonderful meal at one of these places to cost anywhere between US$3 and US$8, depending on what you order and how much they think you're willing to pay. If you comment on how cheap it is, the price will be 25% higher the next day. Always check the price beforehand as some paladares in heavily touristed areas ask exorbitant prices in dollars. If a paladar doesn't have a written menu with prices listed, it is a negative signal.

Many paladares have no sign outside and some operate clandestinely. Almost any Cuban will know if there's a paladar in the neighborhood; just don't ask your hotel receptionist as they usually view the paladares as competition. We have listed a few paladares in this book, but the situation is changing fast and you really do have to ask '¿Hay un paladar cerca de aquí?' Some paladares are open only in the evening, while others are happy to have your business at any time of night or day. As small-time capitalists, the paladar owners are often eager for additional business and may be able to help you find a private room, hire private car and driver for sightseeing, and so on.

Grocery Stores & Markets Unless you bring your own camping stove and cooking utensils there will be few opportunities to prepare your own meals in Cuba. Buying groceries is also difficult as hotel shops sell only cookies, candies, soft drinks, and alcohol. However, Servi-Cupet gasoline stations usually have some pasta and canned meats for sale in the office, and there are dollar supermarkets in the main towns. A chain of dollar bakeries called Doña Neli has opened recently, and these often have cakes, pastries, and even pizza in addition to bread.

On the Menu

If deciphering menus in Spanish seems a bit daunting, refer to the list of food terms

Puerco asado in the making

in the Food section under Language in the Facts about Cuba chapter.

Main Dishes It's unlikely you'll receive many (or indeed any) gourmet meals in Cuba. The absence of haute cuisine is not merely a result of the shortages and inefficiencies of the present – it simply isn't in the Cuban tradition. The *cocina criolla* (Creole kitchen) developed under Spanish and American influence and its heavy, fatty, or sweet dishes are often inappropriate to the tropical climate.

The most common Cuban foods are pork, beef, rice, beans, eggs, tomatoes, and lettuce. The Spanish influence is apparent in the use of rice, lemons, and oranges. *Yuca* (manioc or cassava) is a native root vegetable shaped like a large carrot that can be boiled or baked, and *malanga* is a large-leafed root vegetable like taro. Hot spices and chili peppers are not used in Cuban cooking; instead, the dishes are seasoned with garlic and onions. The Cubans are avid meat eaters and many tourists are disappointed to find so little fish *(pescado)*. Fresh vegetables are scarce, even at the luxury hotels.

The most common dish offered at Cuban restaurants is *carne asada* (roasted meat), usually *puerco asado* (roast pork) or *carne de cerdo* (pork). State-run restaurants should also have *carne de res* (beef), *picadillo* (ground beef), and *arroz con pollo* (chicken and rice).

The lobster is becoming an endangered species, a result of so many being slaughtered for tourist plates or exported for hard currency. It's still readily available at restaurants, however, and if you won't eat it, the next guy certainly will. Sea turtles have already been eaten into near extinction, and it's rare to see them on Cuban menus anymore (during the 1970s large tour groups would be fed turtle steak as one of their regular weekly meals).

Ajiaco is a typical Cuban meat, garlic, and vegetable stew. *Congrí oriental* (rice cooked with red kidney beans) was introduced by French coffee planters from Haiti during the 19th century. It's similar to *moros y cristianos* (rice with black beans), a dish that has often been compared to the racial mix in Cuba itself. *Fufú* (boiled green bananas mashed into a paste and seasoned with salt) is usually eaten with meat.

A tasty treat to watch for at street stalls is *fritura de maíz* (corn fritters).

Desserts Cuban ice cream *(helado)* is of high quality, and almost every Cuban town has a Coppelia ice-cream parlor with long lines of Cubans waiting to pay in pesos (foreigners pay in dollars). Cubans love to have their ice cream with caramel cream or *natilla* (vanilla pudding). Unfortunately, ice cream has become a lot scarcer due to the chronic milk shortages.

Granizado is shaved ice with a sugary syrup, sold in the street by a person pushing a cart. *Flan* is a small Spanish caramel pudding.

Fried green banana chips are called *tachinos* or *tostones* if they're thick, or *chicharitas* when thinner. Fried ripe banana is *plátano frito*.

DRINKS
Nonalcoholic Drinks
The Cubans usually take their coffee strong and black in a small cup loaded with sugar, an energy hit called a *cafecito* or *café cubano*. A morning favorite is *café con leche*, a mixture of strong black coffee and hot milk in a large cup. *Café americano* is weak coffee in a large cup. *Té* or *yerba buena* (tea) is often taken with *limón* (lemon).

Street stalls often sell a sweet water-based drink called *refresco* or *limonada*, which is certain to eventually give you Batista's revenge if you drink it regularly. A better bet is a *jugo* (juice) or *batido* (milkshake) made in a mixer from whole fruit before your very eyes, although the ice may be dubious. Hotel shops sell cartons of quality fruit juice produced in Cuba by a Chilean company under the brand name Tropical Island.

Guarapo is the juice pressed from whole stalks of sugar cane right on the spot, cooled with ice. If your stomach is strong enough to take the ice, it's a great refreshing drink often available on the street.

In Oriente you can often get *prú*, a nonalcoholic drink made from various root vegetables and herbs that are left to ferment for three days. Canned *malta* (malt beverage) and soft drinks are sold at hotel shops.

The tap water in Cuba is often questionable, and it's better to drink *agua mineral* (mineral water), which you can easily purchase at hotel shops in plastic 1½-liter bottles.

Alcoholic Drinks
Cuba is famous for its rum *(ron)*, a by-product of the sugar industry. To produce rum, distilleries dilute high-quality molasses *(miel de caña)* with water, add yeast, and allowed the mixture to ferment for 30 hours. The fermented brew is heated by a jet of compressed vapor and the condensed liquid is fed into a copper distillation vat and strengthened until it is 75 proof. This young rum is pumped into oak barrels and allowed to mature for three years. Then the rum is diluted with water, filtered, and various ingredients may be added to influence the taste. Some is returned to the oak barrels for further aging, after which caramel may be added to produce a deeper color.

A crude type of rum has been made in Cuba since the 16th century, but only during the sugar boom of the mid-19th century were modern distilleries set up in Havana, Matanzas, and Cárdenas to produce large quantities of quality rum for export. Bacardí rum was first brewed at Santiago de Cuba in 1878, and although the Bacardí trademark departed for Puerto Rico in 1960, the original factory is still there producing Caney rum and other brands. The quality remains excellent.

Cuba's most famous brand is Havana Club, either Carta Blanca (a three-year-old light, dry white rum), Carta de Oro (a five-year-old golden dry rum), or Añejo (a seven-year-old brown rum). Carta Blanca is used in mixed drinks, but Carta de Oro and Añejo are best taken straight or on the rocks. Havana Club was founded at Cárdenas in 1878, but the main factory is now at Santa Cruz del Norte, east of Havana. The figure of the Giraldilla statue from Havana's Castillo Real de la Fuerza appears on every bottle.

Havana Club also produces a large variety of exquisite liqueurs, including banana, chocolate, chocolate mint, cocoa, coffee, creme de menthe, guava, lemon, lime, maraschino, pineapple, and triple sec. Ponche Kuba is an egg liqueur manufactured in Cuba by the Dutch distiller Lucas Bols, maker of the famous Advokaat of Curaçao.

Cuban workers and farmers often snap back glasses of *aguardiente,* or 'fire water,' a cane brandy.

If you're a wine or champagne lover, you had better bring a couple of bottles of duty-free wine with you on the plane as what is available in Cuba is poor quality and expensive. Some wine is produced locally from tropical fruits and imported raisins, but Cuba really isn't a wine country.

On the other hand, Cuba produces some outstanding beer. Among the best brands are Mayabe (3.8% alcohol), made by Holguín's Mayabe Brewery, and Hatuey (5.4% alcohol), bottled at Santiago de Cuba since 1927. The Lagarto and Cristal beers brewed in Havana just can't compare to soft, gentle, full-bodied Mayabe.

Cuban Cocktails

The official bartender's guide produced by Havana Club includes the recipes of 100 Cuban cocktails, including 10 'Cuban classics,' five 'imaginative' drinks, 10 winter cocktails, 20 long drinks, and 55 short drinks.

The most famous of the classic cocktails are probably the Cuba libre (rum, cola, and ice cubes, stirred), invented to toast Cuban independence in 1902, and the daiquirí (rum, lemon juice, sugar, maraschino, and crushed ice, shaken). The daiquirí was created in Oriente around the turn of the century and improved during the 1920s with the introduction of the electric blender at Havana's El Floridita bar, where American writer Ernest Hemingway was said to have imbibed vast quantities. The daiquirí can also be made with strawberries, oranges, pineapples, bananas, or peaches.

Another Hemingway favorite was the mojito (rum, lemon juice, sugar, soda, mint leaf, and ice cubes, stirred), a refreshing drink often ordered at beach bars. The presidente (rum, red vermouth, grenadine, and pieces of ice, stirred) is named for President Mario García Menocal, whose love of drink was surpassed only by his fondness for dipping into the public purse.

The roaring '20s witnessed the birth of many new cocktails: the ron collins (rum, sugar, lemon juice, soda, and ice cubes, stirred), the Havana special (rum, pineapple juice, maraschino, and pieces of ice, shaken), the Mary Pickford (rum, pineapple juice, grenadine, and pieces of ice, shaken), and the Isla de Pinos (rum, grapefruit juice, and ice cubes, stirred). During the 1940s Cuban bartenders came up with the mulata (rum, lemon juice, cacao liqueur, and crushed ice, shaken) and the saoco (rum, water of a green coconut, and ice cubes, stirred).

After you've tried the 10 classics, Cuban bartenders still have plenty to offer. On a hot summer day order a planter's punch (similar to the daiquirí but larger and including tropical fruit) or a piña colada (rum, pineapple juice, coconut cream, and crushed ice, shaken). In Cuba a bloody mary is called a Cubanito (rum, tomato juice, lemon juice, Worcestershire sauce, Tabasco sauce, salt, and ice cubes, stirred).

Other popular drinks are the Cuban Manhattan (rum, angostura, red vermouth, and pieces of ice, stirred), the highball (rum, water, soda, or ginger ale, and ice cubes, stirred), the Cuba bella (daiquirí with grenadine, chocolate syrup, and creme de menthe), the stinger (rum and creme de menthe, shaken), and the zombie (three types of rum with lemon juice, pineapple or orange juice, grenadine, tropical fruit, and pieces of ice).

Whenever a cold front moves in, drown your troubles in grog (rum, hot water, lemon juice, and sugar, stirred). Other winter drinks include ron toddy (rum, hot water, sugar, and spices, shaken) and hot buttered rum (rum, butter, sugar, and spices, boiled). A shot of rum in a cup of tea, coffee, or hot chocolate is also very good. ∎

ENTERTAINMENT

An old marketing slogan of the Cuban tourism authorities is *Cuba, alegre como su sol* (Cuba, happy as its sun). You'll usually have a good choice of entertainment options including folk music and jazz clubs, Afro-Cuban dancing, cabaret shows, discos, classical music recitals, dramatic theater, puppet shows, and movies. The Cubans themselves love to have a good time and you'll find them as enthusiastic about it all as you are.

Cinemas

Most cinemas are open from 3 pm until 10 pm, although the larger cinemas in Havana (such as the Yara and Payret) open earlier. Tickets cost only about a peso and most foreign films are in the original language with Spanish subtitles. Some cinemas show videos in small rooms.

Discos

All of the main hotels have discos that often open around 9 pm. Foreign tourists are usually admitted promptly without reservations if they pay the cover charge in dollars. Cubans wishing to pay in pesos must make advance reservations through an official booking office. Cubans can spend pesos at nonhotel discos intended for the general population, but foreigners may be expected to pay dollars here too. At least the price will be lower than at a hotel. Some of the top discos have dress requirements such as a long-sleeved shirt with a collar and no jeans, shorts, or sneakers. It's best not to take items that can be easily stolen to a disco.

Nightclubs

As a holdover from the fifties, many Cuban cabarets present gala floorshows with big bands, leggy, bosomy dancers, smooth singers, acrobats, and all the glamour and excitement you could ask for. The most famous cabaret is presented outdoors at Havana's Tropicana, 'paradise under the stars,' and a second Tropicana is now operating in Santiago de Cuba. In Havana, the Nacional, Capri, Havana Libre, and Riviera

hotels all have cabarets. The Cabaret Continental at Varadero's Hotel Internacional and the Cabaret San Pedro del Mar in Santiago de Cuba are also famous. Cabaret shows are staged at nightclubs in most towns and resorts with admission costing US$5 to US$30 per person. Drinks in these establishments cost US$3 to US$5 each (small groups should order a bottle of rum and mix). Most large hotels have excursion packages to the cabarets that include transfers, admission, and one drink.

Theater

All of the provincial capitals have theaters where plays in Spanish are presented, and in Havana and Santiago de Cuba there are several to choose from. Children's theater is very popular, and puppet shows are staged in some cinemas and theaters every Saturday and Sunday morning.

We provide the phone numbers for some theaters, but they are all but irrelevant. Public phones are hard to find in Cuba and one would need to be fluent in Spanish to be understood. Even then the person at the theater probably wouldn't pick up the receiver or might give incomplete or misleading information. Relying on a telephoned reservation would be extremely foolish as 99 times out of 100 the person at the theater door would have no record of it. In all such cases the only real way of obtaining reliable information is to go to the theater beforehand and buy advance tickets if possible.

Classical Music & Ballet

Classical music is often performed at the Casa de la Cultura in every Cuban town. Leading theaters presenting musical programs include the Gran Teatro de La Habana and the Teatro Nacional de Cuba in Havana, the Teatro José Jacinto Milanés in Pinar del Río, the Teatro Sauto in Matanzas, the Teatro Tomás Terry in Cienfuegos, Teatro La Caridad in Santa Clara, the Teatro Principal in Sancti Spíritus, the Teatro Principal in Camagüey, the Teatro Suñol in Holguín, the Sala Teatro José Joaquín Palma in Bayamo, and the Sala de

Conciertos Dolores and the Teatro José María Heredia in Santiago de Cuba. The Havana Symphony Orchestra was founded in 1922, the Havana Philharmonic Orchestra in 1924, the Ballet Nacional de Cuba in 1948, the National Symphony Orchestra in 1960, and the Ballet de Camagüey in 1971.

Folk & Traditional Music

Most Cuban cities have a Casa de la Trova, an informal sort of club where Cubans get together to hear everything from *la nueva trova* to traditional *sextetos* and *septetos* (turn to Music under Arts in the Facts about Cuba chapter for a discussion of these genres). Local amateurs with a musical knack get up to play and sing here, especially on weekends. At other times semi-professionals will come to practice or try out a new act. Cuba's social system has prevented most of these clubs from becoming commercialized or being spoiled by tourism, and they're great places to feel the local pulse. It's fine to tip the musicians (usually the only compensation they'll receive), but don't allow yourself to be hustled for drinks by hangers-on.

III FESTIVAL NACIONAL DE AFICIONADOS CAMPESINOS
MATANZAS, DICIEMBRE 1972
CNC-ANAP

LUIS ALVAREZ
COURTESY CUBA POSTER PROJECT

Some Afro-Cuban folkloric groups such as the Conjunto Folklórico Nacional in Havana and Ballet Folkórico Cutumba in Santiago de Cuba present weekly preview shows at their dance workshops. These are excellent and worth every effort to attend.

You'll run across quite a bit of free entertainment, especially on the weekends with rumba parties and salsa music in the streets and squares.

Bars

Virtually every hotel will have a bar and drinks are reasonably priced. Rumbos has set up a number of tourist bars in places usually frequented by visitors, and these are fine places to take a break with a can of beer or a soft drink. Peso bars intended for the local population usually have only straight shots of rum. Cuba's most famous tourist bars are La Bodeguita del Medio and El Floridita in Havana, both former Ernest Hemingway haunts.

SPECTATOR SPORTS

After the revolution all sporting facilities were taken over by the government and professional sport was abolished. Instead, huge investments were plowed into physical education and amateur sport, and by 1975 the number of participants in organized sport had increased from 15,000 before the revolution to about three million, over half of them students.

Modern sporting facilities are found throughout the country and Cuban athletes have won honors at international competitions all out of proportion to the country's size. Cuba is a leader in world amateur boxing, as indicated by the Olympic gold medals won by Cuban heavyweight Teófilo Stevenson in 1972, 1976, and 1980. In 1991 Cuba hosted the Pan-American Games, an imposing legacy of which is the Estadio Panamericano near Cojímar just outside Havana. Cuba placed first in those games and was fifth at the 1992 Barcelona Olympics. Javier Sotomayor currently holds the world high-jump record, and track star Ana Fidelia Quirot has medaled in many international competitions, including the 1996 Olympics. At the Atlanta games, Cuba finished 9th among the 197 countries competing, winning 25 of the 271 medals awarded during the games. Cuba took a total of nine gold medals, including four in boxing and one each in baseball, judo, volleyball, weightlifting, and wrestling.

Cuba's national sport is baseball, which has been played here since the late 19th century. Even before the Spanish conquest of Cuba the Taino Indians played a similar game called *batos*, and the Cuban national team is easily the best in Latin America. Baseball is a civilized sport, unmarred by the violence of soccer and football. Until recently admission to all matches and sporting events was free, and although a few pesos are now collected, attendance at a Cuban baseball game is well worth the effort. The main baseball season runs November to March and matches usually take place Tuesday, Wednesday, and Thursday at 8 pm, Saturday at 1:30 and 8 pm, and Sunday at 1:30 pm (Monday and Friday are traveling days). Ask at your hotel if there's a stadium anywhere near where you're staying, then go there in person during business hours to check the schedule. As a foreigner, you'll have no trouble getting a ticket (and in Cuba you needn't worry about hooliganism). Basketball, volleyball, and soccer are also popular in Cuba.

THINGS TO BUY

Dollar shops at the hotels sell things like dolls, woodcarvings, jewelry, leather goods, books, musical instruments, Cuban stamps and coins, Che Guevara posters, T-shirts, and cigars. The *guayabera*, a men's pleated tropical shirt with buttons, is almost the national dress on formal occasions. All hotel shops have bottles of rum and many sell bags of the outstanding Cuban ground coffee.

It's always a good idea to hang onto the receipts whenever you purchase Cuban goods for dollars at a hotel shop as these give you the right to export the items duty-free without question. This is especially true in the case of cigars: Cubans on the street often sell foreigners contraband cigars, and these could raise questions if found by Cuban customs upon departure. In practice, however, the Cuban authorities are highly unlikely to check your bags as you're leaving Cuba.

It's worth knowing that the goods (including alcohol) sold for dollars at Intur and Caracol tourist shops in the hotels are tax free and just as cheap as anything in the duty-free shops at the airports. There's no advantage to waiting until the last minute to do all your shopping.

Cuba's state recording company, Egrem, produces quality compact discs and cassettes of Cuban music. Most are made under license in Canada and clearly marked as such, so it should be no problem importing them into the US.

Numerous galleries in Havana and around the country sell artwork by Cuban artists. If you buy an original painting, print, or sculpture, be sure to ask for a receipt to prove you bought the object at an official sales outlet; otherwise, it could be confiscated by customs upon departure. Original works of art purchased in the street or directly from the artist require an export permit costing US$10. The smuggling of Cuban art works has received considerable publicity recently and customs officials are on the lookout.

To preserve the natural environment, visitors should refrain from purchasing souvenirs made from wild plants, animals, birds, sea shells, or coral. Customs regulations intended to protect endangered species prohibit the import/export of items containing turtle shell, black coral, some butterflies, and reptiles. Crocodile-skin souvenirs could raise questions if found by the customs authorities in Canada or Europe, and it would be necessary to have documentation proving they originated at the Guamá crocodile farm. Conch shells could also cause problems.

Before purchasing any dried or mounted specimens of Cuban flora and fauna, make sure you'll be allowed to take them out of Cuba as sanitary and export documents may be required. Items sold in hotel shops are usually OK.

Cigars

Hand-rolled cigars in cedar boxes are a favorite souvenir. The price of some of the better brands (per sealed box of 25 cigars) are as follows:

Bolívar (US$65)
Cohiba Coronas Especiales (US$206)
Cohiba Espléndidos (US$295)
Diplomáticos (US$67)
Larrañaga (US$30)
Montecristo No 3 (US$71)
Montecristo No 4 (US$55)
Montecristo Cabinet Selection (US$107)
Partagás (US$50 to US$86)
Punch (US$62)
Romeo y Julieta (US$62 to US$80)

The giant *panatela larga* Cohiba cigars sold individually are popular. Before he gave up smoking, President Castro's favorite cigars were double Corona Montecristo and Cohiba (named for the original Taino word for tobacco). With all the best tobacco going into cigars, Cuban cigarettes are terrible and the super-strong Popular brand is guaranteed to choke even seasoned Gitane smokers.

Black-market cigars sold on the street are often of dubious quality and even sealed boxes of known brands may have been tampered with. It's best to pay a bit more to be sure of what you're getting, and an official purchase receipt from a hotel shop eliminates the possibility of problems with Cuban customs at the airport. The export of over 200 cigars per person is not allowed. Cuban cigars are prohibited entry into the US and will be confiscated by US customs if found.

Getting There & Away

AIR

Almost all visitors arrive by air and there's a wide choice of airlines, airports, and air fares. Direct scheduled flights arrive in Cuba from Canada, the Caribbean, Central and South America, and Europe, and there are special charter flights from the US.

Airlines & Airports

Cuba's national airline, Cubana de Aviación, dates back to the inauguration of air service between Havana and Santiago de Cuba in October 1929. By 1945 there were scheduled flights from Havana to Miami, and these were extended to Madrid in 1948. Nationalized in May 1959 and merged with several other airlines, Cubana launched flights to Eastern Europe in 1961 and subsequently acquired a fleet of sturdy Ilyushins, Antonovs, Tupolevs, and Yakolevs.

Today Cubana carries about a million passengers a year to Havana from Barcelona, Berlin-Schönefeld, Bogotá, Brussels, Buenos Aires, Cancún, Caracas, Cologne, Costa Rica, Fort de France, Gran Canaria, Grand Caiman, Guayaquil, Kingston, Lima, London-Stansted, Madrid, Mexico City, Montego Bay, Montreal, Moscow-Sheremetyevo, Nassau, Panama City, Paris-Orly, Pointe-a-Pitre, Quito, Rio de Janeiro, Santiago de Chile, Santo Domingo, Sao Paulo, and Toronto. There are also Cubana flights to Varadero from Cancún, Lima, London-Stansted, Montreal, Paris-Orly, and Toronto; to Ciego de Ávila from Montreal; to Holguín from Cologne; and to Santiago de Cuba from Santo Domingo.

By flying Cubana your Cuban experience begins the moment you board the plane. Unfortunately, however, Cubana has a reputation similar to that of the Russian carrier Aeroflot, so be prepared for uncomfortable Soviet-era aircraft, slow inflight service, poor food, and occasional delays.

On the other hand, fares on Cubana are often cheaper than those of competitors, especially on the long hauls from Europe, and saving a hundred dollars or more may be worth the possible inconvenience. Another advantage to Cubana is their offices throughout Cuba where you can easily reconfirm flight times and get information; all of the foreign airlines have only an office in Havana, and the charter companies are often represented by an elusive tour representative at Varadero. Some Cubana flights have free seating, in which case you should board quickly to have a choice of seats.

Other international airlines flying into Havana include:

Aerocaribbean
(from Puerto Plata and Managua)
Aeroflot-Russian Airlines
(from Lima, Luxembourg, Managua, Moscow-Sheremetyevo, Santiago de Chile, and Shannon)
Aerolíneas Argentinas
(from Buenos Aires)
Aeropostal
(from Caracas)
ALM Antillean Airlines
(from Curacao)
AOM French Airlines
(from Paris-Orly)
Iberia
(from Barcelona and Madrid)
Lacsa
(from San José)
Ladeco Airlines
(from Bogotá, San José, and Santiago de Chile)
LTU International Airways
(from Düsseldorf and Munich)
Mexicana de Aviación
(from Cancún, Mérida, Mexico City, Oaxaca, Tuxtla Gutierrez, and Villahermosa)
TAAG
(from the Cape Verde Islands and Luanda)
Viasa
(from Caracas)

These are only the direct flights – all of these airlines offer transfer connections to/from the other cities they serve.

Cuban cities other than Havana receiving direct international flights include Varadero, Santiago de Cuba, Holguín, Ciego de Ávila, Camagüey, Manzanillo, and Cienfuegos. You can fly directly to Varadero on Aeroperu (from Lima); Air Transat, Royal Airlines, and Skyservice (all from Toronto); Cubana (from Cancún, Lima, London-Stansted, Montreal, Paris-Orly, and Toronto); LTU International Airways (from Düsseldorf and Munich); Martinair Holland (from Amsterdam); and SAM (from Bogotá and San Andrés Island).

Direct flights to Santiago de Cuba are available on Aeropostal (from Aruba, Caracas, and Santo Domingo); Cubana (from Santo Domingo), Air Transat, Canadian Airlines, and Royal Airlines (all from Toronto); and LTU International Airways (from Düsseldorf and Munich).

Direct flights to Holguín are offered by Air Transat, Canadian Airlines, and Royal Airlines (all from Toronto); Martinair Holland (from Amsterdam); Cubana (from Cologne); and LTU International Airways (from Düsseldorf and Munich).

Ciego de Ávila is served by Canadian Airlines and Royal Airlines from Toronto and Cubana from Montreal. Royal Airlines has charter flights to Camagüey and Manzanillo from Toronto. Cienfuegos is served from Toronto by Royal Airlines.

Buying Tickets

The plane ticket will probably be the single most expensive item in your budget, and buying it can be an intimidating business. There's likely to be a multitude of airlines, tour companies, and travel agents hoping to separate you from your money, and it's always worth putting aside a few hours to research the current state of the market. Start early: Some of the cheapest tickets have to be bought months in advance, and some popular flights sell out early. Look at the ads in newspapers and magazines, consult reference books, and watch for special offers. Then phone round the travel agents for bargains. (Airlines can supply information on routes and timetables; however, except at times of inter-airline war, they do not supply the cheapest tickets.) Find out the fare, the route, the duration of the journey, and any restrictions on the ticket. Then sit back and decide which is best for you.

Travel agencies vary widely and you should ensure that you use one that suits your needs. Some simply handle tours, while full-service agencies handle everything from tours and tickets to car rental and hotel bookings. A good one will do all these things and can save you a lot of money. However, if all you want is a ticket at the lowest possible price, then you really need an agency specializing in discounted tickets. A discounted ticket agency, however, may not be useful for things like hotel bookings.

Some officially discounted fares vary with the time of year. There's often a low (off-peak) season and a high (peak) season. Sometimes there's an intermediate or shoulder season as well. At peak times when everyone wants to fly, not only will the officially discounted fares be higher but so will unofficially discounted fares, or there may simply be no discounted tickets available. Usually the fare depends on your outward flight – if you depart in the high season and return in the low season, you pay the high-season fare.

If you must cancel or change a discount ticket, you'll often incur heavy penalties. No changes at all may be allowed on charter tickets. Some airlines impose penalties on regular tickets as well, particularly against 'no show' passengers.

At least 72 hours prior to the departure time of an onward or return flight, you must contact the airline and 'reconfirm' that you intend to be on the flight. If you fail to do this, the airline can delete your name from the passenger list and you could lose your seat. You don't have to reconfirm the first flight on your itinerary or if your stopover is less than 72 hours. Many charter flights also don't require reconfirmation (ask your travel agent). Only Cubana Airlines is represented outside Havana; all other airlines have offices in Havana only (see Getting There & Away in the City of Havana chapter for addresses and phone numbers).

Airlines ask you to check in a certain time ahead of the flight departure (usually two hours on scheduled international flights and three hours on charters). If you fail to check in on time and the flight is overbooked, the airline can cancel your booking and give your seat to somebody else.

Airlines hate to fly empty seats, and since every flight has some passengers who fail to show up, they often book more passengers than they have seats. Usually the excess passengers balance those who fail to show up, but occasionally somebody gets bumped. If this happens, guess who it's most likely to be? The passengers who check in late.

Legally an airline is entitled to treat a ticket like cash, and if you lose it, it's gone forever. Sometimes, however, the airline will treat it like a traveler's check and, after inquiries, issue you another one. Once you have your ticket, photocopy it or write down its number and also jot down the flight number and other details. Keep the information somewhere separate from your ticket. If the ticket is lost or stolen, this will help you get a replacement.

Use the fares quoted in this book as a guide only. They are approximate and based on the rates advertised by travel agents at press time. Quoted airfares do not necessarily constitute a recommendation for the carrier.

Travelers with Special Needs

If you have special needs of any sort – you've broken a leg, you're a vegetarian, traveling in a wheelchair, taking a baby, terrified of flying – you should let the airline know as soon as possible so that they can make arrangements accordingly. You should remind them when you reconfirm your booking (at least 72 hours before departure) and again when you check in at the airport. It may also be worth ringing round the airlines before you make your booking to find out how they can handle your particular needs.

Airports and airlines can be surprisingly helpful, but they do need advance warning. Most international airports will provide escorts from check-in desk to plane where needed, and there should be ramps, lifts, accessible toilets, and reachable phones. Aircraft toilets, on the other hand, are likely to present a problem; travelers should discuss this with the airline at an early stage and, if necessary, with their doctor.

Deaf travelers can ask for airport and in-flight announcements to be written down for them.

Children under two travel for 10% of the standard fare (or free, on some airlines), as long as they don't occupy a seat. They don't get a baggage allowance either. 'Skycots' should be provided by the airline if requested in advance; these can hold a child weighing up to about 10 kg. Children between two and 12 can usually occupy a seat for half to two-thirds of the full fare, and they do get a baggage allowance. Strollers can often be taken as hand luggage.

Baggage

Two pieces of luggage are allowed on flights to/from Canada. On all other flights the limit is 20 kilograms in economy. If you plan to take along something bulky such as a bicycle, golf bag and clubs, surfboard, water skis, fishing tackle box, or portable musical instrument, you should check the airline's policy before you book your ticket. Such items will usually be considered one of your two pieces or part of your 20 kilograms, but check. It's wise to securely lock your baggage before checking in and to carry valuable items in your hand luggage. Cases of baggage handlers pilfering items from unlocked suitcases at Havana's José Martí International Airport are not unknown.

The USA

There are no scheduled flights from the USA to Cuba, and the US offices of airlines such as Mexicana de Aviación that fly to

Cuba from third countries aren't allowed to book flights to Cuba. You must work through their offices or a travel agent outside the US. Air services to Cuba from Canada, Mexico, and the Bahamas are discussed below, and gateway cities like Cancún, Mexico City, Montreal, Nassau, and Toronto are just a short hop away. Turn to Organized Tours near the end of this chapter for a list of Canadian and Mexican travel agencies that are happy to take your booking and obtain your Cuban tourist card.

US citizens able to obtain US government permission to visit Cuba can use special charter flights from Miami to Havana (via Cancún). These semisecret flights aren't listed on the electronic displays at Miami Airport and depart from an obscure terminal gate. Officially they're open only to Cuban nationals resident in Cuba or the US, diplomats and their families, government officials, US citizens with a Treasury Department license to visit Cuba, and accredited journalists. At last report the flights went twice weekly via Cancún, Mexico, and the fare was US$399 roundtrip. Direct charter flights between Miami and Havana were suspended on February 26, 1996. For more information call Marazul Tours (mentioned under Organized Tours) or Airline Brokers Co (☎ 305-871-1260).

Canada

Cubana flies an Ilyushin IL-62 nonstop from Montreal and Toronto to Varadero weekly (four hours). Another Cubana flight goes from Montreal to Ciego de Ávila. Royal Airlines flies from Toronto to Varadero, Cienfuegos, Ciego de Ávila, Camagüey, Holguín, Manzanillo, and Santiago de Cuba. There are flights on Canadian Airlines from Toronto to Ciego de Ávila, Holguín, and Santiago de Cuba. Air Transat has flights to Varadero, Holguín, Manzanillo, and Santiago de Cuba. During the winter season Canadian Airlines' charter flights operate direct to Varadero from Vancouver and Halifax. Virtually all flights from Canada other than those of Cubana

are charters and – surprisingly – few of the Canadian carriers fly to Havana.

The Cubana flights depart Varadero in the morning and return from Canada in the afternoon; Air Transat, Canadian Airlines, and Royal Airlines do the reverse. If you live in Montreal or Toronto, or plan to overnight there en route, the Canada-based carriers are preferable as you get two extra half days in the sun. Cubana may be more convenient if you want to schedule a same-day connection in Montreal or Toronto to some other point.

Reduced advance-purchase excursion (APEX) fares are available allowing a maximum stay of one month; and these must be purchased 14 days in advance. The fares vary according to season with the high seasons at Christmas and Easter, the shoulder seasons just before and after Easter and in July and August. At last report, the regular return APEX fare from Montreal to Varadero was about CDN$500/600/700 low/shoulder/high.

These are Cubana's *published* fares, and you can obtain a better price by working through a Canadian travel agent who books charter flights to Cuba. Some of these companies are listed under Organized Tours at the end of this chapter. On these expect to pay around CDN$400 return (more at Christmas, Easter, and on weekends), plus CDN$55 Canadian departure tax and CDN$14 for a Cuban tourist card. If you wish to stay in Cuba over two weeks, the charter prices increase considerably. Flight dates cannot be changed and there are heavy cancellation penalties. Always compare the price of a tour package as it may only cost a few hundred dollars more and airport transfers, accommodations, and often meals will be included.

Australia

The most direct route to Cuba from Australia and New Zealand is to Toronto via Hawaii on Air New Zealand. There one can board one of the Canadian flights previously mentioned.

Aerolíneas Argentinas (☎ 9650-7111 or 800-333-609) runs two flights each week from Sydney to Buenos Aires, from which passengers can make connections to Havana on sister carrier Viasa. These flights pass through Caracas, Mexico. The entire route costs around A$3100.

Mexico

For most US citizens (and Mexicans), Cancún, Mexico, is the least expensive gateway to Cuba (US$185 to US$222 return plus US$24 tax), and unlike Canada, there are many flights straight to Havana. Both Cubana and Mexicana cover the 500 km from Cancún to Havana. Cubana's Yakovlev YAK 42s and Fokker F27s fly four times a week, while Mexicana's DC-9s go six times a week. Cubana also has nonstop weekly flights from Cancún to Varadero. Call the Cubana and Mexicana offices mentioned below for their current fares between Cancún and Havana. Cancún itself is easily accessible on cheap charter flights from cities all across the US.

In addition to the Cancún services, Mexicana has direct flights to Havana from Mérida, Mexico City, Oaxaca, Tuxtla Gutierrez, and Villahermosa once or twice a week. Cubana flies to Havana from Mexico City twice a week.

From Mexico City to Havana, Mexicana charges US$260 one way or US$411 return on a 30-day excursion basis. From Mérida it costs US$143 one way, US$222 30-day return. For information on Mexicana flights to Cuba call the reservations offices in Mexico City (☎ 52-5-325-0990) or in Cancún (☎ 52-98-874444); Mexicana offices in the US are not allowed to help with these flights.

The Cubana office in Mexico City is accessible over ☎ 52-5-255-3776, fax 52-5-255-0835, while Cubana's Cancún office is ☎ 52-98-877333. Also check the Organized Tours section below.

Other Caribbean Islands

Cubana has flights to Havana from Fort de France, Grand Caiman, Kingston, Montego Bay, Nassau, Pointe-a-Pitre, and Santo Domingo. Aerocaribbean flies between Puerto Plata, Dominican Republic, and Havana twice a week (US$180/250 one way/return). The Venezuelan carrier Aeropostal has a twice weekly flight to Santiago de Cuba from Aruba and Santo Domingo. The Colombian airline SAM flies to Varadero from San Andrés Island weekly.

Cubana's Nassau-Havana flight operates three times a week (US$130/175 single/return, plus US$15/27 tax) – a useful connection for blockade runners from the eastern US. Book through Havanatur Bahamas (☎ 809-328-7985, fax 809-361-1336), PO Box N-10246, Nassau, Bahamas. Cuban tourist cards are sold at the airline desk in Nassau.

ALM Antillean Airlines has flights twice a week between Havana and Curacao, connecting in Curacao to/from Amsterdam. ALM offers a one-week package from Aruba, Bonaire, or Curacao to Havana at 2699/4258 Antillean guilders single/double including airfare and accommodations.

Central America

Four airlines fly between Havana and Central America. Cubana runs flights twice a week from Panama City and a 21-day excursion roundtrip fare is available for US$496. The Costa Rican airline Lacsa operates a Boeing 737 from San José to Havana twice a week; the 21-day roundtrip excursion fare is US$484. Cubana and Ladeco also fly out of San José. Aeroflot Russian Airlines has a weekly flight from Managua to Havana with a 21-day excursion fare of US$437. The weekly Aerocaribbean Managua-Havana flight is cheaper at US$235/378 one way/return.

South America

From Caracas, Venezuela, Aeropostal flies twice weekly to both Havana and Santiago de Cuba. Viasa's Boeing 727-200s link Caracas to Havana six times a week. On both airlines the 21-day roundtrip excursion fare between Caracas and Havana is US$480. There's also a seven-day excursion fare of US$351 that must be paid immediately upon booking (not for sale in Colombia). Cubana also flies from Caracas to Havana.

The Medellín-based carrier SAM flies a Boeing 727 weekly from Bogotá to Varadero. The Chilean company Ladeco Airlines flies a Boeing 727 twice weekly to Havana from Santiago, via Bogotá or San José. Ladeco has a two-month roundtrip excursion fare of US$576 from Bogotá to Havana (not available to US citizens). Ladeco also has a US$350 21-day excursion fare from Bogotá that can only be purchased in Colombia (other strange rules apply). A third option is a one-month excursion fare of US$522 return. From Santiago, Chile, expect to pay about twice as much. Cubana flies to Havana from Bogotá, Quito, and Guayaquil.

Aeroperu flies a Boeing 727-200 weekly from Lima to Varadero. Aeroflot Russian Airlines has twice weekly flights to Havana from Lima, weekly from Santiago de Chile. You're looking at US$1020 for a 21-day roundtrip excursion from Lima to Havana, or about US$200 more from Santiago de Chile. Cubana also links Lima to both Havana and Varadero.

Further afield, Aerolíneas Argentinas flies an Airbus A310 to Havana weekly from Buenos Aires. The two-month roundtrip excursion fare costs US$1368. Cubana also has flights to Havana from Buenos Aires weekly, from Santiago de Chile twice a week, and from Rio de Janeiro and Sao Paulo, Brazil, weekly (US$1225 return).

Europe

Several European airlines fly to Cuba. Iberia flies a DC-10 to Havana from Barcelona and Madrid four times a week. AOM French Airlines flies another DC-10 widebody jet to Havana from Paris-Orly twice a week. In France, call AOM reservations at ☎ 33-01-4979-1234.

Martinair Holland has weekly Boeing 767 flights from Amsterdam to Varadero and Holguín. A 28-day return ticket to either is about 1235 Dutch guilders when booked through an agent such as Havanatour Benelux (☎ 31-10-411-2444, fax 31-10-411-4749) in Rotterdam. To get this fare, you must book at least three hotel

nights through Havanatour, but the Cuban tourist card and Dutch airport tax are included. Grand Travel/Flyworld (☎ 31-20-657-0000, fax 31-20-648-0477) in Amsterdam sells the same tickets without hotel arrangements for slightly different prices. There are reductions for persons under 25 or over 60, but around Christmas prices are higher. Flying KLM-Royal Dutch Airlines from Amsterdam to Havana via Curacao is about 400 guilders more expensive. ACA Latina Travel (☎ 31-20-663-3379, fax 31-20-663-4216), Veeteeltstraat 19, 1097 WL Amsterdam, claims to sell everything their competitors sell at a lower price. It should be possible to book your Martinair flights into one Cuban airport and out of the other, making it possible to travel overland from Holguín to Varadero without having to backtrack.

From Germany, Düsseldorf-based LTU International Airways flies weekly from Düsseldorf to Havana, Varadero, Holguín, and Santiago de Cuba, with connections in Düsseldorf to/from Munich. A six-month return fare from Düsseldorf to any of LTU's four Cuban destinations is DM 1469/1569/1669/1749 low/shoulder/high/peak season (the exact periods are complicated, so check). Agencies specializing in discount airfares can often sell you these tickets for less. One such agency is Walther-Weltreisen (☎ 49-228-661-239, fax 49-228-661-181), Hirschberger Strasse 30, D-53119 Bonn, Germany.

Cubana also flies to Havana from Barcelona, Berlin-Schönefeld, Brussels, Cologne, Gran Canaria, London-Stansted, Madrid, Moscow-Sheremetyevo, and Paris-Orly, and to Varadero from London-Stansted and Paris-Orly. Another Cubana flight goes from Cologne to Holguín. Most operate weekly, except Havana-Madrid, which runs four times weekly. Cubana's fares are often lower than those charged by the Western European airlines and reduced last-minute fares are often available. Brussels to Havana on Cubana is 1135 Dutch guilders return when booked through Havanatour Benelux (see above). Amber Reisbureau (☎ 31-20-685-1155, fax

31-20-689-0406), Da Costastraat 77, 1053 ZG Amsterdam, the Netherlands, has cheaper tickets from Brussels to Havana for two people traveling together. (Amber also carries an excellent selection of maps of Cuba.)

Finally, Aeroflot Russian Airlines flies to Havana once or twice a week from Luxembourg, Moscow, and Shannon with connections to/from St Petersburg and Stockholm.

SEA

Thanks to the US blockade very few cruise ships call at Cuban ports. There are no scheduled passenger services by ship to Cuba.

Access by private yacht or cruiser is easy, and there are numerous yacht harbors around Cuba, such as the Marina Hemingway at Havana, the three marinas at Varadero, and the Marina Bahía de Naranjo at Guardalavaca. On the south coast yachts can call at Santiago de Cuba, Manzanillo, Cienfuegos, Ancón, Cayo Largo, and the Colony Hotel on Isla de la Juventud. For more information turn to Yacht under Visas & Documents and Yachting under Activities, both in the Facts for the Visitor chapter.

DEPARTURE TAX

The Cuban departure tax of US$15 is paid directly in cash at the airport upon departure. The stamp is checked just as you're boarding the aircraft, so don't bother trying to escape without paying.

ORGANIZED TOURS
The USA

US citizens eligible for a US government 'license' to visit Cuba should contact Marazul Tours Inc. (☎ 201-319-9670, fax 201-319-9009), Tower Plaza, 4100 Park Ave, Weehawken, NJ 07087, which books charter flights direct to Havana from Nassau (US$145/200 one way/roundtrip, plus US$22 tax) and Cancún (US$180/260, plus US$21 tax). Marazul also makes hotel reservations throughout Cuba – its brochure is most informative. Due to US regulations,

land arrangements in Cuba cannot cost over US$100 per person per day.

In cooperation with Marazul Tours, the Center for Cuban Studies (☎ 212-242-0559, fax 212-242-1937), 124 West 23rd St, New York, NY 10011, organizes one-week special interest tours to Cuba focusing on the environment, education, museums, African culture, and other subjects. These cost around US$1000 including airfare, double-occupancy accommodations (single supplement US$200), some meals, and transportation in Cuba. In addition, the center sends fact-finding and donation-carrying expeditions to Cuba on a regular basis.

Global Exchange (☎ 415-255-7296, fax 415-255-7498, email globalexch@igc.apc.org), 2017 Mission St, Room 303, San Francisco, CA 94110, USA, operates monthly 'Cuba travel seminars' to Cuba that examine topics such as public health, sustainable agriculture, women's issues, and the political and economic situation. These 10-day trips cost about US$1200 including airfare from Miami, double-occupancy accommodations, visas, transportation in Cuba, and half board.

About five times a year CamBas Associates LC (☎ 500-446-1234 or 319-354-3189, fax 319-337-2045), 25 West 43rd St, Suite 1603, New York, NY 10036, offers 'Contemporary Cuban Society' study tours to Cuba. According to the leaflet they cater to 'members of all professional disciplines and associations interested in comparative research and journalistic pursuits, such as psychologists, artists, journalists, educators, attorneys, physicians, etc.' A typical one-week package to the Hotel Inglaterra in Havana will cost US$1295 including airfare from Canada and all meals.

Other US groups organizing trips to Cuba includes:

Brigada Antonio Maceo
  Box 441803, Miami, FL 33144
  (☎ /fax 305-757-3113)
Freedom to Travel Campaign
  Box 401116, San Francisco, CA 94140
  (☎ 415-558-9490, fax 415-255-7498)

Music & Dance Programs
1611 Telegraph Ave, No 808,
Oakland, CA 94612
(☎ 510-444-7173, fax 510-444-5412)
National Venceremos Brigade
PO Box 7071, Oakland, CA 94601
(☎ 510-267-0606)
Office of the Americas
8124 West 3rd St, No 201,
Los Angeles, CA 90048
(☎ 213-852-9808)
Pastors for Peace
331 17th Ave, SE, Minneapolis, MN 55414
(☎ 612-870-7121, fax 612-870-7109)
Promoting Enduring Peace
112 Beach Ave, Woodmont, CT 06460
(☎ 203-878-4769, fax 203-876-7349)
Radical Philosophy Association
1443 Gorsuch Ave, Baltimore, MD 21218
(☎ 410-243-3118, fax 410-235-5325)
US/Cuba Labor Exchange
PO Box 39188, Redford, MI 48239
(☎ 313-836-3752, fax 313-836-3752)

Canada

A list of Toronto-area wholesalers offering package tours to Cuba is provided below. US citizens should call or fax these companies directly to request their brochures, although travel industry etiquette prevents them from dealing directly with the public. Thus you must work through a Canadian travel agent, and two Toronto agencies specializing in tours to Cuba are Sun Holidays (☎ 416-322-0333 or 800-387-0571) and Bel Air Travel (☎ 416-699-8833 or 800-465-4631). Many more advertise in the travel section of the Saturday edition of the *Toronto Star*, available at major newsstands throughout the US. Otherwise, ask one of the tour companies to give you a number.

Air Transat Holidays
5915 Airport Rd, Suite 1000, Mississauga,
Ontario L4V 1T1
(☎ 905-405-8600, fax 905-405-8587)
Alba Tours
790 Arrow Rd, Weston, Ontario M9M 2Y5
(☎ 416-746-2488, fax 416-746-0397)
Canadian Holidays
191 The West Mall, 6th Floor, Etobicoke,
Ontario M9C 5K8
(☎ 416-620-8687, fax 416-620-9267)

Delta Hotels and Resorts
350 Bloor St East, Suite 300, Toronto,
Ontario M4W 1H4
(☎ 416-926-7800 or 800-268-1133)
Hola Sun Holidays
146 West Beaver Creek Rd, Unit 8,
Richmond Hill, Ontario L4B 1C2
(☎ 905-882-9445, fax 905-882-5184)
Magna Holidays Inc
50 Alness St, Room 200C, Downsview,
Ontario M3J 2G9
(☎ 416-665-7330, fax 416-665-8448)
Quest Nature Tours
36 Finch Ave West, Toronto, Ontario
M2N 2G9
(☎ 416-221-3000, fax 416-221-5730)
Regent Holidays
300-6205 Airport Rd, Building A,
Mississauga, Ontario L4V 1E1
(☎ 905-673-3343, fax 905-673-1717)
Signature Vacations
111 Avenue Rd, Suite 500, Toronto,
Ontario M5R 3J8
(☎ 416-967-1112, fax 416-967-3862)
Sunquest Vacations
130 Merton St, Toronto, Ontario M4S 1A4
(☎ 416-482-3333, fax 416-485-2089)

Alba Tours has the largest selection of tours with some of the lowest prices on packages to the Mar del Sur and Hotel Bellamar at Varadero, Hotel Ancón near Trinidad, Hotel Atlántico at Guardalavaca and Bucanero Beach near Santiago de Cuba. Such a package with transfers, meals, and accommodations sometimes costs only a few hundred dollars more than airfare alone. Alba Tours produces the most informative Cuba brochure of any of the Canadian tour companies (although we've heard they often switch confirmed passengers from one hotel to another at the last minute and complaints voiced after arrival in Cuba have little effect). Regent Holidays also has cheap packages to Hotel Bellamar at Varadero.

Alba Tours and Canadian Holidays offer a 'Cuba Ecotour' program involving stays at three mountain resorts around Santiago de Cuba. Quest Nature Tours offers much the same thing for a considerably higher price. Canadian Holidays also has tour packages to Cuba direct from Halifax and

Vancouver (a good bet for US citizens living in adjacent states). Signature Vacations deals only in upmarket resorts at Varadero and Guardalavaca. Air Transat Holidays has a better selection of destinations and some medium-priced choices. Always note carefully if meals and a private bathroom are included. 'All inclusive' tours include all meals, unlimited local drinks, nonmotorized water sports, and some other activities.

Be aware that the Canadian packages are designed for Canadian 'snowbirds' who want to spend a week or two at Varadero or another beach resort. Tours based in Havana and other cities are rare, and none of the Canadian companies list car-rental rates in their brochures. If you want to stay somewhere other than at the beach, you must book an 'air only' package, and Air Transat Holidays, Alba Tours, Canadian Holidays, Regent Holidays, and Signature Vacations all sell cheap air tickets on their charters. Expect to pay about CDN$400 roundtrip from Toronto to Varadero with a two-week maximum stay.

If you're a bit adventurous, you could easily have your Canadian travel agent book only the flights and arrange the rest of your stay upon arrival in Cuba. In this case, write the name of one of the hotels listed in a brochure (or this book) on your tourist card. Upon arrival at Varadero walk straight out of the airport terminal and take a taxi to Matanzas or Varadero (US$20). Otherwise rent a car at one of the three car rental agencies in the airport parking lot (if they don't happen to have any vehicles, their offices in Varadero certainly will).

Add CDN$69 to all prices to cover Canadian airport tax and the Cuban tourist card. On some packages you can get a discount of CDN$35 to CDN$50 if you book 60 days in advance or before December 15 for the winter season. Special bonuses are offered to honeymooners who have their travel agent advise the tour company's reservations department when booking. Children under 12 receive free accommodations on some tours.

If you'll be transiting through Toronto, ask your travel agent to check on special stopover rates at Toronto airport hotels when booking. At last report the International Plaza Hotel near Toronto's Pearson International Airport had double rooms at CDN$67 plus 12% tax when booked in conjunction with an Alba Tours package. Included were an early breakfast, free accommodations for children under 12, free airport shuttle, free coat check until you get back from Cuba, and free parking for 21 days. The Best Western Carlton Place Hotel offers a similar deal that must be booked in conjunction with an Air Transat package.

Australia
The Cuba Company (☎ 03-9867-1200), a tour operator based in Melbourne, offers a variety of theme trips including one for Hemingway fanatics.

Mexico
If you live in the southern or western US, the easiest way to get to Cuba is via Mexico, and the Mexican tour companies offer lots of packages based in Havana itself. Due to US government regulations, you cannot book trips to Cuba through travel agencies or airline offices in the US itself. However, the Mexican companies listed below offer a variety of package tours to Cuba from Mexico City and Cancún. All of them can obtain your Cuban tourist card together with package tour or flight bookings. A one-week package including return airfare to Havana from Mexico City, double-occupancy accommodations with breakfast, and airport transfers in Cuba will cost around US$500 plus tax. Check where they'll be sending you as some Havana hotels are inconveniently far from the city center. The following agencies are all based in or near Mexico City:

AS Tours
   Insurgentes Sur 1188–602, 03200 México, DF (☎ 52-5-575-9814, fax 52-5-559-5097)
Asis Tours
   Baja California No 46, Colonia Roma (☎ 52-5-574-2355, fax 52-5-574-5876)

Cubamar
    Eje Lázaro Cárdenas No 623, Colonia
    Portales, 03300 México, DF
    (☎ 52-5-601-1302, fax 52-5-604-6215)
Taino Tours/Havanatur
    Avenida Coyoacán No 1035, Colonia del
    Valle CP, 03100 México, DF
    (☎ 52-5-559-3907)
Tip's Travel
    Baja California No 218 – 401, Colonia
    Roma Sur, 06760 México, DF
    (☎ 52-5-584-1557, fax 52-5-264-1767)
Viajes Sol y Son
    Temístocles No 246, Colonia Polanco,
    11550 México, DF
    (☎ 52-5-250-6355, fax 52-5-255-0835)
Viñales Tours
    Oaxaca No 80, Colonia Roma, México, DF
    (☎ 52-5-208-9900, fax 52-5-208-3704)

South America

For a package tour from Colombia try
Asis Tours (☎ /fax 57-1-621-1594), Car-
rera 14 No 79–20, Segundo Piso, Bogotá,
Colombia.

Europe

Many European tour companies offer
beach holidays to Cuba, usually at Varadero, Trinidad, Santa Lucía, Cayo Coco,
Guardalavaca, and Santiago de Cuba. In
addition, the European companies run
one-week bus tours around Cuba (not available from Canada), which can be combined
with a week or more at the beach.

The bus trips involve a flight between
Havana and Santiago de Cuba or vice versa.
Beginning in Varadero, you might spend
three days visiting Havana and Pinar del Río
before flying to Santiago, returning to
Varadero by bus via Camagüey and
Trinidad. If you start in Holguín, you'll first
be driven to Santiago and then flown to
Havana. After a visit to Pinar del Río you'll
be bused back to Holguín via Guamá,
Trinidad, and Camagüey. Transportation,
accommodations, meals, and admissions are
included, so it's an easy way to get a glimpse
of the country in a short time provided you
don't mind being shepherded around.

A variation on this are the 'fly and drive'
programs that provide a car and hotel
accommodations along a fixed route for

one or two weeks (gasoline, car insurance,
guided tours, and meals not included). One
can also rent a car alone with gasoline and
insurance paid directly in Cuba itself.

Companies offering package tours and
cheap flight tickets from the UK to Cuba
include the following:

Havanatur UK
    Interchange House, 27 Stafford Rd,
    Croydon, Surrey CR0 4NG
    (☎ 44-181-681-3613, fax 44-181-760-0031)
Journey Latin America
    14–16 Devonshire Rd, Chiswick, London
    W4 2HD
    (☎ 44-181-747-3108, fax 44-181-742-1312)
Progressive Tours
    12 Porchester Place, Marble Arch, London
    W2 2BS
    (☎ 44-171-262-1676)
Regent Holidays
    15 John St, Bristol BS1 2HR
    (☎ 44-117-921-1711, fax 44-117-925-4866)
South American Experience
    47 Causton St, Pimlico, London SW1P 4AT
    (☎ 44-171-976-5511, fax 44-171-976-6908)

The following companies are based in
continental Europe:

Havanatour Benelux
    Hofplein 19, 3032 AC Rotterdam, the
    Netherlands
    (☎ 31-10-411-2444, fax 31-10-411-4749)
Fietsvakantiewinkel
    Spoorlaan 19, 3445 AE Woerden, the
    Netherlands
    (☎ 31-0348-421844, fax 31-0348-423839)
Tropicana Touristik
    Berliner Strasse 161, D-10715 Berlin,
    Germany
    (☎ 49-30-853-7041, fax 49-30-853-4070)
Meier's Weltreisen GmbH
    Parseval Strasse 7b, D-40468 Düsseldorf,
    Germany
    (☎ 49-211-907-801, fax 49-211-907-8350)
Havanatur Paris
    24 Rue Quatre Septembre, 75002 Paris,
    France
    (☎ 33-01-4451-5085; fax 33-01-4265-1801)
Havanatur Italia
    Via San Anselmo 40, 10125 Torino, Italy
    (☎ 39-11-669-0632, fax 39-11-650-4608)
Guamá SA, Paseo de La Habana 28, 28036
    Madrid, Spain
    (☎ 34-1-411-2048, fax 34-1-564-3918)

Australia
An Australian travel agency specializing in Cuba is Dorothy Button's Cubatours (☎ 61-3-9428-0385), 235 Swan St, Richmond, Victoria 3121.

WARNING
The information in this chapter is particularly vulnerable to change: Prices for international travel are volatile, routes are introduced and canceled, schedules change, special deals come and go, and rules and visa requirements are amended. Airlines and governments seem to take a perverse pleasure in making price structures and regulations as complicated as possible. You should check directly with the airline or a travel agent to make sure you understand how a fare (and ticket you may buy) works. In addition, the travel industry is highly competitive and there are many pitfalls and perks.

The upshot of this is that you should get opinions, quotes, and advice from as many airlines and travel agents as possible before you part with your hard-earned cash. The details given in the chapter should be regarded as pointers and are not a substitute for your own careful, up-to-date research.

Getting Around

AIR
Domestic Air Services

Cubana de Aviación has domestic flights from Havana to:

Baracoa (US$78 one way)
Bayamo (US$59)
Camagüey (US$51)
Ciego de Ávila (US$43)
Guantánamo (US$73)
Holguín (US$79)
Las Tunas (US$77)
Manzanillo (US$59)
Moa (US$73)
Nueva Gerona (US$16)
Santiago de Cuba (US$68)

The weekly flight between Santiago de Cuba and Baracoa (US$17 and currently on Tuesdays) is a good one to know about.

Check-in is 60 minutes before flight time and the baggage limit is 20 kilos.

Most of Cubana's flights are on Antonov AN-24 propeller aircraft, although Yakovlev YAK 42 jets are often used to Camagüey, Holguín, and Santiago de Cuba, and a Fokker F27 Friendship jet is used for one of the flights to Holguín.

Domestic flights are 25% cheaper when booked in conjunction with an international flight on Cubana. Ask your travel agent to check with Cubana about this. Inside Cuba you can often book through your hotel tour desk or a local travel agency for the same price that you'd pay at the disorderly local Cubana office. Reserve as far in advance as possible if you want to be sure of a seat, although dollar-paying foreigners do get some preference.

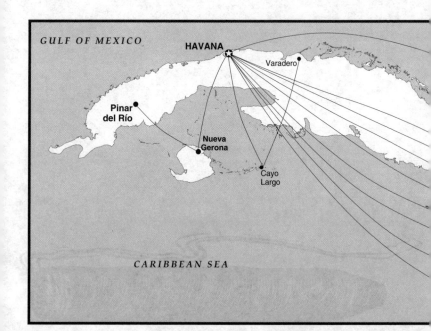

Aerocaribbean has scheduled flights from Havana's Terminal No 1 to Holguín (US$60) and Santiago (US$68) on Wednesday and Sunday; and to Nueva Gerona (US$17) on Wednesday, Friday, and Sunday.

For information on Aerotaxi flights between Pinar del Río and Nueva Gerona on Isla de la Juventud, turn to the Pinar del Río chapter.

At the Airport

If you haven't prearranged airport transfers, metered tourist taxis are always available. A cheaper way to go is to look for a private car with yellow license plates. Private car owners interested in the chance to earn a few extra dollars often park a bit away from the area with the official taxis, and they'll take you into town for about 60% of what you'd pay for a regular taxi. Make sure the price is well understood before you depart. Private cabs aren't available at Varadero Airport where the police enforce the monopoly of the official taxis, but here (and perhaps elsewhere) you can often hitch a ride on a tour bus for a US$5 per person tip to the driver.

BUS

Since 1991 long-distance bus services around Cuba have been slashed and getting a ticket on one of the remaining routes has become very difficult. Although it's now easier to travel by train, some important routes are only covered by *ómnibus*; these include Cienfuegos-Trinidad, Trinidad-Sancti Spíritus, Sancti Spíritus-Ciego de Ávila, and Guantánamo-Baracoa.

Tickets for intercity buses have to be purchased at the office in advance, and reservations must be reconfirmed at the terminal about two hours prior to departure. Ask about getting on the *lista de fallos* (waiting list), and if you have real difficulty obtaining a ticket, ask for the *jefe de turno*

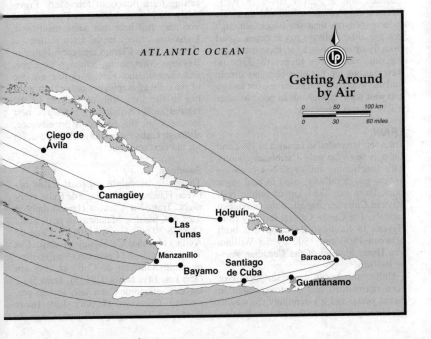

(dispatcher), who may be willing to put you on the first available bus for a dollar gratuity. It's usually easier to catch a bus on a weekday than on weekends or holidays. Travel by public transport is most difficult between Christmas and New Year's, and during July and August when most Cubans take their holidays. Even when you've managed to get aboard a long-distance bus, you must be prepared for breakdowns, in which case you'll have to hitch from wherever it is you happen to be. Buses marked *flete* are chartered for private use.

Most provincial capitals have two bus stations, a Terminal de Ómnibus Nacionales or Interprovinciales for long-distance services and a Terminal to Ómnibus Intermunicipales for local buses within the province. These are often far apart, so make sure you go to the correct one.

Given the shortage of buses, private entrepreneurs have converted large trucks *(camiones)* into public transportation vehicles, sometimes with long wooden benches and a canvas cover in back. Because they're not subsidized these are more expensive than the buses, although you can almost always pay in pesos. Apart from flying or renting a car, these trucks are the only other way to get to Baracoa. Reservations are not possible; you simply find out where the trucks leave from and go and wait with the Cubans. In good weather it'll be a great adventure.

TRAIN

Train service ended in Jamaica in 1992 and Cuba is now the only Caribbean country with functioning railways. Not counting narrow-gauge railways used to haul sugar cane, there are 4881 km of public railways in Cuba serving all of the provincial capitals. The Cuban Central Railway from Havana to Santiago de Cuba was built between 1900 and 1902 by Sir William Van Horn, founder of the Canadian Pacific Railway.

Unlike the buses, train services have been maintained and even expanded in recent years, and it's definitely the way to go. Getting a ticket with a seat reservation is usually painless and the trains are far less crowded than the buses. Some trips are even relaxed. In addition, the train stations tend to be closer to the city centers than the bus stations.

Services are fairly frequent with at least one train a day on all major routes and often more. Foreigners must pay for their tickets in hard currency, but prices are fairly low and the carriages, though old and worn, are comfortable, offering lots of local color. Carriages on the air-conditioned *especial* trains are often quite cold. Vendors come through the train selling coffee (you must have your own cup with you) and sandwiches, and snacks can also be purchased through the window at stations. Going by train can be great fun and eliminates all the stress of trying to go by bus.

Reservations

Ladis (from 'larga distancia') is the railway tourism organization in charge of selling train tickets to foreigners. Previously they were known as Ferrotur and you may still hear that name mentioned. Ladis has offices in the train stations at Havana, Santa Clara, Camagüey, Holguín, Bayamo, Manzanillo, Santiago de Cuba, and Guantánamo. Elsewhere just ask one of the railway employees rather than waiting in the long line of Cubans at the regular ticket window. It's always best to check on the procedure in advance, although Ladis can usually sell you a ticket for the next train out.

Services

There are overnight *especial* trains between Havana and Santiago de Cuba every night. Train No 1 leaves Havana daily at 4:25 pm, passing Matanzas (6 pm), Santa Clara (8:30 pm), Guayos (10 pm), Ciego de Ávila (11 pm), Camagüey (1 am), Las Tunas (3 am), and Cacocum (4 am) before reaching Santiago de Cuba at 6:45 am (856 km, 14½ hours, US$35). Train No 2 leaves Santiago de Cuba daily at 4:35 pm, passing Cacocum (7 pm), Las Tunas (8:15 pm), Camagüey (10 pm), Ciego de

RICK GERHARTER

All smiles at the Tropicana Nightclub

DAVID STANLEY

Mechanical organ at El Patio Colonial on
Havana's Plaza de Armas

DAVID STANLEY

Hands-on performance by the Ballet Folklórico
Cutumbá in Santiago de Cuba

DAVID STANLEY

Orchestra Casino de la Playa in Holguín

RICK GERHARTER

Living large at a private Havana cabaret

RICK GERHARTER

An impeccable performance at Manila,
a private cabaret

DAVID STANLEY

Tobacco fields

DAVID STANLEY

Inspecting

DAVID STANLEY

Harvesting

DAVID STANLEY

Hauling

DAVID STANLEY

Drying tobacco in sheds (*vegas*)

RICK GERHARTER

RICK GERHARTER

Rolling cigars at the Partagás Cigar Factory

Ávila (midnight), Guayos (1:25 am), Santa Clara (2:30 am), and Matanzas (5:30 am) before reaching Havana at 7:05 am. In the center of the country between Santa Clara and Las Tunas most other long-distance trains also pass in the middle of the night, so boarding or alighting in those areas is rather inconvenient.

Other services of interest to travelers include Havana-Pinar del Río-Guane, Havana-Matanzas, Havana-Cienfuegos, Cienfuegos-Santa Clara-Sancti Spíritus, Santa Clara-Morón-Nuevitas, Camagüey-Nuevitas, Camagüey-Bayamo, Bayamo-Manzanillo, Manzanillo-Bayamo-Santiago de Cuba, and Santiago de Cuba-Holguín. Many additional local trains operate at least daily and some more frequently.

CAR

Cuba's road network is among the most highly developed in Latin America. There are almost 20,000 km of paved highways, the most important of which is the Carretera Central, built by the Machado government between 1926 and 1931 and stretching 1119 km from Pinar del Río to Guantánamo. Since the revolution this two-lane highway has been complemented by the Autopista Nacional or 'Ocho Vías,' so named for its eight lanes. The autopista (freeway) is already complete from Pinar del Río to Taguasco beyond Sancti Spíritus, and it will eventually link up with existing sections around Santiago de Cuba and

Guantánamo. Other famous roads are the Vía Blanca along the north coast between Havana and Varadero and 'La Farola' between Guantánamo and Baracoa. Most large cities have a bypass ring road (circunvalación) that allows one to avoid the city centers.

Unfortunately the signposting is often poor, especially around Havana. In early 1996 highway tolls were announced for the road between Varadero and Matanzas and the causeway to Cayo Coco. Additional tolls can be expected in the future and foreigners will have to pay in dollars.

Road Rules

As is the case in most of the rest of the Americas and continental Europe, driving is on the right-hand side of the road. Speed limits for cars are 20 km/hour in driveways and parking lots, 40 km/hour around schools, 50 km/hour in urban areas, 60 km/hour on dirt roads and in tunnels, 90 km/hour on paved highways, and 100 km/hour on the autopista. Low beams must be used in towns, within 150 meters of an approaching vehicle or within 50 meters of a vehicle being overtaken. The use of seat belts is optional.

Road signs are similar to those used in Europe. A circular white sign with a red border indicates a road closed to vehicles in both directions, whereas a white bar across a red circle means simply 'no entry.' A red-bordered white circle containing

Distances between Cuban Cities (in kilometers)

Pinar del Río	Havana	Matanzas	Varadero	Cienfuegos	Santa Clara	Sancti Spíritus	Ciego de Ávila	Camagüey	Las Tunas	Holguín	Bayamo	Santiago de Cuba	Guantánamo
Pinar del Río													
186	Havana												
284	98	Matanzas											
326	140	42	Varadero										
439	253	191	192	Cienfuegos									
473	287	199	192	74	Santa Clara								
559	373	285	278	152	86	Sancti Spíritus							
634	448	360	353	227	161	75	Ciego de Ávila						
744	558	469	463	337	271	185	110	Camagüey					
867	681	592	586	460	394	308	233	123	Las Tunas				
944	758	669	663	537	471	385	310	200	77	Holguín			
943	757	668	662	536	470	384	309	199	76	71	Bayamo		
1070	884	797	789	663	597	511	436	326	203	143	127	Santiago de Cuba	
1119	933	844	838	712	646	560	485	375	252	197	176	86	Guantánamo

two vehicles means no passing (a black-bordered white circle with a diagonal line between the two vehicles means you may pass again). A yellow diamond indicates that you have priority at a crossroads; otherwise, the vehicle approaching from the right has priority if the roads are of equal importance. A blue circle with a red diagonal bar across it means parking is prohibited.

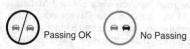

Passing OK   No Passing

Safety

The traffic is refreshingly light and the highway police leave foreigners alone. Women drivers can expect to arouse curiosity in Cuba. As everywhere, the ratio of women behind the wheel is often a good indication of the real status of the local women.

There are a number of driving hazards to bear in mind. Away from the Carretera Central and the Autopista Nacional it's dangerous to drive fast, as smooth paved highways can deteriorate without warning and unmarked potholes or railway crossings may appear at any time. The worst roads are in eastern Cuba. Excessive speed can invalidate the insurance on a rental car.

People on bicycles are a constant danger: You'll often see cyclists riding two abreast down the middle of a highway, oblivious to traffic approaching from the rear. For their safety and yours, it's often necessary to gently toot your horn at them before passing. Routinely sound the horn on blind curves and always honk loudly when passing a truck as many are without rear-view mirrors. Also be on guard against slow-moving horse-drawn carriages, ox carts, and tractors, and at night watch out for trucks with only one headlight, bicycles without lights or reflectors, free-ranging animals, and pedestrians who feel they own the road. If at all possible, avoid driving at night.

Use your low-beam headlights during fog; otherwise, don't drive with your lights on during the day because in Cuba this is the sign of an emergency vehicle. If an oncoming vehicle flashes its lights during the day, it could mean the police or a dangerous situation is ahead. After nightfall, truck drivers seem to delight in blinding you by flipping on their high beams just as you are about to pass.

As always, the driver's golden rule: It's better to lose a minute of your life than to lose your life in a minute.

Gasoline

Obtaining fuel is no problem as 40 hard-currency Servi-Cupet gas stations are scattered around Cuba, selling gasoline at US$0.90 a liter (which works out to US$3.40 per US gallon). We provide the addresses of Servi-Cupet service stations in the regional chapters; most are open 24 hours a day. Even so, it's always wise to keep the tank at least half full to avoid unnecessary detours to obtain fuel. There are almost never lines at Servi-Cupet and foreign tourists no longer have to buy gasoline vouchers. Aside from selling fuel, Servi-Cupet gas stations are often good places to buy cold drinks and stock up on groceries.

Cuban motorists buy their gasoline for pesos at local gas stations that take ration coupons. The local stations are often out of fuel or have only regular gas, not the super *(especial)* required for most rental vehicles. When there's no electricity, the pumps don't work. Beware of pumps that provide a reading in gallons as these are often defective, and sometimes they appear to have been tampered with to bilk motorists. Individuals will occasionally offer to sell you black-market fuel at US$0.50 a liter, but accepting such an offer would violate your car-rental agreement, and unless you know what you're doing you could easily receive watered-down gas and end up damaging the vehicle.

Picking Up Hitchhikers

An excellent way to find someone to guide you into a strange town or along a confusing route is to pick up a couple of Cuban hitchhikers. You'll get to meet the people in an informal way, although you'll need to speak a little Spanish as your passengers will almost never understand English. However, it's wise to exercise care when deciding who to take. Women and elderly people are unlikely to cause problems. As for young men, it's probably better to pick them up only when they're already out on the highway waiting at a spot where they'd never expect to receive a ride from a tourist. Giving rides to people in front of tourist sites, restaurants, bars, hotels, or Servi-Cupet stations involves the risk of getting a troublesome or dangerous person in the car (unless it's clearly a hotel employee, in which case it's fine). Also avoid taking people from junctions where hitchhiking is organized by government officials in yellow uniforms (see the Hitchhiking section below) as they may unload their worst complainers on you and you'll have no choice over who you get. Of course, you're not obliged to take anyone at all.

Rental

Renting a car is definitely the easiest if not the cheapest way to see Cuba. (Foreigners aren't allowed to purchase regular cars in Cuba. They may, however, purchase vintage cars and have them shipped home.) The main car-rental companies are Transautos (☎ 33-5532, fax 33-4057), Havanautos (☎ 33-2369, fax 33-1416), Cubanacán/Cubacar, and National/Gaviota (☎ 81-0357, fax 33-0742). Transautos and Havanautos are the best companies to deal with as they have numerous branch offices at hotels (serving both guests and nonguests) and Servi-Cupet stations throughout Cuba offering good service facilities in case of problems. In contrast, Cubanacán/Cubacar and National/Gaviota have only a few offices in the main centers. Cars can be picked up and delivered at most airports, but it's essential to reserve a car except in Havana.

Transautos is the cheapest company, followed by National/Gaviota and Havanautos. Rates at Havanautos begin at US$45 a day for a Daihatsu/Suzuki soft-top jeep or a Renault/Peugeot hard-top sedan (the first 100 km included; additional kilometers US$0.30 each). You can also pay US$55 daily with unlimited kilometers – a good idea as Cuba is a *big* country and 100 kilometers go fast. Discounts are available on a weekly/fortnightly basis. Transautos charges US$46/42/38 per day on a daily/weekly/fortnightly basis for a Daihatsu soft-top jeep with unlimited kilometers. National/Gaviota asks US$50/46/42 and Havanautos US$55/50/45 for the same. Once you have the car for six days you can extend the rental period at the discount rate. The jeeps are highly recommended for their rugged build, and the 4WD traction can come in handy on mountain or muddy roads.

The rental fee must be paid in advance and a refundable US$200 to US$250 cash deposit is required, although a credit card imprint is also acceptable. It's better to put up a cash deposit, however, in case you decide to return the car in another city. Delivery charges are relatively low (for example, US$17 from Santiago de Cuba to Holguín). Don't lose your copy of the rental agreement; otherwise, you'll have to take the car back to the office where you originally obtained it and pay a penalty. Your home driver's license or an international driver's license will be accepted but you must be at least 21 years of age.

Check the car carefully before accepting it, making sure there's a jack, wrench, and windshield cleaning fluid. Agents often will attempt to give you a car that isn't completely full of gas, and if you return it the same way you'll be charged for the 'missing' liters. If the fuel gauge isn't on full, ask them to fill it up. It's much cheaper to refill the tank yourself just before returning the car rather than letting them calculate how much fuel you owe.

Insurance Two optional insurance plans are available. Plan 'A' (US$8 to US$10 a day) covers accidents but not theft; plan 'B' (US$15 daily) covers all risks except the loss of one wheel. Under both plans you're still responsible for the first US$250 to US$350 in damage or loss, so plan 'A' is quite sufficient. If you do have an accident, get a copy of the police report (*denuncia*) for the car rental agency. Drive carefully: If the police determine that you are the party responsible for an accident, you may have to pay full damages, insurance or no insurance.

Precautions To avoid being stuck with an unwelcome charge when you return the car, you should take precautions against small parts being stolen, such as the windshield wipers, rear-view mirrors, spare tire, and so on (notice how most older Cuban cars lack rear-view mirrors. Most large hotels have guarded parking lots where you pay US$1 a night; otherwise, you can tip the hotel security guard a similar amount to protect your car. Avoid parking anywhere panhandlers congregate as they could scratch the sides or cut the top unless you've been generous with chewing gum, pens, soap, or money. Vagrants who pretend to wash your car with a dirty rag will also demand payment. All of this makes it cheaper to use paid parking. During the day in places where no large hotel is convenient seek out one of the ubiquitous bicycle parking facilities, indicated by signs reading *se cuidan bicicletas* or *parqueo* on the front of houses, and offer the person in charge a dollar to mind your vehicle.

If the car breaks down on the road contact the car-rental company or at least try get the vehicle to a tourist hotel. The Cubans are masters of improvised repairs and passersby will invariably stop to help. Never abandon the vehicle as you'll be responsible for stolen parts. If you notice a mechanical defect in the offing, take the car to any branch of the rental company and ask for a replacement vehicle.

MOTORCYCLE & SCOOTER

You can't rent real motorcycles in Cuba, but scooters and mopeds are available at many tourist resorts. These are only useful for local sightseeing and are not especially cheap.

BICYCLE

Since 1991 the number of bicycles on Cuba's streets and roads has increased dramatically as tens of thousands of sturdy Phoenix and Flying Pigeon bicycles were assembled from parts imported from China. Cubans use their bicycles to go to work and school or to run errands, but it's unlikely you'll see a Cuban touring the country by bicycle. However, an experienced foreign cyclist could easily do exactly that. In Cuba as elsewhere, cycling is a cheap, convenient, healthy, environmentally sound, and above all fun way of traveling.

You'll have to bring your own bicycle with you as the Chinese bicycles are sold only to Cubans who earn one by being a model worker. Before you leave home, go over your bike with a fine-tooth comb and fill your repair kit with every imaginable spare. You'll need a supply of parts as none will be available in Cuba. Even the smallest village will have a place repairing punctured tires at a peso apiece, but you certainly won't be able to buy a crucial part when your bike breaks down.

Travelers arriving by plane can easily bring their bikes. You *can* take them to pieces and put them in a bike bag or box, but it's much easier to simply wheel your bike to the check-in desk, where it should be treated as a piece of baggage. You may have to remove the pedals and turn the handlebars sideways so that it takes up less space in the aircraft's hold; check all this with the airline well in advance, preferably before you pay for your ticket.

Be sure to bring a strong lock, as bicycle theft is rampant. There are plenty of bicycle parking facilities in the towns where you can safely leave your cycle for a small peso fee.

Cuba's roads are reasonable and the country is flat. The lack of traffic is another advantage. On the down side, black smoke from heavy trucks and buses will often leave you gasping, and it's unsafe to cycle after dark. When planning a route, be aware that bicycles are usually not permitted on trains. Check with a Ladis railway ticket office about this as they might make an exception.

HITCHING

Cuban men and women hitchhike all the time, an activity known as *hacer botella*, literally 'to make a bottle' (with the hand, of course). There's even a law requiring government vehicles with empty space to carry passengers whenever they can. At major highway junctions and the exits from towns, officials called *amarillos* clad in yellow uniforms and carrying clipboards arrange rides for ordinary Cubans. Government vehicles that fail to stop can be fined. There's always a crowd of Cubans waiting at these places, and although it looks disorderly, there will be a line *(cola)* and rides are supposed to be first come, first served. In some places there's even a metal stairway to assist passengers in getting into the back of trucks.

Foreigners almost never travel this way and you'd be the object of considerable curiosity if you did. You'd also probably get priority and end up taking rides away from the locals.

Cuban license plates convey considerable information to hitchhikers and the *amarillos*. The vehicles obliged to give rides are those belonging to state entities, and these will have red license plates in the case of cars and small trucks or blue plates on larger trucks and buses. Trucks belonging to cooperatives have white plates, those of the Ministry of the Interior or Revolutionary Armed Forces have green plates, private vehicles and mixed corporations have yellow plates, and tourism vehicles and the diplomatic corps have black plates. None of these four types are required to carry riders, although drivers of cars with yellow plates will often be happy to take you for a negotiable price.

The license plate also bears a letter that indicates the province in which the vehicle is registered: A (Ciego de Ávila), B (Province of Havana), C (Camagüey), F (Cienfuegos), G (Granma), H (City of Havana), M (Matanzas), N (Guantánamo), O (Holguín), P (Pinar del Río), S (Sancti Spíritus), T (Las Tunas), U (Santiago de Cuba), and V (Villa Clara).

BOAT
Hydrofoil

A hydrofoil operates twice daily between Surgidero de Batabanó, 60 km south of Havana, and Nueva Gerona on Isla de la Juventud. For details turn to Getting There & Away under Nueva Gerona in the Isla de la Juventud chapter and Batabanó in the Province of Havana chapter.

Chartered Yacht

If you were planning to spend a considerable amount to stay at an upmarket resort, it won't cost a lot more to charter a yacht if you can get a few friends together. The most reliable company offering 'bareboat' charters to experienced sailors and 'crewed' charters to everyone else is KP Winter SA (☎ 34-71-490900, fax 34-71-491605), Club Marítima, E-07610 Ca'n Pastilla, Mallorca, Spain. In Germany the address is KP Winter GmbH (☎ 49-5043-98060, fax 49-5043-98061), Am Bohlenkamp 5, D-31867 Messenkamp. In Cuba KP Winter operates Cubanáutica bases at Varadero for crewed and day charters and at Cayo Largo for bareboat charters.

Like the Bahamas, Cuba is an ideal cruising area for boats with low draft and most of KP Winter's 30 boats are catamarans. A four-cabin cat will cost about US$2450/2730/3500 low/shoulder/high season a week and up for the boat, and divided among eight people it's not as expensive as you might think. A 5% discount is available on a two-week charter, 10% on three weeks. The low season is May to mid-July and September to mid-October, shoulder mid-July to August and mid-October to mid-December, and high January to April. Considerably higher prices apply around Christmas.

Scuba divers can rent a diving bottle and lead weights at US$7 a day, a diving compressor US$35 a day. If necessary, crew can be hired at US$45 a day for a skipper or diving instructor, US$30 a day for a host or sailor. Of course, food is extra and KP Winter offers a complete provisioning and catering service. If you've never chartered before, here's your chance to start.

LOCAL TRANSPORT
Bus
Since 1991 city bus services have been seriously affected by shortages of gasoline and spare parts, and in some towns they have been completely replaced by horse-drawn carriages that shuttle along fixed routes carrying passengers at one peso per person a ride.

Those city buses *(guaguas)* still operating have route numbers and only stop at bus stops *(paradas)*. Although it may not appear so, there's often a line *(cola)* at the bus stop and you must find out who you're behind by calling out *el último?* (the last one?). You wave to the next person who shows up and asks the same question, and your place in the invisible queue is marked. Professionals who put in time in line on behalf of others for small fees are called *coleros*.

On most city buses you either pay the driver or toss the exact fare into a fare box next to the door. Those boarding through the back doors pass their coins up to the front via other passengers. City buses cost anywhere between 10 centavos and one peso depending on whether it's an ordinary bus, a special bus, an express bus, or a taxi bus. The price is often marked on a sign in the window; otherwise, the person next to you in line will be able to tell you. On local buses to points just outside the towns the fare is often collected by a conductor. Try to have small change. When you want to get out, you must shout '*Parada!*' (Stop!) or bang on the roof.

Using the city buses can involve long waits and they're almost always extremely crowded, so it's better not to depend on them. If possible, stay somewhere in the center of town and plan on doing a lot of walking.

Taxi
There are several types of taxis. Tourist taxis cluster at large hotels and they often have a blue T on the front door. Passengers must pay in dollars; if the taxi doesn't have a meter, ask the price beforehand.

Taxis intended for Cubans are generally old American cars called *máquinas*. These are cheaper, but they'll often want dollars from you. You can usually find them at a *piquera* (taxi stand) in the center of town or in front of the train or bus station. These never have a meter and the price must always be agreed upon in advance.

A *colectivo* is a collective taxi that charges per seat and travels long distances, such as between towns. They usually park in front of the train or bus station and leave when full. It may seem unfair the way they charge foreigners much more than Cubans, but one should realize that the driver is risking a heavy police fine by accepting tourists.

Other forms of taxis are motorcycles with a double seat, bicycles with an extra seat behind, and peddle-powered rickshaws. These are the cheapest way to go, but assume the quoted price is per person. Motorized vehicles usually want dollars, but the cycles should take pesos.

Private pirate taxis have yellow license plates and charge US$1/2 for short/long trips in town with the price negotiable for longer trips. The drivers of private cars *(coches particulares)* will often agree to drive you around all day for US$10 to US$25, gasoline included. You can often organize your own excursions in this way at a price far below what the hotel tour desks ask.

Boat
Some towns such as Havana, Cienfuegos, and Santiago de Cuba have local ferry services across their harbors. Details of these are provided in the respective chapters.

City of Havana

Havana (La Habana), the largest city in the Caribbean, is Cuba's political, cultural, and economic hub. Havana suffered little or no damage during the wars and revolutions of the past 200 years, and the old town is easily the finest surviving Spanish colonial complex in the Americas. Millions of dollars have gone into restoration work since La Habana Vieja was declared a UNESCO World Heritage Site in December 1982, but this process had begun two decades earlier when some of Havana's finest buildings were converted into museums in the wake of the revolution.

Conservation efforts have benefited from a deliberate government policy of diverting resources to the countryside and limiting growth in the capital. Although many of Havana's houses are run down, the heavy traffic, rampant commercialization, and extensive slums that choke many other Latin American cities are absent. Even the US blockade helps in a way by keeping out the cruise ships that clog most other Caribbean ports and by limiting US consumer tourism. Enjoy it while it lasts.

Aside from being the country's leading center of government, education, medicine, research, communications, tourism, and trade, Havana has much of Cuba's light and heavy industry, including thermoelectric power plants, a petroleum refinery, metallurgical and chemical plants, paper mills, printing plants, textile factories, food processing, cigarette and cigar factories, shipyards, and the bulk of the fishing fleet. Unfortunately, Havana's inner harbor is one of the most polluted in the world: An oil slick covers the water's surface, and thick black smoke billows from several chimneys just across the bay. Havana also suffers from deteriorating sewage and waste disposal systems and dwindling water supplies due to antiquated, leaky plumbing. Nearly half the housing in the city is in bad repair and thousands of

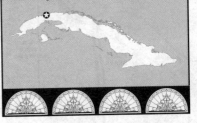

HIGHLIGHTS

- Wonderful colonial churches, palaces, and museums
- Colorful handicraft markets and used-book markets in La Habana Vieja
- Formidable Spanish castles of El Morro and La Cabaña
- Intriguing revolutionary monuments, including the Pavillón Granma, the Museo de la Revolución, and the Memorial José Martí
- Gran Teatro de La Habana, the oldest functioning theater in the Americas
- Sizzling 1950s-style nightclubs

city residents have had to be evacuated for safety reasons. Each year about 300 buildings collapse, and it's estimated that 88,000 Havana dwellings will have to be demolished.

As a visitor you'll doubtless become aware of some of these problems, but you'll also be overwhelmed by the wealth of historical monuments and the exuberant friendliness of the Cuban people. It would be difficult to exhaust the things to see and do, and you shouldn't even try. Instead, savor the city's flavor to the full, and then get out and see a bit more of Cuba. Your real adventure will begin when you board that train or plane and set out to discover what this country is really all about. Havana is only a gateway, not the beginning and end.

135

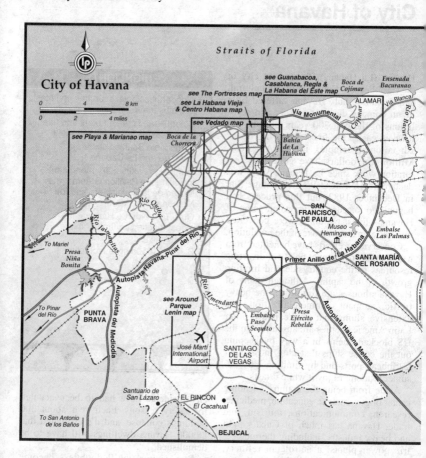

History

In 1514 San Cristóbal de la Havana was founded on the south coast of Cuba near the mouth of the Río Mayabeque, which today is a swampy, sparsely inhabited area. A few years later the settlement shifted to the mouth of the Río Almendares between present-day Vedado and Miramar, and only in 1519 did the town reestablish itself next to the mouth of the harbor, an area presently referred to as La Habana Vieja.

Although Havana was one of the seven original towns established in Cuba by Diego Velázquez, no one ever intended for it to be the capital. The town's remote location in the far northwest made it a poor site from which to administer the center and east of the island, and it's not coincidental that almost every rebellion against the Havana authorities since the early 19th century has broken out in Oriente.

It took the Spanish conquest of Mexico and Peru to swing the pendulum in Havana's favor. The town's strategic location, at the mouth of the Gulf of Mexico facing a coastline washed by the northeast-bound Gulf Stream, made it a perfect gathering point for the annual treasure fleets.

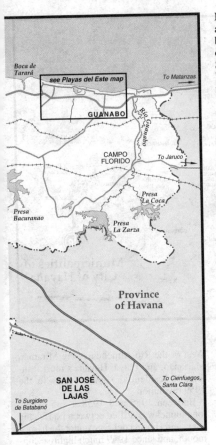

The colonial authorities also channeled trade through the town, and in 1556 Havana replaced Santiago de Cuba as seat of the Spanish captains general. The first combined *flota* sailed to Spain from here in 1564, and for the next two hundred years Havana was the most important port in the Americas, the 'key' to the vast Spanish colonial empire. In 1592 Havana was declared a city and in 1607 the capital of the colony was officially moved here.

After Havana was sacked by French privateers led by Jacques de Sores in 1555, the castles of La Fuerza, La Punta, and El Morro were built between 1558 and 1630, and from 1674 to 1740 a strong wall was built around the city. These defenses kept out the pirates but proved ineffective when Spain became embroiled in the Seven Years' War with Britain, the strongest maritime power of the time.

On June 6, 1762, a British army under the Earl of Albemarle attacked Havana, landing at Cojímar and striking inland to Guanabacoa. From there they drove west along the northeast side of the harbor and on July 30 they attacked El Morro Castle from the rear. Other troops landed at La Chorrera, west of the city, and by August 13 the surrounded Spanish were forced to surrender. The British held Havana for 11 months. (The same war cost France almost all its colonies in North America, including Quebec and Louisiana.)

When the Spanish regained the city a year later in exchange for Florida, they began a crash program to upgrade the city's defenses so it would never fall again. A new fortress, La Cabaña, was built along the ridge from which the British had shelled El Morro, and by the time the work was finished in 1766, Havana had become the most strongly fortified city in the New World, the 'bulwark of the Indies.'

The British occupation resulted in Spain opening Havana to freer trade. In 1765 the city was granted the right to trade with seven Spanish cities instead of only Cádiz, and beginning in 1818 Havana was allowed to ship its sugar, rum, tobacco, and coffee directly to any part of the world. The 19th century was an era of steady progress: First came the railway in 1837, and then public gas lighting in 1848, the telegraph in 1851, an urban transportation system in 1862, telephones in 1888, and electric lighting in 1890. At the end of the 16th century Havana had around 4000 inhabitants; by 1774 it had grown to 76,000, half the population of the island. The city was physically untouched by the devastating wars of independence, and by 1902 it had a quarter million inhabitants. The present population is 2,100,000, or about one in every five Cubans.

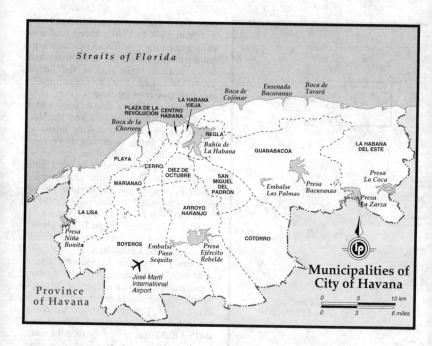

Municipalities of City of Havana

Orientation

Completely surrounded by the Province of Havana, the 727-sq-km City of Havana is divided into 15 municipalities: La Habana Vieja, Centro Habana, Plaza de la Revolución, Playa, La Lisa, Marianao, Cerro, Diez de Octubre, Boyeros, Arroyo Naranjo, San Miguel del Padrón, Cotorro, Regla, Guanabacoa, and La Habana del Este.

La Habana Vieja, or 'colonial Havana,' sits on the west side of the harbor in an area once bounded by 17th-century city walls that ran along present Avenida de Bélgica and Avenida de las Misiones. In 1863 these walls were demolished and the city spilled west into an area called Centro Habana, bisected by busy Calle San Rafael. West of this lies Vedado, the 20th-century hotel and entertainment district that only developed after independence in 1902. Near Plaza de la Revolución and between Vedado and Nuevo Vedado, a huge government complex was erected in the 1950s.

West of the Río Almendares are Miramar, Marianao, and Playa, Havana's most fashionable residential suburbs prior to the 1959 revolution.

Between 1955 and 1958 a 735-meter-long tunnel was drilled between La Habana Vieja and Havana del Este under the harbor mouth, and since 1959 much highrise construction has taken place in La Habana del Este, Cojímar (a former fishing village), and Alamar, northeast of the harbor. South of East Havana's endless blocks of flats are the old colonial towns of Guanabacoa, San Francisco de Paula, and Santa María del Rosario. On the east side of the harbor are the old towns of Regla and Casablanca.

The bulk of Havana's working-class population lives in industrial areas south of Centro Habana and the harbor such as Cerro, Diez de Octubre, and San Miguel del Padrón. South of that is Boyeros with the golf course, zoo, and international airport, and Arroyo Naranjo with Parque Lenin.

Visitors spend most of their time in La Habana Vieja, Centro Habana, and Vedado, and they should become familiar with important street names: Obispo, which cuts through the center of La Habana Vieja; Paseo de Martí (or Paseo del Prado), an elegant 19th-century promenade in Centro Habana; Avenida de Italia (or Galiano), Centro Habana's main shopping street for Cubans; Malecón, Havana's broad coastal boulevard; and Calle 23 (or La Rampa), the heart of Vedado's hotel district.

Confusingly, many main avenues around Havana have two names in everyday use, a new name that appears on street signs and in this book, and an old name still commonly used by local residents and provided in parentheses below :

Agramonte (Zulueta)
Aponte (Someruelos)
Avenida Carlos Manuel de Céspedes (Avenida del Puerto)
Avenida de Bélgica (Egido and Monserrate)
Avenida de España (Vives)
Avenida de Italia (Galiano)
Avenida de la Independencia (Avenida de Rancho Boyeros)
Avenida de las Misiones (Monserrate)
Avenida de México (Cristina)
Avenida Salvador Allende (Carlos III)
Avenida Simón Bolívar (Reina)
Brasil (Teniente Rey)
Calle 23 (La Rampa)
Calle G (Avenida de los Presidentes)
Capdevila (Cárcel)
Enrique Barnet (Estrella)
Leonor Pérez (Paula)
Malecón (Avenida de Maceo)
Máximo Gómez (Monte)
Padre Varela (Belascoaín)
Paseo de Martí (Paseo del Prado)
San Martín (San José)

Throughout this chapter we've tried to organize the listings in geographical order, beginning in La Habana Vieja, then Centro Habana, and finally Vedado. Separate sections that follow are devoted to Miramar, Marianao, Playa, Parque Lenin, Santiago de las Vegas, and all of the areas east of the harbor.

Maps Your best guide to the old city is *La Habana Vieja Guía Turística* published by the Instituto Cubano de Geodesia y Cartografía in 1991. It contains 35 maps of the old town, plus 222 pages of references and description in Spanish, English, French, and German. It's available at many hotel shops.

The Instituto also publishes *Ciudad de la Habana Mapa Turístico*, which covers all 15 municipalities in adequate detail, including detailed street maps of the central city and Playas del Este. It's another invaluable resource. Highway signs around Havana are poor to nonexistent, and this map is almost essential for drivers.

Map Stores Tienda El Navegante, Mercaderes No 115 between Obispo and Obrapía (Monday to Saturday 8 am to noon and 1 to 5 pm), has maps of many parts of Cuba. It also sells Cuban nautical charts at US$16 each.

Geotech, Calle 13 No 409 at F in Vedado (weekdays 9 am to 5 pm), sells maps, guidebooks, and atlases.

Downtown Havana

Information

Tourist Offices Surprisingly, there's no tourist information office in Havana. Travel agencies such as Rumbos and Havanatur do exist, but like their counterparts in other countries their main aim is to sell services such as excursions and no one is paying them to supply free information. Be prepared to fend for yourself.

Foreign Embassies Many countries maintain embassies in Havana. Check the listings in the Facts for the Visitor chapter under Foreign Embassies in Cuba.

Money To change money in La Habana Vieja, try the Banco Internacional, Aguiar No 411 (weekdays 8 am to 5 pm).

Most of the commercial banks are in Vedado. The Banco Nacional de Cuba, Calle

23 between O and P (weekdays 8:30 am to noon), changes traveler's checks for 2% commission, but it doesn't make cash advances. The International Branch of the Banco Nacional de Cuba is at Calle M and Línea (weekdays 8:30 am to noon).

The privately run Banco Financiero Internacional, inside the Hotel Habana Libre with a street entrance off Calle 25 (weekdays 8 am to 3 pm), charges 3% commission on traveler's checks. It'll give cash advances on Visa and MasterCard only. The Banco Financiero Internacional branch at Línea No 1 and O (weekdays 8 am to 3 pm) has lengthy lines.

You can buy Cuban pesos (moneda nacional) for cash dollars at Casas de Cambio (Cadeca), inside Almacenes Ultra at Bolívar No 109 near Avenida de Italia in Centro Habana (Monday to Saturday 9 am to 6 pm, Sunday 9 am to 1 pm). There's another Cadeca branch next to the market on Calle 19 between A and B in Vedado (Monday to Saturday 8 am to 6 pm, Sunday 8 am to 1 pm). Moneychangers on the street nearby give a slightly lower rate to those unwilling to waste time in line.

Post & Communications The post office and telephone center in the lobby of the Hotel Habana Libre, Calles 23 and L, accepts dollars only.

Peso post offices serving the local population are at the Estación Central de Ferrocarriles, Avenida de Bélgica and Arsenal in La Habana Vieja; at Calle 23 at C in Vedado (weekdays 8 to 11:30 am and 2 to 6 pm, Saturday 8 to 11:30 am); and in the Ministry of Communications building on Avenida de la Independencia between Plaza de la Revolución and the bus station (Monday to Saturday 8 am to 6 pm).

DHL Worldwide Express courier service is available at Aerocaribbean (☎ 33-4543, fax 33-5016), Calle 23 No 64 at P in Vedado.

Havana's telephone code is 7.

Travel Agencies Havanatur (☎ 33-1758), inside the airline building on Calle 23 between P and Infanta in Vedado (weekdays

8:15 am to 5:30 pm), is a full-service travel agency. On the outer side of the same building is Sol y Son, a travel agency owned by Cubana Airlines (☎ 33-3271, fax 33-5150), Calle 23 No 64 between P and Infanta in Vedado.

Cubamar (☎ 30-5536), Paseo No 306 at 15 in Vedado, is the travel agency of the Empresa Nacional de Campismo Popular. They specialize in youth tourism at seaside or mountain resorts such as El Abra at Playa Jibacoa and Aguas Claras in Pinar del Río. The reservations office is open daily from 8:30 am to 8 pm.

Bookstores Librería La Bella Habana in the Palacio del Segundo Cabo on Plaza de Armas, O'Reilly No 4 at Tacón (Monday to Saturday 10 am to 5:30 pm), carries numerous books in English (payable in dollars). The best selection of books old and new is available at the secondhand book market held on the Plaza de Armas on Saturdays and to a lesser extent on Sundays.

Two good bookstores are just off the Parque Central: Librería Internacional, Obispo No 526 (Monday to Saturday 10 am to 5:30 pm), and Librería Cervantes, an antiquarian bookstore. It's at Obispo and Bernaza (weekdays 10 am to 5 pm, Saturday 8 am to 3 pm).

Also in this area are Librería Rubén Martínez Villena, Paseo de Martí No 551 opposite the Capitolio Nacional, and Librería Abel Santamaría, Máximo Gómez at Cárdenas, opposite the Fuente de la India. These cater mostly to the local Cuban market.

Centro Habana has a number of specialized bookstores. Librería Luis Rogelio Nogueras, Avenida de Italia No 467 between Barcelona and San Martín (weekdays 10 am to 5 pm, Saturday 8 am to 2 pm), is good for literary magazines and Cuban literature in Spanish. Librería Viet Nam, San Rafael No 256 near Avenida de Italia (weekdays 8 am to 5 pm, Saturday 8 am to 3 pm), also has Cuban literature and some political books. Librería El Siglo de las Luces, Neptuno No 263 (weekdays 10 am to 5 pm, Saturday 8 am to 3 pm), is also

DAVID STANLEY

Second-hand book market on Plaza de Armas

strong on politics and literature; it's also the best source of books in Russian.

In Vedado, check Librería Internacional Alma Mater for textbooks; it's at San Lázaro and L, next to the university stairway (weekdays 9 am to 1 pm and 4 to 4:30 pm). Librería Fernando Ortíz, Calle L No 202 at 27 (Monday to Saturday 9 am to 8:30 pm, Sunday 9 am to 4 pm), has books in Spanish on politics and economics, essays, and books for children. Librería Centenario del Apóstol, Calle 25 No 164 at O (weekdays 10 am to 5 pm, Saturday 9 am to 3 pm), has a great assortment of used books.

Librería Rayuela, Calle 3 and G inside the Casa de las Américas (weekdays 8 am to 4:30 pm), is good for contemporary literature and compact discs. Payment is in dollars.

Libraries The main city library is the Biblioteca Pública Provincial Rubén M Villena, Obispo No 160 at San Ignacio (weekdays 8:30 am to 6 pm).

The Biblioteca Nacional José Martí, Avenida de la Independencia on the Plaza de la Revolución (Monday to Saturday 8 am to 5:45 pm), is also open to the public, but you must leave your bags in a cloak room.

Photography Photo Service, Avenida de Italia No 572 at Avenida Simón Bolívar in Centro Habana (daily 9 am to 9:45 pm), offers one-hour development service on film.

One of Havana's only public photocopy machines is available at Photo Service, Calle 23 at O in Vedado (open 24 hours).

Medical Services Most medical problems can be addressed at the Hospital Nacional Hermanos Ameijeiras (☎ 70-7721, fax 33-5036), San Lázaro No 701 just off Malecón in Centro Habana. This modern 900-bed hospital specializes in plastic surgery and other cosmetic operations on foreign patients who pay in hard currency. The hospital bed charge here is US$75 a night (US$40 for accompanying persons).

Two old-fashioned pharmacies in the old town are Drogería Johnson, Obispo No 260 (daily 8 am to 9 pm), and Drogería Sarrá, Brasil No 261 at Compostela (daily 8 am to 9 pm), which offers service after hours through a small side window.

In Centro Habana there's a pharmacy

at San Rafael No 108 behind the Hotel Inglaterra (Monday to Saturday 8 am to 6 pm).

In Vedado try the pharmacy at Calle 23 at M (daily 8 am to 9 pm), which also takes requests through a small window after hours.

All of these cater to the Cuban public and the range of medicines offered is limited. If they can't help you, consult the Playa & Marianao section of this chapter for a listing of pharmacies serving the diplomatic community.

Emergency The friendly English-speaking staff at Asistur (☎ 62-5519, fax 33-8087), Paseo de Martí No 254 (open 24 hours), can help in getting money sent from most countries (except the USA), changes American Express traveler's checks, expedites insurance claims, organizes repatriation, and arranges medical or dental treatment. This is the place to come first if you lose your passport or tourist card, are a victim of crime, or need legal advice.

The Policía Nacional Revolucionaria is on Calle Picota between Leonor Pérez and San Isidro near Estación Central. In an emergency, dial ☎ 116 (this number works anywhere in Cuba).

Public Toilets All large tourist hotels have public toilets, but some restaurants don't. Since you won't find restrooms on every corner, use them when you see them or at least note the location for future use.

Public toilets are available in La Habana Vieja in the courtyard at El Patio Colonial, Obispo and Baratillo off the southeast corner of the Plaza de Armas; at the rear of Lluvia de Oro, Obispo and Habana; in the cloister of the Iglesia de Nuestra Señora de la Merced, Calle Cuba No 806 at Merced; and at Dragones No 57 near the Capitolio. Give a small tip to the attendant.

Dangers & Annoyances Havana is an amazingly safe city and the heavy police presence on the streets is reassuring. You can walk through areas here in the middle of the night that you wouldn't dare enter at midday in places like Los Angeles or New York. However, watch out for young men on bicycles who try to snatch purses, handbags, or cameras. Other cyclists who seem to be giving chase to the thief are probably his accomplices.

La Habana Vieja Walking Tour

Colonial Havana contains far too many museums, memorials, art galleries, churches, castles, and other historical monuments to see in a day. For an introduction to the city you could walk the following loops through La Habana Vieja and Centro Habana in one day without spending too much time at any one place, and then go back on subsequent days to see the museums at leisure. Expect most of the printed information and verbal guidance along the way to be in Spanish only. In any case, this city offers such a sumptuous banquet you're certain to come away sated.

Begin with the **Catedral de San Cristóbal de La Habana**, the two unequal towers of which dominate the Plaza de la Catedral, framing a theatrical baroque facade designed by the Italian architect Francesco Borromini. When the Jesuits began construction of the church in 1748, Havana was still under the ecclesiastical control of Santiago de Cuba. Work continued despite the expulsion from Cuba of the conspiratorial Jesuits in 1767, and when the building was finished in 1787 the diocese of Havana was created. A year later the city became the seat of a bishop, elevating the church to a cathedral. Unfortunately the marble high altar and other works of art inside the cathedral are hard to visit as the building remains closed except for Sundays between 9 am and noon.

Many other noble buildings face the Plaza de la Catedral. One is the **Palacio de los Marqueses de Aguas Claras** (1760), San Ignacio No 54 at Empedrado, which is now Restaurante El Patio. The **Centro Wilfredo Lam**, San Ignacio No 22 next to the cathedral (Monday to Saturday 10 am to 5 pm, admission US$1), displays the works of one of Cuba's leading modern painters and presents exhibitions by Third

World artists. A Cuban of Chinese and African ancestry, Lam was strongly influenced by Pablo Picasso, who he met in 1936. On the opposite side of the square are the 18th-century **Casa de Lombillo**, presently the Museo de la Educación (Tuesday to Saturday 8:30 am to 5:30 pm, admission US$1), and the **Palacio del Marqués de Arcos** (1746), today housing a Telecorreo Internacional office. During the mid-19th century this palace served as Havana's main post office and the stone mask mailbox in the wall is still in use.

The **Museo de Arte Colonial** at San Ignacio No 61 on the south side of the square (Wednesday to Monday 10 am to 4:45 pm, Sunday 9 am to noon, admission US$2) displays colonial furniture and decorative arts in the Palacio de los Condes de Casa Bayona (1720), the oldest house on the Plaza de la Catedral. Just up Callejón del Chorro from the southwest corner of Plaza de la Catedral is the **Taller Experimental de Gráfica** (weekdays 9 am to 4 pm, admission free), where you can see original prints being made. Daily except Monday and Friday, the whole square becomes an open-air handicraft market.

Continue one block south on San Ignacio and turn left on O'Reilly. Two blocks ahead is the **Plaza de Armas**, the seat of authority and power in Cuba for 400 years. A square has existed on this site since 1582, although the present Plaza de Armas dates only from 1792. In the center of the park surrounded by stately royal palms is a marble statue (1955) of Carlos Manuel de Céspedes, the man who set Cuba on the road to independence in 1868. A large secondhand book market takes place here on weekends.

The baroque **Palacio de los Capitanes Generales** on the west side of the Plaza de Armas is one of Cuba's most majestic buildings. Construction began on the site of the old parochial church in 1776, and from 1791 until 1898 this was the residence of the Spanish captains general. From 1899 until 1902 the US military governors were based here, after which the building became the presidential palace. In 1920 the president moved to the building now housing the Museo de la Revolución and this palace became the city hall. The municipal authorities moved out in 1967 and since 1968 it has been home to the **Museo de la Ciudad** (daily 9:30 am to 6 pm, admission US$3, guided tour US$1, photos US$2, video camera US$30). The rooms are richly decorated, and a white marble statue of Christopher Columbus stands in the courtyard.

The baroque **Palacio del Segundo Cabo** (1772), O'Reilly No 4 at the northwest corner of the Plaza de Armas, is the former headquarters of the Spanish vice-governor. Later it became the Supreme Court and today the building houses the Instituto Cubano del Libro. It's worth glimpsing into the arcaded inner courtyard and visiting the art gallery and bookstore here.

On the northeast side of the Plaza de Armas is oldest extant colonial fortress in the Americas, the **Castillo Real de la Fuerza**, built between 1558 and 1577 on the site of an earlier fort destroyed by French privateers in 1555. The west tower is crowned by the famous bronze weathervane called La Giraldilla, cast in Havana in 1632 by Jerónimo Martínez Pinzón and popularly believed to be Doña Inés de Bobadilla, the wife of explorer Hernando de Soto, awaiting his return from the quest for the 'fountain of youth' in Florida. (The original Giraldilla is in the Museo de la Ciudad and the figure also appears on the Havana Club rum label.) The Spanish captains general resided in the castle for two hundred years until they finally got around to constructing a palace of their own across the square. La Fuerza now shelters the **Museo de la Cerámica Artística Cubana** downstairs (Thursday to Monday 9:15 am to 4:45 pm, admission US$1) and it's free to go upstairs to the pizzeria/bar (10 am to midnight) from which you'll get a great view of the harbor entrance, only slightly diminished by black smoke rising from the oil refinery to the right.

In 1519 the Villa de San Cristóbal de la Habana was founded on the spot marked

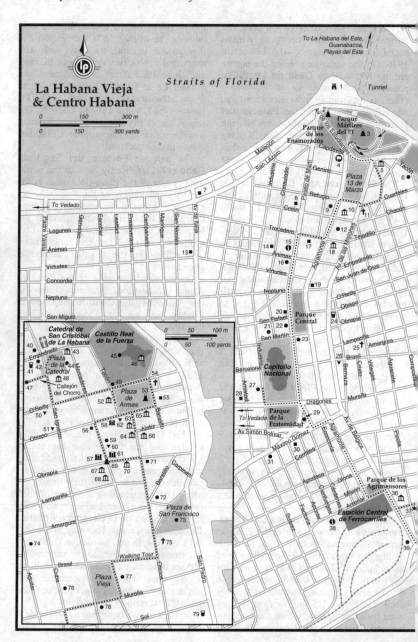

La Habana Vieja & Centro Habana

Straits of Florida

To La Habana del Este,
Guanabacoa,
Playas del Este

Tunnel

To Vedado

Parque Mártires
del 71

Parque de los
Enamorados

Plaza
13 de
Marzo

Malecón

San Lázaro

Industria

Consulado

Paseo de Martí

Genios

Refugio

Colón

Capdevila

Tacón

Cuarteles

Chacón

Trocadero

Tejadillo

Av de las Misiones

Animas

Agramonte

Empedrado

Virtudes

San Juan de Dios

Neptuno

O'Reilly

Obispo

Obrapía

Lamparilla

Amargura

Brasil

Cristo

Villegas

Aguacate

Compostela

Parque
Central

San Rafael

San Martín

Barcelona

Amistad

Industria

Capitolio
Nacional

Dragones

Parque de la
Fraternidad

Av Simón Bolívar

Máximo Gómez

Corrales

Apodaca

Gloria

Misión

Arsenal

Factoría

Suárez

Cienfuegos

Economía

Parque de los
Agrimensores

Estación Central
de Ferrocarriles

Padre Varela

Gervasio

Escobar

Lealtad

Perseverancia

Campanario

Manrique

San Nicolás

Av de Italia

Lagunas

Animas

Virtudes

Concordia

Neptuno

San Miguel

Catedral de
San Cristóbal
de La Habana

Plaza
de la
Catedral

Callejón
del Chorro

Empedrado

O'Reilly

Obispo

Obrapía

Lamparilla

Amargura

Brasil

Aguiar

Cuba

Castillo Real
de la Fuerza

Tacón

Plaza
de
Armas

Baratillo

Justiz

San Ignacio

Mercaderes

Oficios

San Pedro

Baratillo

Carpineti

Plaza de
San Francisco

Walking Tour

Plaza
Vieja

Muralla

Sol

To Vedado

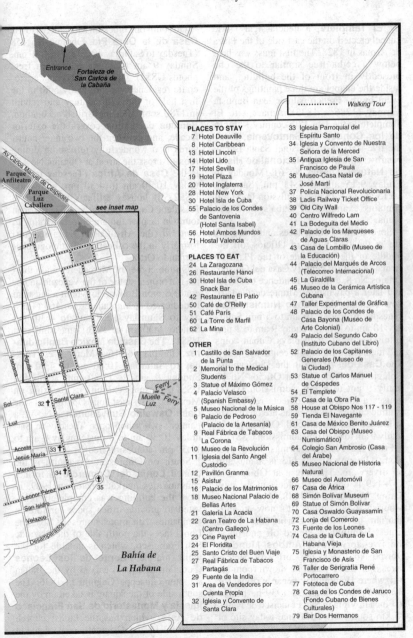

.... Walking Tour

PLACES TO STAY
7 Hotel Deauville
8 Hotel Caribbean
13 Hotel Lincoln
14 Hotel Lido
17 Hotel Sevilla
19 Hotel Plaza
20 Hotel Inglaterra
28 Hotel New York
30 Hotel Isla de Cuba
55 Palacio de los Condes
   de Santovenia
   (Hotel Santa Isabel)
56 Hotel Ambos Mundos
71 Hostal Valencia

PLACES TO EAT
24 La Zaragozana
26 Restaurante Hanoi
30 Hotel Isla de Cuba
   Snack Bar
42 Restaurante El Patio
50 Café de O'Reilly
51 Café París
60 La Torre de Marfil
62 La Mina

OTHER
1 Castillo de San Salvador
   de la Punta
2 Memorial to the Medical
   Students
3 Statue of Máximo Gómez
4 Palacio Velasco
   (Spanish Embassy)
5 Museo Nacional de la Música
6 Palacio de Pedroso
   (Palacio de la Artesanía)
9 Real Fábrica de Tabacos
   La Corona
10 Museo de la Revolución
11 Iglesia del Santo Angel
   Custodio
12 Pavillón Granma
15 Asistur
16 Palacio de los Matrimonios
18 Museo Nacional Palacio de
   Bellas Artes
21 Galería La Acacia
22 Gran Teatro de La Habana
   (Centro Gallego)
23 Cine Payret
24 El Floridita
25 Santo Cristo del Buen Viaje
27 Real Fábrica de Tabacos
   Partagás
29 Fuente de la India
31 Area de Vendedores por
   Cuenta Propia
32 Iglesia y Convento de
   Santa Clara

33 Iglesia Parroquial del
   Espíritu Santo
34 Iglesia y Convento de Nuestra
   Señora de la Merced
35 Antigua Iglesia de San
   Francisco de Paula
36 Museo-Casa Natal de
   José Martí
37 Policía Nacional Revolucionaria
38 Ladis Railway Ticket Office
39 Old City Wall
40 Centro Wilfredo Lam
41 La Bodeguita del Medio
42 Palacio de los Marqueses
   de Aguas Claras
43 Casa de Lombillo (Museo de
   la Educación)
44 Palacio del Marqués de Arcos
   (Telecorreo Internacional)
45 La Giraldilla
46 Museo de la Cerámica Artística
   Cubana
47 Taller Experimental de Gráfica
48 Palacio de los Condes de
   Casa Bayona (Museo de
   Arte Colonial)
49 Palacio del Segundo Cabo
   (Instituto Cubano del Libro)
52 Palacio de los Capitanes
   Generales (Museo de
   la Ciudad)
53 Statue of Carlos Manuel
   de Céspedes
54 El Templete
57 Casa de la Obra Pía
58 House at Obispo Nos 117 - 119
59 Tienda El Navegante
61 Casa de México Benito Juárez
63 Casa del Obispo (Museo
   Numismático)
64 Colegio San Ambrosio (Casa
   del Árabe)
65 Museo Nacional de Historia
   Natural
66 Museo del Automóvil
67 Casa de África
68 Simón Bolívar Museum
69 Statue of Simón Bolívar
70 Casa Oswaldo Guayasamín
72 Lonja del Comercio
73 Fuente de los Leones
74 Casa de la Cultura de La
   Habana Vieja
75 Iglesia y Monasterio de San
   Francisco de Asís
76 Taller de Serigrafía René
   Portocarrero
77 Fototeca de Cuba
78 Casa de los Condes de Jaruco
   (Fondo Cubano de Bienes
   Culturales)
79 Bar Dos Hermanos

by **El Templete**, a neoclassical Doric chapel erected on the east side of the Plaza de Armas in 1828. The first mass was held below a ceiba tree similar to the one presently in front of the building, and inside the chapel are three paintings of the event by the French painter Jean Baptiste Vermay (1786 – 1833). Adjacent to El Templete is the late-18th-century **Palacio de los Condes de Santovenia**, today the five-star, 28-room Hotel Santa Isabel. Nearby is the **Museo Nacional de Historia Natural**, Obispo No 61 (Monday to Friday 9:15 am to 3:45 pm, Saturday 10:15 am to 1:45 pm, admission US$1). It contains examples of Cuba's flora and fauna.

Several more old palaces and museums are in the first block of Oficios, off the middle of the south side of the Plaza de Armas. The 17th-century Casa del Obispo, Oficios No 8, a former residence of clerics and later a pawnshop (Monte de Piedad), now contains the **Museo Numismático** (Tuesday to Friday 10 am to 5 pm, Saturday 10 am to 4 pm, Sunday 9 am to 1 pm, admission free). It displays Cuban coins and medals from the 16th century to today. The **Casa del Árabe** in the 18th-century Colegio San Ambrosio at Oficios No 12 (daily 9 am to 6 pm, admission US$1) houses a museum of objects relating to Islamic culture. Classic cars are on display at **Museo del Automóvil**, Oficios No 13 (daily 9 am to 6:30 pm, admission US$1).

From the Plaza de Armas, head west along Obispo. At No 113 is a museum of silverware. The house at Obispo No 117–119 is one of the oldest in the city, dating from around 1648, with several Moorish-style ceilings (it's now an antiquarian bookstore). During the 1930s Ernest Hemingway stayed off and on at the five-story **Hotel Ambos Mundos**, Obispo No 153 at the corner of Mercaderes. For US$1 you'll be shown room No 511 where Hemingway began writing *For Whom the Bell Tolls*. (In 1939 he moved to Finca la Vigía in San Francisco de Paula, 15 km southeast of Havana, today site of the Hemingway Museum.)

Go south one block on Mercaderes to the **Casa de la Obra Pía**, Obrapía No 158 (Tuesday to Saturday 10:30 am to 4:30 pm, Sunday 9 am to 1 pm, admission free, photos US$2). This typical Havana aristocratic residence was originally built in the first half of the 17th century and rebuilt in 1780 soon after the British occupation. Baroque decoration covers the exterior facade, and between the two inner courtyards is a wonderfully refreshing dining room. Across the street at Obrapía No 157 is the **Casa de África** (Tuesday to Saturday 10:30 am to 4:30 pm, admission US$2). It houses artifacts presented to President Castro during his 1977 African tour. On display too are objects relating to *santería* (the Afro-Cuban religious cult) formerly in the collection of ethnographer Fernando Ortíz.

On the corner of Mercaderes and Obrapía is a bronze statue of the Venezuelan liberator Simón Bolívar, to whom a museum is dedicated at Mercaderes No 160 (Tuesday to Saturday 10:30 am to 4:30 pm, Sunday 9:30 am to 12:30 pm, admission US$1). The **Casa de México Benito Juárez**, Obrapía No 116 at Mercaderes (Tuesday to Saturday 10:30 am to 4:30 pm, Sunday 9 am to 12:30 pm, admission US$1), presents exhibitions focusing on Mexico. Just east on Obrapía is the **Casa Oswaldo Guayasamín** at No 11, a painter's workshop open Tuesday to Saturday 10:30 am to 5 pm, Sunday 9 am to 12:30 pm (admission free).

South on Oficios at Amargura is the domed **Lonja del Comercio**, a former commodities market erected in 1909. In 1996 the building was completely renovated to provide office space for foreign companies with joint ventures in Cuba. The Lonja faces the north side of the Plaza de San Francisco, which is notable for the white marble **Fuente de los Leones** (Fountain of Lions) carved by the Italian sculptor Giuseppe Gaginni in 1836. The south side of the square is taken up by the **Iglesia y Monasterio de San Francisco de Asís**, which has the tallest church tower in Havana. Originally constructed in

1608 and rebuilt in the baroque style from 1719 to 1738, San Francisco de Asís ceased to be a consecrated church in 1841, and it's now a concert hall and museum (daily 9:30 am to 6:30 pm, admission US$2). The crypt was a favorite burial place of local 18th-century aristocrats.

Continue south on Oficios one block to Brasil and go west one block to La Habana Vieja's third historic square, the **Plaza Vieja** dating from the 16th century. It served as an open-air marketplace until 1835. Later the Batista regime constructed an ugly underground parking lot there that army engineers demolished in 1996. Several historic buildings surround the restored square, including Mercaderes No 307 (the Fototeca de Cuba, a photo gallery open Tuesday to Saturday 10 am to 5 pm) and San Ignacio No 352 (an art gallery). The **Casa de los Condes de Jaruco**, Muralla No 107 at San Ignacio, has a wide covered gallery typical of aristocratic residences built around 1737. It now contains various shops and art galleries belonging to the Fondo Cubano de Bienes Culturales (open Monday to Friday 10 am to 5 pm, Saturday 10 am to 1 pm, admission free).

Continue west on Muralla one block and then go south on Cuba another block into the poorer southern section of old Havana. The **Iglesia y Convento de Santa Clara** (1638 – 1643), Cuba No 610, stopped being a convent in 1920, and the team in charge of the restoration of colonial Havana is presently based there. Weekdays between 9 am and 3 pm you can visit the large cloister and nun's cemetery for US$2 admission. Heading south again to the corner of Cuba and Acosta, you'll find Havana's oldest surviving church, the **Iglesia Parroquial del Espíritu Santo** (1640, rebuilt in 1674), with many burials in the crypt; it's open daily from 8 am to noon. The **Iglesia y Convento de Nuestra Señora de la Merced** (1755), Cuba No 806 at Merced (daily 8 am to noon and 3 to 6:30 pm), was reconstructed in the 19th century. Altars, frescoed vaults, and a number of old paintings are inside and a quiet cloister is adjacent.

Continue one block further south on Cuba, go right on Leonor Pérez, and walk five blocks west to the **Museo-Casa Natal de José Martí** at No 314 (Tuesday to Saturday 10 am to 5 pm, Sunday 9 am to 1 pm, admission US$1). The apostle of Cuban independence was born in this humble dwelling on January 28, 1853, and the museum displays letters, manuscripts, photos, books, and other mementos of his life. Nearby, to the west across Avenida de Bélgica, is the longest remaining stretch of the old city wall. A bronze map shows the outline of the original layout. To the right is Havana's huge **Estación Central de Ferrocarriles** (Central Railway Station) where *La Junta*, the locomotive that inaugurated the line to Matanzas in 1843, is on display inside.

If you're continuing the walking tour into Centro Habana, take Calle Agramonte from the park on the north side of the train station north five blocks. Turn left on Máximo Gómez and from the next corner you'll see the **Fuente de la India** in the center of a major boulevard.

Centro Habana Walking Tour

Begin this walk at the **Fuente de la India**, which is east of Parque de la Fraternidad between Máximo Gómez and Dragones. This white Carrara marble fountain, carved by Guiseppe Gaginni in 1837, portrays an Indian girl seated above four dolphins, a famous symbol of Havana. She holds in her hand the city's coat of arms.

Across the street to the west is **Parque de la Fraternidad**, originally a Spanish military parade ground. The first park was laid out here in 1892 to commemorate the fourth centenary of the Spanish discovery of America, and in 1928 the park was remodeled to mark a Pan-American Conference held in Havana that year. The ceiba tree presently protected by a high iron fence was planted in a mixture of soil from all the countries of the Americas and busts of prominent Latin Americans and North Americans were set up around the park.

The huge white marble building north of the park is the Capitolio Nacional. Before

visiting it, have a look at the **Real Fábrica de Tabacos Partagás**, Industria No 520, one of Havana's oldest cigar factories, along the west side of the Capitolio. Today some 400 workers roll cigars in this factory founded in 1845 by a Spaniard named Jaime Partagás. Factory tours take place weekdays at 10 am only (admission US$5), but the sales room with its large display of Havana cigars and demonstration roller is accessible free of charge Monday to Saturday from 9 am to 5 pm.

Dominating this entire area is the marble-covered **Capitolio Nacional**. It's similar to the US Capitol Building in Washington, DC, but richer in detail. Initiated by the US-backed dictator Gerardo Machado in 1929, the Capitolio took 5000 workers three years, two months, and 20 days to build at a cost of US$17 million in the dollars of those days. It was the seat of the Cuban Congress until 1959 and it now houses the Cuban Academy of Sciences and the National Library of Science and Technology. The main entrance is at the top of the monumental stairway on the east side of the building. Comprehensive guided tours are offered Monday to Saturday from 9 am to 4:30 pm (the US$3 fee includes a soft drink in the cafe).

Visitors enter through huge bronze doors bearing plaques illustrating the history of Cuba. Opposite the entrance is a 49-metric-ton, 17-meter statue of Jupiter, the third largest indoor bronze statue in the world (after a statue of the Buddha in Japan and the Lincoln Memorial in Washington).

Directly below the Capitolio's 62-meter-high dome a copy of a 24-carat diamond is set in the floor. Highway distances between Havana and all sites in Cuba are calculated from this point. The 120-meter-long entry hall is known as the Salón de los Pasos Perdidos. Visitors are also shown the mahogany-covered library and the former chambers of the Senate and Deputies. Don't miss the opportunity to tour this impressive building.

On the north side of the Capitolio is the ornate neobaroque **Centro Gallego**, Paseo de Martí and San Rafael, erected as a Galician social club between 1907 and 1914. The center was built around the existing Teatro Tacón, which had itself opened in 1846 with a series of Verdi operas. This connection is the basis of claims by the present 2000-seat **Gran Teatro de La Habana** that it's the oldest operating theater in the Western Hemisphere. The National Ballet of Cuba and the State Opera are based here. Guided tours of the theater are offered Tuesday to Sunday 10 am to 7 pm (admission US$2).

Parque Central, across Paseo de Martí from the Centro Gallego, has long been a popular meeting point between old and new areas of Havana. The park was expanded to its present size after the city walls were knocked down in the late 19th century, and the marble statue of José Martí (1905) in its center was the first statue of Martí to be erected in Cuba. One of Havana's finest grand hotels, the **Inglaterra**, faces the west side of the square. José Martí made a speech advocating independence at a banquet here in 1879, and much later US journalists covering the so-called Spanish-American War stayed at this hotel. Bar La Sevillana just inside the Inglaterra is a great place for a break, and the 4th floor terrace offers a view of central Havana.

The most memorable section of Paseo de Martí (also called the Paseo del Prado) is to the north of Parque Central. Construction of this stately boulevard began outside the city walls in 1770, and the work was completed in the mid-1830s during the term of

Captain-General Miguel Tacón, who ruled from 1834 to 1838. He also constructed the original Parque Central. The figures of lions along the promenade were added in 1928. At Paseo del Martí No 302 at the corner of Ánimas is the neo-Renaissance **Palacio de los Matrimonios**, the former Casino Español dating from 1914. On Saturday mornings passersby can see many couples being married here.

A block north on Paseo de Martí is the sumptuous old **Hotel Sevilla**, Trocadero No 55, the former Sevilla-Biltmore (erected 1908) where Enrico Caruso stayed when he came to perform in Havana during the 1920s. One of Cuba's most famous cocktails, the Mary Pickford (rum, pineapple juice, and grenadine), was invented at this hotel's bar. Also on Trocadero, just east across Agramonte, is the **Museo Nacional Palacio de Bellas Artes** (Thursday to Monday 10 am to 5 pm, admission US$3). This building erected in 1955 houses Cuba's most important fine-arts collection, with European painting downstairs and Cuban painters from the 18th to 20th centuries and ancient art upstairs. Notice the sexuality apparent in the paintings of mulatto women, especially *El Rapto de las Mulatas* (1938) by Carlos Enríquez (1900 – 1957). (Turn to Painting in Facts about Cuba chapter for a brief discussion of some of the Cuban artists represented in this museum.)

Since 1976 the square in front of the Palacio de Bellas Artes has accommodated the **Pavillón Granma**, housing the 18-meter motor vessel *Granma* that carried Fidel Castro and 82 others from Tuxpán, Mexico, to Cuba in 1956. Today this glass-encased memorial is one of the holiest shrines of Cuban Communism, the equivalent of Mao's mausoleum in Beijing. The pavilion is accessible from the Museo de la Revolución (see below).

Walk up Calle Agramonte on the west side of the *Granma* to Calle Refugio, where you'll find the **Real Fábrica de Tabacos La Corona** founded in 1842. During the weekday tour at 9:30 am (admission US$5) you'll see the hundreds of workers busy hand-rolling such famous cigars as Romeo and Julieta, Montecristo, and Cohiba (President Castro's favorite brand until he gave up smoking). The factory sales room just inside to the left is worth a look Monday to Saturday from 9 am to 5 pm (free).

The **Museo de la Revolución**, opposite La Corona at Refugio No 1 (Tuesday 10 am to 6 pm, Wednesday to Sunday 10 am to 5 pm, admission US$3, children US$1.50, photos US$3, video cameras US$5), is housed in the former Presidential Palace constructed between 1913 and 1920. Tiffany's of New York decorated the interior. This palace was the site of an unsuccessful assassination attempt against Fulgencio Batista in March 1957 (see History in the Facts about Cuba chapter for details). The exhibits inside provide a complete documentary and photographic account of the Cuban Revolution, and it's a must for anyone with a taste for history – allow yourself plenty of time. In front of the building are a SAU-100 tank used by Fidel Castro during the 1961 Battle of the Bay of Pigs and a fragment of the former city wall.

On the east side of this museum up narrow Calle Cuarteles is the **Iglesia del Santo Angel Custodio** (daily 9 am to 1 pm and 3 to 7 pm), rebuilt in neo-Gothic style in 1871. This church has many literary and historical connotations due to the famous people who have passed through its doors (including Cirilo Villaverde, who set the main scene of his novel *Cecilia Valdés* in the church, and José Martí, who was baptized here in 1853).

Continue east on Cuarteles another block, and then head north on Habana through a picturesque corner of old Havana to the **Museo Nacional de la Música**, Capdevila No 1 (Monday to Saturday 9 am to 4:45 pm, admission US$2). Its collection of Cuban musical instruments is exhibited in the eclectic residence (1901) of a wealthy Havana merchant. The museum shop sells recordings of Cuban music, and concerts (admission US$1 to US$3) take place in the music room a couple of nights a week (check the showcase in front of the museum for schedules of events).

From here walk west on Capdevila keeping the entrance to the harbor tunnel and the tall equestrian statue of General Máximo Gómez (1935) on your right. On the corner of Capdevila and Agramonte is the Art Nouveau **Palacio Velasco** (1912), the present Spanish Embassy, easily distinguishable by the yellow and red flag. Just beyond in Parque de los Enamorados is a surviving section of the colonial **Cárcel** (1838) where many Cuban patriots, including José Martí, were imprisoned. On the opposite side of Avenida de los Estudiantes, beyond a long line of cyclists waiting to be carried by bus through the tunnel, is a fragment of wall encased in marble where eight Cuban medical students chosen at random were shot by the Spanish in 1871 as a reprisal for allegedly desecrating the tomb of a Spanish journalist (in fact, they didn't do it).

Across the street is the **Castillo de San Salvador de la Punta**, designed by the Italian military engineer Giovanni Bautista Antonelli and built between 1589 and 1600. During the colonial era a chain was stretched 250 meters over to El Morro Castle every night to close the harbor mouth to shipping.

Vedado Walking Tour

The name Vedado means 'forest reserve'; during the colonial era cutting down trees was forbidden here. Havana's American community established itself in this area after 1898, and within a few decades Vedado was thick with highrise hotels, office buildings, restaurants, nightclubs, and other businesses. Vedado boomed during the Batista era and the East Coast mafia of the US had a hand in it all. The Hotel Capri was a favorite haunt of mafia notables such as Lucky Luciano and Meyer Lanski, the same mob that was supposedly behind the Las Vegas-style Hotel Riviera. The cheap sex, liquor, and gambling were big attractions for US tourists, and Batista's thugs made sure everything ran smoothly. The party ended in January 1959 when Fidel Castro and his *barbudos* arrived from the Sierra Maestra and set up headquarters on the 22nd floor of the 25-story Havana Hilton (now called the Habana Libre).

An ideal place to begin a visit is the neocolonial-style **Hotel Nacional** (1930) at Calles 21 and O. In August 1933 the US-backed dictator Gerardo Machado was overthrown during a popular uprising, and a month later Fulgencio Batista, an army sergeant, seized power. On October 2, 1933, some 300 army officers displaced by Batista's coup sought refuge in the newly opened Hotel Nacional where the US ambassador Sumner Wells was staying. Aware that the reins of power had changed hands, Ambassador Wells found urgent business elsewhere and Batista's troops attacked the officers, many of whom were shot after surrendering. The Nacional still manages to convey the atmosphere of a bygone era and it's worth a look around. From the main entrance go straight ahead through the lobby and out into the park behind the hotel.

As you leave the Nacional, turn left and go down Calle O one block to Calle 23, Vedado's famous 'La Rampa.' The futuristic **Pabellón Cuba** is between N and M, one block up the slope (or 'ramp') to your right, and most of Havana's airline offices and travel agencies are in a long office building one block down Calle 23 to your left.

Cross Calle 23 and continue southeast two blocks on Calle O to Calle 25 No 164, where you'll find the **Casa Museo Abel Santamaría** on the 6th floor (weekdays 10 am to 4 pm, Saturday 9 am to noon, admission free). If the door to this apartment building is locked, knock until someone opens it. Apartment No 603 belonged to Abel Santamaría and his sister Haydée Santamaría, early associates of Fidel Castro, and the 1953 attack on the Moncada barracks in Santiago de Cuba was planned here.

Walk west on Calle 25 three blocks and turn left on Calle L just after the Habana Libre Hotel. Face the point where Calle L swings east as San Lázaro, and you'll see the monumental central stairway of the **Universidad de La Habana**, founded by

Dominican monks in 1728 after the reforming Bourbon kings assumed the Spanish throne. In 1842 the university was secularized. The present neoclassical complex dates from the second quarter of this century, and today some 30,000 students (2000 of them foreigners) follow courses taught by 1700 professors in the social sciences and humanities, natural sciences, mathematics, and economics. Across the street from the university stairway is the **Monumento a Julio Antonio Mella**, the student leader who founded the first Cuban Communist Party in 1925. In 1929 the dictator Machado sent an assassin to Mexico City and Mella was murdered.

Go up the stairway and through the monumental gateway into Plaza Ignacio Agramonte, the university's central square. In front of you will be the **Biblioteca** (library) and to your left the Edificio Felipe Poey with two unusual museums. The **Museo de Ciencias Naturales** downstairs is the oldest museum in Cuba, founded in 1874 by the Royal Academy of Medical, Physical, and Natural Sciences, and many of the stuffed specimens of Cuban flora and fauna date from the last century. Upstairs is the **Museo Antropológico Montané**, established in 1903, with a rich collection of pre-Columbian Indian artifacts. The most important objects are the wooden 10th-century Ídolo del Tobaco, discovered in Guantánamo Province, and the stone Ídolo de Bayamo. The exhibits are color-coded to indicate the three periods of Indo-American civilization in Cuba: Pre-Ceramic (red), Proto-Ceramic (green), and Ceramic (yellow). Both museums are open weekdays from 9 am to noon and 1 to 4 pm, and admission costs US$1.

Go down through the park on the north side of the Edificio Felipe Poey and exit the university compound via a small gate to reach the **Museo Napoleónico**, San Miguel No 1159 at Ronda (Tuesday to Saturday 10 am to 5:30 pm, Sunday 9 am to 12:30 pm, admission US$2, guided tour an additional US$1). The museum's four-story Italian-style mansion, built in 1928, contains objects associated with Napoleon Bonaparte that were amassed by a Cuban collector. The 10,000-seat **Estadio Universitario Juan Abrahantes** is just up the hill from this museum.

If you've still got time after the Vedado walk, you could continue south on Avenida de la Universidad alongside the stadium to Avenida Salvador Allende. If you wish to continue on this walking tour, follow the course described in the next section.

Plaza de la Revolución

Beginning at the Museo Napoleónico (see above), walk 200 meters down Avenida de la Universidad. To the left is the **Quinta de los Molinos**, a former residence of General Máximo Gómez and now a museum (Tuesday to Saturday 9 am to 5 pm, Sunday 9 am to noon, admission US$0.50) set in the university's former botanical gardens.

If time is short, skip the Quinta and walk south on Avenida de la Independencia past

RENÉ MEDEROS
COURTESY CUBA POSTER PROJECT

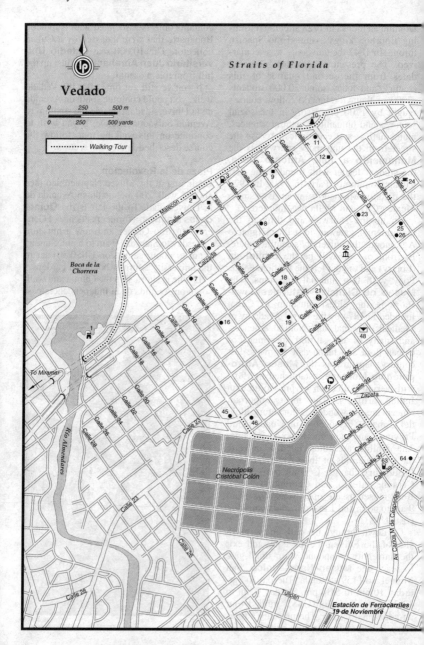

Vedado

Straits of Florida

Walking Tour

Boca de la Chorrera

To Miramar

Río Almendares

Necrópolis Cristóbal Colón

Zapata

Tulipán

Estación de Ferrocarriles
19 de Noviembre

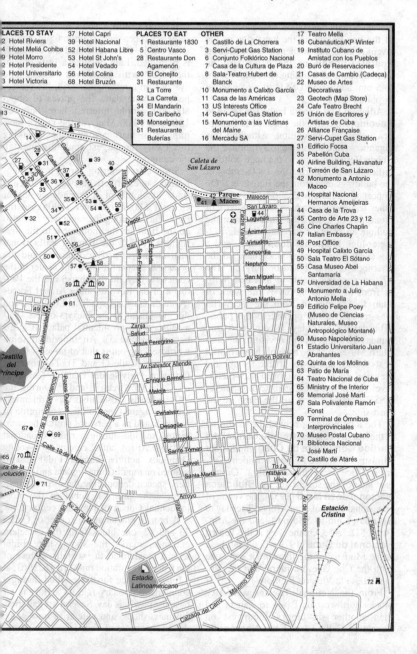

PLACES TO STAY
2 Hotel Riviera
4 Hotel Meliá Cohiba
9 Hotel Morro
2 Hotel Presidente
3 Hotel Universitario
3 Hotel Victoria
37 Hotel Capri
39 Hotel Nacional
52 Hotel Habana Libre
53 Hotel St John's
54 Hotel Vedado
56 Hotel Colina
68 Hotel Bruzón

PLACES TO EAT
1 Restaurante 1830
28 Restaurante Don Agamenón
30 El Conejito
31 Restaurante La Torre
32 La Carreta
34 El Mandarin
36 El Caribeño
38 Monseigneur
51 Restaurante Bulerías

OTHER
1 Castillo de La Chorrera
3 Servi-Cupet Gas Station
6 Conjunto Folklórico Nacional
7 Casa de la Cultura de Plaza
8 Sala-Teatro Hubert de Blanck
10 Monumento a Calixto García
11 Casa de las Américas
13 US Interests Office
14 Servi-Cupet Gas Station
15 Monumento a las Víctimas del *Maine*
16 Mercadu SA
17 Teatro Mella
18 Cubanáutica/KP Winter
19 Instituto Cubano de Amistad con los Pueblos
20 Buró de Reservaciones
21 Casas de Cambio (Cadeca)
22 Museo de Artes Decorativas
23 Geotech (Map Store)
24 Cafe Teatro Brecht
25 Unión de Escritores y Artistas de Cuba
26 Alliance Française
27 Servi-Cupet Gas Station
31 Edificio Focsa
35 Pabellón Cuba
40 Airline Building, Havanatur
41 Torreón de San Lázaro
42 Monumento a Antonio Maceo
43 Hospital Nacional Hermanos Ameijeiras
44 Casa de la Trova
45 Centro de Arte 23 y 12
46 Cine Charles Chaplin
47 Italian Embassy
48 Post Office
49 Hospital Calixto García
50 Sala Teatro El Sótano
55 Casa Museo Abel Santamaría
57 Universidad de La Habana
58 Monumento a Julio Antonio Mella
59 Edificio Felipe Poey (Museo de Ciencias Naturales, Museo Antropológico Montané)
60 Museo Napoleónico
61 Estadio Universitario Juan Abrahantes
62 Quinta de los Molinos
63 Patio de María
64 Teatro Nacional de Cuba
65 Ministry of the Interior
66 Memorial José Martí
67 Sala Polivalente Ramón Fonst
69 Terminal de Ómnibus Interprovinciales
70 Museo Postal Cubano
71 Biblioteca Nacional José Martí
72 Castillo de Atarés

Havana's main bus station. One block south of the bus station on the west side of the Avenida de la Independencia is the **Museo Postal Cubano** in the Ministerio de Comunicaciones building (weekdays 9 am to 5 pm, admission US$1). It's of interest to philatelists.

Adjacent to the south is the **Plaza de la Revolución**, called the Plaza de la República before the revolution. Although this gigantic square has come to symbolize the Cuban Revolution due to the huge political rallies held here during the 1960s, most of the buildings date from the Batista era. On important occasions President Castro and other leaders have addressed hundreds of thousands of assembled Cubans from the podium in front of the star-shaped, 142-meter-high **Memorial José Martí**, and a big event usually takes place here on the afternoon of May 1 and on July 26. The 17-meter marble statue of a seated Martí in front of the memorial is the work of Juan José Sicre. In 1996 the memorial was renovated and opened to the public (Tuesday to Saturday 10 am to 6 pm, Sunday 10 am to 2 pm). A visit to the José Martí Museum at the base of the memorial costs US$5, and if you'd like to take the elevator up to the enclosed 129-meter-level viewpoint, it's US$10 total (cameras US$5 extra). Entry is up the ramp on the west side.

The long building behind the memorial is the heavily guarded **Comité Central del Partido Comunista de Cuba**, the former Ministry of Justice (1958). President Castro's office is in this building. On the east side of the square are the **Biblioteca Nacional José Martí** (1958), the venue of occasional cultural events (open Tuesday to Saturday 8 am to 5:45 pm), and the Ministry of Defense. On the west is the **Teatro Nacional de Cuba** (1979). Between these is the Ministry of the Interior (it's the one with the Che Guevara mural and the slogan 'Hasta la Victoria Siempre').

From the National Theater walk five blocks northwest on Paseo to Zapata and then another six blocks southwest on Zapata to Calle 12 and the **Necrópolis Cristóbal Colón**, Cuba's most important cemetery (open daily 6 am to 6 pm, admission US$1). Driving around the cemetery is permitted. Laid out like a little city of the dead with numbered streets and avenues on a rectangular grid, the Necrópolis accommodates the graves of about 800,000 people interred here between 1868 and 1982. Many of the graves have impressive marble tombstones, making this easily the largest sculpture park in the country.

Soon after entering through the neo-Romanesque northern gateway (1870), one finds the tomb of independence leader General Máximo Gómez (1905) on the right. Further along the same way and also on the right are the monument to the firefighters (1890), the Familia Falla Bonet mausoleum (of artistic interest), and the octagonal chapel (1886) in the center of the cemetery. Beyond the chapel are the Pantheon of the Revolutionary Armed Forces (Avenida Obispo Espada and Calle L) and the monument to the martyrs of the 1957 assault on the presidential palace (Calle J between 3 and 5). An individual tomb worth seeking out is that of novelist Cirilo Villaverde (Calle G and 3). The tomb of Orthodox Party leader Eduardo Chibás is on Calle 8 between E and F. During the '40s and early '50s Chibás was a relentless crusader against the political corruption of his time, and as a personal protest he committed suicide during a radio broadcast in 1951. At his burial ceremony a young Orthodox activist named Fidel Castro jumped on top of Chibás' grave and made a fiery speech denouncing the old establishment – the political debut of the most influential Cuban of the 20th century.

A bronze plaque at the corner of Calles 23 and 12, one block from the cemetery entrance, marks the spot where Fidel Castro proclaimed the socialist nature of the Cuban Revolution on April 16, 1961, at a funeral service for those killed during a counterrevolutionary raid on a Havana air base the previous day. Several art galleries, cinemas, shops, and cafeterias now grace this lively corner of Vedado.

Along the Malecón

Most visitors to Havana take a stroll along the **Malecón**, also called Avenida de Antonio Maceo, constructed soon after Cuban independence in 1902. From the Castillo de la Punta in La Habana Vieja the Malecón extends along the coast to the Río Almendares. The Malecón dives under the river in tunnels, continuing southwest through Miramar as Avenida 5 and eventually becoming the autopista to Mariel. Instead of walking east into town as most tourists do, consider walking west past some lesser-known sights. It's about eight km from La Punta to La Chorrera, another castle at the mouth of the Río Almendares. Just be aware that some rather shady characters hang out on the Malecón after dark.

The 24-story **Hospital Nacional Hermanos Ameijeiras** (1980), the highest building in Havana, undeniably dominates this part of the city. The clinics inside specialize in treating foreigners. Opposite the hospital is a monument to Antonio Maceo (1916), the mulatto general who cut a blazing trail across the entire length of Cuba during the 1895 War of Independence. Nearby is the 18th-century **Torreón de San Lázaro**, built as a watchtower by the Spanish.

West beyond the Hotel Nacional is a stretch of the Malecón known as Avenida Washington because the old US Embassy was here. In the center of the boulevard is the **Monumento a las Víctimas del Maine** (1926), which had an American eagle on top until the 1959 revolution. The current inscription on the side of the monument alludes to a Cuban theory that US agents deliberately blew up their own ship to create a pretext for declaring war on Spain: '*A las víctimas de El Maine que fueron sacrificados por la voracidad imperialista en su afán de apoderarse de la Isla de Cuba*' (To the victims of the *Maine* who were sacrificed by voracious imperialism in its desire to gain control of the island of Cuba). The rectangular seven-story building at the west end of this square is the former US Embassy. It now houses the US Interests Office.

Walk 10 minutes west along the Malecón. At Calle G you'll see the **Monumento a Calixto García** (1959), the Cuban general that US military leaders in Santiago de Cuba prevented from attending the Spanish surrender in 1898. The Cubans have never forgotten that slight. Twenty-four bronze plaques around the equestrian statue provide a history of García's 30-year struggle for Cuban independence. On Calle G just behind the monument is the **Casa de las Américas**, a major cultural institution sponsoring literary and artistic seminars, conferences, and exhibitions. Inside there's an art gallery (weekdays 10 am to 4:30 pm, admission US$2) and bookstore.

Two blocks southeast of the Casa de las Américas on Avenida G (formerly Avenida de los Presidentes) is the 10-story **Hotel Presidente** (1928), where foreign entertainers often stay while appearing in Havana. In the middle of the avenue next to the hotel is a former monument to Cuba's first president, Tomás Estrada Palma, who is now looked upon as a US puppet. His statue was toppled and all that remains of the monument is his shoes.

On the other side of Avenida G is the neo-baroque **Ministerio de Relaciones Exteriores**.

Continue one kilometer southwest along the Malecón toward the most recent bow to tourism, the 22-story **Hotel Meliá Cohiba** (1994) at the west end of Paseo. Overshadowed by this luxurious Spanish-operated establishment is the Hotel Riviera (1957), once a playground for US gangsters. In those days the large circular hall (on the right as you enter the lobby) was a gambling casino.

If you're still game, continue another 15 minutes southwest to the **Castillo de**

Santa Dorotea de La Luna de La Chorrera (1646) at the mouth of Río Almendares. A deluxe restaurant, the Mesón La Chorrera (daily 2 pm to 2 am), now occupies the castle's vaulted halls, and nearby you can get snacks and drinks at Los Jardines del 1830 (daily from noon to 4 pm). Two one-way tunnels dive under the river here.

On your way back to town you might stop at the **Museo de Artes Decorativas**, Calle 17 No 502 between D and E (Wednesday to Sunday 10 am to 4:45 pm, admission US$2). The sumptuous rooms of this stately mansion (1927), formerly owned by the Countess of Revilla de Camargo, are decorated in various styles: rococo, Regency, neoclassical, empire, English, oriental, and art deco.

Activities

Cubanáutica/KP Winter (☎ 33-4546, fax 33-4545), Paseo No 309 between 13 and 15, is a yacht charter operation, and their business is usually prebooked from abroad. You might be able to line up some yachting on the spot at a cheaper price, assuming a boat is available. They also arrange deep-sea fishing at the marinas Hemingway and Tarará. All-day trips (9 am to 6 pm) cost US$340 for up to six persons including lunch and transfers.

Language Courses

Mercadu SA (☎ 33-3893, fax 33-3028), Calle 13 No 951 at 8 in Vedado, organizes language and culture courses at La Universidad de Habana.

The Centro de Idiomas para Extranjeros José Martí, Calle 16 No 109 between Calles 1 and 3 in Miramar, offers language courses that should be booked ahead through the Grupo de Turismo Científico Educacional (☎ /fax 53-7-33-1697), Avenida 3 No 403 in Miramar. For more information turn to Courses in the Facts for the Visitor chapter.

Organized Tours

Rumbos Buro de Turismo at Obispo No 358 (daily 8:30 am to 5:30 pm) in La Habana Vieja and at Calle 23 at P in Vedado (daily 8:30 am to 6 pm), offers organized sightseeing excursions to Soroa (US$29), Cayo Levisa (US$69), Playas del Este (US$10), Guamá (US$39), Trinidad (US$89), Cayo Coco (US$89), Cayo Largo (US$94), Santiago de Cuba (US$139), and Baracoa (US$159). The company's city tour is US$10 and it organizes visits to the Tropicana Nightclub for US$35 and up.

Havanatur, Calle 23 and M below the Hotel Havana Libre in Vedado, offers similar excursions for about the same prices. Both companies routinely cancel their trips when not enough people sign up, so it's a good idea to check with both to get an idea which tour has the best chance of actually taking place.

Special Events

Annual events in Havana include: the Havana International Jazz Festival, which occurs every other even-numbered year in February; a two-week International Guitar Festival every other year in May; carnival during the last two weeks of July and the first week of August (presently suspended); the International Theater Festival every other year in late August or early September; the Festival of Contemporary Music in October; the International Ballet Festival in late October; the Havana Marathon in November; and the International Festival of Latin American Film in December. Since its inception in 1983 the Feria Internacional de La Habana, held at ExpoCuba in October or November, has been Cuba's largest annual trade fair.

There's no easy way to get reliable advance information on special events. In the US, Marazul Tours Inc. (mentioned under Getting There & Away) would be a good place to try. Otherwise, an office of the Cuban Tourist Board listed under Tourist Offices Abroad in Facts for the Visitor might be willing to help, although general printed information from them on events should be used with caution. If you try writing the organizers in Cuba, you may never get a response, so it's better to have a Spanish-speaker phone.

Places to Stay

Although we provide phone numbers for many hotels, calling ahead is not necessarily the best way to get a room. Rather, walking from hotel to hotel to see what's available is usually a better idea. Rarely are hotels full, and you'll gain a sense of the place when you see it. These hotel listings are ordered with this strategy in mind. Hotels in Miramar, Cojímar, Playas del Este, and elsewhere appear later in this chapter.

Budget travelers looking for a double room costing US$40 or less in the high season have a choice of the Caribbean, Lido, New York, Isla de Cuba, and Lincoln hotels in Centro Habana; the Universitario, Bruzón, and Morro hotels in Vedado; the Residencia Universitaria Ispjae and Villa Universitaria Miramar in Miramar; and Motel La Herradura in Parque Lenin. A number of places near the beach at Playas del Este also fit into this price range. In Vedado, the St John's and Vedado hotels are only a few dollars more. Touts around town offer private rooms (often misleadingly called 'apartments') in La Habana Vieja for US$15 to US$20 double, but they provide less privacy than the hotels just mentioned and some are rather basic. Have a look before committing yourself. (We can't mention specific addresses in this book as any home so listed would soon be overwhelmed by travelers.)

La Habana Vieja Havana's finest hotel may be the 28-room *Hotel Santa Isabel* on the east side of the Plaza de Armas. Originally the Palacio de Santovenia and a hotel only since the mid-19th century, this three-story edifice was upgraded to five-star standards in 1996 and the new rate was still unknown at press time (if you have to ask, the Santa Isabel probably isn't for you). The location is splendid.

Similar but less expensive is the *Hostal Valencia* (☎ 62-3801), Oficios at Obrapía. The 12 rooms in this mid-18th-century colonial mansion are US$27/42 single/ double (or US$35/46 with balcony) year-round. The Valencia reopened after renovations in 1989 and is presently under Spanish management, which explains why the hotel restaurant (daily noon to 10 pm) specializes in paella. The Valencia's courtyard is charming, but be aware that this hotel is heavily booked and you'd be lucky to get a room.

During his stays in Havana during the 1930s, author Ernest Hemingway put up at the five-story *Hotel Ambos Mundos* (☎ 61-4887), Obispo No 153 at Mercaderes. In 1996 the 54 rooms were undergoing a complete renovation and future prices were unknown.

Centro Habana Since the 1970s 'individual tourists' on something of a budget have been sent to the 14-story *Hotel Deauville* (☎ 62-8051, fax 33-8148), Avenida de Italia and Malecón. The 144 rooms with bath, TV, and balcony are US$43/50 single/ double in the low season, US$51/60 in the high season. Facilities include a swimming pool and cafeteria with a view of Havana on the roof of the six-story section, a good souvenir shop, hairdresser, disco, and Transautos car rental desk.

Hotel Lincoln (☎ 33-8209), Avenida de Italia between Virtudes and Ánimas, has 135 rooms with bath and TV at US$25/33 single/double in the low season, US$27/40 in the high season. This nine-story hotel was the second highest building in Havana at the time of construction in 1925. A bar is on the roof, and although most of the guests are Cuban, you'll also be welcome.

A good budget choice is the six-story *Hotel Lido* (☎ 62-2046), Consulado No 210 between Ánimas and Trocadero. It's quieter than the Caribbean and the 65 rooms with shower cost exactly the same price: US$19/25 single/double in the low season, US$26/35 in the high season. The Lido has a medium-priced restaurant.

The five-story *Hotel Caribbean* (☎ 33-8233), Paseo de Martí No 164 between Colón and Refugio, is one of the cheapest Havana hotels regularly catering to foreigners. The 35 rooms with bath and TV go for US$19/25 single/double in the low season, US$26/35 in the high season. It's a good value considering the location.

The *Hotel Sevilla* (☎ 33-8560, fax 33-8582), Trocadero No 55 between Paseo de Martí and Agramonte, is a colonial-style hotel that lives up to the Old World aura of its name. This 1908 structure was completely renovated in 1993, and in a city brimming with unique hotels this is another of the greats. In 1996 the French Accor chain assumed management of the Sevilla and further upgraded the property. The 178 rooms with bath and satellite TV are US$62/90 single/double in the low season, US$71/108 in the high season. It's the only hotel in the old town with a swimming pool, and there's also a sauna and fitness club. Its Patio Sevillano cafe off the lobby is open 24 hours a day, and the hotel restaurant near the front door lays out a breakfast buffet daily from 7 to 10 am (US$6). For an admirable view take the elevator up to the 9th-floor rooftop restaurant. Havanautos and Transautos car-rental agencies and several shops are also here.

The yellow-colored *Hotel Plaza* (☎ 33-8583, fax 33-8592), Agramonte No 267 at Neptuno, is an elegant four-story hotel built in 1908 with Spanish touches such as tile floors and neoclassical columns. The 188 rooms with shower and satellite TV are US$54/72 single/double in the low season, US$68/90 in the high season, and you can't beat the location. A 24-hour bar, rooftop terrace, and Transautos car-rental office are on the premises.

The neoclassical *Hotel Inglaterra* (☎ 33-8593, fax 33-8254), Paseo de Martí No 416 at San Rafael opposite Parque Central, is Havana's oldest functioning hotel and perhaps also its most charming. Erected in 1875, the Inglaterra was renovated in 1989. The 83 rooms with shower, satellite TV, mini-fridge, and neoclassical balconies are US$55/79 single/double in the low season, US$65/89 in the high season. The rooms with balconies overlooking the square can be noisy. The Inglaterra's rooftop La Terraza bar offers entertainment nightly.

Hotel New York (☎ 62-7002), Dragones No 156, has 94 rooms at US$18 single with bath and fan, US$34 double with bath and air-con (US$22 single in the high season).

This old five-story hotel is patronized mostly by Cubans.

The cheapest regular hotel in Havana is the four-story *Hotel Isla de Cuba* (☎ 62-1031), Máximo Gómez No 169. Erected in the 1880s, this is the second oldest hotel in Havana after the Inglaterra. Elegant wrought-iron railings highlight this little-known hotel, and the 67 fan-cooled rooms with bath are just US$14/17 single/double year-round. It's mostly Cubans who stay here, but they'll probably give non-Cubans a room.

Vedado The *Hotel Nacional* (☎ 33-3564, fax 33-5054), Calles 21 and O, is Havana's most opulent hotel. The hotel opened in 1930 and was renovated in 1992. Famous former guests include Winston Churchill, Ava Gardner, and Frank Sinatra. This huge eight-story edifice has 467 rooms with bath and satellite TV for US$105 to US$125 singles, US$152 to US$175 doubles in the low season; US$120 to US$155 singles, US$170 to US$220 doubles in the high season. (The presidential suite is US$1055.) The price for all rooms includes breakfast. The 6th floor has been designated the executive floor with its own reception, telex, fax, meeting rooms, and secretarial staff for business travelers. Among the Nacional's many facilities are two swimming pools, tennis courts, a pharmacy, barber shop, post office, shopping, Havanautos car-rental agency, guarded parking lot, taxi stand, and the Cabaret Parisién (closed Thursday). The hotel's Cadeca exchange office will give cash advances on Visa and Master-Card. Although not quite up to its advertised five stars, the Nacional remains an unforgettable Havana landmark.

The 17-story *Hotel Capri* (☎ 33-3747, fax 33-3750), Calle 21 between N and O, retains the flavor of the '50s even though the gambling casino closed in 1959 and mafia notables no longer frequent the rooftop swimming pool. The 214 rooms with bath and TV are US$45/60 single/double in the low season, US$53/70 in the high season. The main Transautos car-rental office is next door.

The five-story *Hotel Victoria* (☎ 33-3510, fax 33-3109), Calles M and 19, has 31 rooms with bath and satellite TV for US$80/100 single/double year-round. This mini deluxe hotel erected in 1928 and renovated in 1987 caters to business travelers. There's a small swimming pool.

The four-story *Hotel Universitario* (☎ 32-5506, fax 33-3022), Calle 17 at L opposite the Servi-Cupet gas station, has 21 rooms for US$30/40 single/double. Part of the income is used to buy textbooks for students.

The least expensive of the main Vedado tourist hotels is the 13-story *Hotel St John's* (☎ 33-3740), Calle O No 216 between 23 and 25. The 97 rooms with bath and TV are US$24/32 single/double in the low season, US$32/43 in the high season. There's a swimming pool, 24-hour snack bar, and 14th-floor Pico Blanco nightclub.

The eight-story *Hotel Vedado* (☎ 33-4072), Calle O No 244 between 23 and 25, is more of a package-tour place. At US$26/34 single/double in the low season, US$34/45 in the high season, the 192 rooms with bath and TV are reasonable, and the Vedado has a swimming pool and El Cortijo nightclub (closed Tuesday, US$5 minimum, couples only).

Havana's largest hotel, the *Habana Libre* (☎ 33-4011, fax 33-3141), Calles L and 23, was completed just prior to the 1959 revolution. Once part of the Hilton chain, it's now managed by Spain's Tryp Hotels. The 579 rooms with bath, satellite TV, and balcony cost US$55/88 single/double year-round. Even if you don't stay there, this hotel is useful for its many facilities, including a post office/telephone center, Photo Service branch, shops, Havanautos office, and taxi stand. Also here are a 2nd-floor swimming pool, a cafeteria (8 am to midnight), a bakery (next to the cafeteria), the Turquino bar on the 25th floor, and the 2nd-floor Cabaret Caribe (closed Monday). Foreign journalists and business travelers often stay here.

Near the university is the six-story *Hotel Colina* (☎ 32-3535), Calles L and 27, with 79 rooms with shower and TV at US$30/40 single/double in the low season, US$39/62 in the high season. It runs a 24-hour snack bar.

Cubans waiting to catch a bus out of town often stay at the *Hotel Bruzón* (☎ 70-3531), Bruzón No 217 between Pozos Dulces and Avenida de la Independencia next to the Terminal de Ómnibus Interprovinciales. This four-story hotel belonging to the Islazul chain has 48 rooms with bath at US$18/22 single/double.

The 10-story *Hotel Presidente* (☎ 33-4394), Calzada and G, wouldn't be out of place on a street just off Times Square in New York. Built in 1928 just before the Great Depression hit Cuba, it has 148 rooms with shower at US$39/54 single/double in the low season, US$48/72 in the high season (36 rooms are presently occupied by offices). The Presidente has a swimming pool, a 10th-floor bar, and a car-rental office.

The three-story *Hotel Morro* (☎ 33-3907), Calle 3 at D just off the Malecón, has 20 rooms with bath, fridge, and TV at US$21/28 single/double in the low season, US$29/38 in the high season. It's a good value if a little out of the way.

Overlooking the Riviera is the soaring 22-story *Meliá Cohiba* (☎ 33-3636, fax 33-4550), Paseo between 1 and 3, which is part of the Spanish Sol Meliá hotel chain. Opened in 1994, the hotel has 462 rooms with bath and satellite TV beginning at US$150/180/215 single/double/junior suite year-round. Rooms on the executive (20th) floor are US$195/225/275. Facilities include a swimming pool, fitness center, sauna, business center, shopping arcade, art gallery, the Ache Disco (open at 10:30 pm, admission US$15), bars, and restaurants. Fussy travelers should ask their agents to book them into this shiny five-star marble palace.

The 17-story *Hotel Riviera* (☎ 33-4051, fax 33-3739), Paseo and Malecón, opened in 1957. The 330 rooms with bath and TV are US$60/90 single/double year-round, although prices may increase in 1997 when renovations are complete. There are lots of facilities, including a swimming pool, buffet restaurant (downstairs), 24-hour coffee shop (near the pool), and Havanautos car-rental desk (downstairs). The Cadeca exchange office downstairs gives cash advances on Visa and MasterCard. Top salsa orchestras play in the Riviera's Palacio de la Salsa daily except Wednesday from 10 pm to 4 am. However, it's a long walk from here to the Vedado tourist district and even farther to old Havana.

Places to Eat

Most of the places mentioned below are run by state enterprises, but Havana also has many *paladares* (private restaurants of12 seats or less) where the food is often of a higher quality. However, the locations of these tend to change frequently. Below we describe the state-run restaurants first and then the paladares.

Beware of Havana paladares that charge high prices in dollars yet claim to be cheaper than the regular restaurants. Ask to see a printed menu and if you get the feeling you're being hustled, say you'll be back later and split.

If you tire of the hassle of finding a decent meal at a restaurant, consider hopping into a supermarket, produce market, or bakery. In La Habana Vieja, the supermarket at Brasil No 461 is open daily from 9 am to 9 pm. Fresh loaves of bread are sold for dollars at *Panadería San José*, Obispo No 161 (daily 8 am to 8 pm).

For a decent supermarket in Centro Habana, try *Almacenes Ultra*, Bolívar No 109 at the corner of Rayo (Monday to Saturday 9 am to 6 pm, Sunday 9 am to 1 pm). The main public market is the *Mercado Agropecuario Egido* on Avenida de Bélgica between Corrales and Apodaca.

In Vedado, you'll find a supermarket below the Edificio Focsa, Calle 17 at N (Monday to Saturday 9 am to 6 pm, Sunday 9 am to 1 pm). The *agromercado* at Calles 19 and A has fresh fruits, vegetables, and meats at local prices. Some stalls sell cooked food in cardboard boxes and picnic tables are nearby. Fresh loaves of bread are sold for dollars at *Panadería Karla*, Calle 21 No 52 and N (Monday to

Saturday 7 to 11 am and 3 to 7 pm). Bread is also sold through a window next to the cafeteria at the back of the lobby of the Hotel Habana Libre.

La Habana Vieja *Restaurante El Patio*, San Ignacio No 54 at Empedrado (daily noon to midnight), occupies the romantic inner courtyard of an old colonial palace on the Plaza de la Catedral. A complete meal (Cuban and international cuisine) costs around US$16. You can also get sandwiches, ice cream, and drinks on their pleasant terrace (open 24 hours) facing the Plaza de la Catedral.

Similar but less pretentious is *Restaurante Don Giovanni*, Tacón No 4 at Empedrado (noon to midnight) in the Moorish-style Casa de Aróstegui, erected in 1759. The menu consists mostly of Italian dishes such as pizza and spaghetti.

Much cheaper pizza and roast chicken is available at *Doña Isabel*, Empedrado between Tacón and Mercaderes (open 24 hours), just around the corner from Don Giovanni. This open-air venue is just off the Plaza de la Catedral. Even cheaper fried chicken (US$1.50) is served at a small open-air bar called *El Bosquecito* at the corner of O'Reilly and San Ignacio.

Two upmarket restaurants near the Plaza de Armas specialize in exotic oriental cuisine. *La Torre de Marfil*, Mercaderes No 111 between Obispo and Obrapía (daily noon to 10 pm), offers Cantonese food, while *Al Medina*, Oficios No 12 between Obrapía and Obispo (daily noon to 11 pm), serves Arab lamb and mutton dishes.

El Patio Colonial, Baratillo at the corner of Obispo just off Plaza de Armas, serves chicken and pork dishes on the terrace daily from 10 am to midnight. A fashion show is presented on Monday, Wednesday, and Friday nights, and from 11 pm to 3 am a disco operates in the adjacent hall. All day there's live music on the terrace.

Perfect for those on a tight budget, *Cafetería Torre La Vega*, Obrapía No 114a (daily 9 am to 7 pm), next to the Casa de México, serves large bowls of spaghetti at a high wooden bar for about one dollar.

DAVID STANLEY
Havana's skyline from El Castillo del Morro

DAVID STANLEY
Havana santero Rubén Gonzalez

RICK GERHARTER
Looking up in Havana

RICK GERHARTER
A sweet for your sweet?

RICK GERHARTER
Flowers say it all.

RICK GERHARTER

Construction of La Catedral de San Cristóbal de La Habana began in 1748.

DAVID STANLEY

Crafts market, Plaza de la Catedral

RICK GERHARTER

It took 5000 workers over three years to build El Capitolio Nacional.

RICK GERHARTER

Taking it all in at Plaza de Armas in La Habana Vieja

Cafe París, Obispo No 202 at San Ignacio (open 24 hours), specializes in light chicken meals and drinks, and there's often live music. Filling slices of pizza are dispensed from a takeout window on the side of the building.

La Lluvia de Oro, Obispo at Habana (open 24 hours), has a good selection of inexpensive light meals including spaghetti, pizza, chicken, hot dogs, sandwiches, ice cream, and beer. The atmosphere is nice with a long wooden bar and overhead fans. There's a public toilet at the rear of the restaurant.

La Zaragozana, Avenida de Bélgica between Obispo and Obrapía (daily noon to 11 pm), serves international cuisine and seafood amid air-conditioned splendor. Established in 1830, La Zaragozana is next door to the celebrated El Floridita of Hemingway fame but manages to be less snobbish.

Restaurante Hanoi, Brasil and Bernaza (daily noon to 11 pm), serves what any Cuban would expect at a good Vietnamese restaurant: typical Cuban dishes with a few pseudo-Vietnamese selections for the flavor. The Hanoi is not promoted as a tourist restaurant, and complete meals are available for under US$4.

Cafe de O'Reilly, O'Reilly No 203 between Cuba and San Ignacio, serves snacks and drinks 24 hours a day. Go up the stairway inside. *Doña Teresa* next to La Mina at Obispo No 109 (no sign) sometimes has caramel pudding *(natilla)*. *El Naranjal*, Obispo and Cuba (daily 10 am to 10 pm), is recommended for its Italian-style ice cream.

Centro Habana The Hotel Isla de Cuba on the south side of the Capitolio has a cheap *snack bar* open daily from noon to midnight.

Arabian cuisine is offered at the *Oasis Restaurant* in the Centro Cultural Cubano Arabe, Paseo de Martí No 258 (open daily 11 am to midnight). The menu is reasonable and there's a floorshow at 9 pm, 11 pm, and 1 am (US$5 minimum).

Cafetería Vea, San Rafael and Avenida de Italia (open 24 hours), serves up chicken, hot dogs, and beer. It's fast, easy, and unappetizing. *Burgui*, Neptuno and Avenida de Italia (open 24 hours), specializes in American fast food: hamburgers, chicken, and french fries.

El Pacífico, San Nicolás No 518 at Cuchillo (Tuesday to Sunday noon to 7 pm), serves authentic Chinese food in the heart of Havana's small but lively Chinatown. It's a bit hard to find, but look west of the Capitolio off Zanja, two blocks west of Avenida Italia. A disco cranks up in the evening.

Among the paladares worth trying is *Bar Restaurante La Esmeralda*, upstairs at Avenida de Bélgica No 653 near the train station (daily 1 pm to 1 am) – just be sure to clarify the prices when ordering.

Las Delicias de Consulado, upstairs at Consulado 309 between Neptuno and Virtudes (daily 1 pm to 1 am), has pork dishes for US$5. There's a nice terrace overlooking the street.

Vedado *Rumbos Cafetería*, Calle 23 and P (open 24 hours), has cold drinks and fast food (chicken, pizza, and so on).

Several inexpensive restaurants are near the Hotel St John's. *Restaurante Wakamba*, Calle O between 23 and 25 (daily 10 am to midnight), is an old-fashioned lunch counter serving pizza, spaghetti, and chicken. Across the street is *Maraka's Cafeteria* (daily 7 am to 5 am) with plastic models of their dishes including pizza, chicken, and sandwiches. *Disco-Pop El Cortijo*, Calles O and 25, operates as a budget restaurant. Open daily except Tuesday from noon to 10 pm, it offers pizza, hamburgers, chicken, and a few other meat dishes.

Vedado is full of upmarket tourist restaurants, such as *El Mandarín*, upstairs at Calle 23 No 34 at M, serving Chinese food. *Restaurante Bulerías*, on Calle L between 23 and 25 opposite the Hotel Habana Libre (noon to 7 pm), has Spanish cuisine; a lively disco operates here from 10 pm to 4 am (US$3.50 cover, US$1 for a beer).

Three upmarket state-run restaurants are on Calle 21: *Monseigneur*, Calles O and 21 opposite the Hotel Nacional (daily noon to midnight), has international cuisine; *El Caribeño*, Calles 21 and N (Wednesday to Monday noon to 10 pm), serves seafood; and *La Carreta*, Calle 21 at K (Friday to Wednesday noon to 6 pm), has Cuban cuisine. Clientele dressed in T-shirts or shorts are not appreciated at any of these.

El Conejito, Calle M No 206 at the corner of 17 (daily noon to midnight), is the place to taste rabbit, and most dishes sell for under US$10. If you can't handle the somber Tudor decor, check out the cheap beer garden behind the restaurant.

Restaurante La Torre, Calle 17 No 55 at the corner of M (daily noon to 11:30 pm), is on the top floor of the Edificio Focsa, 125 meters above the city. This 36-story apartment building – the highest in Havana – once housed Soviet technicians, and you get the best view of Havana from here. For such an upmarket place, the menu is surprisingly reasonable, consisting mostly of lobster, fish, and chicken dishes. The restaurant side of La Torre faces the city, while the bar (daily 11:30 am to 4 am) faces the sunset. The excellent view from the restaurant makes the leisurely service bearable.

Across the street from the Edificio Focsa is *Restaurante Don Agamenón*, Calle 17 No 60 between M and N (daily 9 am to 2 am), offering cheap pizza and chicken in the back courtyard and more expensive meals inside this old eclectic mansion.

Not far from the Riviera and Meliá Cohiba hotels is the *Centro Vasco*, Calles 3 and 4 (daily noon to 2 am), serving Spanish dishes. Also in this part of town is *Restaurante 1830*, Calzada No 1252 near the Almendares tunnels (daily noon to 10 pm), one of Havana's most elegant restaurants. In the evening there's live music and salsa dancing in the garden behind the restaurant (don't come on a windy night). The *Mesón La Chorrera* (daily 2 pm to 2 am) is in the old tower nearby, and light snacks are served in the garden daily from noon onwards.

As you might expect, there are many paladares around Vedado. *Restaurant-Cafeteria D'Oscar*, San Lázaro No 1061 between San Francisco and Espada, lies between Vedado and Centro Habana. *Paladar Hurón Azul*, Humboldt No 153 at P (daily noon to midnight), serves typical Cuban dishes.

Paladar Los Helechos de Trinidad, Calle 25 No 361 between K and L (daily noon to midnight), is one block south of the Hotel Havana Libre. *Restaurant Bar Bon Appetit*, Calles 21 and M (daily 12:30 to 11:30 pm), offers pork, fish, and chicken dishes for about US$3 a plate. *Restaurante Escorpión*, Calle 17 No 105 between L and M near the Hotel Universitario (daily 8 am to 2 am), sells pork, chicken, lobster, and shrimp dishes.

One reader recommends *Eddie's Paladar*, Calle B No 514 between 21 and 23 (no sign). You can get a full fish dinner here including a beer, dessert, and coffee for US$6. Not quite as good but cheaper is *Paladar La Última Instancia*, Calle D No 557 between 23 and 25.

Cubans trying to buy ice cream with pesos form tremendous lines at *Coppelia*, Calle 23 at L (daily 10 am to 2 am) in the park diagonally opposite Hotel Habana Libre. It's one of Havana's most popular meeting places.

Entertainment

The free *Cartelera* entertainment newspaper published every Thursday carries comprehensive listings of cinema programs, theatrical presentations, musical events, TV schedules, art galleries, museums, hotels, restaurants, bars, nightclubs, and general services. You can often pick up a copy at the reception or tour desk of the large hotels (such as the Habana Libre); otherwise visit the newspaper office at Calle 15 No 602 at C in Vedado.

Cinemas There are about 200 cinemas in Havana. Some have an 5 pm screening, and most have a screening at 8 pm.

In Centro Habana, *Cine Payret*, Paseo de Martí No 505 at San Martín opposite the

Capitolio, presents five showings daily in a building erected in 1878. On the opposite side of the Capitolio from the Payret is *Cine El Mégano*, Industria and San Martín. *Cinecito*, San Rafael and Consulado behind the Hotel Inglaterra, shows mostly films for children.

Also try *Cine Actualidades*, Avenida de Bélgica No 262 behind the Plaza Hotel, and *Cine Jigüe*, Avenida de Italia No 255 at Concordia.

In Vedado, film festivals are often held at *Cine La Rampa*, Calles 23 and O. *Cine Yara*, Calle 23 and L, opens at noon and offers five showings daily in three halls. (Cine Yara and the streets nearby are reputed to be frequented by gays and lesbians.) Further afield is *Cine Riviera*, Calle 23 No 507 near G.

Cine Charles Chaplin, Calle 23 between 10 and 12, is a venue for previews and special screenings daily except Tuesday at 5 and 8 pm. The International Festival of Latin American Film is held here in December. Nearby try *Cine 23 y 12*, Calle 23 and 12 (open Tuesday to Sunday from 2 to 9 pm).

If you're staying at the Riviera, Meliá Cohiba, Morro, or Presidente hotels, you could check *Cine Trianón* on Línea between Paseo and A (closed Monday).

Theaters The *Gran Teatro de La Habana*, Paseo de Martí and San Rafael in Centro Habana, is the seat of the acclaimed Ballet Nacional de Cuba, founded in 1948 by Alicia Alonso. The National Opera also performs here. The building also contains the Teatro García Lorca and several smaller concert halls where art films are often shown. You can count on some type of live musical performance almost every night (check the notices posted outside the theater). The ticket office is open Tuesday to Saturday from 10 am to 5 pm and on Sunday from 5 pm until the performance begins. Concert tickets average US$10, and you can request a tour of the theater throughout the day for US$2. Don't overlook the good bar inside.

Lighter fare is presented at *Teatro América*, Avenida de Italia No 253 between Concordia and Neptuno in Centro Habana. The vaudeville variety shows staged Saturday at 8:30 pm and Sunday at 4 pm can be fun.

The theater scene in Vedado is quite active. Important foreign groups usually appear at the *Teatro Nacional de Cuba* (☎ 79-6011), Paseo and 39 on the Plaza de la Revolución. The National Symphony Orchestra sometimes plays in the main hall or the smaller Sala Avellaneda or Sala Covarrubias.

If you understand Spanish, it's well worth attending a performance of the Grupo Teatro Rita Montaner in the *Sala Teatro El Sótano* (☎ 32-0630), on Calle K between 25 and 27 not far from the Habana Libre. Cuban contemporary theater is often presented here from Wednesday to Saturday at 8:30 pm, Sunday at 5 pm. The box office is open Wednesday to Saturday from 5 to 8:30 pm, Sunday 3 to 5 pm, and tickets cost around US$3.

The *Teatro Nacional de Guiñol* (☎ 32-6262), on Calle M between 17 and 19 near Hotel Victoria, presents puppet shows for children Saturday at 5 pm and Sunday at 10 am and 5 pm. From Tuesday to Thursday at 8:30 pm there are comedy shows (in Spanish) for adults.

Also be sure to check *Cafe Teatro Brecht* (☎ 32-9359), Calle 13 at I, where varied performances often take place on Friday and Sunday at 7 pm, Saturday at 8 pm. Tickets go on sale one hour before the performance, and obtaining them will be no problem unless an internationally known group is appearing.

Teatro Mella (☎ 3-8696), Línea No 657 between A and B, is noted for its Cuban contemporary theater and dance. Other times there are guest performances. If you have kids come to the children's show Sunday at 10 am.

Sala-Teatro Hubert de Blanck (☎ 3-6447), Calzada No 657 between A and B, is named for the founder of Havana's first conservatory of music (in 1885). Today you'll see variety shows in Spanish, often on weekends at 5 pm (admission US$3). Advance tickets are sold Wednesday to Friday from 3 to 6 pm, Saturday and Sunday 3 to 5 pm.

Cabarets The *Cabaret Nacional*, San Rafael and Paseo de Martí below the Gran Teatro de La Habana opposite Hotel Inglaterra, is open daily except Monday from 9 pm to 3 am (admission US$5). As at all the cabarets, minimum dress regulations apply (definitely no shorts or T-shirts, and preferably pants other than jeans and a proper shirt).

Cabaret Parisién in the Hotel Nacional (at the west end of the lobby), 21 and O, opens at 9 pm daily except Thursday (admission US$20).

Cabaret Caribe in the Hotel Habana Libre, Calles 23 and L, opens daily except Monday at 10 pm (admission US$10). The theater is on the 2nd floor up the circular stairway from the hotel's reception desk.

The *Palacio de la Salsa* in the Hotel Riviera, Paseo and Malecón (daily except Wednesday 10 pm to 4 am, admission US$10, beers US$3), is patronized mostly by foreigners and nouveau-riche Cubans. To get a table, you will have to arrive early or make a reservation in person. Though touristy and expensive, top salsa musicians such as Los Van Van, Isaac Delgado, and Manolín perform regularly at the Palacio, and it's a must if you go for this kind of thing.

Nightclubs The following three clubs are in Centro Habana. *Palermo*, San Miguel y Amistad (daily except Wednesday from 9 pm), is a local disco with live music. The disco at the *Hotel Deauville*, Avenida de Italia and Malecón (admission US$3), has operated for gays on Thursday nights, although this has changed in the past and should be double-checked.

La Pampa Disco, Malecón and Vapor opposite the Torreón de San Lázaro (daily except Monday from 10 pm to 4 am), has a show at 11 pm (US$1 cover charge).

The following clubs are in Vedado. *Cabaret Las Vegas*, Infanta No 104 between 25

and 27, presents dance music and a show daily from 10 pm to 6 am (US$5 a couple).

The *Pico Blanco* on the 14th floor of the Hotel St John's, Calle O between 23 and 25, opens nightly at 9 pm (US$3 cover). Monday is salsa night, and rumba music fills the room Saturday and Sunday from 3 to 6 pm.

Club 21, Calles 21 and N opposite the Hotel Capri, is a disco that opens daily from 8 pm to 6 am. Other clubs in this general area include *Club La Red* (☎ 32-5415), Calles 19 and L (closed Monday), and *Karachi Club*, Calles 17 and K (daily from 10 pm to 5 am, US$2 cover).

Two local discos west of here are *Discoteca Amanecer*, Calle 15 between N and O (daily except Monday from 10 pm to 4 am), and *Ecodisco*, Calles Línea and F (daily from 9 pm to 2 am).

Cabaret Rinconcito Disco Salsa, also known as the Rincón del Tango or El Pampero, draws many locals. It's in the Hotel Bruzón, Bruzón No 217, near the Plaza de la Revolución (daily except Monday from 9 pm to 3 am).

Rock *Patio de María* on Calle 37 between Paseo and 2 near the Teatro Nacional de Cuba, is a local youth hangout run by María Gattorno. Here you'll find Disco Mix (live salsa music) on Friday and Saturday from 9 pm to 2 am, and there are rock concerts every Sunday from 6 pm to midnight. Dancing lessons can be arranged. This unpretentious counterculture scene has received considerable media coverage in Cuba and abroad, partly due to Gattorno's AIDS-prevention educational work.

Folk & Traditional Music The *Casa de la Cultura de La Habana Vieja*, Aguiar No 509 between Amargura and Brasil, presents Afro-Cuban dancing Tuesday at 8 pm (free), folk singing by local residents Friday at 8 pm (free), and rumba dancing Saturday at 4 pm (US$2). More traditional folk music is played at the *Casa de la Trova*, San Lázaro No 661 near Parque Maceo, on Saturday afternoons.

It's worth visiting *El Hurón Azul*, the social club of the Unión de Escritores y Artistas de Cuba (UNEAC), Calles 17 and H in Vedado, on Saturday from 9 pm to 2 am. At that time you'll see and hear authentic Cuban *boleros* (ballads) performed in this open-air setting (admission US$3). Numerous Cuban intellectuals associated with UNEAC are usually in attendance.

Also outstanding is the Sábado de Rumba dancing held every other Saturday at 3 pm at the workshop of the *Conjunto Folklórico Nacional*, Calle 4 No 103 between Calzada and 5 in Vedado (admission US$3). The troupe specializes in Afro-Cuban dancing (all of the drummers are *santeros*), but performances don't happen every week, so check ahead.

Cafes The *Cafe Cantante*, below the Teatro Nacional de Cuba at Paseo and 39 (side entrance), is open daily from 10 am to 6 am as a bar. Nightly from 9 pm to 5 am there's disco dancing or live salsa music (admission US$10). No shorts, short-sleeved shirts, or hats may be worn inside.

Facing the Plaza de Armas, *La Mina*, Obispo No 109 between Oficios and Mercaderes (daily 9 am to 9 pm), is a popular place to sit on the terrace and sip drinks while enjoying live music and the passing parade. *Al Cappuccino* next door is similar (both are very much geared to tourists).

Cultural Centers Cultural events often take place at the *Fundación Alejo Carpentier*, Empedrado No 215 near the Plaza de la Catedral (weekdays 8 am to 5 pm). The foundation's home is a baroque palace built in the 1820s.

Also ask about cultural activities at the *Instituto Cubano de Amistad con los Pueblos*, Paseo No 406 between 17 and 19 in Vedado (open daily except Monday from 11 am to 11 pm). This elegant mansion constructed in 1926 contains a cafeteria.

French-speaking visitors may wish to visit the *Alliance Française* (☎ 33-3370), Calle G No 407 between 17 and 19 in Vedado. French films are shown on video Saturdays at 2 pm (free) and this would be

Keeping the beat on a güiro

a good place to meet Cubans interested in French culture. The Alliance organizes French courses for local students.

The *Casa de las Américas*, Calle 3 and G in Vedado, organizes conferences and exhibitions relating to the music, literature, and art of Latin America. Each year the Casa hosts one of the Spanish-speaking world's most prestigious literary contests with awards in the categories of novel, short story, poetry, essay, narrative, Brazilian literature, and Caribbean literature in English or Creole. An international seminar on Afro-Cuban culture is held here in August. Literary events take place here quite frequently.

Many important festivals are held at the *Casa de la Cultura de Plaza*, Calzada at 8 in Vedado. Most events begin at 4 pm.

Pubs/Bars Havana's most celebrated bar is *La Bodeguita del Medio*, Empedrado No 207 off Plaza de la Catedral (daily noon to 1 am), a favorite Havana haunt of

Ernest Hemingway. Since Hemingway's time a visit to La Bodeguita has become de rigueur, and notables such as Salvador Allende, Fidel Castro, Harry Belafonte, and Nat 'King' Cole have left their autographs on the wall. You should order a *mojito* (US$4), just as Papa used to do. The staff claim to serve the best *lechón asado* (roast suckling pig) in Cuba, though it's hard to get a table.

El Floridita, Obispo No 557 at Avenida de Bélgica (daily 11 am to midnight), also cashes in on the Hemingway legend as best it can. A bartender named Constante assured El Floridita's place in Cuban drinking history when he began using an electric mixer to make frozen daiquiris here in the 1920s. A decade later Hemingway arrived and the Ernest Hemingway Special (rum with grapefruit juice, lemon juice, and crushed ice) was created in his honor. If you'd like to order either at the long wooden bar, they're US$6 apiece. Resist the temptation to eat at El Floridita, as the food is mediocre and overpriced, and the service pretentious and slow.

Rather than rubbing elbows with the tour-bus crowd in El Floridita, you'd do better heading south on Avenida de Bélgica one block to Calle Obrapía where you can have a daiquiri at the *Monserrate Bar* for a sixth of the price quoted by the red-coated waiters in El Floridita.

Better yet, repair to *Bar Dos Hermanos*, Calle San Pedro No 304 at Sol near Muelle Luz (open 24 hours), a favorite hangout of the Spanish poet Federico García Lorca during his three months in Cuba in 1930. As at any good pub there are snacks such as oyster cocktails, meatballs, hamburgers, and chicken to go with the drinks. The salty atmosphere only adds to what is arguably the best bar in Havana.

The *Unión Francesa de Cuba*, Calle 21 and 6 in Vedado, has a public bar open 24 hours a day.

The *Casa de los Infusiones*, Calles 23 and G (10 am to 10 pm), is a bit of a nocturnal hangout for nonconformist youth, and often all you can get to drink is shots of rum straight.

Spectator Sports

Baseball games are held Tuesday, Wednesday, and Thursday at 8 pm, Saturday at 1:30 and 8 pm, and Sunday at 1:30 pm at the 58,000-seat *Estadio Latinoamericano*, Patria and Pedro Pérez in Cerro just south of Centro Habana. Entry costs three pesos.

Wrestling, boxing, weightlifting, volleyball, and basketball matches are held at the *Sala Polivalente Ramón Fonst* opposite the main bus station on Avenida de la Independencia.

Things to Buy

Shops & Markets The Palacio de la Artesanía, Cuba No 64 at Tacón (daily 9:15 am to 7 pm), housed in the Palacio de Pedroso erected in 1780, is the place to buy souvenirs, crafts, musical instruments, compact discs, clothing, and jewelry at fixed prices. You can haggle at the open-air handicraft market on nearby Plaza de la Catedral and Calle San Ignacio daily except Monday and Friday.

The Fondo Cubano de Bienes Culturales, Muralla and San Ignacio at Plaza Vieja (weekdays 10 am to 5 pm, Saturday 10 am to 1 pm), also sells original handicrafts and works of art. The Unidad de Filatelía, Obispo No 516 (Monday to Saturday 8 am to 2 pm), is Havana's philatelic bureau with stamps for collectors. Aborígenes, Calle Bernaza between Obispo and O'Reilly (weekdays 10:30 am to 7 pm, weekends 10:30 am to 5 pm), has T-shirts, ceramics, tapestries, and woodcarvings with Indian themes.

Gallería La Acacia, San Martín No 114 between Industria and Consulado behind the Gran Teatro de La Habana (weekdays 10 am to 4 pm, Saturday 10 am to 2 pm), sells antiques with export permits.

The main shopping streets for Cubans are San Rafael and Avenida de Italia in Centro Habana. Variadades Galiano, San Rafael and Avenida de Italia (Mònday to Saturday 10 am to 5:30 pm), is the former Woolworth, as you could guess from the lunch counters inside. You can pay in Cuban pesos here. Several similar stores are north along Avenida de Italia.

The Area de Vendedores por Cuenta Propia, Máximo Gómez No 259 at Suárez (Monday to Saturday 7 am to 6 pm, Sunday 7 am to 1 pm), is a permanent flea market where you can pick up santería beads, old books, leather belts, and so on. Much more of the same is available at the large open-air market at the corner of Bolívar and Aguila (daily).

The Artex shop opposite the Hotel Habana Libre, Calles L and 23 in Vedado (Monday to Saturday 9 am to 9 pm, Sunday 10 am to 4 pm), has a good selection of compact discs, cassettes, posters, books, crafts, and souvenirs.

Art Galleries When buying art at an official outlet always ask for a receipt to show Cuban customs, especially if the object won't fit in your suitcase and will be obvious. To control black marketeering, officials sometimes confiscate undocumented artwork at the airport. Art objects legally purchased at any of the hard-currency galleries mentioned below may be exported duty free when validated by receipts.

The following galleries are in La Habana Vieja. The Taller Experimental de Gráfica in Callejón del Chorro off Plaza de la Catedral (weekdays 10 am to 4 pm) sells engravings and prints that you can watch being made on the premises. The Galería Víctor Manuel is on the corner of the square nearby.

The Galería Horacio Ruiz in the Palacio del Segundo Cabo, O'Reilly No 4 on Plaza de Armas (Monday to Saturday 10 am to 4 pm), has colorful papier-mâché objects, jewelry, and tie-dyed clothing.

Galería Roberto Diago, Muralla No 107 at San Ignacio (weekdays 10 am to 5 pm, Saturday 10 am to 1 pm), specializes in naive paintings.

The Taller de Serigrafía René Portocarrero, Cuba No 513 between Brasil and Muralla (weekdays 9:30 am to 6 pm), has paintings and prints by young Cuban artists in the US$100 to US$200 range. You can see the artists at work here.

The following galleries are in Centro Habana. Galería Orígenes in the Gran Teatro de La Habana on Paseo de Martí opposite Parque Central (daily 10 am to 6 pm) exhibits paintings and sculpture for sale.

Galería La Acacia on San Martín between Industria and Consulado (weekdays 10 am to 4 pm, Saturday 10 am to 2 pm) has paintings by leading artists.

Also have a look at the paintings and sculpture at Galería Galiano, Avenida de Italia No 258 at Concordia opposite Teatro América (Tuesday to Saturday 10 am to 5 pm). If you see something you like, you must negotiate a price directly with the artist.

These galleries are in Vedado. Galería Ciudades del Mundo, Calle 25 at L (weekdays 8:30 am to 5 pm), presents expositions on Havana and other cities of the world.

The Centro de Arte 23 y 12, Calle 12 at 23 (Tuesday to Saturday 10 am to 5 pm), features contemporary Cuban art.

Other art galleries are at the Casa de las Américas, Calles 3 and G (weekdays 10 am to 4:30 pm, admission US$2), and at the Unión de Escritores y Artistas de Cuba, Calles 17 and H.

Getting There & Away

Air Cubana's head office (☎ 33-4949), Calle 23 No 64 at Infanta at the Malecón end of the Airline Building (no sign), deals with international flights. It's open weekdays from 8:30 am to 4 pm, Saturday 8:30 am to noon. For domestic flights you must go to the Cubana office at the corner of Infanta and Humboldt in Vedado (weekdays 8:15 am to 2 pm).

Other airline offices are either in the Airline Building, Calle 23 No 64 between P and Infanta in Vedado, or at the Hotel Habana Libre, Calle 23 and L, also in Vedado:

Aerocaribbean
    Airline Building (☎ 33-4543, fax 33-5016)
Aerocaribe
    Airline Building (inside), entrance between
    Aeroflot and LTU

Aeroflot-Russian Airlines
    Airline Building (☎ 33-3200)
Aerolíneas Argentinas (represented by Iberia)
ALM Antillean Airlines
    Airline Building (inside), entrance between
    Aeroflot and LTU (☎ 33-3730, fax 33-3729)
AOM French Airlines
    Airline Building (inside), entrance between
    Aeroflot and LTU (☎ 33-3997, fax 33-3783)
Condor (represented by LTU)
    Airline Building (☎ 33-3524)
Iberia
    Airline Building (☎ 33-5041)
Lacsa
    Hotel Habana Libre (☎ 33-3114)
Ladeco Airlines
    Hotel Habana Libre (☎ 33-3252)
LTU International Airlines
    Airline Building (☎ 33-3524)
Martinair
    Airline Building (inside), entrance between
    Aeroflot and LTU (☎ 33-4364, fax 33-3729)
Mexicana de Aviación
    Airline Building (☎ 33-3531, fax 33-3077)
TAAG
    Airline Building (inside), entrance between
    Aeroflot and LTU (☎ 33-3527)
Viasa
    Hotel Habana Libre (☎ 33-3228)

Bus Buses to all parts of Cuba depart from the Terminal de Ómnibus Interprovinciales, Avenida de la Independencia and Calle 19 de Mayo near the Plaza de la Revolución. You can ask about tickets at the Lista de Fallos (waiting list) office upstairs; just be aware that there are long lines and no special preference for dollar-paying foreigners. In short, you're better off taking a train.

The Buró de Reservaciones, Calles 21 and 4 in Vedado (weekdays 7 am to 2:15 pm, Saturday 7 to 10:45 am), is supposed to issue bus reservations, but again foreigners and Cubans are treated the same and you'll face large crowds. Just get a number and wait in line for your turn. If you wish to try the buses, come as far in advance of your preferred departure date as possible.

Train Trains to most parts of Cuba depart from the Estación Central de Ferrocarriles, Avenida de Bélgica and Arsenal on the south side of La Habana Vieja. Foreigners must buy tickets for dollars at the Ladis office at the back side of the station near the corner of Arsenal and Cienfuegos (daily 8 am to 5 pm). Here you'll be given priority and offered a ticket with a seat reservation. Services include:

Bayamo	daily, 14 hours, US$26
Camagüey	three daily, 537 km, 8½ hours, US$22
Ciego de Ávila	three daily, 435 km, 6½ hours, US$18
Cienfuegos	daily, seven hours, US$11
Holguín	daily, 747 km, 13 hours, US$31
Las Tunas	two daily, 657 km, 9½ hours, US$27
Manzanillo	daily, 16 hours, US$28
Matanzas	seven daily, 92 km, 1½ hours, US$3.50
Pinar del Río	daily, seven hours, US$6.50
Sancti Spíritus	daily, eight hours, US$13.50
Santa Clara	four daily, 281 km, four hours, US$12
Santiago de Cuba	daily, 856 km, 14½ hours, US$35

The Estación de Ferrocarriles 19 de Noviembre, Calle Tulipán in Nuevo Vedado, has trains to points in the Province of Havana, including two to Artemisa (three hours), two to Surgidero de Batabanó (2½ hours), six to San Antonio de los Baños (one hour), and four to Wajay (one hour). Twice daily from Wednesday to Sunday there's railcar service to ExpoCuba (40 minutes). Expect long lines at this station and no priority for dollar-paying tourists.

For information about the electric train from Casablanca to Matanzas, turn to the Casablanca section below.

Taxi Collective taxis take passengers from Calle 19 de Mayo opposite Terminal de Ómnibus Interprovinciales to Pinar del Río (US$5), Cienfuegos (US$10), and Varadero (US$8). Out of fear of being fined by the police, most drivers are reluctant to accept foreign passengers, but it's always worth a try. To use a metered tourist taxi for such a trip would be prohibitively expensive (over US$100 to Varadero for the car).

Boat Tickets for the ferry and hydro-foil from Surgidero de Batabanó to Nueva Gerona on Isla de la Juventud are sold upstairs in the Terminal de Ómnibus Inter-provinciales, Avenida de la Independencia and Calle 19 de Mayo near the Plaza de la Revolución. The same office handles tickets for the connecting bus from Havana. Turn to the Isla de la Juventud chapter for more information.

Getting Around
To/From the Airport José Martí Inter-national Airport is at Rancho Boyeros, 25 km southwest of Havana via Avenida de la Independencia. There are three terminals here. Terminal No 1 on the southeast side of the runway handles all Cubana flights, both domestic and international, scheduled Aerocaribbean flights, and Iberia flights. Opposite on the north side of the runway but three km around by road is Terminal No 2, which receives all other international flights. Charter flights to Cayo Largo and elsewhere use the Terminal Caribbean at the northwest end of the runway, five km west of terminal No 2.

A tourist taxi to most Havana hotels will cost about US$10 for the car from the arrivals door of any of these terminals. Private taxis (with yellow license plates) parked outside the departures door at Terminal No 1 begin by asking US$10 for the trip into town but will come down to US$8 after bargaining. A taxi between Terminal No 1 and Terminal No 2 should cost about US$2.

Buses marked 'Aeropuerto' to the Parque Central and Vedado depart Terminal No 1 about 15 minutes after the arrival of all domestic Cubana flights. Rides cost one peso and take about an hour to reach town. To catch this bus from the Parque Central to Terminal No 1, look for the line of people seated on stone benches near the José Martí statue and ask for *el último* (the last in line). Service is infrequent, but there's usually one around noon.

If you don't mind walking a bit under a kilometer east from Terminal No 1 or 2 to the main highway, you can use bus No M-2, which runs from Santiago de las Vegas to Calle Bolívar between Industria and Amistad on the west side of Parque Fraternidad in Centro Habana. If you're boarding at Parque Fraternidad, note that there are two separate lines here, one for persons who want seats (*sentados*) and another for those willing to stand (*de pie*). Of course, the line of standers moves faster, but if you're not in a hurry, it's best to continue waiting in the line of sitters as it's a long trip.

Transautos and Havanautos have offices open 24 hours a day outside Terminal No 1. Havanautos, Transautos, National/Gaviota, and Cubanacán/Cubacar all have kiosks beyond the parking lot outside Terminal No 2. The Banco Nacional de Cuba branches in Terminals No 1 and 2 give cash advances on Visa and MasterCard.

Bus As a result of fuel shortages and a lack of spare parts, Havana's bus service has been greatly reduced. City buses are called *guaguas* (pronounced 'wawas'), but some prefer the term *aspirinas* for the relief their arrival provides after a long wait. In the city center the fare is usually a flat 10 centavos, which you must toss into a box near the driver. Unfortunately there is no bus-route map available.

There are lines (*colas*) at most bus stops (*paradas*) even though it may not appear so at first glance. To mark your place ask for *el último* (the last in line), and when the bus arrives get behind that person. This excellent system, which reduces pushing, is rigorously followed.

To take a bus to places outside town such as Cojímar, Alamar, Guanabo, and Guana-bacoa, you should try to board at the origi-nating point of the bus (listed below under the sections dealing with those destina-tions), as the buses are often so full they don't stop at subsequent stops. Many of the older buses to Miramar and Guanabo leave from near the train station. Buses No 67 and 264 run between Centro Habana and Vedado.

Since 1995 the public transportation crisis in Havana has been eased by the introduction of Metro buses, popularly called *camelos* (camels) for their two humps. These huge buses are hauled by trucks and all have the prefix M before their number:

M-1	Alamar-Vedado via Fraternidad
M-2	Fraternidad-Santiago de las Vegas via the airport
M-4	Fraternidad-San Agustín via Marianao
M-6	Calvario-Vedado
M-7	Fraternidad-Alberro via Cotorro

As you can see, many of the Metro buses leave from Parque de la Fraternidad on the south side of the Capitolio in Centro Habana.

Train The Estación Cristina, Avenida de México and Arroyo, Cuatro Caminos, lies south of Centro Habana and about a kilometer southwest of the Estación Central de Ferrocarriles. It handles local trains within the city limits. At last report there were eight trains a day to Boyeros; these could be used to reach Parque Lenin (Galápago de Oro Station) and airport Terminal No 1. Four times a day trains run to Cotorro, passing near the Museum Hemingway and Santa María del Rosario. Wednesday to Sunday one train a day leaves for ExpoCuba around noon. In July and August only, there's a train from here to Guanabo (1½ hours). Cristina was the first train station built in Havana and in 1996 it was completely renovated. It's worth checking out if you're spending some time in Havana and want to get around cheaply.

Car To rent a car, try Havanautos (☎ 33-2369, fax 33-1416), Calle 36 No 505 between 5 and 5a in Miramar. It also has offices open 24 hours a day at both terminals of José Martí International Airport and desks at the Habana Libre, Nacional, Riviera, and Sevilla hotels. The main Transautos office is next to the Hotel Capri, Calle 21 between N and O in Vedado, and there are desks at the Deauville, Plaza, and Sevilla hotels.

Guarded parking is available at the Parqueo Parque El Curita, Avenida de Italia and Bolívar in Centro Habana (US$1 should be enough).

In Vedado use the guarded parking lot at the Hotel Nacional, which charges a set fee of US$1 to park from 7 am to 7 pm or 7 pm to 7 am. If you overlap another 12-hour period you must pay a second fee.

There are three Servi-Cupet gas stations in Vedado: at Calle L at 17; at Malecón and 15; and at Malecón and Paseo near the Riviera and Meliá Cohiba hotels. All are open 24 hours a day. South of the center, there's a Servi-Cupet station at Santa Catalina and Vento in La Víbora.

Taxi Metered tourist taxis are readily available at all of the upmarket hotels, with the air-conditioned Nissan taxis charging slightly higher tariffs than the non-air-conditioned Ladas. The cheapest official taxis are operated by Panataxi (☎ 81-0153). Tourist taxis can be ordered from Turistaxi (☎ 33-5539), Cubanacán (☎ 33-6312), Gaviota (☎ 33-1730), and Cubalse (☎ 33-6558).

Private pirate taxis with yellow license plates are a bit cheaper, but you must agree on the fare before getting into the car and carry exact change. A whole row of private taxis is always parked in the middle of the street on the east side of Parque Central in Centro Habana.

Bicycle Panaciclos (☎ 81-0153), Avenida de la Independencia and Santa Ana, southwest of the Plaza de la Revolución (open 24 hours), rents bicycles at US$1 an hour, US$10 a day (24 hours), or US$50 a week. They'll deliver bicycles to your hotel for US$1 per bicycle, plus another US$1 to pick them up. You can buy a used bicycle from Panaciclos for US$60 (the same amount you'll be charged if you lose the bicycle). Call and ask for Santiago.

It's much cheaper to rent a bicycle privately from a local resident and this is easily arranged if you're staying in a private room. Always use the ubiquitous bicycle *parqueos* and lock the bike securely.

Boat Passenger ferries across the harbor to Regla and Casablanca leave every 10 or 15 minutes from Muelle Luz, San Pedro and Santa Clara on the southeast side of La Habana Vieja. The fare is a flat 10 centavos. Since the ferries were hijacked to Florida in 1994 (and later returned), security has been tightened.

Outer Havana

PLAYA & MARIANAO

The municipality of Playa, west of Vedado across the Río Almendares, includes the prestigious residential neighborhoods of Miramar, Cubanacán, Flores, Siboney, Atabey, Barlovento, and Santa Fe. To the south is the more proletarian municipality of Marianao.

Most of Havana's foreign embassies are in Miramar, and business travelers could consider staying at one of large resort hotels there to have easy access to the many facilities originally created to serve the diplomatic community. Those interested primarily in sightseeing and entertainment, however, will find commuting to Vedado or the old town a continual nuisance or expense.

Many of Havana's business or scientific fairs and conventions take place at Cubanacán where there are also several specialized medical institutes. Despite the austerity of the período especial, vast resources have been plowed into biotechnological and pharmaceutical research institutes in this area. Yachties, anglers, and scuba divers will find themselves using the Marina Hemingway at Playa's west end. Marianao is noted mostly for the Tropicana Nightclub, Cuba's most famous cabaret.

Information

Immigration Travelers should arrange extensions of stay at the 'Control de Extranjeros' immigration office on Calle 20 between 3 and 5 in Miramar (weekdays 8 am to 4:30 pm).

Money The various foreign banks in this area deal only in commercial transactions and are closed to the public. You must change money at your hotel or use the banks in Vedado.

Post & Communications A post office is at Calle 42 No 112 between 1 and 3 near Hotel Copacabana (weekdays 8 to 11:30 am and 2 to 6 pm, Saturday 8 to 11:30 am).

Courier service is available from DHL Worldwide Express (☎ 33-1578), nearby at the corner of Avenidas 1 and 42 in Miramar (weekdays 9 am to 6 pm, Saturday 9 am to noon).

Another local post office is on Calle 110 between 3 and 5 in Miramar (Monday to Saturday 8 am to 6 pm).

Travel Agencies Cubanacán Express (☎ 33-2331, fax 33-2584), Avenida 5 No 8210 between 82 and 84, Miramar (weekdays 8 am to 12:30 pm and 1:30 to 5 pm), sells plane tickets and offers a courier service.

The Grupo de Turismo Científico Educacional (☎ 33-1697), Avenida 3 No 402 at 4 in Miramar, runs the Centro de Idiomas para Extranjeros José Martí, a well-known language school described under Courses in Facts for the Visitor.

Laundry Aster Tintorería y Lavandería (☎ 33-1622), Calle 34 No 314 between 3 and 5 in Miramar (Monday to Saturday 8 am to 5 pm), charges per piece, and there's a 12% surcharge for pickup and delivery.

Medical Services Top-quality medical attention is available at the Clínica Central Cira García (☎ 33-2811, fax 33-1633), Avenida 41 and Calle 18A in Miramar, a 42-room clinic that specializes in treating foreigners. This is one of the only places in Havana where you can buy foreign patent medicines (the pharmacy is open 24 hours). Cira García also has a dental section.

Imported patent medicines are also available at the Farmacia Internacional,

PLACES TO STAY
1 Villa Paraíso
2 Hotel El Viejo y el Mar
10 Hotel Biocaribe
14 Hotel El Comodoro
16 Hotel Sol Habana
17 Complejo Neptuno-
    Tritón
20 Hotel Chateau Miramar
22 Villa Universitaria
    Miramar
24 Hotel Copacabana
32 Residencia Universitaria
    Ispjae
37 Hotel Sierra Maestra
45 Hotel El Bosque
46 Hotel Kohly

PLACES TO EAT
3 La Ferminia
4 Supermercado Flores
5 El Ranchón
13 La Cecilia
17 Supermercado 70
26 Panadería Doña Neli
28 Morambón
30 El Aljibe
34 Restaurante El Tocororo
38 Media Noche
39 El Pavo Real
40 La Casa de 5 y 16

OTHER
5 Pabexpo
6 Palacio de las
    Convenciones
8 Centro Nacional de
    Investigaciones Científicas
9 Centro de Ingeniería Genética
    y Biotecnología
11 Instituto Superior de Arte
12 Servi-Cupet Gas Station
15 Cubanacán Express
18 Museo Marcha del Pueblo
    Combatiente
21 Russian Embassy
23 Acuario Nacional
25 Post Office
27 British Embassy
29 Canadian Embassy
31 Pabellón para la Maqueta
    de la Capital
33 Immigration Office
35 French Embassy
36 Teatro Karl Marx
41 Tienda La Maison
42 Servi-Cupet Gas Station
43 Casa de la Música, Max Music
44 Clínica Central Cira García
47 Estadio Pedro Marrero
49 Tropicana Nightclub
49 Servi-Cupet Gas Station
50 Museo de la Alfabetización

Playa & Marianao

0   .5   1 km
0   .25   .5 miles

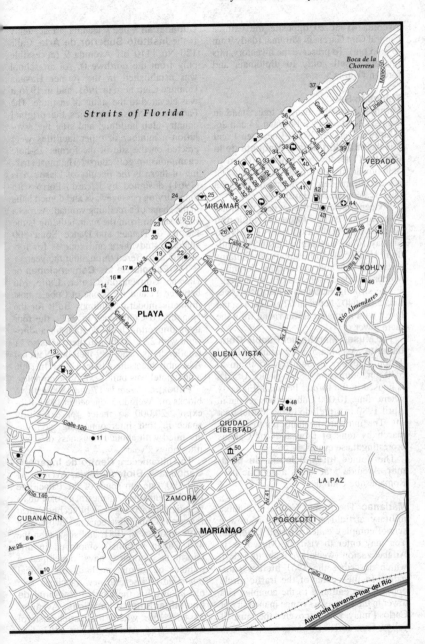

Avenida 41 at 20 opposite the Clínica Central Cira García in Miramar (daily 9 am to 8:45 pm). To preserve the inventory, this pharmacy sells only to diplomats and foreign visitors.

Things to See

Miramar Immense banyan trees stand in the park on Avenida 5 between 24 and 26. Nearby at Calle 28 No 113 between 1 and 3 is the **Pabellón para la Maqueta de la Capital** (Tuesday to Saturday 10 am to 5:30 pm, admission US$3, students US$1); it's an ultramodern pavilion containing a huge scale model of Havana.

Sixteen blocks southwest near the Hotel Copacabana is the **Acuario Nacional**, Avenida 1 No 6002 at Calle 60 (Tuesday to Sunday 10 am to 6 pm, adults US$2, children US$0.50). This aquarium contains saltwater fish and performing dolphins. Videos on related subjects can be viewed.

The striking **Russian Embassy**, Avenida 5 No 6402 between 62 and 66, is a tall tower with a smaller tower rising from the main tower.

The **Museo Marcha del Pueblo Combatiente**, Avenida 5 at 72 near the Hotel Tritón (Monday to Saturday 9:30 am to 5:30 pm, admission US$1, photos US$1), is housed in the former Peruvian Embassy where some 10,000 Cubans took refuge in April 1980 in a prelude to the Mariel boat lift. The museum contains photos of the march by tens of thousands of Cubans protesting these events.

The domed **Iglesia Jesús de Miramar**, Avenida 5 at 82, is a gigantic neo-Romanesque church.

Marianao The former Cuartel Colombia military airfield at Marianao is now a school complex called **Ciudad Libertad**. You may enter to visit the Museo de la Alfabetización (weekdays 8 am to 5 pm), which describes the 1961 literacy campaign. In the center of the traffic circle opposite the entrance to the complex is a tower in the form of a syringe in memory of Carlos Finlay, who discovered the cause of yellow fever in 1881.

Cubanacán Cuba's leading art academy is the **Instituto Superior de Arte**, Calle 120 No 1110 off Avenida 9 (accessible only from the northwest). An art school was established in the former Havana Country Club here in 1961, and in 1976 it was elevated to the status of institute. The Faculty of Music occupies the original country-club building, and after the revolution a number of other facilities were erected on the site of the former 18-hole championship golf course. The most striking of these is the Faculty of Plastic Arts (1961) designed by Ricardo Porro with long curving passageways and domed halls in the shape of a reclining woman. Across a small stream from the main building is the Faculty of Theater and Dance. Some 800 students study here and courses for foreigners are offered throughout the year.

The **Palacio de las Convenciones** or Havana Convention Center, Calle 146 between 11 and 13, is one of Cuba's most dramatic modern buildings. Built for the Nonaligned Conference in 1979, the four interconnecting halls contain an auditorium with 2200 seats, and there are also 11 smaller halls. The 589-member National Assembly meets here twice a year. In 1996 a new hotel was built next to the complex.

Pabexpo, Avenida 17 and 180, just two blocks off Avenida 5, opened in 1987. Pabexpo's 20,000 sq meters of exhibition space in four interconnecting pavilions are filled with about 15 business or scientific shows a year.

The ultramodern **Centro de Ingenieria Genética y Biotecnología**, Avenida 31 and 190, one km south of the Palacio de las Convenciones, is the focus of Cuba's genetic engineering and biotechnological research. Cuba first became involved in biotechnology in 1981, and since then the 400 Cuban scientists employed in this enormous complex have developed a number of unique methods of medical treatment and several new vaccines. Two blocks away is the **Centro Nacional de Investigaciones Científicas**, Avenidas 25 and 158, where the anticholesterol wonder drug Ateromixol, or PPG, was created. This remarkable work has been conducted without foreign assistance, and it possibly holds the key to a world-class pharmaceutical industry of the future.

Activities

The **Marina Hemingway** (☎ 33-1150, fax 33-1149), Avenida 5 and Calle 248 in Barlovento, 20 km west of central Havana, has four channels each 15 meters wide, 4½ meters deep, and one km long. Each channel has berths capable of accommodating 100 cruisers or yachts. Several restaurants, a shopping center, a telecommunications center, and various upmarket hotels are at Marina Hemingway. The port office is near Papa's Restaurant but cruising yachts clear customs at a wharf near Villa Paraíso two km west of Marina Hemingway. You can call the marina over channel 72 (VHF). Cruising yachts are not allowed to stay in Havana Harbor itself.

Scuba diving and deep-sea fishing can be arranged in the small office labeled Renta de Yates (☎ 33-6848 or 21-5277) upstairs in the building marked 'Watersports' next to Papa's Restaurant at the Marina Hemingway. Scuba diving costs US$25 a dive including equipment (initiation US$15). Three hours of deep-sea fishing for up to five persons costs US$110, US$170, or US$210 depending on the boat (extra hours US$30 to US$50 each) with a captain, sailor, and tackle included. The same office offers water-skiing or jet-ski rentals at US$15 for 15 minutes. Hotel tour desks should also be able to arrange these things.

For information on the Ernest Hemingway International Marlin Fishing Tournament held here in May, turn to Fishing in the Activities section of the Facts for the Visitor chapter.

Places to Stay

Kohly *Hotel Kohly* (☎ 33-0240), Calle 49 and Avenida 36A, just across the Río Almendares from Nuevo Vedado, is in a quiet neighborhood, but it's rather remote from everything. The 136 rooms with bath and satellite TV all cost US$52/62 single/double year-round, but get one well away

from the loud recorded music at the swimming pool. This modern five-story hotel contains two tennis courts, a sauna, and a gymnasium. A National Rent-a-Car desk is in the lobby, and the Kohly's Pizzería Mi Patio (accessible from the parking lot) serves inexpensive pizza and beer daily from noon to midnight.

Hotel El Bosque (☎ 33-9232, fax 33-5637), Calle 28A between 49A and 49B, only opened in 1995. In this five-story building on the hillside, the 62 rooms with bath, mini-fridge, and satellite TV cost US$42/54 year-round including breakfast (this introductory price could increase). There's a swimming pool, tennis court, cabaret, and National Rent-a-Car office. Secretarial services are available for business travelers.

Miramar The 13-story, 80-room *Hotel Sierra Maestra* (☎ 23-6561), on the coast at Avenidas 1 and 0, was being converted into an office building in 1996, but the final project may also include hotel rooms.

Hostal Icemar (☎ 33-0043), Calle 16 No 104, has 40 rooms at US$32/52 single/double including breakfast. This three-story student residence is in a nice area, but it's overpriced for what it offers.

A better value is the *Residencia Universitaria Ispjae* (☎ 23-5370), Avenida 1 at 22. Its eight rooms with bath cost US$25/36 single/double with breakfast, US$30/46 with breakfast and lunch, or US$35/56 with all three meals. These twin two-story buildings facing the ocean bear no sign; the reception is in the bar inside.

The five-story *Hotel Copacabana* (☎ 33-1037, fax 33-2846), Avenida 1 and Calle 44, is a 168-room hotel complex charging US$76/100 single/double year-round for a room with bath and TV. A room with a balcony goes for US$8 extra. It's right on the coast, and although there's no beach, a seawall creates a protected pool. There's also a regular swimming pool. Aquascooters can be hired to explore the coast and there are tennis courts. The Ipanema Disco and a Transautos car rental agency are also on the premises.

The *Hotel Chateau Miramar* (☎ 33-1952, fax 33-0224), Avenida 1 between 62 and 64, is a stylish five-story hotel. The 50 rooms with bath, fridge, and satellite TV are US$106/130 single/double year-round. There's a post office at the reception, and a swimming pool next to the sea.

The *Villa Universitaria Miramar* (☎ 33-1034), Calle 62 No 508 at Avenida 5A, has 25 rooms with bath for US$14/15 single/double. Ask at the *gerencia* upstairs in the restaurant building between 9 am and 3 pm. The guest rooms themselves are in another two-story building one block away.

The dismal, characterless *Complejo Neptuno-Tritón* (☎ 33-1606, fax 33-0042), on the coast at Avenida 3 and Calle 70, features two 22-floor hotel towers built in 1979. Each tower contains 261 overpriced rooms with bath and TV at US$90 single or double in the low season, US$110 in the high season. A large swimming pool stands next to the rocky shore, and Havanatur, Cubana Airlines, Rumbos, and Transautos all have booking offices at the reception. The Neptuno-Tritón was closed for renovations in 1996.

Presently under construction next to the Neptuno-Tritón is the 420-room *Hotel Sol Habana*, Avenida 3 between 78 and 80, to be managed by the Spanish Sol Meliá hotel chain. Its grand opening is scheduled for November 1997.

Hotel El Comodoro (☎ 33-5551, fax 33-2028), Avenida 1 and Calle 84, is right on the coast but 15 km west of La Habana Vieja. The 124 rooms with bath and satellite TV in a main four-story building dating from before the revolution are US$67/90 single/double in the low season, US$83/110 in the high season. Another 10 rooms in a two-story cabaña block facing the ocean cost the same as rooms in the main block. In 1990 the complex was expanded with 163 two-story, tile-roof bungalows with sitting room, TV, kitchenette, and fridge at US$120/153/204 single/double/triple in the low season, US$141/183/284 in the high season. A further 165 bungalows should open in 1996. The hotel's small sandy beach is protected from the waves by a large iron seawall. The Comodoro has a leisurely resort atmosphere with lots of chic facilities, including a tennis court, shopping mall, Karaoke club, and the Havana Club disco. The main Cubanacán/Cubacar car rental office is here.

Cubanacán Five km southwest of Hotel El Comodoro is the modern four-story *Hotel Biocaribe* (☎ 33-6495), Avenida 31 and Calle 158, in a poorly marked location next to the huge Centro de Ingenieria Genética y Biotecnología. The 120 rooms with shower, satellite TV, and balcony are overpriced at US$43/67 single/double in the low season, US$54/77 in the high season. This inconvenient hotel is far from the beach and the small swimming pool is often dry. It's used by foreigners undergoing treatment at the nearby medical facilities.

Barlovento *Hotel El Viejo y el Mar* (☎ 33-6336, fax 33-6823), or 'The Old Man and the Sea,' is adjacent to the Marina Hemingway, 20 km west of colonial Havana. This boring six-story coastal hotel, managed by Canada's Delta hotel chain, has 140 rooms with bath, fridge, and satellite TV in the main building at US$123/143 single/double year-round, plus 46 rooms in a long row of two-story units called 'cabañas' at US$160/180. There's a swimming pool. A grocery store (with bread), Papa's Nightclub, a Cubanacán/Cubacar car-rental agency, and water-sports facilities are nearby. This expensive hotel is only recommended for travelers whose main interest is yachting, deep-sea fishing, or scuba diving as it's a poor base from which to tour Havana.

Residencial Turístico Marina Hemingway (☎ 33-1150, fax 33-1149) is at the Marina Hemingway, Avenida 5 and Calle 248. The 70 rooms are in a variety of houses and bungalows of one to four bedrooms, each with a bath, fridge, kitchenette, and satellite TV. There are 36 one-bedroom bungalows at US$140 double, plus 12 houses of one bedroom (US$200), two bedrooms (US$227), three bedrooms

(US$274), or five bedrooms (US$400). Additional units are under construction. The same reception (down the road past Pizzería Pizza Nova) controls 22 villas at *Villa Paraíso* in a much nicer (though more remote) location along the seawall, two km beyond El Viejo y El Mar. These cost US$140 double and Villa Paraíso has a swimming pool. You'd need to rent a car, but it's an adequate place to stay if you want privacy and don't mind spending a bit of money.

La Lisa *Hotel Mariposa* (☎ 33-6131 or 33-9136) is in La Lisa, west of Playa and Marina Hemingway beside the highway before San Antonio de los Baños. At this modern four-story building the 50 rooms with shower and satellite TV cost US$26/40 single/double year-round, and there's a swimming pool. You'd definitely need a car here and the price is too high to make it a hot option.

Places to Eat

Miramar Buy groceries at *Supermercado* in the former Hotel Sierra Maestra, Avenida 1 and Calle 0 (Monday to Saturday 9 am to 6 pm, Sunday 9 am to 1 pm). *Supermercado 70*, Avenida 3 at Calle 70 between the Russian Embassy and the Complejo Neptuno-Tritón (Monday to Saturday 9 am to 6 pm, Sunday 9 am to 1 pm), is a large supermarket also known as the 'Diplomercado.' *Supermercado Flores*, Calle 176 between 1 and 3 in Flores (Monday to Saturday 10 am to 6 pm, Sunday 10 am to 2 pm), sells out of bread early. The Mini-Soda at the end of the building has hamburgers.

Panadería Doña Neli, Avenida 5A and Calle 40 (open 24 hours), is a hard-currency bakery.

Cafetería Kasalta, Avenida 5 and O near the entrance to the Almendares tunnel (daily from 11 am to midnight), serves light snacks. *El Pavo Real*, Avenida 7A and 4 close to the bicycle bridge over the river (Monday to Saturday from noon to midnight), has an extensive medium-priced Chinese menu.

La Casa de 5 y 16, Avenida 5 at Calle 16 (Monday to Saturday noon to 10:30 pm), is an upmarket garden restaurant (it's also known as Restaurant El Ranchón). It offers international cuisine, while *El Tocororo*, Calle 18 and Avenida 3 (daily 12:30 to 11:30 pm), features seafood. It's one of Havana's top restaurants.

El Aljibe, on Avenida 7 between 24 and 26 (noon to midnight), specializes in chicken. Tour groups often have lunch under the thatched roof of this open-air establishment. Nearby is *Dos Gardenias*, Avenida 7 at 28 (daily noon to midnight), an upmarket complex with several restaurants, bars, and shops. You'll have a choice of pizza or Chinese food here. Dos Gardenias is also called 'El Rincón del Bolero' for the musicians in the courtyard.

Morambón, Avenida 5 at 32 (daily noon to 1 am), is housed in an elegant old mansion. To maintain appearances, the restaurant serves well-dressed people in a different room from those in 'street clothes.' A cheaper terrace is next to the rear parking lot. *Media Noche*, Calle 4 between 3A and 5 (daily from noon to midnight), is an elegant garden cafe behind El Siglo gallery.

Cubanacán The following restaurants cater mostly to diplomats and business-people on expense accounts. *La Cecilia*, Avenida 5 No 11010 between 110 and 112 opposite Servi-Cupet (daily noon to midnight), is an upmarket garden restaurant featuring Cuban cuisine, especially steak and lobster. There's a floorshow Wednesday at 9 pm (US$10 cover) and live salsa music Thursday to Sunday from 9:30 pm.

Another upmarket place, not to be confused with another restaurant of the same name in Miramar, is *El Ranchón*, Avenida 19 and Calle 140, in a forest near the Palacio de las Convenciones (daily noon to 11 pm). The Cuban cooking is served under a thatched roof.

La Ferminia, Avenida 5 No 18207 at 184 (noon to 11 pm), is another very elegant upmarket restaurant serving international cuisine.

Entertainment

Teatro Karl Marx, the former Teatro Blanquita, Avenida 1 and 10 in Miramar, presents Cuban and international guest performers. Programs for adults are usually Saturday and Sunday at 7:30 pm, and there's a children's show Sunday at 10 am.

The *Salsateca Río Club*, Calle A No 314 between 3 and 3A, La Puntilla in Miramar, opens at 10 pm. This disco claims to offer *el sonida más duro de la ciudad* (the hardest sound in town).

A more upmarket place is *Discoteca La Maison*, Calle 16 No 701, at Avenida 7 in Miramar, which opens daily except Sunday at 10 pm. The US$5 minimum charge per person includes three drinks.

The *Casa de la Música* (☎ 33-0447), Avenida 35 and Calle 20 in Miramar, is one of Havana's top venues, launched with a concert by renowned jazz pianist Chuchu Valdés in 1994. Salsa concerts begin daily at 10 pm (tickets US$5 to US$15, drinks available).

Cuba's most famous nightclub is the *Tropicana* (☎ 33-0110), Calle 72 No 4504 at Avenida 43 in Marianao (closed Monday). Since the Tropicana opened in 1939 famous artists such as Benny Moré, Nat 'King' Cole, and Maurice Chevalier have performed here. Over 200 dancers perform during Tropicana's 1950s-style cabaret show 'paradise under the stars.' The doors open at 8 pm and the show begins at 9:30 pm. Admission including one drink is US$35 to US$55 per person, depending on the table. Additional drinks are US$3 for a beer or US$5 for cocktails. To avoid struggling to get the attention of the server during the show, small groups can order a bottle of rum (US$30) and a selection of mix. Tropicana bookings can be made through any hotel tour desk with hotel transfers included.

Spectator Sports

You can see soccer matches on weekends at 3 pm at the 15,000-seat *Estadio Pedro Marrero*, Calle 41 and 46 near Hotel Kohly. The Cristal Brewery, located directly behind the field, does not give tours.

Things to Buy

La Habanera, Calle 12 No 505 between 5 and 7 in Miramar (weekdays 9 am to 5:45 pm), sells upmarket jewelry. La Maison, Calle 16 No 701 at Avenida 7 in Miramar, is a large specialty store with designer clothing, shoes, jewelry, cosmetics, and souvenirs. A fashion show is held here Monday to Saturday at 10 pm (US$10 admission). La Maison's upmarket hairdresser works from noon to 7 pm.

Max Music, Avenida 33 No 2003 between Calles 20 and 22 in Miramar (weekdays 1 to 7:30 pm, Saturday 10 am to 4:30 pm), has a good selection of compact discs, cassettes, videos, and magazines. Special orders for musical materials are accepted. Also check the shop in the Casa de la Música around the corner at Calle 35 and 20 (open Monday to Saturday 10 am to 6:30 pm). The Casa de la Música, a musical instruments sales room, is open Monday to Saturday from 10 am to 6:30 pm.

The Diplotienda, Calle 42 and Avenida 5A in Miramar near Hotel Copacabana, is a dollar department store with cheap clothing, consumer goods, and liquor eagerly sought after by long lines of Cubans.

Getting There & Away

To get to Playa, take bus No 64, 232, or 264 from Calle Arsenal next to the central train station or bus No 132 from Dragones and Industria beside the Capitolio.

To reach the Marina Hemingway take bus No 9 or 420 from near the Kasalta Restaurant in Miramar (close to the tunnel under the Río Almendares).

Getting Around

There are Servi-Cupet gas stations at Avenida 31 between 18 and 20 in Miramar; at Calle 72 and Avenida 41 in Marianao (near Tropicana); and on the traffic circle at Avenida 5 and Calle 112 in Cubanacán. All are open 24 hours a day.

AROUND PARQUE LENIN

The city's largest recreational area is **Parque Lenin**, off the Calzada de Bejucal in Arroyo Naranjo, 20 km southeast of central Havana. Constructed between 1969 and 1972, this is one of the few developments in Havana from that era. These 670 hectares of green parkland and beautiful old trees surround an artificial lake, the Embalse Paso Sequito, just west of the much larger Presa Ejército Rebelde formed by damming the Río Almendares. The main things to see are south of the lake, including the Galería de Arte Amelia Peláez (admission US$1). Opposite is the Bosque Martiano, with a small library under a bridge (closed Monday and Tuesday).

Up the hill there's a dramatic white marble monument (1984) to Lenin by the Soviet sculptor LE Kerbel, and west along the lake is an overgrown amphitheater and an aquarium with freshwater fish and crocodiles (admission US$1). The bronze monument (1985) to the late Celia Sánchez, a longtime associate of Fidel Castro who was instrumental in having Parque Lenin built, is rather hidden beyond the aquarium. A ceramics workshop is nearby. Most of these attractions are open Wednesday to Sunday from 9 am to 5 pm and admission to the park itself is free. Wednesday to Sunday from 10 am to 2 pm a nine-km narrow-gauge railway with four stops operates inside the park.

A visit to Parque Lenin can be combined with a trip to **ExpoCuba** at Calabazar on the Carretera del Rocío in Arroyo Naranjo, three km south of Restaurante Las Ruinas. Opened in 1989, this large permanent exhibition showcases Cuba's economic and scientific achievements in 25 pavilions. There's a revolving restaurant atop a tower. The Feria Internacional de La Habana, Cuba's largest trade fair, is held here in October or November. ExpoCuba is open Wednesday to Sunday from 9 am to 5 pm, admission US$1.

Directly across the highway from Expo-Cuba is the **Jardín Botánico Nacional** (Wednesday to Sunday 8:30 am to 4:45 pm, admission US$0.60). There's a Japanese garden. The tractor train ride around the park departs four times a day and costs US$3.

The extensive **Parque Zoológico Nacional**, off Calzada de Bejucal on Avenida Zoo-Lenin in Boyeros, is two km west of the Parque Lenin riding school. It's cheaper to come by car as that way you'll pay US$5 for up to four persons, guide included, whereas on foot it's US$3 for adults, US$2 for children. The zoo is open Wednesday to Sunday from 9 am to 3:15 pm.

Activities

In the northwestern corner of Parque Lenin is the Club Hípico Iberoamericano (☎ 44-1058; daily 8 am to 6 pm). Horseback riding through the park on a horse rented from the club is US$15 an hour, although it's much cheaper to rent horses from boys at the nearby amusement park. The club's Escuela de Equitación offers riding classes at US$12 an hour or US$108 for a course of 12 one-hour lessons.

The Club de Golf La Habana (☎ 33-8919, fax 33-8820), Carretera de Venta km 8, Reparto Capdevila in Boyeros lies between Vedado and the airport. It's a bit hard to find the first time as the signposting is poor and the course itself is on a back road not visible from nearby highways. It's also called the 'Diplo Golf Club,' but most Cubans know it as 'golfito' (ask directions frequently). The course is open Tuesday to Sunday from 8:30 am to 5 pm and starting time reservations are not usually necessary. There are nine holes with 18 tees to allow 18-hole rounds. Green fees are US$20 for nine holes, US$30 for 18 holes; clubs and cart cost an extra US$10. In addition, the club has five tennis courts (US$2), a bowling alley (Tuesday to Sunday noon to 11 pm), and a swimming pool (US$3.50 for nonmembers). This par-35 course is patronized mostly by diplomats and resident businesspeople, making it a good place to make contacts.

Places to Stay & Eat

Motel La Herradura (☎ 44-2810), next to the riding school in the northwest corner of Parque Lenin, six km from the international airport, has six rooms with bath, TV, and mini-fridge in a single-story block

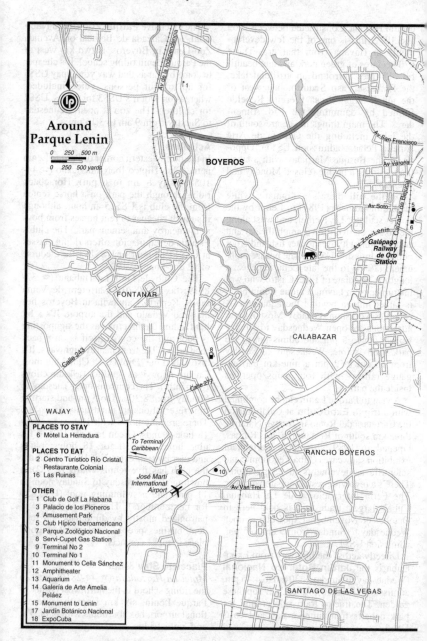

Around Parque Lenin

0   250   500 m

0   250   500 yards

BOYEROS

FONTANAR

CALABAZAR

WAJAY

RANCHO BOYEROS

SANTIAGO DE LAS VEGAS

Av de la Independencia

Av San Francisco

Av Varona

Calzada de Bejucal

Av Soto

Av Zoo-Lenin

Galápago Railway de Oro Station

Calle 243

Calle 277

To Terminal Caribbean

José Martí International Airport

Av Van Troi

PLACES TO STAY
6   Motel La Herradura

PLACES TO EAT
2   Centro Turístico Río Cristal,
    Restaurante Colonial
16 Las Ruinas

OTHER
1   Club de Golf La Habana
3   Palacio de los Pioneros
4   Amusement Park
5   Club Hípico Iberoamericano
7   Parque Zoológico Nacional
8   Servi-Cupet Gas Station
9   Terminal No 2
10 Terminal No 1
11 Monument to Celia Sánchez
12 Amphitheater
13 Aquarium
14 Galería de Arte Amelia
    Peláez
15 Monument to Lenin
17 Jardín Botánico Nacional
18 ExpoCuba

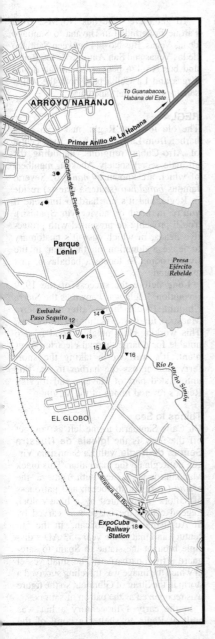

for US$17 single or double. The guarded parking lot makes this a good base if you have a car, and there are eight daily trains between Cristina Station in Havana and Galápago de Oro Station adjacent to the motel. The only drawback is the smell of cooking from the attached restaurant. A terrace bar with pizza is opposite the motel.

Havana's most celebrated restaurant is *Las Ruinas*, Cortina de la Presa, on the southeast side of Parque Lenin, a striking combination of the ruined walls of an old sugar mill engulfed in modern architecture highlighted by René Portocarrero's stained-glass windows. The antique furnishings enhance the elegant atmosphere. The most expensive item on the menu here is lobster (US$25), but there are several Cuban and Italian selections for under US$10. It's open for leisurely dining Tuesday to Sunday from 11 am to midnight.

A useful stop on your way back to Havana from an outing south of the city is the *Centro Turístico Río Cristal*, Avenida de la Independencia between the airport and Havana. Access is from the northbound lane only: Be prepared to turn off sharply soon after you see the sign. It's a nice picnic spot next to the Río Almendares, with a good cafeteria/bar open Monday to Thursday 9 am to 10 pm, Friday to Sunday 9 am to midnight. The Restaurant Colonial on the grounds is an old slave barracks dating from 1790; it's now open daily from noon to 9 pm.

Getting There & Away

The easiest way to get to Parque Lenin is by train from Cristina Station in Havana to Galápago de Oro Station on the northwest side of the park. It runs about eight times a day. Bus No 88 from Víbora and No 113 from Marianao run right through the park; otherwise, there's bus No 31 to Galápago de Oro and bus No 473 to El Globo just south of the park.

Access to ExpoCuba is also easy: From Wednesday to Sunday a three-wagon railcar departs the Estación de Ferrocarriles 19 de Noviembre on Calle Tulipán in Nuevo Vedado for the exhibition at 9:06 am and leaves ExpoCuba for Cristina Station at 10:50 am; it again departs Cristina at 12:36 pm and leaves ExpoCuba at 3:50 pm (US$1 each way). Otherwise, buses No 88 and 113 also serve ExpoCuba.

Getting Around

There's a Servi-Cupet gas station at Avenida de la Independencia and 271 in Boyeros near the Hospital Psiquiátrico north of the airport. It's accessible only from the northbound lane and is open 24 hours a day.

AROUND SANTIAGO DE LAS VEGAS

On a hilltop at **El Cacahual**, eight km south of José Martí International Airport via Santiago de las Vegas, is the open-air mausoleum of the hero of Cuban independence, General Antonio Maceo, who was killed in the Battle of San Pedro near Bauta on December 7, 1896. An open-air pavilion next to the mausoleum shelters an historical exhibit.

Western Cuba's most important pilgrimage center is the **Santuario de San Lázaro** at El Rincón four km southwest of Santiago de las Vegas. Up to 50,000 Cubans come here during the night of December 16 to exorcise evil spirits, and Sunday is always a busy day with large crowds having their children baptized. Lazarus, a black saint, is paralleled in Afro-Cuban santería by Babalú Ayé, the Yoruba god of sickness. It's the statue wearing a red cape to the left of the church entrance.

Devotees come from afar to fill their bottles with holy water from a fountain in front of the leprosy sanatorium directly behind the church. Another feature of this area is the well-kept AIDS sanatorium occupying buildings on both sides of the road midway between Santiago de las Vegas and El Rincón. Cubans found to be HIV-positive were once required to stay here indefinitely, but the norm is now a couple of weeks after which they're free to leave provided they're considered sexually responsible. In practice many stay because medical and housing conditions here are often better than at home.

To get there, take bus No M-2 from Parque Fraternidad in Havana to Santiago de las Vegas. Bus No 444 between Santiago de las Vegas and San Antonio de los Baños and bus No 476 between Santiago de las Vegas and La Ceiba pass both the AIDS sanatorium and the sanctuary.

REGLA

The old town of Regla, just across the harbor from La Habana Vieja, is a center of Afro-Cuban religions, including the all-male secret society Abakúa, members of which are known as *ñáñigos*. Several famous *babalawo* (santería priests) reside in Regla, and it's not hard to find one if you're in need of advice (in Spanish). You'll probably be presented with protective beads, in which case it's customary to leave a donation on the altar in the living room. To locate a babalawo, just ask around.

Long before the success of the 1959 revolution, Regla was known as the Sierra Chiquita (Little Sierra, after the Sierra Maestra) for its revolutionary traditions. This working-class neighborhood is also notable for a large thermal electric power plant. It's well worth taking the short ferry ride across the harbor to see this untouristed part of Havana and to visit Regla's revered image of the Virgin.

Things to See

On Calle Santuario to the left as you get off the ferry is the **Iglesia de Nuestra Señora de Regla** with La Santísima Virgen de Regla on the main altar. This black Madonna is associated with Yemayá, the *orisha* (spirit) of the ocean and patroness of sailors (represented by a blue color). Legend claims the image was carved by St Augustine, 'The African,' in the 5th century and that in the year 453 AD a disciple brought the statue to Spain to safeguard it from barbarians. The small vessel in which the image was traveling survived a storm in the Strait of Gibraltar, so the figure was recognized as the patron of sailors.

In the early 17th century a hut was built at Regla to shelter a copy of the image, and when this was destroyed during a hurricane, a new Virgen de Regla was brought from Spain in 1664. In 1714 Nuestra Señora de Regla was proclaimed patroness of Havana Bay. A pilgrimage is celebrated here on September 8. The church is open daily from 7:30 am to 6 pm. Mass is said at 8 am Tuesday to Sunday, and on Sunday a second mass is said at 5 pm. A branch of the Museo Municipal de Regla is next to the church.

The main section of the **Museo Municipal de Regla** is at Calle Martí No 158 (Tuesday to Saturday 9:30 am to 6 pm, Sunday 9 am to 1 pm, admission US$2 to all sections). A couple of blocks straight up the main street from the ferry, this museum records the history of Regla and its Afro-Cuban religious cults. Don't miss the small exhibit on Remigio Herrero, first babalawo of Regla, complete with his shackles of slavery and *elegguá* (idol). An Observatorio Astronómico was established in the museum building in 1921.

From the museum head straight east on Calle Martí past the square, and turn left on Albuquerque and right on 24 de Febrero, the road to Guanabacoa. About 1½ km from the ferry you'll see a high metal stairway that gives access to **Colina Lenin**. In 1924 Antonio Bosch, the socialist mayor of Regla, created a monument to mark the death of Lenin, one of the first of its kind outside the USSR. The olive tree that Bosch planted at the top of the hill is surrounded by seven figures, and a huge image of Lenin is below. A small exhibition on the history of Colina Lenin is in a pavilion on the back side of the hill, and although it's usually closed, much is visible through the windows. When it's open, Colina Lenin accepts the ticket from the Museo Municipal de Regla for entry. Colina Lenin offers a good view of the harbor.

Getting There & Away

Regla is easily accessible on the regular passenger ferry that departs every 10 minutes (10 centavos) from Muelle Luz, Calles San Pedro and Santa Clara in La Habana Vieja.

THE FORTRESSES

The **Castillo de los Tres Santos Reyes Magnos del Morro** was erected between 1589 and 1630 on an abrupt limestone headland to protect the entrance to the harbor. In 1762 the British captured El Morro by attacking from the landward side and digging a tunnel under the walls. The castle's gallant Spanish commander, Don Luís de Velasco, was killed in the battle, and the British buried him with full military honors. In 1845 a lighthouse was added to the castle. Today the castle contains a maritime museum (daily 9 am to 6 pm, admission US$2 for the museum only or US$4 if you also want to climb the lighthouse, photography another US$2).

The **Fortaleza de San Carlos de la Cabaña** was built between 1763 and 1774 to deny the long ridge overlooking Havana to attackers. It's one of the largest colonial fortresses in the Americas. Carlos III of Spain supposedly tried to spy it through a telescope because it cost so much money he was sure it must be visible from Madrid. During the 19th century Cuban patriots faced firing squads in the Foso de los Laureles outside La Cabaña's southeast wall. Dictators Machado and Batista used the fortress as a military prison, and immediately after the revolution Che Guevara set up his headquarters here. Later it served as a military academy, and only in recent years have visitors been allowed inside to see the collection of armaments at the Museo Fortificaciones y Armas (daily 10 am to 10 pm, admission US$3, photos US$2, video cameras US$5). Nightly at 9 pm a cannon is fired on the harbor side of La Cabaña by a squad attired in 19th-century uniforms, a holdover from Spanish times when such a shot signaled that the city gates were about to close. The ceremony begins at 8:30 pm and is included in the regular admission price.

Surprisingly, almost no tourists visit La Cabaña, while El Morro is always jammed. This is because the tour buses unload their masses at El Morro but never have time for La Cabaña even though it's a much larger and more interesting fortress. Around mid-morning it's chaos at El Morro as the tour buses from Varadero stop there on their way to Havana. If you're on your own, first tour La Cabaña in relative peace and then head to El Morro. If you run out of time, just skip El Morro.

Places to Eat

Parts of the fortresses have been converted into restaurants and bars. The *Cafetería Batería del Sol* below El Morro serves drinks and light snacks daily from 10 am to 5 pm, and the *Restaurante Los Doce Apóstoles*, so named for the battery of 12

cannons atop its ramparts, is open daily from 12:30 to 11 pm. Back below La Cabaña, just beyond the Dársena de los Franceses where the launch from Havana landed before the harbor tunnel was built, is another battery of huge 18th-century cannons. The upmarket *Restaurante La Divina Pastora* behind the guns is open daily from 12:30 to 11 pm.

Getting There & Away

To get to the fortresses from Havana, take the bicycle bus through the tunnel from Avenida de los Estudiantes near the

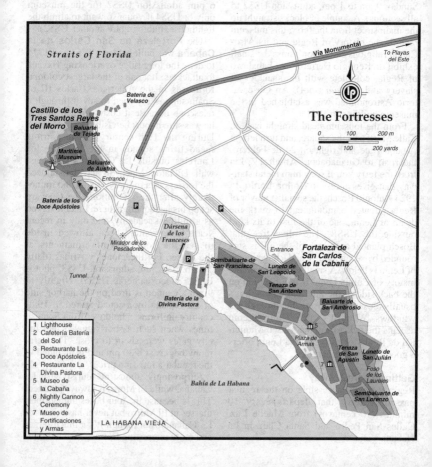

The Fortresses

Straits of Florida

Via Monumental — To Playas del Este

Batería de Velasco

Castillo de los Tres Santos Reyes del Morro
Baluarte de Tejada
Maritime Museum
Baluarte de Austria
Entrance

Batería de los Doce Apóstoles

0   100   200 m
0   100   200 yards

Mirador de los Pescadores

Dársena de los Franceses

Tunnel

Entrance

Semibaluarte de San Francisco
Luneto de San Leopoldo

Fortaleza de San Carlos de la Cabaña

Tenaza de San Antonio

Baluarte de San Ambrosio

Batería de la Divina Pastora

Plaza de Armas

Tenaza de San Agustín
Luneto de San Julián

Foso de los Laureles

Bahía de La Habana

Semibaluarte de San Lorenzo

1 Lighthouse
2 Cafetería Batería del Sol
3 Restaurante Los Doce Apóstoles
4 Restaurante La Divina Pastora
5 Museo de la Cabaña
6 Nightly Cannon Ceremony
7 Museo de Fortificaciones y Armas

LA HABANA VIEJA

large equestrian statue of General Máximo Gómez. If you don't have a bicycle, you can walk to the head of the line and get on the first bus (ask the person selling bus tickets). From where this bus drops you it's only a five-minute walk back to either fortress, and you can easily return the same way. Otherwise, a metered tourist taxi from Habana La Vieja should cost only a couple of dollars.

If you're driving, note that the parking attendant at La Cabaña charges US$1, and it's a good, safe place to leave a car while visiting this area.

GUANABACOA

In the 1540s the Spanish conquerors concentrated the few surviving native Indians at Guanabacoa, five km east of central Havana. A town was founded here in 1607 and this later became a center of the slave trade. In 1762 the British occupied Guanabacoa, but not without a fight from its mayor, José Antonio Gómez Bulones, better known as Pepe Antonio, who attained almost legendary status by conducting a guerrilla campaign behind the lines of the victorious British.

Guanabacoa today is a lively, colorful town well worth a wander around. (Guanabacoa is also the name of the municipality that surrounds the town.) There are no hotels here, access on public transport is not easy, and the town is surrounded by ugly industrial suburbs, but it's still worth making the effort if you have time.

Things to See

The **Iglesia de Guanabacoa**, also known as the Iglesia de Nuestra Señora de la Asunción, Calle Pepe Antonio at Cadenas on Parque Martí in the center of town, was designed by Lorenzo Camacho and built between 1728 and 1748. A painting of the Assumption of the Virgin is inside and the main altar is worth a look. If the main doors are closed (as they usually are), try getting in through the parochial office on Calle Enrique Guiral on the back side of the church (open 8 to 11 am and 2 to 5 pm).

The town's main sight is the **Museo Municipal de Guanabacoa**, Calle Martí No 108 between San Antonio and Versalles, two blocks west of Parque Martí (Monday and Wednesday to Saturday 10:30 am to 6 pm, Sunday 9 am to 1 pm). Founded in 1964, most of the exhibits relate to the history of Cuba during the 18th and 19th centuries. The museum is most famous for its rooms on Afro-Cuban culture, but these are often closed and if they are the main reason for your visit, you might ask before paying your US$2.

The **Bazar de Reproducciones** at Martí No 175 (Monday to Saturday 9 am to 4:30 pm), two blocks west of the museum, sells artwork with Afro-Cuban themes, including orishas, ceramics, textiles, metalwork, and graphics. A bar is in the courtyard.

Conspicuous for its Moorish arch, the eclectic **Teatro Carral** at Pepe Antonio No 364 off Parque Martí now houses a cinema. From here go north one block on Pepe Antonio to Rafael de Cárdenas, and then head east three blocks to the **Iglesia de San Francisco** (1748), also called the Monasterio de Santo Domingo. This former Franciscan monastery is the second most important church in Guanabacoa, but it's often closed.

Getting There & Away

Bus No 3 to Guanabacoa leaves from Máximo Gómez and Aponte near the Hotel Isla de Cuba in Centro Habana. You can also get there on buses No 5, 105, and 295 from Havana and bus No 195 from Vedado. Bus No 29 arrives infrequently from Regla.

SAN FRANCISCO DE PAULA

In 1939 US novelist Ernest Hemingway rented a villa called Finca la Vigía on a hill at San Francisco de Paula, 15 km southeast of central Havana. A year later he bought this building, erected in 1888, and he lived there continuously until 1960, when he moved back to the US. Each morning Hemingway would rise at dawn and spend six hours standing in oversized moccasins

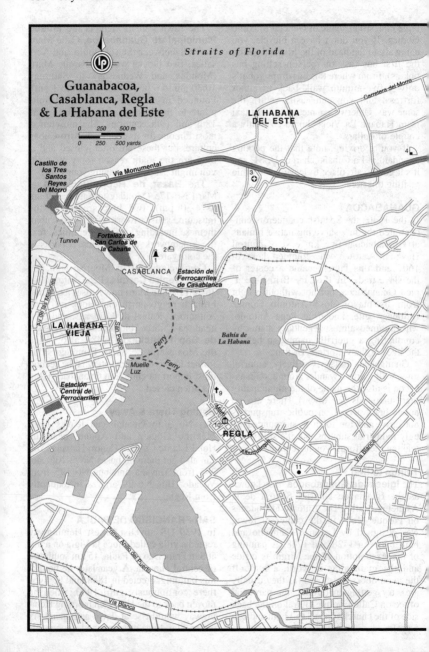

Straits of Florida

Guanabacoa, Casablanca, Regla & La Habana del Este

0   250   500 m
0   250   500 yards

LA HABANA DEL ESTE

Carretera del Morro

Via Monumental

Castillo de los Tres Santos Reyes del Morro

Tunnel

Fortaleza de San Carlos de la Cabaña

Carretera Casablanca

CASABLANCA

Estación de Ferrocarriles de Casablanca

LA HABANA VIEJA

Avda. las Misiones

San Pedro

Ferry

Bahía de La Habana

Ferry

Muelle Luz

Estación Central de Ferrocarriles

REGLA

Martí

Albuquerque

Via Blanca

Primer Anillo del Puerto

Calzada de Guanabacoa

Via Blanca

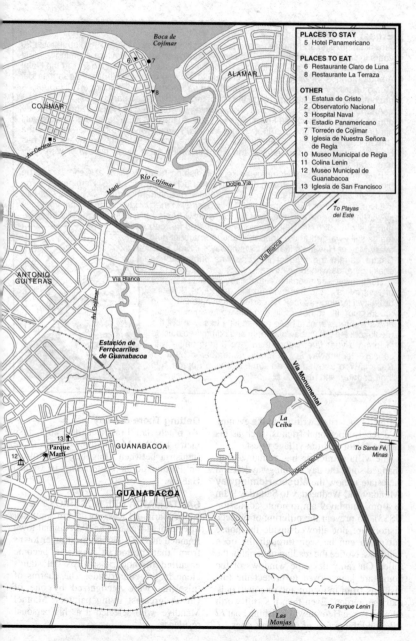

PLACES TO STAY
5 Hotel Panamericano

PLACES TO EAT
6 Restaurante Claro de Luna
8 Restaurante La Terraza

OTHER
1 Estatua de Cristo
2 Observatorio Nacional
3 Hospital Naval
4 Estadio Panamericano
7 Torreón de Cojímar
9 Iglesia de Nuestra Señora de Regla
10 Museo Municipal de Regla
11 Colina Lenin
12 Museo Municipal de Guanabacoa
13 Iglesia de San Francisco

Ernest Hemingway

American novelist and short-story writer Ernest Hemingway (1899 – 1961) spent over 20 years in Cuba and a 'Hemingway Trail' can be followed around Havana. Hemingway first visited Cuba in 1928, and during the 1930s he often stayed in room No 511 at the Hotel Ambos Mundos in La Habana Vieja. Graffiti he wrote on the wall of La Bodeguita del Medio near Havana Cathedral – *mi mojito en La Bodeguita, mi daiquirí en El Floridita* – put both those places squarely on the list of the world's 'great' bars.

After covering the Spanish Civil War, Hemingway returned to Havana and in 1939 he purchased an estate called Finca Vigía just outside the city. Here he lived and wrote until his departure for Idaho in 1960. Before leaving, Hemingway donated his estate to the Cuban people and since 1962 it has housed the Museo Hemingway. Everything has been carefully preserved exactly the way the writer left it, as if the owner were only temporarily absent.

Ever the sportsman, Hemingway kept his fishing boat, *El Pilar*, at Cojímar, and he himself named a six-km stretch of sea off Havana 'Hemingway's Mile.' Hemingway's *The Old Man and the Sea* (1952), based on the life of a fisherman from Cojímar, won him the Nobel Prize for Literature in 1954. His *Islands in the Stream*, three stories about life in wartime Havana and the hunt for German U-boats off Cuba, was published post-

humously in 1970. In 1950 Hemingway donated the cup that is still awarded at the annual fishing tournament held every May at Havana's Marina Hemingway. In 1960 Fidel Castro caught the biggest fish and was photographed shaking hands with the writer.

Hemingway's relationship with the revolution is a matter of controversy, and although he did denounce Batista's brutality, Hemingway took no part in the events unfolding around him. It's rather ironic that this world-class traveler and adventurer should have had so little to say about the revolution. He left Cuba voluntarily and committed suicide in Idaho a year later rather than face a long battle with cancer. Hemingway is still fondly remembered by most Cubans who see him as an American who approached their country with respect. ■

---

before a typewriter, writing. In the evening he'd receive personal friends, such as his family doctor and the village priest.

The villa's interior has remained unchanged since the day Hemingway left and the estate is now the **Museo Hemingway** (Monday and Wednesday to Saturday 9 am to 4 pm, Sunday 9 am to noon, admission US$3). To prevent the pilfering of objects, visitors are not allowed inside the house but much can be seen through the open windows. Notice the reading material in the toilet. On rainy days the windows of the house are kept closed to protect the furnishings from moisture and one may only tour the garden. Even then it's still worth coming to see Hemingway's fishing boat *El Pilar* and the graves of four of his dogs.

Getting There & Away

To reach San Francisco de Paula, take metro bus No M-7 (Cotorro) from Calle Industria between Dragones and Bolívar on Parque de la Fraternidad in Centro Habana.

SANTA MARÍA DEL ROSARIO

Santa María del Rosario, 19 km southeast of central Havana, is an old colonial town founded in 1732. Unlike most other towns from that period it has not become engulfed in modern suburbs but stands alone in the countryside. The charms of this area were recognized by one of Cuba's greatest living painters, Manuel Mendive, who selected it as his personal residence.

Things to See

The **Iglesia de Nuestra Señora del Rosario**, also called the 'Catedral de los Campos de Cuba,' on Santa María del Rosario's old town square, was built in 1720 by the Conde de Casa Bayona near the Quiebra Hacha Sugar Mill, nothing of which remains today. Inside are a gilded mahogany altar and a painting by Veronese. Unfortunately the church only opens Sunday from 5:30 to 7:30 pm.

On a rear wall of the **Casa de la Cultura** opposite the church is a mural by Manuel Mendive depicting the legends of this region.

The **Balneario**, in a pleasant location one km northeast of the church, is a mineral spring with a bathhouse open weekdays from 8 am to 3 pm.

Getting There & Away

Bus No 97 runs from Guanabacoa to town. From Havana, take Metro bus No M-7 to Cotorro and then bus No 97.

CASABLANCA

Casablanca, just across the harbor from La Habana Vieja, is best known for its towering white marble **Estatua de Cristo** created in 1958 by J Madera. As you disembark the harbor ferry, turn right and go up the first stairway on the left. Follow the road on the left to the statue – an easy 10-minute walk. There's a splendid view of Havana from the statue and a 24-hour snack bar at its base, but it's not possible to reach La Cabaña Fortress from this side as a military zone blocks the way. Behind the statue is the **Observatorio Nacional** (not open to tourists).

Getting There & Away

Passenger ferries to Casablanca depart Muelle Luz, San Pedro and Santa Clara in La Habana Vieja, about every 15 minutes (10 centavos).

The Estación de Ferrocarriles de Casablanca next to the ferry wharf is the western terminus of the only electric railway in Cuba. In 1917 the Hershey Chocolate Company of the US state of Pennsylvania built this line to Matanzas, and trains still depart for Matanzas four times a day (at 4 am, 9:35 am, 2:45 pm, and 9 pm). The train usually leaves Casablanca on time but often arrives an hour late. It's a wonderfully scenic four- to five-hour trip, and tickets are easily obtainable at the station (except on weekends and holidays when it could be crowded).

COJÍMAR

Cojímar was founded in 17th century at the mouth of the Río Cojímar. In 1762 an invading British army landed here. During the 1940s and 1950s Ernest Hemingway kept his boat, *El Pilar*, in the harbor of this picturesque little village, 10 km east of Havana, and Cojímar became the prototype of the fishing village in Hemingway's novel *The Old Man and the Sea*, which won him the Nobel Prize for Literature in 1954. Hemingway's old captain, Gregorio Fuentes, after whom Hemingway is thought to have modeled the protagonist in his novel, still lives five blocks up the hill from Restaurante La Terraza in Cojímar. He's 96 years old and charges visitors US$10 for consultations. Everyone knows his home. In 1994 Cojímar was a departure point for thousands of rafters lured to Florida by US radio broadcasts and US promises of political asylum.

Money

The Banco Nacional de Cuba, just down the road from the Aparthotel Las Brisas (weekdays 8:30 am to 3:30 pm, Saturday 8:30 am to noon), changes traveler's checks for 2% commission (no commission on foreign cash). Cash advances on Visa and MasterCard are possible.

Things to See

The huge concrete **Estadio Panamericano** on the Vía Monumental between Havana and Cojímar was built for the 1991 Pan-American Games. Other sporting facilities are nearby.

Overlooking the harbor is the **Torreón de Cojímar**, an old Spanish fort presently occupied by the Cuban coast guard. Next to this tower and framed by a neoclassical archway is a gilded bust of Ernest Hemingway erected by the residents of Cojímar in 1962. East across the river from Cojímar is **Alamar**, a large housing estate of pre-fabricated five-story apartment blocks built by *microbrigadas* beginning in 1971.

Places to Stay
The four-story *Hotel Panamericano* (☎ 33-8810, fax 33-8580), on Avenida Central at the entrance to Cojímar, was built in 1991 to house athletes attending the 11th Pan-American Games. The 80 rooms with bath and TV go for US$33/40 single/double in the low season, US$50/60 in the high season. There's a swimming pool, disco (closed Tuesday), and Transautos car rental agency. This chaotic hotel is far from the coast and a poor choice as a place to stay.

Better values are *Aparthotel Las Brisas* and *Aparthotel Vista al Mar* (☎ 33-8545, fax 33-8580), twin four-story complexes on opposite sides of the main road into Cojímar, across the street from the Hotel Panamericano. Both use the same reception desk and the 500 apartments are US$38/41 in the low/high season for a two-bedroom apartment with fridge and TV (up to four persons) or US$46/57 for a three-bedroom (up to six persons). A unit with cooking facilities is about 20% more. Havanautos has an office here.

Places to Eat
Self-Catering Beside the Aparthotel Las Brisas, a bakery is open daily from 8 am to 8 pm. Across the street is a grocery store, the *Mini-Super Caracol*, open daily from 9 am to 6:45 pm.

Restaurants The *Restaurante La Terraza de Cojímar*, Calle Real No 161 (daily noon to midnight), serves seafood on an enclosed terrace overlooking the bay. Photos of Hemingway adorn the walls.

Restaurante Claro de Luna, three blocks from the Hemingway bust toward the open ocean (ask for directions), is a private restaurant open Wednesday to Sunday noon to midnight.

Getting There & Away
Bus No 58 runs from the Hospital Calixto García near Havana University in Vedado reaches Cojímar, as does bus No 65 or 265 from near the entrance to the tunnel.

Alternatively catch Metro bus No M-1 (Alamar) on Calle Bolívar between Amistad and Industria at Parque de la Fraternidad in Centro Habana, and ask to be let out on the highway below the Hotel Panamericano in Cojímar. From there it's just over one km on foot to the Hemingway bust.

PLAYAS DEL ESTE
Havana's pine-fringed riviera, Playas del Este, begins at Bacuranao, 18 km east of central Havana, and continues east through Tarará, El Mégano, Santa María del Mar, and Boca Ciega to the small town of Guanabo, 27 km from the capital. Santa María Loma stands on the hillside above El Mégano and Santa María del Mar. About a dozen large resort hotels are scattered along this nine-km stretch of Atlantic sand with the largest concentration at Santa María del Mar. Most of the facilities for Cubans are in Guanabo and this would be the place to look for a private room. In general, you'll find the food and lodgings much less expensive at Guanabo than at Santa María del Mar.

Cheap tour packages to Santa María del Mar are readily available in Canada and Europe, and the resorts provide a base from which you can visit Havana while enjoying a seaside holiday. As elsewhere in Cuba, high-season rates usually apply from November to March and in July and August. Access is easy: The Vía Blanca runs right along the backside of the seaside strip and there are buses between Havana and Guanabo. However, those interested mostly in museums and historical sites would do better to stay in Havana itself.

Information
Post & Communications The main post office is at Avenida 5 and 492 in Guanabo (Monday to Saturday 8 am to 6 pm).

The telephone center is in the Edificio

Los Corales on Avenida de las Terrazas between Calles 10 and 11 in Santa María del Mar (daily 8 am to 6:30 pm).

Most of the telephone numbers at Playas del Este fall under the 687 area code.

Photography Photo Service is on Avenida 5 between 480 and 482 in Guanabo.

Medical Services The Clínica Internacional Habana del Este, Avenida de las Terrazas between Aparthotel Las Terrazas and Hotel Tropicoco in Santa María del Mar, charges US$20 for consultations from 8 am to 7 pm or US$30 from 7 pm to 8 am. Hospitalization here costs US$40 a day.

The Hospital Naval (☎ 62-6825), off the Vía Monumental in Habana del Este, has a decompression chamber accessible 24 hours a day.

Activities

Marinas Puertosol (☎ 33-5510, fax 33-5499) at Villa Marina Tarará, 22 km east of Havana, offers yacht charters and deep-sea fishing with KP Winter/Cubanáutica, and scuba diving with Marsub. Ask about this at your hotel tour desk.

Places to Stay

Guanabo Hotel Vía Blanca and Villa Marea Blanca on Avenida 5 at 486 are closed to foreigners, but in a pinch you could always make inquiries.

Hotel Miramar (☎ 2507), Avenida 7B and Calle 478, a small four-story hotel 400 meters from the beach, has 24 rooms with bath, TV, and balcony at US$17/22 single/double in the low season, US$21/28 in the high season. There's a rectangular swimming pool behind the building.

Villa Playa Hermosa (☎ 2774), on Avenida 5D between 472 and 474, has 47 rooms in small single-story bungalows with shared bath and TV at US$14/18 single/double in the low season, US$17/22 in the high season. The high season here is May 15 to September 15. There's a swimming pool and the beach is nearby.

Villa del Mar (☎ 4234), Avenida 13 and Calle 466, is on the hillside five blocks in from the beach. The 100 noisy rooms in two-story blocks are for Cubans only.

Hotel Gran Vía (☎ 2271), Avenida 5 and 462, is a good budget choice. The 10 rooms with bath were recently renovated and the exact tariff was still unknown at press time, although it should be reasonable.

Playa Santa María del Mar The modern Hotel Itabo (☎ 2575), on the Laguna Itabo between Boca Ciega and Santa María del Mar, has 198 rooms with shower at US$29/38 single/double in the low season, US$36/48 in the high season. The Itabo's four two-story blocks are set around the swimming pool and the ground-floor rooms have small patios. The beach is just 150 meters away via a wooden footbridge suspended over the lagoon (which you can explore by rented rowboat). The Itabo Disco (closed Tuesday) and a Transautos car rental agency are off the lobby.

Hotel Atlántico (☎ 2375), Avenida de las Terrazas and Calle 11, is a solid four-story hotel right on the beach. The 192 rooms with bath and TV are US$32/42 single/double year-round. A swimming pool, tennis court, disco, Havanautos car rental agency, and three conference rooms are on the premises. Deep-sea fishing and scuba diving can be arranged.

Across the street from Hotel Atlántico is four-story Aparthotel Atlántico (☎ 2188), on Avenida de las Terrazas between 11 and 12. It caters to vacationing families, offering 180 apartments with cooking facilities and fridge. Eighty-two of the rooms are in two four-story blocks that have been closed for renovations, but the remaining 98 apartments go for US$23/30 in the low/high season for a one-bedroom, US$35/50 for a two-bedroom (four persons), or US$50/75 for a three-bedroom (six persons). A swimming pool is next to the hotel and tennis courts are available (bring your own rackets and balls). As at the Aparthotel Las Terrazas mentioned below, some budget-tour arrangements at Aparthotel Atlántico involve different guests being assigned separate bedrooms in the same two- or three-bedroom apartment in which they are required to share the bathroom and other facilities. To get a private bathroom, you may have to pay a bit more. In any case, it's a good budget choice just 100 meters from the beach.

Aparthotel Las Terrazas (☎ 3829), on Avenida de las Terrazas between Calles 9 and 10, has 154 apartments with cooking facilities, fridge, and TV at US$28/36 in the low/high season for a one-bedroom apartment, US$42/52 for a two-bedroom, or US$58/72 for a three-bedroom. This five-story building is just 100 meters from the beach, and the disco is in a separate building from the guest rooms so noise isn't a problem. Las Terrazas has a split-level swimming pool.

Hotel Tropicoco (☎ 2531), formerly called Hotel Marazul between Avenida Sur and Avenida de las Terrazas, is a formidable six-story complex 100 meters from the beach. The 189 rooms with shower go for US$25/30 single/double in the low season, US$29/38 in the high season for room only; otherwise, their all-inclusive deal (room, meals, drinks, etc) is US$40/47 low/high season per person. There's a small inside swimming pool, a post office, tennis courts, and a Havanautos car rental agency. The disco is on the beach across the street.

Playa El Mégano *Villa Los Pinos* (☎ 2591), Avenida de las Terrazas No 21 between 5 and 7, offers more privacy than the other hotels if you're willing to spend the money. The 59 rooms in 27 small villas with cooking facilities, fridge, and TV cost from US$76 to US$170 for a two-bedroom apartment, US$111 to US$200 for a three-bedroom, or US$180 to US$400 for a four-bedroom. These prerevolution holiday homes vary in style, and two of the more expensive units even have private swimming pools.

Villa El Mégano (☎ 4441), opposite the Campamento de Pioneros José Martí up the hill from the beach, has 51 cabañas with bath and TV. Only some of the units have a fridge. It's a bit overpriced at US$28/32 single/double in the low season, US$35/38 in the high season for a small room in a

long block of five, or US$30/35 in the low season, US$41/45 in the high season for a larger room in a duplex. There's a rectangular swimming pool.

Santa María Loma *Villa Los Marinos* (☎ 80-2642 or 0687-3901), on the Vía Blanca at Calle 20, has 38 rooms in 10 houses at US$36/40 low/high season for a one-bedroom house, US$52/57 for a two-bedroom, US$76/89 for a three-bedroom, or US$96/117 for a four-bedroom. All units have a fridge, TV, and cooking facilities shared between all the rooms. It's far from everything and too expensive.

Villa Las Brisas (☎ 80-2793), on Calle 11 between 1 and 3, is also way up on the hillside one km from the beach. The 86 rooms are in 20 one- or two-story units. A room in one of the large two-story 12-room buildings is US$30/39 low/high season double (no singles) with TV. Individual houses are US$65/71 with two bedrooms, US$95/111 with three bedrooms, or US$120/137 with four bedrooms. Better units with a private cook cost US$85/100 for two bedrooms, US$140/160 for three bedrooms, US$170/200 for four bedrooms, or US$190/210 for five bedrooms. All units have a fridge and TV. There's a swimming pool but Las Brisas is a poor choice considering the price and location.

Motel Las Vistas (tel 80-2361), previously called Motel El Valle, on Calle Balcón de Bacuranao between Avenidas 4 and 5, is south of the Vía Blanca and far from the beach. This pleasant, three-story hotel with excellent views on both sides is a bit hard to find the first time. Look for it next to a large circular water tank at the top of the hill. Formerly reserved for foreign technicians, Las Vistas makes a good base if you have a car. The seven rooms with TV are US$23/30 low/high double (no singles). Two of the rooms have shared bath. There's a swimming pool with a bar alongside, and this motel is small enough to have a family atmosphere.

Playa Tarará You reach *Villa Marina Tarará* (☎ 33-5510 or 33-5501, fax 33-5499),

RICK GERHARTER

Bikers and beaters in La Habana Vieja

RICK GERHARTER

Iglesia San Francisco de Asís, La Habana Vieja

RICK GERHARTER

Heavy metal in La Habana Vieja

RICK GERHARTER

Land shark in Vedado

RICK GERHARTER

Hydrant hoppers in La Habana Vieja

RICK GERHARTER

Iglesia San Martín de Porres in Vedado

RICK GERHARTER

Farmer's market in Vedado

RICK GERHARTER

Monumento a las Víctimas del *Maine*

RICK GERHARTER

Ministerio del Interior at Plaza de la Revolución

RICK GERHARTER

Art and life and Che

through the Campamento de Pioneros José Martí off the Vía Blanca, 22 km east of Havana. The entrance is poorly marked, so be alert. The 125 units with bath, kitchen, and TV in 45 one- and two-story villas near the marina cost US$60/76 low/high season for a two-bedroom, US$93/119 for a three-bedroom, or US$200/250 for a five-bedroom. There's a one-time US$12 charge for cooking gas. A good if small beach is near the marina, but Tarará is rather isolated unless you rent a car (which must be ordered from Hotel Tropicoco). Scuba diving, deep-sea fishing, and yachting are readily available at the marina, and there's a disco.

Since February 1989 some 13,500 radiation-affected children and 2500 adults from Ukraine have received medical treatment at a sanitarium at Tarará. Cuba has provided more assistance to the victims of the 1986 Chernobyl accident than all the rich countries of the Group of Seven combined.

Playa Bacuranao *Villa Bacuranao* (☎ 65-7645), on the Vía Blanca 18 km east of Havana, is the closest beach resort to Havana. There's a long sandy beach between the resort and mouth of the Río Bacuranao, across which is the old Torreón de Bacuranao (inside the compound of the Military Academy and inaccessible). The 51 units with bath are all US$23/28 single/double in the low season, US$28/33 in the high season, although 30 are in long five-room blocks and the other 21 in much larger duplex units. Built in the 1970s, this older resort is rather shabby but undergoing renovation.

Places to Eat

Guanabo The local farmer's vegetable market is at Avenida 5 and 494. For ice cream head to *Heladería Los Almendros* (next to Heladería El Betty), Avenida 5 between 478 and 480 (daily 10 am to 2 am).

Very good pizza at US$1 a portion is available in the back yard of *Pizzería al Mare*, Avenida 5 and Calle 482 (open 24 hours). *Restaurante Bélic*, Avenida 5 and Calle 478 (daily noon to 6 pm), is a state-run peso restaurant with a regular menu.

Cafetería d'Prisa, opposite Villa Playa Hermosa on Avenida 5D between 472 and 474, has reasonable pizza and spaghetti. It's open daily from 10 am to 6 am – in other words, all night. A cheap chicken place is on Avenida 5 on the opposite side of Villa Playa Hermosa. *Snack Bar Parrillada* next to the Hotel Gran Vía (open 24 hours) serves inexpensive chicken, hamburgers, and grilled meats.

Playa Boca Ciega The *Casa del Pescador*, Avenida 5 and Calle 442 (daily noon to 10:45 pm), is a good medium-priced seafood restaurant worth seeking out if you like to dine in style.

Playa Santa María del Mar Among the many small grocery stores at Santa María del Mar are *Mini-Super Caribe Caracol*, at the Puente de Boca Ciega near Hotel Itabo (daily 9 am to 7 pm and until 11 pm on Tuesday, Thursday, and Saturday); *Mini-Super Las Terrazas*, beside Discoteca Havana Club at Aparthotel Las Terrazas (daily 9 am to 6 pm); *El Grocery*, on Avenida del Sur behind Aparthotel Atlántico (daily 9 am to 7 pm); and *Mini-Super Santa María*, on Avenida de las Terrazas and 7 opposite Hotel Tropicoco (daily 9 am to 6:30 pm).

Most of these have no bread but check *Cafetería Pinomar*, Avenida del Sur and 7 in nearby El Mégano, which sells loaves of bread at US$1 each from 9 am to 5 pm only.

Mi Cayito, on a tiny island in the Laguna Itabo (daily 10 am to 10 pm), serves lobster, shrimp, and grilled fish in an open-air locale.

Restaurante Mi Casita de Coral, Avenida del Sur and Calle 8 (open 24 hours), is a medium-priced seafood restaurant.

Playa El Mégano Bread is hard to come by, but check *Cafetería Pinomar*, Avenida del Sur and 7, which sells loaves of bread at US$1 each from 9 am to 5 pm only.

The least expensive place to eat in

this part of Playas del Este is *Cafetería Pinomar*, Avenida del Sur and 7 (open 24 hours). Pizza, chicken, hot dogs, and beer are served on their outdoor terrace and inside.

El Rinconcito is at Avenida de las Terrazas and Calle 4 near Villa Los Pinos (daily 11:45 am to 9:45 pm). It has inexpensive pizza and spaghetti.

Entertainment

For a movie try *Cine Guanabo*, Calle 480 off Avenida 5 in Guanabo. *Cabaret Guanimar*, Avenida 5 and 468 in Guanabo (open Tuesday to Saturday 9 pm to 3 am, admission US$2), is an open-air nightclub with a show from Thursday to Sunday at 11 pm.

On a hillside with sea views, five blocks straight up the hill from the Guanimar, is the *Guanabo Club*, on Calle 468 between 13 and 15. The open-air disco here cranks up daily from 10 pm to 5 am (admission US$5 per couple). Sunday at 3 pm there's live music in the disco. The club's bar is open daily from noon to midnight, and Pizzería Acércate on the premises is open daily except Monday from noon to 10 pm. The Guanabo Club attracts many locals.

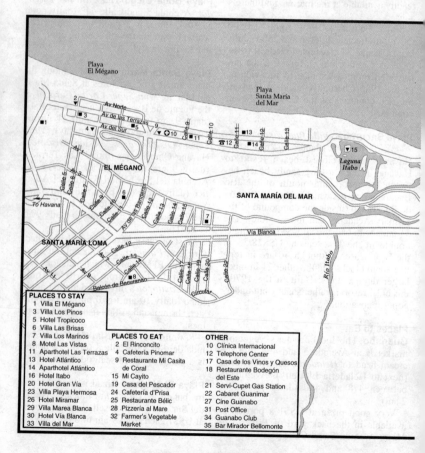

PLACES TO STAY
1　Villa El Mégano
3　Villa Los Pinos
5　Hotel Tropicoco
6　Villa Las Brisas
7　Villa Los Marinos
8　Motel Las Vistas
11　Aparthotel Las Terrazas
13　Hotel Atlántico
14　Aparthotel Atlántico
16　Hotel Itabo
20　Hotel Gran Vía
23　Villa Playa Hermosa
26　Hotel Miramar
29　Villa Marea Blanca
30　Hotel Vía Blanca
33　Villa del Mar

PLACES TO EAT
2　El Rinconcito
4　Cafetería Pinomar
9　Restaurante Mi Casita de Coral
15　Mi Cayito
19　Casa del Pescador
24　Cafetería d'Prisa
25　Restaurante Bélic
28　Pizzería al Mare
32　Farmer's Vegetable Market

OTHER
10　Clínica Internacional
12　Telephone Center
17　Casa de los Vinos y Quesos
18　Restaurante Bodegón del Este
21　Servi-Cupet Gas Station
22　Cabaret Guanimar
27　Cine Guanabo
31　Post Office
34　Guanabo Club
35　Bar Mirador Bellonmonte

Discoteca Habana Club at the Apart-hotel Las Terrazas in Santa María del Mar (Tuesday to Saturday 8 pm to 3 am) is more of a tourist disco. There's also a disco opposite Hotel Tropicoco.

The *Restaurante Bodegón del Este*, on Avenida 1 between Avenidas 1 and 2 (open 24 hours), is a local drinking place. Another good bar is the *Casa de los Vinos y Quesos*, on Avenida 1 near Hotel Itabo (daily 10 am to 10 pm), with light snacks and drinks.

Getting There & Away
Bus & Taxi Bus No 400 from Calle Gloria and Agramonte near Havana's central train station will bring you here eventually. To mark your place in line, ask for *el último*. Otherwise, you could bargain with the collective taxis parked across the street. Bus No 462 runs between Guanabacoa and Guanabo.

Train In July and August only, you can catch a train from Havana's Estación Cristina south of Centro Habana to the Estación de Ferrocarriles next to the road to Campo Florido at the far east end of Guanabo (four a day, 1½ hours).

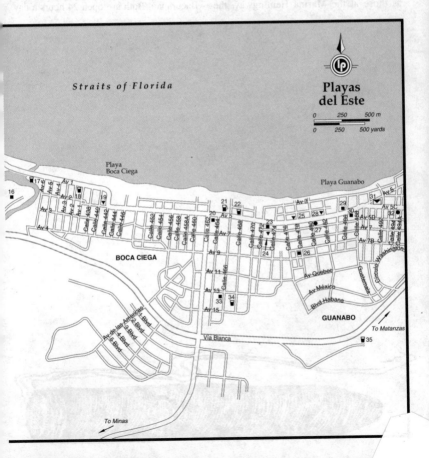

Car If you're driving from Havana to Playas del Este, be prepared for some very confusing road signs between the Havana Harbor tunnel and Bacuranao. Even after you know the way you could still get lost the second time.

Yacht Many cruising yachts moor Mediterranean-style at the Marina Tarará (☎ 33-5510, fax 33-5499), 22 km east of Havana. This well-protected anchorage is just opposite a good beach, and Discoteca Sirena and a large swimming pool are 300 meters away. Although the facilities aren't as good as those at the Marina Hemingway, the surroundings are a bit nicer and it's a viable alternative for yachties who want to be near Havana.

Getting Around

To rent a car, try the Transautos main office on Avenida de las Terrazas between Aparthotel Atlántico and Aparthotel Las Terrazas. Havanautos has offices at Hotel Atlántico and Hotel Tropicoco.

Servi-Cupet gas stations are at the Rotonda de Guanabo, Avenida 5 and 464 in Guanabo, and on the Vía Blanca opposite the Military Academy just west of Bacuranao. Both are open 24 hours a day.

Province of Havana

Squashed between Pinar del Río and Matanzas Provinces with the City of Havana cut out of its heart to the north, the 5731-sq-km Province of Havana is an area most tourists see only in passing. All roads seem to lead to the capital or somewhere far away. Yet hotels such as El Abra and El Salado make excellent stopovers on the way to neighboring provinces, and two resorts – Villa El Trópico and Hotel Las Yagrumas – provide fixed bases for those interested in experiencing the unspoiled countryside while enjoying the convenience of a package tour. Laid-back Surgidero de Batabanó in the south is a gateway to Isla de la Juventud.

Along the province's north coast from Arroyo Bermejo to Santa Cruz del Norte is an uplifted limestone ridge offering occasional excellent views to hikers; to the south of these hills lie the plains of western Cuba extending into Pinar del Río and Matanzas. The south coast facing the shallow Golfo de Batabanó is swampy.

There's dairy cattle ranching in the hillier areas and market gardening of potatoes, sweet potatoes, mangos, tomatoes, and cucumbers on the plains. Large pig farms provision Havana. During the 16th and 17th centuries the fertile red soils of the lowlands were used to cultivate tobacco, and only in the 18th and 19th centuries did sugar cane come to dominate. Today nearly half the cane is grown on private farms and the use of irrigation is widespread.

The Province of Havana has 19 municipalities, the largest number of any province in Cuba. In 1837 a 72-km railway line was laid southeast from Havana to Güines via Bejucal, the first in the Western Hemisphere outside the US. More recent historical events, such as the 1896 independence campaign led by Antonio Maceo and the 1980 Mariel boat lift,

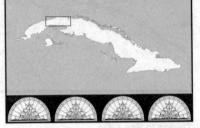

appear only as footnotes to Cuban history. Overshadowed by Havana, this province is off the beaten track.

AROUND PLAYA JIBACOA

Playa Jibacoa, 60 km east of central Havana, is a favorite recreational region for ordinary Cubans who can't afford the more upmarket resorts of Playas del Este and Varadero. Not only is it cheaper, but the high limestone terrace overlooking the coast is an excellent hiking area and there's good snorkeling offshore. The Vía Blanca from Havana to Matanzas runs along this coast, and just inland are many picturesque farming communities linked by the Hershey Electric Railway. Although Playa Jibacoa is a good place to stop between Havana and Matanzas, getting there can be a struggle unless you have your own transportation.

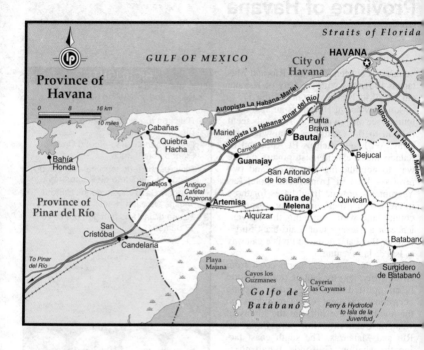

Things to See & Do

Above the Vía Blanca on the border of Havana and Matanzas Provinces is the **Mirador de Bacunayagua** overlooking Cuba's longest bridge (313 meters long and 110 meters high). All of the tour buses between Varadero and Havana stop here for a morning break.

The tour buses then continue west to **Santa Cruz del Norte** where three factories are pointed out. The most famous is the Ronera Santa Cruz, the original Havana Club rum factory, which is the oldest and largest of its kind in Cuba. Founded in 1919, a new Havana Club distillery was built in 1973, and this produces 30 million liters of rum a year. Some 50 million liters of rum is constantly aging in 20 large halls. Unfortunately the slothful Havana Club management still hasn't recognized the advertising value of their Santa Cruz del Norte factory, and tourist visits are not allowed. Also at Santa Cruz del Norte are a cardboard factory using cane fiber as a raw material and a thermal electric power station burning oil extracted from wells along the road near Boca de Jaruco, just to the west.

Five km above Santa Cruz del Norte is one of Cuba's largest sugar mills, the **Central Camilo Cienfuegos,** formerly owned by the Hershey Chocolate Company of the US state of Pennsylvania. During the cane crushing season it's discernible from the Vía Blanca only by a cloud of black smoke. The headquarters of the Casablanca-Matanzas electric railway built by Hershey in 1917 is still here. The four daily trains between Havana and Matanzas cross nearby, and there are also trains from Hershey (as Camilo Cienfuegos is still commonly called) to Santa Cruz del Norte five times a day and to Jaruco six times a day.

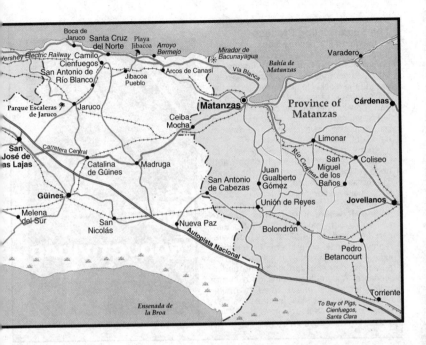

Places to Stay & Eat

Near the center of Santa Cruz del Norte is the 27-room *Hotel Río Mar* (☎ 0692-8-3313). To give the staff a day off the Río Mar closes from Monday at 2 pm to Tuesday at 4 pm. The nightclub operates Tuesday to Sunday from 9 pm to midnight. The Río Mar's small swimming pool is on a terrace overlooking the Havana Club rum factory and the bay. If you can't get a room in this peso hotel, the locals may know of private rooms for rent in Santa Cruz del Norte, and there are several places to buy food for pesos (but no hiking possibilities or beach).

As you head east, the first hotel regularly accepting foreigners is on a hill overlooking a small beach near the mouth of the Jibacoa River, just off the Vía Blanca nine km east of Santa Cruz del Norte. *Villa Loma de Jibacoa* (☎ 0692-8-3612) has 29 rooms in 12 stone houses of one to four rooms each for US$15/20 single/double low season, US$19/24 high season. The TV, fridge, and bath are common space, but it's OK for families or small groups willing to share an entire house. Villa Loma has a small swimming pool (often dry).

East of Villa Loma are two resorts for Cubans, *Villa Los Júcaros* with wooden A-frame huts, and a collection of cabañas called *Campismo Las Caletas*.

Backpackers and foreigners on budget 'ecotours' often stay at *Campismo El Abra* (☎ 0692-8-3612), where the 84 simple fan-cooled concrete bungalows with toilet and cold shower go for US$9/16 single/double with bath year-round. This is an officially designated 'camp for youth' run by Cubamar, the unofficial Cuban equivalent of Hosteling International. El Abra welcomes guests of all ages, but foreigners are not allowed to share rooms with Cubans or even invite them over. The bar overlooks

The Sugar-Milling Process

In the mid-18th century sugar replaced tobacco as Cuba's main crop. During the crushing season (zafra) from January to May the country's 156 sugar mills operate around the clock. Nothing is wasted in the sugar refining process. The cane is cut by hand or machine, and the cane leaves are fed to animals. The harvested cane must be brought to the mill within two days of being cut, or it ferments.

At the mill the cane is cut up into Chips, shredded, and crushed between huge rollers that squeeze out the juice. The fibers, or bagasse, are used for fuel or to make paper. Milk of lime is added to the juice, and the mixture is fed into a clarifier where it is heated. Impurities settle out, making a mud juice that can be used as fertilizer. Evaporators remove excess water from the purified juice and sugar crystals begin to form in a vacuum pan after further boiling under pressure. A centrifuge spins off a syrup called molasses (miel), used to make rum or animal feed. Hot air dries the raw sugar crystals that are now ready for export or for refining into white sugar. ■

MARCOS PÉREZ
COURTESY CUBA POSTER PROJECT

a large rectangular swimming pool, and there's good snorkeling on the reef just off the rocky shore. Hiking trails scale the high hills right behind the resort. El Abra could be crowded in July and August, but it's usually empty all winter (though still open). Expect spartan accommodations in a lovely setting.

Next to El Abra on the east side is *Campismo La Laguna* with more concrete cabins for Cubans and another large swimming pool. A hiking trail runs directly up the hill from opposite the main entrance.

Five hundred meters east of El Abra is *Villa El Trópico* (☎ 33-8004 from Havana, ☎ 66-7585 from Varadero), an upmarket resort marketed to Italian tour groups as 'Venta Club.' There are 121 units with shower, fridge, and TV for US$90/140/165 single/double/triple including all meals and drinks. Twenty-five of the rooms are in five long five-unit blocks, 52 in superior duplex units with a separate living room, and 44 in several new three-story blocks at the entrance. It's on Playa Arroyo Bermejo, a small stream named for the torrents of muddy red water it carries through the property after heavy rains (it's usually dry). There's a swimming pool, and several picturesque farming villages are accessible by bicycle (a car-rental desk is also at the hotel). A high limestone ridge encloses much of the resort, although a level coastal road runs five km west to Villa Loma and four km east to Peña Blanca. It makes a good package destination for nature lovers, as the snorkeling is reasonable off the small beach and there's the possibility of hikes along the coast or up into surrounding hills (of course, El Abra offers much the same at a fraction the price). El Trópico is five km off the Vía Blanca from Arcos de Canasí. Coming from Matanzas, watch for the turnoff 13 km west of the Bacunayagua Bridge.

Just east of El Trópico is *Campismo Playa Amarilla* and four km east of that, at the east end of the paved coastal road, *Campismo Peña Blanca* with two-story concrete units. These two and La Laguna are intended for Cubans only, and they're usually closed outside the Cuban holiday season (July and August).

Getting There & Away

To reach Playa Jibacoa, take crowded and infrequent bus No 669 from Calle Apodaca near Havana's Central Railway Station to Santa Cruz del Norte. You might also be able to pick up bus No 669 in Guanabo (Playas del Este), 30 km west of Santa Cruz del Norte, but from Santa Cruz to Jibacoa you must hitch or take a taxi.

It's more colorful to take the electric train from Casablanca Station in Havana to Jibacoa Pueblo, five km from Villa Loma, or to Arcos de Canasí, six km from El Abra. There's no bus service to the beach from either of these and traffic is sporadic, so be prepared to walk.

JARUCO

Jaruco, halfway between Havana and Matanzas, is a potential day trip destination for sightseers who have their own transportation and are staying at the hotels of Playas del Este. It's a scenic 32-km drive southeast from Guanabo via Campo Florido, and one can make it a circle trip by returning through Santa Cruz del Norte, 18 km northeast of Jaruco via Central Camilo Cienfuegos. The **Parque Escaleras de Jaruco**, six km west of Jaruco village, features somewhat interesting forests, caves, rock formations, and limestone cliffs, but the picturesque countryside along the way to Jaruco itself more than justifies the trip.

The 36-room *Hotel Escaleras de Jaruco* (☎ 3-2925) in the park is for Cubans only. *Restaurante El Árabe*, at the entrance to the park from Jaruco, is a state-run establishment open only on Saturday and Sunday from noon to 3 pm. It's mostly of interest for the excellent view of the coast from the terrace.

SURGIDERO DE BATABANÓ

The small town of Batabanó (population 8000), 51 km south of central Havana, has few attractions for visitors other than perhaps its Museo Municipal at Calle 64 No 7502 (closed Monday). The main attraction of this area is the pleasant fishing village of Surgidero de Batabanó, five km south, where the boats from Isla de la Juventud dock. Fidel Castro and the other Moncada prisoners disembarked here on May 15, 1955, after being granted amnesty by Batista.

Surgidero de Batabanó is a surprisingly picturesque settlement of ramshackle wooden houses with covered porches lining the streets. There are lots of little places to eat and fried fish is fairly easy to obtain. If you can't connect with the ferry to Isla de la Juventud right away, it's no great hardship to hang around here for the night, provided you have the time.

Places to Stay & Eat

The old four-story *Hotel Dos Hermanos* (☎ 062-8-8975 or 062-8-8955), Calle 68 No 315 in Surgidero de Batabanó, is a huge 29-room peso hotel looming near the port and train station.

Another option is the 20 small prefabricated cabañas with bath on the beach at La Playita, two km east by road from the ferry terminal (or less on foot via the beach). From the Dos Hermanos it would be around 10 minutes on foot. How foreigners are received at these places and how much they'll be charged could vary. In a pinch, ask around for a private room.

Getting There & Away

The train station in Surgidero de Batabanó is just down the street from the Hotel Dos Hermanos and less than a kilometer from the ferry wharf. Trains from the Estación de Ferrocarriles 19 de Noviembre in Havana should arrive/depart here twice a day (2½ hours), but they're often canceled due to problems with the locomotives.

The hydrofoil (*kometa*) from Surgidero de Batabanó to Isla de la Juventud leaves twice daily at 10 am and 4 pm (two hours,

US$15). In addition, a normal ferry leaves at 7:30 pm on Tuesday, Wednesday, Friday, and Sunday (six hours, US$8). Dollar-paying foreigners can buy ferry or boat tickets for cash right at the wharf; otherwise, check the office controlling the ferry waiting list *(lista de fallos)* next to the post office between the train station and Hotel Dos Hermanos. For information on direct bus connections from Havana, turn to Boat in Getting There & Away in the City of Havana chapter.

Vehicles are shipped over by barge daily with loading at 1 pm (US$20 each way for a jeep). No passengers are allowed on the cargo barge; and drivers must take the hydrofoil or ferry and pick up their vehicles the next day. Call ☎ 8-5355 in Surgidero de Batabanó for hydrofoil, ferry, or barge reservations.

Getting Around
There's a Servi-Cupet gasoline station in the center of the town of Batabanó on Calle 64 between 71 and 73. The next Servi-Cupet station to the east is in Güines.

SAN ANTONIO DE LOS BAÑOS
San Antonio de los Baños, a market town of 30,000 inhabitants, lies 35 km southwest of central Havana. Founded in 1775, it sits in the middle of a citrus- and tobacco-growing area. Although there's really nothing to warrant a special trip, the townspeople are very friendly, and the predominantly Canadian clientele at the nearby Hotel Las Yagrumas will find it an interesting place to poke around.

Post & Communications
The post office is at the corner of Calles 41 and 64. Photo Service is across the street. The telephone code of San Antonio de los Baños is 650.

Things to See
The Río Ariguanabo flows through San Antonio de los Baños and goes underground below a huge ceiba tree opposite a yeast mill *(molina de levadura)*, just 100 meters from the train station.

San Antonio de los Baños has several attractive squares, such as the one containing an old church at the corner of Calles 66 and 41. Nearby is the **Museo Municipal**, Calle 66 between 41 and 43 (Tuesday to Friday 10 am to 6 pm, Saturday 1 to 5 pm, Sunday 9 am to 1 pm).

The collection of cartoons, caricatures, and other humorous objects at the **Museo del Humor**, Calle 60 at Avenida 45, is unique in Cuba (Tuesday to Saturday 11 am to 6 pm, Sunday 9 am to 1 pm, admission US$2). Among the drawings exhibited in this old colonial house are a few pornographic cartoons.

The work of local artists is on display at the **Galería Provincial Aduardo Abela**, Calle 58 No 3708 between 37 and 39 (Tuesday to Saturday 10 am to 5 pm, admission US$1).

Places to Stay
The *Hotel Las Yagrumas* (☎ 650-33-5238, fax 650-33-5011), also called the Yagrumas Park Hotel, overlooks the picturesque Río Ariguanabo, three km north of San Antonio de los Baños. Each of the 120 rooms with shower and satellite TV (US$37/50 single/double) of this tile-roof two-story building has a balcony or terrace. For peace and quiet ask for a room facing the river rather than the L-shaped swimming pool. Rowboat rentals are US$1 per person an hour (included in some tour packages); otherwise, a one-hour motorboat ride six km along the river costs US$3 per person in a large slow boat or US$5 per person per hour in a speedboat. The hotel also offers tennis courts, squash courts, and bicycling.

Entertainment
The *Taberna del Tío Cabrera*, Calle 56 No 3910 between 39 and 41, is an attractive garden nightclub open Saturday and Sunday from 8:30 pm to 1 am. Foreigners are welcome. A local peso restaurant called *La Quintica*, just past the baseball stadium next to the river two km north of town, has live music on Friday and Saturday nights (closed Tuesday). A footbridge across the river leads to a hiking area.

Getting There & Away

There are six trains a day to Havana ($1) from the train station at Calles 53 and 54 on the south side of town.

ARTEMISA

Artemisa, 60 km southwest of Havana, is a bustling town of 35,000 in a lush sugarcane growing area. Artemisa is worth an hour or two of your time if you happen to be passing this way.

Things to See

The local **Museo de Historia**, Calle Martí No 2307 (Tuesday to Sunday 9 am to 5 pm, Sunday 9 am to noon), is next to the Casa de Cultura Municipal, one block from the large church on the main square.

Those interested in the history of the revolution may wish to visit the **Mausoleo a las Mártires de Artemisa**, Avenida 28 de Enero east of the Carretera Central (Tuesday to Saturday 8 am to 5 pm, Sunday 8 am to noon). Of the 119 revolutionaries who accompanied Fidel Castro in the 1953 assault on the Moncada Barracks, 28 were from Artemisa or this region. Of the 17 men presently buried below the cubic bronze mausoleum, 14 died in the assault itself or were killed soon after by Batista's troops. The other three Moncada veterans buried here died later in the Sierra Maestra. If you're curious, the mausoleum guides can tell you the life history of each individual.

The **Antiguo Cafetal Angerona**, 17 km west of Artemisa on the road to Cayajabos and the Autopista de Pinar del Río, has been preserved as a museum. Angerona was erected between 1813 and 1820 by Cornelio Sauchay, who had 450 slaves tending 750,000 coffee plants. After Sauchay died in 1835 the plantation was divided among his heirs and sugar eventually replaced coffee as the main crop. A white Grecian statue stands in front of the ruined mansion and further back lie the slave barracks near an old watchtower, from which their comings and goings were monitored. The estate is mentioned in novels by Cirilo Villaverde and Alejo Carpentier, and James A Michener devotes several pages to it in *Six Days in Havana*.

Places to Stay

Motel Los Laureles (☎ 3-2157), 1½ km south of town on the Carretera Central, has six fan-cooled rooms. This is a peso hotel, but it's worth inquiring after a room.

Getting There & Away

The train station is five blocks west of the center along Avenida Héroes del Moncada. There are four morning trains to Havana (2½ hours, $2.50) and three afternoon trains to Pinar del Río (3½ hours, $4).

The bus station is on the Carretera Central in the center of town.

BAUTA

Bauta is the provincial capital. Stretching along the old highway to Pinar del Río, the town offers nothing to travelers other than a few places to stay.

Motel El Lago (☎ 0680-3434), beside the Carretera Central 500 meters south of Bauta, has seven rooms with bath, fridge, and TV in a garden setting. Only Cubans are admitted.

Five-story *Hotel Machurrucuto* (☎ 0680-2971) is just off the Autopista de Pinar del Río, three km north of Punta Brava. The 42 rooms with bath and TV are US$10/20 single/double, but it's a dilapidated concrete building and not a pleasant place to stay. Most of the guests are Cuban workers, although foreigners are accepted.

There are Servi-Cupet stations on the Carretera Central at the south exit from Bauta toward Caimito and in Punta Brava.

MARIEL

Mariel (population 14,000), 45 km west of Havana, is known mostly for the 120,000 Cubans who left here for Florida in April 1980. Founded in 1762, Mariel is a major industrial town and port with the largest cement factory in Cuba, a thermal power plant, and shipyards. A duty-free industrial zone is to be developed here over the next few years. It sits on the Bahía de Mariel at Cuba's narrowest point, just 31 km north of the Caribbean at Playa Majana. The town is mostly a draw for journalists looking for a story.

A huge castle-like mansion stands on a hilltop overlooking Mariel. The building formerly housed a naval academy, but it is now in a dilapidated state and inaccessible due to a nearby military zone.

Places to Stay & Eat

Motel La Puntilla (☎ 9-2548), on a point near the center of town, has 21 rooms with bath. The rates in this three-story peso hotel could vary, but it's friendly if noisy. There's a saltwater swimming pool and a bar shaped like the bridge of a ship.

The nicest place to stay in these parts is *Villa El Salado* (☎ 80-5089) on the Autopista La Habana-Mariel, 20 km east of Mariel on the way to Havana. There are 41 rooms with bath, TV, and fridge costing US$18/25 single/double for a room in a single-story five-room block or US$30/40 in a larger duplex unit. El Salado is in a beautiful location on the coast just off the highway. Good snorkeling is available right off the beach, and a complete range of nautical activities, including scuba diving, is offered. You can rent a rowboat and paddle along the coast or lounge by their swimming pool. The motel's nightclub is open on Saturday only.

Province of Pinar del Río

In area, 10,925-sq-km Pinar del Río is Cuba's third-largest province, bounded by Havana Province to the east, the Gulf of Mexico to the north, and the Caribbean Sea to the south. The 175-km-long Cordillera de Guaniguanico is Pinar del Río's spine. To the north of this range is an undulating lowland and to the south a continuation of the level plains of western Cuba. Most of the province's towns and villages are on this southern plain.

The Valle de Viñales is embraced by two arms of the Guaniguanico, the Sierra de los Órganos to the west and the Sierra del Rosario to the east. These eroded hills reach 699 meters at El Pan de Guajaibón, in the Sierra Chiquita south of La Mulata. At Viñales the conical limestone hills *(mogotes)* rising out of the fertile plains have been eroded into fantastic shapes by karst action. (Karst geology describes an area of irregular limestone in which erosion, usually by water, has created sinkholes, fissures, caverns, and other irregular formations.) The province's limestone bedrock is riddled with caves up to 26 km long, and many rivers dive underground and flow through tunnels in the limestone rock. The longest river is the 112-km Cuyaguateje, which drains the western half of the Sierra de los Órganos into the Bahía de Cortés.

Pine forests predominate in the west, semideciduous forests in the east. The primeval forests of western Cuba were cleared long ago and most of what you see now is subsequent growth. Much of Pinar del Río's coastline is swampy. The Archipiélago de los Colorados off the north coast of the main island is slowly being developed for tourism.

The plains of eastern Pinar del Río are planted in sugar cane, giving way to rice paddies south of Los Palacios. There's also beef cattle ranching in the foothills and orange or grapefruit trees around Sandino

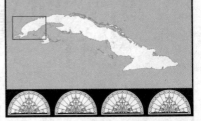

HIGHLIGHTS

- Charming Viñales with its caves, cliffs, and hills affording excellent walks
- Fantastic scuba diving and yachting at María la Gorda
- Fishing, swimming, and scuba diving at Cayo Levisa
- Hot springs at San Diego de los Baños
- Bird watching and hiking at Villa Turística Los Pinos
- Ecotourism center at Las Terrazas

in the west. Copper is mined at Minas de Matahambre in the northwest.

Pinar del Río contains some of Cuba's loveliest scenery, reminiscent of southern China, and yet the entire province is largely untouristed. The Valle de Viñales north of the city of Pinar del Río is a photographer's paradise highlighted by lovely cliffs and caves. To the east is the more rugged beauty of the Sierra del Rosario; some of Cuba's finest mountain resorts are Villa Turística Los Pinos near La Güira, Hotel Moka at Las Terrazas, and Villa Soroa just south of Las Terrazas. Hotel María la Gorda in the west is a scuba-diver's paradise, with excellent anchorage for yachts, clear waters, spectacular corals, and kilometers of unfrequented white sands. The tobacco-growing area around San Juan y Martínez is one of

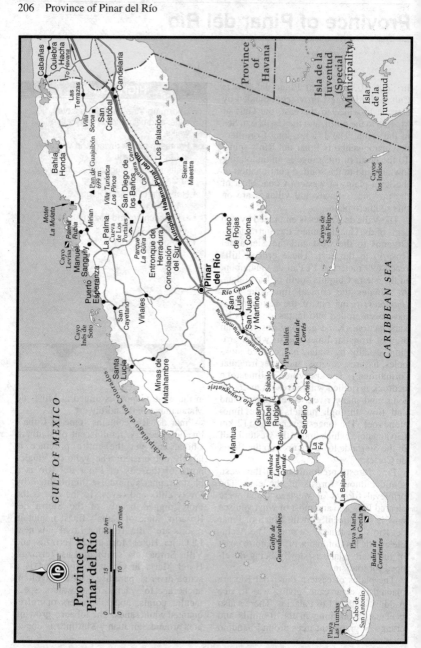

Pinar del Río: La tierra del mejor tabaco del mundo

Cuban Cigars

On his first visit to Cuba, Christopher Columbus encountered Indian medicine men who used a reed pipe called a *tobago* to inhale smoke from the burning dried leaves of the *cohiba* (tobacco) plant through their nostrils. The Indians termed the act of smoking *sikar* and it was only done as part of a fortune-telling ritual.

Later the Spaniards began rolling the leaves into cigars that could be smoked in the mouth. Tobacco *(Nicotiana tabacum)* was grown commercially in Cuba after 1580, and by 1700 it was the largest export. Tobacco requires careful attention and it's a common belief that the plants grow best when the farmer talks to them. Corn is often rotated with tobacco to maintain the fertility of the soil.

After seeding at a nursery it takes about a month until the tobacco seedlings are ready for transplanting. Planting usually takes place between the end of October and the beginning of December, and in two to four months the plants grow about 1½ meters high with leaves 30 cm long and 25 cm wide. The finest tobacco is grown under cheesecloth coverings to protect the leaves from the sun's rays. Rather than damage the taste of the tobacco with pesticides, farmers place elaborate nets above the fields to keep insects away. The tobacco is harvested by hand and the leaves are hung to dry for one or two months in special curing houses *(vegas)*, which are oriented to catch the maximum amount of sunlight. The cured leaves are then packed in bales and shipped to the cigar factories of Havana, which produce 65 million cigars a year for export.

At the factory the leaves are shaken out, moistened, and again dried in a special room. After sorting, the stalks are cut out and the leaves are flattened. To make a cigar, a roller encloses a body of cut filler tobacco in a binder leaf and puts it in a press for half an hour. He then covers the cigar by hand, wrapping it in a high-quality wrapper leaf. The color of the leaves has little bearing on the strength of the tobacco, although darker leaves are slightly sweeter and stronger. All the cigars packed in a cedar cigar box must have a uniform appearance. Only the best tobacco leaves are used for cigars; the rest are shredded for cigarettes. ■

the most picturesque in Cuba. The capital city has its sights, and the hot springs at San Diego de los Baños are ideal places to linger, but the province of Pinar del Río appeals most to nature lovers and those with the time to get off the beaten track.

Tobacco

Pinar del Río is the source of 80% of Cuba's tobacco, with 17,400 metric tons produced in 1995. The first tobacco factory opened here in 1760 and it's still the main industry. Private farms account for a majority of the crop and considerable irrigation is employed. Recently the government has tried to stimulate tobacco production by turning state farms over to cooperatives and granting land to farming families. Today most of the tobacco leaves are actually rolled into cigars or shredded into cigarettes at factories in Havana (hence the name Havana cigars).

It's said that Cuba's best cigars are made of tobacco from the Vuelta Abajo region along the Río Cuyaguateje, due to the sandy soil and humid climate. Tobacco has been cultivated there since the 18th century. Others claim the finest leaves come from Hoyo del Monterray near San Juan y Martínez, southwest of the city of Pinar del Río, one of the most picturesque parts of the province.

PINAR DEL RÍO

Pinar del Río (population 124,000) stands on the Río Guamá at 60 meters elevation below the Alturas Pizarrosas del Sur, 186 km southwest of Havana. The city was founded as Nueva Filipina in 1669, one of the last of the major cities of Cuba to be established. In 1896 General Antonio Maceo brought the Second War of Independence to Pinar del Río.

This bustling, appealing town was once sadly neglected by the central government, but since the revolution an excellent autopista from Havana has been built and much new development has been channeled in. Large schools, apartment blocks, and sporting facilities stand on the northeast side of town near the entrance to the autopista, and there are also lots of military bases and Communist Party facilities around the city.

Pinar del Río seems to have more bicycles per capita than any city in Cuba, and it sometimes looks almost like China for the masses of cyclists crowding the roads. Long neoclassical colonnades line the city streets, and there's a good choice of things to see, places to stay, and places to eat. The better-than-average transportation facilities make it a good base for touring this colorful province.

Orientation

Martí is Pinar del Río's main street, and many facilities are also on Máximo Gómez and Antonio Maceo, which run parallel to Martí just to the south. An important cross street is Isabel Rubio, which leads into the Carretera Central north of the city toward Havana and into the road to San Juan y Martínez to the south. It's easy to find your way around the center.

Information

Tourist Offices There's no regular tourist information office, but Islazul, Maceo No 119 Oeste, may have information on the fishing resort at Laguna Grande.

Campismo Popular, Isabel Rubio No 22 near Adela Azcuy, takes room reservations for Cabañas Aguas Claras located on the road to Viñales and Campismo El Salto near Guane.

Money The Banco Nacional is at Martí No 32 opposite Photo Service (weekdays 8 am to 1 pm, Saturday 8 to 11 am).

The money changers wait on Gerardo Medina at Martí next to Guamá Tiendas Panamericanas.

Post & Communications The post office is at Martí No 49 at Isabel Rubio opposite Hotel Globo (Monday to Saturday 8 am to 10 pm). The telephone center, Martí No 33 next to Photo Service, is open 24 hours.

The city of Pinar del Río's telephone code is 82. Elsewhere in the province the codes vary (Viñales is 8).

Bookstores The main bookstores are Librería Viet Nam Heroica, Martí No 28 (Monday to Saturday 1 am to 5 pm), and Librería La Internacional, Avenida Colón at Martí (weekdays 8 am to noon and 1 to 5 pm, Saturday 8 am to 4 pm).

Library Biblioteca Ramón González Coro, Avenida Colón No 3 next to the Teatro Milanés, is open weekdays 8 am to 6 pm, Saturday 8 am to 4 pm.

Photography Photo Service is at Martí No 35 near Hotel Globo.

Medical Services Farmacia Martí, Martí 50 at Isabel Rubio below Hotel Globo, is open daily from 8 am to 11 pm. After hours you can still make purchases through a small window on Isabel Rubio.

Annoyances Young men around town will try to attach themselves to you with the intention of becoming your paid guide. Be aware that they'll want to take you to a private restaurant in anticipation of a commission from the proprietor.

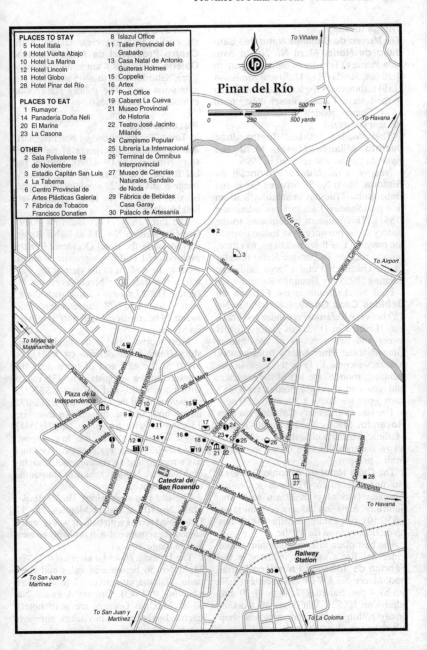

PLACES TO STAY
5 Hotel Italia
9 Hotel Vuelta Abajo
10 Hotel La Marina
12 Hotel Lincoln
18 Hotel Globo
28 Hotel Pinar del Río

PLACES TO EAT
1 Rumayor
14 Panadería Doña Neli
20 El Marina
23 La Casona

OTHER
2 Sala Polivalente 19 de Noviembre
3 Estadio Capitán San Luis
4 La Taberna
6 Centro Provincial de Artes Plásticas Galería
7 Fábrica de Tabacos Francisco Donatien

8 Islazul Office
11 Taller Provincial del Grabado
13 Casa Natal de Antonio Guiteras Holmes
15 Coppelia
16 Artex
17 Post Office
19 Cabaret La Cueva
21 Museo Provincial de Historia
22 Teatro José Jacinto Milanés
24 Campismo Popular
25 Librería La Internacional
26 Terminal de Ómnibus Interprovincial
27 Museo de Ciencias Naturales Sandalio de Noda
29 Fábrica de Bebidas Casa Garay
30 Palacio de Artesanía

Pinar del Río

To Viñales
To Havana
To Airport
To Minas de Matahambre
To Havana
To San Juan y Martínez
To San Juan y Martínez
To La Coloma

Eliseo Caamaño
San Luis
Carretera Central
Río Guamá
Solano Ramos
Alameda
González Coro
Rafael Morales
20 de Mayo
Plaza de la Independencia
Antonio Guiteras
R. Ajete
Antonio Tarafa
Gerardo Medina
Isabel Rubio
Martí
Adela Azcuy
Colón
Juan Gómez
Pinares
Maceo González
Máximo Gómez
Catedral de San Rosendo
Antonio Maceo
Quintín Banderas
Gerardo Medina
Isabel Rubio
Ceferino Fernández
Primero de Enero
Colón
Rafael Ferro
Pachecho
González Alcorta
Autopista
Frank País
Ferrocarril
Railway Station
Frank País

Things to See
The **Museo de Ciencias Naturales Sandalio de Noda**, Martí No 202 at Avenida Pinares (Tuesday to Saturday 9 am to 4:30 pm, Sunday 8 to 11:30 am, admission US$1), showcases the local flora and fauna in the eclectic Palacio Guasch dating from 1914. Cement models of dinosaurs are in the rear courtyard.

The wooden 500-seat **Teatro José Jacinto Milanés** (1845), Martí and Avenida Colón, was restored in 1996.

Nearby is the **Museo Provincial de Historia**, Martí No 58 between Colón and Isabel Rubio (Tuesday to Saturday 8:30 am to 4 pm, Sunday 9 am to 1 pm, admission US$1). This museum is dedicated to the history of the province from Indian times to the present. You'll see paintings, furniture, objects relating to Enrique Jorrín (creator of the chachachá) and a large landscape painting (1955) by Domingo Ramos.

Four blocks south is the **Fábrica de Bebidas Casa Garay**, Isabel Rubio No 189 between Ceferino Fernández and Frank País. Erected in 1892, this factory distills sweet and dry versions of the famous Guayabita del Pinar brandy from guavas. You're welcome to taste the brew in the sampling room to the left of the entrance, and you can purchase bottles for US$5 each (open weekdays 8:30 am to 4:30 pm).

The late-19th-century **Catedral de San Rosendo**, Maceo No 2 Este at Gerardo Medina, is usually closed, but you may be let in through the side office weekdays from 2 to 6 pm.

The **Casa Natal de Antonio Guiteras Holmes**, Maceo No 52 Oeste at Ormani Arenado (weekdays 8:30 am to 5 pm, Saturday 8:30 am to noon, admission US$0.50), has exhibits on the life of this revolutionary from the 1930s.

The best place to learn something about Pinar del Río's tobacco industry is the **Fábrica de Tabacos Francisco Donatien**, Maceo No 157 Oeste (weekdays 7:30 am to 4 pm, Saturday 7:30 to 11:30 am, admission US$2). You'll see 80 workers busily rolling cigars and there's a shop where you can buy the products.

On Plaza de la Independencia around the corner from the cigar factory is the **Centro Provincial de Artes Plásticas Galería** (weekdays 8 am to noon and 1 to 7 pm, Saturday 8 am to noon and 1 to 5 pm, admission free). The gallery presents art exhibits of local interest.

Places to Stay
In Town The nicest budget hotel regularly accommodating foreigners is the three-story *Hotel Globo* (☎ 4268), Martí at Isabel Rubio. The 42 rooms with bath and fridge cost US$19/22 single/double. Spanish tiles highlight the lobby of this lively hotel built in 1917.

The three-story *Hotel Italia* (☎ 3049), Gerardo Medina No 213 at Isabel Rubio, was formerly the Hotel Occidente. It's the pink-colored building opposite a monument to José Martí at the start of the Carretera Central, four blocks north of the center. The 27 rooms – some with shared bath – are US$17/23 single/double year-round. The rooftop nightclub is closed on Monday.

Most tourists stay at the modern four-story *Hotel Pinar del Río* (☎ 5071), on Martí at the east end of town near the entrance to the autopista. The 136 rooms with bath, radio, and TV run US$20/27 single/double in the low season, US$24/32 in the high season. In addition there are 13 cabañas with fridge for US$27/35/42 single/double/triple in the low season, US$32/42/50 in the high season. The hotel has a rectangular swimming pool, a nightclub (closed Monday), and a Transautos car-rental office.

The old two-story *Hotel Vuelta Abajo*, Martí No 101 at Rafael Morales, has 37 fan-cooled rooms with bath. It was recently closed for repairs but will probably reopen before long.

The 14-room *Hotel La Marina* (☎ 2558), Martí No 56 between Morales and Arenado, and the attractive, 12-room *Hotel Lincoln* (☎ 4643), Ormani Arenado No 52 at Máximo Gómez, are peso hotels intended only for Cuban visitors, although you can always try.

Outside Town One of the nicest hotels in Cuba is *Cabañas Aguas Claras* (☎ 2722), on the Viñales highway, six km north of town. It's accessible by bus No 7 from Pinar del Río six times a day. The 50 duplex or two-story bungalows with private bath (US$19 single or double) are arranged around a rectangular swimming pool. Built in 1989, Aguas Claras is run by Cubamar, Cuba's 'youth tourism' enterprise. Although not luxurious, the accommodations are adequate, the landscaping lovely, and the staff congenial. A large park down toward the river below the motel has several pavilions where *fiestas campesinas* present the food and lore of Cuban country folk. Horseback riding is US$3 an hour and you can arrange a half-day horseback excursion for US$7 per person. Other optional tours are posted at the reception desk.

The two-story *Hotel del Partido* (☎ 6-2716), four km out on the Carretera Central toward Havana, doesn't accept foreigners in its 32 rooms.

Places to Eat
Self-Catering *Panadería Doña Neli*, Gerardo Medina at Máximo Gómez, has bread from 6:30 am to 6 pm. The adjacent cafeteria stays open until 2 am, and it continues selling bread until the day's supply is gone. There's also a good selection of pastries.

Long lines of peso-paying Cubans characterize *Coppelia* on Gerardo Medina north of Martí (Tuesday to Sunday noon to midnight).

State-Run Restaurants Two state-run peso restaurants are *El Marino*, Martí and Isabel Rubio (daily except Wednesday 10 am to midnight), and the colonial-style *La Casona*, Martí at Colón (Wednesday to Monday noon to 1 am). Both serve what is known as Creole or Cuban cuisine.

Pinar del Río's top government-operated restaurant is *Rumayor*, one km out on the road to Viñales (daily except Thursday noon to 10 pm). The specialty here is *pollo ahumado* (smoked chicken). Nightly except Thursday Rumayor functions as a cabaret with a floorshow (US$5 cover).

Paladares Privately operated *Restaurant El Mesón*, Martí No 205 opposite the Museo de Ciencias Naturales (Monday to Saturday noon to midnight), serves chicken, pork, and fish. Their menu is priced in pesos.

You'll have to pay in dollars at *Casa Don Miguel*, Gerardo Medina No 108; a pork meal costs about US$3 and fish dishes US$5. There's no written menu and it's rather touristy.

Entertainment
Cine Praga is next to Coppelia (see above in Places to Eat) on Gerardo Medina. Nearby is the *Casa de la Música*, Gerardo Medina No 21 at Antonio Rubio, which occasionally has live music. The *Casa de la Cultura Pedro Junco*, Martí No 65 at Rafael Morales, is also worth checking for evening events.

Cabaret La Cueva, Máximo Gómez near Isabel Rubio (closed Tuesday), has a bar open from 10 am to 5 pm. Recorded music is played from 6 pm to 2 am, but there's no show. *Cabaret El Patio*, Maceo No 62 Oeste at Rafael Morales (Wednesday to Sunday 9 pm to 2 am), sometimes offers live music.

The *cafeteria/bar* in the courtyard behind Artex, Martí No 36 (daily 7 am to 1 am), is great for a beer break, and the bar's public toilet is accessible for a small tip.

La Esquinita Coctelería, Isabel Rubio at Juan Gualberto Gómez (Tuesday to Sunday 6 pm to 1:30 am), is a local bar. *La Taberna*, González Coro No 101 at Solano Ramos (Tuesday to Sunday 5 to 11:30 pm), is a large Spanish-style pub well worth seeking out.

Spectator Sports
Be sure to ask about baseball games at the Estadio Capitán San Luis on the north side of town. Your best chance of seeing a game is Tuesday to Thursday at 8:30 pm, Saturday at 5 pm if it's a double-header or at 8:30 pm if it's only a single, and Sunday at 1:30 pm.

The *Sala Polivalente 19 de Noviembre*

on nearby Rafael Morales is the venue for wrestling, boxing, weight lifting, volleyball, and basketball.

Things to Buy

Artex, Martí No 36 (Monday to Saturday 9 am to 6 pm), sells souvenirs, crafts, compact discs, and T-shirts.

Visit the Taller Provincial del Grabado, Ormani Arenado No 7 (Monday to Saturday 8:30 am to 5 pm), to see prints being made. If you buy anything here, ask for a receipt to present to Cuban customs.

The Palacio de Artesanía, on Avenida Rafael Ferro at Frank País, has a craft shop upstairs (9 am to 5 pm) and an upmarket restaurant and disco downstairs (9 am to midnight).

Getting There & Away

Air There are direct flights to Nueva Gerona on Isla de la Juventud from the Aeropuerto Álvaro Barba off Avenida Aeropuerto on the northeast side of town, only two km from central Pinar del Río. These flights previously left from the military airfield at La Coloma, 13 km southeast of Pinar del Río, so beware of confusing references to it.

There are morning and afternoon Aerotaxi flights on Monday, Wednesday, and Friday, and one flight on Saturday. The price is US$20 one way, and Aerotaxi is happy to have a few dollar-paying foreign passengers aboard in addition to peso-paying Cubans. However, passage is officially by waiting list only and there's usually quite a crowd. However, if you call ☎ 6-3248 to request seats a day or two before, they'll be expecting you and will try to get you on. You'll fly in an old Antonov AN-2 biplane, which is really quite an experience. It's an excellent connection to 'la isla.'

There are no other scheduled flights to/from Pinar del Río.

Bus The Terminal de Ómnibus Interprovincial, Adela Azcuy between Avenida Colón and Avenida Pinares, has three buses a day to Havana (186 km, three hours). Ask

to have your name added to the *lista de fallos* (waiting list) at the information counter one day before. If things don't look good, consider taking one of the unreserved buses that leave for Artemisa eight times a day and try to continue from there.

A better bet are the colectivos parked in front of the bus station. They take passengers to Havana for US$5 a seat. You could also rent a car and driver here to take you to Viñales for US$10 and up for the car for one day.

Train The Estación de Ferrocarriles, Ferrocarril between Avenida Rafael Ferro and Avenida Pinares, has trains northeast to Havana (three daily, six hours, US$6.50) and southwest to Guane (three daily, two hours, US$1.85). This service tends to be rather slow and unreliable, but it's less crowded than the buses.

Car Guarded parking is available at the corner of Martí and Rafael Morales, diagonally opposite Hotel Vuelta Abajo (US$1 a day). Otherwise, park at Hotel Pinar del Río (tip the guard a dollar if there's no charge for parking).

Getting Around

There's a Transautos car-rental office at the Hotel Pinar del Río. The Servi-Cupet gas station is two km out on the Carretera Central toward Havana.

CARRETERA PANAMERICANA

Southwest of the city of Pinar del Río is the picturesque tobacco-growing area around the town of San Juan y Martínez. Several inexpensive local beach resorts are on the Bahía de Cortés and a budget mountain resort is at El Salto just north of Guane. To the west is the freshwater Embalse Laguna Grande stocked with largemouth bass.

Three trains a day shuttle between Pinar del Río and the train station near the cinema a few blocks from the center of **Guane** (two hours). A Servi-Cupet gas station is at Isabel Rubio. Be sure to tank up here if you intend to drive to Cabo de San Antonio as fuel is difficult to find further west.

Motel Yaguas (no phone), 500 meters off the Carretera Panamericana, 12 km southwest of San Juan y Martínez, has five cabañas and four rooms with bath, and a swimming pool (often dry). It usually accommodates Cubans only.

Backpackers and budget travelers should head to *Villa Boca de Galafre* (☎ 3-3410) on the Bahía de Cortés. The turnoff from the Carretera Panamericana is on the left, 1½ km beyond Motel Yaguas or 36 km southwest of Pinar del Río; then it's three km down to the beach. The train to Guane stops on the access road two km from the resort, so this place is accessible to those without a car. Villa Boca de Galafre has 32 basic fan-cooled cabañas with bath, TV, and fridge. A small unit capable of accommodating three persons costs US$10/11 low/high season, while a larger unit for up to six is US$17/20 low/high. All rooms are right on a sandy beach that's OK for swimming but without any coral reef for snorkelers. Two small local restaurants are nearby, but you should bring basic food supplies with you from Pinar del Río. Boca de Galafre is a tiny Cuban fishing village well suited to those who like solitude. Expect lots of local atmosphere but no luxuries. Foreigners are always welcome, but it could be fully booked during the Cuban holiday season in July and August.

A much larger version of the same is *Villa Playa Bailén* (☎ 3-3401), also on the Bahía de Cortés, 44 km from Pinar del Río. It's eight km off the main highway and six km from the nearest train station on the Pinar del Río-Guane railway. (Playa Bailén might be a better choice if you're driving, but Boca de Galafre is more easily accessible to backpackers.) Villa Playa Bailén has 163 cabañas with bath and fridge costing US$12/15 low/high season for a small A-frame bungalow housing up to three persons or US$22/27 for a larger beach bungalow holding up to four persons. Concrete houses with cooking facilities cost US$25/33 for a two-room house housing up to four persons or US$34/41 for a three-room house holding six persons. It's probably better to take a smaller A-frame unit

right on the beach. The cabañas stretch for two km along the beach with the larger houses at the far end. Several restaurants are available and it can be very crowded in summer. Villa Playa Bailén caters mostly to Cubans, and although foreigners are accepted, one should expect everything to be rather basic. What you sacrifice in convenience you gain in local color. The beach is somewhat wider and sandier than at Boca de Galafre, but these shallow, murky waters are also no good for snorkeling as coral growth is inhibited by the nearby Río Cuyaguateje. Surfing might be an option here in August and September (please let us know), but you'll have to bring your own board as there are none for rent. A crocodile farm is two km from the resort back along the road to the main highway.

The 29-room *Hotel 26 de Julio* (☎ 9-7310) in the center of the town of Guane is a peso establishment intended mostly for Cubans. There's a local nightclub here.

Campismo El Salto (no phone), five km north of Guane, is in a pretty location next to the Río Los Portales at the southwest end of the Cordillera de Guaniguanico. It's right below a high hill with hiking trails to various caves. Each of the 46 individual cabins at El Salto has a private bath but no air-con or fan. It's all very basic but adequate for hikers, campers, and cyclists. To be guaranteed easy admittance, reserve ahead through the Campismo Popular office in Pinar del Río. Unless you're lucky enough to find a taxi or hitch a ride, you will have to walk the six km from the train station in Guane.

The *Hotel Cocibolca* (☎ 2275) in the center of Sandino, 89 km southwest of Pinar del Río, has 48 rooms with bath at about US$10 double. The Cocibolca's prefabricated four-story concrete building is basic. Foreign visitors are rare, so there's no guarantee that you'll be accommodated at all. Give it a try if you're stuck.

Four km south of the crossroads at Bolívar, 29 km southwest of Guane or 84 km southwest of Pinar del Río, is the fishing resort of *Villa Laguna Grande* (no phone). The 12 thatched cabañas with bath and fridge are US$20/26/33 single/double/triple. The resort is located directly below the dam that raised this natural lake, which is presently stocked with bass. You can swim in the lake, but the fishing facilities are unreliable (at last report there were no rods, reels, or boats). If fishing is your main aim, inquire at the Islazul office in Pinar del Río before coming here.

PENÍNSULA GUANAHACABIBES

The flat Península Guanahacabibes begins at La Fé, 94 km southwest of Pinar del Río. This tail end of Cuba is rocky along the south coast, swampy along the north. Few people live here as the soils are poor for agriculture, but it's a good bird-watching area populated with many parrots and partridges, and the occasional bee hummingbird. The splendid beach at Hotel María la Gorda was named for a plump Venezuelan marooned here by pirates. She turned to prostitution to survive and her ample charms are still fondly recalled in these parts. The scuba diving is excellent.

In 1987 the whole peninsula west of La Bajada was declared a biosphere reserve by UNESCO. To enter the park and drive to Cabo de San Antonio, you must pay a fee of US$10 per vehicle at the Hotel María la Gorda. Coastguards check permits at La Bajada, where they string a rope across the road. You may chafe at paying this fee, but it's good that the peninsula is being protected and Playa Las Tumbas near Cabo de San Antonio really is lovely. The waters off this cape are always rough as the Caribbean Current squeezes through the Estrecho de Yucatán into the Gulf of Mexico.

Scuba Diving & Snorkeling

The dive center at Hotel María la Gorda sends out their scuba diving boat daily at 9:30 am and 3:30 pm. Diving costs US$25 per dive, plus US$15 for equipment (night diving US$30). The center offers a brief scuba initiation course for US$30, but full scuba certification is not yet available. In his *Cruising Guide to Cuba*, Simon Charles says 'I have never dived in a more beautiful environment below the surface.'

Places to Stay & Eat

The *Hotel María la Gorda* (☎ 04-3121) is on the Bahía de Corrientes near the point where the Caribbean Sea becomes the Gulf of Mexico, 150 km southwest of Pinar del Río. From the coastguard post at La Bajada where the highway meets the Caribbean, Hotel María la Gorda is 14 km to the left, and Cabo de San Antonio is 54 km to the right. Although only a few hours from Pinar del Río by car, this is the most remote hotel on the main island of Cuba. It's right on the beach and over 50 dive sites are in the vicinity, including a vertical drop-off just 200 meters from the hotel. There are lots of nice picnic and snorkeling spots along the road to the hotel if you only want to make it a day trip.

Hotel María la Gorda has 20 rooms at US$15/30/45 single/double/triple year-round. Sixteen of the rooms are in two eight-room, two-story blocks with every two rooms sharing a TV, bath, and fridge. Four more rooms are in two wooden duplex bungalows near the wharf (all rooms cost the same price). Buffet meals are another US$5/15/15 for breakfast/lunch/dinner. Credit cards are not accepted. The lure of thewhite sandy beach, crystal clear water, and coral reef is strong, but just don't expect a posh hotel – this is something of a scuba camp. Many cruising yachts moor offshore in this fantastic location.

VIÑALES

Tucked away in the Sierra de los Órganos, 27 km north of Pinar del Río, is one of the prettiest natural areas in Cuba. Viñales is a fertile plain of several valleys separated by pincushion or 'haystack' hills called *mogotes*, similar to the limestone hills of Quilin in southern China (Viñales is also the name of a village).

This whole area was once several hundred meters higher, but during the Cretaceous Period a hundred million years ago, a network of underground rivers ate away at the limestone bedrock, creating vast caverns. Eventually the roofs collapsed leaving only the eroded walls we see today.

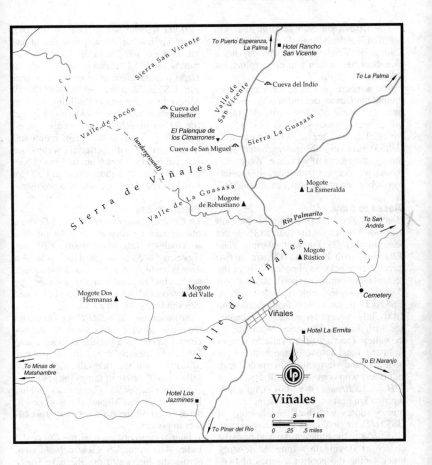

Viñales

0   .5   1 km
0   .25   .5 miles

It's lovely, but the tourist brochure hype is such that visitors occasionally come away considering Viñales slightly overrated. Bus tourism to the province focuses almost exclusively on this area.

The area code in Viñales is 8.

Things to See

The village of Viñales (4000 inhabitants) in the southern part of the Viñales region was founded in 1607. The **Casa de la Cultura** in an old mansion beside the church on the main square has a full program of cultural activities, and an art gallery is next door.

Four km west of the village is **El Mural de la Prehistoria** on a cliff at the foot of the 617-meter-high Sierra de Viñales, the highest portion of the Sierra de los Órganos. This 180-meter-long painting on the side of Mogote Dos Hermanas was designed in 1961 by Leovigildo González Morillo, a follower of the Mexican artist Diego Rivera. Unless you eat at the site restaurant, which specializes in grilled pork (noon to 7 pm), you'll pay US$1 per person to view the mural up close.

The **Cueva de San Miguel**, four km north of Viñales village, is now Disco-Bar Cuevas de Viñales. During the day it's a nice cool bar, which you can explore for the price of a drink.

The northern portion of the Viñales area around the **Cueva del Indio** is the prettiest part. This cave 5½ km north of Viñales village was previously inhabited by Indians. In 1920 it was rediscovered. Boat trips (US$3) now ply the underground river through the electrically-lit cave. You go 300 meters on foot and then travel 400 meters by rowboat, emerging near a small waterfall.

Places to Stay

Hotel Los Jazmines (☎ 3-3404) is four km south of Viñales on the road to Pinar del Río, another 25 km to the south. The 72 rooms with bath and TV are in two three-story blocks on opposite sides of the rectangular swimming pool. Rooms cost US$21/30 single/double in the low season, US$26/35 in the high season. In addition 16 slightly cheaper rooms called 'cabañas' are in a long single-story block facing the valley. The view of the Valle de Viñales from the hotel is one of the best, so the pool area and viewpoint are crowded with sightseers who come and go all day.

Hotel La Ermita (☎ 93-6071), on a hilltop two km east of Viñales village, has 62 breezy rooms with bath and balcony at US$21/28 single/double in the low season, US$29/38 in the high season. You have the choice of staying in a long single-story block facing the pool or a series of two-story blocks facing the valley. This modern, relaxing hotel offers a swimming pool with an excellent view of the valley, tennis courts, and horseback riding (US$5 an hour). This is the only official accommodation within easy walking distance of the varied eating and entertainment possibilities in the village.

The *Casa del Marisco* (☎ 9-3202), directly across the highway from the Cueva del Indio entrance, has two rooms for rent at US$16 single or double. Both have a mini-fridge, but only one of the rooms has a private bath.

Hotel Rancho San Vicente (☎ 9-3201), seven km north of Viñales village and one km north of the Cueva del Indio, has 29 rooms and 34 cabañas with bath at US$17/23 single/double in the low season, US$24/32 in the high season. The 29 rooms in a three-story building next to the highway have been closed recently, but the 34 small cabañas are nicely spaced around a large lawn. Five individual thermal pools with sulfurous waters are accessible daily from 9 am to 5 pm (US$1 per half-hour, 15-minute massage US$15). Loud recorded music could be a problem.

Places to Eat

La Casa de Don Tomás (☎ 9-3114), in an old colonial mansion at the south entrance to Viñales village (daily 9 am to 10 pm), serves a plate called 'las delicias de Don Tomás,' which includes rice, lobster, fish, pork, chicken, and sausage with an egg as the central decoration (US$10). Fried chicken here costs US$5.50.

Restaurante Valle-Bar/Casa Dago, on the main street a block south of Viñales central square, is a paladar offering cheap food and expensive drinks. Inside you pay in dollars, but the sidewalk stall outside sells a good variety of things for pesos.

El Palenque de los Cimarrones, behind La Cueva de San Miguel along a one-km access road off the main highway, specializes in poultry.

Four restaurants are near the Cueva del Indio. The upmarket *Casa del Marisco*, across the highway from the cave (daily 9 am to 10 pm), serves seafood dishes in an ad-hoc venue that looks like an office.

The *Restaurante Cueva del Indio*, at the entrance to the cave (daily 9 am to 4 pm), is a tour-group–style restaurant with long communal tables where travelers are served baked chicken with manioc cakes.

Ranchón y Finca San Vincente, near the exit from the Cueva del Indio (11 am to 4 pm), is also on the tour-bus circuit. A country-style lunch here will cost about US$10, and you may get salsa music with your grilled pork.

Paladar Los Antonios, beside the highway next to the main building of Hotel Rancho San Vicente, is a private place cheaper than the official tourist restaurants in this area.

Getting There & Away
No local buses operate between Viñales and Pinar del Río. You must walk to the edge of town and from there try to hitch a ride in a truck.

An *especial* bus to Havana (188 km) via Pinar del Río departs the main square of Viñales daily at 2:30 pm (fully booked on weekends).

Getting Around
The only gas station on the north coast of Pinar del Río selling the super gasoline required by most rental vehicles is Servi-Cupet Las Brisas at San Cayetano, 12 km northwest of Rancho San Vicente toward Puerto Esperanza.

CAYO LEVISA
This small coral key off the north side of Pinar del Río is part of the Archipiélago de los Colorados, which sits in the Gulf of Mexico. It's known for its white coral beaches, thick mangroves, abundant seabirds, and seas rich in red snapper, sea bass, lobster, marlin, and other species.

Recently an exclusive tourist resort has been built on the island. From the early 1940s, American author Ernest Hemingway had a fishing camp on Cayo Paraíso, a smaller coral island 10 km east of Cayo Levisa.

Places to Stay & Eat
Cayo Levisa's 20 cabañas with private bath are US$59/82/123 single/double/triple for a room only, plus US$2/8/9 per person for buffet breakfast/lunch/dinner. Most guests arrive on a package tour and the resort is often full, usually with groups from Italy. However, Havanatur offices around Cuba should be able to reserve rooms at Cayo Levisa. There's a scuba-diving center on the island and sport fishing can be arranged.

Getting There & Away
The landing for Cayo Levisa is 21 km northeast of La Palma or 40 km west of Bahía Honda. Take the turnoff to Mirian and proceed four km through a large banana plantation to reach the coastguard station at Palma Rubia, from which the boat to the island departs. Boat transfers to Cayo Levisa are US$10 per person return and you can make it a day trip for the same price (plus US$15 for a lobster lunch). From the dock you cross the mangroves on a wooden walkway to the resort on the island's north side.

AROUND BAHÍA HONDA
Northern Pinar del Río Province is an alternative transit route to/from Havana. A scenic road winds along a ridge with many sea views over the cane fields, pine forests, tobacco fields, and banana plantations. Rice paddies lie in the river valleys and you pass a succession of picturesque thatched

Tobacco thrives throughout the province.

farmhouses. In 1901, when the US was trying to decide whether Cuba was worthy of independence, there were congressional calls for Bahía Honda to be seized for use as a US naval base. Luckily the Americans settled for Guantánamo alone.

Motel La Mulata, 27 km west of Bahía Honda and one km off the main road, has six duplex units with bath in a long single-story block for US$13 single or double. A terrace overlooks the bay. It's a friendly place, but there's no beach suitable for swimming.

The *Motel Punta de Piedra* (☎ 341) is on a hilltop three km north of the town of Bahía Honda, on a sideroad to Punta de Piedra. The 19 rooms, each with bath and fridge in a long single-story block, are US$15 double in May, June, September, October, and November, or US$19 the rest of the year. There's a nice view of the bay but no real beach. Power and water failures are routine and mosquitoes abound. It's overpriced for what you get.

AROUND SAN DIEGO DE LOS BAÑOS

San Diego de los Baños, 130 km southwest of Havana, is a pretty little resort town worthy of a day of relaxation if you enjoy thermal baths. The Río San Diego on which this lowland village sits separates the Sierra de los Órganos to the west from the higher Sierra del Rosario to the east. The Sierra de Güira to the west of San Diego de los Baños is a nature reserve with pine, mahogany, and cedar forests, a favorite bird-watching area.

Things to See & Do

The **Balneario San Diego** is a modern bathing complex where thermal waters of 30°C to 40°C are used to treat muscular and skin afflictions. Mud from the mouth of the Río San Diego is used here in beauty treatments. The sulfurous waters of these mineral springs are potent and immersions of only 15 minutes per day are allowed. The baths are open Monday to Saturday from 8 am to 5 pm, Sunday 8 am to noon. Fifteen minutes in the collective bath costs US$4; a private 15-minute bath

is US$6. Massage is available at US$15 and many other health services are offered. These facilities are among the finest and most accessible of their kind in Cuba.

Five km west of San Diego de los Baños is **Parque La Güira**, the former Hacienda Cortina, a large sculpture park built by wealthy landowner Manuel Cortina. This public park is often misleadingly nicknamed a 'national park' in Cuban tourism brochures. There are artificial ruins, a Chinese pavilion, and clusters of bamboo. A huge modern restaurant called *Restaurante Mirador* (closed Monday) is just above Parque La Güira, but the cabins here are reserved for vacationing military personnel.

During the 1962 Cuban Missile Crisis, Che Guevara transferred the headquarters of the Western Army to **Cueva de Los Portales**, 11 km west of Parque La Güira and 16 km north of Entronque de Herradura on the Carretera Central. The cave is in a pretty area, one km off the main road, and the Río Caiguanabo runs right through it.

Places to Stay

Camping At Cueva de Los Portales, there's a camping area in the forest near the cave and six basic cabañas. A stairway up the mountainside is available to those who stay.

Hotels There are three functioning hotels a couple of blocks apart in the center of San Diego de los Baños. Foreigners are expected to stay at the two-story *Hotel Mirador* (☎ 33-5410), adjacent to the hot springs. The 30 air-conditioned rooms with bath and TV cost US$27/34 single/double year-round. There's a rectangular swimming pool. Don't confuse this hotel with Restaurante Mirador five km away at La Güira.

Hotel Saratoga (☎ 3-7821), two blocks over from Hotel Mirador, is a gracious old hotel erected in 1924, complete with rocking chairs on the porch. Unfortunately the 35 fan-cooled rooms with bath and radio are for Cubans only.

Two-story *Hotel Libertad* (☎ 3-7820), a block away at Calle 33 No 3805, has 20 fan-cooled rooms with bath, also officially for Cubans only.

Resorts Cuba's most intriguing mountain resort is without doubt *Villa Turística Los Pinos* in the Sierra de Güira, 12 km west of San Diego de los Baños via Parque La Güira. Los Pinos was built in the early 1960s by Fidel Castro's secretary, the late Celia Sánchez, whose cabin stands in the center of the complex. In recent years the resort has fallen on hard times and there's no telephone or regular supply of electricity. The single generator is used only on special occasions, leading to water problems since there's no pump to fill the tanks. If you come here, don't expect more than a bed and a roof over your head.

This bed will be in one of the 23 rustic wooden cabins on stilts scattered through the pine forest and connected by wooden walkways. This idyllic resort stands on a ridge directly below the mountain peaks, and it's an ideal base for bird watching if you don't mind roughing it. The Cueva de los Portales is just five km further west. Expect to pay about US$12 single or double and bring a few food supplies. For more information call the office in San Diego de los Baños (☎ 9-6813). Los Pinos would make a perfect 'ecotourism' resort if it were ever restored. For better or for worse, this is unlikely to happen soon, so you'll probably have the place to yourself.

A striking contrast to Los Pinos is *Villa Maspotón*, a base camp for khaki-clad sharpshoots who are taken out to slaughter the local wildlife. As you drive down a poorly marked dirt road to this dismal spot, you're engulfed in dust. The resort's also known as the Club de Caza y Pesca, but no fishing facilities are available.

The rooms are in prefabricated cement blocks. The swimming pool is usually dry, but there's a bar exhibiting the mounted carcasses of dead birds and photos of those responsible for the carnage. For merely US$10 a day you can rent a gun and another US$10 gets you 25 cartridges. The

daily schedule includes hunting for duck (up to 15), pigeon (up to 50), partridge (up to 30), and guinea fowl (up to five). Carlo Gébler's book *Driving through Cuba: An East-West Journey* includes a lengthy chapter about his misadventures at Maspotón. It's sad that there are places like this in Cuba.

Getting Around

There's a Servi-Cupet gas station at the entrance to San Diego de los Baños from Havana.

SOROA

Soroa, 95 km west of Havana, is the closest mountain resort area to the capital. It's above Candelaria in the Sierra del Rosario, the easternmost and highest section of the Cordillera de Guaniguanico. Soroa is known as the 'rainbow of Cuba,' and the region's heavy rainfall promotes the growth of tall trees and orchids. The park was created in the 1920s by Ignacio Soroa as a personal retreat, and only since the revolution has this lovely area been developed for tourism.

Things to See

All of the sights of Soroa are conveniently near Villa Soroa. Next door to the motel is an **Orquidareo** established in 1943 where 350 species of orchids are on display (daily 9 am to noon and 1 to 4 pm, admission US$2).

Just across the road from here is the entrance to a park featuring the **Salto de Soroa**, a magnificent waterfall on the Arroyo Manantiales. You can swim at the foot of the falls. Regular admission to the falls is US$2, but it's free if you're staying at Villa Soroa.

Across the stream from the waterfall parking lot are the **Baños Romanos**, a stone bathhouse with a pool of sulfurous water. It's rather primitive, but you can get the key from the Villa Soroa reception if you might like to take a dip. It's a half-hour hike up the hill from the bathhouse to the **Mirador**, a rocky crag with a sweeping view of all Soroa.

The **Castillo de la Nubes**, on the hilltop above the Orquidareo, has an excellent view of the Valle de Soroa and coastal plain. The bar is open daily from 8 am to 5 pm. Ignacio Soroa's personal residence on the ridge beyond the bar is empty, but several luxury villas on the hillside can be rented through the Villa Soroa reception.

Places to Stay

Villa Soroa (☎ 2041) nestles on spacious grounds in a valley among stately trees and verdant hills. There are 24 cabañas with bath and fridge in four-unit single-story blocks at US$21/28 single/double in the low season, US$24/38 in the high season. The standard of comfort here is high, with good beds in every room. Ask for a room on the front row high above the rather dirty swimming pool. The loud recorded music broadcast from the bar beside this pool is one of the few blights on this complex.

Campismo La Caridad (no phone) is on the Arroyo Manantiales, 2½ km west of Villa Soroa. The 23 tiny cement cubicles are US$11 double, and although it's mainly for Cubans, you should be allowed to stay. A large cave is about one km away.

Getting There & Away

The nearest train station is at Candelaria, nine km southeast of Villa Soroa. The station is on Calle 34, a few blocks south of Candelaria's central square. Three trains arrive daily from Havana's Central Station and Pinar del Río. Once you arrive, you'll have to look for a taxi to Soroa.

LAS TERRAZAS

The community of Las Terrazas in eastern Pinar del Río, near the border of the Province of Havana, originated as a reforestation project in 1968. The surrounding mountains had been denuded by fire and shortsighted agricultural techniques, and the inhabitants lived in poor conditions. A reservoir was created in 1971, and alongside it a model settlement was built taking its name from the hillside terraces planted with pines. The scheme was so successful that in 1985 this area was declared the Reserva Sierra del Rosario, Cuba's first UNESCO-sanctioned biosphere reserve.

Cuba's present minister of tourism, Osmani Cienfuegos (brother of the revolutionary hero Camilo Cienfuegos), was involved in the original reforestation project, and in 1990 an upmarket tourist resort was built just above the community to provide employment for the 850 inhabitants. Between 1992 and 1994 a hotel was built and all of the present workers are from Las Terrazas. A few small art galleries and textile or pottery workshops have been set up in the village. This is Cuba's main center for 'ecotourism.'

Las Terrazas is 17 km northeast of Villa Soroa and 13 km west of the Havana-Pinar del Río autopista at Cayajabos. There are gates at both entrances to the reserve. About 1½ km up the hill from the gate on the Cayajabos side, six km from the hotel by road, are the ruins of the 19th-century Buenavista coffee plantation. The main building is now a restaurant (closed Monday), and the coffee drying platforms here are typical of many such ruins in this area. You can hike there from Las Terrazas in under an hour on Las Delicias Trail. In the same general area is La Serafina Trail, a favorite of bird watchers. Another good hike from Las Terrazas is the three-km trail up the Río San Juan to a small falls and a natural swimming hole.

Places to Stay

The comfortable *Hotel Moka* (☎ 085-2996 or 085-2921, fax 33-5516) has 26 rooms with bath, fridge, and satellite TV for US$58/72 single/double. This two-story building with colonial touches blends into the surrounding woods, and there's a swimming pool and tennis court. Guests can rent rowboats and rods to fish black bass from the reservoir or mountain bikes for touring. Horseback riding is also available.

On a hill just east of Las Terrazas, off the road to Cayajabos, is *Campismo El Taburete* with 54 concrete cabañas intended mostly for Cubans. No further information was available at press time.

Province of Matanzas

Matanzas is Cuba's second largest province (11,978 sq km). The province of Havana lies to the west and Villa Clara and Cienfuegos Provinces to the east. In the 18th and 19th centuries this was the heartland of the Cuban sugar industry, and towns like Matanzas and Cárdenas were built with sugar money. Since the 1959 revolution huge grapefruit and orange plantations have been created in the center of the province between Varadero and the Bay of Pigs. The fruit from 300 sq km of orange trees around Jagüey Grande is processed into high-grade concentrate and packed in cartons of juice by Chilean and Israeli companies.

The province's highest point is the Pan de Matanzas (381 meters) to the west of the city of Matanzas. Other low hills lie to the south between Havana Province and Coliseo – this is cattle country. Cane fields fill the fertile plains of western Matanzas. The southern half of the province is mostly marsh and bog: The Ciénaga de Zapata around the Bay of Pigs is Cuba's largest swamp. The terrain on the north-coast varies from rocky around the city of Matanzas to sandy at Varadero to muddy east of Cárdenas.

Matanzas Province hosts much of Cuba's tourist industry, both at Playa de Varadero and around the Bay of Pigs. Varadero is Cuba's biggest resort center with 43 hotels and all the facilities you could hope for. Boca de Guamá in Parque Nacional Ciénaga de Zapata in the south is a Cuban-style ecotourism resort. Scuba divers and history buffs will love Playa Girón on the Bay of Pigs. Other towns such as Matanzas and Cárdenas have museums and colonial buildings but no official accommodations, so they're visited mostly by tourists in transit.

Note: In addition to the Servi-Cupet stations at Matanzas, Varadero, and Cárdenas, there are gas stations on the Carretera

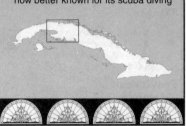

HIGHLIGHTS

- Unique handmade books at Ediciones Vigía in the city of Matanzas
- Entertaining boat ride up the Río Canímar
- Sky diving, yachting, scuba diving, and golf at fantastic Playa Varadero
- Timeworn town of Cárdenas, where the Cuban flag was first flown
- Exotic Boca de Guamá and the Laguna del Tesoro with its crocodile farm and reconstructed Indian village
- Historic Bay of Pigs invasion site, now better known for its scuba diving

Central at Jovellanos and Colón and at Jagüey Grande off the Autopista Nacional.

MATANZAS

Matanzas (population 115,000) is a large industrial city with a sugar refinery, mechanized sugar-exporting facilities, a paper mill using crushed cane fiber *(bagazo)*, a shoe factory, a textile mill, two fertilizer factories, a chemical plant, a base for unloading supertankers, oil storage facilities, and two thermal power stations. These installations are on the northeast side of the bay well outside the historic city center, and it's certainly worth stopping for a look around downtown. Unfortunately the lack of a city-center hotel forces you into a substandard private room should you care to linger.

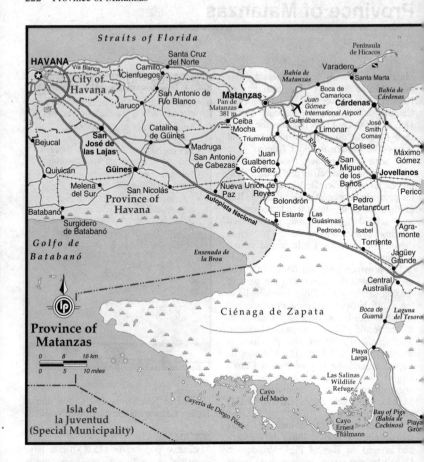

History

In 1508 Sebastián de Ocampo sighted a bay the Indians called Guanima and which we now know as Bahía de Matanzas. In 1628 the Dutch pirate Piet Heyn captured a Spanish treasure fleet carrying 12 million gold florins in this bay. Later Carlos II of Spain ordered that a settlement be established, so in 1693 immigrants from the Canary Islands founded the town of San Carlos y Severino de Matanzas on a site between the Yumurí and San Juan rivers. The original fort has long since disap-

peared, but the original Plaza de Armas remains as Plaza de la Vigía.

Matanzas only began to flourish after large sugar mills were established in the region between 1817 and 1827. Coffee also began to be exported and in 1843 the railway arrived from Havana. By the second half of the 19th century, this was the second largest city in Cuba boasting a newspaper, public library, high school, theater, and philharmonic society. Due to the number of artists, writers, musicians, and intellectuals living here at that time,

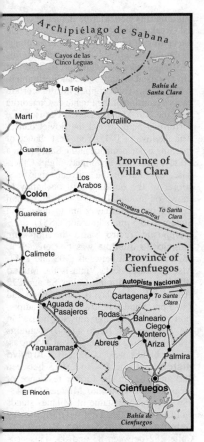

Matanzas came to be known as the 'Athens of Cuba.' The most famous 19th-century resident was the mulatto poet Gabriel de la Concepción Valdés, better known as Plácido, who was executed by the Spanish in 1844.

Orientation

The compact old town lies between the Yumurí and San Juan rivers with the historic Versalles quarter just to the north. Most of the industry is east of Versalles. The Hershey Railway terminates in

Versalles, but all of the other transportation facilities are south of the Río San Juan.

Matanzas' streets suffer from a capricious numbering system. In the old town the north-south streets bear even numbers beginning at Calle 268 near the bay and rising. The streets on either side of the main square, Parque Libertad, are 288 and 290. The east-west streets increase from Calle 75 at the Yumurí bridge to Calle 97 along the banks of the San Juan. House numbers give an indication of the location: Building No 28813 on Calle 85 is west of Calle 288, and shop No 8311 on Calle 288 is south of Calle 83.

Matanzas residents just ignore these arbitrary numbers and continue using the old colonial street names. However, we use the numbers because that's all you'll find posted on street corners.

Information

Tourist Offices There's no tourist information office in Matanzas. The Dirección Provincial de Campismo Popular, Calle 290 between 83 and 85 (weekdays 8 am to noon and 1 to 5 pm), reserves accommodations at a variety of low-budget resorts such as Canímar Abajo (eight km east of Matanzas), Faro de Maya (on the old road to Varadero), Victoria de Girón (beyond Playa Larga), and Las Carolinas (at Limonar).

Money You can change traveler's checks or get cash advances at the Banco Nacional, Calles 83 and 282 diagonally opposite cathedral, or the Banco Financiero Internacional, Calles 85 and 298.

Post & Communications The post office, Calle 85 No 28813 at Calle 290, is open Monday to Saturday from 7 am to 8 pm. The telephone center, Calles 83 and 288 just off Parque Libertad, opens daily from 6:30 am to 10 pm. Matanzas' telephone code is 52.

Bookstore Try Librería Viet Nam, Calle 85 No 28612 near Calle 288.

Library Biblioteca Gener y Del Monte, Calles 79 and 290 on Parque Libertad (weekdays 8:30 am to 10 pm, Saturday 8:30 am to 3:30 pm, Sunday 8:30 am to 12:30 pm), is housed in the former Casino Español. Founded in 1835, this is one of the oldest libraries in Cuba.

Photography Photo Service is at Calle 288 No 8311 between Calles 83 and 85.

Medical Services A new hospital was recently under construction on the outskirts of town. Ask for directions if you need aid. The old-fashioned Farmacia Central, Calles 85 and 280 (open 24 hours), was founded in 1838.

Things to See

In Town The steel **Puente Calixto García** (1899) spans the Río San Juan and leads directly into **Plaza de la Vigía** from the south. Three centuries ago the original settlement of Matanzas was established on this site. In the center of the square is a marble statue (1919) of a 19th-century independence fighter with a quotation from Antonio Maceo. The Matanzas fire brigade still has its headquarters in the neoclassical **Parque de los Bomberos** (1897) opposite the statue.

On the opposite side of the statue is the **Galería de Arte Provincial**, Calle 272 between 85 and 91 (Monday 9 am to 5 pm, Tuesday to Saturday 9 am to 6 pm, admission US$1). Next door is **Ediciones Vigía** (weekdays 8 am to noon and 1 to 5 pm, Saturday 8 am to noon), one of Matanzas' most intriguing attractions. Founded in 1985, this unique institution produces handmade first-edition books on a range of topics. The books are typed, stenciled, and pasted in editions of 200 copies. You can see books being made in workshops downstairs and upstairs, and purchase numbered signed copies for a mere US$5 to US$10 each. Many famous libraries have ordered these genuine collector's items.

The **Teatro Sauto** (1862), diagonally across Plaza de la Vigía from the art gallery, is one of the finest neoclassical buildings in Cuba. Marble statues of classical Greek goddesses stand in the lobby and the ceiling of the main hall bears paintings of the muses. Three balconies enclose this 775-seat theater, which features a floor that can be raised to convert the auditorium into a ballroom. The original theater curtain bears a painting of the Puente de Concordia over the Río Yumurí. Enrico Caruso once performed here, as did the Soviet dancer Ana Pavlova in 1945. Your best chance of catching a performance at the Sauto is on a Friday, Saturday, or Sunday night. Otherwise, the staff of the souvenir shop in a corner of the building will be happy to show you around Tuesday to Friday 9 am to 4:30 pm, Saturday 9 am to noon, and Sunday 2 to 5 pm (admission US$1).

Opposite Teatro Sauto the imposing **Palacio de Justicia** was first erected in 1826 and rebuilt between 1908 and 1911. Also on Plaza de la Vigía is the **Museo Histórico Provincial**, Calles 83 and 272 (Tuesday to Saturday 10 am to noon and 1 to 5 pm, Sunday 8:30 am to noon, admission US$1). This large museum housed in the Palacio del Junco (1840) contains exhibits relating to the history of Matanzas.

Two blocks west is the city's **Archivo Histórico**, Calle 83 No 28013 between 280 and 282, in the former residence of local poet José Jacinto Milanés (1814 – 1863). A bronze statue of Milanés stands on Plaza de la Iglesia in front of the nearby **Catedral de San Carlos Borromeo**, Calle 282 between 83 and 85. This neoclassical cathedral was first constructed in 1693 and rebuilt in 1878. Unfortunately the magnificent frescoes are moldy and peeling. The cathedral's front doors are open Monday to Friday from 8 am to noon and 3 to 5 pm, Sunday 9 am to noon (donation suggested).

The city's main square is **Parque Libertad**. A bronze statue of José Martí (1909) stands in its center. The east side of the square on Calle 288 is dominated by the orderly **Palacio de Gobierno** (1853), now the seat of Poder Popular (Popular Power). The first performance of the danzonette *Rompiendo La Rutina* by Anceto Díaz took

Neoclassical Iglesia San Pedro Apóstol in Matanzas

RICK GERHARTER

Deluxe Hotel Sol Palmares in Varadero

RICK GERHARTER

Playa Varadero

DAVID STANLEY

The oldest statue of Christopher Columbus
in the Americas (in Cárdenas)

DAVID STANLEY

The former Dupont Mansion in Varadero

DAVID STANLEY

Discoteca El Galeón in Varadero

place in the former **Casino Español**, Calles 79 and 290, on the northwest side of Parque Libertad. These days the building houses a library.

The **Museo Farmacéutico**, Calle 83 No 4951 on the south side of Parque Libertad, is the former Botica La Francesa founded in 1882 by the Triolett family. Since 1964 this has been a museum preserving the original furnishings, equipment, porcelain jars, and medical recipes (Monday to Saturday 10 am to 5 pm, Sunday 10 am to 2 pm, admission US$1).

From this square it's worth continuing three blocks west to Calle 298 and then four blocks south to the **Puente Sánchez Figueras** (1916) over the Río San Juan. Bustling **Mercado La Plaza** is adjacent to the bridge.

For an excellent view of Matanzas and the picturesque Valle de Yumurí march north up Calle 306 to the ruined **Iglesia de Monserrate** (1875).

The **Versalles quarter** north of the Río Yumurí was colonized by French refugees from Haiti in the 19th century. From just north of Plaza de la Vigía head north on Calle 272 across the graceful **Puente de la Concordia** with its tall pillar in each corner. The neoclassical **Iglesia de San Pedro Apóstol**, Calles 57 and 270, is worth seeking out. Four blocks east at Calles 63 and 260 stands the sinister-looking **Cuartel Goicuría**, a former barracks of Batista's army that was assaulted on April 29, 1956, by a group of rebels led by Reinold T García. Today it's a school.

In an industrial area above the port a little over one km northeast of here is the 18th-century **Castillo de San Severino**, erected by the Spanish. Entry is via the Centro Politécnico Ernest Thälmann on Calle 230 at the end of Calle 57, but in reality the castle is often closed.

Outside Town The **Cuevas de Bellamar** on Finca La Alcancía, five km southeast of Matanzas, is the city's most promoted tourist attraction. These 2500-meter-long caves were discovered in 1850 by a shepherd searching for a lost sheep. An underground stream is inside, a restaurant and snack bar outside. Tour groups descend into the caves for one-hour visits every 45 minutes daily from 9 am to 5 pm (admission US$3, cameras US$2, video camera US$4, parking US$1). Due to a railway realignment that blocks the former access road, the caves are now hard to find. Take Calle 276 south from Calle 171 near the old railway station and just keep watching for signs and asking along the way.

On your way from Matanzas to Varadero you'll pass the **Universidad de Matanzas Camilo Cienfuegos**, six km east of town. Founded in 1972, some 3000 students are taught here by 450 professors.

The Río Canímar, one km beyond the university, feeds into the Bahía de Matanzas. It is one of deepest rivers in Cuba. Just before the highway bridge a road runs one km down the west (Matanzas) side of the river to a cove where the four guns of the **Castillo del Morrillo** (1720) overlook a small beach at the river mouth. This two-story castle is now a museum (Tuesday to Sunday 9 am to 5 pm) dedicated to the student leader Antonio Guiteras Holmes (1906 – 1935) who founded the revolutionary group Joven Cuba (Young Cuba) in 1934. After serving briefly in the post-Machado government, Guiteras was forced out by army chief Fulgencio Batista, and on May 8, 1935, he and 18 others had come to Matanzas in hope of finding a yacht that would take them into exile in Mexico. Before they could board, Guiteras and Venezuelan revolutionary Carlos Aponte Hernández (1901 – 1935), who had served with Sandino in Nicaragua, were discovered by Batista's troops and shot. Bronze busts of the pair now mark the spot where they were executed, under a caoba (mahogany) tree down some steps from a cement gate back near the bridge.

Boat trips on the **Río Canímar** depart from Bar Cubamar below the bridge on the Varadero side of the river. This excellent excursion runs daily from noon to 5:30 pm, costing US$21 per person with lunch and horseback riding included. You must call ☎ 6-1516 one day ahead to make a

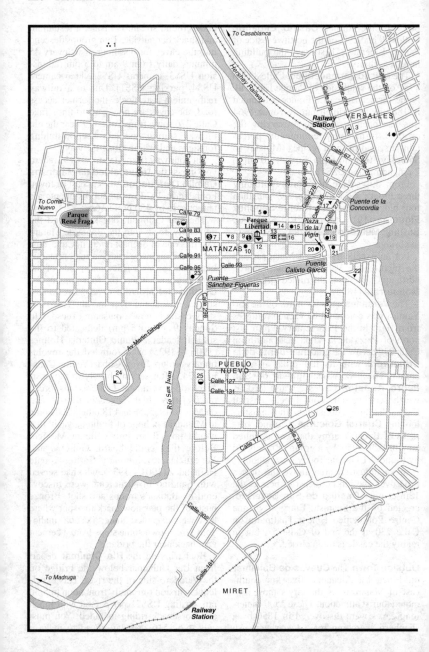

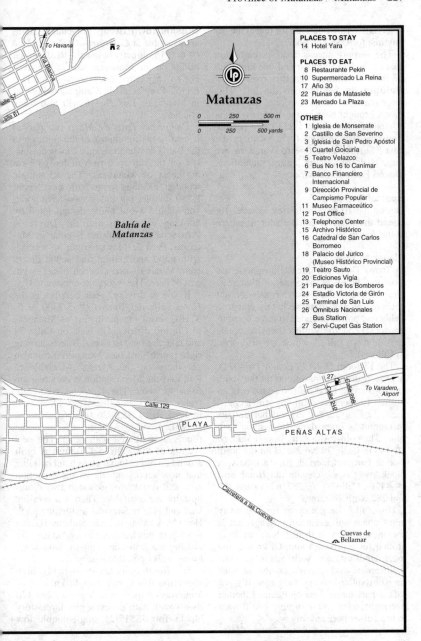

PLACES TO STAY
14 Hotel Yara

PLACES TO EAT
8 Restaurante Pekin
10 Supermercado La Reina
17 Año 30
22 Ruinas de Matasiete
23 Mercado La Plaza

OTHER
1 Iglesia de Monserrate
2 Castillo de San Severino
3 Iglesia de San Pedro Apóstol
4 Cuartel Goicuría
5 Teatro Velazco
6 Bus No 16 to Canímar
7 Banco Financiero Internacional
9 Dirección Provincial de Campismo Popular
11 Museo Farmaceútico
12 Post Office
13 Telephone Center
15 Archivo Histórico
16 Catedral de San Carlos Borromeo
18 Palacio del Jurico (Museo Histórico Provincial)
19 Teatro Sauto
20 Ediciones Vigía
21 Parque de los Bomberos
24 Estadio Victoria de Girón
25 Terminal de San Luis
26 Ómnibus Nacionales Bus Station
27 Servi-Cupet Gas Station

reservation. Rowboats are for rent at the bar anytime for US$2 an hour.

The airport access road is eight km east of the Río Canímar and one km south of the Vía Blanca. On this road is the **Refugio de Saturno** to the left. This large cave is often explored by scuba divers brought here by the Varadero scuba companies for about US$33 per person. You can also just go for a swim in the cave. Further east toward Varadero are large sisal-producing agave plantations around Boca de Camarioca.

Special Events

During the 10 days following October 10, attend the Festival del Bailador Rumbero at the Teatro Sauto.

Places to Stay

In Town There are three atmospheric old two-story hotels in the center of Matanzas. Unfortunately non-Cuban visitors are not accepted at any of these hotels due to a deliberate policy intended to force foreigners to stay at the more expensive hotels outside town (all of which are also open to Cubans).

The 17-room *Hotel El Louvre* (☎ 4074), next to Museo Farmacéutico on the south side of Parque Libertad (no sign), is in an elegant 19th-century building with a courtyard. El Louvre has a good bar and its restaurant is open daily from noon to 8 pm. The old-fashioned *Hotel Velazco* (☎ 4443), Calle 79 No 28803 on the north side of Parque Libertad, has 18 rooms. A block away is the elegant old *Hotel Yara* (☎ 4418), Calle 79 No 28216 between 288 and 282, with 16 rooms.

Hopefully the policy of turning away non-Cubans will eventually change, but in the meantime you'll just have to look around for a private room. Of course, the local landlords are well aware of your predicament and demand exorbitant rates for substandard, noisy lodgings. It's not safe to park a rental car on Parque Libertad overnight, so if you're driving you'll want to head elsewhere anyway.

Outside Town Twenty low-budget cabins are available at *Campismo Canímar Abajo* (☎ 6-1516) directly below the Río Canímar bridge on the Matanzas side of the river. For an easy entry, book ahead at the Dirección Provincial de Campismo Popular in Matanzas. Bus No 16 will also bring you here.

Campismo Faro de Maya (no phone) is next to the lighthouse at the entrance to the Bahía de Matanzas on a tiny peninsula. It's on the old road to Varadero, 17 km northeast of Matanzas. The 85 simple wooden cabañas with bath cost about US$9 double, but unless you have a car, you should avoid being disappointed by booking ahead through the Dirección Provincial de Campismo Popular in Matanzas. Faro de Maya is right on a beach with good snorkeling, and scuba divers from Varadero use a beach just 1½ km east of here. The resort has a restaurant.

If you're driving, your best bet is the *Hotel Valle del Yumurí* (☎ 5-3300 or 5-3118), seven km northwest of Matanzas in Chirino district. Go west on Calle 79 and take the road to Corral Nuevo, turning right (north) just past Mena. You can also get there on the Matanzas-Casablanca Railway; the Mena station is only two km from the hotel. The 42 rooms with bath, fridge, and TV in a three-story block built in 1985 cost US$20/26 single/double low season, US$24/32 high season. Some rooms have shared bath (ask). The new section of the Valle del Yumurí is built around an old colonial-style hotel building that now serves mostly as the reception area and restaurant, although two rooms upstairs are available. There's a bowling lane and nice rectangular swimming pool. Horseback riding is US$3 an hour. Hidden in a forest, this hotel makes a good base for visiting the Valle del Yumurí, with some lovely walks possible nearby.

The *Hotel Canimao* (☎ 6-1014), high above the Río Canímar eight km east of Matanzas on the way to Varadero, has 120 rooms with bath in seven new three-story blocks for US$17/21 single/double low season, US$21/28 high season. There's a swimming pool. The cabaret is open daily except Monday from 10:30 pm to 2:30 am (admission US$10). Boat trips are offered on the Río Canímar on Saturday (US$30 including lunch); on Thursday there's a trip to Cuevas de Bellamar (US$5). Bus No 16 from Calle 300 at 83 in Matanzas (see map) will drop you at the bridge near the hotel. The Canimao is 14 km from Juan Gualberto Gómez International Airport, but no taxis are stationed at the hotel so it's of no use as a stepping stone in reaching the airport. There's a guarded parking lot.

Places to Eat
Self-Catering The snack bar at the corner of Calles 83 and 294 (open 24 hours) sells loaves of bread.

Groceries and more bread are available at *Supermercado La Reina*, Calle 85 No 29006 between Calles 290 and 292 (Monday to Saturday 9 am to 5 pm, Sunday 8:30 am to 12:30 pm).

Matanzas' colorful vegetable market is near the Puente Sánchez Figueras, Calles 97 and 298. Many peso-accepting food stalls are here if you have a strong stomach.

Restaurants The restaurant situation in Matanzas is pretty poor. Most transit tourists eat at *Cafe Atenas*, Calles 83 and 272 opposite the Teatro Sauto on Plaza de la Vigía (open 24 hours). It offers pizza, spaghetti, sandwiches, chicken, ice cream, and drinks, and the overhead fans and old metal chairs look good. Unfortunately the food is uninspiring and the waiters will probably try to overcharge, so be sure to check the menu carefully before ordering.

Another unfriendly place with a meager choice of sandwiches, beer, and soft drinks available for dollars is *Cafe Velasco*, Calle 79 on the north side of Parque Libertad (open 24 hours). *Cafeteria El Rápido*, Calles 85 and 282 next to the cathedral, has absolutely nothing to recommend it except the cheap prices. Even McDonald's tastes good after this!

Two places catering to the local peso-paying crowd are *Restaurante Pekin*, Calle 83 No 29214 between 292 and 294 (daily noon to 2 pm and 6 to 9 pm), and *Año 30*, Calle 272 near the Puente de la Concordia (Monday to Saturday noon to 2 pm). You'll be expected to pay in dollars.

The *Ruinas de Matasiete* (open 24 hours) is a dollar bar housed in the ruins of a 19th-century warehouse next to the bay. It's near the entrance to town if you're coming from Varadero. Drinks and grilled meats are served on an open-air terrace, and there's sometimes live music on weekend evenings. The place is named after a famous bandit who committed seven murders.

Mesón La Viña, Calles 83 and 290 next to the Museo Farmacéutico on the south side of Parque Libertad, may be worth checking out (Monday to Saturday 10 am to 5 pm). This 19th-century grocery store is now a noted (though badly managed) cafe.

Entertainment
The *Teatro Velazco*, Calle 79 at 288 on Parque Libertad, is actually a cinema. Musical events often take place at the *Casa de la Cultura José White*, Calle 79 between 288 and 290. This is the former Lyceum Club and it was here in 1879 that the danzón was danced for the first time.

Your best bet for live theater and music is the *Teatro Sauto* previously mentioned under Things to See. Opposite the service station behind Teatro Sauto is the *Centro Nocturno Antillano*, Calles 83 and 268 (daily from 8 pm), where you're sure to find locals hanging out.

Spectator Sports
Baseball games take place at the Estadio Victoria de Girón, near the Río San Juan one km southwest of the market. Games are usually Tuesday, Wednesday, and Thursday at 3:30 or 8 pm, Saturday at 1:30 pm (if broadcast by radio) or 5 pm (if televised), and Sunday at 1:30 pm. Admission costs one peso.

Things to Buy

Try the Casa de Bienes Culturales La Vigía, Calle 272 No 8501 at 85 on Plaza de la Vigía. For highly original handmade books, go to Ediciones Vigía nearby (turn to Things to See for more information).

Getting There & Away

Matanzas is on the Vía Blanca between Varadero and Havana, 42 km west of Varadero and 98 km east of central Havana. The Carretera Central from Pinar del Río to Santiago de Cuba also passes through the city.

Matanzas is connected to the outside world through Juan Gualberto Gómez International Airport, 20 km east (turn to Getting There & Away in the Varadero section for details). All trains between Havana and Santiago de Cuba call here.

Bus Long-distance buses use the Ómnibus Nacionales bus station in the old train station at Calles 131 and 272 in Reparto Pueblo Nuevo south of the Río San Juan. There are buses to Varadero (daily, 42 km), Cárdenas (daily, 51 km), Havana (four daily, 98 km, two hours), Santa Clara (daily, 199 km, 4½ hours), Camagüey (daily, 469 km), and Santiago de Cuba (daily, 797 km).

Buses within Matanzas Province to Varadero, Cárdenas, Jovellanos (54 km), Colón (89 km), and Jagüey Grande (90 km) use the Terminal de San Luis, Calles 298 at 127. Private taxis park outside this station.

Train The new Estación de Ferrocarriles is on Calle 181 in Reparto Miret at the southern edge of the city. Since foreigners must pay the peso price in dollars, the staff will do its best to get you a ticket. There are seven early morning trains to Havana (US$3.50 regular, US$4 express), a morning train to Sancti Spíritus, an afternoon train to Los Arabos (via Jovellanos and Colón), other afternoon trains to Santa Clara (US$7 ordinary) and Cienfuegos, a night train to Camagüey (US$16 ordinary) and Las Tunas (US$20.50 ordinary), and a late night train to Bayamo and Manzanillo. The nightly express train that runs to/from Santiago de Cuba (764 km, 13 hours, US$32) goes via Santa Clara (189 km, 2½ hours, US$8), Ciego de Ávila (343 km, five hours, US$15), Camagüey (445 km, seven hours, US$19), Las Tunas (565 km, nine hours, US$24), and Cacocum (638 km, 10 hours, US$24).

The Hershey Railway uses a different station at Calles 55 and 67 in Versalles, an easy 10-minute walk from Parque Libertad. There are four trains a day to Casablanca Station in Havana (four hours, $2.80) via Hershey ($1.35). At last report the departure times from Matanzas were 4 am, 9:40 am, 2:55 pm, and 9 pm. The sale of tickets begins an hour before the scheduled departure time, and except on weekends and holidays there's no problem getting aboard. Though the train usually leaves on time, it often arrives in Havana one hour late. This is the only electric railway in Cuba and during thunderstorms the train must stop. It's a very scenic trip if you're not in a hurry.

Hitching Cubans often try to hitch to Havana from opposite the former Cuartel Goicuría, Calles 63 and 260 in Versalles. For Varadero take bus No 16 from Calle 300 between Calles 81 and 83 to Canímar and hitch from there.

Getting Around

Weekends from 9 am to 6 pm bus No 12 operates every hour to the Cuevas de Bellamar and Ermita de Monserrate. Catch it on Calle 298 (or just take a private taxi from the Terminal de San Luis on the same street).

The Servi-Cupet gas station is at Calles 129 and 208, four km out on the road to Varadero. A soda bar with snacks is attached.

VARADERO

At the end of the Vía Blanca, 140 km east of Havana, is Varadero, the largest resort complex in the Caribbean. Although a Cuban holiday center existed here as early as 1872, international development only began in 1930 when the US chemical millionaire Irenee Dupont Nemours built an estate complete with a large mansion, golf course, airstrip, and yacht harbor. Other wealthy Americans soon followed and Varadero became a millionaires' hideaway. Even Chicago mafia boss Al Capone used to holiday at Varadero.

In March 1959 all private beaches in Cuba were declared public, and since the mid-1970s Varadero has accommodated tens of thousands of Canadians and western Europeans. One foreign tourist in three visiting Cuba spends his or her vacation here. Foreign companies have arrived in growing numbers in recent years to build huge resorts along the eastern peninsula. Varadero caters mostly to visitors who come for the sun, sand, blue-green water, and everything that goes with it. In addition, some 10,000 Cubans live here year-round.

Orientation

Varadero begins at the west end of the Península de Hicacos where a channel called the Laguna de Paso Malo links the Bahía de Cárdenas to the Atlantic Ocean. After crossing the Puente Bascular over this waterway the Vía Blanca becomes the Autopista Sur and runs up the peninsula's spine to the Marina Gaviota at Varadero's easternmost point. From the same bridge Avenida Kawama heads west along the channel toward several new resorts. In general, the Atlantic side of the peninsula is devoted to tourism, while the Bahía de Cárdenas side is where local Cubans live (they also live in Santa Marta at the western end of the peninsula).

Parallel to Autopista Sur on the ocean side are avenues 1, 2, 3, and 4, which are transversed at right angles by a series of short streets numbered 1 to 69. The center of town is Parque Central, at Avenida 1 between Calles 44 and 46. Avenida de la Playa runs along the beach in the center of Varadero and, at the east end of downtown, Avenida Las Américas branches off Avenida 1 and continues east to the largest and most expensive resorts.

The 20 km of white sands for which Varadero is famous stretch along the Atlantic side of the peninsula. The rolling breakers and shifting sands here inhibit coral growth, making the snorkeling unspectacular. Yet Varadero is a joy for those with the time to stroll kilometer after kilometer along these pure white sands, and tractors clean the beach each morning Beach chairs cost US$2 a day.

The hotel and restaurant listings that follow are organized in geographical order from west to east from one end of the peninsula to the other.

Information

Immigration The immigration office, Avenida 1 and Calle 39 (weekdays 8 to 11:30 am and 1 to 4 pm, Saturday 8 to 11:30 am), has no sign, but it's the green building beyond a parking lot diagonally opposite the United Colors of Benetton store. You can pay your US$25 visa extension fee at the nearby Club Herradura.

Tourist Offices The Centro de Información Turística Rumbos, Avenida 1 at Calle 23 (daily 8 am to 8 pm), sells excursion tickets and maps but has little information about anything else.

Money The easiest place to change money is the Caja de Ahorros, Calle 36 between Avenida 1 and Autopista Sur (weekdays 8 am to noon and 1:30 to 4:30 pm). It charges 2% commission to change traveler's checks into cash dollars and it also makes cash advances. The somewhat more crowded Banco Nacional de Cuba, Avenida 1 at 36 (weekdays 8 am to 12 pm), charges the same commission.

The privately operated Banco Financiero Internacional, Avenida de la Playa and Calle 32 (upstairs), takes 3% commission on traveler's checks and makes cash advances on Visa and MasterCard. Although its hours are better (daily 8 am to 12:30 pm and 1:30 to 7 pm), this office is usually extremely crowded, so come early or late. Those staying at the upmarket resorts in eastern Varadero can use the

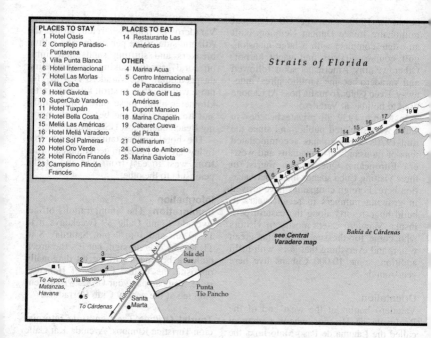

PLACES TO STAY	PLACES TO EAT
1 Hotel Oasis	14 Restaurante Las
2 Complejo Paradiso-	Américas
Puntarena	
3 Villa Punta Blanca	**OTHER**
6 Hotel Internacional	4 Marina Acua
7 Hotel Las Morlas	5 Centro Internacional
8 Villa Cuba	de Paracaidismo
9 Hotel Gaviota	13 Club de Golf Las
10 SuperClub Varadero	Américas
11 Hotel Tuxpán	14 Dupont Mansion
12 Hotel Bella Costa	18 Marina Chapelín
15 Meliá Las Américas	19 Cabaret Cueva
16 Hotel Meliá Varadero	del Pirata
17 Hotel Sol Palmeras	21 Delfinarium
20 Hotel Oro Verde	24 Cueva de Ambrosio
22 Hotel Rincón Francés	25 Marina Gaviota
23 Campismo Rincón	
Francés	

Straits of Florida

see Central Varadero map

Bahía de Cárdenas

Banco Financiero Internacional branch next to the reception desk at Villa Cuba (weekdays 9:30 am to noon and 1 to 4 pm; Saturday 8:30 am to noon).

Hotel reception desks are the worst places to change money, as the cashiers take around 4% commission to cash US dollar traveler's checks or to change foreign banknotes into greenbacks.

You can buy Cuban pesos for cash dollars at the Casas de Cambio (Cadeca), Avenida de la Playa and Calle 41 (daily 9 am to 6 pm). It offers as much or more than the unofficial moneychangers hanging around nearby. If you don't intend to go beyond Varadero or the tour bus circuit, you won't need any *moneda nacional* as foreign tourists can't buy much for pesos around here.

It's a good idea to always keep a supply of small Cuban coins in your pocket or purse; otherwise, the cashiers at hotel shops will give you candies as change.

Post & Communications The local Correos y Telégrafos office is on Avenida de la Playa between Calles 39 and 40 (Monday to Saturday 8 am to 6 pm).

Many of the larger hotels have convenient branch post offices in the reception area, and these accept only dollars. Card phones accepting magnetic telephone cards are available here. These cards are the easiest way to make calls.

The Centro Telefónico Nacional, Avenida 1 and Calle 30 (Monday to Saturday 8 am to 10 pm, Sunday 8 am to 8 pm), sells cards of US$10 and US$25 that can be used to place local, national, and international calls through phones in its office.

The Centro Telefónico Internacional, Calle 64 between Avenida Las Américas and Avenida 2 (daily 8 am to 10 pm), is the top communications office at Varadero and the DHL Express courier service representative.

Direct-dial telephones at Varadero use

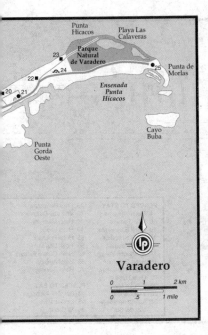

Punta Hicacos
Playa Las Calaveras
Parque Natural de Varadero
23
24
22
25 Punta de Morlas
20 21
Ensenada Punta Hicacos
Cayo Buba
Punta Gorda Oeste

Varadero

0   1   2 km
0   .5   1 mile

addition to the local tours and excursions, it offers horseback riding (US$12 an hour), glass-bottom boat rides (US$25), and overnight yacht cruises.

A third choice is Gaviotatours, Avenida 1 between Calles 25 and 26.

Bookstore Librería Hanoi, Avenida 1 and Calle 44 (9 am to 9 pm), has a fair selection of books in English, cassettes, compact discs, and T-shirts.

Library Visitors are welcome at the Biblioteca José Smith Comas, Calle 33 No 104 between Avenidas 1 and 3 (Monday to Saturday 9 am to 8 pm). To take books out, you must present your hotel guest card. The service is free of charge, but most of the books are in Spanish.

Photography Cubanacán Photo Express and Photo Service both have offices on Avenida 1 between Calles 41 and 42. Farther east, another Photo Service branch is on Calle 63 between Avenidas 2 and 3 at the entrance to the Centro Commercial Copey (9 am to 10 pm).

the international access code 119. Varadero's own telephone code is 5.

Travel Agencies Varadero's most important travel agency is Havanatur Tour & Travel (☎ 66-7154, fax 66-7026) with a central office on Avenida de la Playa between Calles 36 and 37 (daily 8 am to 7 pm). Its branch offices are at Avenida Kawama and Calle 0 (Zero) near Hotel Kawama; at Avenida 1 and Calle 31 opposite Villa Caribe (daily 8 am to 8 pm); on Calle 64 near Hotel Siboney; and on Avenida Las Américas near Hotel Tuxpán. They arrange bus transfers to Havana (US$20) or the Havana airport (US$25) and local sightseeing excursions. Booking hotel rooms outside Varadero through them is risky, as the reservations are often not passed along.

Agencia de Viajes Playazul (☎ 6-3897), Avenida 1 and Calle 13 opposite the Hotel Acuazul (daily 8 am to 8 pm), is similar. In

Medical Services If you need to see a doctor or dentist, you'll receive immediate attention at the Clínica Internacional Servimed (☎ 66-7710), Avenida 1 and Calle 60. Varadero's best pharmacy is on the premises and all facilities are accessible around the clock. A medical or dental consultation will cost US$20, and it's US$10 an hour if you're hospitalized on these premises. Serious cases are referred to the new hospital in Matanzas.

Many large hotels have infirmaries that provide basic first-aid service free of charge.

The Policlínico Doctor Mario Muñoz Monroy, Calle 27 near Avenida 1 (open 24 hours), is a local clinic intended mostly for Cubans. The Clínica Estomatológico, Avenida 1 and Calle 49, is a dental clinic for Cubans. Whether they'll see you probably depends on who you are and who you get, but as always the care will be good.

A local pharmacy open 24 hours is on

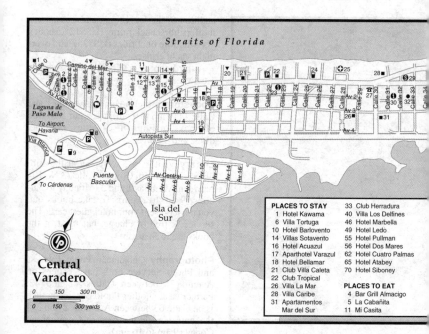

Straits of Florida

Central Varadero

0   150   300 m
0   150   300 yards

PLACES TO STAY
1 Hotel Kawama
6 Villa Tortuga
10 Hotel Barlovento
14 Villas Sotavento
16 Hotel Acuazul
17 Aparthotel Varazul
18 Hotel Bellamar
21 Club Villa Caleta
22 Club Tropical
26 Villa La Mar
28 Villa Caribe
31 Apartamentos Mar del Sur

33 Club Herradura
40 Villa Los Delfines
46 Hotel Marbella
49 Hotel Ledo
55 Hotel Pullman
56 Hotel Dos Mares
62 Hotel Cuatro Palmas
65 Hotel Atabey
70 Hotel Siboney

PLACES TO EAT
4 Bar Grill Almacigo
5 La Cabañita
11 Mi Casita

Avenida 1 between Calles 28 and 29, opposite the Communist Party offices. A better and friendlier pharmacy for Cubans is at the corner of Avenida de la Playa and Calle 44 (daily 8 am to 10 pm). There's no sign.

Emergency If you have any legal or financial problems, turn to Asistur, Calle 31 No 101 behind Havanautos (weekdays 8:30 am to 5 pm, Saturday 8:30 am to noon). It can help you out with insurance claims, change American Express traveler's checks, have money sent from overseas (except from the USA), organize repatriation, report a lost passport or tourist card, give advice if you become a victim of crime, and so on.

A Canadian Consulate (☎ 6-2078) is on Calle 7 across from Villa Tortuga (Monday, Tuesday, Wednesday, and Friday 5 to 7 pm).

Dangers & Annoyances Strangely, some electrical outlets in Varadero hotels oper-ate on 110 volts while others are 220 volts. Adjacent hotels belonging to the same hotel chain can have conflicting currents, and some rooms even have different currents in different outlets! Be sure to check carefully before plugging in any appliance you brought with you; a North American 110-volt shaver or hair dryer will burn out in minutes when fed a European-style 220-volt current.

A red flag on the beach means swimming is not allowed due to the undertow or some other danger. A blue jellyfish known as the Portuguese man-of-war will leave burning welts across your body if you come in contact with its long tentacles. They're most common in summer and you can usually determine whether any are present by looking for examples washed up on the beach. Be aware that the theft of unguarded shoes, sunglasses, and towels is routine along this beach (ask another visitor to watch your stuff while you're in the water).

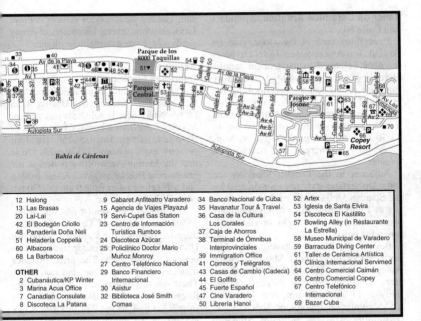

12 Halong	9 Cabaret Anfiteatro Varadero	34 Banco Nacional de Cuba
13 Las Brasas	15 Agencia de Viajes Playazul	35 Havanatur Tour & Travel
20 Lai-Lai	19 Servi-Cupet Gas Station	36 Casa de la Cultura
42 El Bodegón Criollo	23 Centro de Información	Los Corales
48 Panadería Doña Neli	Turística Rumbos	37 Caja de Ahorros
51 Heladería Coppelia	24 Discoteca Azúcar	38 Terminal de Ómnibus
60 Albacora	25 Policlínico Doctor Mario	Interprovinciales
68 La Barbacoa	Muñoz Monroy	39 Immigration Office
	27 Centro Telefónico Nacional	41 Correos y Telégrafos
OTHER	29 Banco Financiero	43 Casas de Cambio (Cadeca)
2 Cubanáutica/KP Winter	Internacional	44 El Golfito
3 Marina Acua Office	30 Asistur	45 Fuerte Español
7 Canadian Consulate	32 Biblioteca José Smith	47 Cine Varadero
8 Discoteca La Patana	Comas	50 Librería Hanoi

52 Artex	
53 Iglesia de Santa Elvira	
54 Discoteca El Kastillito	
57 Bowling Alley (in Restaurante	
La Estrella)	
58 Museo Municipal de Varadero	
59 Barracuda Diving Center	
61 Taller de Cerámica Artística	
63 Clínica Internacional Servimed	
64 Centro Comercial Caimán	
66 Centro Comercial Copey	
67 Centro Telefónico	
Internacional	
69 Bazar Cuba	

Twenty-four hours a day long tongues of flame shoot up from two tall chimneys just southwest of Varadero as superfluous natural gas from oil wells in the vicinity is burned off. Unfortunately the hotels of western Varadero are occasionally subjected to a horrible stench in the middle of the night as sulfurous gas is released from the wells. It usually doesn't last long but is worth remembering when booking a tour package (in other words, try for a hotel east of Hotel Bellamar). Varadero itself may be sitting on top of the richest oilfield of all, and wells may one day sprout from the hotel gardens. Notice the huge overwater drilling platform in the Bahía de Cárdenas south of the peninsula.

Things to See

Although Varadero's main sight is the beach itself, there's lots more to see along the peninsula. The **Fuerte Español**, Calle 43 No 106 off Avenida 1, is a two-story Spanish fort dating from 1897. It appears on the official Varadero coat of arms but is presently a private residence. The **Parque Central** and adjacent Parque de las 8000 Taquillas, both between Calles 44 and 46, are a bit rundown these days. Just east at Avenida 1 and Calle 47 is the colonial-style **Iglesia de Santa Elvira**.

A kilometer further east, the **Museo Municipal de Varadero**, Calle 57 off Avenida 1 (Tuesday to Saturday 9 am to 6 pm, Sunday 9 am to noon, admission US$1), displays Indian artifacts and paintings in a large two-story mansion erected in 1921. This is one of the few Cuban museums with captions in English, and there's a fine view of the beach from the upstairs balcony.

Parque Josone, Avenida 1 and Calle 58 (admission free), features a lake set among manicured lawns and artificial hills. The Retiro Josone on the grounds is now a romantic villa/restaurant and other pavilions are scattered around the park. You can see pottery being made at the

Taller de Cerámica Artística, Avenida 1 and Calle 60.

Everything east of the stone gate on Avenida Las Américas near Hotel Las Morlas once belonged to the Dupont family. Here they built a green-roofed, three-story mansion called Xanadu overlooking the coast and laid out a nine-hole golf course. Today the **Dupont Mansion** contains a restaurant downstairs (daily 10 am to 11:30 pm) and a bar on the top floor. Non-diners may be charged US$3 admission to enter.

Adjacent to the Dupont Mansion are three Disneyland-style resorts managed by the Spanish Meliá chain, each worth visiting as a holy shrine of contemporary consumer tourism. Walk right in and stroll around at will.

Beyond the Marina Chapelín, five km northeast of the Dupont Mansion along Autopista Sur, is Varadero's **Delfinarium**. Here you can witness dolphin shows daily at 11 am, 2:30 pm, and 4 pm for US$5 admission (photos another US$4). Swimming with the dolphins yourself costs US$25.

Another two km east on Autopista Sur beyond the Hotel Rincón Francés is the **Cueva de Ambrosio**. In 1961 some 72 Indian drawings were discovered in the cave. These feature the same concentric circles seen in similar Indian painting on the Isla de la Juventud, perhaps a form of solar calendar. Later the cave was used as a refuge by escaped slaves. A sign outside the cave claims it's open Tuesday to Sunday from 10 am to noon and 2 to 4 pm (admission US$2), but the attendants only bother to come when a group has booked a visit.

From the Hotel Rincón Francés, a road heads northeast toward Punta Hicacos. This entire eastern portion of the peninsula has been designated the **Parque Natural de Varadero** to preserve a bit of the local flora and fauna. After about three km you'll pass a giant cactus tree nicknamed 'El Patriarca' on the right and then some flatlands known as the Laguna Mangón, where sea water was once evaporated to produce salt. The big attraction for visitors is Playa Las Calaveras, several kilometers of empty sands where you can really be alone.

Activities

Deep-Sea Fishing Varadero's three marinas also offer many nautical activities and facilities. For instance, the *Marina Acua* (☎ 66-8063), near Hotel Oasis just west of Varadero, provides a boat for four hours of deep-sea fishing for US$250 for four persons, extra persons US$20 each. (Note that the Marina Acua office is across the bridge near Hotel Kawama.) A line fishing and snorkeling safari from 9 am to 4:30 pm costs US$50 per person.

The *Marina Chapelín* (☎ 66-7093 or 66-7550), near the Hotel Oro Verde, offers deep-sea fishing from 9 am to 2:30 pm for US$240 for one to four persons, extra persons US$30 each. The price includes transfers and an open bar, but not lunch. Their most popular trip is the 'Jolly Roger' safari to Cayo Blanco, which lasts from 9 am to 4:30 pm. For this you'll pay US$60 on a catamaran or US$65 on a yacht, including drinks, lunch, and hotel transfers. Private groups of between four and 10 persons can hire a yacht for the Cayo Blanco excursion for US$70 per person.

The *Marina Gaviota* (☎ 6-3712), at the east end of Autopista Sur, is less expensive but more remote. Deep-sea fishing from this marina costs US$200 for four anglers (extra persons to seven maximum cost US$20 each). You leave at 9 am, return at 3 pm, and have four hours of fishing (only two can fish at a time). The price includes hotel transfers and welcoming drink but no lunch (US$15 per person extra if required). A seven-hour motor-yacht tour including a lobster lunch on a coral key and hotel transfers, snorkeling, swimming, and line fishing is US$50 per person (on a sailing yacht US$55).

Scuba Diving Varadero's largest scuba facility is the Barracuda Diving Center (☎ 6-3481, fax 66-7072), Avenida 1 and

Calle 58. Diving is US$35 (or US$30 if you bring your own equipment). Cave diving or night diving costs US$40, a package of four dives US$105, and a package of seven dives US$175. You can go out snorkeling with the divers for US$21. Barracuda conducts introductory resort courses for US$70 and complete scuba certification courses for US$365. A popular seafood restaurant is on the center's premises.

In western Varadero, the Marina Acua office (☎ 66-8064), Avenida Kawama between Calles 3 and 4, charges US$35 for a single dive or US$50 for two dives (US$10 discount if you have your own equipment). (The office is not at the marina itself, which is off the Vía Blanca.) Five-dive packages cost US$150, ten-dive packages US$200. When a north wind is blowing and diving isn't possible in the Atlantic, they can transfer you over to the Caribbean coast in a minibus (1½-hour drive); this costs a total of US$55/60 for one/two dives.

Marina Gaviota (☎ 6-3712), at the east end of Autopista Sur, also offers scuba diving at similar prices and also has snorkeling trips. A three-hour snorkeling trip will run US$25 per person. Marina Chapelín (☎ 66-7093) also has snorkeling.

A decompression chamber is available at nearby Cárdenas.

Yachting Cubanáutica/KP Winter (☎ /fax 66-7403), Calle 3 near the Hotel Kawama, offers yacht or cabin-cruiser day trips by sailing (ask which) to Cayo Piedras at US$60 per person including hotel transfers, a lobster lunch, open bar, snorkeling, and line fishing. Trips depart at 9:30 am and return by 5 pm. Chartering a 10-passenger yacht for this trip costs US$750 all-inclusive. Overnight yacht trips (lasting from 9:30 am the first day to 5 pm the second day) are US$135 per person (four-person minimum/eight-person maximum). For three days the trip costs US$210. Drinks are not included on the overnight trips, but almost everything else is. A trip of this kind is highly recommended.

Golf Golfers will certainly want to test their swing at the Club de Golf Las Américas (☎ 66-7749) along Avenida Las Américas. The original nine holes created by the Duponts are between the Hotel Bella Costa and the Dupont Mansion, and in 1996 the course was extended to 18 holes by building another nine holes along the south side of the three Meliá resorts. At last report bookings were made through a small office in a corner of the Dupont Mansion, and green fees were US$10 (club and cart rentals available), although things could change as the course is upgraded.

It's also fun to play miniature golf at El Golfito, Avenida 1 and Calle 42 (open 24 hours). The charge is US$1 per person.

Skydiving Perhaps the greatest thrill Varadero offers is skydiving at the Centro Internacional de Paracaidismo (☎ 66-7256, fax 66-7260), based at the old airport just west of Varadero. The terminal is one km up the dirt road opposite Marina Acua. Sky divers take off in an Antonov AN-2 biplane (of WWII design but recently built) and jump from 3000 meters using a two-harness parachute with an instructor strapped in tandem to your back. After 40 seconds of free fall the parachute opens and you float another 10 minutes before landing on the beach right in front of your hotel.

The price is US$135 per person and that includes hotel transfers, a T-shirt, and a diploma. You can pay another US$45 to have photos taken of yourself during the dive or get a video of it all for US$50. The photographer will be an instructor who has the camera strapped to his head! Four pairs of divers jump from a single flight, and a dive offers all the excitement of starring in an old James Bond movie.

The parachuting center opened in 1993 and although they do about 250 jumps a month, there have been no accidents. Jumps are only scheduled in good weather when the wind is exactly right, so start inquiring as soon as you get to Varadero if you're keen.

Other There's a bowling alley in Restaurante La Estrella (☎ 66-2649, open daily 9 am to 9 pm) at the back of Parque Josone, Avenida 1 and 56. It's US$2 a lane. You can also play billiards here.

Surfboard rentals can be problematic at Varadero, so you'd better bring your own.

Special Events
The carnival formerly held at Varadero in late January and early February has been discontinued. At last report there was still an International Marathon at the end of November.

Organized Tours
Tour desks at the main hotels book most of the nautical or sporting activities mentioned above and arrange organized sightseeing excursions from Varadero. Among the many trips offered are a half-day trip to the Cuevas de Bellamar near Matanzas (US$15); a 10-hour bus tour to the Bay of Pigs and the crocodile farm at Boca de Guamá (US$43 including lunch); bus tours to Trinidad (US$59) and Soroa (US$74); a full-day tour of Havana (US$49 including lunch); an 18-hour tour of Havana including the evening show at the Tropicana Nightclub (US$115 including lunch and dinner); an overnight trip to Havana (US$159 including accommodations); and an evening trip to the Tropicana Nightclub (US$89). Excursions by air are possible to Trinidad (US$89), Santiago de Cuba (US$118), Baracoa (US$129), Pinar del Río (US$94), Cayo Coco (US$89), and Cayo Largo (US$94).

A visit to colonial Havana is a must and the Bay of Pigs trip is a good second choice, if only because you get to see the Cuban countryside. Only the Havana trips operate daily. The other trips are often canceled if the minimum number of participants fail to sign up, so it's wise to decide early and make advance bookings at your hotel desk. The day before your scheduled departure date, ask the booking clerk to reconfirm that the tour will actually operate. This will allow time to make alternate plans if it falls through.

Boat Tours Marina Gaviota's pride and joy is the 'underwater viewer' glass-bottom boat *Nautilo*, which has 56 viewing windows and a capacity for 90 passengers. It's US$25 for the four-hour trip, including hotel transfers and a welcoming drink. Make a reservation either at your hotel desk or through Havanatur. The 48-passenger *Varasub* based at Villa Punta Blanca offers similar underwater viewing possibilities six times a day for US$20/35 for children/adults (one hour). Local Havanatur offices handle bookings.

Places to Stay
Varadero is an extremely popular destination for foreign tourists. If you're picky about your accommodations or you intend to stay a while, consider making advance reservations. On the other hand, hotels are numerous and rooms number in the thousands, so you probably won't have trouble finding an adequate room even without a reservation. It may just take you longer.

Camping The least expensive regular accommodations are at *Campismo Rincón Francés* (no phone), two km east of the new Hotel Rincón Francés at the far east end of Varadero. The 38 A-frame cabañas facing the beach are US$5 for up to four persons (shared bath), or US$15 with bath for up to three persons. You could also pitch your own tent. The restaurant here is expensive, so it's best to bring food. Unless you've rented a car or have a bicycle, the only easy way to get there is by taxi.

Private Rooms Cheaper and less policed than the hotels are the private rooms rented to visitors by local residents. It's usually possible to rent a small apartment with private bath in central Varadero for US$25 a day, with reductions for long stays. The rooms vary in quality, so it pays to shop around. Sometimes you'll have a private entrance; other times you'll have to walk in through the living room past the family. Government restrictions prevent the owners from posting signs or turning their places into regular guest houses.

We're unable to provide any addresses because things change fast and any place mentioned here might disappear quickly. Despite this, many repeat visitors to Varadero always find a place to stay by seeking out a private room.

Villas & Hotels The accommodations listings that follow are arranged in geographical order from west to east. At the risk of going overboard, we've tried to describe every hotel to ensure that the place you're considering booking is included. Almost all rooms are air-conditioned, but on some of the cheaper tours you get a bedroom in an apartment and must share the TV room, toilet, and shower with another couple or individual. The only way to be sure of a private bathroom is to have your travel agent clarify this point with the tour operator before booking. Trying to correct this mistake after you've arrived at heavily booked Varadero is difficult. Even the deluxe hotels often charge extra to use the mini-fridge, safety deposit box, beach towels, beach chairs, sauna, and satellite TV.

Hotels with low-occupancy levels often reduce their rates to fill their rooms. Other than the Campismo Rincón Francés, the least expensive hotels regularly accepting foreigners are Villa Tortuga, Villas Sotavento, Aparthotel Varazul, Hotel Bellamar, Villa La Mar, Apartamentos Mar del Sur, Club Herradura, Hotel Pullman, and the Hotel Dos Mares. If you're traveling independently, ask for one of the places in central Varadero between Calles 7 and 53. Many of the more expensive resorts are beyond Hotel Internacional in eastern Varadero, 12 km from downtown Varadero and about 26 km east of Varadero International Airport. Head to these pricier resorts if you don't care about the price and want a quality vacation.

Virtually all of the hotels are owned by the government and it's officially prohibited to take Cubans you meet on the street or beach back to your room. How strict the doorman is about this varies according to your hotel, who's watching at the time,

whether you might be going to the hotel disco, or the size of your gratuity. The street action late at night around the corner of Avenida 1 and Calle 13 might lead you to surmise that Varadero is a wide open town, but it isn't as simple as that.

The only Varadero hotel west of the access bridge to the peninsula is the *Hotel Oasis* (☎ 66-7380) on the Vía Blanca about five km west of the rest of Varadero. This two-story, motel-style building is wedged around the swimming pool a bit back from the rocky beach. The 147 rooms with bath are US$29/38 single/double low season, US$34/45 high season for the room only, or US$54/88 low season, US$59/95 high season including meals and drinks. Activities include a disco, bicycle and scooter rentals, and horseback riding (US$6 an hour). It's rather isolated and not a good choice.

The *Complejo Paradiso-Puntarena* (☎ 66-7125), Avenida Kawama and Final on the beach at the west end of Varadero, consists of twin eight-story blocks next to the channel linking the Bahía de Cárdenas to the sea. Opened in 1990, the Puntarena is often called the 'Siesta Club' by tour companies selling all-inclusive packages. Together the two towers have 510 rooms with bath, color TV, and balcony at US$65/90 single/double low season, US$85/130 high season. Among the many facilities are impressive two-level atrium lobbies, a huge freshwater swimming pool with swim-up bar, a sauna, fitness room, scooter rentals, and a Transautos car-rental desk. A package at the Puntarena's Discoteca La Salsa offers admission and unlimited drinks for US$15. The bars, shops, and restaurants here are on the expensive side, and the whole complex is rather isolated. It's strictly an affluent foreigner's playground far removed from the realities of Cuban life. Another major drawback is the midnight stink from the oil wells directly opposite the resort.

Villa Punta Blanca (☎ 6-3916), on the beach near the west end of Varadero between the Paradiso-Puntarena and Hotel

Kawama, is a sprawling 316-room complex of 35 red-roofed villas, six two-story buildings, and a big new three-story block. A room with shower runs US$38/58 single/double low season, US$47/72 high season, but the living rooms and verandas of the renovated prerevolution holiday homes here vary from unit to unit. A swimming pool, tennis court, Splash Disco, and other facilities are available.

The *Hotel Kawama* (☎ 6-3015), Calle 0 (Zero) near Avenida Kawama, is a graceful old hacienda-style hotel dating from before the revolution. The 194 rooms and cabins with shower begin at US$45/65 single/double low season, US$55/85 high season, US$70/110 peak season. Only about half the rooms have TV sets. The eight low-rise units of 10 to 12 rooms each are right on the beach.

Villa Tortuga (☎ 6-2243), Calle 7 between Avenida 1 and Camino del Mar, has 264 rooms with shower in 20 two-story villas for US$26/35 single/double low season, US$34/45 high season. This medium-priced hotel is half a block from the beach in an area known for its nightlife. Havanautos has a car-rental office nearby.

The more upmarket *Hotel Barlovento* (☎ 66-7140), Avenida 1 between Calles 9 and 12, has 288 rooms with bath, balcony, and TV in three two- and three-story buildings facing the large swimming pool. It's managed by the Spanish Iberostar chain and is a bit overpriced at US$75/96 single/double low season, US$110 single or double high season.

Villas Sotavento, Calle 13 between Avenida 1 and Camino del Mar, offers a variety of older two-story villas, each with three or four double units. The 108 simple rooms with shower vary considerably as these were once privately owned holiday homes, and the front door, living room, fridge, and patio will be shared with other guests. At US$23/30/40 single/double/triple low season, US$29/38/48 high season, it's a good value if you're lucky with your neighbors. Make inquiries at the Hotel Acuazul reception, which also controls the Sotavento.

The eight-story *Hotel Acuazul* (☎ 66-7132), Avenida 1 and Calle 13, has 75 rooms with bath, TV, and balcony at US$35/50 single/double low season, US$45/60 high season. It's two blocks from the beach, but there's a small triangular swimming pool. Disco La Pachanga is in a corner of the hotel and the street-level bar next to the disco has happy hour from 4 to 6 pm. This area is usually thick with prostitutes and hustlers late into the night, although the action doesn't necessarily spill over into the hotel rooms.

The Hotel Acuazul reception desk also takes care of the seven-story *Aparthotel Varazul*, Avenida 1 between Calles 14 and 15, where the 65 one-bedroom apartments with shower, kitchenette, TV, and small balcony are US$28/38 single/double low season, US$36/48 high season. The grocery store next door makes cooking your own food possible. You can use the pool of the adjacent Hotel Acuazul, and the beach is just a five-minute walk away. The Varazul is getting a little old and tired, but it's still popular among visitors who prebook long stays.

Hotel Bellamar (☎ 6-3014), Calle 17 between Avenidas 1 and 2, one block back from the beach, is a 'no frills' budget hotel. The Bellamar's eight- and 12-story blocks contain 282 dimly lit rooms with shower and satellite TV costing US$29/38 single/double low season, US$32/43 high season. Many of the units are small apartments that share a bathroom between two rooms. There are many facilities, including a swimming pool, 24-hour cafeteria, and Discoteca El Eclipse (on the 12th floor). You get what you pay for and it isn't a lot.

Club Villa Caleta (☎ 66-7080, fax 66-7194), Avenida 1 and Calle 20, has 46 rooms with bath and satellite TV in two-story bungalows facing the beach or a long three-story block at US$45/60 single/double low season, US$55/72 high season. This intimate resort, often patronized by Italian groups, has a swimming pool and National car-rental desk.

A slightly more upmarket choice is *Club Tropical* (☎ 6-3915), Avenida 1 between

Calles 22 and 23. The 70 rooms with shower and TV in several new two-, three-, and four-story buildings on the beach in the heart of Varadero are US$47/63 single/double low season, US$60/80 high season. Cheaper rooms in an older annex called *Villa Los Cocos* next door are US$30/40 single/double low season, US$38/50 high season in two-bedroom apartments with shared facilities. A circular swimming pool and a Transautos car-rental office are on the premises.

About two hundred meters inland from the beach and without a swimming pool is budget-priced *Villa La Mar* (☎ 6-3130), Avenida 3 and Calle 29. The 260 rooms with bath and TV are in a series of newish four-story blocks. The rates are US$23/29 single/double low season, US$29/35 high season.

Pink-colored *Apartamentos Mar del Sur* (☎ 6-2246), Avenida 3 and Calle 30, formerly known as Villa Granma, consists of 10 scattered four-story blocks. The 318 rooms with shower and TV go for US$25/30 single/double low season, US$33/38 high season – a good value. Cooking facilities and a living room are available in the one- and two-bedroom units for US$38 double low season, US$40 high season. It's all several hundred meters away from the beach, but the complex features a large swimming pool.

Villa Caribe (☎ 6-3310), Avenida 1 and Calle 31, is on the beach in the center of Varadero. The 124 rooms for US$35/47/57 single/double/triple high season are in 53 apartments. In some cases you'll be expected to share the bathroom. There's a swimming pool hidden in the core of this complex of green, three-story blocks.

Club Herradura (☎ 6-3703), Avenida de la Playa between Calles 35 and 36, is a four-story, crescent-shaped hotel overlooking the beach. The 78 rooms in shared apartments with bath and TV are US$29/35 single/double low season, US$34/45 high season. Once again, check whether the bathroom is private or shared. There's a small grocery store here and next door is a military holiday camp called Playa Azul.

Villa Los Delfines (☎ 6-3815), Avenida de la Playa and Calle 38, is on the beach in central Varadero. There are 47 rooms, 11 of them in an older main building and 36 in a new four-story block. Singles/doubles cost US$49/98 year-round including breakfast and dinner.

The three-story *Hotel Marbella* (☎ 6-3206), Avenida 1 and Calle 42, is intended mostly for Cubans. In 1996 it was gutted and closed. Also closed for renovations in 1996 was the *Hotel Ledo* (☎ 6-3206), Avenida de la Playa and Calle 43, a two-story motel in the center of Varadero. The Ledo's 20 rooms with bath used to be among the cheapest on this beach, but the new prices are still unknown.

The *Hotel Pullman* (☎ 66-7161), Avenida 1 between Calles 49 and 50, is a small colonial-style pension 150 meters back from the beach. The 15 fan-cooled rooms with bath are US$26/36 single/double low season, US$30/40 high season.

The hotel school operates the *Hotel Dos Mares* (☎ 6-2702), Avenida 1 and Calle 53, an attractive old three-story building about 70 meters from the beach. The 34 rooms with bath are US$32/43 single/double high season. Both the Pullman and the Dos Mares are a bit overpriced for what they offer but perhaps OK for a couple of nights.

On the beach the upmarket *Hotel Cuatro Palmas* (☎ 66-7040), Avenida 1 between Calles 60 and 62, has 200 rooms with bath and satellite TV in a huge Spanish-style complex of two- and three-story blocks enclosing the swimming pool. Another 112 rooms with shower, fridge, and satellite TV are in a series of shared villas jammed together across the street, a block back from the beach, so what you get can vary. Expect to pay US$83/96 single/double low season, US$96/114 high season. In early 1996 the French Accor chain took over management of the Cuatro Palmas.

If unlimited shopping, eating, and drinking are your major concerns, you won't go wrong at the hotels Atabey or Siboney, huge complexes collectively known as the *Copey Resort*. These twin hotels are on opposite sides of a big shopping arcade and both share a large swimming pool, a sauna, the Havana Club disco, Havanautos and Transautos car-rental offices, and many other facilities. Signs on the doors of the Atabey and Siboney restrict entry to hotel guests, so don't try inviting in friends. It's a four-block walk to the beach through a crowded mall, across a busy road, and past another resort, but the Copey's grounds are spacious if you decide to stay put and socialize with other guests.

The *Hotel Atabey* (☎ 6-3013 or 66-7505, fax 66-7509), Avenida 3 and Calle 60, has 136 rooms with shower and balcony in a main five-story building plus 43 cabañas, all on the Bahía de Cárdenas side of the peninsula. Ask for a room facing away from noisy Autopista Sur, which passes behind the hotel. Unlike the neighboring Siboney, which will rent you a room only, the Atabey requires that you take the all-inclusive deal, which costs US$62/101 single/double high season or about US$45 per person in the low season. All the food and drink you care to push or pour into your mouth is included.

The *Hotel Siboney* (☎ 66-7500, fax 66-7503), Avenida 2 and Calle 64, consists of two four- and five-story hotel blocks with 179 rooms with shower, TV, and balcony for US$29/34 single/double low season, US$34/45 high season. Both the Siboney and Atabey are extremely popular, but, frankly, they are low-class mass-consumer tourism meccas, and this combined with distance from the beach makes them only worth considering if the tour package is really cheap (as it often is).

The *Hotel Internacional* (☎ 66-7038, fax 66-7246), Avenida Las Américas, is Varadero's most famous hotel. Opened in December 1950 as a sister hotel to Miami's Fontainebleau, the four-story Internacional today offers 163 rooms with shower, balcony, and satellite TV at US$51/87 single/double low season, US$87/100 high season. The front side of the hotel faces a spacious lawn, while the back is right on the beach. It's a huge complex with various bars, the Cabaret/Disco Continental, a swimming pool, tennis courts, and many

other facilities. Havanautos maintains a desk at the Internacional. It may not have the flashy glamour of its newer competitors, but it's overflowing with '50s charm.

The Hotel Internacional reception desk also controls motel-style *Villa Solymar* next door on Avenida Las Américas. The 55 rooms with bath and TV are in two long two-story blocks facing the pool. On the opposite (east) side of the Internacional is *Cabañas del Sol* with another 66 one- or two-story villas, each with one to four rooms, at US$50/76 single/double low season, US$51/87 high season. Some rooms in the villas have shared baths.

The *Hotel Las Morlas* (☎ 66-7230), Avenida Las Américas and Calle A, is a good medium-priced hotel efficiently managed by Spain's Riu chain. There are 148 rooms with bath, mini-fridge, and satellite TV in this new three- and four-story hotel. Rooms go for US$43/57 single/double low season, US$63/65 high season. The outstanding breakfast/dinner buffet is US$7/15. This Mediterranean-style complex shares a swimming pool, unisex beauty salon, and bicycle and scooter rentals with adjacent Villa Cuba.

Villa Cuba (☎ 6-2975), Avenida 1 and Calle C, has 137 rooms in 30 villas with communal living areas, refrigerator, TV, and patio for US$37/54 single/double low season, US$46/72 high season. Some cheaper rooms in the older villas have shared baths. The three-story hotel blocks here each have 32 rooms with shower and fridge. Villa Cuba has long been a favorite of Canadian package tourists, and it's only as nice as your neighbors (one visitor reported that it was noisy and dirty and that the food was mediocre). A Banco Financiero Internacional branch is next to the reception desk.

The *Hotel Gaviota* (☎ 66-7240, fax 66-7194), Avenida 1 between Calles G and J, consists of a mass of three-story hotel blocks and villas crowded around the central swimming pool. Unlike most of its neighbors, this is not a planned resort but a hotel that has been expanded over the years. Adding to the confusion are the similar names of the various wings: Caracol, Caribe, and Cascada. In 1994 the five-story Coral section was added to the front side of this dense complex. All 260 rooms have bath, mini-fridge, and satellite TV, and full resort facilities are available. Rates average US$65/77/103 single/double/triple low season, US$78/90/115 high season, with breakfast/dinner US$5/15 extra (be forewarned that the long lines at the buffet are annoying). The karaoke singalongs in the hotel's Disco Salsa from 11 pm to 2:30 am are great fun. It's package-tour paradise.

In July 1996 the four-story 250-room *Hotel Las Sirenas* opened between Hotel Gaviota and SuperClub. Managed by the Spanish Sol Melía chain, this upmarket resort operates on an all-inclusive basis, but exact prices were not available at press time.

SuperClub Varadero (☎ 66-7030), Avenida Las Américas Km 3, is managed by a Jamaican hotel chain. It's similar to Club Med with all meals, drinks, and activities included in the tariff. The 98 rooms (US$198/264 single/double) and 172 suites (US$222/296) are in 12 two- and three-story buildings. Facilities include a piano bar, disco, fitness center, three hot tubs, four floodlit tennis courts, and a big swimming pool. SuperClub tries to be Varadero's most pretentious resort and only hotel guests are allowed through the well-guarded gate. Children under the age of 16 are also not admitted. It's great if you want to play the big shot for a week.

The five-story *Hotel Tuxpán* (☎ 66-7560, fax 66-7561), Avenida Las Américas, opened in 1990 and is presently managed by Germany's LTI chain. The 233 rooms with bath, satellite TV, and balcony or terrace (US$80/130 single/double low season, US$100/150 high season) are complemented by good facilities such as an attractive swimming pool, hot tub, floodlit tennis courts, and Discoteca La Bamba. The food is reputedly excellent. Varadero's wide white beach is down two long flights of stairs right in front of this world-class resort.

The expensive *Hotel Bella Costa* (☎ 66-7210, fax 66-7205), on Avenida Las Américas at the west end of the golf course, has 306 rooms with bath, mini-fridge, and satellite TV for US$110/138 single/double. Opened in 1993, this huge six-story, propeller-shaped building has three wings, and the rooms facing the swimming pool also face the beach. Tennis and watersports facilities are shared with the adjacent Hotel Tuxpán (both are managed by Germany's LTI hotel chain).

The Spanish-operated *Meliá Las Américas* (☎ 66-7600, fax 66-7625), just east of the Dupont Mansion, has 225 rooms and 25 suites in a main four-story building built in 1994. In 1996 a long two-story zigzag wing with another 125 rooms was added on the east side of the split-level swimming pool. Rooms with bath, balcony, and satellite TV in either section begin around US$86/116 single/double low season, US$101/146 high season. A suite costs US$215/240 low/high. In 1996 the Varadero golf course was extended east alongside this and the other two neighboring Meliá hotels.

The *Hotel Meliá Varadero* (☎ 66-7013, fax 66-7012) overlooks the new section of the golf course at the east end of the Varadero strip. The 490 rooms with bath, balcony, mini-fridge, and satellite TV (US$82/108 single/double low season, US$95/132 high season) are in seven five-story wings protruding from the circular central core of a gigantic star-shaped building erected in 1991. Three glass-cabin elevators go up and down one side of the magnificent seven-story central atrium, which also features a fountain and luxuriant vegetation. This ostentatious resort also has a fitness center and a large swimming pool with a safe end for children. The Meliá Varadero sits on a rocky headland and you have to walk a bit to reach the beach.

The deluxe *Hotel Sol Palmeras* (☎ 66-7009, fax 66-7008) is 500 meters beyond the Meliá Varadero and nine km east of the bridge into Varadero. The Sol Palmeras opened in May 1990 as a joint venture between the Spanish Sol Meliá Group and

Cubanacán, the first of its kind in Cuba. The three- and four-story wings of this horseshoe-shaped hotel encircle a large swimming pool open to a great beach. The 407 rooms with bath, satellite TV, and balcony in the main building cost US$69/95 single/double low season, US$81/119 high season. Another 200 rooms in bungalows with living room and mini-fridge go for US$84/111 low season, US$96/135 high season. A hotplate and utensils can be supplied in the bungalows at an additional charge (the beach in front of the bungalows isn't as good as the one near the main building). The hotel's huge lobby with its bars, restaurants, caged birds, vegetation, and many places to sit down is worth a walk around, and outside are two floodlit tennis courts. The pharmacy in unit No 314 is open 24 hours.

Though recently under construction the upmarket *Hotel Arenas Doradas* and *Hotel Oro Verde* to the east of the Sol Palmeras should soon be accepting guests. Also under construction in 1996 was the 331-room *Hotel Rincón Francés*, a long four-story complex on the site of the former pioneer camp. It's all part of a massive development program intended to ensure that Varadero remains the Caribbean's biggest tourist resort well into the 21st century.

Places to Eat

The following restaurants are listed within each section roughly west to east along the peninsula.

Aside from the established restaurants mentioned below, a few local residents serve lobster meals to tourists in their private homes for about US$10 a plate. These places are unofficial and none post signs outside, so you'll have to ask around. They're usually a better value than the regular restaurants, and only government efforts to protect the state tourism monopoly have prevented this sector from flourishing. Unfortunately, the sort of privately operated paladares active in other parts of Cuba aren't allowed here, and we suggest that you approach all of the following state-run restaurants with caution. If they don't have many customers seated at their tables, it could be for a good reason.

Self-Catering There are grocery stores at Calle 13 No 9 between Avenida 1 and Camino del Mar (daily 9 am to 5:30 pm); beside Aparthotel Varazul, Calle 15 off Avenida 1 (daily 9 am to 7:20 pm); at Club Herradura, Avenida de la Playa and Calle 36 (daily 9 am to 7 pm); and at Cabañas del Sol on Avenida Las Américas near Hotel Internacional (9 am to 6:45 pm).

The only place where you can always find bread and pastries is *Panadería Doña Neli*, Avenida 1 and Calle 43 (open 24 hours).

Heladería Coppelia in Parque Central, Avenida 1 between Calles 44 and 46 (Monday to Saturday 10 am to 5 pm), serves ice cream at US$1 a scoop.

Cafeterias *Bar Grill Almacigo*, also known as Don Pepe's Ranchón, Camino del Mar between Calles 6 and 7 (daily 9 am to 10 pm), is right on the beach and crowded all day. Meat sizzles on the grill as prostitutes size up the clientele. *Snack Bar Lagarto*, Camino del Mar and Calle 9 (daily 10 am to 2 am), is similar. The inexpensive hamburgers, pizza, chicken, and beer are served on an open terrace and a trio often plays in the afternoon. *El Rincón*, Camino del Mar between Calles 11 and 12 (8 am to 5 pm), has hamburgers, sandwiches, and omelets.

The cafeteria next to the lower swimming pool at *Hotel Bellamar*, Calle 17 between Avenidas 1 and 2 (open 24 hours), has cheap hamburgers, omelets, spaghetti, pizza, and sandwiches.

Ranchito Criollo, Avenida 1 and Calle 40 (open 24 hours), offers chicken, hot dogs, hamburgers, and beer.

Restaurants At the far western end of Varadero, *La Casa de Al*, next to Hotel Punta Blanca (daily 11 am to 10 pm), occupies a mansion once owned by Chicago gangster Al Capone. The house specialty is paella (US$20 for two persons with a

30-minute wait). but you can also get shrimp and meat dishes.

There are lots of unpretentious places in central Varadero where you can order light meals. Many also serve as social centers, and they're often crowded with people tossing back can after can of Hatuey in an open-air environment.

A good place for pizza is *Kiki's Club*, Avenida 1 and Calle 5 (open 24 hours). You can observe the street action from the terrace overlooking Paso Malo. *La Sangría*, Avenida 1 and Calle 7 (open 24 hours), is another pizza place that also serves spaghetti and grilled meats.

Castel Nuovo, Avenida 1 and Calle 11 opposite Hotel Barlovento (daily noon to 10:45 pm), features chicken, beef, fish, spaghetti, and pizza also served Italian style.

Over on the beach is *La Cabañita*, Camino del Mar and Calle 9 (daily 9 am to 10 pm), with shellfish and meat dishes.

Camino del Mar between Calles 11 and 14 could almost be called Restaurant Row for its concentration of places to eat. Elegant *Mi Casita*, Camino del Mar between Calles 11 and 12 (daily noon to 10:30 pm), is right on the beach. It's a good spot for splurging on chicken (US$12), steak (US$14), shrimp (US$18), or lobster (US$25). For Asian cuisine there's *Halong*, Camino del Mar and Calle 12 (daily 3 to 11 pm). *Las Brasas*, Camino del Mar and Calle 12 (daily noon to 10 pm), has grilled meats, while *El Arrecife*, Camino del Mar and Calle 13 (daily noon to 10 pm), specializes in shellfish and fish. *La Taberna*, Camino del Mar between Calles 13 and 14 (daily noon to 10 pm), usually features Italian cuisine but there's also a sign proclaiming the *Taberina Dortmunder Kneipe* to cater to the German market.

Restaurante El Criollo, Avenida 1 and Calle 18 (open 24 hours), has typical Cuban dishes. *Lai-Lai*, in a two-story mansion on the beach across the street (daily noon to 10:45 pm), has Chinese cuisine.

Further east, *El Bodegón Criollo*, Avenida de la Playa and Calle 40 (daily noon to midnight), is a takeoff on La Bodeguita del Medio in Havana. Typical Cuban dishes are listed on a blackboard.

Pizzería Capri, Avenida de la Playa and Calle 43 opposite Hotel Ledo, has inexpensive Italian pizza and pasta, and it's one of the few regular Varadero restaurants we're prepared to recommend. If an evening floorshow is staged here, it will probably be good and they cater to individuals rather than prepackaged groups.

There are several expensive restaurants in Parque Josone, Avenida 1 and Calle 56. These include *El Retiro* with international cuisine; *Dante* (Monday to Saturday 12:30 to 4 pm and 7 pm to midnight) with Italian food; and *Mesón y Parrillada La Campana* with Cuban dishes. On the edge of the park is *La Casa de Antigüedades*, Avenida 1 and Calle 59, where red-meat, fish, and shellfish dishes are served beneath the chandeliers of the old mansion.

Barracuda Grill El Anzuelo, Avenida 1 and Calle 58, in a thatched pavilion on the beach of the grounds of the Barracuda Diving Center, is better regarded than the stuffy restaurants in Parque Josone. It serves grilled meats, fish, and shellfish. Fish, squid, shrimp, and lobster are also on the menu at *Albacora*, on the beach near Avenida 1 and Calle 59 (daily 10 am to midnight).

A few more upmarket restaurants are opposite the Hotel Cuatro Palmas, Avenida 1 and Calle 62, including *Mallorca* (daily noon to midnight) with Spanish and international cuisine, and *Restaurante La Fondue* (daily noon to 11 pm) with Swiss French cuisine. A good cheap snack bar is on Calle 62 beside La Fondué. Also try *La Barbacoa*, Avenida 1 and Calle 64 (daily noon to midnight), a big Cuban steak house with grilled meats.

Among the few non-hotel restaurants out this way is *El Mesón del Quijote* on a hill near the old water tower above Hotel Las Morlas (daily 3 to 11 pm). A metal statue of Don Quijote stands next to this tavern, and reservations are recommended if you want to sample their Spanish-style cooking.

Restaurante Las Américas in the library of the former Dupont Mansion on Avenida

Las Américas (daily 10 am to 11:30 pm) serves upmarket international cuisine. The main draw is the chance to dine in this historic site.

Entertainment

The *Casa de la Cultura Los Corales*, Avenida 1 and 34, has an art gallery and open-air theater. You should be able to find a music teacher here if you'd like to learn to play Cuban instruments or study Cuban music.

Cinemas *Cine Varadero*, Avenida de la Playa between Calles 42 and 43, presents a film nightly at 6:30 pm (admission US$2).

Discos The fanciful *Discoteca El Galeón* is in a full-size reconstructed pirate ship currently tied up at the Marina Acua, 1½ km west of the bridge into Varadero. The restaurant is open from 8 pm, the disco from 11 pm.

Discoteca La Patana, just across the bridge from central Varadero, is on a barge in Laguna de Paso Malo behind the Anfiteatro Varadero (open Thursday to Tuesday 9 pm to 3 am). The US$4 admission includes two beers. The open-air setting is nice and it's less touristy than many of the other places.

Discoteca La Salsa, above the reception desk at Complejo Paradiso-Puntarena at the west end of Varadero (11 pm to 3 am), is geared mostly toward foreign tourists.

Several places in central Varadero are open to everyone. *Discoteca La Pachanga* at Hotel Acuazul, Avenida 1 and Calle 13, is one of Varadero's hottest clubs. *Discoteca El Eclipse* on the 14th floor at Hotel Bellamar, Avenida 1 and Calle 17, exacts a US$5 cover charge, except on Sunday from 5 to 8 pm, when the cover is a mere US$1. Another place popular with the locals is *Discoteca Azúcar*, also known as La Cancha, Avenida 1 and Calle 25 (daily from 10 pm, admission US$3).

Further east, *Discoteca El Kastillito*, Avenida de la Playa and Calle 49 (daily 11 pm to 3 am), offers free admission, and the beach bar is open all day.

Discoteca Havana Club at the Centro Comercial Copey, Avenida 3 at Calle 62, is another tourist disco.

Varadero's most modern video disco is *Discoteca La Bamba* at the Hotel Tuxpán in eastern Varadero (daily 10 pm to 4 am). Admission is US$10, but it's free for guests staying at the Tuxpán.

Cabarets *Cabaret Anfiteatro Varadero*, Vía Blanca and Carretera Sur just west of the bridge into Varadero, is open Wednesday to Sunday from 9 pm to 2:45 am (admission US$5). The gala open-air floorshow here is similar to that of the Tropicana Nightclub in Havana.

Cabaret Continental in the Hotel Internacional on Avenida Las Américas stages a 2½-hour floorshow Tuesday to Sunday. It costs US$40 for dinner at 8 pm followed by the show or US$25 including one drink for the show alone at 10 pm. Make reservations through your hotel tour desk.

Cabaret Cueva del Pirata (☎ 66-7751) on Autopista Sur one km east of the Hotel Sol Palmeras (open Monday to Saturday 9 pm to 2:45 am), presents more leggy dancers in a Cuban-style floorshow inside a natural cave. Admission costs US$15 and most hotel tour desks can arrange return hotel transfers for another US$3.

Bars *Bar Beny*, Camino del Mar between Calles 12 and 13 (daily 9 am to 3 am), is a beach bar with a slight bohemian atmosphere. *El Paso*, on Avenida 1 between Calles 6 and 7, is very active at night, as is *Snack Bar Calle 13*, Avenida 1 at Calle 13, which is packed all evening with people on the make. The bar diagonally across the street has a happy hour from 4 to 6 pm.

Coffee Shop 25, Avenida 1 and Calle 25, and *Bar El Caribeño*, Avenida 1 and Calle 31, both have open-air terraces where the beer goes down very nicely.

Bar Mirador on the top floor of the Dupont Mansion on Avenida Las Américas in eastern Varadero has a happy hour from 5 to 7 pm daily (US$1 admission and two drinks for the price of one). Dress up a bit and enjoy the sunset.

Things to Buy

Caracol shops in the main hotels sell souvenirs, postcards, T-shirts, clothes, alcohol, and some snack foods. The prices are usually as good as those elsewhere. Beware of guys on the street selling black-market cigars, as the boxes are often full of sand or low-quality cigars. It's better to pay more and be sure of what you're getting, but insist on a receipt to prove to Cuban customs that you purchased your cigars at an official outlet.

Boutique Glamour, Avenida 1 and Calle 29 (Monday to Saturday 10 am to 7 pm, Sunday 9 am to 1 pm), sells clothes, footwear, and jewelry and has a nice bar in the back yard.

El Encanto, Avenida 1 and Calle 41 (Monday to Saturday 9 am to 5 pm, Sunday 9 am to noon), is a dollar department store intended for Cubans.

Bazar Varadero Publicigraf in Parque Central, Avenida 1 and Calle 44 (daily 9 am to 7 pm), is good for ceramics, reproductions of famous paintings, artistic postcards, wall hangings, T-shirts, and books. There is an adjacent clothing boutique.

For compact discs, cassettes, souvenirs, and more books try Artex, Avenida 1 between Calles 46 and 47.

Kawama Sport, Avenida 1 and Calle 60 (9 am to 7 pm), sells beach clothing and snorkeling gear.

Varadero's main tourist shopping malls are the Centro Comercial Caimán, Avenida 1 and Calle 62 opposite Hotel Cuatro Palmas, and the Centro Comercial Copey, Avenida 2 between Calles 61 and 63 next to the Atabey and Siboney hotels. Both are open daily from 9 am to 7 pm.

You can see cigars being rolled at the Casa del Habano, Avenida Las Américas and Calle 63 (daily 9 am to 7 pm). This is a good place to buy genuine cigars if you want a specific brand, but check the prices at your own hotel shop before coming here.

Bazar Cuba, also known as the Casa de la Artesanía, Avenida Las Américas and 64 (9 am to 7 pm), has the best selection of souvenirs and crafts at Varadero. They also sell beach clothing, jewelry, and books.

Getting There & Away

Air Juan Gualberto Gómez International Airport (airport code VRA) is at Carbonera, six km off the main highway between Matanzas and Varadero. Flights arrive here on Aeroperu from Lima, Air UK from London-Gatwick; Cubana from Cancún, Lima, London-Stansted, Montreal, Paris-Orly, and Toronto; LTU International Airways from Düsseldorf; Martinair Holland from Amsterdam; Royal Airlines from Toronto; and SAM from Bogotá and San Andrés Island. Details of these are provided in the Getting There & Away chapter. The check-in time at Varadero is 90 minutes before flight time.

If you're catching a chartered flight from Varadero and want a choice of seats (assigned at the airport), consider taking a taxi to the airport even if the hotel bus is included in your package. This will cost US$20, but you'll be first in line and able to get a window seat near the front. It's a good value when compared to the surcharge for business class on other airlines.

Havanautos, Transautos, and National all have car-rental offices in the airport parking lot.

The Cubana agent (☎ 66-7593) is Sol y Son at the entrance to Hotel Barlovento, Avenida 1 between Calles 10 and 12 (daily 8 am to 6 pm).

Bus Tourists are not encouraged to use the public buses departing the Terminal de Ómnibus Interprovinciales, Calle 36 and Autopista Sur, and long-distance services such as those to Havana (two daily, 140 km, three hours, $5.50) and Santa Clara (daily, 192 km, $8) must be reserved two weeks in advance. Reservations are not required for the bus to Matanzas (10 daily, 42 km, $2): Just go into the waiting room beyond the public toilets and ask for *el último* (the last in line). Have Cuban pesos ready for the fare. If you have the time, you can get to Havana by taking this bus to Matanzas and continuing on another bus or the Hershey Electric Railway from there, although a day trip is not possible in this way.

The collective taxis *(colectivos)* to Matanzas parked outside the bus station are not allowed to take foreigners (who are supposed to use regular tourist taxis). Private drivers who carry tourists are subject to heavy fines if detected by the police. Once again, the Cuban government is anxious to protect its tourism monopoly.

Getting to Cárdenas by local bus is fairly straightforward if you're prepared to wait. Bus No 236 departs every hour or so from next to a small tunnel marked 'Ómnibus de Cárdenas' outside the main bus station. You can also catch this bus up at the corner of Avenida 1 and Calle 13, but have your 50 centavos in exact change ready.

By far the easiest way to get to Havana is on one of the regular tourist buses booked through the tour desk at your hotel or at any Havanatur office. It's possible to purchase transportation only between Varadero and Havana for US$25/30 one way/round-trip, lunch and sightseeing not included. These buses collect passengers right at your hotel door.

Train The nearest train stations are 18 km southeast in Cárdenas and 42 km west in Matanzas.

Yacht Cruising yachts can tie up at the marinas Chapelín and Gaviota at the far east end of the peninsula. The crowded Marina Chapelín (☎ 66-7093, 66-7550, or channel 72 VHF) charges US$0.45 per foot a day (although they often don't have space available), while the more distant Marina Gaviota (☎ 6-3712) is cheaper at US$0.35 per foot, electricity and water included.

The Marina Acua (☎ 66-8063), on the Vía Blanca just west of central Varadero, can be contacted over channel 68 VHF. Marina Acua handles customs clearance and is more conveniently located for land-based sightseeing than the other marinas. Less appealing aspects of this marina are the overpowering sulfur fumes from the nearby oil wells, acidic fallout generated as worthless natural gas is burned in enormous chimneys, and noise from loudspeakers broadcasting local radio reports.

Getting Around
To/From the Airport
A tourist taxi to/from Varadero (or Matanzas) is about 20 km each away and costs US$20 for the car. If you're able to negotiate in Spanish, the driver of one of the Varadero tour buses may agree to take you for around US$5 per person. The police try to prevent unlicensed private taxis from picking up or delivering passengers to the airport.

Bus There are three local bus routes costing 10 centavos a ride: Nos 47 and 48 from Calle 54 to Santa Marta, south of Varadero on the Autopista Sur; No 220 from Santa Marta to Hotel Las Morlas; and No 222 from the Terminal de Ómnibus Interprovinciales to Boca de Camarioca, west of Varadero on the Vía Blanca. These buses are very infrequent and in practice you won't find them useful.

Most municipal buses around Varadero don't bear a number and many are special services for hotel employees only. If you're able to converse in Spanish, get information from the Cubans waiting at the bus stops.

Car Cars are readily available from Havanautos at Avenida 1 and Calle 8 and at Avenida 1 and Calle 31, or Transautos at Avenida 1 and Calle 21. There are also Transautos rental offices at Complejo Paradiso-Puntarena and Club Tropical hotels, a National office at Club Villa Caleta, and a Havana autos desk at the Hotel Internacional. The Copey Resort has both Transautos and Havanautos desks.

Servi-Cupet has gas stations on the Vía Blanca at the entrance to Marina Acua (7 am to 11 pm) and at Autopista Sur and Calle 17 near Hotel Bellamar (open 24 hours).

Bike & Moped Moped rentals are available at many locations around Varadero. They cost US$9/12/15 for one/two/three hours with additional hours US$5 each. No insurance or helmets are available. Far fewer places rent bicycles (US$1 an hour). If you do get a bicycle, you'll need a secure lock if you intend to leave it unattended.

Taxi Tourist taxis charge a US$1 starting fee plus US$0.55 per km (same tariff day and night). To call a Turistaxi, dial ☎ 6-3763 or 6-3563. Tourists are not supposed to use the older state-owned taxis, only the shiny new 'tourist' taxis.

Private cars with yellow license plates often serve as unofficial taxis although they're not allowed to carry foreigners (1500 peso fine for the driver if caught). To earn dollars, many drivers are willing to take the risk and you can usually negotiate a price of US$25 per day for the whole car, gas included, for trips to Cárdenas, Matanzas, and so on. It's a much better value than the organized sightseeing tours sold at the hotels. Of course, your driver will speak no English and he may ask you to duck as you're passing the police post on the bridge into Varadero.

A horse and buggy around Varadero will be US$3 per person per hour.

CÁRDENAS
The city of Cárdenas (75,000 inhabitants) stands on the Bahía de Cárdenas, 18 km southeast of Varadero. Founded in 1828, this was the heart of Cuba's richest sugar-growing area in the 19th century. Cárdenas is best remembered for the first raising of the Cuban flag by General Narciso López in 1850, and the revolutionary hero José Antonio Echeverría also hails from here. Nineteenth-century houses with stained-glass windows still grace the streets, and if you want to see real Cuban life, Cárdenas makes a good outing from Varadero. A small shipyard and a rum factory are among the industries here.

Orientation
The northeast-southwest streets are called avenidas and the northwest-southeast streets are calles. Avenida Céspedes is Cárdenas' main drag with the avenues to the northwest called *oeste*, those to the southeast *este*. The calles are numbered consecutively beginning at the bay.

Information
There are no tourist information offices or travel agencies for visitors in Cárdenas.

Money The unofficial moneychangers are stationed near the hard-currency stores on Avenida Céspedes at Calle 13.

Post & Communications Correos y Telégrafo is on Parque Colón at the corner of Avenida Céspedes and Calle 8 (Monday to Saturday 8 am to 6 pm). The local telephone center is on Avenida Céspedes near Calle 13 (daily 7 am to 10:30 pm).

Bookstore Librería La Concha de Venus, Céspedes and Calle 12 (weekdays 9 am to 5 pm, Saturday 8 am to noon), has books in Spanish only.

Photography Photo Service is at Avenida Céspedes No 568.

Medical Services A Soviet decompression chamber dating from 1981 is at the Centro Médico Sub Acuática (☎ 52-2114, or channel 16 VHF) at Hospital Julio M Aristegui on Calle 13, four km northwest on the road to Varadero. The attendant is on duty from Monday to Saturday 8 am to 4 pm, and the names and addresses of doctors on call 24 hours are posted on the door. A US$10 fee is charged to use the decompression chamber.

The pharmacy at Calle 12 No 60 is open daily from 8 am to 8 pm.

Things to See
Parque Colón, on Avenida Céspedes between Calles 8 and 9, contains the oldest statue of Christopher Columbus in the Western Hemisphere. Dating from 1862, it's the work of a Spanish sculptor named Piquier. The **Catedral de la Inmaculada Concepción** (1846) behind the statue is noted for its stained glass (but it's usually closed).

Nearby at the corner of Avenida Céspedes and Calle 9 is the **Hotel Dominica**, a former sugar warehouse rebuilt in the neoclassical style as a hotel in 1919. A

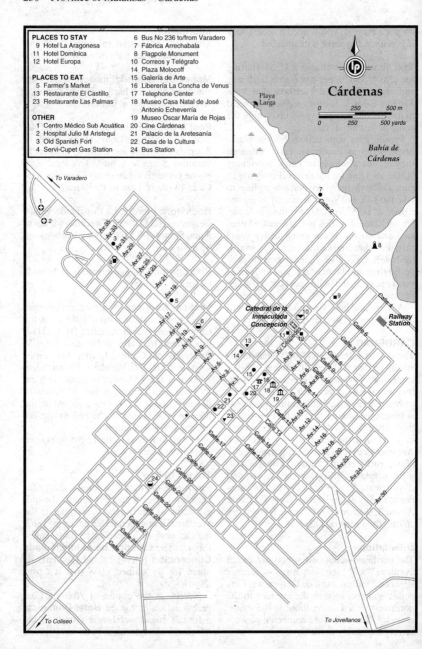

PLACES TO STAY
9 Hotel La Aragonesa
11 Hotel Dominica
12 Hotel Europa

PLACES TO EAT
5 Farmer's Market
13 Restaurante El Castillo
23 Restaurante Las Palmas

OTHER
1 Centro Médico Sub Acuática
2 Hospital Julio M Aristegui
3 Old Spanish Fort
4 Servi-Cupet Gas Station

6 Bus No 236 to/from Varadero
7 Fábrica Arrechabala
8 Flagpole Monument
10 Correos y Telégrafo
14 Plaza Molocoff
15 Galería de Arte
16 Librería La Concha de Venus
17 Telephone Center
18 Museo Casa Natal de José
     Antonio Echeverría
19 Museo Oscar María de Rojas
20 Cine Cárdenas
21 Palacio de la Aretesanía
22 Casa de la Cultura
24 Bus Station

Cárdenas

Playa Larga

Bahía de Cárdenas

0   250   500 m
0   250   500 yards

To Varadero

Catedral de la Inmaculada Concepción

Railway Station

To Coliseo

To Jovellanos

plaque on the building recalls the first raising of the Cuban flag.

The local **Galería de Arte** is at Céspedes No 560 between Calles 12 and 13.

The **Museo Oscar María de Rojas**, on Parque Echeverría at Avenida 4 Este and Calle 12 (Tuesday to Saturday 8 am to 4 pm, Sunday 8 am to noon, admission US$1), is housed in the former town hall erected in 1861. Founded in 1900, this was one of Cuba's first museums. Here you'll see displays of minerals, butterflies, insects, shells, armaments, numismatics, and Indian artifacts, plus an ornate funeral carriage.

Across the street is the **Museo Casa Natal de José Antonio Echeverría**, Avenida 4 Este No 560 (Tuesday to Saturday 8 am to 4 pm, Sunday 8 am to noon, admission free, tip the guide). The rich historical collection includes the original *garrote* used to execute Narciso López by strangulation in 1851. Objects relating to the 19th-century independence wars are downstairs, while the 20th-century revolution is covered upstairs. A spiral staircase with 36 steps links the two floors of this house dating from 1703. In 1932 Echeverría was born here, and a monument to this student leader slain by Batista's police in 1957 is outside on Parque Echeverría.

Another Cárdenas curiosity is **Plaza Molocoff**, Avenida 3 Oeste and Calle 12, a two-story cast-iron market hall with a 16-meter-high dome.

At the northeast end of Avenida Céspedes, look for a monument with a huge **flagpole** commemorating the first raising of the Cuban flag on May 19, 1850. There's a good view of the bay and Varadero from here. To the northwest near the port is the **Fábrica Arrechabala** rum factory where Varadero and Bucanero rums are distilled. The Havana Club rum company was founded here in 1878.

Places to Stay

The only functioning hotel in Cárdenas is the *Hotel Dominica* (☎ 52-1502), Avenida Céspedes at Calle 9 on Parque Colón. This old two-story hotel has 25 rooms for US$15/23 single/double with bath year-round. Only two or three of the rooms have air-con. The hotel's rather poor restaurant serves meals sharply at 7:30 am, noon, and 6 pm daily except Tuesday (closed at other times).

Nearby are two other old two-story hotels, both lacking signs and presently closed. Both are for sale and will again be good places to stay if buyers willing to renovate can be found. The 32-room *Hotel Europa*, Avenida Céspedes No 365 on Parque Colón, is occupied by resort entertainers, while the 16-room *Hotel La Aragonesa* (☎ 52-4667), Avenida Céspedes and Calle 6, has been taken over by the restaurant-workers union.

Places to Eat

The farmer's market on Calle 13 between Avenidas 17 and 19 Oeste is open Tuesday to Sunday from 8 am to 5:30 pm.

The choice of places to eat is poor. *Restaurante El Castillo*, Avenida 3 Oeste at Calle 12 (daily except Friday 6 to 9 pm), is your typical state-run peso restaurant with limited hours and food.

Restaurante Las Palmas, Céspedes and Calle 16 (Tuesday to Sunday noon to 2 pm and 6 to 9 pm), is a large Spanish-style villa surrounded by high walls. This impressive mansion contains an imposing dining room and there's a bar outside on the porch. On Friday, Saturday, and Sunday from 9 pm to 2 am Las Palmas becomes a cabaret with a show at 10:30 pm (admission US$5).

For sandwiches and beer you can always go to *Cafetería El Rápido*, Calle 12 and Avenida 3 Oeste (daily 9 am to 3 am), an open-air snack bar that offers unappetizing fast food at low prices. The same chain has another location known as *Cafetería Los Almendros* at the corner of Calle 8 and Avenida Céspedes opposite the post office (open 24 hours). Their yellow and red fence desecrates Parque Colón, and the food is awful.

Entertainment

For a movie try *Cine Cárdenas*, Avenida

Céspedes and Calle 14, or the privately run *Sala de Video*, Avenida Céspedes No 807.

If you're lucky, a performance will be happening at the *Casa de la Cultura*, Avenida Céspedes No 706 between Calles 15 and 16.

Things to Buy
The Palacio de la Artesanía, Avenida Céspedes No 660 between Calles 14 and 15 (weekdays 9 am to 6 pm, Saturday 10 am to 4 pm, Sunday 10 am to 1 pm), has crafts, pottery, puppets, dolls, straw hats, clothes, purses, and shoes.

Getting There & Away
Bus Services depart the bus station, Avenida Céspedes and Calle 22, to Matanzas (56 km, daily), Colón (68 km, twice a day), Jagüey Grande (66 km, daily), Havana (152 km, three daily), and Santa Clara (174 km, daily).

Bus No 236 to/from Varadero leaves hourly from a different station at the corner of Avenida 13 Oeste and Calle 13 (50 centavos in exact change). The private taxis with yellow license plates parked across the street from this station are hesitant to take foreigners for fear of heavy fines from the police. In a pinch you might be able to convince them to drop you off just before the bridge into Varadero for US$10, provided you can negotiate in Spanish.

Train Rail cars leave the Estación Terminal de Ferrocarriles, Avenida 8 Este near the bay, to Pedroso via Jovellanos (daily), Guareiras via Colón (daily), and Los Arabos (twice daily).

Getting Around
The main horse-cart route through Cárdenas is northeast on Avenida Céspedes from the bus station and then northwest on Calle 13 to the hospital, passing the stop of bus No 236 (to Varadero) on the way. The fare is one peso a ride.

The Servi-Cupet gas station is on Calle 13 at Avenida 31 Oueste, opposite an old Spanish fort on the northwest side of town out on the road to Varadero.

BOCA DE GUAMÁ
The 4230-sq-km Península de Zapata in southern Matanzas is a vast wetland of mangroves, marshes, and swamps, home to 160 species of bird, 31 types of reptile, and 12 species of mammal, plus countless amphibians, fish, and insects (including mosquitoes). It's home to the occasional manatee seacow *(manatí)* and the alligator gar *(manjuarí, Atractosteus tristoechus)*, Cuba's most primitive fish. From sunset to sunrise, May to August, tens of thousands of land crabs swarm across the one road through the swamp *(ciénaga)*. The Zapata is the place to come to see cormorants, ducks, flamingos, ibis, herons, partridges, parrots, sparrows, wrens, bee hummingbirds (the smallest bird in the world), and trogons (Cuba's national bird). Numerous migratory birds from North America overwinter here.

Very few people live on the peninsula as the land is unsuitable for agriculture, and until the revolution communications were almost nonexistent. Charcoal makers burn wood from the region's semideciduous forests, and *turba* (peat) dug from the swamps is an important source of fuel. The main industry today is tourism. Ecotourists are arriving in increasing numbers to visit Parque Nacional Ciénaga de Zapata.

The main center for visitors is Boca de Guamá, halfway between the Autopista Nacional at Jagüey Grande and the famous Bay of Pigs (or Bahía de Cochinos, as the Cubans call it). Here you'll find a crocodile farm, restaurant, snack bar (expensive), handicraft shop, ceramics workshop, and boats waiting to take you to the Laguna del Tesoro.

Things to See
In Town Boca de Guamá's principal sight is the **Criadero de Cocodrilos** where two species of crocodiles are raised: the native Rhombifer *(cocodrilo)* and the Acutus *(caimán)*, which is found throughout the tropical Americas. (At present only Rhombifer crocodiles are kept at the farm.) Prior to the establishment of a breeding program here in 1962, these two species of

Mermaid or Manatee?

The slow-moving Caribbean manatee *(manatí, Trichechus manatus)* is descended from a land mammal that returned to life in the water. The Atlantic manatee can grow up to 4½ meters long and weigh as much as 600 kilograms. (A similar but smaller 'sea cow' called a dugong is found in the Indian Ocean.) It has a small head with only a little hair, a thick neck, and a wide bristly snout with two nostrils that can close. Its poorly developed eyes have glands that secrete an oily substance for protection against salt water. Although ears are not visible, the manatee has excellent hearing.

Adult manatees have a thick tapered body ending in a wide horizontal tail flipper. It uses two front flippers to swim and to bring food to its mouth, but it has no back legs. The manatee's ribs aren't attached to a rib cage, so its lungs are crushed if the animal lies on its belly on dry land. To avoid suffocating, a manatee caught by low tide will flip over onto its back and wait for the water to return. Manatee couples remain together year-round and the gestation period is one year. The animal lives 30 to 60 years.

Unlike whales and seals, this marine mammal never takes to the open ocean. It prefers to linger around thick plant growth and grazes on seaweed in brackish coastal waters, estuaries, and rivers, where it consumes up to 50 kilograms of plant life a day. Before eating, the manatee 'washes' the plants by shaking them in the water. While grazing in shallow water with its head and shoulders above the water, it resembles a human figure, which perhaps gave rise to mermaid legends. Although the manatee has no natural enemies except man, it has become endangered due to hunting, injury from boat propellers, and habitat destruction. ■

marsh-dwelling crocodiles were almost extinct, but today they're abundant enough that there's even a barbecue serving crocodile steaks for US$7 a small portion (lunch only). You can also see the jutía and other examples of Cuba's flora and fauna in this attractive park. The farm is open daily 9 am to 6 pm, admission US$3.

If you buy anything made from crocodile leather at Boca de Guamá's handicraft shop, be sure to get an invoice for the customs authorities proving that the material came from a crocodile farm and not wild crocodiles. A less controversial purchase would be one of the attractive ceramic bracelets sold at the nearby **Taller de Cerámica** (closed Sunday) where you can see five kilns in operation.

Aside from the crocodile farm, this area's main attraction is the **Laguna del Tesoro**, eight km east of Boca de Guamá via the Canal de la Laguna and accessible only by boat (see the Getting Around section below). On the east side of this eight-sq-km lake is a tourist resort named Villa Guamá built to resemble an Arawak village on a dozen small islands. A sculpture park has been set up next to the mock village with 32 life-size figures of Indians in a variety of idealized poses. The lake is called 'treasure lake' due to a legend about a treasure the Indians are said to have thrown into the water just prior to the Spanish conquest. Guamá himself was a chief who fought bravely against the Spanish. All of this has a strong appeal to the Cuban honeymooners who flock to the resort, and it's sort of worth a visit. Those who stay can try the freshwater fishing for largemouth bass.

Around Boca de Guamá About 1½ km south of the Autopista Nacional at Jagüey Grande, on the way to Boca de Guamá, is a large sugar mill called Central Australia, built in 1904. During the 1961 Bay of Pigs invasion battle Fidel Castro had his headquarters in the former office of the sugar mill. Today it's the **Museo de la Comandancia** (Tuesday to Saturday 8 am to 5 pm, Sunday 8 am to 1 pm, admission US$1). This municipal museum right next to the mill contains a few stuffed birds and animals, and a good historical collection ranging from prehistory to the present. Outside is the wreck of an invading aircraft shot down by Fidel's troops.

Places to Stay & Eat
Villa Guamá (☎ 59-2979) was built in 1963 on the east side of the Laguna del Tesoro. There are 45 thatched cabañas with bath and TV on piles over the shallow waters. These cost US$25/35 single/double low season, US$31/44 high season. The six small islands bearing the units are connected by wooden footbridges to other islands with a bar, cafeteria, overpriced restaurant, gift shop, and a swimming pool containing chlorinated lake water. Rowboats are for rent. Noise from the disco occasionally cancels some of the nocturnal tranquility, and day-trippers come and go by speedboat throughout the day. Your best chance of seeing any bird life here is at dawn. You'll need insect repellent if you decide to stay.

Getting There & Away
In theory the public bus between Jagüey Grande and Playa Girón passes three times a day and there's service to/from Havana (178 km) three times a week on Friday, Saturday, and Sunday afternoons. In practice almost all tourists arrive by rental car or tour bus. Day tours from Varadero to Boca de Guamá occur daily, and if you're traveling independently, you might be able to negotiate a ride back there by speaking to the driver (US$10 per person should be enough).

Getting Around
A large passenger ferry departs Boca de Guamá for Villa Guamá daily at 10:10 am, noon, 1 pm, and 3 pm. It's a 20-minute ride. The ferry returns immediately, so time your stay accordingly. If a quick visit is enough, there's no need to wait for this boat, as speedboats will whisk you across to the pseudo-Indian village in just 10 minutes anytime during the day for US$7 per person (with 45 minutes waiting time at Villa Guamá). Since foreigners must also pay US$7 per person return to use the ferry, it's the same price either way.

PLAYA LARGA
Continuing south across the peninsula from Boca de Guamá you reach the famous Bay of Pigs at Playa Larga after 13 km (or 32 km from where you left the Autopista Nacional). US-backed landings occurred here on April 17, 1961, but the main museum dedicated to these events is at Playa Girón, 35 km further south. Playa Larga is a rather unappealing little village with a dirty black beach and the usual throng of young men trying to sell you conch shells, stuffed crocodiles, and contraband cigars. If you're hungry, they'll take you to a paladar where you can consume lobster for US$10 – expensive but a better deal than anything offered at the official restaurants. The one tourist resort here does provide a base for visiting the unspoiled western part of the peninsula, but you'll need a rental car, and an official guide is mandatory.

Things to See
About 25 km southwest of Playa Larga is the **Laguna de las Salinas**, now part of Las Salinas Wildlife Refuge where large numbers of migratory birds can be seen from November to May. Another wildlife refuge, the **Corral de Santo Tomás**, is west of Playa Larga. At the western outskirts of Playa Larga is a checkpoint and a chain across the road, and tourists are not allowed to enter the refuges without an official guide. Before going, inquire at the reception desk of Villa Playa Larga.

A more accessible sight is the **Cueva de los Peces**, a huge flooded tectonic fault, or *cenote*, about 70 meters deep on the inland side of the road almost exactly midway between Playa Larga and Playa Girón. Watch for Restaurante El Cenote, which is between the road and the pool. Numerous fish ply the pool's waters, and the dive shops at both Playa Larga and Playa Girón bring scuba divers here. The snorkeling is also good.

Activities

About 200 meters west along the beach from Villa Playa Larga is the Club Octopus International Diving Center, offering full scuba facilities.

Places to Stay & Eat

Villa Playa Larga (☎ 59-7294), on a small beach by the road just east of the village, has 41 rooms in small bungalows with bath, sitting room, fridge, TV, and hot water for US$15/20 single/double low season, US$19/25 high season. There are also eight two-bedroom family bungalows costing a bit more. A well-stocked shop sells groceries, clothes, and souvenirs. Unfortunately there's poor security, and beach boys in the parking lot and along the waterfront hassle you with various scams. Frankly, you're better off staying at Playa Girón.

Getting There & Away

The hypothetical bus between Playa Girón and Jagüey Grande is supposed to pass here three times a day, but don't be surprised if it doesn't. Another bus runs to/from Havana (191 km) on Friday, Saturday, and Sunday afternoons.

PLAYA GIRÓN

If you're driving, Playa Girón on the eastern side of the famous Bay of Pigs (Bahía de Cochinos), 48 km south of Boca de Guamá, makes a good base. The CIA-sponsored landing here on April 17, 1961, was defeated within 72 hours, as a museum and many monuments proclaim. In all, 200 invaders were killed, 1197 captured, and

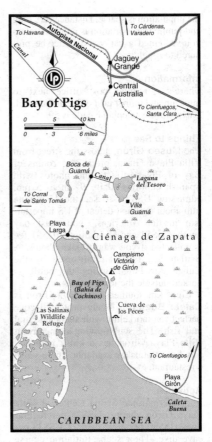

11 hostile planes shot down (for more details, see the Conflict with the USA section under History in the Facts about Cuba chapter). You really get the feel of reliving history by coming here, and the clear Caribbean waters washing these shores make Playa Girón a favorite destination for scuba divers.

The main resort is rather pleasant and a huge seawall provides a protected swimming area. Another long white beach without a wall is just a five-minute walk along the shore. The rocky soils of this region are of little use for agriculture and the population is sparse. Distances are long and public transportation is poor, so unless you've rented a car you'd better be prepared to rough it.

Information
There's a regular post office next to museum and tourist post office at the hotel. Playa Girón's telephone code is 59.

Things to See
The **Museo Girón**, across the street from Villa Playa Girón, offers two rooms of Bay of Pigs artifacts and photos with Spanish captions (daily 9 am to 5 pm, admission US$2). To see the 15-minute film about the 'first defeat of US imperialism in the Americas,' you must pay another US$1 and an additional US$1 fee is collected if you want to take photos. A British Sea Fury aircraft used by the Cuban Air Force during the battle is parked outside the museum.

Eight km southeast of Playa Girón is **Caleta Buena**, a lovely protected cove perfect for snorkeling with abundant coral and fish. The scuba-diving company at Villa Playa Girón has a kiosk here and row-boat rentals are available. There's also a restaurant.

Activities
The International Scuba Center at Villa Playa Girón charges US$25 per regular dive, US$30 per night dive, or US$35 per cave dive. Their scuba initiation course in the swimming pool costs US$10, a snorkeling course US$30, and open-water scuba certification US$300 all-inclusive. A special package including two dives, accommodations, and three meals is available for US$60 per night. Fax Ángel Roca Gálvez at ☎ 53-7-33-6013 for information. Ángel can pick you up at Varadero Airport. A special feature of the diving in this area are the underwater caves with a blind species of fish.

Places to Stay & Eat
Villa Playa Girón (☎ 59-4110) has 150 rooms in small concrete bungalows with bath and TV for US$19/25 single/double low season, US$25/33 high season. Another 28 rooms are available in two long 14-room blocks called 'Motel La Fermina' and 'Motel La Gaviota,' but all cost the same so take an individual unit. Despite the many names all accommodations are controlled by the same reception desk. This unpretentious beach resort has a swimming pool, bar, disco, and telephone center. The meals in the restaurant are best when a tour group is present and a buffet is laid out. Otherwise, it's the usual hit-or-miss. You're unlikely to be pestered by hustlers around here.

Getting There & Away
The bus to/from Jagüey Grande is supposed run three times a day. On Friday, Saturday, and Sunday afternoons there should be a bus to/from Havana (215 km). No bus is scheduled to connect Playa Girón to Cienfuegos (94 km), as the many Cuban hitchhikers will confirm. If any tour buses are at the hotel, find the driver and try to arrange to be taken somewhere for a negotiable fee.

Getting Around
Three car-rental companies have branches at Playa Girón: Transtour, Transautos, and Havanautos. If you decide to patronize them, be sure you get a vehicle with the tank full of gas as the local gas station is often sold out. (Remember this if you're driving down from elsewhere.)

There's a Servi-Cupet gas station on the Autopista Nacional at Jagüey Grande and another at Aguada de Pasajeros in Cienfuegos Province.

East of Caleta Buena (southeast of Playa Girón), the coastal road toward Cienfuegos becomes very bad and only passable by a tractor, so you must backtrack and take the inland road via Rodas.

Standing tall in Villa Clara

Private food stall in Santa Clara

Embalse Hanabanilla in the mountainous
southern region of Villa Clara Province

The evocative Bella Durmiente statue in
Cementerio La Reina in Cienfuegos

The tower of Iglesia de Santo Tomás and rooftops of Santiago de Cuba

Tomb of national hero Carlos Manuel de Céspedes at Cementerio Santa Ifiguenia

Monument to mulatto general Antonio Maceo in Santiago de Cuba

Santiago de Cuba poet and painter Efraín Nadereau

Province of Cienfuegos

Cienfuegos Province (4178 sq km) was part of Las Villas until 1975 and aside from the City of Havana it is Cuba's smallest province. It's surrounded by the provinces of Matanzas to the west, Villa Clara to the north, and Sancti Spíritus to the east. The Caribbean forms its southern border.

Cienfuegos Province shares the Sierra del Escambray with Villa Clara and Sancti Spíritus, but it contains the range's highest peak, Pico San Juan (1156 meters), also called 'La Cuca.' Much of central Cienfuegos is devoted to the cultivation of sugar cane. Coffee is grown in the mountains to the southeast, while cattle range the plains to the northwest.

The province's attractions are concentrated in a small area. These include the stately 19th-century cityscape of the capital, the second most important colonial fortress on Cuba's south coast at the mouth of the bay, a couple of big beach resorts to the south, and the country's largest botanical garden to the east. Some of Cuba's finest mineral water comes from Balneario Ciego Montero north of the city of Cienfuegos.

CIENFUEGOS

The city of Cienfuegos sits on the lovely Bahía de Cienfuegos, which opens into the Caribbean Sea. After the US purchased the territory of Louisiana from Napoleon in 1803, numerous French refugees from that area moved here in 1819. Just two years later they were forced to rebuild their settlement after it was destroyed by a hurricane. The settlement's name, Fernandina de Jagua, changed in 1829 to Cienfuegos (for Captain-General José Cienfuegos who ruled from 1816 to 1819).

Cienfuegos today is one of Cuba's largest industrial centers. A surprising number of the city's 125,000 residents have very light skin, blue eyes, and blond hair. The port was rebuilt in the early 1970s, and

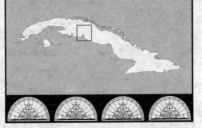

the Tricontinental sugar container terminal north of town is reportedly the world's largest sugar-exporting facility, handling the production of the fertile Las Villas Plain. Much of Cuba's shrimp fishing fleet is also based here, and there's shipbuilding, a fertilizer factory, a major cement works, a paper mill, an oil refinery, and a thermal power plant. A proposal for a duty-free industrial zone at Cienfuegos is presently being studied. The Soviets once maintained a submarine base here.

In 1980 construction of a Soviet-designed nuclear power plant began at Juraguá southwest of Cienfuegos, but work stopped in September 1992 when Cuba was unable to meet new Russian financial demands. Juraguá is now 75% complete with 20% of the equipment installed, and regular maintenance is being carried out to prevent the facility from deteriorating.

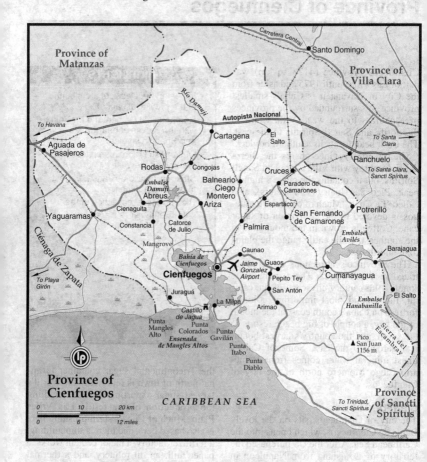

Province of Matanzas

Carretera Central

Santo Domingo

Province of Villa Clara

Río Damují

Autopista Nacional

To Havana

Aguada de Pasajeros

Cartagena

El Salto

To Santa Clara

Ranchuelo

To Santa Clara, Sancti Spíritus

Rodas

Congojas

Cruces

Embalse Damují

Abreus

Balneario Ciego Montero Ariza

Paradero de Camarones

Cienaguita

Espartaco

San Fernando de Camarones

Potrerillo

Yaguaramas

Constancia

Catorce de Julio

Palmira

Embalse Avilés

Barajagua

Mangrove

Caunao

Ciénaga de Zapata

To Playa Girón

Bahía de Cienfuegos

Cienfuegos

Jaime Gonzalez Airport

Guaos

Pepito Tey

Cumanayagua

San Antón

El Salto

Juraguá

La Milpa

Arimao

Embalse Hanabanilla

Castillo de Jagua

Punta Mangles Alto

Punta Colorados

Punta Gavilán

Ensenada de Mangles Altos

Punta Itabo

Punta Diablo

Pico San Juan 1156 m

Sierra del Escambray

Province of Cienfuegos

CARIBBEAN SEA

To Trinidad, Sancti Spíritus

Province of Sancti Spíritus

0   10   20 km
0   6   12 miles

In 1995 a consortium led by Russia and Cuba conducted a feasibility study on the completion of the two VVER-440 reactors, and if the additional estimated US$750 million required can be found, Cuba could be receiving 417 megawatts of its electricity requirements from Juraguá by the year 2000 – 15% of the nation's entire electricity demand. If so, safety will have to be a major consideration as pressurized-water VVER-440-type reactors are considered even riskier than the Chernobyl-style RBMK reactor.

Apart from all the industry, this 'pearl of the south' has some fine neoclassical architecture, well laid-out streets, and a number of interesting places nearby to visit on day trips. Getting there from Havana, Santa Clara, and Sancti Spíritus is fairly easy by train, and if you're driving, it's a straight run along the coast to/from Trinidad.

Orientation

Cienfuegos is laid out on a grid: All the east-west streets are known as avenidas (even numbered) and all the north-south streets are called calles (odd numbered). Downtown Cienfuegos, or 'Pueblo Nuevo,' is the area bounded by Avenidas 46 and 62, bisected by Calle 37. Most of the things to see are on or near the Parque Martí in the center of Pueblo Nuevo. Calle 37 (popularly called the Paseo del Prado or Malecón) runs three km south to Punta Gorda where the town's top hotel, best restaurants, and most elegant villas are found. The adjacent train and bus stations are at the corner of Avenida 58 and Calle 49, seven blocks east of Calle 37. The big beach resorts are about 20 km south via Avenida 5 de Septiembre.

Information

Tourist Office For general tourist information try Intur, Avenida 56 and Calle 33, or ask the staff in the tourist shop at Teatro Tomás Terry. For information on cheaper places to stay in remote areas, ask at Reservaciones de Campismo, Calle 31 No 5402 at Avenida 54.

Money The unofficial moneychangers hang out near the corner of Avenida 60 and Calle 35.

Post & Communications The post office is in an unmarked building at the corner of Avenida 56 and Calle 35. The telephone center is at Avenida 54 No 3512 between Calles 35 and 37 (open 24 hours). DHL Express courier service is available here. Cienfuego's telephone code is 432.

Bookstores The main bookstores are Librería La Edad de Oro, Avenida 54 No 3309 opposite Restaurante La Verja; Librería Dionisio San Román, Avenida 54 No 3526 between Calles 35 and 37, and Librería Bohemia, Avenida 56 No 3318 between Calles 33 and 35.

Library The Biblioteca Provincial Roberto García Valdés is at Calle 37 No 3615 between Avenidas 56 and 58.

Medical Services The Clínica Internacional, Calle 37 No 202 near Hotel Jagua, caters to foreigners and charges reasonable fees in dollars.

Farmacia Santa Elena, Calle 37 and Avenida 60, is open 24 hours.

Dangers & Annoyances Unfortunately, Cienfuegos is one of the towns where you'll encounter some of the most determined panhandlers in Cuba, young and old alike. Their zeal is the result of the thoughtlessness of package tourists on quick bus tours from Varadero who often amuse themselves by throwing pens and candies to the throng. Luckily both the mendicants and their benefactors seldom stray far from the tour bus stop in front of the Teatro Tomás Terry on Parque Martí, and away from there Cienfuegos is an appealing city to explore.

Things to See

Most visitors begin their explorations on **Parque José Martí**. Two marble lions stationed opposite the cathedral lead into an impressive park that is centered around a white marble statue of José Martí. At the opposite end is a triumphal arch dedicated to Cuba independence won in 1902, and all around are stately trees. It's a nice place to sit if the folks in hot pursuit of chewing gum and soap will agree to leave you alone.

On the east side of the square is the neoclassical **Catedral de la Purísima Concepción**, Avenida 56 No 2902. Erected in 1870, it has twin towers and French stained-glass windows. The south side of Parque Martí is dominated by the 19th-century **Palacio de Gobierno**, formerly the Ayuntamiento and now the Poder Popular Provincial. Nearby at the corner of Avenida 54 and Calle 27 is the **Museo Histórico** in a building formerly occupied by the Club Jesús Menéndez. On the west side of Parque Martí stands the former Palacio de Ferrer, now the **Casa de la Cultura Benjamín Duarte**, Calle 25 No 5403, where you can climb up the *mirador* (tower) upon payment of US$1. Occasional live musical performances take place here in the evening.

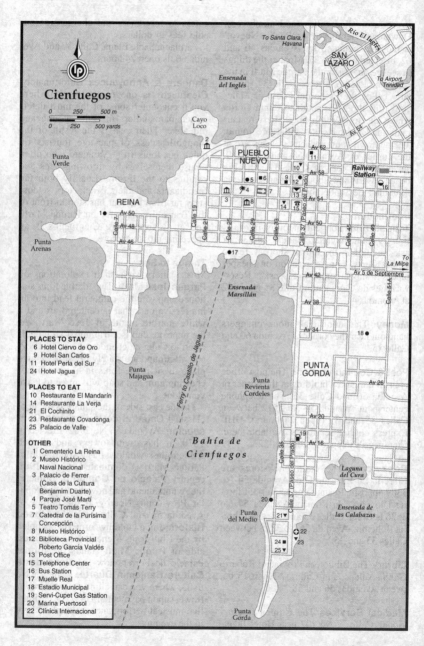

Cienfuegos

0   250   500 m
0   250   500 yards

To Santa Clara, Havana

Río El Inglés

SAN LÁZARO

To Airport Trinidad

Ensenada del Inglés

Cayo Loco

Punta Verde

PUEBLO NUEVO

Railway Station

REINA

Punta Arenas

Ensenada Marsillán

Punta Majagua

Ferry to Castillo de Jagua

To La Milpa

Av 5 de Septiembre

Punta Revienta Cordeles

PUNTA GORDA

Bahía de Cienfuegos

Laguna del Cura

Ensenada de las Calabazas

Punta del Medio

Punta Gorda

PLACES TO STAY
6 Hotel Ciervo de Oro
9 Hotel San Carlos
11 Hotel Perla del Sur
24 Hotel Jagua

PLACES TO EAT
10 Restaurante El Mandarín
14 Restaurante La Verja
21 El Cochinito
23 Restaurante Covadonga
25 Palacio de Valle

OTHER
1 Cementerio La Reina
2 Museo Histórico Naval Nacional
3 Palacio de Ferrer (Casa de la Cultura Benjamín Duarte)
4 Parque José Martí
5 Teatro Tomás Terry
7 Catedral de la Purísima Concepción
8 Museo Histórico
12 Biblioteca Provincial Roberto García Valdés
13 Post Office
15 Telephone Center
16 Bus Station
17 Muelle Real
18 Estadio Municipal
19 Servi-Cupet Gas Station
20 Marina Puertosol
22 Clínica Internacional

One of the city's most famous buildings is the **Teatro Tomás Terry** on the north side of Parque Martí. Between 1887 and 1889 the sons of Venezuelan industrialist Tomás Terry built this 950-seat auditorium. in his honor. An 1889 statue of Terry carved from Carrara marble rests in the lobby. The theater opened in 1895 with a performance of Verdi's *Aïda*. Famous performers who have appeared here include Enrico Caruso and Sarah Bernhardt. The seats are carved from Cuban hardwoods and there's an impressive ceiling fresco. Daily from 9 am to 6 pm brief tours begin at the Artex gift shop in a corner of the theater for US$1 per person.

Several blocks northwest of here at the corner of Avenida 60 and Calle 21 is the **Museo Histórico Naval Nacional** (daily 8 am to 4 pm) with exhibits on the abortive naval revolt against Batista that took place here on September 5, 1957. At last report this museum was closed for renovations.

Another interesting sight is the **Cementerio La Reina**. To get there, head to the far west end of Avenida 48 and then turn to the right. This route takes you through a seedy part of town, so be prepared for the supplications of chewing-gum-crazed kids. The rundown cemetery is rather evocative. The graves of Spanish soldiers who died in the wars of independence line the sides. Look for the marble statue of the 'Bella Durmiente,' a young woman who died in 1907 of a broken heart at the age of 24.

The aristocratic quarter of Cienfuegos is Punta Gorda, which lies three km south down Calle 37. You can't miss the Moorish-style **Palacio de Valle** right in front of the Hotel Jagua. It was built in 1917 by Oclico Valle Blanco, a Spaniard from Galicia. Batista planned to turn the building into a casino, but today it's an upmarket restaurant with a small one-room museum upstairs (daily 8 am to 4 pm). The US$1 museum admission charge includes a drink in the terrace bar on the third floor (open until 11 pm), but even if the museum is closed, it's worth going up for the drink. You should also go around behind the palace and the Hotel Jagua to

glimpse the large villas on the point. Pelicans are sometimes visible from the promenade.

Two km east of town on Avenida 5 de Septiembre (the road to Hotel Rancho Luna and La Milpa) is the **Necrópolis Tomás Acea**, an impressive cemetery entered through a huge neoclassical pavilion (1926) surrounded by 64 Doric columns. Among the many historic graves inside is a monument to the martyrs of September 5, 1957.

Activities

The Marina Puertosol, or 'Base Náutica' (☎ 8195), Avenida 8 and Calle 35, a few blocks north of Hotel Jagua, offers fishing trips for US$13 per person for four hours (four persons minimum) and motorboat rentals for sightseeing purposes for US$5 per person an hour. Verify all prices carefully as the staff running this marina seem uncharacteristically enthusiastic about dreaming up tricks to separate you and your money.

Special Events

Local festivals include carnival in July and the Benny Moré International Festival of Popular Music in August.

Places to Stay

Near the Center One of the top hotels in central Cuba, the seven-story *Hotel Jagua* (☎ 3021, fax 33-5056), Calle 37 No 1 at Punta Gorda, three km south of the center, was erected in the 1950s by Batista's brother. There are 145 rooms with bath and TV for US$34/45 single/double. Amenities include a rectangular swimming pool, tennis courts, cabaret, telephone center, post office, Transautos office, and tourist taxi stand.

Three peso hotels are in Pueblo Nuevo. Foreigners are not accepted at the flea-ridden *Hotel Ciervo de Oro* (☎ 5757), Calle 29 No 5614 between Avenidas 56 and 58. This old three-story 32-room establishment is intended to accommodate Cuban workers in transit, as the staff will point out if you request a room.

At last report 67-room *Hotel San Carlos* (☎ 8455), Avenida 56 No 3305 between Calles 33 and 35, was closed. This grand old hotel with its neoclassical facade could again be a fine place to stay if investors would fix it up.

Perhaps the only peso hotel where you have a remote chance of staying is the two-story *Hotel Perla del Sur* (☎ 2-1531), Calle 37 at Avenida 62. If that fails and you don't wish to shell out big bucks at the Hotel Jagua, ask the guys in front of the Artex shop at the Teatro Tomás Terry if they know anyone offering private rooms. Insist on something in the center of town.

South of Town Foreign tour groups often stay at the *Hotel Rancho Luna* (☎ 048-120), Carretera a Rancho Luna, 19 km southeast of Cienfuegos. There are 225 rooms with bath in two long two-story buildings. Singles/doubles cost US$21/28 low season. Travel agents prefer to book the Rancho Luna because the small Playa Rancho Luna is only 150 meters away (none of the other hotels have a beach), and there's also a rectangular pool. This is the only hotel in the province offering scuba diving, and there's also a Havanautos desk.

Several kilometers beyond the turnoff to Rancho Luna stands the *Hotel Faro de Luna* (☎ 048-165), Carretera a Rancho Luna, a three-story building overlooking a rocky coast. The 27 rooms are a bit overpriced at US$35/45 single/double, but the accommodations are good. Faro de Luna has a rectangular swimming pool.

The *Hotel Pasacaballo* (☎ 096-280), Carretera a Rancho Luna, about 29 km south of Cienfuegos and seven km beyond Hotel Faro de Luna, stands dramatically on a headland on the opposite side of the harbor mouth from the Castillo de Jagua. The 188 rooms with bath in this huge five-story hotel cost US$20/24 single/double low season, US$25/30 high season. There's running water only at certain times of day (ask while checking in). The long narrow rooms have balconies overlooking a figure-eight-shaped swimming pool with a bridge

across the middle. You get an excellent view of the castle and unfinished nuclear power plant from the 6th-floor terrace. There's a reasonable cafeteria in the basement offering pizza and spaghetti, but it closes at 5 pm. Also in the basement is a disco. The Pasacaballo has more of a Cuban atmosphere than Rancho Luna, and it's preferable for one-night stays. However, there's no beach, so Rancho Luna is better for an extended stay. In theory all of these hotels are accessible by local bus from Cienfuegos bus station four times a day except on weekends.

Places to Eat
Near the Center As usual, you'll receive better food for less at one of the private paladares that come and go at a dizzying pace. Ask someone on Calle 37 to point them out. All of the places below are state-run and should be approached with caution. Expect to be charged dollars for food and drink that Cubans can get for pesos.

El Palatino, Avenida 54 No 2514, on the south side of Parque Martí, serves drinks and snacks for dollars only.

Polinesio, Calle 29 No 5410 on the east side of Parque Martí (open Tuesday to Sunday from 6 to 9 pm only), serves Chinese and Cuban food. *Pizzería Aire Libre*, Avenida 56 No 2904 between Calles 29 and 31 behind the cathedral, seldom has any pizza. *Cafeteria Juragüe*, Avenida 56 and Calle 33, is an active local snack bar where you may be able to pay in pesos. *Restaurante La Verja*, Avenida 54 No 3306 (daily except Tuesday noon to 2 pm and 7 to 9 pm), offers upmarket seafood and meat dishes in a typical Cuban setting.

Several other official establishments lie along Calle 37. *Restaurante El Pollito*, Calle 37 and Avenida 56 (daily noon to 2 pm and 7 to 9:30 pm, closed Monday), has chicken and beer. Cuban cuisine is the specialty at *Restaurante 1819*, Calle 37 No 5609 at Avenida 58 next to El Pollito. You'll dine under elegant glass chandeliers. *Restaurante El Mandarín*, Calle 37 at Avenida 60 (daily noon to 2:30 pm and 7 to 9:30 pm), has mock Chinese.

Coppelia, Calle 37 and Avenida 52, is the local ice cream place.

Punta Gorda With the exception of the Palacio del Valle, we don't especially recommend any of the following.

The *Palacio de Valle*, next to the Hotel Jagua (daily from 9:45 am to 11 pm), serves upmarket seafood (including lobster), but nothing costs over US$20. It's one of the most imposing restaurants in Cuba and perhaps worth the splurge; otherwise, just have a drink at the rooftop terrace bar.

Opposite Hotel Jagua is *Restaurante Covadonga* with Spanish paella, and nearby is *Restaurante La Cueva del Camarón*.

For something different there's *El Cochinito*, Calle 37 and Avenida 4 (daily except Tuesday from noon to 2 pm and 7 to 10:30 pm), with pork dishes.

Entertainment

Theater Check to see if anything's happening at the *Teatro Tomás Terry* and the *Casa de la Cultura Benjamin Duarte* mentioned above in Things to See.

The *Sala del Centro Dramático*, Avenida 56 No 3306 between Calles 33 and 35, presents plays in Spanish. The *Teatro Guiñol*, Calle 37 No 5416 at Avenida 56, presents children's puppet shows on Saturday and Sunday at 10 am – they're fun for everyone. Also check the *Casa de la Cultura*, Calle 37 and Avenida 58.

Folk Music The *Casa de la Trova*, Avenida 16 at Calle 35, near the Servi-Cupet gas station on the way to Hotel Jagua at Punta Gorda, presents Cuban folk music in the evening.

Cinemas There are three movie houses to check out: *Cine-Teatro Luisa*, Calle 37 No 5001 at Avenida 50; *Cine Prado*, Calle 37 No 5402 at Avenida 54; and *Cine-Teatro Guanaroca*, Calle 49 at Avenida 58 opposite the bus station.

Discos Two nontourist discos in the center are *Tropizul*, Calle 37 and Avenida 48 – it's

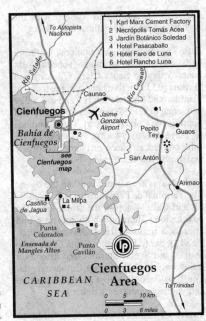

1	Karl Marx Cement Factory
2	Necrópolis Tomás Acea
3	Jardín Botánico Soledad
4	Hotel Pasacaballo
5	Hotel Faro de Luna
6	Hotel Rancho Luna

the place with a pink-and-blue wall around it (no sign). *Discoteca Costa Sur* is at Avenida 46 west of Calle 37.

Things to Buy
Avenida 54 is Cienfuego's pedestrian shopping street, and it's well worth a stroll. Have a look at the Galería de Arte, Avenida 54 No 3310 at Calle 33.

The Fondo Cubano de Bienes Culturales, Avenida 54 No 2506 on the south side of Parque Martí, has one of Cuba's best collections of colorful folk art for sale. The Artex shop in a corner of the Teatro Tomás Terry carries a good selection of compact discs.

Getting There & Away
Air Jaime Gonzalez Airport is five km northeast of Cienfuegos on the road to Caunao. Royal Airlines operates charter flights from Toronto weekly in summer and three times a week in winter. Round-trip fares vary between CDN$349 and

CDN$559 according to season, with the highest prices at Christmas and Easter.

Bus The Terminal de Ómnibus, Calle 49 between Avenidas 56 and 58, schedules six buses a day to Santa Clara (74 km) and Havana (253 km, five hours), three a day to Trinidad (82 km, two hours), and one a day to Camagüey (337 km, seven hours) and Santiago de Cuba (663 km). There's no bus to Playa Girón (94 km). All services are fully booked, so check early and accept any assistance you're offered.

Train Trains are a better bet than the buses. The Terminal de Ferrocarriles is at Avenida 58 and Calle 4 across the street from the bus station. There are both morning and afternoon trains to Havana (seven hours, US$11), Santo Domingo, Santa Clara (two hours), and Sancti Spíritus, and afternoon trains only to Aguada and Cumanayagua. You'll pay in dollars, but it's not expensive and you're guaranteed a ticket.

Yacht Cruising yachts are required to report to the Guarda Frontera post near the Castillo de Jagua at the mouth of the Bahía de Cienfuegos, where a mandatory (and unnecessary) pilot must be hired for US$30 to accompany you on the straightforward run up to the Marina Puertosol, or 'Base Náutica' (☎ 8195), near the Hotel Jagua. Although this marina makes a convenient base for visiting Cienfuegos or purchasing provisions, be aware of the possibility of thieves swimming from the nearby public beach.

Getting Around
Car The Hotel Rancho Luna has a Transautos desk. Havanautos is adjacent to the Servi-Cupet gas station on Calle 37 at the corner of Avenida 16, 800 meters north of the Hotel Jagua. Another Servi-Cupet gas station is near Hotel Rancho Luna.

In addition to the Servi-Cupet stations in Cienfuegos, there's a Servi-Cupet station at Km 172 on the Autopista Nacional at the turnoff to Aguada de Pasajeros.

Boat There's a 120-passenger ferry to the Castillo de Jagua three times a day from the Muelle Real, Avenida 46 and Calle 25 (40 minutes, 50 centavos). It leaves Cienfuegos at 7 am, 1 pm, and 5:30 pm, departing Jagua for the return at 6 am, 10 am, and 3 pm. The wharf is near the castle.

Taxi To call a Turistaxi, dial ☎ 9-6256 or 9-6212.

Horse & Carriage Horse carts charging a peso per person per ride shuttle up and down Calle 37.

AROUND CIENFUEGOS
Castillo de Nuestra Señora de los Ángeles de Jagua
The Castillo de Jagua, on the west side of the narrow mouth of the Bahía de Cienfuegos, was designed by José Tontete in 1738 and completed in 1745 (long before the city of Cienfuegos was founded). The original purpose was to deny the bay to pirates who had been using it as a refuge; the castle now shelters a government-run seafood restaurant serving lunch only (open daily). You can get there via a roundabout road from Cienfuegos, but the easiest access is on the launch across the mouth of the bay from a landing just below the Hotel Pasacaballo. It operates frequently throughout the day, charging one peso per person per ride, but unfortunately someone in the local tourism establishment has given orders to the launch operators not to carry foreign passengers, who are expected to order a special launch from the Marina Puertosol in Cienfuegos. You can always try using the local ferry from Cienfuegos mentioned under Getting Around above; otherwise, the excellent view of the castle from the 6th-floor terrace of the Hotel Pasacaballo may have to suffice.

Jardín Botánico Soledad
The 90-hectare Jardín Botánico Soledad near the Pepito Tey sugar mill, 17 km east of Cienfuegos near Guaos, has 2000 species of plants including 23 bamboo species,

65 fig species, and 280 palm species. The botanical garden was founded by Edwin F Atkins, a US sugar millionaire, in 1901 on land belonging to the old Colonia de Limones sugar estate, formerly known as the Central Soledad. Atkins originally intended to use the garden to study different varieties of sugar cane, but he soon began planting exotic tropical trees from around the world and in 1919 Harvard University took over the garden, which they managed until 1961. Today it's run by the Instituto de Ecología y Sistemática.

You'll need a car to get the garden. Coming from Cienfuegos, turn right (south) just beyond the Karl Marx cement factory. The garden is open from 8 am to 4 pm daily, admission US$2.

Province of Villa Clara

With its 8662 sq km, Villa Clara is the fifth largest province in Cuba, bordering Matanzas Province to the west, Cienfuegos Province to the southwest, and Sancti Spíritus to the east. Prior to the political/administrative reorganization of Cuba in 1975, Las Villas Province included within its boundaries what is now Villa Clara as well as Cienfuegos, Sancti Spíritus, and the Península de Zapata.

The main economic activity is the planting, cutting, and crushing of sugar cane grown on the fertile red plains of northern Villa Clara. Beef cattle range across the rolling terrain south of the provincial capital. The Río Sagua la Grande in the north of the province is the largest river on Cuba's northern watershed. It drains the Embalse Alacranes, Cuba's second largest artificial reservoir. The Embalse Hanabanilla in the mountainous south of the province is the third largest.

Tourism here is mostly stopover traffic in the provincial capital of Santa Clara, where a number of monuments and museums commemorate the historic battle of late December 1958 that led to the downfall of Fulgencio Batista. Here the dictator's fate was sealed when guerrillas led by the legendary Che Guevara descended on the city from the Sierra del Escambray. Further afield, the old town of Remedios near the Atlantic coast contains some of the finest colonial architecture in Cuba, and it's still far enough away from large tourist complexes like Cayo Coco to the east so as not to be overrun with visitors. In the far northwest are the sulfurous baths of Elguea, and in the south a resort hugs the shores of Embalse Hanabanilla.

Future tourism development in Villa Clara will probably be focused on Cayo Santa María, an idyllic Atlantic island east of Cayo Fragoso boasting 14 km of sandy white beach. Between 1989 and 1996, a massive 48-km causeway of 45 bridges that

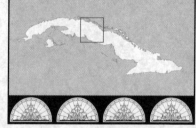

HIGHLIGHTS

- Impressive monuments to the legendary Ernesto 'Che' Guevara in Santa Clara
- Early colonial architecture in the unspoiled town of Remedios
- Scenic 48-km causeway to idyllic Cayo Santa María
- Fishing and mountain scenery at the Embalse Hanabanilla in the Sierra del Escambray

allow an exchange of tidal waters was constructed across the Bahía Buena Vista from the port of Caibarién at a cost of a hundred million pesos. It's expected that 28 beach hotels with a total of 10,000 rooms will be built on previously inaccessible Ensenacho, Las Brujas, and Santa María. Foreign investors are being courted.

SANTA CLARA

Santa Clara stands at 112 meters elevation about midway between Havana and Camagüey, 196 km southeast of Varadero. Christopher Columbus believed that Cubanacán, an Indian village once located in this area, was the seat of the khans of Mongolia. Santa Clara was founded in 1689 by settlers from Remedios who wanted to be less accessible to pirates, and the town grew quickly after a fire at Remedios in 1692. In 1867 Santa Clara became capital of Las Villas Province and in 1873 the railway arrived from Havana. Santa Clara

was the first major city to be liberated from Batista's army in December 1958.

Santa Clara today is a vibrant city of 200,000 with lots of street life, yet it lacks the array of historical monuments of Camagüey or Santiago de Cuba. There's some industry in the suburbs, including a cigarette factory, a textile mill, and plants producing domestic electrical appliances and heavy equipment for industry and agriculture. Founded in 1948, the Universidad Central de Las Villas, eight km east of town on the road to Remedios, is one of Cuba's largest universities.

Orientation

The city's best architecture and downtown hotels are all on or near Parque Vidal, Santa Clara's central square. Monuments relating to the culminating battle of the Cuban Revolution are on the east and west sides of the city. The train station is seven blocks north of Parque Vidal; the two bus stations are less conveniently located out on the Carretera Central west of town.

Information

Tourist Office There isn't any regular tourist information office. The Intur Oficina

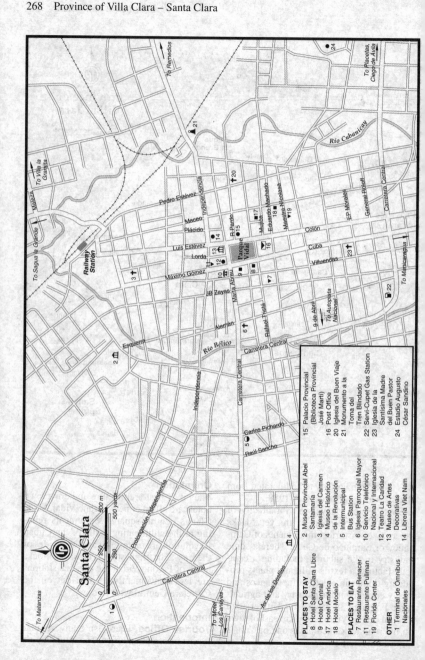

Santa Clara

To Matanzas

To Motel
Los Canejyes

Av. de los Desfiles

Carretera Central

To Sagua la Grande

Maleza

To Villa la
Grahjita

Railway
Station

To Remedios

Río Cubanicay

To Placetas,
Ciego de Ávila

To Maticaragua

PLACES TO STAY
8 Hotel Santa Clara Libre
17 Hotel Central
18 Hotel Modelo

PLACES TO EAT
1 Restaurante Renacer
11 Restaurante Pullman
19 Florida Center

OTHER
1 Terminal de Omnibus
   Nacionales

2 Museo Provincial Abel
   Santamaría
3 Iglesia del Carmen
4 Museo Histórico
   de la Revolución
5 Intermunicipal
   Bus Station
6 Iglesia Parroquial Mayor
10 Servicio Telefónico
   Nacional y Internacional
12 Teatro La Caridad
13 Museo de Artes
   Decorativas
14 Librería Viet Nam

15 Palacio Provincial
   (Biblioteca Provincial
   José Martí)
16 Post Office
20 Iglesia del Buen Viaje
21 Monumento a la
   Toma del
   Tren Blindado
22 Servi-Cupet Gas Station
23 Iglesia de la
   Santísima Madre
   del Buen Pastor
24 Estadio Augusto
   César Sandino

de Reservaciones, Lorda 6 beside Teatro La Caridad, makes hotel reservations for Cubans, and the staff will probably do so for you too. It's open weekdays from 8 to 11:30 am and 1 to 3:45 pm.

Money Moneychangers range along Calle Independencia, one block north of Parque Vidal.

Post & Communications The main post office is at Calle Colón No 10. The Servicio Telefónico Nacional y Internacional, Alfredo Barrero No 6 (daily from 7 am to 11:45 pm), is rather hidden down a side street behind Teatro La Caridad. Santa Clara's telephone code is 422.

Bookstores Santa Clara's best bookstore, Librería Viet Nam, Independencia between Plácido and Luis Estévez, requires 50% payment in hard currency. There's also Librería Pepe Medina, Parque Vidal No 18.

Library The Biblioteca Provincial José Martí, on the east side of Parque Vidal, is a nice place to take refuge when it's raining.

Medical Services Farmacia Campa, Independencia and Luis Estévez, is open daily from 8 am to 8:40 pm.

Public Toilets The public toilets on the Plaza de Intercambio Cultural, Independencia and Luis Estévez, are open 24 hours a day.

Dangers & Annoyances Various hustlers and panhandlers hang around on the sidewalk outside the Hotel Santa Clara Libre offering various services and stories. They leave you alone once you get away from the hotel.

Things to See
Begin your visit on **Parque Vidal**, named for Colonel Leoncio Vidal y Caro, who was killed here on March 23, 1896, as a small monument attests. During the colonial era twin sidewalks circled the park with a fence separating blacks and whites. Today there's a bandstand in the center of the park and lots of shady benches where you can sit and watch the world go by.

The city's most impressive building is **Teatro La Caridad** (1885) on Calle Máximo Gómez in the northwest corner of Parque Vidal, with frescoes by Camilo Zalaya. The opera singer Enrico Caruso once performed here. The **Museo de Artes Decorativas**, Parque Vidal No 27 just east of Teatro La Caridad on the same side of the park, is an 18th-century building packed with period furniture. It's open Monday, Wednesday, and Thursday 9 am to 6 pm, Friday and Saturday 1 to 6 and 7 to 11 pm, and Sunday 6 to 10 pm, admission US$1, or US$3 if you want a guided tour. On the east side of Parque Vidal is the neoclassical **Palacio Provincial**, built between 1902 and 1912. A garrison during the Batista period, it now houses the provincial library and an art gallery.

Uncharacteristically, the churches are scattered around the city rather than on or near the main square. The **Iglesia de Nuestra Señora del Buen Viaje**, Pedro Estévez and Pardo, is an eclectic mix of Gothic, Romanesque, and neoclassical.

On Parque Tudurí, north of the center on the way to the train station, is the **Iglesia de Nuestra Señora del Carmen** (1748) with a tower added in 1846. A large monument in front of the church commemorates the foundation of Santa Clara in 1689.

West of the center is the early 20th-century **Iglesia Parroquial Mayor de las Santas Hermanas de Santa Clara de Asís**, Calle Marta Abreu No 113 and Alemán. Facing a square south of the center is the **Iglesia de la Santísima Madre del Buen Pastor**, EP Morales No 4 between Cuba and Villuendas.

East on Calle Independencia just over the river is the **Monumento a la Toma del Tren Blindado**. Here on December 29, 1958, 18 men under the command of Che Guevara and equipped with rifles and grenades captured an armored train containing 408 heavily armed Batista troops in a battle lasting an hour and a half. A small museum (Tuesday to Saturday 9 am

From Doctor to Revolutionary to Hero

Ernesto 'Che' Guevara was born to a middle-class family in Rosario, Argentina, on June 14, 1928. The family moved to Buenos Aires in 1945, and it was there that Ernesto finished medical school in 1953. He traveled widely in Latin America, both before and after graduation, and the widespread poverty he saw convinced him that he had a mission in life more important than medicine.

In December 1953 he arrived in Guatemala, where an elected government led by Jacobo Arbenz was working to solve social problems. Six months later Guevara witnessed the CIA-backed invasion that overthrew Arbenz and unleashed a wave of pitiless repression that has continued to this day.

Guevara fled to Mexico City where he met Fidel Castro in mid-1955, and he was among the first to sign up for the *Granma* expedition to Cuba a year later. The Cubans nicknamed him 'Che' for the interjection *che* meaning 'say!' or 'hey!' that Argentines frequently insert into their sentences. Although wounded during an initial engagement with Batista's troops, Guevara was among the small band that escaped into the Sierra Maestra.

In July 1957 Guevara was made *comandante* of a second rebel column, and in August 1958 he and his men set out on an epic trek to spread the revolution to central Cuba. In October they reached the Sierra del Escambray, where they linked up with other revolutionaries, and by December they had captured several small towns, effectively cutting Cuba in two. The Battle of Santa Clara began on December 28, and the next day they captured an armored train Batista had sent to reinforce the city. With the capital of

to 6 pm, Sunday 8 am to noon, admission US$1) has been installed inside five wagons of the 22 that comprised the original armored train. The bulldozer that the guerrillas used to cut the railway line has been set up on a pedestal nearby.

The **Museo Provincial Abel Santamaría** is on a hilltop north of the center, just across the Río Bélico in Reparto Osvaldo Herrera. It's at the north end of Calle Esquerra and a bit hard to find, so be prepared to ask. The unmarked museum building is a former military barracks where Batista's troops surrendered to Che Guevara on January 1, 1959. The revolutionary police now have a new headquarters just opposite. The museum presents natural history downstairs, history upstairs. It's open weekdays 8 am to noon and 1 to 6 pm, Saturday 8 am to noon, admission US$1.

One sight not to be missed is the **Museo Histórico de la Revolución** on Avenida de los Desfiles, two km west of Parque Vidal via Calle Rafael Tristá (just keep heading west). Here in the center of the Plaza de la Revolución stands a massive statue of Che Guevara erected in 1987 to mark the 20th anniversary of Guevara's murder in Bolivia. In the museum directly below the monument (entry from the rear) are exhibits about the life of this colorful figure and the Battle of Santa Clara. The museum is open Monday to Saturday 8 am to 5 pm, Sunday 8 am to noon, and it's worth the US$1 admission price.

Places to Stay

In Town The *Hotel Santa Clara Libre* (☎ 2-7548), Parque Vidal No 6 between Marta Abreu and Tristá, has 131 rooms with bath

Las Villas Province falling to the rebels, Batista fled into exile, and on January 2, 1959, Guevara and other *barbudos* (bearded guerrillas) entered Havana.

Guevara was granted Cuban citizenship in February 1959, and he soon assumed a leading role in Cuba's economic reforms as head of the Industry Department of the National Institute of Agrarian Reform (October 1959), president of the National Bank of Cuba (November 1959), and Minister of Industry (February 1960). Guevara made several long trips to Europe, Asia, and Africa, arranging trade agreements and promoting Cuban interests. In time he became convinced that the poverty he had witnessed throughout Latin America could only be corrected by a continentwide revolution.

In March 1965, Guevara withdrew from public life and secretly returned to Africa, where he helped organize left-wing rebels in the Congo. By December 1965 he was back in Cuba making preparations for a guerrilla campaign that would convert the Andes into a new Sierra Maestra. In November 1966 Guevara arrived in Bolivia and there his group established a base. After the successful ambush of a Bolivian detachment in March 1967, he issued a call for 'two, three, many Vietnams.' This alarmed the US, which quickly sent military advisors to Bolivia, and thousands of Bolivian troops began combing the area where Guevara's small band of guerrillas was operating. On October 8, 1967, Guevara was captured by the Bolivian army, and after consultation with military leaders in La Paz and Washington, DC, he was murdered before the eyes of US advisors.

Despite a debilitating asthma condition, Che Guevara personified the heroic guerrilla willing to confront the most powerful forces of imperialism without any thought for personal safety or profit. By leaving Cuba on a mission that he knew could easily lead to his death, he gave up an assured position and expressed his solidarity with oppressed peoples around the world. After Guatemala, Che had become a determined Marxist, and he wrote several influential books about the art of guerrilla warfare and Communist theory in the Latin American context. Through his writings and example he left an indelible mark on the 1960s.

'Revolutions rarely, if ever, emerge fully ripe, and not all their details are scientifically foreseen. They are products of passion, of improvisation by human beings in their struggle for social change, and are never perfect. Our revolution was no exception.'
– Ernesto 'Che' Guevara, 1961

at US$15/20 single/double low season, US$18/24 high season. Only a few of the rooms have air-con. The front of this 11-story hotel built in 1956 is still pocked with bullet holes from one of the last battles of the revolution. There's a pleasant restaurant on the 10th floor, a rooftop bar with good views on 11th floor, and a smelly, dungeonlike cafeteria in the basement. The disco is also in the basement. If you're driving, you'll have to pay someone to guard your car; otherwise, one of the numerous indigents hanging around outside will scratch lines in the paint unless you've been generous with soap, pens, chewing gum, and money. Cubans waiting to get into the disco will sit on the hood, and overnight the vehicle will receive an unsolicited car wash.

The nearby 30-room *Hotel Central* (☎ 2-2369), Parque Vidal No 3, a stately two-story building erected in 1929, has been closed for renovations.

A peso hotel worth trying is the decrepit four-story *Hotel América* (☎ 5451), Calle Mujica No 9 off Calle Colón, a block east of Parque Vidal. The 28 rooms cost about US$10 single or double without air conditioning, US$12 with. Farther south is the four-story, 80-room *Hotel Modelo* (☎ 2-6744), Calle Maceo No 210, which doesn't usually accept foreigners.

Outside Town Most tourists on package bus tours are accommodated at *Motel Los Caneyes* (☎ 4512), Avenida de los Eucaliptos and Circunvalación de Santa Clara, five km west of the town center. The thatched bungalows were built in 1966 to resemble an Indian village. The 90 cabañas with bath, fridge, and TV are US$21/28 single/double low season, US$24/33 high season. There's a swimming pool, post office, Havanautos office, and a guarded parking lot, which makes this the best place to stay if you're driving.

Less known and a bit overpriced is *Villa la Granjita* (☎ 2-6052), Carretera de Maleza beyond the train station six km northeast of town. The 40 thatched units cost US$35/45 single/double. It's in an orange grove with a variety of fruit trees around, and there's a swimming pool, bowling alley, and some other sporting facilities.

Places to Eat

Of the state-run restaurants, *Restaurante Colonial 1878*, Calle Máximo Gómez between Marta Abreu and Independencia, serves Cuban cuisine Tuesday to Sunday from 11 am to 2:30 pm and 7 to 11 pm. This colonial-style building once housed a school.

Nearby on the corner of Independencia and Máximo Gómez, a block north of Parque Vidal, is *Restaurante Pullman* (closed Thursday), which has one section for peso-paying Cubans and another where everyone pays dollars. Go into the dollar section as you'll get better food and service for less money (they won't accept pesos from you anyway).

Hamburguesa El Recreo, Parque Vidal No 31 at Lorda, is another anomaly. The Cuban queue is discreetly across the street next to Teatro La Caridad. Of course, you'll be allowed to walk right in but in dollar terms the prices are rather high.

Another government-operated eatery is *Restaurante El Nuevo Artesano*, Parque Vidal No 19 at Calle Colón (closed Tuesday, otherwise open 24 hours).

Rather than eating at any of the official establishments you'll eat better for less money at a privately operated paladar, of which there are many in Santa Clara. These places open and close from week to week. Most don't have a sign, but you'll know them by the bare light bulb hanging outside. Otherwise, just ask anyone.

If the *Florida Center*, Maestra Nicolasa No 56 between Colón and Maceo (daily 7 to 11 pm), is still open, you'll probably get a tasty meal for a low price. The portions aren't large, so order a few extras from the menu. This attractive old house has a nice garden and the friendly staff provides excellent service.

Another private place to try is *Restaurante Renacer* (☎ 2-2272), JB Zayas No 111 between Eduardo Machado and Tristá. This old colonial house is attractive, but be prepared for two menus, one in pesos and a more expensive menu in dollars. Sometimes they have lobster (US$5) and other prohibited dishes; if you order one of these, you'll be ushered into a back room to enjoy them.

If all you need is a snack, try *La Marquesina Tea Shop* in a corner of the Teatro La Caridad building. Santa Clara's ice cream parlor is *Coppelia*, Calle Colón opposite the post office.

Entertainment

The *Casa de la Cultura Juan Marinello*, Parque Vidal No 5 on the west side of Parque Vidal near the Hotel Santa Clara Libre, presents concerts and art exhibitions in a former private club.

Disco Villa Clara, Parque Vidal No 11, diagonally opposite Hotel Santa Clara Libre (closed Monday), caters to young locals.

Things to Buy

Calle Independencia between Maceo and Zayas is Santa Clara's pedestrian shopping mall, locally known as the 'Boulevard.'

Getting There & Away

There's no airport at Santa Clara.

Bus The intermunicipal bus station on the Carretera Central, just west of the center via Calle Abreu, has buses to Remedios (45 km) three times a day.

The more important Terminal de Ómnibus Nacionales is 2½ km out on the Carretera Central toward Matanzas, beyond the intermunicipal station. Here you'll find buses to Cienfuegos (two daily, 74 km), Sancti Spíritus (two daily, 86 km), Trinidad (daily, 90 km, three hours), Camagüey (daily, 271 km, six hours), Havana (two daily, 287 km, four hours), Holguín (daily, 471 km, eight hours), and Santiago de Cuba (daily, 597 km, 12 hours). As usual, it's difficult to get a ticket as demand far outstrips supply.

Train Rather than trekking way out to the bus station and hassling for a ticket, consider going by train. The Estación de Ferrocarriles is on the north side of town straight up Calle Luis Estévez from Parque Vidal. The crowded railway reservations office for locals is at Luis Estévez 323, just across the park from the train station, but foreigners must use the Ladis ticket office inside the station where you receive immediate personal attention and pay dollars.

There are trains to Havana (six daily, 281 km, four hours, US$12), Matanzas (189 km, seven hours, US$8), Cienfuegos (two daily), Sancti Spíritus (two daily), Camagüey (daily, 256 km, four hours), and Santiago de Cuba (daily, 10 hours, US$24).

Getting Around

The main form of local transportation is horse and carriage with an important route along Calle Marta Abreu, west toward the bus station. Rides are one peso per person.

There's a Havanautos desk at the Motel Los Caneyes just outside town. The Servi-Cupet gas station is on the Carretera Central, corner of General Roloff, just south of the town center.

To call a tourist taxi, dial ☎ 4512.

EMBALSE HANABANILLA

South of Santa Clara rises the Sierra del Escambray, running west into Cienfuegos Province. Surrounded by the northern foothills of the Sierra del Escambray, nine km below Barajaguá, is the Embalse Hanabanilla, a sizable reservoir supplying Cuba's largest hydroelectric generating station. A large tourist hotel stands on the northwest shore of the lake and there's fishing for largemouth bass. Hanabanilla

is a centrally located stopover for motorized tourists traveling between Cienfuegos 58 km to the west, Santa Clara 80 km to the north, Sancti Spíritus 80 km to the east, or Trinidad 58 km to the south. Theoretically there are three buses a day from Manicaragua, but the only practical access is by car.

The four-story *Hotel Hanabanilla* (☎ 8-6932) has 156 rooms with bath, fridge, and balcony overlooking the lake for US$17/22 single/double low season, US$23/30 high season. Facilities include a rectangular swimming pool, post office, and the Bar Mirador on the top floor. Speedboat rentals are US$20 an hour and horseback riding can be arranged. It's a peaceful spot although the loud music broadcast through the hotel cancels some of its charm. The Hanabanilla is crowded with Cubans on the weekend. *Restaurante Río Negro*, seven km across the lake and accessible only by boat, offers Creole cuisine.

REMEDIOS

San Juan de los Remedios was founded in 1524 by Vasco Porcallo de Figueroa, who is also famous for having fathered over 200 children. It served as the main center of the region until the founding of Santa Clara in 1689, but after a fire in 1692 the town's importance declined. Today Remedios (population 20,000) retains a 17th-century air, and it's certainly one of the prettiest towns in Cuba. Remedios' current peace and quiet will likely end soon as tourism is developed on nearby Cayo Santa María, across the causeway from Caibarién.

Things to See

The **Parroquia de San Juan Bautista de Remedios** (1545), Camilo Cienfuegos No 20 on Parque Martí, is one of the finest churches in Cuba. The gilded high altar and mahogany ceiling are worth seeing. If the front doors are closed, go around to the rear doors where sightseers are admitted from 9:30 to 11 am and 3:30 to 5:30 pm. Also on Parque Martí is the 18th-century **Iglesia de Nuestra Señora del Buen Viaje**,

Alejandro del Río No 66. Between these churches is the **Museo de Música Alejandro García Caturla**, Parque Martí No 5, which commemorates García, the Cuban composer who lived here from 1920 until his murder in 1940.

The **Museo de las Parrandas Remedianas**, Máximo Gómez No 71, two blocks off Parque Martí (Tuesday to Saturday 9 am to noon and 1 to 5 pm, Sunday 9 am to 1 pm, admission US$1), has displays about the noisy processions called *parrandas* (see Special Events below).

The **Museo de Historia Francisco Javier Balmaseda**, Maceo No 56 between Fe del Valle and Avenida General Carrillo, about four blocks from Parque Martí, opened in 1933.

Special Events

Parrandas take place from December 24 through 26 as neighborhoods compete for the honor of having the best *carroza* (float). Processions are accompanied by fireworks and street music (see Things to See above).

Places to Stay

The only hotel in town is the two-story *Hotel Mascotte* (☎ 39-5481) on Parque Martí, a beautiful 19th-century building with 14 rooms costing from US$9/12 single/double up to US$22 for a suite.

If the Mascotte is full, try the seven-room *Hotel Brisas del Mar* (☎ 8-6932) or the 11-room *Hotel España* (☎ 3-3191), both in Caibarién on the coast eight km east. The rooms cost about the same.

Getting There & Away

Theoretically there are buses to/from Santa Clara (45 km) three times a day.

ELGUEA

Elguea, 136 km northwest of Santa Clara near the border with Matanzas Province, is a health resort where medicinal sulfur springs are used to treat arthritis, rheumatism, and skin diseases.

The *Hotel Elguea* (☎ 9-6240), Circuito Norte in nearby Corralillo, has 139 rooms with bath, fridge, and TV in a series of large two-story blocks at US$15/20 single/double. Facilities include a swimming pool, tennis courts, gymnasium, and many other sporting facilities. Fishing trips can be arranged.

Province of Sancti Spíritus

With Villa Clara and Cienfuegos Provinces to the west and Ciego de Ávila Province to the east, the 6744-sq-km Province of Sancti Spíritus is the historical heartland of central Cuba. Much of the province is a lowland dedicated to the cultivation of sugar cane or the raising of cattle. In the southwest two branches of the Sierra del Escambray are divided by the Río Agabama. Rice paddies are near the coast in the far south and a considerable amount of tobacco is still grown in the center of the province.

For visitors Sancti Spíritus has two wonderful colonial towns, the provincial capital, Sancti Spíritus, and the old sugar-growing center of Trinidad. Among the many attractions of the Trinidad area are the fabulous beaches and diving possibilities of the Península de Ancón, the Valle de los Ingenios with its 19th-century sugar estates and the health-resort town of Topes de Collantes. The northern portion of the province is less visited, although Yaguajay is notable as the headquarters of the revolutionary hero Camilo Cienfuegos whose exploits are detailed at a museum in the town. Cabaiguán, 19 km north of the city of Sancti Spíritus, has ethnographic and municipal museums.

SANCTI SPÍRITUS

Sancti Spíritus (population 80,000) is near the geographical center of Cuba along the Carretera Central between Santa Clara and Ciego de Ávila Provinces. Founded in 1514 on the banks of the Río Tuinicú, this is the oldest city in the Cuban interior. Moved to its present location on the Río Yayabo in 1522, it was sacked by pirates in 1665. The Río Yayabo has lent its name to two items closely associated with Cuba, the loose-fitting *guayabera* shirt invented in this area, and the *guayaba* (guava), a fruit that still grows prolifically along the river's banks.

Sancti Spíritus became the provincial capital in 1975. Though not lacking in

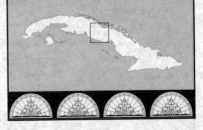
quaint colonial churches, squares, and streets, Sancti Spíritus is not promoted as a tourist center and it's refreshingly free of visitors. It's still mainly an agricultural market town for the surrounding region. Just southeast of Sancti Spíritus is the 127-sq-km Embalse Zaza, Cuba's largest reservoir, created by damming the Río Zaza. The 1020 million cubic meters of water in this vast reservoir are stocked with large-mouth bass.

Orientation

The bus and train stations are on opposite sides of Sancti Spíritus. Of the two the train station is the more convenient: It's an easy five-minute walk to the old Puente Yayabo and then another five minutes to Parque Serafín Sánchez in the center of town. The

Province of Sancti Spíritus

main tourist hotel in the area is on the Embalse Zaza, 10 km southeast of town.

Information
There are no tourist information offices or travel agencies for foreigners in Sancti Spíritus.

Money It should be possible to change cash on Calle Independencia Sur near the large hard-currency department store with reflecting glass on the corner of Parque Serafín Sánchez.

Post & Communications The post office is at Independencia Sur No 8 off Parque Serafín Sánchez. Sancti Spíritus' telephone code is 41.

Bookstores Try Librería Julio Antonio Mella, Independencia Sur No 29 near the post office. Nearby at No 25 is a good used bookstore.

Medical Services There's a pharmacy at Independencia Sur No 15 opposite the post office.

Things to See

The city's most renowned monument is the **Puente Yayabo**, a brick bridge built by the Spanish in 1815. The **Teatro Principal** next to the bridge dates from 1876, and the old cobbled streets just below here were restored in the late 1980s, but are still pleasantly uncommercialized. You can stroll here without seeing another tourist!

Up the hill from the Teatro Principal is the **Museo de Arte Colonial**, Calle Plácido Sur No 74 (Tuesday to Saturday 8:30 am to 5 pm, Sunday 8 am to noon, admission US$1), with colonial furniture displayed in an imposing 17th-century building. Farther up the same way is the yellow **Iglesia Parroquial Mayor del Espíritu Santo**, Agramonte Oeste No 58 on Plaza Honorato. Originally constructed of wood in 1522 and rebuilt in stone in 1680, it's said to be the oldest church in Cuba still standing on its original foundations. There's a splendid ceiling inside if you're lucky enough to be able to enter.

Other museums include the **Museo de Historia Natural**, Máximo Gómez Sur No 2 off Parque Serafín Sánchez; the **Museo Provincial**, Céspedes Sur No 11; and the **Museo Casa Natal de Serafín Sánchez**, Céspedes Norte No 112. Serafín Sánchez was a local patriot who participated in both wars of independence and died fighting in November 1896. Also visit the **Iglesia de Nuestra Señora de la Caridad**, Céspedes Norte No 207.

Special Events

In early September the Copa Internacional de Pesca de Black Bass is held at the Hotel Zaza on Embalse Zaza.

Places to Stay

In Town All of the following are peso hotels patronized mostly by Cubans, but you'll probably be admitted if you ask. The old *Hotel Colonial* (☎ 2-5123), Máximo Gómez Norte No 23, has 20 rooms for US$7/9 single/double. The two-story *Hotel Plaza* on the opposite side of Parque Serafín Sánchez has 27 rooms for

US$20/30 single/double, US$38 *especial*. At these prices ask to see the room before agreeing to stay.

The three-story *Hotel Perla de Cuba*, Parque Serafín Sánchez, is a stately 19th-century building decorated with Spanish tiles. It has been closed for reconstruction.

If you can't find a room in a hotel, a local taxi driver, Ricardo Rodríguez, rents rooms at US$12 double in his house at Independencia Norte No 28, just off Parque Serafín Sánchez. Ask around for other folks willing to do the same.

Two more peso hotels are on the Carretera Central one km east of the center. The *Hotel Las Villas* (☎ 2-6989), Bartolomé Masó No 11, has 20 rooms, and a block away is *Hospedaje Flor de Cuba*, Bartolomé Masó No 63. Expect them to be extremely basic.

Outside Town Three better hotels are along the Carretera Central as you head north out of town toward Santa Clara. The four-story *Hotel Deportivo* (☎ 2-6019), right next to the highway three km north of town, has 48 rooms. It's a sports hotel where visiting teams often stay. *Villa Rancho Hatuey* (☎ 2-6015), a modern complex on a hilltop just off the Carretera Central four km north of town, is a 'protocol' hotel used mostly by top government officials and party leaders. Tourists are also accommodated in the 38 overpriced rooms for US$37/54/71 single/double/triple for a room in the main building or US$68/80/100 for a cabaña. There's a swimming pool. A more local place intended for ordinary Cubans is *Motel Los Laureles* (☎ 2-3913), five km north of town. The 50 rooms cost US$20/25 single/double. It's a pleasant, shady spot with a swimming pool and Cabaret Tropi (closed Monday).

Most bus tours stop at the *Hotel Zaza* (☎ 2-6012, international calls ☎ 66-8001) in Finca San José on the huge Embalse Zaza 10 km southeast of town. Go east five km on the Carretera Central toward Ciego de Ávila and then south five km to the lake. The 128 rooms with bath are US$14/19

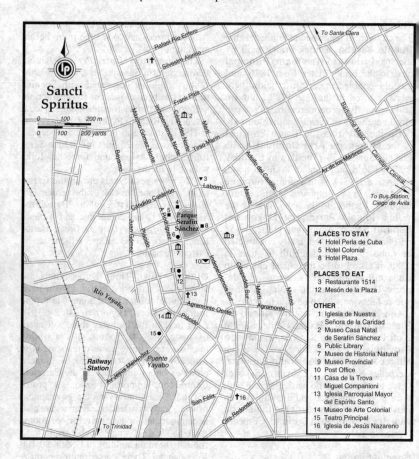

Sancti Spíritus

PLACES TO STAY
4 Hotel Perla de Cuba
5 Hotel Colonial
8 Hotel Plaza

PLACES TO EAT
3 Restaurante 1514
12 Mesón de la Plaza

OTHER
1 Iglesia de Nuestra
   Señora de la Caridad
2 Museo Casa Natal
   de Serafín Sánchez
6 Public Library
7 Museo de Historia Natural
9 Museo Provincial
10 Post Office
11 Casa de la Trova
   Miguel Companioni
13 Iglesia Parroquial Mayor
   del Espíritu Santo
14 Museo de Arte Colonial
15 Teatro Principal
16 Iglesia de Jesús Nazareno

single/double low season, US$20/26 high season – a good value if you have your own transportation. A swimming pool and a nightclub are on the premises.

Places to Eat

Restaurante 1514, Céspedes Norte No 52 (no sign), serves shots of rum for US$2 and meals for US$4 (daily except Thursday from noon to 2 pm and 6:30 to 8:30 pm). The *Mesón de la Plaza*, Plaza Honorato (closed Monday), specializes in meat dishes. It's near the Iglesia Parroquial Mayor.

A paladar would be a better bet than either of the state-run restaurants, so ask around. Also watch for homemade pizza being sold at stalls along the city's streets.

Entertainment

For folk music it's the *Casa de la Trova Miguel Companioni*, Máximo Gómez Sur No 26 off Parque Honorato.

Rumbos Bar, Independencia Norte No 32 a block off Parque Serafín Sánchez, sells cold canned beer for about a dollar. The drunken Cubans you see in there are probably émigrés on visits from the US.

Getting There & Away

Bus The Terminal Provincial de Ómnibus on the Carretera Central, two km east of town, has buses to Trinidad (12 daily, 70 km, two hours), Ciego de Ávila (six daily, 75 km), Santa Clara (five daily, 86 km), Camagüey (daily, 185 km, five hours), Havana (three daily, 373 km, five hours), Holguín (daily, 385 km), and Santiago de Cuba (daily, 511 km). Colectivos parked outside the station will take you to Trinidad for US$5 for one seat or US$15 for the whole car.

Train To go anywhere other than Trinidad or Ciego de Ávila, you're better off arriving or departing by train. The train station is at the end of Avenida Jesús Menéndez, southwest of the Puente Yayabo, an easy 10-minute walk from town.

There's a train every afternoon to Santa Clara (two hours) and Cienfuegos (four hours), and every evening to Havana (eight hours, US$13.50). Since Sancti Spíritus isn't right on the main railway line between Havana and Santiago de Cuba, passengers on the cross-country express trains must change at Guayos, 15 km north of Sancti Spíritus. With advance reservations you should be able to pick up the eastbound train to Santiago de Cuba at Guayos around 10 pm – ask at the station. Train tickets must be purchased with dollars (US$21 from Guayos to Santiago de Cuba).

TRINIDAD

In December 1988 Trinidad and the nearby Valle de los Ingenios were declared a World Heritage Site by UNESCO, and today this 'museum town' of 50,000 inhabitants on the coastal road between Cienfuegos and Sancti Spíritus offers travelers all the colonial atmosphere they could desire. To boot, plenty of other interesting sights await exploration in the hinterland.

History

In 1514 the first governor of Cuba, Diego Velázquez, founded La Villa de la Santísima Trinidad, the third settlement established in Cuba (after Baracoa and Bayamo). The first mass was said by Fray Bartolomé de las Casas, Apostle of the Indies. In 1518 the future conqueror of Mexico, Hernán Cortéz, recruited people here for his expedition. Despite this early start Trinidad remained a backwater frequented by smugglers until the late 18th century. Slaves and goods were surreptitiously imported from British-controlled Jamaica, and cattle ranching and tobacco growing were the main agricultural activities.

Things changed in the early 19th century when Trinidad became capital of the Departamento Central and hundreds of French refugees fleeing a slave rebellion in Haiti arrived to set up over 50 small sugar mills in the Valle de los Ingenios northeast of town. Sugar soon replaced leather and salted beef as the most important products, and by the mid 19th century the region around Trinidad was producing a third of Cuba's sugar, creating the wealth that financed the townscape still lovely today.

The boom ended during the two wars of independence when the sugar plantations around Trinidad were devastated, and by the late 19th century the focus of the sugar industry and trade had shifted to Cienfuegos and Matanzas Provinces. Trinidad wallowed in a time warp and its baroque church towers, Carrara marble floors, wrought-iron grills, red-tile roofs, and cobblestone streets have changed little in a century and a half.

Orientation

Trinidad turns on two hubs. The museums and churches of the old town are focused around the Plaza Mayor, while the everyday facilities serving the local people are on or near Parque Céspedes in the lower town. The bus station is a bit west of Plaza Mayor.

Be aware that most of the streets in Trinidad have two names, the new name used on the street sign (and in this book) and an old colonial name still preferred by many local residents. For example, Bolívar is also called Desengaño, Echerri is also Cristo, etc. Some crusty old-timers pretend they don't even know the new names.

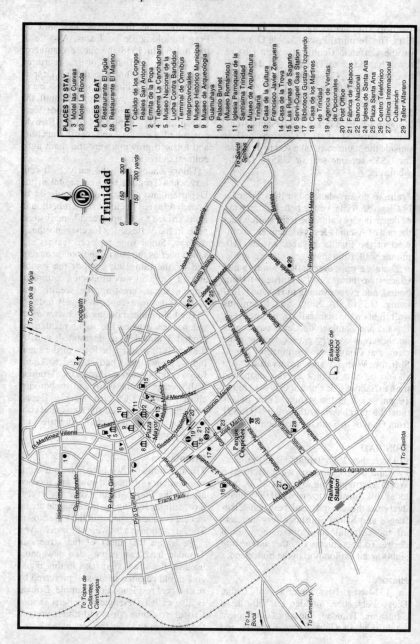

PLACES TO STAY
3   Motel las Cuevas
23 Motel La Ronda

PLACES TO EAT
6   Restaurante El Jigüe
28 Restaurante El Marino

OTHER
1   Cabildo de los Congos
    Reales San Antonio
2   Ermita de la Popa
4   Taberna La Canchánchara
5   Museo Nacional de la
    Lucha Contra Bandidos
7   Terminal de Omnibus
    Interprovinciales
8   Museo Histórico Municipal
9   Museo de Arqueología
    Guamuhaya
10 Palacio Brunet
    (Museo Romántico)
11 Iglesia Parroquial de la
    Santísima Trinidad
12 Museo de Arquitectura
    Trinitaria
13 Casa de la Cultura
14 Casa de la Trova
15 Las Ruinas de Segarte
16 Casa de la Cultura
    Francisco Javier Zerquera
17 Biblioteca Gustavo Izquierdo
18 Casa de los Mártires
    de Trinidad
19 Agencia de Ventas
    de Opcionales
20 Post Office
21 Fábrica de Tabacos
22 Banco Nacional
24 Iglesia de Santa Ana
25 Plaza Santa Ana
26 Centro Telefónico
27 Clínica Internacional
    Cubanacán
29 Taller Alfarero

Trinidad

0   150   300 m
0   150   300 yards

To Cerro de la Vigía

footpath

To Sancti
Spíritus

To Topes de
Collantes,
Cienfuegos

To Casilda

To La
Boca

To Cemetery

Railway
Station

Paseo Agramonte

Estadio de
Beísbol

Parque
Céspedes

Plaza
Mayor

Information
Tourist Office For general tourist information try the Agencia de Ventas de Opciones (☎ 4414) at the corner of Maceo and Zerquera.

Money The Banco Nacional is at Calle Martí No 264. Changing money elsewhere involves discreetly asking around, and it's a buyer's market.

Post & Communications The post office is at Maceo No 418. The Centro Telefónico, General Lino Pérez No 274, is diagonally opposite the church on Parque Céspedes. Trinidad's telephone code is 419.

Library The Biblioteca Gustavo Izquierdo is at Martí No 265 between Colón and Zerquera.

Photography Photo Service, Martí No 222 on Parque Céspedes, sells film and batteries.

Medical Services The Clínica Internacional Cubanicán, General Lino Pérez No 103 at Anastasio Cárdenas, offers emergency consultations for US$20 and specialist consultations at US$25. It's open 24 hours. The English-speaking personnel specialize in treating foreigners.

Things to See
If you can only visit one museum in Trinidad, make it the **Museo Histórico Municipal**, Bolívar No 423 just off Plaza Mayor, in a mansion that belonged to the Borrell family from 1827 to 1830. Later the building passed into the hands of a German planter named Kanter, and it's still called Casa Cantero. Reputedly Dr Justo Cantero acquired vast sugar estates by poisoning an old slave trader named Pedro Iznaga and marrying his widow (who also suffered an untimely death). Cantero's ill-gotten wealth is well displayed in the stylish neoclassical decoration of the rooms. There's a splendid view of Trinidad from the tower.

The **Iglesia Parroquial de la Santísima Trinidad** on the northeast side of Plaza Mayor was rebuilt in 1892 on the site of an earlier church. The venerated Christ of the True Cross (1731) is among the many sacred objects sheltered inside. It's open for sightseeing from 11:30 am to 12:30 pm and for mass at 7:30 pm.

Across the street is the **Museo Romántico**, Echerri No 52 (Tuesday to Sunday from 8 am to 5 pm, admission US$2), in the Palacio Brunet, the ground floor of which was built in 1740, the upstairs in 1808. In 1974 the mansion was converted into a 13-room museum equipped with locally made 19th-century furnishings.

The **Museo de Arquitectura Trinitaria**, on the southeast side of Plaza Mayor (daily 8 am to noon to 5 pm, admission US$1), is housed in buildings erected in 1738 and 1785 that were joined together in 1819. The museum showcases upper-class domestic architecture of the 18th and 19th centuries.

On the northwest side of Plaza Mayor is the **Museo de Arqueología Guamuhaya**, Bolívar No 457 (Sunday to Friday 9 am to 5 pm, admission US$1), with natural history exhibits and Indian artifacts. The famous German explorer Alexander von Humboldt stayed in this 18th-century house during his visit to Trinidad in 1801.

Admission is free at the 19th-century Palacio Ortíz, which today houses the **Galería de Arte Universal**, Rubén Martínez Villena at Bolívar on the southwest side of Plaza Mayor. Displays showcase the work of local artists. The upstairs rooms are sometimes closed suddenly, so it's best to see them first.

The **Museo Nacional de la Lucha Contra Bandidos**, Echerri No 59 at Piro Guinart (Tuesday to Sunday 9 am to 5 pm, admission US$1), is housed in the 18th-century ex-convent of San Francisco de Asís, of which only the bell tower remains. The displays are mostly photos, maps, weapons, and other objects relating to the struggle against the various counterrevolutionary gangs that operated in Sierra del Escambray between 1960 and 1965. An American U-2 spy plane shot down over

Cuba is also on display. Here, too, you can climb the tower and there's a pleasant square in front of the museum.

The **Casa de los Mártires de Trinidad**, Zerquera No 254 between Maceo and Martí (weekdays 8 am to 5 pm, admission by donation), is dedicated to 72 Trinidad residents who died in the struggle against Batista, the campaign against the counter-revolutionaries, and the war in Angola (for more about Cuba's involvement in Angola, see the Cuban Internationalism section under History in the Facts about Cuba chapter).

Visit the nearby **Fábrica de Tabacos**, Maceo No 403 at Colón, to see cigars being rolled. There's also a large cigarette factory in town.

A few additional sights are on the east side of town. Of the **Iglesia de Santa Ana** only the shell remains, but just across the square on Calle Camilo Cienfuegos is a former Spanish prison that has been converted into a cultural center, the **Plaza Santa Ana**. The complex includes an art gallery, handicraft market, ceramics shop, cafeteria, and restaurant. The Trinidad Folk Ensemble occasionally performs here.

Five blocks south is the **Taller Alfarero**, Calle Andrés Berro near Abel Santamaría (weekdays 7 am to 5 pm), a large workshop where teams of workers make ceramics using the traditional potter's wheel.

If you're interested in Cuba's African traditions you should seek out the **Cabildo de los Congos Reales San Antonio**, Isidro Armenteros No 168 on the north side of town, founded in 1856. An image of San Antonio de Paula (the parallel saint of the African deity Hogún) is on the altar before the congo drums.

For a view of Trinidad from above, walk straight up Calle Simón Bolívar (the street between the Iglesia Parroquial and the Museo Romántico) to the destroyed 18th-century **Ermita de Nuestra Señora de la Candelaria de la Popa** on a hill to the north of the old town. There's also a footpath directly to the hermitage from Motel Las Cuevas. The Cueva de Ayala behind the Ermita de la Popa is a nightclub built in a natural cave, and from here it's a 30-minute hike up the hill to the radio transmitter atop 180-meter-high **Cerro de la Vigía**, which overlooks the entire area.

Organized Tours

The Agencia de Ventas de Opcionales (☎ 4414) at the corner of Maceo and Zerquera runs day tours to Topes de Collantes (US$30 per person, three-person minimum) and Cienfuegos (US$25, five-person minimum). A Havana overnight excursion costs US$188 (five-person minimum). Guides around Trinidad are US$12 per person for four hours. Of course, all of this is very expensive and you can easily hire a private car sporting a yellow license plate to drive you around for much less.

Special Events

The Fiestas Sanjuaneras are a sort of local carnival that takes place from June 20 to 24. The Semana de la Cultura Trinitaria is in the second half of November.

Places to Stay

Camping Along a small stream 10 km out on the road to Topes de Collantes, the basic *Base de Campismo Manacal* has 28 small cabins that are rented mostly to Cubans. It's crowded with Cubans on Friday, Saturday, and Sunday nights but empty the rest of the time.

Private Rooms The Gil Lemes family (☎ 3142), Calle Martí No 263 between Zerquera and Colón, has two rooms in an old colonial house right in the center of town for US$10 single or double. If they can't accommodate you, they'll probably know of another family that can. Avoid allowing the hustlers who will immediately flock to you to offer their services when you arrive in Trinidad. If you let them lead you to this house, they'll demand a commission that will be added to your bill. Pablo Dalmán Montesinos (☎ 4450), Calle Martí No 335, also accommodates visitors. You could also ask the people at Taberna La Cancháchara about private rooms. Otherwise, rely on the hustlers but insist on something in the center and clarify all prices beforehand. Your host will probably be happy to cook your dinner for US$5.

Hotels Most independent travelers stay at *Motel las Cuevas* (☎ 4013), one km northeast of town beyond the Iglesia de Santa Ana. There are 112 rooms with bath for US$17/22 single/double low season, US$22/29 high season. Some rooms are in older one-story duplex units on the hillside, while others are in newer two-story units overlooking the valley. Avoid the noisy 12-unit block facing the swimming pool near the top of the hill. You get good views of Trinidad and the sea from the motel, but it fills up fast when the tour buses pull in. Cueva La Maravillosa is accessible down a stairway near a pit where you see a huge tree growing out of the cave.

If you're driving, an excellent alternative to Las Cuevas is the *Casa del Campesino* (☎ 3581) at Finca María Dolores by the Río Guaurabo six km west on the road to Cienfuegos and Topes de Collantes. There are 18 rooms in duplex cabañas for US$8/15/20 single/double/triple. Some nights when groups are present there's a 'fiesta campesina' with real country-style Cuban folk dancing at 9 pm (free for diners, US$4 per person for others). Horseback riding costs US$4 an hour. One km west of the Casa del Campesino is a monument to Alberto Delgado, a teacher murdered by the counterrevolutionaries.

The two-story *Motel La Ronda*, Calle Martí No 238, has closed but renovations will likely be underway soon.

Places to Eat

Cafeteria Siboney, Calle Martí No 208 on Parque Céspedes, is a basic lunch counter taking pesos. Nearby is *Merendero El Agro*, Calle Martí No 198 at General Lino Pérez (8 am to 8 pm). The *Casa del Caldo*, Maceo and Cienfuegos (daily 8 am to 7 pm), serves bowls of bone soup.

Several state-run restaurants cater to tourists. At *Restaurante El Jigüe*, Rubén Martínez Villena at Piro Guinart (daily 11 am to 5 pm), the specialty is 'Pollo al Jigüe' (US$12). For Italian cuisine try *Restaurante Villa Real*, Rubén Martínez Villena No 74 between Piro Guinart and Pablo Pichs Girón. The *Mesón del Regidor*, Bolívar No 424 (daily 9 am to 9 pm), serves grilled meats. *Restaurante Las Begonias*, Maceo at Bolívar (daily 9 am to 5 pm), features seafood and lobster (the sign says 'Casa Mimbre'). *Trinidad Colonial*, Maceo No 402 at Colón, serves upmarket international cuisine in the elegant 18th-century Casa Bidegaray. You could also take a look at *Pizzería Tosca*, Calle Martí No 226 at Parque Céspedes (daily 6 am to 8:30 pm).

As usual, we cannot specifically recommend any of the restaurants listed above as far too often their prices don't necessarily translate to good service and food. You'll almost always do better at a privately operated paladar, for example, *Restaurante Paladar Bastida* (☎ 2151), Maceo No 537 between Bolívar and Pino Guinart. *Paladar Inés*, Martí No 160, has also been recommended. Such places come and go from week to week, so ask around.

Entertainment

The *Casa de la Trova*, Echerri No 29 at Jesús Menéndez, presents Cuban folk music. *Las Ruinas de Sagarto*, on Calle Jesús Menéndez a block up from the Casa de la Trova, is a 24-hour bar that often has live music in the evening (admission free). Also check the *Casa de la Cultura Francisco Javier Zerquera*, Zerquera No 406 at Ernesto Valdés Muñoz.

More of a tourist scene revolves around *Taberna La Cancháchara*, housed in a 17th-century building at Rubén Martínez Villena at Ciro Redondo. The house cocktail is the cancháchara (US$2), made from rum, honey, lemon, and water. The local musicians playing here are often quite good, and it's not unusual for the crowd to break into dancing and clapping.

One reader recommends a bar called *Daiquirí* at Lino Pérez and Calle Martí and a disco on a patio across the street.

Check what the locals are up to at *Restaurante El Marino*, Cienfuegos and

Frank País. It functions as a disco Saturday from 9:30 pm to 2 am and Sunday from 9:30 pm to midnight.

Things to Buy

There's an excellent open-air arts-and-crafts market on Calle Colón between Maceo and Martí. It's the place to buy souvenirs – just avoid the black coral and turtle-shell items that are prohibited entry into many countries. Caracol Tienda Trinidad, Maceo No 442, is a hard-currency tourist shop with maps, postcards, and compact discs.

Getting There & Away

The Terminal de Ómnibus Interprovinciales, Piro Guinart No 224 at Gustavo Izquierdo, has buses to Topes de Collantes (three daily, 18 km, one hour), Sancti Spíritus (nine daily, 70 km, two hours), Cienfuegos (four daily, 82 km, two hours), Santa Clara (daily, 90 km, three hours), and Havana (daily, 462 km, six hours). A bus leaves for Casilda from a nearby street around 10 am.

Getting Around

National Rent a Car (☎ 4101) is at Martí No 166 near Cienfuegos. The Transautos desk is at Motel Las Cuevas. Servi-Cupet, Frank País No 353 at Zerquera, is open 24 hours. Ice cream and some groceries are sold in the office.

To call a tourist taxi, ☎ dial 2479.

PLAYA ANCÓN

Playa Ancón, 12 km south of Trinidad, got its name from a black rock on Punta María Aguilar that once served as a landmark for sailors. Because it seemed to resemble the leg of a horse, it was nicknamed *ancón* (hind leg). Over the centuries ocean currents have built up four km of soft, white beach here, and just a few hundred meters offshore is an excellent reef for snorkeling and scuba diving.

Since the late 1980s Playa Ancón has been developed for international tourism and there are several large hotels facing the warm Caribbean. Most visitors to this region arrive on package tours and stay at one of these resorts, and indeed, Playa Ancón makes an ideal base from which to explore the architectural treasures of nearby Trinidad and the forested Sierra del Escambray. Not as overwhelmed by tourism as Varadero or Guardalavaca, it's an excellent choice for a Cuban holiday.

Things to See

From Hotel Ancón it's 18 km to Trinidad via Casilda, or 16 km on the much nicer coastal road via La Boca. It makes a pleasant circle trip by rental bicycle.

The decrepit old fishing port of **Casilda**, six km due south of Trinidad, is used mostly for exporting refined sugar. The road from Ancón to Casilda crosses a tidal flat with abundant bird-life in the early morning.

Activities

Fishing The Marina Cayo Blanco, run by Marinas Puertosol, is a few hundred meters east of Hotel Ancón. Its specialty is deep-sea fishing at a cost of US$150/200/250 for four/six/eight hours for the whole boat (four anglers). Fishing from a launch is US$50 a day. The marina also offers excursions to the Archipiélago de los Jardines de la Reina for US$350 for four persons including three meals. A 'safari' to Cayo Blanco costs US$25 per person including lunch, or US$35 per person including lunch and open bar.

Scuba Diving Cayo Blanco, a reef islet 25 km southeast of Playa Ancón, has eight marked scuba diving sites where you'll see black coral and bountiful marine life. Both of the big hotels organize trips there. The Marina Cayo Blanca's scuba-diving center charges US$30 a dive or US$230 for a 10-dive package.

Places to Stay & Eat

The only low-budget place is the run-down *Hotel Brisas de Ancón* (☎ 5124) in the port of Casilda, an old two-story peso hotel with six rooms. Its restaurant serves basic meals.

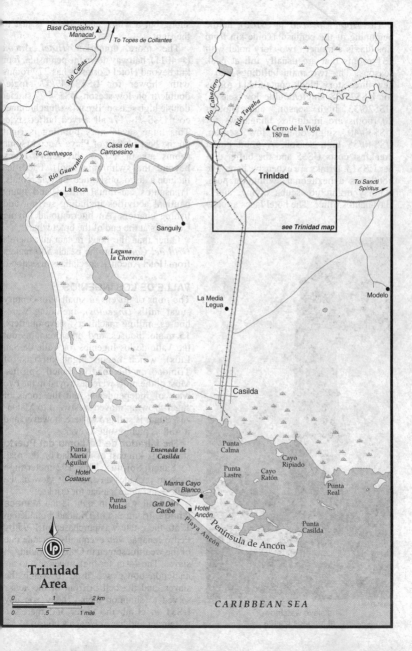

Base Campismo
Manacal
To Topes de Collantes

Río Cañas

Río Caballero

Río Tayaba

To Cienfuegos

▲ Cerro de la Vigía
180 m

Casa del
Campesino

Río Guaurabo

Trinidad

To Sancti
Spíritus

La Boca

Sanguily

see Trinidad map

Laguna
la Chorrera

Modelo

La Media
Legua

Casilda

Punta
María
Aguilar

Ensenada de
Casilda

Punta
Calma

Cayo
Ripiado

Hotel
Costasur

Punta
Lastre

Cayo
Ratón

Marina Cayo
Blanco

Punta Mulas

Grill Del
Caribe

Hotel
Ancón

Punta
Real

Punta
Casilda

Playa Ancón

Península de Ancón

Trinidad
Area

0   1   2 km
0   .5   1 mile

CARIBBEAN SEA

The *Hotel Costasur* (☎ 6100), at the beginning of the peninsula, nine km from Casilda, is a modern two-story hotel with 131 rooms that are usually full at peak seasons. The two main buildings and a new three-story block contain 111 rooms for US$21/28 single/double low season, US$26/35 high season, and another 20 rooms are in duplex bungalows for US$30/40 single/double low season, US$40/55 high season. A good buffet breakfast costs US$5 and the buffet dinner US$15. Drinks are expensive here. The hotel has a hexagonal swimming pool, a noisy nightclub, scuba diving, and a Havanautos office. The hotel faces a rocky shore, but a white sandy beach is just to the right.

The more upmarket *Hotel Ancón* (☎ 4011), halfway down the peninsula, four km beyond Hotel Costasur, has 279 rooms with shower for US$37/49/57 single/double/triple low season, US$54/77 single/double high season. Breakfast/lunch/dinner cost US$4/14/17, all served buffet style. This huge seven-story building is right on the best section of Playa Ancón (some rooms are in a new three-story block beyond the swimming pool). Facilities include a disco, post office, bicycle rentals, Transautos car-rental office, and many nautical activities including surfing and fishing charters. An International Diving Center is at the end of the hotel wharf.

Other than the hotel restaurants there's *Grill del Caribe* on the beach 500 meters from Hotel Ancón. It specializes in seafood.

VALLE DE LOS INGENIOS

The ruins of dozens of small 19th-century sugar mills *(ingenios)*, including warehouses, milling machinery, slave quarters, 15 manor houses, and other remains dot the Valle de los Ingenios (or Valle de San Luis), which begins eight km east of Trinidad on the road to Sancti Spíritus. Most of the mills were destroyed in the two wars of independence and the focus of sugar-growing moved westward to Matanzas. Sugar is still grown here, however, and it's all as picturesque as ever.

The **Mirador de La Loma del Puerto** stands six km east of Trinidad on the road to Sancti Spíritus. This 192-meter-high lookout provides an excellent view of the valley, and there's a bar for drinks.

The valley's main sight is the **Manaca Iznaga**, 16 km east of Trinidad. Founded in 1750, the estate was purchased in 1795 by Pedro Iznaga, who eventually became one of the wealthiest men in Cuba by trading in slaves. The 44-meter-high tower next to the hacienda house was used to watch the slaves, and the bell in front of the house served to summon them. Today you pay US$1 to climb the tower and there's a restaurant and bar in Iznaga's house.

DAVID STANLEY

The slave watchtower
at Manaca Iznaga

Five km beyond the Manaca Iznaga on the road inland through the valley is the **Casa Guachinango**, an old hacienda built by Don Mariano Borel toward the end of the 18th century. If you want to do some horseback riding here, call the Manaca Iznaga restaurant (☎ 271) beforehand. Today the Casa Guachinango is occasionally used as a dining room by tour groups and the friendly manager might allow you to pitch a tent somewhere. The Río Ay is just below, and the landscape around here is very pleasant.

Places to Stay
One of Cuba's best centers for horseback riding is *Hacienda Los Molinos*, two km off the main highway between Trinidad and Sancti Spíritus, 38 km from Trinidad and 40 km from Sancti Spíritus. Watch for the small bar by the highway several kilometers west of La Güira that marks the turnoff. There are four fan-cooled rooms for guests in a pleasant wooden house surrounded by flowers. Two of the rooms are doubles and two are triples, and the tariff is US$15/20 double/triple. Meals are about US$15 extra per person for all three. This is an operating cattle ranch, and the main reason to come is to ride horses in the adjacent forest that extends up into the foothills of the Alturas de Sancti Spíritus. Saddled horses cost US$3 for the first hour, US$2 for the second hour, and US$1 for additional hours. Highly recommended.

Getting There & Away
Luckily, it's easy for those without their own transportation to visit the valley. On Wednesday, Friday, and Sunday a reconstructed railway carriage takes passengers on a full-day excursion through the valley. The train is pulled by steam engine No 52204, built by the Baldwin Locomotive Company of Philadelphia in August 1919. The price is US$10 per person if you pay direct at the old Trinidad train station (check at the station the day before). Tourists staying at the beach resorts can arrange trips on the train through their hotel tour desks. Passengers have a no-host lunch at the Manaca Iznaga and visit the Casa Guachinango. (Incidentally, this is the only train service that still operates out of Trinidad.)

TOPES DE COLLANTES
The 90-km-long Sierra del Escambray just northwest of Trinidad culminates in Pico San Juan (1156 meters) in neighboring Cienfuegos Province. The largest settlement in the range is Topes de Collantes, a health resort town standing at 771 meters elevation, 18 km north of Trinidad. En route to Topes de Collantes you'll pass Pico de Potrerillo (931 meters), the highest peak in Sancti Spíritus Province. Coniferous forests, vines, lichens, mosses, and giant ferns flourish in this cool, foggy climate, and Arabica coffee plantations thrive on the slopes.

The various sanatoriums and hotels of Topes de Collantes serve mostly for vacationing government officials, trade unionists, military personnel, and university students, but several hotels are also open to foreigners.

Hiking
Ecotourists come on organized tours to hike here. It's an excellent two-hour walk from Topes de Collantes to **Hacienda Codina**, where the groups have lunch. A more ambitious hike is the four-hour walk down to the **Salto del Caburní**. Ask about these trips at the Carpeta Central information office near the sundial at the entrance to Topes de Collantes.

Places to Stay & Eat
The eight-story *Kurhotel Escambray* (☎ 4-0180, ext 2268) stands on a hilltop overlooking the resort town like a futuristic neo-Stalinist dream. The 210 rooms with bath and satellite TV are US$28/40 single/double low season, US$30/42 high season. This hotel is actually a sanatorium, and it has elaborate facilities for the treatment of various ailments.

A better bet for the fit and healthy is the three-story *Hotel Los Helechos*

(☎ 4-0180, ext 2222). Its 48 rooms with bath cost US$19/25 single/double low season, US$27/31 high season. Los Helechos has a covered thermal swimming pool, gym, sauna, and steam baths.

The three-story, 88-room *Hotel Los Pinos* (☎ 4-0180, ext 2268) is under partial renovation and accepts Cubans only. Other hotels, such as Hotel Serano and Motel Las Dracenas, are also for Cuban guests only.

Getting There & Away

In theory a bus leaves Trinidad for Topes de Collantes at 6 am and 3 pm, but in practice it usually fails to report for duty.

If you're driving, there's a spectacular 44-km road that continues right over the mountains from Topes de Collantes to Manicaragua via Jibacoa. It's also possible to drive straight to/from Cienfuegos via San Blas.

Province of Ciego de Ávila

The 6910-sq-km Province of Ciego de Ávila, between Sancti Spíritus and Camagüey Provinces, stretches across Cuba's narrow waist from the Atlantic to the Caribbean. Most of the province is a flat savanna with some low hills in the northwest reaching 443 meters. Mangrove swamps line the north and south coasts. The center of the province is devoted to cattle ranching, and sugar cane is grown along both coasts. The sugar industry in Ciego de Ávila is highly mechanized with irrigation widely used. There are also citrus and pineapple plantations.

The saline Laguna de la Leche (67 sq km) north of Morón is Cuba's largest lake. Three natural channels allow seawater to enter creating the milky appearance that gives the lake its name. The Archipiélago de Camagüey off the north coast includes coral keys, such Cayo Coco and Cayo Guillermo, on which the province's main resorts and sandy beaches are found. Also within Ciego de Ávila's boundaries is the western half of the Archipiélago de los Jardines de la Reina, offering more glorious beaches and excellent scuba diving.

The province's name derives from a type of forest-fringed savanna called a *ciego* found on the original estate of Jácome de Ávila, a Spaniard who was granted the *encomienda* of San Antonio de la Palma in 1538. Only in the 17th century did towns such as San Fernando de Morón begin to appear in this region. During the independence wars of the latter half of the 19th century, Morón was the terminus of a defensive line built by the Spanish to prevent Cuban patriots from carrying their independence struggle to western Cuba. The line extended 67 km from Morón in the north to Júcaro in the south. Despite this, rebel forces under Antonio Maceo and Máximo Gómez managed to break through in 1896, a feat repeated 62 years later by Ernesto 'Che' Guevara and Camilo

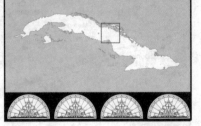

HIGHLIGHTS

- Terrific freshwater fishing in Laguna La Redonda
- Impressive 27-km causeway across to Cayo Coco
- Resorts of Cayo Coco facing high white-sand beaches
- Outstanding deep-sea fishing from the resorts of Cayo Guillermo
- Challenging shore casting and scuba diving in the secluded Archipiélago de los Jardines de la Reina

Cienfuegos during their historic march on Santa Clara. In 1975 Ciego de Ávila separated from Camagüey to become a province in its own right.

Ciego de Ávila's only real attractions for tourists are the freshwater fishing possibilities in the northern lakes, the deep-sea fishing and scuba diving off the north and south coasts, and the splendid beaches on the keys. The massive causeway over to Cayo Coco is worth the drive if you have a car. On the other hand, the provincial capital, Ciego de Ávila, and the northern town of Morón are rather dismal places unworthy of a special trip.

CIEGO DE ÁVILA

Situated between the cities of Santa Clara and Camagüey, Ciego de Ávila (population 85,000) has little to offer tourists. Only founded in 1840, the city has no important

colonial monuments. There is, however, a thermal power plant. The Carretera Central cuts across the center of town as Calle Chicho Valdés, providing a glimpse of this dreary agricultural market town. You won't miss much if you breeze on through.

Information

Tourist Office For general information try the Intur Buro de Turismo, Joaquín Agüero No 85. Campismo Popular in the 12-story building on the west side of Parque Martí may know about budget accommodations in isolated areas.

Post & Communications The post office is at the corner of Chicho Valdés and Marcial Gómez.

Long-distance telephone calls can be placed at the Salón de Llamadas Nacional y Internacional. The office is below the 12-story building on the west side of Parque Martí. Ciego de Ávila's telephone code is 33.

Library The Biblioteca Provincial Roberto Rivas Fragas, Calle Serafín Sánchez between Calles 1 and 2, is on Plaza Camilo Cienfuegos northwest of the center.

Things to See

The centerpoint of Ciego de Ávila is **Parque Martí** around the inevitable monument to José Martí (1925). The old **Ayuntamiento** (1911), now the headquarters of the provincial government, is next to the church on the south side of the park. The only other notable building is the **Teatro Principal** (1927), Joaquín Agüero at Honorato del Castillo between Parque Martí and the Hotel Santiago-Habana.

If you have time, you could visit the **Galería de Arte Provincial**, Calle Independencia between Honorato del Castillo and Maceo, or the **Parque Zoológico** on Calle Independencia east of the center.

The **Museo Provincial**, Jose Antonio Echevarría No 25 (Tuesday to Saturday 8 am to noon and 1 to 5 pm, Sunday 8 am to noon, admission US$1), is in a former school building marked 'Instituto de Segunda Enseñanza' west of the center along Avenida Libertad. The exhibits recount the student struggle against Batista.

Places to Stay

The five-story *Hotel Santiago-Habana* (☎ 2-5703), Chicho Valdés and Honorato del Castillo, has 76 overpriced rooms for US$26/30 single/double. Erected in 1957, the Santiago-Habana suffers from traffic noise, poor furnishings, and lumpy pillows, but at least it's conveniently located and friendly.

The *Hotel Ciego de Ávila* (☎ 2-8013) on the Carretera de Ceballos, four km northwest of the center, is a modern five-story hotel containing 144 rooms with bath and TV for US$23/30 single/double low season, US$29/39 high season. There's a rectangular swimming pool, taxi stand, and the local Havanautos office. It's a much better hotel for about the same price but far from the center.

If you're driving, you could also try *Motel Las Cañas* (☎ 8180), off the Carretera Central at the west entrance to town, about five km west of the center. There are 74 rooms in prefabricated cabañas costing US$16 per room in a block of six or US$21 for an individual unit. It's mostly frequented by local Cubans, and foreigners seldom stay there. Just across a small bridge is a nice park where you'll find Cabaret Las Piñas.

Places to Eat

Ciego de Ávila has its share of state-run restaurants, such as *Restaurant Solaris* (☎ 2-3424), on the top floor of the 12-story building facing the west side of Parque Martí. Rather than sample its 'Cuban cuisine,' look for the 24-hour hard-currency bar called *Rumbos 12* at street level in one corner of the same building. There you can obtain reasonable fried chicken and terrible pizza at low prices, and the beer is cold. Knock if the door is locked.

Other official restaurants around town include *El Colonial*, Independencia No 110 (daily 6 to 11:45 pm), which serves more 'Cuban cuisine' in a pleasant courtyard; *Restaurant La Romagnola* (☎ 2-5989), Chicho Valdés at Marcial Gómez opposite the post office (daily 6 pm to midnight), where the specialty is Italian cuisine; and *Restaurante Moscú*, Chicho Valdés No 78 opposite the Cubana office (daily except Wednesday 6 pm to midnight).

The *Mesón El Fuerte* (daily 6 to 11:45 pm) occupies an authentic two-story Spanish blockhouse on Avenida Las Palmas opposite Plaza Camilo Cienfuegos on the northwest side of town. This building once formed part of the 19th-century Spanish defensive line from Morón to Júcaro.

Instead of taking your chances at any of the above, you ought to ask a local to recommend a privately operated paladar.

Entertainment

Cuban folk singing is the staple at the *Casa de la Trova*, Libertad No 130 at Simón Reyes.

Getting There & Away

Air Ciego de Ávila's new Máximo Gómez Airport (airport code AVI) is at Ceballos, 25 km north of town. Cubana flies here nonstop from Havana five times a week (one hour, US$43 one way). The Cubana

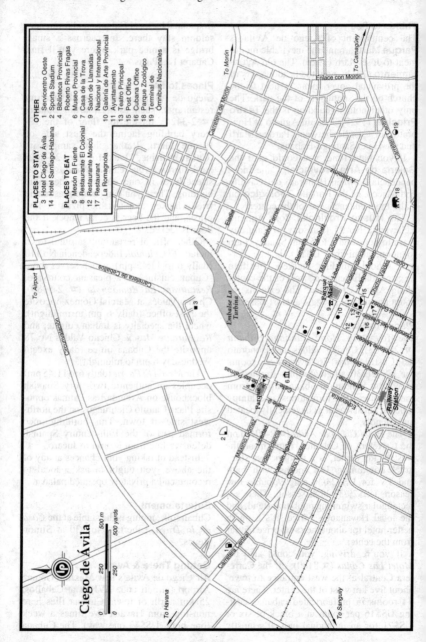

Ciego de Ávila

PLACES TO STAY
3 Hotel Ciego de Ávila
14 Hotel Santiago-Habana

PLACES TO EAT
5 Mesón El Fuerte
8 Restaurante El Colonial
12 Restaurante Moscú
17 Restaurant
La Romagnola

OTHER
1 Servicentro Oeste
2 Sports Stadium
4 Biblioteca Provincial
Roberto Rivas Fragas
6 Museo Provincial
7 Casa de la Trova
9 Salón de Llamadas
Nacional y Internacional
10 Galería de Arte Provincial
11 Ayuntamiento
13 Teatro Principal
15 Post Office
16 Cubana Office
18 Parque Zoológico
19 Terminal de
Omnibus Nacionales

office (☎ 2-5316) in Ciego de Ávila is at Chicho Valdéz No 83 between Maceo and Honorato del Castillo.

Canadian Airlines and Royal Airlines have weekly charter flights to Ciego de Ávila from Toronto, and Cubana arrives from Montreal. Virtually all of the foreign passengers have prebooked package tours at one of the coral keys off the north coast.

Bus The Terminal de Ómnibus Nacionales, about 1½ km east of the center on the Carretera Central, has buses to:

Sancti Spíritus (six daily, 75 km)
Camagüey (three daily, 110 km, two hours)
Santa Clara (two daily, 161 km, three hours)
Cienfuegos (daily, 227 km, four hours)
Holguín (daily, 310 km, five hours)
Manzanillo (daily, 327 km, eight hours)
Matanzas (daily, 360 km, six hours)
Niquero (daily, 399 km)
Havana (two daily, 448 km, seven hours)

Most of the long-distance buses are already full when they pass through Ciego de Ávila. Colectivos outside the station leave occasionally for Sancti Spíritus and Camagüey.

Train It's easier to arrive and depart from town through the Estación de Ferrocarriles, six blocks southwest of the center. There are nightly trains to Holguín (312 km, six hours, US$13), Matanzas (343 km, five hours, US$15), Santiago de Cuba (421 km, eight hours, US$18), and Havana (three daily, 435 km, seven hours, US$18).

Getting Around
There's a Havanautos office at the Hotel Ciego de Ávila. The Servi-Cupet gas station is on Carretera de Morón just before the bypass road, northeast of the center. Servicentro Oeste is on the Carretera Central at the west entrance to town.

MORÓN
Morón is a town of 45,000, about 40 km north of Ciego de Ávila via a flat road through the cane fields. Founded in 1750, Morón is called the 'ciudad del gallo' for a verse about a cock that continued to crow

after being defeathered, as recalled by the bronze rooster on a pedestal at the entrance to the Hotel Morón. It's a rather uninteresting place where you'll be hassled by chewing-gum–crazed kids as you wander around (a result of the earlier largesse of tourists from Cayo Coco). If you're stuck for something to do, check the **Museo Municipal** at Calle Castillo No 164.

Information
Viajes Fantásticos (☎ 3161, fax 33-5026), Cristóbal Colón No 49, sells excursions to Cayo Coco and makes hotel reservations throughout Cuba at slightly reduced prices.

Moron's telephone code is 335.

Fishing
There's good fishing for largemouth bass at the Marina Fluvial La Redonda on Laguna La Redonda, 18 km north of Morón off the road to Cayo Coco. Fishing from a launch costs US$70 a half day (3½ hours) for two persons, plus US$3 per fishing rod. There's also a nice bar here if you only want to stop for a drink and a view of the lake.

Places to Stay
Most tourists stay at the *Hotel Morón* (☎ 3901), Avenida de Tarafa at the south entrance to town, a large, modern four-story hotel. The 136 rooms cost US$30/39 single/double low season, US$38/44 high season, and the eight cabañas or 'junior suites' are US$60 double. There's a swimming pool and a disco open daily from 9:30 pm to 2 am. Persistent children in the hotel parking lot will hassle you for chewing gum and pens.

The *Club de Caza y Pesca* (☎ 4563), Cristóbal Colón No 41 just east of the train station, is an attractive two-story villa with seven rooms for US$29/39 single/double.

The old *Hotel Perla del Norte* (☎ 3961) on Avenida de Tarafa just west of the train station has 54 rooms for US$7/10/13 single/double/triple. If they won't accommodate you at this peso hotel, ask around for a private room.

Entertainment

The *Casa de la Trova* is on Calle Libertad between Martí and Narciso López.

Getting There & Away

Daily trains to Camagüey via Ciego de Ávila depart from the Estación de Ferrocarriles between Hotel Morón and the center of town. The line from Santa Clara to Nuevitas also passes through Morón.

Getting Around

The Servi-Cupet gas station near Hotel Morón is open 24 hours.

CAYO COCO

Cayo Coco, the main tourist island of the Archipiélago de Camagüey, lies in the Atlantic Ocean about 400 km due south of Nassau in the Bahamas. This 370-sq-km coral key is about 37 km long, and 21 km of snowy white beach runs along the Atlantic side. The interior is heavily forested and the whole island is a wildlife refuge that is home to many sea birds, including pelicans and flamingos. Since 1988 Cayo Coco has been connected to the mainland by a formidable 27-km causeway across the Bahía de Perros (Bay of Dogs), and there are additional causeways from Cayo Coco to Cayo Guillermo in the west and Cayo Romano in the east. Pelicans and flamingos are often visible from the causeways. This entire area is being developed for upmarket tourism, and the hotels meet high standards of comfort and service. Sixty km from Morón, 90 km from Ciego de Ávila Airport, and 100 km from Ciego de Ávila, Cayo Coco is a rather isolated location best suited to those who intend to stay put.

Activities

The Marina Puertosol at Casasa, 13 km southeast of the Hotel Cayo Coco, offers deep-sea fishing outings. Hotel Cayo Coco itself offers scuba diving.

Places to Stay & Eat

The Spanish-operated *Hotel Cayo Coco* (☎ 33-5388, fax 33-5166) is a sprawling complex of 23 two- and three-story mock-colonial buildings erected in 1993. The 458 rooms offering bath, mini-fridge, satellite TV, and balcony or terrace are expensive at US$86/116/166 single/double/triple with breakfast low season, US$94/132/174 high season. Using the safe in the room costs an extra US$2 per day. The resort's facilities include the Salsa Cafe Disco (daily from 10 pm), two swimming pools, four floodlit tennis courts, car rentals, and a full range of nautical activities including scuba diving. It's a little city by the sea, and the high white beach adjacent to the hotel is certainly one of Cuba's best.

In 1996 the 514-room *Hotel Caribe* was under construction on a site adjacent to Hotel Cayo Coco – its grand opening is scheduled for 1997. The architecture is similar except that the roofs are green instead of red, and the Caribe will strive for three-star status rather than the Cayo Coco's four. In addition, the French Accor hotel chain has announced plans to build 1200 rooms on Cayo Coco over the next few years.

Getting There & Away

There's a small airstrip off the road between Cayo Coco and Cayo Guillermo, 21 km west of the Hotel Cayo Coco and 24 km east of Villa Cojímar. It's only used by an air-taxi service catering to tourists. Quaint little biplanes shuttle high rollers around the country on excursions or to the international airports for connecting flights.

There are no public buses to Cayo Coco as ordinary Cubans aren't allowed to go there without special permission (there's a checkpoint at the beginning of the causeway where foreigners are waved through). In early 1996 it was announced that a toll would be imposed on traffic crossing the causeway from the main island to Cayo Coco.

CAYO GUILLERMO

Just west of Cayo Coco is 13-sq-km Cayo Guillermo, a much smaller coral key than Cayo Coco, to which it's connected by a 17-km causeway. The mangroves off the south coast of Cayo Guillermo are home to

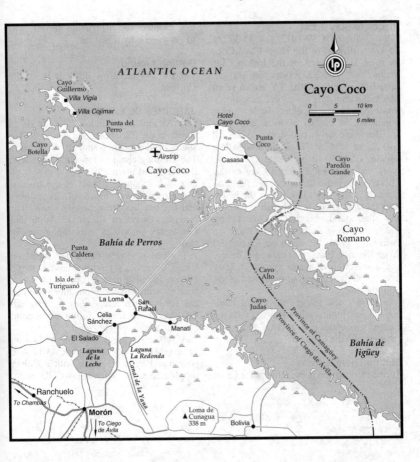

flamingos and pelicans, and there's a great diversity of tropical fish and crustaceans on the key's Atlantic reef.

This was a favorite fishing spot of US writer Ernest Hemingway, who mentioned it in his book *Islands in the Stream*, and the local tourism authorities have decided to play on this. The main hotel is named Villa Cojímar for the fishing village near Havana where Hemingway kept his boat, and the resort's restaurant is called the Bodeguita de Guillermo after Hemingway's favorite Havana bar, the Bodeguita del Medio. In

a way, the analogy is justified because Cayo Guillermo is probably the best destination in Cuba for those who want to fish. The deep-sea fishing facilities are suberb, and several freshwater lakes on the mainland are within commuting distance.

Activities
The Marina Puertosol at Villa Cojímar offers deep-sea fishing for mackerel, pike, and marlin on boats that depart from the wharf right at the hotel. The resort also offers snorkeling and scuba diving.

Places to Stay & Eat
Villa Cojímar (☎ 30-1012, fax 33-5221), 45 km northwest of the Hotel Cayo Coco by road, is managed by the Italian Club Venta chain. The 200 rooms with shower, mini-fridge, and satellite TV are in small Mediterranean-style tile-roofed bungalows. Some rooms are in older duplex units, others are in blocks of four, and there are also some larger two-story blocks. All cost about US$75/100 single/double low season, US$85/110 high season, for the room and three meals (drinks are extra). This resort is more spread out and less dramatic than the Cayo Coco, and the beach isn't quite as good (though still superb by any other standards), but the snorkeling and scuba diving are better here. There's a swimming pool, the open-air Cueva del Pirata Disco, a Transautos car-rental office, and a selection of water sports. A long wooden pier stretches out over the lagoon from the disco.

In 1996 a new resort called *Villa Vigía* (named for Hemingway's Havana villa, of course) was under construction about two km west of Villa Cojímar.

Getting There & Away
Access information is the same as for Cayo Coco: Unless you're on a tour the only way to get there is by rental car.

Getting Around
There's a Transautos desk at the Villa Cojímar.

JARDINES DE LA REINA
The Archipiélago de los Jardines de la Reina in the Caribbean Sea, about 80 km south of the main island of Cuba, is a 160-km-long chain of low coral keys with the reefs and marine life you'd expect on any such group of islands in the tropics. Mangroves cover much of these keys and the beaches are generally small. The boundary between Ciego de Ávila and Camagüey provinces cuts the group in two.

Tourism is slowly being developed on Ciego de Ávila's territory, and a *motel flotante* (floating motel) is being used as a base by scuba divers. From shore one can cast for bonefish, a legendary fighting fish that has a dedicated following among amateur anglers worldwide.

At last report access was via the Marina Júcaro, 24 km south of Ciego de Ávila. Ask your travel agent to check with a Cuban supplier about the current possibilities.

Province of Camagüey

The largest of Cuba's 14 provinces, Camagüey occupies a 15,990-sq-km chunk of central Cuba between Ciego de Ávila and Las Tunas Provinces. It was even bigger until 1975, when Cuba's political/administrative reorganization sliced away Ciego de Ávila and a bit of Las Tunas.

Most of Camagüey is flat and the highest hill reaches only 330 meters in the Sierra de Cubitas north of the capital. Partly because of this, Camagüey's cloud formations can be spectacular. Off the north coast are the huge coral keys of Cayo Romano and Cayo Sabinal, as yet undeveloped for tourism. A long swamp extends along the south coast facing the shallow Golfo de Ana María, itself bounded on the south by the uninhabited eastern half of the Archipiélago de los Jardines de la Reina, also a part of Camagüey.

Much of Cuba's livestock ranges across the grasslands of this ancient peneplain (flattened by erosion) where stately royal palms provide shade for close to a million animals. Camagüey is Cuba's largest producer of beef and its most productive dairy region as well. Sugar cane grows in the north and south, and rice in the southwest.

The province's only important port is Nuevitas, and tourism revolves around the large hotels of Playa Santa Lucía to the northeast. The main attraction here is scuba diving on the spectacular reefs. The city of Camagüey harbors a wealth of colonial monuments and museums, animated by the exuberant activity of the citizenry, yet surprisingly few foreigners manage a visit. For the independent budget traveler, this is one city not to miss.

CAMAGÜEY

Camagüey (population 300,000) is Cuba's third largest city and its biggest interior center. Approximately midway between Santa Clara and Santiago de Cuba, Camagüey is a city of white colonial buildings

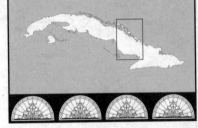

HIGHLIGHTS

- Untouristed colonial monuments and museums in the lively city of Camagüey
- Huge colonial hospital on Plaza San Juan de Dios, Camagüey's most picturesque square
- Appealing vintage hotels in the city of Camagüey
- Fantastic scuba diving at Playa Santa Lucía

with lush green gardens hidden away in their courtyards. It's known as the city of *tinajones* for the large clay pots originally kept in the courtyards to provide a supply of cool water during droughts. The Universidad de Camagüey, founded in 1975, is one of Cuba's five universities.

History

In February 1514 Santa María del Puerto Príncipe was founded near the site of present Nuevitas, one of the seven original towns established by Diego Velázquez. Soon after the town was moved twice, mostly because of Indian rebellions and the poor farmland around Nuevitas. In 1528 the present site was selected because it was less vulnerable to attack, and as a defensive measure Camagüey was deliberately laid out in a confusing, irregular way in the hope that assailants would become disoriented. Despite these precautions the

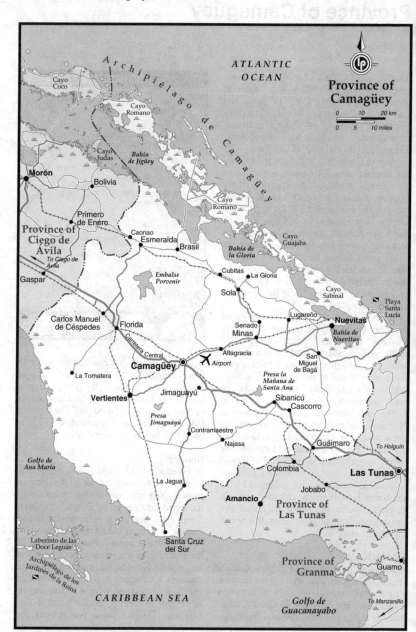

English pirate Henry Morgan attacked the town in 1668, followed in 1679 by François Granmont.

Orientation

The irregular street grid, so unlike the grid of most Cuban towns, makes getting around town as confusing to visitors as it was to invaders in years past. The train station is on the north side of town, and several inexpensive hotels are nearby. The city's north-south axis is República, which meets Avenida Agramonte at the historic church of La Soledad. Most of the other hotels, churches, and museums are just southwest of here in the city center. The Río Hatibonico crosses the southern side of the city center and the main bus station is on the Carretera Central about three km southeast of the river.

Information

Tourist Offices For tourist information try Islazul on Avenida Agramonte behind Iglesia de la Merced (weekdays 8 am to noon and 1 to 4:30 pm, Saturday 8 to 11:30 am).

Money The unofficial moneychangers work Maceo between Iglesia de la Soledad and the Gran Hotel.

Post & Communications The main post office is on Avenida Agramonte at Plaza de los Trabajadores opposite Iglesia de la Merced.

The Centro Para Llamadas de Larga Distancia telephone center, Avellaneda No 270, is open 24 hours. The philatelic bureau is at the same address.

Camagüey's telephone code is 332 (most other parts of the province use telephone code 32).

Bookstores Librería Mariana Grajales, República No 300, has a good selection of used books.

Libraries The Biblioteca Provincial Julio A Mella is on the west side of Parque Agramonte.

Medical Services Farmacia Álvarez Fuentes, Oscar Primelles and Avellaneda, is open 24 hours with service through a small window after 10 pm.

Walking Tour

Due to the irregular street pattern, finding sights in town can be difficult. Consider taking this walking tour if you wish to get in most of the main sights.

Just to the north of the train station is one of Cuba's largest museums, the **Museo Provincial Ignacio Agramonte**, Avenida de los Mártires No 2 at Calle Ignacio Sánchez (Tuesday to Saturday 9 am to 5 pm, Sunday 8 am to noon, admission US$1). Erected in 1848, this former Spanish cavalry barracks became the Hotel Camagüey after independence in 1902. In 1948 the present museum was installed with collections relating to history, natural history, decorative arts, and fine arts. There are three paintings by the local turn-of-the-century artist Fidelio Ponce. Notice the big tinajones in the courtyard.

South of the railway line Avenida de los Mártires becomes República. At the corner of Avenida Agramonte is the massive red-brick structure of the **Iglesia de Nuestra Señora de la Soledad** (1775) with baroque frescoes inside.

Two blocks west along Avenida Agramonte is another imposing colonial church, the **Iglesia de Nuestra Señora de la Merced** (1748, rebuilt 1848), with a small museum below the main altar. There's an active convent in the cloister attached to the church.

The **Museo Casa Natal de Ignacio Agramonte**, Avenida Agramonte No 59 at Independencia opposite La Merced (Tuesday, Wednesday, and Saturday 10 am to 6 pm, Thursday and Friday 10 am to 10 pm, Sunday 8 am to noon, admission US$1), is the birthplace of Ignacio Agramonte (1841 – 1873), the cattle rancher who led the revolt against Spain in this area in 1868. In July 1869 rebel forces under Agramonte bombarded Camagüey, and four years later he was killed in action against the Spanish. This early hero of

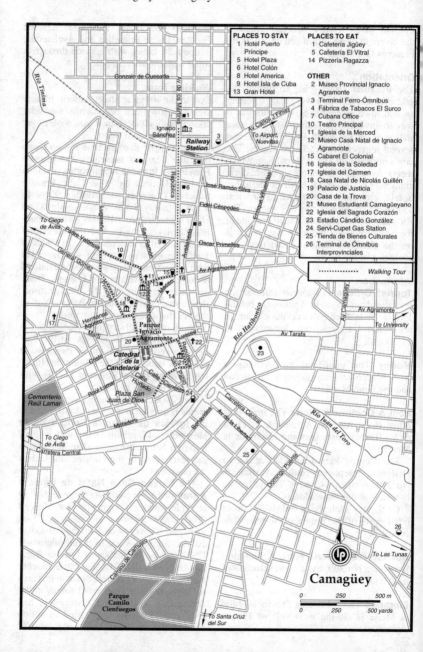

PLACES TO STAY
1 Hotel Puerto Príncipe
5 Hotel Plaza
6 Hotel Colón
8 Hotel America
9 Hotel Isla de Cuba
13 Gran Hotel

PLACES TO EAT
1 Cafetería Jigüey
5 Cafetería El Vitral
14 Pizzería Ragazza

OTHER
2 Museo Provincial Ignacio Agramonte
3 Terminal Ferro-Ómnibus
4 Fábrica de Tabacos El Surco
7 Cubana Office
10 Teatro Principal
11 Iglesia de la Merced
12 Museo Casa Natal de Ignacio Agramonte
15 Cabaret El Colonial
16 Iglesia de la Soledad
17 Iglesia del Carmen
18 Casa Natal de Nicolás Guillén
19 Palacio de Justicia
20 Casa de la Trova
21 Museo Estudiantil Camagüeyano
22 Iglesia del Sagrado Corazón
23 Estadio Cándido González
24 Servi-Cupet Gas Station
25 Tienda de Bienes Culturales
26 Terminal de Ómnibus Interprovinciales

················· Walking Tour

Camagüey

0   250   500 m
0   250   500 yards

Cuban independence is well remembered in the city today.

Cross triangular Plaza de los Trabajadores in front of Iglesia de la Merced and head west on Padre Valencia to the **Teatro Principal** at No 64. It's worth entering this impressive theater erected in 1850 to see the chandeliers and stained glass. You can often see performances by Cuba's second most important ballet company, the Ballet de Camagüey, formed in 1971 and presently directed by Fernando Alonso.

Continue west on Padre Valencia and turn left (south) at the first corner. Follow Lugáreño two short blocks south to General Gómez, cross it, and continue south on Calle Príncipe, the street branching off General Gómez just east of Lugáreño. Príncipe ends at Hermanos Agüero, and right on the corner at No 58 you'll find the **Casa Natal de Nicolás Guillén** in the house where the mulatto poet Nicolás Guillén was born on July 10, 1902. During the 1930s Guillén founded the school of Afro-Cuban poetry and until his death in 1989 he was Cuba's poet laureate. The house is open weekdays 8 am to 4:30 pm, Saturday 8 am to noon. The door is always shut, but just knock.

Go east on Hermanos Agüero a block and turn left on Cisneros to the 19th-century **Palacio de Justicia** at No 253, originally La Real Audiencia Primada de Puerto Príncipe founded in 1800. Opposite is the Centro de Promoción Cultural Ibero Americano, a cultural center housed in the former Spanish Club.

A block and a half south on Cisneros is **Parque Ignacio Agramonte** with an equestrian statue (1950) of Camagüey's hero. On the south side of the square is the **Catedral de Nuestra Señora de la Candelaria**, Cisneros No 168 at Luaces, rebuilt in the 19th century on the site of an earlier church dating from 1530. The cathedral is closed for renovations until 1997.

From Cisneros take Luaces three blocks east and go right on República. At República No 69 you'll find the **Museo Estudiantil Camagüeyano** (closed Monday). This museum is also known as the Casa

Jesús Suárez Gayol, for the revolutionary who once lived here. He died fighting alongside Che Guevara in Bolivia in 1967.

Turn right at the next corner to the south and go west four short blocks to Hurtado. Just to the right is **Plaza San Juan de Dios**. (The way is rather confusing – as the city's founders intended – so ask directions.) This square is easily Camagüey's most picturesque colonial corner. The **Hospital de San Juan de Dios** is a large complex with a front cloister dating from 1728 and a triangular rear patio from 1840 (soon to become a deluxe hotel). San Juan de Dios functioned as a children's hospital until 1972, when it became a nursing school. In 1991 the building was taken over by the Centro Provincial de Patrimonio, which is directing the restoration of Camagüey's monuments. You may enter and look around Monday to Saturday from 8 am to 5 pm, admission US$1.

Special Events

The Jornadas de la Cultura Camagüeyana take place during the first two weeks of February in commemoration of the founding of the city. Carnival is around July 26. The 10 days beginning on October 10 are also days of culture during which many musical events take place.

Places to Stay

In Town Camagüey has one of the best selections of reasonably priced hotels in Cuba. *Hotel Puerto Príncipe* (☎ 8-2403), Avenida de los Mártires No 60, is near the train station on the north side of the city center. This old five-story hotel has 77 rooms for US$15/30 single/double. The main hotel restaurant (which accepts pesos from Cubans but not from you) is crowded, more expensive than the decent hotel cafeteria, and unbelievably slow, so avoid it like the plague. The nightclub on the roof is open from 9 pm to 1:30 am with a show at 10:30 pm nightly (admission US$1). Expect some noise if you're staying on an upper floor.

Also good is the three-story *Hotel Plaza* (☎ 8-2413), Van Horne No 1 opposite the train station, a gracious old colonial-style hotel built at the turn of the century. The 67 rooms cost US$17/24 single/double. The Hotel Plaza's lobby is a nice place to relax, but the hotel gets a lot of traffic noise, so ask for a room at the back. The hotel does have a cafeteria, but the one at the nearby Hotel Puerto Príncipe is much nicer.

Three blocks down Avellaneda from the Hotel Plaza is *Hotel America* (☎ 8-2135), an older two-story hotel with 14 rooms for 20 pesos double, or 35 pesos with fridge and TV. Foreigners are always told it's 'full,' but this could change.

Hotel Colón (☎ 8-3346), República No 472, has 48 rooms for US$12/14 single/double low season, US$16/18 high season. This two-story hotel built in 1927 even has rocking chairs in the lobby.

The three-story *Hotel Isla de Cuba* (☎ 9-1515), Oscar Primelles No 453 off República, has 43 rooms for US$15 double or US$22 *especial*.

The friendly *Gran Hotel* (☎ 9-2093), Maceo No 67 between Agramonte and General Gómez, really tries to live up to its name. This old five-story hotel in the heart of the city has 72 rooms for US$17/20 single/double low season, US$18/22 high season – a good value. On the 5th floor is an elegant restaurant with a great view of the city, and just off the lobby is a cabaret that opens at 8 pm nightly except Monday.

If none of the above takes your fancy, guys on the street around Camagüey offer private rooms from US$10 double.

Outside Town The city center hotels don't provide guarded parking – for that you must stay outside the city. Most tourists are booked into the *Hotel Camagüey* (☎ 7-2015) on the Carretera Central, five km southeast of the center. This modern but rather shabby four-story hotel has 136 rooms with bath for US$26/35 single/double low season, US$35/42 high season. Some of the rooms are without TV, but there are also six cabañas with TV and fridge at US$34/46 low season, US$42/56 high season. Facilities include a swim-

ming pool, a wretched restaurant, the Centro Nocturno Tradicuba nightclub, and the main Havanautos car-rental office.

Motel Maraguan (☎ 7-2017 or 7-1813), 1½ km up Camino de Guanabaquilla off Circunvalación Este, is just off the Carretera Central at the southeast entrance to town, five km from the center. The 35 rooms with TV in long brick buildings with red tiles are a bit overpriced at US$43/55 single/double. If you're on a bus tour cross your fingers that the tour operator booked you here rather than at the dismal Hotel Camagüey. When tour groups are present, there's entertainment by the pool.

Your best bet if you're driving is *Villa Tayabito* (☎ 7-1939), 10 km out of Camagüey on the road to Las Tunas. The 20 motel rooms in two long 10-room blocks are US$18/20 single/double, and there are also 10 cabañas for US$20/30. Prices are the same year-round. Tayabito's spacious gardens are beautiful and there's a swimming pool. This is a former drug-addiction treatment center that now operates as a regular hotel, so there are lots of sporting facilities such as bowling, sauna, billiards, gymnasium, and horseback riding. There are also two bars, a restaurant, and a grill.

Places to Eat
Self-Catering *Panadería La Espiga de Oro*, Independencia No 304, is the only hard-currency bakery in town.

Camagüey's ice-cream parlor is *Coppelia*, Independencia near Iglesia de la Merced (Tuesday to Sunday 3 to 10 pm).

Restaurants Two peso pizza places, both with long lines whenever food's available, are *Pizzería La Piazza*, Avenida Agramonte opposite La Soledad, and *Pizzería Ragazza* on Maceo opposite the Gran Hotel. Two other state-run restaurants are *Rancho Luna*, Maceo at Hermanos Agüero (daily noon to 2 pm and 6 to 10 pm), and *La Volante* in a colonial building on the east side of Parque Agramonte (daily noon to 11 pm). Both claim to offer 'Cuban cuisine,' but inspect the menu before sitting down and expect to pay in dollars.

A better bet are two restaurants in old colonial houses on Plaza San Juan de Dios. *La Campana de Toledo* (daily 10 am to 10 pm) serves meals from US$7 and beer for US$1. You can dine under the trees in the patio as a local quartet serenades you. Nearby is the *Paladar de los Tres Reyes*.

The cafeterias at the Hotel Puerto Príncipe and Hotel Plaza are cheaper and easier places to eat. Cafeteria Jigüey (daily 9 am to 9 pm) back behind the Puerto Príncipe's elevator serves good meals for low prices (Creole chicken with yuca is US$2). It only accepts dollars, so you'll have the place to yourself. Cafetería El Vitral (daily 10 am to 10 pm) inside the Hotel Plaza has a very limited menu of fried chicken (US$2), hot dogs (US$0.40), and omelettes (US$0.35). Of these two cafeterias, the first is the better choice.

Entertainment

The *Teatro Principal*, Padre Valencia No 64, often hosts performances by the Ballet de Camagüey. The former *Teatro Guerrero* on Plaza de los Trabajadores opposite Iglesia de la Merced is now a cinema and cultural center with art exhibitions and cultural events.

Folk musicians play at the *Casa de la Trova Patricio Ballagas*, Cisneros No 171 between Martí and Cristo on the west side of Parque Agramonte (closed Monday).

Cabaret El Colonial, Avenida Agramonte No 406 (daily except Wednesday 9 pm to 2 am), is an open-air bar and disco with a show at 10:30 pm.

Cine Encanto, Ignacio Agramonte No 428, is nearby.

Things to Buy

The Galería de Arte Universal Alejo Carpentier, Luaces No 153, is near the cathedral.

The Tienda de Bienes Culturales, Avenida de la Libertad No 112, south of the Río Hatibonico (weekdays 8 am to 3:20 pm), has a good selection of musical instruments, compact discs, ceramics, paintings, T-shirts, dolls, and furniture.

Getting There & Away

Air Ignacio Agramonte International Airport (airport code CBG) is nine km northeast of town on the road to Nuevitas and Playa Santa Lucía.

Cubana flies nonstop from Havana to Camagüey daily (one hour, US$51 one way). The local Cubana office (☎ 9-1338) is at República No 400.

Royal Airlines has charter flights to Camagüey from Toronto (CDN$349 to CDN$519 return depending on the season). Air UK operates weekly charter flights from London-Gatwick.

Bus The Terminal Ferro-Ómnibus, Avenida Carlos J Finlay near the train station, has regional buses to Nuevitas (twice daily, 87 km) and Santa Cruz del Sur (three a day, 82 km).

Long-distance buses depart the Terminal de Ómnibus Interprovinciales Álvaro Barba on the Carretera Central, three km southeast of the center. There are first-class buses to Holguín (daily, 200 km, five hours), Manzanillo (daily, 217 km, five hours), Santiago de Cuba (daily, 326 km, seven hours), Cienfuegos (daily, 337 km, seven hours), Guantánamo (daily, 375 km), Matanzas (daily, 469 km), Baracoa (daily, 490 km), and Havana (three a day, 558 km, 10 hours). Second-class buses leave for Ciego de Ávila (three a day, 110 km, two hours), Las Tunas (daily, 123 km, three hours), Puerto Padre (daily, 173 km), Sancti Spíritus (daily, 185 km, five hours), and Bayamo (daily, 199 km, five hours). There's often a large crowd of people waiting at the station and no buses in sight.

Train Rather than fight for a scarce bus ticket, try going by train. The Estación de Ferrocarriles, Avellaneda and Finlay, is also much more conveniently located than the bus station. Foreigners buy tickets for dollars in the special Ladis office upstairs above the main ticket office in the station building opposite Hotel Plaza. The luggage-storage office downstairs in this building is open 24 hours a day. The trains themselves, however, actually leave from another terminal a block away on Jorge Rodríguez. Check on this and arrive early.

There are trains to Holguín (every other day, 210 km, four hours, US$9), Manzanillo (daily), Bayamo (daily), Santa Clara (256 km, four hours), Santiago de Cuba (twice daily, 319 km, 5½ hours, US$11.50 regular or US$13 especial), Matanzas (445 km, seven hours, US$19), and Havana (three a day, 537 km, nine hours, US$20 regular or US$22 on the *especial*). Most long-distance services pass through Camagüey in the late evening or middle of the night.

Getting Around
To/From the Airport Theoretically bus No 6 runs to Ignacio Agramonte International Airport every 30 minutes or so from Parque Finlay opposite the Terminal Ferro-Ómnibus.

Car There's an Havanautos car-rental desk at the Hotel Camagüey. Servi-Cupet, Avenida de la Libertad at the Carretera Central next to the Río Hatibonico, is open 24 hours.

Taxi To call a tourist taxi, dial ☎ 7-2428.

FLORIDA
The small sugar mill town of Florida, 46 km northwest of Camagüey on the way to Ciego de Ávila, is a potential place to spend the night if you're driving around central Cuba.

The modern, two-story *Hotel Florida* (☎ 5-3011), right next to the Carretera Central, two km west of the center of town, has 74 rooms with bath and TV for US$20/24 single/double low season, US$24/28 high season. There's a swimming pool. Kids in the parking lot harass you for money (the tour buses have been here before you).

GUÁIMARO
Guáimaro (population 20,000) between Camagüey and Las Tunas has its place in Cuban history as the site of the constituent assembly of April 1869, which approved the first Cuban constitution. The same assembly elected Carlos Manuel de Céspedes as president. These events are commemorated by a large monument erected in 1940 on Parque Constitución in the center of town. Around the base of the monument are bronze plaques bearing the likenesses of José Martí, Máximo Gómez, Carlos Manuel de Céspedes, Ignacio Agramonte, Calixto García, and Antonio Maceo, the forefathers of Cuban independence.

Every October an agricultural fair is held in the Feria Exposición Ganadera in Guáimaro.

The *Hotel Guáimaro* (☎ 8-2102), on the Carretera Central just outside Guáimaro on the way to Las Tunas, has 40 rooms in a modern two-story building. They go for US$10/17 single/double. Foreigners rarely stay there.

MINAS
Minas, 60 km northeast of Camagüey on the road to Nuevitas, is notable only for the musical-instrument factory that opened here in 1976. The Fábrica de Instrumentos Musicales on Calle Camilo Cienfuegos is at the eastern entrance to town and might be worth visiting if you're a musician (closed Sunday, admission US$2).

The *Hotel Minas* (☎ 9-6361) on Calle Cisneros just across the train tracks in town is a small 10-room peso hotel.

NUEVITAS
Nuevitas (population 37,000), just off the main road to Playa Santa Lucía 87 km northeast of Camagüey, is a sugar exporting port and industrial city with fertilizer and cement factories, and a huge thermal power plant. Actually, it's not quite as bad as that; the industrial area is well outside the old town, which was founded in 1775. It's a pleasant little place with old wooden houses lining the two main streets, although it's not worth a major detour.

Things to See
The only specific sight is the **Museo Histórico Municipal** on Martí in the center of town.

Cayo Sabinal to the north of Nuevitas is a 30-km-long coral key with marshes accommodating considerable bird life, including flamingos. You must show your passport at the entrance to the key as this is considered a frontier zone. (The Cuban government restricts access to sites that might be departure points for fleeing Cubans.)

Places to Stay

The friendly *Hotel Caonaba* (☎ 4-4265) is a three-story hotel on a slight hill overlooking the sea at the entrance to town as you arrive from Camagüey. The 48 rooms are US$12/14 single/double or US$16/20 with TV and fridge. This establishment caters mostly to a local clientele, but you'll be welcome if they have a room.

Getting There & Away

Nuevitas is the terminus of railway lines from Camagüey via Minas and Santa Clara

via Morón. Trying to come or go by bus is dicey, as the masses of Cuban hitchhikers on the roads attest.

PLAYA SANTA LUCÍA

The province's main tourist resort is Playa Santa Lucía, 112 km northeast of Camagüey. Most people come here to scuba dive on the nearby Atlantic reefs and several dive shops service the trade. Otherwise, this out-of-the-way area shouldn't be your first choice for a beach holiday. The 20-km-long beach is one of Cuba's most extensive, but it's backed by kilometer after kilometer of flatlands and swamps. To experience more of Cuba than the sand and sun, you'll have to travel far.

Of course, the swimming, snorkeling, and diving are great, and the excellent hotels lay on plenty of activities. At least ordinary Cubans are allowed to come here (unlike resorts such as Cayo Coco and Cayo Largo, which are in areas closed

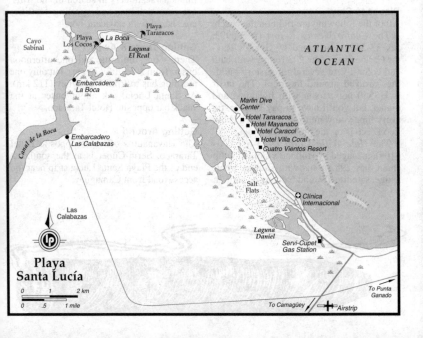

to Cubans without special permits). You will be able to meet some locals. Playa Santa Lucía is slowly developing, and there's perpetual construction work on new hotels. Frankly, it doesn't have much atmosphere.

Activities

Skark's Friends Dive Center (☎ /fax 33-5533), on the beach between Cuatro Vientos and Villa Coral, has snorkeling trips to the reef daily at 11 am (US$13 per person). Scuba diving is at 9 am and 1:30 pm (US$32 a dive). Their open-water course costs US$365, a resort course US$95. The Marlin Dive Center (or 'Divers Den') across from Hotel Tararacos is similar.

Hotel tour desks arrange trips to see the flamingos in the lagoon behind **Playa Los Cocos** at the far northwest end of Playa Santa Lucía, seven km from the hotels. There are also excursions by boat to Nuevitas.

Places to Stay

All of the following are right on the beach.

The *Cuatro Vientos Resort* (☎ 3-6993, fax 33-5433), managed by Spain's Raytur Caribe chain, has 203 rooms with bath and color TV in several three-story buildings arrayed around the pool. The tariff is US$50 per person with breakfast and dinner, but you'll have to pay US$1 extra every time you want to sit in a beach chair. Eco Disco is on the premises.

The *Hotel Villa Coral* (☎ 3-6265, 3-6109), managed by Holland's Golden Tulip chain, has 298 rooms with shower, minifridge, satellite TV, and balcony or patio in a series of tile-roofed two-story blocks built in 1989. There's a swimming pool with a safe end for children.

Golden Tulip also operates the slightly more upmarket *Hotel Caracol* (☎ 3-6302 or 3-6402, fax 33-5043) right next door. The 500 rooms with bath, satellite TV, and balcony or terrace in two-story blocks are US$53/72 single/double. There's a swimming pool with a swim-up bar, horseback riding, bicycles (US$1 an hour), and water sports including scuba diving.

The *Hotel Mayanabo* (☎ 3-6184, fax 33-5533) is a two-story hotel with 225 rooms with shower at US$73 per person all inclusive. Facilities include a rectangular swimming pool, two tennis courts, water sports, and a post office.

Hotel Tararacos (☎ 3-6222) is at the northwest end of the hotel strip beside a public beach where Cubans are allowed. The 31 rooms with shower and color TV in single-story blocks cost US$23/30 single/double. It's designed for budget-minded vacationers in search of 'no frills' accommodations, and sporting facilities are shared with adjacent hotels.

Getting There & Away

There's one morning and one afternoon bus to/from Nuevitas (70 km), but only one morning bus to/from Camagüey (112 km). At Santa Lucía, ask about buses at the snack bar opposite Hotel Tararaco.

Getting Around

The Havanautos office is opposite Hotel Tararaco. Servi-Cupet is at the southeast end of the Playa Santa Lucía strip near the access road from Camagüey.

Province of Las Tunas

Bordering Camagüey Province to the west, Holguín Province to the east, and Granma Province to the south, 6589-sq-km Las Tunas is the Cuban province with the least to interest tourists. Despite this, the provincial capital Las Tunas has a certain vitality and is a potential stopover on your way across the country. The four-km-long beach at Punta Covarrubias on the Atlantic Coast is as yet undeveloped.

This territory belonged to Bayamo until 1847, and only in 1975 was Las Tunas Province carved out of Oriente. Beef cattle ranching is the main activity in the center of the province, while sugar cane is grown in the north and west. It's all sort of off the beaten track. The telephone code for the whole of Las Tunas Province is 31.

LAS TUNAS

The city of Victoria de Las Tunas (population 120,000) was founded in 1752. During the Second War of Independence it was burned to the ground and until 1975 it was just a small market town for the surrounding cattle ranching area. Today it's a provincial capital with an exuberant populace that will be pleased to see you.

Orientation

The train station is on the northeast side of town, and the bus station is east of the center. The Río Hormiguero runs north-south through the center of town with a park on both banks. Most of the things to see are near here. A bypass road runs around the south side of the city if you want to avoid Las Tunas altogether.

A new road not marked on most maps runs from Las Tunas 93 km northwest to Playa Santa Lucía via Manatí. It begins near the train station and passes the airport.

Information

Tourist Offices Campismo Popular, on the corner of Ángel Guardia near Hotel

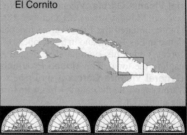

HIGHLIGHTS

- Poignant memorial to the victims of aviation terrorism in the city of Las Tunas
- Undeveloped Covarrubias Beach on the Atlantic
- Colorful folk festival at Motel El Cornito

Santiago, should have information about basic accommodation possibilities in remote areas.

Post & Communications The Centro Telefónico is on Ángel Guardia just off Parque Vicente García in the center of town.

Library The Biblioteca José Martí is at Vicente García No 4 between Francisco Vega and Francisco Varona.

Medical Services Hospital Che Guevara is not far from Hotel Las Tunas, one km from the highway exit toward Holguín.

Things to See

One of the more unusual sights of Las Tunas is the **Memorial a los Mártires de Barbados** in the park next to the river in the center of town. A small museum (admission US$0.50) has been set up in the relocated home of one of the victims of a 1976 plane crash that killed 73 people, including the entire Cuban fencing team. The Cubana plane was on a routine flight from Venezuela to Havana when a bomb exploded just after aircraft had taken off from Barbados. The killer left the bomb in a package beneath his seat when he disembarked during the stopover on Barbados. The individual photos of the victims lining the museum walls are a poignant condemnation of this sort of indiscriminate terrorism.

A few blocks northeast is the **Memorial Vicente García**, Vicente García No 5 (closed Monday, free). In October 1868 García initiated the First War of Independence in Las Tunas, and in September 1876 forces under his command managed to capture the town. The **Museo Provincial General Vicente García** is on Francisco Varona opposite the church a block up from the memorial.

The **Casa Museo Juan Cristóbal Nápoles y Fajardo** on Lucas Ortíz memorializes the Las Tunas poet Juan Nápoles y Fajardo (1829 – 1862), nicknamed 'El Cucalambé,' who had a farm at El Cornito just outside town where the motel of that name exists today.

Special Events

Lovers of Cuban country music gather at Motel El Cornito in June or July for the Cucalambé Folklore Festival. An agricultural fair is held in Las Tunas at the beginning of December.

Places to Stay

Most foreigners stay at the *Hotel Las Tunas* (☎ 4-5014), Avenida 2 de Diciembre, on a hill east of the center. It's not far from Hospital Che Guevara and one km from the highway exit toward Holguín.

This modern four-story hotel has 142 poorly lit rooms with bath and TV for US$15/22 single/double. If a huge, noisy, empty Soviet refrigerator is blocking your air conditioner and filling a quarter of the room, unplug it and wheel it aside. The menus in the Restaurante Majibacoa on the 2nd floor and the cafeteria downstairs are identical, but the latter is less formal and

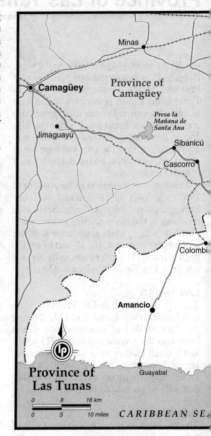

less crowded. Facilities include a swimming pool and a Havanautos car-rental office.

You might try one of the city's peso hotels. The 32-room *Hotel Santiago* (☎ 4-3396), Ángel Guardia No 112, just off Parque Vicente García in the center of town, is the former Hotel Casino.

Nearby is the 19-room *Hotel Managua* (☎ 4-2743), Ángel Guardia No 143. A third peso hotel is the old two-story *Hotel Ferroviario* (☎ 4-2601), opposite the train station. It has 20 small rooms with fan for US$10 or suites for US$25.

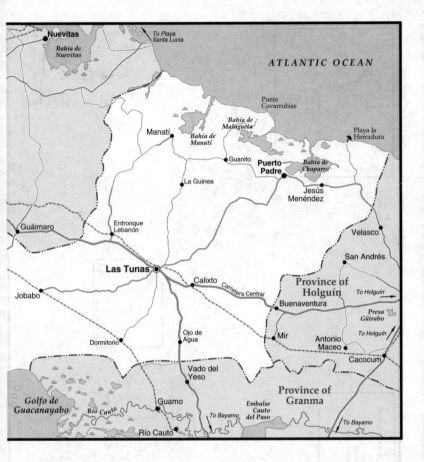

Motel El Cornito (☎ 4-5015), seven km west of Las Tunas toward Camagüey, lies two km southwest of the Carretera Central. El Cornito has 129 rooms for US$13/15 single/double, but there are three types of accommodations: individual bungalows with fridge, musty 'colonial-style' brick rooms, and rooms in blocks of four. Ask for one of the individual bungalows as all rooms cost the same; just don't expect luxury at these prices. The motel is located in a large park surrounded by bamboo groves with a reservoir at the back. There's a large thatched restaurant and a cabaret. In June or July a famous folk festival is held at the motel. Foreigners seldom stay at El Cornito, but it's an option worth considering, and there are hiking possibilities in the vicinity. Three times a day there's a local train from Las Tunas direct to an amusement park right near the motel.

Places to Eat

Restaurante 1876, on Vicente García not far from the riverside park, serves pork dishes from noon to 11 pm daily. Ask around for a privately run paladar.

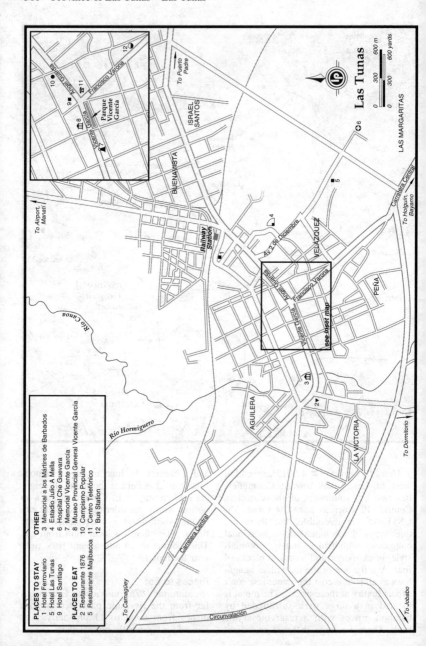

Las Tunas

PLACES TO STAY
1 Hotel Ferroviario
4 Hotel Las Tunas
9 Hotel Santiago

PLACES TO EAT
2 Restaurante 1876
5 Restuarante Majibacoa

OTHER
3 Memorial a los Mártires de Barbados
4 Estadio Julio A Mella
6 Hospital Che Guevara
7 Memorial Vicente García
8 Museo Provincial General Vicente García
10 Campismo Popular
11 Centro Telefónico
12 Bus Station

Entertainment

Check the *Casa de la Cultura*, Vicente García No 8 between Francisco Vega and Francisco Varona, and *Sala-Teatro Raúl Gómez García*, Vicente García No 267 between Lara and Heredia.

Cine Disco Luanda is on Francisco Varona a block from the bus station.

Getting There & Away

Air Las Tunas has a nice new airport terminal (airport code VTU) three km north of the train station, and Cubana flies there nonstop from Havana four times a week (608 km, two hours, US$77 one way). The Cubana office (☎ 4-2702) in Las Tunas is on Lucas Ortíz at 24 de Febrero.

Bus The main Terminal de Ómnibus is on Francisco Varona, one km southeast of the main square. Local buses use the Terminal de Ferro-Ómnibus near the train station.

Train The Estación de Ferrocarriles is near Estadio Julio A Mella on the northeast side of town. There are daily trains to Holguín (90 km, two hours, US$4), Santiago de Cuba (199 km, 3½ hours, US$9), Matanzas (565 km, nine hours, US$24), and Havana (657 km, 10 hours, US$27).

Getting Around

There's an Havanautos car-rental desk at Hotel Las Tunas. Servi-Cupet on the Carretera Central at the exit toward Camagüey is open 24 hours.

Province of Holguín

With four other provinces flanking it on the west and south, 9301-sq-km Holguín embraces much of eastern Cuba's Atlantic coastline. This is Cuba's fourth largest province, and after the City of Havana it's the most populous province with about a million inhabitants, just slightly more than Santiago de Cuba Province.

It's claimed that on October 28, 1492, Christopher Columbus landed at Bariay near Playa Blanca, just west of Playa Don Lino, although no one knows for sure. Columbus did note in his journal that this was the most beautiful land he had ever seen – not surprising considering that his impatient crew had been on the brink of mutiny just a few weeks earlier. Columbus encountered Seboruco Indians whose ancestors had lived in Cuba for several thousand years. This fact didn't prevent Diego Velázquez from giving the area first to Bartolomé de Bastidas, and later to Captain García Holguín.

Today much of Cuba's corn and beans are grown in the eastern part of the province, with sugar dominating in the center. Cattle ranching is important around the city of Holguín. Plantations grow coffee on the higher hills in the east where the Río Mayarí separates the Altiplanicie de Nipe from the Sierra del Cristal. The province's highest point is Pico de Cristal (1231 meters) and farther east are the Cuchillas de Moa, which attain 1175 meters at Pico del Toldo. The economy of this eastern region is based on minerals. Iron is mined in the Altiplanicie de Nipe, and there's a chrome processing plant in Mayarí; nickel, iron, and steel works at Nicaro; and nickel and cobalt processing facilities at Moa.

Tourism is increasingly important around Guardalavaca, one of Cuba's largest beach resorts. New hotels are popping up all the time at nearby beaches such as Ciego Estero, Bahía de Naranjo, and Don Lino.

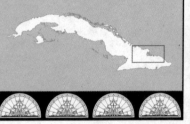

HIGHLIGHTS

- Unique organ factory and mechanical organ bands in the city of Holguín
- Hedonistic resorts on the white sands of Estero Ciego near Guardalavaca
- Intriguing archaeological remains at Museo Chorro de Maita
- Former estate of the Castro family at low-key Finca Las Manacas near Birán village
- High-altitude ecotourism resort at Pinares del Mayarí

'Ecotourism' is being developed at Pinares del Mayarí in the Altiplanicie de Nipe, and the provincial capital of Holguín is an interesting, relaxed city for the culture-oriented traveler. It's also not without significance that President Castro hails from Holguín.

The telephone code for the whole of Holguín Province is 24.

HOLGUÍN

Holguín (population 225,000) is Cuba's fourth largest city, a pleasant, prosperous place with many public parks. San Isidoro de Holguín was founded as early as 1523, and in 1752 it became a municipal seat. This was the setting of much fighting during the two wars of independence in the late 19th century. With the division of

Oriente into five separate provinces in 1975, the city of Holguín became a capital.

As tourism develops and Holguín's international airport becomes increasingly important, more and more travelers are finding Holguín an agreeable first stop in Cuba. The locally brewed Mayabe beer is Cuba's best.

Orientation

Parque Calixto García is Holguín's most important central square and just to the north and south of it are Parque Céspedes and Parque Peralta, either of which would do any city proud. Manduley and Maceo are the main north-south thoroughfares running between the train station and the hills bordering the city on the north. The main bus station is on the west side of town, and main tourist hotels are in the far east.

Information

Tourist Offices Many tourism-related offices are in the Edificio Pico de Cristal, Manduley No 199 at Martí in the southeast corner of Parque Calixto García. The Oficina de Reservaciones Islazul is at street level. Upstairs are the offices of Cubana and the Carpeta Central hotel reservations office (with the Campismo Popular representative). There's also the Cadena de Turismo Islazul, Manduley No 126 at Aguilera. These offices make hotel, restaurant, and cabaret bookings mostly for Cubans (foreigners can book directly at the hotels), but the staffers are generally friendly and will steer you in the right direction if they can. Just don't expect them to speak fluent English.

Immigration Immigration is at Frexes No 76 (Monday to Saturday 8 am to 2 pm).

Money The local unofficial moneychangers are on Frexes behind La Luz de Yara department store.

Post & Communications The post office is at Maceo No 114 on Parque Céspedes (Monday to Saturday 8 am to 6 pm).

To place long distance and local calls, go to the Servicio Telefónico, Frexes at Rastro (daily 7 am to 7 pm).

Bookstores Librería Pedro Rojena Camayd, Manduley No 193 on Parque Calixto García, has an excellent selection of books, maps, and compact discs that it sells for dollars. Also try Librería Villena Botev, Frexes No 151 at Máximo Gómez.

Library Biblioteca Alex Urquiola, Maceo on the west side of Parque Calixto García, has a very pleasant modern reading room.

Photography Try Photo Service at Manduley No 132.

Medical Services Holguín's main medical facility is Hospital Lenin, Avenida VI Lenin on the west side of town. Both the Hotel Pernik and Motel El Bosque have infirmaries.

Things to See

In the center of **Parque Calixto García** is a statue (1912) of General Calixto García, who captured Holguín from the Spaniards in December 1872. In 1898 he was about to repeat his feat when the US intervention

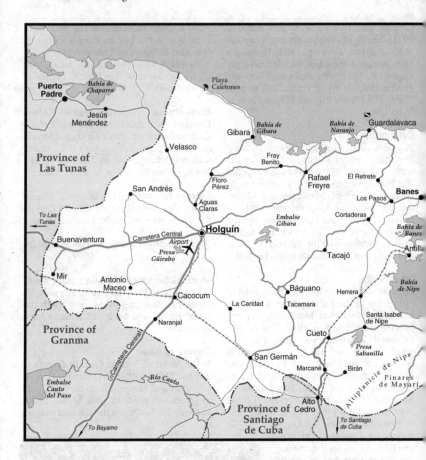

forced him to rush to Santiago de Cuba where his support made the quick US military victory over the Spanish possible. That done, Calixto García came back and occupied Holguín.

The **Museo de Historia Provincial** is at Frexes No 198 on the north side of Parque Calixto García (Monday to Friday 9 am to 5 pm, Saturday 9 am to 1 pm, admission US$1). Housed in a structure built between 1860 and 1868 that later became a Spanish army barracks, it was nicknamed La Periquera ('the parrot cage') for the red, yellow, and green uniforms of the Spanish

soldiers who stood on guard outside. The museum's prize exhibit is an old axe head carved in the likeness of a man. It's known as the Hacha de Holguín (Holguín axe). Discovered in 1860 and kept in Havana for many years, it was only returned to Holguín in 1981.

Information about Holguín's liberator can be found in the **Casa Natal de Calixto García**, Miró No 147 two blocks east of Parque Calixto García (weekdays 8 am to 5 pm, Saturday 8 am to 1 pm, admission US$0.50). García was born here in 1839.

In the southwest corner of Parque

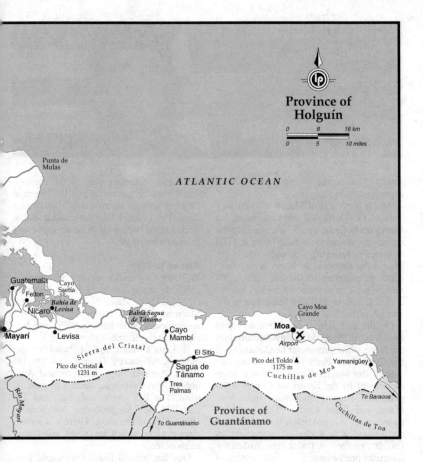

Calixto García is the **Centro Provincial de Artes Plásticas Moncada**, Maceo No 180 at Martí (Tuesday to Saturday noon to 8 pm, Sunday 3 to 7 pm, admission free).

The **Museo de Ciencias Naturales Carlos de la Torre**, Maceo No 129 between Martí and Luz Caballero (Sunday to Thursday 9 am to 5 pm, Saturday 1 to 5 pm, admission US$1), showcases stuffed examples of Cuban wildlife.

The **Catedral de San Isidoro**, Maceo No 122 on Parque Peralta, dates from 1720 but is heavily restored. The square is named for Julio Grave de Peralta, who led

the uprising against Spain in Holguín in October 1868.

Four blocks north on the opposite side of Parque Calixto García is the **Iglesia de San José**, Manduley No 116 in the middle of Parque Céspedes. Founded in 1820, it was recently reconstructed using reinforced concrete.

At the corner of Manduley and Cuba is the workshop of **Casino de la Playa**, a mechanical-organ band, one of eight professional organ groups in Holguín. The group often practices here. If they're present, you'll be welcome to stop and

watch. This is one of eight professional organ groups in Holguín.

At the north end of Maceo is a stairway built in 1950 with 460 steps ascending **La Loma de la Cruz**, the hill overlooking the entire city. A cross was raised here in 1790 in hopes of relieving a drought, and every May 3 the Romería de Mayo brings hundreds of pilgrims to the hill. It's a 20-minute walk from town; otherwise, bus No 3, 5, 14, 200, or 210 will bring you to the foot of the hill.

On the east side of town behind Hotel Pernik is the **Plaza de la Revolución** with the large white provincial headquarters of the Communist Party of Cuba facing one side of the square. Opposite it is a huge monument to the heroes of Cuban independence, bearing quotations from José Martí and Fidel Castro. The tomb of Calixto García is just below this monument and behind it is a smaller monument to García's mother. A forest crisscrossed by footpaths lies beyond.

Holguín contains the only mechanical music organ factory in Cuba, the **Fábrica de Órganos**, Taller Polivalente, Carretera de Gibara No 301 (weekdays 7 am to 3:30 pm). The 36-employee factory produces about six organs a year, as well as guitars and other instruments. A good organ costs around US$15,000. You can see and hear one playing on Parque Céspedes every Saturday at 8 pm.

Special Events

During the Romería de Mayo in the first week of May, hundreds of pilgrims come to town and orchestras play in the squares. The Fiesta Iberoamericana de la Cultura in October features theater, dance, and street fairs. The Festival Internacional de Ballet occurs at the beginning of November every even-numbered year.

Places to Stay

In Town City-center accommodations are available at the five-story *Hotel Turquino* (☎ 46-2124), Martí No 40 at General Marrero. The 40 rooms are US$13/15 single/double with bath and TV, and foreigners are welcome.

Holguín's main tourist hotel is the modern, three-story *Hotel Pernik* (☎ 48-1011), Avenida Jorge Dimitrov and Avenida XX Aniversario, three km east of town. The 202 rooms with bath and TV cost US$26/35 single/double low season, US$32/45 high season. There's a swimming pool, nightclub, taxi stand, and Transautos office.

One km beyond Hotel Pernik and four km east of town is *Motel El Bosque* (☎ 48-1012), Avenida Jorge Dimitrov in Reparto Pedro Diaz Cello. The 69 duplex bungalows with fridge and TV are US$17/23 single/double low season, US$20/27 high season. The extensive motel grounds are attractive and there's a nice bar beside the swimming pool. Holguín's Havanautos car-rental office is at this motel. El Bosque has a pleasant, spacious restaurant with the usual slow service, poor food, and high prices. The motel's cafeteria serves breakfast at half the price, but it doesn't open until 10:30 am (and close at 5:30 pm).

There's a disco open daily except Tuesday (US$9 minimum consumption), but most of the rooms are far enough away that there's no noise.

The three other peso hotels in central Holguín are supposedly for Cubans only, though this could change. The *Hotel Praga* (☎ 42-2665), López No 148 between Frexes and Aguilera, has 29 rooms in a pink three-story building.

Four-story *Hotel Santiago* (☎ 42-3113), Maceo No 134 near Parque Céspedes, has 21 rooms at under US$10 double, and it occasionally admits foreigners.

The old two-story *Hotel Majestic* (☎ 42-4322), Frexes No 139 at Mártires, has 18 rooms. Fidel Castro stayed in room No 13 during one of his trips through Holguín in 1951 (this room is now incorporated into suite No 7). The famous Mexican singer Jorge Negrete also stayed at the Majestic during the '50s when he came to Holguín to perform at the Teatro Suñol.

Outside Town The *Motel Mirador de Mayabe* (☎ 42-5347), Loma de Mayabe, 10 km southeast of Holguín, has 24 rooms with bath and TV in a long block of units. Singles/doubles cost US$14/19. There's a good view of the surrounding area from here, although the loud music broadcast over speakers is distracting. The Mirador de Mayabe's main claim to fame is a beer-drinking donkey named Pancho who hangs out in the bar near the swimming pool. Bus No 208 runs to the bottom of the hill, 1½ km from the motel, four times a day.

Villa El Cocal (☎ 46-1902) on the Carretera Central, three km from the airport (and 10 km south of Holguín), is a 'trampoline' hotel where vacationers on package tours stay when they have early or late flights. The 40 rooms in 10 two-story cabañas are arranged around the swimming pool. Singles/doubles cost US$43/55. The rooms are basic for the price asked and you shouldn't stay here unless you have to.

Places to Eat
Self-Catering *La Luz de Yara*, corner of Frexes and Maceo on Parque Calixto García, is a three-floor department store containing a supermarket with a bakery section.

A much better selection of bread and cakes (but fewer groceries) is available at *Panadería Doña Neli*, Manduley No 285 (daily 8 am to 8 pm). It accepts dollars only.

Cremería Guamá, Luz Caballero and Manduley, is Holguín's answer to Coppelia. Notice the long line of Cubans waiting in Parque Peralta across the street.

Restaurants One of the few state-run restaurants left in the center of town is *Pizzería Roma*, Maceo at Agramonte in a corner of Parque Céspedes (Tuesday to Sunday noon to 2 pm, 6 to 8 pm).

Cafetería Tocororo, Manduley No 189 on Parque Calixto García, is mostly a bar serving cold beer, although you can also get spaghetti and sandwiches.

Holguín may have more privately operated paladares per capita than any other city in Cuba. For example, there's *Paladar Adecuado*, Miró No 114; *Paladar Pepesón*, Miró No 181; *Restaurante Mi Salsa*, López No 154 near Hotel Praga; *Paladar La Mora*, Frexes No 160; and *Paladar Ania*, Frexes No 109. *Restaurante Los Sauces*, Martí No 57 near Hotel Turquino, has pleasant decor, and it serves filling meals. Things change fast on the paladar scene, so check these and ask around.

At last report the closest paladar to the Pernik and El Bosque was *Paladar El Elevado*, Avenida de los Libertadores No 125 (2 pm until late). It's the wooden dining room upstairs. Closer to the hotels is *Taberna Pancho*, which is good for burgers and beer.

Entertainment
Holguín's main theater is the *Teatro Comandante Eddy Suñol*, Martí No 111 on Parque Calixto García. Ask about performances by the Holguín comic opera and ballet at the Teatro Lírico office at nearby Martí No 123.

For traditional folk music it's the *Casa de la Trova*, Maceo No 174 on Parque Calixto García (closed Monday). The *Casa*

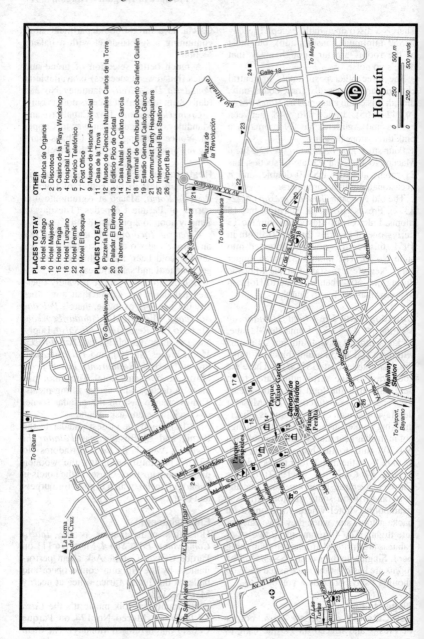

PLACES TO STAY
8   Hotel Santiago
10 Hotel Majestic
15 Hotel Praga
16 Hotel Turquino
22 Hotel Pernik
24 Motel El Bosque

PLACES TO EAT
6   Pizzería Roma
20 Paladar El Elevado
23 Taberna Pancho

OTHER
1   Fábrica de Órganos
2   Discoteca
3   Casino de la Playa Workshop
4   Hospital Lenin
5   Servicio Telefónico
7   Post Office
9   Museo de Historia Provincial
11 Casa de la Trova
12 Museo de Ciencias Naturales Carlos de la Torre
13 Edificio Pico de Cristal
14 Casa Natal de Calixto García
17 Immigration
18 Terminal de Omnibus Dagoberto Sanfield Guillén
19 Estadio General Calixto García
21 Communist Party Headquarters
25 Interprovincial Bus Station
26 Airport Bus

Holguín

de la Cultura, next door at Maceo No 172 (closed Monday), sometimes has exhibitions and classical music.

Cinemas Four cinemas to check are *Cine Martí*, next to the Museo de Historia Provincial on Parque Calixto García; *Cine Bária*, Manduley No 110; *Cine Victoria*, Maceo No 300; and *Cine Frexes*, Frexes No 270.

Bars & Discos Friday to Sunday at 8 am local youths converge on the *Discoteca*, Manduley at Habana. No alcohol is served in the disco, but across the street is the privately run *Bar Acabaret*, Manduley No 57. *El Coctelito*, Manduley No 153 (daily 9 am to 1 am), is a state-run local bar.

Tourists prefer *Taberna Pancho* between Hotel Pernik and Motel El Bosque (daily noon to 11:45 pm), where a trio plays in the evening for patrons consuming hamburgers and beer.

Holguín's Tropicana-style nightclub is *Cabaret Nocturno*, located beyond Servi-Cupet three km out on the road to Las Tunas. There's a show Tuesday to Sunday at 8:30 pm, but this open-air establishment is closed on rainy days (US$10 minimum consumption).

Spectator Sports

Baseball matches take place from November to March at the *Estadio General Calixto García* just off Avenida de los Libertadores not far from Hotel Pernik. The stadium also houses a sports museum.

Things to Buy

The Fondo de Bienes Culturales, Frexes No 196 on Parque Calixto García, sells Cuban handicrafts. The Artex Tienda Holguín, Frexes No 236, has a selection of musical instruments such as guitars, bongo drums, and tambores. Visit the Mercado Artesanal, Martí No 91 on Parque Calixto García, to see local producers selling their own products.

Getting There & Away

Air Several international carriers have flights into Frank País International Airport (airport code HOG), 13 km south of central Holguín. The spacious new airport terminal opened in 1996.

Martinair Holland arrives from Amsterdam weekly, and the German LTU International Airways arrives from Düsseldorf with connections to/from Munich. Cubana runs flights from Cologne. Air Transat, Canadian Airlines, and Royal Airlines have charter flights from Toronto. Details of these are included in the Getting There & Away chapter.

Cubana has nonstop flights from Havana to Holguín once or twice a day (674 km, two hours, US$79 one way). The Cubana office in Holguín (☎ 42-5707) is on the 2nd floor of the Edificio Pico de Cristal, Manduley at Martí on Parque Calixto García (weekdays 8 am to 4 pm).

Bus The Terminal de Ómnibus Dagoberto Sanfield Guillén, Avenida de los Libertadores opposite Estadio General Calixto García, has buses to Guardalavaca (every morning, 54 km) and Moa (four a week, 172 km). To Banes and Antilla the buses operate on alternate days.

Buses for more distant points operate from the Interprovincial Bus Station, Carretera Central at Independencia, west of the center near Hospital Lenin. There are buses to Bayamo (daily, 71 km), Las Tunas (twice daily, 77 km, two hours), Santiago de Cuba (daily, 143 km), and Havana (daily, 758 km, 12 hours).

Train A better bet than a bus would be a train from the Estación de Ferrocarriles, Calle V Pita on the south side of town. Foreigners must purchase tickets with dollars at the special Ladis ticket office opposite the train station.

There's one daily morning train to Las Tunas (90 km, three hours, US$4), a daily afternoon train to Santiago de Cuba (143 km, 3½ hours, US$5), and a daily night train to Havana (747 km, 13 hours, US$31). Other trains go to Antilla (114 km, US$3.20) and Guantánamo. The services are fairly reliable and getting a ticket is usually no problem.

The Santiago-Havana mainline junction is at Cacocum, 17 km south of Holguín, but the trains above are through connections. Other train fares from Holguín are US$9 to Camagüey (210 km), US$13 to Ciego de Ávila (312 km), US$17 to Guayos (393 km), US$20 to Santa Clara (466 km), and US$27 to Matanzas (655 km).

Getting Around

To/From the Airport A tourist taxi into town costs US$10, and a ride in a private car with yellow plates US$6.

The public bus to the airport leaves once or twice a day from General Rodríguez No 84 on Parque Martí near the train station (check the times one day before). For airport information call ☎ 46-2534.

Bus There are three types of public bus in Holguín: regular city buses for 10 centavos a ride, express buses for 40 centavos, and taxi buses for one peso. This is one of the few provincial towns where the city buses actually run on a fairly regular basis.

Car Havanautos has a car-rental office at Motel El Bosque. Transautos has one at Hotel Pernik. Servi-Cupet (open 24 hours) is three km out on the Carretera Central toward Las Tunas.

Taxi To call a tourist taxi, dial ☎ 48-2398.

GIBARA

The town of Gibara (16,000 inhabitants) is near the mouth of the Río Cacoyugüin, 33 km north of Holguín over a winding road through picturesque countryside. Founded in 1827, Gibara was the main port for this part of northern Cuba during the 19th century, and it's called 'la villa blanca' for its stately old mansions with open porches and stained-glass windows. Large *robles africanos* (African oaks) stand on the square in front of the main church. There's a small shipyard and fishing industry here, which accounts for the abundance of seafood including lobster and shrimp.

Things to See

Side by side in the center of town are Gibara's two museums: the **Museo Municipal**, Independencia No 19 (admission US$0.50); and the **Museo de Historia Natural**, Independencia and J Peralta (admission US$1). Both museums keep the same hours (Tuesday to Saturday 8 am to noon and 1 to 5 pm, Sunday 8 am to noon).

For an excellent view of Gibara trek up to **El Cuartelón**, an old Spanish fort on Los Caneyes Hill overlooking the town.

Places to Stay & Eat

In Town The only official place to stay is the *Hotel Bella Mar* (☎ 3-4206) on General Sartorio, a local peso hotel with a dozen rooms. If they don't have any vacancies or won't accept foreigners, ask around for a private room.

The *Restaurante El Faro*, on Parque de las Madres opposite the bus station in the center of town, has a very pleasant dining room facing the sea. *Bar El Cocal* is attached.

Outside Town There's a local tourist resort on the hillside at Silla de Gibara between Floro Pérez and Rafael Freyre, 35 km southeast of Gibara. It's 1½ km off the main road.

There are 42 rooms with two, four, and five beds in duplex units. The resort has a swimming pool. It's a 30-minute hike up the hill to a cave. This is good place to rest for a day or two, but transport along the main road is a mere two buses a day, if that.

Information (and perhaps reservations) should be available from the Campismo Popular representative in Holguín. It's in the Edificio Pico de Cristal, Manduley No 199 at Martí, in the Carpeta Central hotel reservations office, next to Cubana Airlines.

Getting There & Away

Bus service from Holguín is limited to one 18-seat bus every other day, so a visit is only practical if you've rented a car.

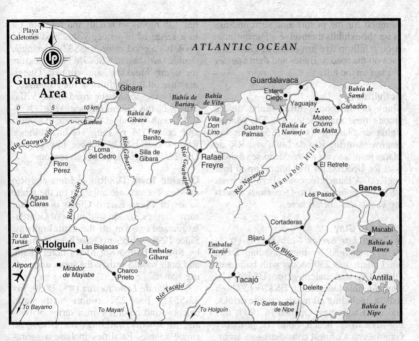

Guardalavaca Area

ATLANTIC OCEAN

Playa Caletones

Guardalavaca

Gibara

Bahía de Bariay

Bahía de Vita

Estero Ciego

Yaguajay

Bahía de Samá

Cañadón

Bahía de Gibara

Villa Don Lino

Museo Chorro de Maita

Río Cacoyugín

Fray Benito

Cuatro Palmas

Bahía de Naranjo

Loma del Cedro

Silla de Gibara

Río Gibara

Río Guabhajatey

Rafael Freyre

Maniabón Hills

El Retrete

Floro Pérez

Río Yabazón

Río Naranjo

Banes

Aguas Claras

Los Pasos

To Las Tunas

Holguín

Las Biajacas

Cortaderas

Bijarú

Río Bijará

Macabí

Bahía de Banes

Airport

Mirador de Mayabe

Embalse Gibara

Embalse Tacajó

Antilla

Charco Prieto

Río Tacajó

Tacajó

Deleite

To Bayamo

To Mayarí

To Holguín

To Santa Isabel de Nipe

Bahía de Nipe

0   5   10 km
0   3   6 miles

GUARDALAVACA

Guardalavaca occupies a three-km-long white beach facing the Atlantic Ocean, 54 km northeast of Holguín. For your convenience the coverage that follows lumps together several subsidiary resorts to the west, including those in Estero Ciego, Bahía de Naranjo, and Don Lino. The many sporting activities available at the resorts include scuba diving, snorkeling, deep-sea fishing, tennis, windsurfing, volleyball, catamaran sailing, and kayaking. There are some appealing places to visit in this part of Cuba if you're willing to rent a car for a day or two, and it's also fun to cycle along the mostly traffic-free country roads. Nearby hills add interest to the landscape, and during Cuba's May-to-October rainy season, this area is one of the driest parts of the country. It's not a bad choice if you're looking for a packaged beach holiday, but we suggest you book a tour that includes breakfast and dinner to avoid having to hassle to find food.

Medical Services

The Clínica Internacional (☎ 3-0291) at Guardalavaca Villa opposite Villas Turey specializes in treating foreigners.

Things to See

The **Parque Natural Bahía de Naranjo**, four km southwest of Estero Ciego and about eight km from the main Guardalavaca strip, features an aquarium on a tiny island in the bay where you can swim with dolphins for US$10. Shows with performing dolphins and sea lions take place daily at 10:30 am and 2 pm. The aquarium is only accessible by boat from a marina on the mainland; the US$6 per person admission fee includes the transfer. All the hotel tour desks sell excursions to the aquarium.

The **Museo Chorro de Maita** is a site-based museum protecting the remains of an excavated Indian village (Tuesday to Saturday 9 am to 5 pm, Sunday 9 am to 1 pm, admission US$1.50). It's worth a visit for anyone staying at Guardalavaca as much for the picturesque surroundings as for the exhibits themselves. The museum is on a hilltop five km south of Guardalavaca on the road to Banes and then another 2½ km up the hill.

Activities

Many of the hotels offer scuba diving among their many activities. The Marina Bahía de Naranjo (☎ 3-0115), four km southwest of the Río de Luna and Río de Mares resorts, rents a large deep-sea fishing boat for US$200 for five hours (up to four anglers). A launch for coastal cruises costs US$55 an hour for up to 15 persons. Cruising yachts can anchor here.

Places to Stay

In Town *Las Brisas Club Resort* (☎ 3-0218), managed by the Canadian Delta hotel chain, has 230 rooms with bath, satellite TV, and balcony for US$65/110 single/double low season, US$70/129 high season, including all meals, on-site drinks, and most activities. Opened in 1994, this big five-story beach hotel is probably Guardalavaca's finest considering its architecture, service, and location. Facilities include a swimming pool, Disco La Dolce Vita, floodlit tennis courts, water sports, horseback riding, and car-rental office. Las Brisas is a good choice for families as a free Kids Kamp for children ages two to 11 operates from 8:30 am to 8 pm.

West along the beach is *Hotel Guardalavaca* (☎ 3-0221). Its 225 rooms with shower and satellite TV in three modern two-story buildings cost US$37/49 single/double low season. Facilities include a swimming pool, disco, and car-rental office.

Hotel Atlántico (☎ 3-0180), near the center of the Guardalavaca complex, has 233 rooms with shower and color TV. This big two- and four-story building facing the pool was built in 1990. Car rentals and tours can be arranged at the hotel tour desk, and there's a scuba-diving center. Some inexpensive package tours use this hotel.

Villas Turey (☎ 3-0195), behind Hotel Atlántico and 200 meters from the beach,

has 135 rooms with bath and satellite TV in a series of two-story villas next to the pool. It's a good value at US$39/51 single/double low season, US$47/63 high season, including breakfast and dinner. Guests may use all the facilities at the Atlántico.

Just west across the road from Villas Turey is the *Guardalavaca Villa* (☎ 3-0212) with 30 budget cabañas with shower and color TV in long six-unit blocks. Rooms cost US$29 double low season, US$29/38 single/double high season.

Outside Town The Río de Luna and Río de Mares resorts are adjacent on the white sands of Playa Estero Ciego in verdant surroundings, six km southwest of Guardalavaca and two km off the main highway. Since 1994 both resorts have been managed by Spain's Grupo Sol Meliá hotel chain, and both should satisfy the most demanding visitor.

The *Rio de Luna Resort* (☎ 3-0030, fax 33-5571) has 222 rooms with bath, balcony, and color TV in a series of two- and three-story buildings for US$40/50 single/double. Facilities include a swimming pool, two tennis courts, and a fitness center with a sauna. Sporting activities include sailing, windsurfing, yachting, catamaran sailing, kayaking, scuba diving, fishing, and bicycling. Havanautos has an office here.

Next door is the *Río de Mares Resort* (☎ 3-0062, fax 3-0065). It has 244 rooms with bath, fridge, and satellite TV in a long three-story building facing the pool and beach. Room rates vary from US$36/44 single/double low season to US$47/65 high season, with much higher prices collected around Christmas and Easter. The buffet breakfast costs US$5, a buffet dinner US$15. Full sporting facilities are available. The diving center at the Río de Mares charges US$30 a dive, US$120 for five dives, or US$225 for 10 dives (equipment extra). The resort course costs US$89, full open-water certification US$350, plus US$90 for books and registration.

The *Marina Bahía de Naranjo* (☎ 3-0115), four km southwest of Playa Ciego

Estero, has one two-story bungalow on a tiny island in the bay for US$70 (up to four persons). Meals at the restaurant are extra and access is by boat.

Villa Don Lino (☎ 2-0443) is 8½ km north of the sugar mill town of Rafael Freyre between Guardalavaca and Holguín. Don Lino has 40 rustic, single-story cabañas with shower, fridge, and terrace, not all of them air conditioned. There's a small white beach, a saltwater swimming pool, and a disco. In early 1996 most of the Don Lino complex was closed with only a section called Villa Sol reserved for government officials (and closed to foreigners) in operation, but it's worth a call.

Three km west of Don Lino is Playa Blanca, with a holiday center for ordinary Cubans. Columbus landed somewhere near here in 1492, as a monument proclaims.

Getting There & Away
The Terminal de Ómnibus Playa opposite Villas Turey has buses to Holguín daily, one of which connects with the train to Havana every other day. The bus to Banes runs twice daily.

If the buses are out of service or you can't get a ticket, Wilfredo Hidalgo, who lives next door to the bus station, has a vintage nine-seater Ford taxi that will do a run to Holguín for US$20 one way for the whole car. Small groups from the nearby hotels can easily organize ad hoc sightseeing tours with Wilfredo for a fraction of the prices the hotel tour desks charge. It's even cheaper than renting a car.

Getting Around
There are car-rental offices at several hotels: Las Brisas Club Resort, Hotel Guardalavaca, and Hotel Atlántico. Servi-Cupet (open 24 hours) is between Villas Turey and Hotel Río de Mares.

BANES
The sugar town of Banes (population 35,000), just north of the shallow Bahía de Banes, was founded in 1887. If you're staying at one of the resorts and want to see how the Cubans really live, this is the

DAVID STANLEY
Wilfredo Hidalgo and his nine-seater Ford taxi

logical place to come. The 33-km road southeast from Guardalavaca to Banes winds between *bohíos* and royal palms through the Maniabón Hills – a really beautiful trip.

Things to See
On October 12, 1948, Fidel Castro Ruz and Birta Díaz Balart were married in the **Iglesia de Nuestra Señora de la Caridad** on Parque Martí in the center of Banes. (After their divorce in 1954, Birta remarried and moved away to Spain, but through their only child, Fidelito, Fidel has several grandchildren.)

Banes is better known for the **Museo Indocubano Bani**, General Marrero No 305 at Avenida José Martí (Tuesday to Saturday 9 am to 5 pm, Sunday 8 am to noon, admission US$1). This museum has one of Cuba's best collections of Indian artifacts.

A few blocks away is the **Museo Histórico Municipal**, Telma Esperanza No 515. Also visit the **Casa de Cultura** between the Museo Indocubano and Hotel Bani. If you're coming from the beach, Banes' biggest attraction may be the street life that you can experience on a leisurely stroll around town.

Places to Stay & Eat

The *Hotel Bani* (☎ 3588), General Marrero No 40, has 17 rooms with shared bath in an old two-story building in the center of town, a block or two from the museums. Sometimes the rooms in this basic peso hotel are without sheets and blankets, so be prepared.

Motel Oasis (☎ 3447), two km west of town on the main road to Guardalavaca and Holguín, has 28 rooms for US$13 double. A cabaret, restaurant, and bar are on the premises. Mostly Cubans stay here.

Getting There & Away

From the bus station at the corner of Tráfico and Los Ángeles, one daily morning bus goes to Holguín (72 km), and another goes in the afternoon bus connecting with the train to Havana.

AROUND MAYARÍ

Mayarí (population 23,000) between Holguín and Moa has little to offer the average tourist, although everyone traveling around this part of Cuba passes through this central point eventually. The most important attractions in the vicinity are mentioned below. Cueto is 30 km west, Pinares de Mayarí 30 km south, and Cayo Saetía 37 km northeast.

Things to See

Fidel Castro Ruz was born on August 13, 1926, at **Finca Las Manacas** near the village of Birán, south of Cueto. The present compound can only be visited with permission from officials at the Communist Party headquarters near Hotel Pernik in Holguín, although quite a lot can be seen from the gate.

To get to the complex, take the turnoff (south) seven km west of Cueto and drive south seven km to the Central Loynaz Hechevarría sugar mill at Marcané. From there a road runs eight km east to Birán, from which it's another three km northeast to Las Manacas. You'll first see the thatched huts of the Haitian laborers, the cockfighting ring, and several large red-roofed wooden houses. The graves of Fidel's parents, Ángel Castro and Lina Ruz, are to the right of the entrance gate, where you'll be met by a guard. Hopefully this intriguing site will eventually be made more accessible to foreign visitors. Birán itself is a model rural settlement with a large school, clinic, and small prefabricated concrete houses for the villagers.

Places to Stay & Eat

Motel Bitiri (☎ 5-2589), in the center of Mayarí a block from the Servi-Cupet gas station, has 21 rooms in two long single-story wings flanking the reception office. There's a swimming pool. This unfriendly peso motel is patronized mostly by Cubans, and it's always 'full' on weekends.

The *Hotel Pinares del Mayarí* (☎ 5-3157) stands at 600 meters elevation in cattle country on the Altiplanicie de Nipe, 30 km south of Mayarí on a rough dirt road. From Santiago de Cuba and Bayamo the easiest access is via Mella. There are 48 spacious fan-cooled rooms with shower in two rustic two-story blocks of seven rooms each, 10 cabañas of three rooms each, and two cabañas with two rooms. The showers are hot and the beds comfortable.

There's a large restaurant/bar with a soaring roof, a swimming pool, and a tennis court. Toads sit on the restaurant windowsills and swim happily in the pool. Pinares del Mayarí is in a pine forest and the mountain-lodge architectural style is pleasant, but for US$48 double and up, it's rather expensive.

Built in the 1970s and presently being marketed as an ecotourism resort, it's a nice stop for groups on tour but not really worth the detour for individuals. The hotel often closes when no groups are present. The nickel and iron deposits of this area are indicated by the red soil.

Villa Cayo Saetía (☎ 2-5350) is a small upmarket resort on a 42-sq-km island at the entrance to the Bahía de Nipe, 37 km northeast of Mayarí over a very rough road. The five cabañas and one suite are expensive at US$70 double, and meals in the restaurant are extra. In contrast to the ecotourists at Pinares del Mayarí, many of

Villa Cayo Saetía's guests come to shoot the local bird life out of the sky or to hunt the wild boar, bulls, zebra, deer, and antelopes that have been introduced on the island's plains. In contrast to this carnage, Cayo Saetía's small curving beaches are lovely.

Getting Around
Don't allow the Servi-Cupet gas station in Mayarí to fill your tank with fuel from the old pump that measures gasoline in gallons; otherwise, you'll pay more than you should for very little gas. If your tank isn't too low, wait until you get to Moa, Holguín, or Guardalavaca to buy fuel.

MOA
Moa is an industrial city of 30,000 inhabitants and home of the Ernesto Guevara nickel smelter on the east side of town. Since 1990 Sherritt International Corporation of Toronto has invested tens of millions of dollars rehabilitating and expanding the Moa refining facilities, and the nickel is shipped to Alberta for further processing. However, there's absolutely no reason to come here unless you're en route to Baracoa or you're a Canadian mining technician. It's one of the most desolate towns in Cuba.

Places to Stay & Eat
The *Hotel Miraflores* (☎ 6-6103) is a modern four-story hotel just above the hospital on a hillside on the west side of Moa, four km west of the airport. It's almost surrounded by highrise apartment blocks where the smelter workers live. The 139 rooms are US$17/23 single/double low season, US$20/27 high season. The local Havanautos office is at this hotel.

Getting There & Away
Air Moa's Orestes Acosta Airport (airport code MOA) is conveniently located beside the highway to Baracoa just two km east of downtown Moa. Cubana has flights from Havana via Camagüey twice a week (816 km, three hours, US$73 one way).

Bus The Terminal de Ómnibus is near the center of town, two km east of the Hotel Miraflores. One early morning bus leaves for Holguín (172 km), but there's no bus to Baracoa (try the *colectivos* just down the hill).

Getting Around
Havanautos has an office at the Hotel Miraflores. The Servi-Cupet gas station is at the entrance to Moa from Mayarí, not far from the Hotel Miraflores.

Province of Granma

Bordered by Las Tunas, Holguín, and Santiago de Cuba Provinces, 8372-sq-km Granma Province has flat plains on the north and rugged mountains on the south. Some 8969 sq km of eastern Cuba are drained by the Río Cauto, Cuba's biggest river, which stretches 343 km from the Embalse Protesta de Baraguá in northern Santiago de Cuba Province to the Golfo de Guacanayabo. The delta of the Cauto consists mostly of mangroves, but paddies on the fertile Cauto Plain produce a third of Cuba's rice. Granma also has extensive beef cattle ranches around Bayamo and sugar fields south of Manzanillo. Coffee is grown in the Sierra Maestra foothills. Pico Bayamesa (1730 meters), due south of Bayamo, is Granma's highest peak (and Cuba's third highest).

The Sierra Maestra dips into the Caribbean at Cabo Cruz near Playa Las Coloradas where Fidel Castro and 81 companions disembarked from the motor vessel *Granma* on December 2, 1956. It's appropriate that the province adopted the name of this historic ship when Oriente split into five provinces in 1975, as the region has a long revolutionary history. It was here in October 1868 that Carlos Manuel de Céspedes launched the revolt that culminated in Cuban independence 30 years later, and during much of his two-year campaign against the Batista dictatorship, Fidel Castro was based at the Comandancia de La Plata high in the mountains of present-day Granma.

For the visitor, Granma offers a charming capital city full of poignant monuments, and the countryside is dotted with numerous historic sites from the place where Carlos Manuel de Céspedes freed his slaves to the bluff where José Martí was shot down. One of Cuba's greatest national parks, Gran Parque Nacional Sierra Maestra, lies south of Bartolomé Masó. It offers challenging hiking and

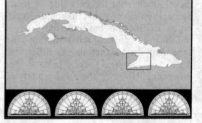

HIGHLIGHTS

- Picturesque Parque Céspedes in the historic city of Bayamo
- Reminiscences of revolution in the Museo Ñico López in Bayamo
- Gran Parque Nacional Sierra Maestra with the Comandancia de La Plata, the mountain headquarters of the revolution
- Historic La Demajagua where the wars of independence began
- World-class resorts of Marea del Portillo and Farallón del Caribe offering scuba diving and horseback riding

mountain-climbing possibilities. Two of Cuba's finest beaches are near Pilón on the south coast. There are abundant options for exploring the beautiful land and sea. Few Cuban provinces have as much variety or as many attractions of national stature as Granma.

The telephone code for the whole of Granma Province is 23.

BAYAMO

In 1975 Bayamo (population 130,000) became capital of Granma Province, and it remains a surprisingly untouristed place with no kids hassling you for chewing gum and no panhandlers. Although right on the Carretera Central between Holguín and Santiago de Cuba, the tour buses don't seem to stop here, and the town's pleasant, relaxed atmosphere is unsullied by tourism. The streets and parks are regularly cleaned, and the Río Bayamo washes through the western suburbs and along it lies a bit of parkland for walks. It's a friendly city that merits a visit.

History

In November 1513 San Salvador de Bayamo became the second Cuban town (after Baracoa) to be founded by Diego Velázquez, and during the colonial era Bayamo was the center of a rich ranching and cane-growing region. This was one of the cradles of Cuban independence: on October 20, 1868, the tenth day of the independence struggle, rebels captured the city under the command of Carlos Manuel de Céspedes. The present Cuban national anthem, composed in 1868 by Perucho Figueredo, begins with the words *'Al combate corred, bayameses'* ('Run to battle, people of Bayamo'). After the defeat of an ill-prepared rebel force by 3000 regular Spanish troops near the Río Cauto on January 12, 1869, the townspeople set their own town on fire rather than see it fall intact to the enemy. The town was also badly damaged in the Second War of Independence in 1895, though you wouldn't know it from the Bayamo you see today.

Orientation

Bayamo is centered on Parque Céspedes. The train station is to the east and the bus station to the southeast about two km apart. Leading off Parque Céspedes is General García, Bayamo's main shopping street. Many of the facilities for tourists – including the bus station, Servi-Cupet gas station, and the main hotel – are along the Carretera Central southeast of town.

Information

Tourist Office For general information try the Buro de Reservaciones Islazul, General García No 207 (weekdays 8:30 am to 5 pm).

Money The Banco Nacional de Cuba is at Saco and General García. The unofficial

---

The Bayamesa

Al combate corred, bayameses,
que la Patria os contempla orgullosa.
No temáis una muerte gloriosa,
que morir por la patria es vivir.
En cadenas vivir es vivir,
en afrenta y oprobio sumido.
Del clarín escuchad el sonido,
a las armas, valientes, corred.

To combat run, bayameses,
for our country looks over you
with pride.
Fear not a glorious death,
for to die for your country is to live.
To live in chains is to live
in insult and drowning shame.
Listen to the bugle calling you
to arms, courageous ones, run.

– Perucho Figueredo, 1868

---

moneychangers linger on General García a bit south of here.

Post & Communications The post office is on the southwest corner of Parque Céspedes, and the Centro de Comunicaciones telephone center (daily 7 am to 11 pm) is just behind it.

Bookstores Try Librería Mardonio Echevarría, General García No 9, and Librería Espejo de Paciencia, General García No 170.

Medical Services Farmacia Piloto, General García 53 just off Parque Céspedes, is open 24 hours.

Things to See

In **Parque Céspedes** stands a bronze statue of Carlos Manuel de Céspedes, hero of the First War of Independence. There's also a marble bust of Perucho Figueredo with the words of the Cuban national anthem. The shady trees and long marble benches make this a nice place to linger. In 1868 Céspedes proclaimed the independence of Cuba in front of the **Ayuntamiento** on the north side of the square.

In 1819 Céspedes was born in the **Casa**

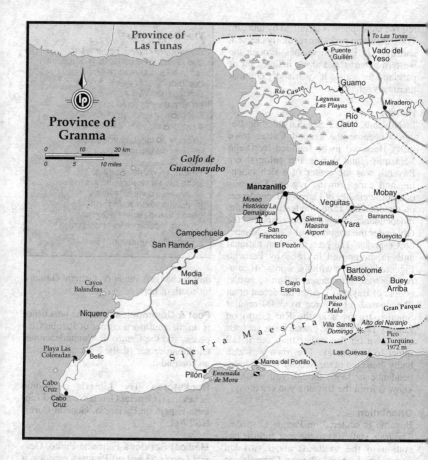

Natal de Carlos Manuel de Céspedes, Maceo No 57 on the west side of Parque Céspedes (Tuesday to Sunday 9:30 am to 5 pm, admission US$1). Next door is the **Museo Provincial**, Maceo No 55 (Tuesday to Sunday 8 am to 6 pm, Saturday 10 am to 2 pm, admission US$1), which houses a historical collection.

The **Iglesia Parroquial Mayor de San Salvador** (1740), a block away on Plaza del Himno Nacional, is notable as the place where *La Bayamesa* was first sung on November 8, 1868. It's open for sightseeing Tuesday to Friday from 3 to 5 pm.

A less known Bayamo sight is the **Casa de Estrada Palma**, Céspedes No 158. Cuba's first president was born here in 1835, but he's now considered a corrupt American puppet, so this building isn't marked on the regular tourist maps. Next door is the place where a forerunner of the national anthem was sung for the first time on March 27, 1851.

Continue southeast to the **Torre de San Juan Evangelista**, José Martí and Amado Estévez. A church dating from the earliest years of Bayamo stood on this spot until it was destroyed in the great

Nearby on Abihail González but a little hard to find (ask around) is the **Museo Ñico López** (Tuesday to Saturday 8 am to noon and 1:30 to 5:30 pm, Sunday 9 am to 1 pm, admission US$0.50), in the former officers club of the Carlos Manuel de Céspedes military barracks. On July 26, 1953, this garrison was attacked by 25 revolutionaries who had hoped to support the abortive assault on the Moncada Barracks in Santiago de Cuba by preventing reinforcements from being sent. Ñico López, who led the Bayamo attack, escaped to Guatemala where he met Che Guevara. It was López who introduced Guevara to Fidel Castro, but López himself was killed after the *Granma* landing in 1956.

Places to Stay

Most tourists stay at the modern four-story *Hotel Sierra Maestra* (☎ 48-1013), three km east on the Carretera Central toward Santiago de Cuba. The 204 rooms with bath and TV are US$26/34 single/double low season, US$31/41 high season, and there's a swimming pool.

A better choice than the Hotel Sierra Maestra would be *Villa Bayamo* (☎ 42-3102), a former military vacation center better known as the 'Casa Central,' three km southwest of the center of town on the road to Manzanillo. The 34 rooms are US$12 double in a two-story block, US$25 in a cabaña, or US$35 for a suite. Foreigners are welcome, and the rooms are generally OK despite the short sheets on the beds and the insect problems. There's a swimming pool with a three-meter-high diving board.

The *Hotel Telégrafo* (☎ 42-5510), Saco No 108, an old two-story hotel in the center of town, has 11 rooms for US$10 single or double. In 1995 it was taken over by the hotel school, and foreigners are accepted although the hotel does have water problems and it's often full. If you stay at the Telégrafo you can safely park a rental vehicle overnight in the private driveway at Saco No 59 for a one-dollar fee.

Another peso hotel that may or may not acceept foreign guests is the three-story, 40-room *Hotel Central* (☎ 42-3636),

fire of 1869. Later the church's tower served as the entrance to the first cemetery in Cuba, which closed in 1919. The cemetery was demolished in 1940, but the tower again survived. A monument to local poet José Joaquín Palma (1844 – 1911) stands in the park diagonally across the street from the tower, and beside the tower is a bronze statue of Francisco Vicente Aguilera (1821 – 1877), who led the independence struggle in Bayamo. There's also a monument to the heroes of the First War of Independence (from 1868 to 1878).

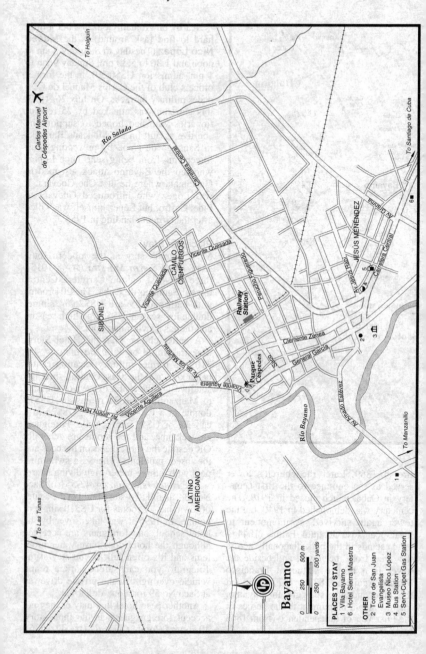

Bayamo

PLACES TO STAY
1 Villa Bayamo
6 Hotel Sierra Maestra

OTHER
2 Torre de San Juan
   Evangelista
3 Museo Nico López
4 Bus Station
5 Servi-Cupet Gas Station

General García No 204. The three-story *Hotel Royalton*, next to the museum on the west side of Parque Céspedes, was closed for renovations in 1996.

Places to Eat

Bayamo's state-run restaurants include *La Casona*, Plaza del Himno Nacional (daily 2 to 10 pm); *El Manegua*, Calle Figueredo No 61 between General García and Céspedes (Tuesday to Sunday noon to 2 pm and 6 to 7 pm); and *Restaurant 1513*, General García No 176 at General Lora (Tuesday to Sunday noon to 2 pm and 6 to 10 pm).

As usual, a privately run paladar would probably be a better bet. You might try *Paladar El Polinesia*, Parada No 125 between Pio Rosado and Cisnero. *Cafe Oriente* on Parque Céspedes serves little cups of lemon tea to those in line at the bar.

Entertainment

Musical events occasionally take place at the *Casa de la Cultura José Fornaris*, General García No 15 on the north side of Parque Céspedes. Also check the *Sala Teatro José Joaquín Palma* in an old church at Céspedes No 164.

Cabaret Bayamo is opposite the Hotel Sierra Maestra.

Getting There & Away

Air Bayamo's Carlos Manuel de Céspedes Airport (airport code BYM) is four km north of town on the road to Holguín. Cubana flies here from Havana nonstop three times a week (two hours, US$59 one way). The Cubana office (☎ 42-3916) in Bayamo is at Martí No 58 at Parada.

Bus The bus station is on the Carretera Central at Avenida Jesús Rabí, one km south of the center. Buses run to Santiago de Cuba (two daily, 127 km) and Havana (one daily, 757 km, 12 hours). Only one bus a day goes to Holguín (71 km) and getting on is hard, so look for a *colectivo*. (The bus station opposite the train station receives only local buses of little use to travelers.)

Train A much better bet than a bus would be a train from the Estación de Ferrocarriles, Saco and Línea, one km east of the center. Foreigners must buy tickets for dollars at the Ladis office inside the station.

There are trains to Havana (daily, 14 hours, US$26), Camagüey (daily), Guamo (two daily), Manzanillo (four daily), Jiguaní (four daily), and Santiago de Cuba (twice daily, US$4.05).

Getting Around

The Servi-Cupet gas station is on the Carretera Central at the entrance to town as you arrive from Santiago de Cuba. It's between Hotel Sierra Maestra and the bus station.

DOS RÍOS

At Dos Ríos, 52 km northeast of Bayamo, a white obelisk overlooking the Río Cauto marks the spot where José Martí was shot and killed on May 19, 1895. The spot is 22 km northeast of Jiguaní on the road

JUAN ANTONIO GOMEZ
COURTESY CUBA POSTER PROJECT

to San Germán (Urbano Noris): Take the unmarked road to the right after crossing the Cauto.

Back toward Jiguaní, 23 km southwest of Dos Ríos, is *Villa El Yarey* (☎ 6-6584), a peaceful, attractive hotel on a ridge with an excellent view of the Sierra Maestra. To get there, go four km west of Baire on the Carretera Central and then six km north on a side road. It would make an ideal stop for anyone driving between Bayamo and Santiago de Cuba. There are 14 rooms in two thatched blocks of six rooms and two rooms attached to the bar. Rooms cost US$20 single or double.

YARA

Yara is a large town of 10,000, 46 km west of Bayamo and 23 km east of Manzanillo. After freeing his slaves at La Demajagua near Manzanillo, Carlos Manuel de Céspedes and his followers arrived here on October 11, 1868, and fought their first battle against the Spanish, as recalled by a monument on Yara's main square. The town is famous for the Grito de Yara ('Yara Declaration') in which Céspedes proclaimed Cuban independence.

Just off the square at Grito de Yara No 107 is the **Museo Municipal** (Tuesday to Saturday 8 am to noon and 2 to 6 pm, Sunday 8 am to noon, admission US$0.50) housing a local historical collection.

GRAN PARQUE NACIONAL SIERRA MAESTRA

This spectacular national park begins 40 km south of Yara, up a very steep 24-km concrete road from Bartolomé Masó. The region is well known as Fidel Castro's base of operations during the Cuban Revolutionary War, and the mountainous park also has the country's highest peak, Pico Turquino, in neighboring Santiago de Cuba Province. The hiking possibilities are unlimited.

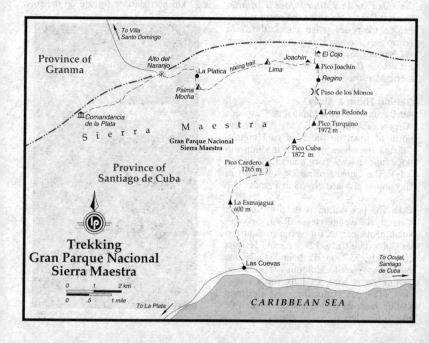

Trekking
Gran Parque Nacional
Sierra Maestra

Things to See

All trips into the park begin at the end of the concrete access road at **Alto del Naranjo**, five km beyond the tourist accommodations at Villa Santo Domingo. There's a good view of the plains of Granma from this 950-meter-high lookout.

The **Comandancia de la Plata**, three km west of Alto del Naranjo along a clearly marked trail, includes a museum, field hospital, command post, the original site of Radio Rebelde, and Fidel's revolutionary residence. It's an easy one-hour walk.

Trekking

The Pico Turquino section of Gran Parque Nacional Sierra Maestra contains 17,450 hectares, including a spectacular trail clear across the Sierra Maestra through a cloud rain forest where daily fogs nourish the luxuriant vegetation. This is a rugged three-day trek and guides should be arranged at either Villa Santo Domingo or in La Platica, the first village on the way. Trekkers must carry sufficient food, warm clothing, and waterproof camping gear. Otherwise, one could just do a day hike up the trail from Alto del Naranjo to get a feel for this spectacular area.

The trail across the mountains from Alto del Naranjo passes the village of La Platica (1½ km), Palma Mocha (campsite), Lima (campsite), Joachín (shelter), El Cojo (shelter), Pico Joachín, Regino, Paso de los Monos, Loma Redonda, Pico Turquino (1972 meters, 13 km), Pico Cuba (1872 meters, with a shelter at 1650 meters), Pico Cardero (1265 meters), and La Esmajagua (600 meters, shelter) before arriving at Las Cuevas on the Caribbean coast. We'd appreciate hearing from any readers who complete the hike.

Places to Stay & Eat

At Bartolomé Masó, *Villa Balcón de la Sierra* (☎ 59-5180), formerly known as El Mirador, has six individual cabañas with fridge and TV for US$22 double. There are also six rooms in a single two-story block for US$15 double. Just above the last cabaña is a swimming pool and a bar featuring extremely loud recorded music, so ask for a cabaña at the other end of the row (farthest away from the bar). Each cabaña has a terrace with an excellent view of the mountains.

The main base for ecotourists visiting Gran Parque Nacional Sierra Maestra is *Villa Santo Domingo* (no phone), 24 km south of Bartolomé Masó. The Villa stands next to the Río Yara at 750 meters elevation. From here a very steep concrete road gains 200 meters elevation during its five-km climb to Alto del Naranjo. There are 20 cabañas with private bath for US$18/26 single/double. Horseback riding is available (US$2.50 an hour), and guides can be hired for birding and hiking trips.

Getting There & Away

There's no public transportation to Alto del Naranjo, so you'll either have to rent a vehicle or hire a private car (with yellow license plates) to drop you off at the trailhead.

MANZANILLO

Founded in 1784, Manzanillo is a city of about 110,000 inhabitants, 65 km west of Bayamo. It's a rather dismal port with shipbuilding and a rice mill. The shallow Golfo de Guacanayabo is a prime source of lobster and shrimp, and much of Cuba's commercial fishing fleet is based here.

Manzanillo has a place in Cuban musical history as the point of entry of the first mechanical organs. During the late 19th century some 200 French street organs were imported through Manzanillo, and from 1920 to 1950 Francisco and Carlos Borbolla built about a dozen full-size organs here. The tradition remains alive in Cuba today, and an organ grinder is often the central player in Cuban rumba bands. Unlike European mechanical organs, Cuban street organs have a second crank the operator uses to control the speed – another unique feature of Cuban music. Your best chance of seeing a mechanical organ in action in Manzanillo is Sunday at 8 pm on Parque Céspedes.

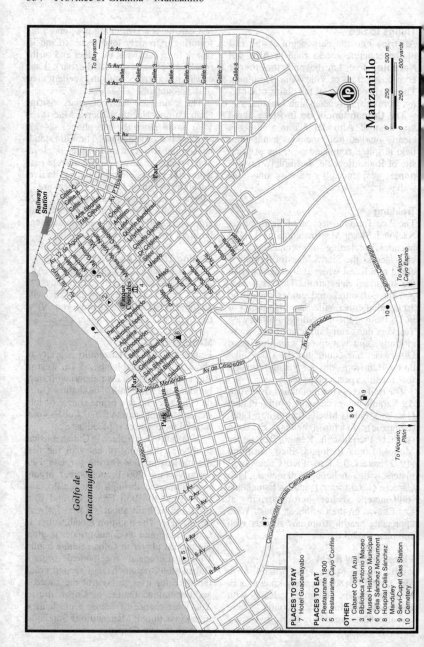

Manzanillo

0   250   500 m
0   250   500 yards

To Bayamo

To Airport, Cayo Espino

To Niquero, Pilón

Railway Station

Golfo de Guacanayabo

PLACES TO STAY
7   Hotel Guacanayabo

PLACES TO EAT
2   Restaurante 1800
5   Restaurante Cayo Confite

OTHER
1   Cabaret Costa Azul
3   Biblioteca Antonio Maceo
4   Museo Histórico Municipal
6   Celia Sánchez Monument
8   Hospital Celia Sánchez
    Manduley
9   Servi-Cupet Gas Station
10 Cemetery

Medical Services

Hospital Ceila Sánchez Manduley is near the intersection of Circunvalación Camilo Cienfuegos and Avenida de Céspedes.

Things to See

Manzanillo's central square, **Parque Céspedes**, is known for its Andalusian Moorish style of architecture, exemplified by the bandstand and some buildings around the square. A plaque on the **Comite Ejecutivo Municipal** on the south side of Parque Céspedes recalls that the *nueva trova* movement was founded here in 1972.

On the east side of Parque Céspedes is the **Museo Histórico Municipal**, Martí No 226 (Tuesday to Saturday 1 am to noon and 2 to 6 pm, Sunday 8 am to noon, admission US$0.50). The **Iglesia de la Purísima Concepción**, José Antonio Saco No 18, is nearby.

The **Museo Histórico La Demajagua**, 10 km south of Manzanillo, is the site of the sugar estate of Carlos Manuel de Céspedes. It was here on October 10, 1868, that Céspedes freed his slaves, setting in motion the process that led to Cuba's independence from Spain 30 years later. To the left of the entrance is a museum flanked by two large *calderas* (kettles) once used to boil cane juice into molasses. Other remains of Céspedes' *ingenio* (sugar mill) are behind the building.

From here a broad walkway leads to a monument bearing a quotation from Fidel Castro: *'Nosotros entonces habriamos sido como ellos, ellos hoy habrían sido como nosotros'* ('We would then have been as they were, they today would be as we are' – that is, without the revolution we would have been slaves, and the revolution has joined us all as one). Below two huge trees next to the monument are the remains of a steam engine that formerly powered the mill, and hanging nearby is the famous Demajagua bell once used to call the slaves to work. On October 10, 1868, it was used to announce Cuba's independence. To get to La Demajagua, go south 10 km from the Servi-Cupet gas station in Manzanillo in the direction of Media Luna and then another 2½ km off the main road toward the sea.

Places to Stay

The three-story *Hotel Guacanayabo* (☎ 5-4012) is south of town on Circunvalación Camilo Cienfuegos, one km straight down the hill from the Servi-Cupet gas station. Built in 1979, the hotel has 112 rooms with bath, and for some strange reason the prices vary for guests of different nationalities: Canadians US$28/34 single/double low season, US$32/34 high season; Dutch US$20/24 low season, US$23/30 high season. The Guacanayabo is high up on the hillside (no beach), but there is a swimming pool. A rather unpleasant atmosphere somehow pervades this overpriced hotel, and the isolated location makes it preferable to ask around in town for a private room.

Places to Eat

On the Malecón two km below the hotel is *Restaurante Cayo Confite* (daily except Wednesday noon to 2 pm and 3 to 6 pm), featuring fish dishes.

Restaurante 1800, Merchan No 243 between Maceo and Saco, is a state-run place just off Parque Céspedes.

Getting There & Away

Air Manzanillo's Sierra Maestra Airport (airport code MZO) is on the road to Cayo Espino, eight km south of the Servi-Cupet gas station in Manzanillo. Cubana has a nonstop flight from Havana once or twice a week (623 km, two hours, US$59 one way). The Cubana office (☎ 2800) in Manzanillo is at Maceo No 70. Air Transat and Royal Airlines fly directly there from Toronto (CDN$399 to CDN$549 return depending on the season).

Bus The Terminal de Ómnibus, two km east of town on the road to Bayamo, has buses to Yara (twice daily, 23 km), Bayamo (twice daily, 65 km), Pilón (daily, 83 km), Santiago de Cuba (daily, 192 km), and Havana (daily, 775 km).

Train It's easier to travel by train. There are services from the Estación de Ferrocarriles on the north side of town. All services are via Yara and Bayamo. Foreigners must purchase tickets for dollars at the Ladis office in the station. Trains go to Bayamo (daily), Jiguaní (two daily), Santiago de Cuba (daily, US$5.75), Guamo (daily), and Havana (daily, 16 hours, US$28).

Getting Around
The Servi-Cupet gas station is opposite the hospital, two km south of the city center on the road to Media Luna. There's a good selection of (expensive) groceries in the shop, and the Havanautos car-rental office is also here.

PILÓN
The sugar town of Pilón (population 12,000) faces the Ensenada de Mora on the Caribbean Sea, 91 km southwest of Manzanillo.

The paved road from Manzanillo to Pilón continues another 17 km east to Marea del Portillo where it soon begins to deteriorate. The next 24 km east of Marea del Portillo are bad, with several rivers to ford and steep grades. After the Río Macío, the pavement suddenly reappears and from here on east it's clear sailing all the way to Santiago de Cuba. This is one of the most scenic drives in Cuba with high mountains on one side and the sea on the other.

Places to Stay & Eat
The two-story *Hotel Caribe* (☎ 59-4264) in Pilón is a local peso hotel with five rooms.

Motel Mirador (☎ 4365) is six km east of Pilón, high up on a hillside at a spot with an excellent view. You could hike up the mountain behind the motel. The four cabins with red-tile roofs are US$10 double and there's a restaurant in a thatched building.

Villa Turística Punta Piedra (☎ 59-4421), on a small brown beach 11 km east of Pilón, has 13 rooms in two single-story blocks for US$25/30 single/double low season, US$30/40 high season.

Getting There & Away
There's a daily bus between Pilón and Santiago de Cuba via Manzanillo. No buses run along the south coast between Pilón and the Río Macío, which forms the border of Santiago de Cuba Province.

Getting Around
Servi-Cupet is by the highway at the entrance to Pilón.

MAREA DEL PORTILLO
This two-km black-sand beach, 108 km south of Manzanillo's airport, is on the drier southern side of the Sierra Maestra, and in winter it's the warmest part of Cuba. It sports two good hotels managed by Canada's Commonwealth hotel chain, both offering every creature comfort and plenty of outdoor activities. Inexpensive package tours are available and this area also makes a nice stop for anyone driving around Cuba in a rental car. Cruising yachts can find protected anchorage near the mangroves on the northeast side of this bay.

Activities
A Canadian company, Dive Adventures Inc. (☎ 416-424-4247, 800-567-6284 in Canada), runs the scuba operation at the Farallón del Caribe and Marea del Portillo hotels. Divers should call Brian Mienser for information about scuba packages.

Both hotels operate an all-day horseback riding and hiking tour to El Salto (a waterfall) for US$35 per person including lunch and four drinks (six persons minimum). Swimming is possible at the falls. Other horseback riding costs US$5 an hour.

Places to Stay & Eat
Right on a dark sandy beach is the *Hotel Marea del Portillo* (☎ 59-4201), built in the 1970s and renovated in 1995. The hotel consists of 72 rooms with shower in a long two-story hotel building and 36 two-story cabaña blocks. There's a swimming pool, one floodlit tennis court, horseback riding, deep-sea fishing for swordfish, and water sports including scuba diving at the

adjacent Albacora Dive Club. Day trips to Cayo Blanco and its secluded white sandy beach cost US$30.

Directly above the Marea del Portillo the *Hotel Farallón del Caribe* (☎ 59-4032) stands on a low hill overlooking the Sierra Maestra. It's one of Cuba's top hotels, and the view across the Sierra Maestra from the beach bar just below the hotel is beautiful. The two three-story buildings built in 1993 contain 140 rooms with shower and satellite TV for US$30 per person low season, US$50 high season, including all meals. The meals are served buffet style, so you can't be held hostage by a surly waiter, and dinner is quite a spread. The all-inclusive price also covers beer and selected national

cocktails served anytime between 10 am and 11 pm, the boat ride to Cayo Blanco with lunch, and nonmotorized sporting activities such as kayaking, catamaran sailing, windsurfing, and snorkeling. Extras such as car rentals, guided hiking and horseback riding tours, and scuba diving are easily arranged. The resort lays on a full program of evening activities (but if you don't appreciate music until 11 pm, avoid the rooms facing the bandshell just below the swimming pool).

Getting Around
The hotels rent scooters at US$10 for five hours including two liters of gas – great for zipping into Pilón.

Province of Santiago de Cuba

The Province of Santiago de Cuba (6170 sq km) nestles between Granma, Holguín, and Guantánamo Provinces in the heart of the Sierra Maestra, a pine-clad mountain range that extends 250 km from Cabo Cruz in the east to the Cuenca de Guantánamo in the west, culminating at Pico Turquino (1972 meters). To the south is the sparkling Caribbean. The city of Santiago de Cuba stands in a horseshoe-shaped basin on the east side of one of only three great natural harbors on the south coast of Cuba (the others are at Cienfuegos and Guantánamo).

The capital is somewhat industrial, and just over the Puerto Boniato ridge from the city is the densely populated Valle Central drained by the headwaters of the Río Cauto and Río Guantánamo, where most of the province's sugar and oranges are grown. Coffee is collected in the Sierra Maestra. There's also mining for copper, commercial fishing, and increasingly, tourism.

For visitors, Cuba's second city, the birthplace of the revolution, offers imposing monuments from almost every era of the city's 500-year history, and only Havana has more museums. The cultural life is rich. Just southeast of the city lies Baconao, the tourist's playground, with one of Cuba's largest collections of resort hotels and a great mountain, La Gran Piedra. Other attractions include Cuba's most important pilgrimage shrine, several ecotourism resorts tucked away in the hills, and a chance to climb Cuba's highest peak.

Most of the province uses the telephone area code 22 (the city of Santiago de Cuba's code is 226).

History

The city of Santiago de Cuba was founded several kilometers fom its present site by Diego Velázquez in 1514 and its first mayor was the future conqueror of Mexico, Hernán Cortés. In 1522 the town moved to its current location. From 1515 until 1607 Santiago de Cuba was the island's capital, although the Spanish captains-general left for Havana in 1556. The Seminario de San Basilio Magno was founded in 1722, several years before the Universidad de Havana. The Bishop of Santiago remained Cuba's leading cleric until 1788 when Havana also received a bishop, but in 1804 the city's ecclesiastical dominance was reestablished when its bishop was promoted to archbishop.

HIGHLIGHTS

- Cuba's oldest palaces and museums including the Casa de Diego Velázquez and the Museo Municipal Bacardí in the city of Santiago de Cuba
- Revolutionary monuments and museums such as the Moncada Barracks and the homes of Antonio Maceo and Frank País in the provincial capital
- Musical traditions that gave rise to unique institutions such as the Casa de la Trova and Ballet Folklórico Cutumba
- Sacred religious sanctuary of the Basílica del Cobre
- Popular resort area of Parque Baconao with nearby La Gran Piedra mountain station
- Challenging trek up Pico Turquino, Cuba's highest mountain

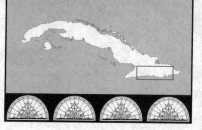

However, Santiago de Cuba's decline began early as the region's meager gold reserves gave out, the Indian laborers died off due to the cruel treatment received from Spanish *encomenderos,* and the colony's population shifted toward Havana. Santiago de Cuba was plundered by the French privateer Jacques de Sores in 1554, sacked by the pirate Henry Morgan in 1662, and hit by an earthquake in 1675.

In 1607 Santiago de Cuba became the capital of the island's Departamento Oriental and a chain of forts was built to strengthen the city's defenses. By this point black slaves from Africa had replaced Indians as the workforce at the region's copper mines and cattle ranches. After a slave uprising in nearby Haiti in 1791, Oriente (eastern Cuba) received an influx of French refugees who developed coffee, cotton, and sugar-cane plantations throughout the region. Increasing numbers of slaves were imported, and today the region that constituted Oriente has the country's highest percentage of black inhabitants.

Oriente's isolation from Havana has given it a distinct history and culture. Under the influence of independence movements elsewhere in the Americas, the Governor of Oriente, Manuel Lorenzo, attempted to throw off the rule of the Spanish captain-general in Havana in 1836, but he failed when the Creole planters withdrew their support out of fear of a slave rebellion.

Much of the fighting in both wars of independence took place in Oriente, and the great mulatto general Antonio Maceo was born in Santiago de Cuba. In 1898, just as Cuba's long struggle for independence was about to culminate in success, the US intervened in Cuba's Second War of Independence and cheated the Cubans of their hard-won victory. At Santiago de Cuba the Spanish fleet was sacrificed to save face for Spain and future US President Theodore Roosevelt managed to cover himself in glory by leading the charge of the 'Rough Riders' up San Juan Hill in a battle the Spanish were happy enough to lose. The triumphant Americans graciously accepted the surrender of the gallant Spanish, but the Cuban general Calixto García and his largely black army were not allowed to attend the ceremony.

The US victory ushered in six decades of neocolonial rule by a succession of corrupt politicians and brutal dictators. Yet despite the poverty, the city's musical and literary life flourished. Batista's 1952 military coup inspired heroic resistance among the Cuban people, and it was at Santiago de Cuba on July 26, 1953, that Fidel Castro and his companions launched an assault on the Moncada Barracks, an event that changed the course of Cuban history. At his trial here Castro made his famous 'History Will Absolve Me' speech, which became the basic platform of the Cuban Revolution.

On November 30, 1956, the people of Santiago de Cuba rose in rebellion against Batista's troops to distract attention from the landing of Castro's guerrillas aboard

Socialism or death, a motto for the masses

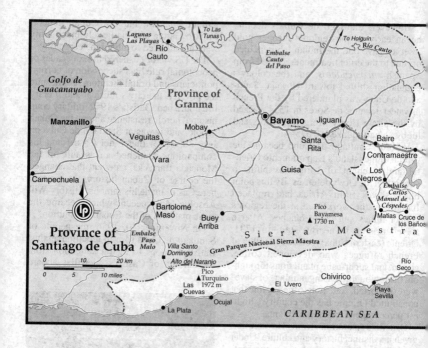

the *Granma* on the western shores of Oriente. An underground movement led by Frank and Josue País continued to support the fighters in Oriente's Sierra Maestra. Despite the death of the País brothers and many others, the struggle continued, and it was in Santiago de Cuba on the evening of January 1, 1959, that Fidel Castro first appeared publicly to declare the success of the revolution. All these events have earned Santiago the title 'Hero City of the Republic of Cuba.'

In 1975 Oriente Province was split into five provinces (Las Tunas, Holguín, Granma, Santiago de Cuba, and Guantánamo), and the amount of territory administered from Santiago de Cuba was much reduced. Yet this great city remains the throbbing heart of a colorful region.

Culture

Santiago de Cuba has a rich cultural history that goes back to the construction of a cathedral in the 1520s and the formation of a church choir. The noted composer Estéban Salas served as the cathedral's *maestro de capilla* from 1764 until his death in 1803, and his numerous Christmas carols and other choral works in both Spanish and Latin rank among the finest of the period.

The French planters from Haiti brought opera with them, and regular performances were staged at various theaters from 1800 onwards. The first philharmonic society was created in 1832, and in 1851 the Teatro de la Reina opened with a series of French operas. In 1871 *La Hija de Jefté* by Laureano Fuentes Matons became the first *zarzuela* (operetta) by a Cuban composer to be staged in Cuba.

Aside from this academic musical culture, Oriente has a distinctive folk culture resulting from 19th-century Haitian immigration. This is the original home of *son*, the forerunner of salsa. The various genres

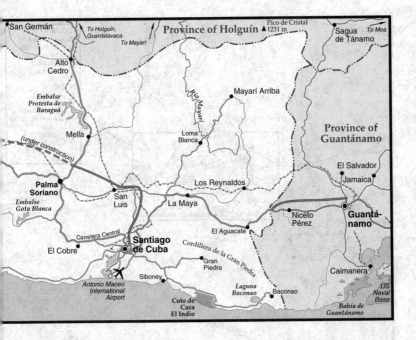

of Cuban popular music from Afro-Cuban drumming to the rumba are alive and well in Santiago de Cuba.

Two of Cuba's foremost 19th-century romantic poets, José María Heredia (1803 – 1839) and his cousin José María de Heredia y Giralt (1842 – 1905), were born here, although both spent most of their adult lives abroad.

SANTIAGO DE CUBA
At 420,000 inhabitants Santiago de Cuba is Cuba's second largest city and a strong rival to Havana in literature, music, and politics. During the 19th century French settlers arrived and contributed to the melting pot of Haitian, African, and Spanish influences that have made this Cuba's most Caribbean city. The Universidad de Oriente (founded 1947) is one of Cuba's leading educational institutions. Santiago de Cuba has a thick Spanish colonial air without the American high-

rise buildings from the 1950s one finds in Havana. This is the cradle of the Cuban revolution and numerous 'political' museums tell the tale.

Architecturally, the 4th Congress of the Communist Party of Cuba in 1991 left an indelible mark on the city in the form of the soaring Hotel Santiago de Cuba, the huge Teatro José María Heredia on Avenida de las Américas, the dramatic Antonio Maceo Monument opposite the Terminal de Ómnibus Nacionales, and the flashy new terminal building at Antonio Maceo International Airport. Unfortunately, the new train station on the northwest side of the city was abandoned half finished.

Santiago de Cuba lies in a partly submerged valley of the Sierra Maestra and the city's large natural harbor has made it an important port for almost five centuries. The Cuban Central Railway from Havana terminates here, and the Carretera Central passes through on its way to Guantánamo.

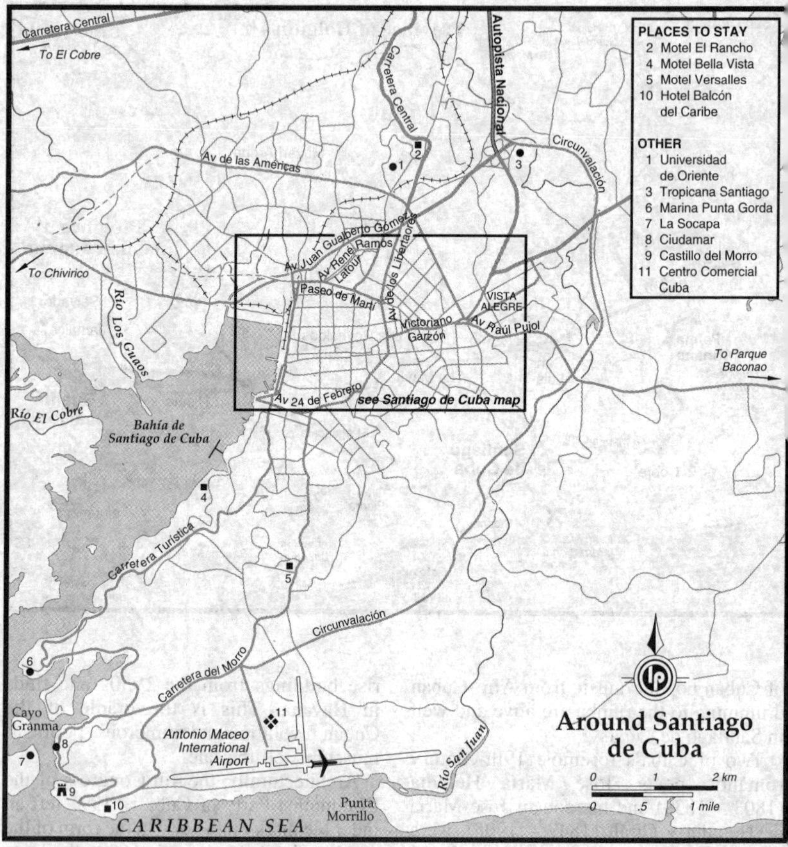

PLACES TO STAY
2 Motel El Rancho
4 Motel Bella Vista
5 Motel Versalles
10 Hotel Balcón
    del Caribe

OTHER
1 Universidad
   de Oriente
3 Tropicana Santiago
6 Marina Punta Gorda
7 La Socapa
8 Ciudamar
9 Castillo del Morro
11 Centro Comercial
    Cuba

Around Santiago de Cuba

Local plants process coffee and sugar, distill rum, construct furniture, make cement, refine petroleum, generate electricity, build ships, and manufacture garments. Yet the industry is well away from the historic center and seldom imposes on the visitor.

Orientation

Most of the regular tourist hotels are in the Vista Alegre and Ampliación de Terrazas neighborhoods, three km east of the train station (via Sánchez Hechavarría and Avenida Victoriano Garzón); 2½ km east of Parque Céspedes (via Aguilera and Avenida Victoriano Garzón); two km southeast of the Terminal de Ómnibus Nacionales (via Avenida de las Américas); and 1½ km southeast of the Terminal de Ómnibus Intermunicipales (via Avenida Céspedes). The airport is seven km to the south.

The main monuments, museums, and restaurants are in a narrow corridor running east from Parque Céspedes to Plaza de Dolores and Plaza de Marte along Calle José A Saco, the city's most important shopping street. The old residential neighborhoods north and south of this strip also contain interesting things to see, while the main monuments to the revolution are along Avenida de los Libertadores.

Maps The best locally available guide is the 255-page *Santiago de Cuba Guía Turística* map book that contains 128 detailed street maps and 10 maps of the Parque Baconao area. It's very handy if you really wish to explore the city, and some hotel shops sell it for US$5. The *Mapa Turístico Santiago de Cuba* contains a good overall map of the city, and threre's a useful map of the province on the back. There's also a *Parque Baconao Mapa Turística* for that area.

Information
Unfortunately, there isn't a general tourist information office in Santiago de Cuba.

Immigration The Immigration Office is conveniently located at Avenida Raúl Pujol No 10 near Hotel Santiago de Cuba (weekdays 8 am to noon and 1:30 to 4 pm). To extend your stay, you must drop into this office and show your tourist card to allow the officials to determine whether you're eligible. If you are, you'll be sent to Hotel Santiago de Cuba where you can pay the US$25 extension fee at the hotel tour desk. Take the receipt to immigration where you will be granted a one-month extension. The procedure is fast and routine.

Money The Banco Financiero Internacional, Felix Peña No 565 off Parque Céspedes (weekdays 8 am to 3 pm), gives cash advances on Visa and MasterCard, and it changes dollar traveler's checks into cash for 2% commission. Other currencies are changed at the daily rate less 2%. As usual, checks issued by American Express or US banks are not accepted. The Banco Nacional de Cuba (International Branch), General Lacret at Aguilera on Parque Céspedes (weekdays 8 am to noon), offers similar services. Exchange facilities are also available at all the main hotels, though their rates are worse.

Unofficial exchanges take place along Avenida de Céspedes between the Servi-Cupet gas station and Fantasía department store and on Plaza de Marte, but you must be discreet. The police often crack down on this activity around Parque Céspedes and you'll seldom be approached there.

Post & Communications The old post office building at Aguilera No 517, dating from 1926, was closed for renovations in 1996. A temporary post office has been operating at the corner of Heredia and Hartmann.

The Centro de Llamadas Internacionales, Heredia at Félix Peña next to the cathedral, is open 24 hours. DHL and EMS courier services are available here.

The city of Santiago de Cuba's telephone code is 226 (most of the rest of the province uses 22).

Travel Agencies Rumbos, General Lacret at Heredia opposite Hotel Casa Granda (daily 8 am to 8 pm), handles Tropicana Santiago bookings, sightseeing excursions, and hotel reservations, and it can arrange air, bus, and train tickets. This is a commercial travel agency that may be able to provide information about state-run tourist facilities such as official hotels, restaurants, and nightclubs – just don't bother asking about privately operated restaurants and taxis that don't pay them commissions.

Across the street is the Carpeta Central, General Lacret between Heredia and Bartolomé Maso below the cathedral (weekdays 8 am to 1 pm and 2 to 7 pm), which makes reservations for Cubans at the cheaper hotels.

To book accommodations at inexpensive Cuban resorts such as Villa Siboney, Verraco, and Juraguá at Baconao, go to Reservaciones de Turismo Parque Baconao, Saco No 455 at Valiente near Plaza de Dolores (weekdays 8 am to 4:30 pm). If you really want to stay at one of those places, making an advance reservation is almost essential.

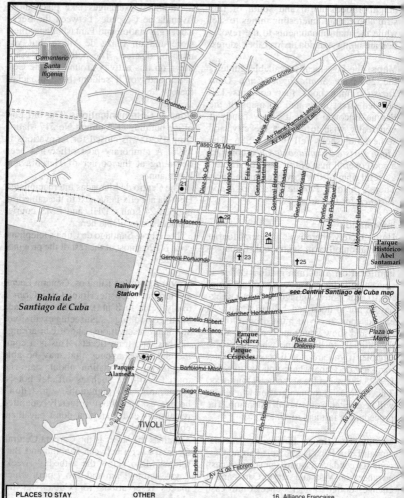

PLACES TO STAY
6 Hotel Deportivo
12 Hotel Santiago de Cuba
14 Hotel Universitario Birret
20 Villa Gaviota
35 Motel San Juan
38 Hotel Las Américas

PLACES TO EAT
9 Restaurante Pekin
28 Coppelia La Arboleda
29 Santiago XXX Aniversario
31 Paladar El Amanecer
39 Restaurante El Tocororo

OTHER
1 Terminal de Ómnibus Nacionales
2 Teatro José María Heredia
3 Club Turey
4 Hospital Provincial Saturnino Lora
5 Estadio de Béisbol Guillermón Moncada
7 Terminal de Ómnibus Intermunicipales
8 Servi-Cupet Gas Station
10 Club Caribe
11 Fantasía
13 Arte Universal
15 Tienda Cubalse

16 Alliance Française
17 Palacio de Pioneros
18 Casa del Caribe
19 Ciroa
21 Bacardí Rum Factory
22 Museo-Casa Natal de Antonio Maceo
23 Iglesia de Santo Tomás
24 Casa Museo de Frank y Josué País
25 Iglesia de la Santísima Trinidad
26 Moncada Barracks
27 Palacio de Justicia
30 Nuevo Lido
32 Parque Zoológico

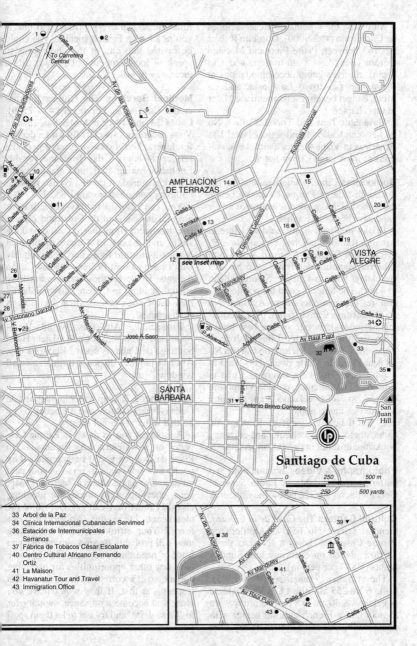

Santiago de Cuba

33 Arbol de la Paz
34 Clínica Internacional Cubanacán Servimed
36 Estación de Intermunicipales
   Serranos
37 Fábrica de Tobacos César Escalante
40 Centro Cultural Africano Fernando
   Ortiz
41 La Maison
42 Havanatur Tour and Travel
43 Immigration Office

Similarly, the Oficina de Reservaciones de Campismo (☎ 2-9000), Cornelio Robert No 163 between Padre Pico and Mariano Corona (weekdays 8 am to noon and 1 to 4 pm), reserves cabin accommodations at Playa Larga, Arroyo La Costa, and La Mula, budget beach resorts mentioned later in this chapter.

Havanatur Tour and Travel, Calle 8 No 54 between Calles 1 and 3 near Hotel Las Américas in Vista Alegre, handles reservations at most large Cuban hotels.

Bookstores Librería Internacional, facing the south side of Parque Céspedes below the cathedral, has a good selection of rather expensive books in English.

Books in Spanish are sold at Librería Amado Ramón Sánchez, Saco No 356 (Monday to Saturday 8 am to 4 pm), and Librería Manolito del Toro, Saco No 413 (weekdays 8 am to 4:30 pm, Saturday 8 am to 4 pm). The latter is good for political literature. Librería Viet Nam, Aguilera No 567 (weekdays 9 am to 5 pm, plus alternating Saturdays), is one of the best bookstores in town. Also try Librería José A Echeverría, Avenida Victoriano Garzón No 18 near Plaza de Marte (weekdays 8 am to 4 pm). Near Hotel Santiago de Cuba is Librería El Estudiante, Avenida Victoriano Garzón No 388 (weekdays 8 am to 4 pm, Saturdays 8 am to noon).

If you'll be flying out of Santiago de Cuba, there's an excellent hard-currency bookstore upstairs in the airport terminal.

Photography & Video Common films and batteries are available at Photo Service, General Lacret No 728 below the cathedral.

Cultural Centers The *Casa de la Cultura*, General Lacret No 651 at Aguilera on Parque Céspedes, hosts a 'Noches de la Terraza' dance on Saturday and Sunday nights (US$4 per person).

The *Alliance Française* (☎ 4-1503), Calle 6 No 253 at Calle 11 in Vista Alegre (weekdays 8:30 am to 8 pm, Saturday 9 am to noon), is a French cultural center with photo exhibitions and a French library. Free films are shown every Friday at 6 pm. If you're a native French speaker, you could be invited into one of the classrooms to speak to local students of French. It's a great way to make friends.

Medical Services The Clínica Internacional Cubanacán Servimed (☎ 4-2589), Calles 13 and 14 near Motel San Juan in Vista Alegre, is a special clinic intended for foreigners. You'll receive prompt personal service 24 hours a day from the capable English-speaking staff, and appointments are not required. A dentist is also present. Ordinary consultations are US$20.

You can also go to any polyclinic or hospital in Santiago de Cuba and receive free treatment from the Spanish-speaking staff, and thanks to Cuba's traditional hospitality toward foreigners you probably won't have to wait in line with the Cuban patients. However, these centers are busy enough tending to Cubans, so you should only use Cuba's free medical facilities in emergencies.

Farmacia Las Américas, Avenida Victoriano Garzón No 422 at Calle 10 near Hotel Santiago de Cuba, is open 24 hours a day. After 11 pm they dispense through a small window.

Annoyances The tap water in Santiago de Cuba is barely potable and it's better to buy bottled water at a hotel shop.

As soon as you sit down in Parque Céspedes or at Cafeteria Las Enramadas on Plaza de Dolores you'll be approached by young men who want to serve as your paid guide and/or panhandlers in search of soap, pens, chewing gum, money, or anything else they think they can get. Get rid of the mendicants by saying *'No moleste, por favor.'* Your attitude toward the young men will probably depend on whether you want or need their services. These people have few other opportunities for obtaining dollars, so it's correct to treat them with respect – at first. If they won't leave you alone and become a nuisance, switch over to *'No moleste'* and try not to let them spoil your day.

City Center

Most visits begin on **Parque Céspedes** where a bronze bust recalls Carlos Manuel de Céspedes, the man who issued the *Grito* declaring Cuban independence in 1868. Some of Santiago de Cuba's most imposing buildings front this former Plaza de Armas. The **Casa de la Cultura Miguel Matamoros**, General Lacret 651 next to the Hotel Casa Granda on the east side of the square, is the former San Carlos Club. The neoclassical **Ayuntamiento** (town hall), General Lacret and Aguilera on the north side of the square, was erected in the 1950s on a design of 1783. Fidel Castro appeared on the balcony of this building on the night of January 1, 1959, immediately after the success of the revolution.

Facing the northwest corner of Parque Céspedes at Felix Peña No 602 is the **Casa de Diego Velázquez** dating from 1522, the oldest house still standing in Cuba. This Andalusian-style building was restored in the late 1960s, and in 1970 the Museo de Ambiente Histórico Cubano opened here (Monday to Saturday 9 am to 5 pm, Sunday 9 am to 1 pm, admission US$1). The ground floor was originally a trading house and gold foundry, while the upstairs was the personal residence of Diego Velázquez. Today period rooms display furnishings and decoration from the 16th to the 19th centuries. Visitors are also shown through an adjacent neoclassical house dating from the 19th century.

The **Catedral de Nuestra Señora de la Asunción** on the south side of Parque Céspedes is only the latest in a series of churches on this spot. Cuba's first cathedral was built here in the 1520s, but the building has suffered repeated destruction. The original church was positioned differently with its facade facing the bay. The present five-nave cathedral with its coffered ceiling and dome was completed in 1922 (the choir stalls date from 1910). It's believed that Diego Velázquez is buried beneath the cathedral, although this has never been proven and there's no marker. Unfortunately the cathedral is usually closed outside of mass hours (Monday, Wednesday, Thursday, and Friday at 6:30 pm, Saturday at 7 pm, and Sunday at 9 am and 6:30 pm).

Behind the cathedral and a block over at Bartolomé Masó and Mariano Corona is the **Balcón de Velázquez**, the site of an old Spanish fort which has a lovely view of the harbor.

Heredia east of the Hotel Casa Granda accommodates many culturally significant buildings, such as the **Casa del Estudiante** at No 204 and the onetime home of composer Rafael Salcedo (1844 – 1917) at No 208. Today it's the Casa de la Trova. On the next corner at No 260 is the **Casa Natal de José María de Heredia** (Tuesday to Friday 9 am to 5 pm, Saturday 9 am to 10 pm, Sunday 8 am to noon, admission US$1), which illustrates the life of the romantic poet born here on December 31, 1803. Heredia is known to all students of Latin American literature for his *Ode to Niagara* and other poems extolling the natural beauty of the Americas. As a result of his espousal of independence, Heredia was forced into exile in the US and Mexico, where he died in 1839.

Nearby on Heredia are the former home of educator Juan Bautista Sagaria (1806 – 1871) at No 262; the Elvira Cape Library (founded in 1899) opposite at No 259; the Provincial Historical Archives (with documents dating back to 1687) on the next block at No 302; and the erstwhile home of the painters Felix and José Joaquín Tejada Revilla at No 304. At No 303 is the **Museo del Carnaval** (Tuesday to Friday 9 am to 5 pm, Saturday 9 am to 11 pm, Sunday 9 am to 5 pm, admission US$1, cultural activities in the patio another US$1).

Pío Rosado, the narrow alley next to the Museo del Carnaval, leads up to the eclectic neoclassical building of the **Museo Municipal Emilio Bacardí Moreau** (Monday 3 to 8 pm, Tuesday to Saturday 9 am to 9 pm, Sunday 9 am to 4 pm, admission US$2), one of Cuba's oldest functioning museums. Founded in 1899 by the famous rum distiller and first mayor of Santiago de Cuba, Emilio Bacardí y Moreau (1844 – 1922), this provincial

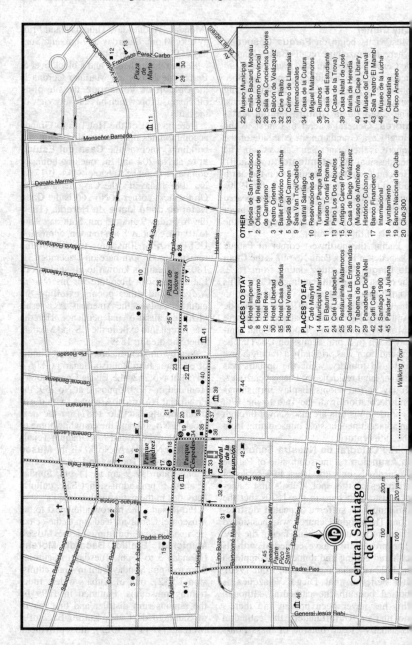

PLACES TO STAY
6 Hotel Imperial
8 Hotel Bayamo
12 Hotel Rex
30 Hotel Libertad
35 Hotel Casa Granda
38 Hotel Venus

PLACES TO EAT
7 Café Marylin
14 Municipal Market
21 El Baturro
24 Café La Isabelica
25 Restaurante Matamoros
26 Cafetería Las Enramadas
27 Taberna de Dolores
29 Panadería Doña Neli
42 Caffi Caribe
44 Santiago 1900
45 Paladar La Juliana

OTHER
1 Iglesia de San Francisco
2 Oficina de Reservaciones de Campismo
3 Teatro Oriente
4 Ballet Folklórico Cutumba
5 Iglesia del Carmen
9 Sala Van Troi/Cabildo Teatral Santiago
10 Reservaciones de Turismo Parque Baconao
11 Museo Tomás Romay
13 Patio Los Dos Abuelos
15 Antiguo Cárcel Provincial
16 Casa de Diego Velázquez (Museo de Ambiente Histórico Cubano)
17 Banco Financiero Internacional
18 Ayuntamiento
19 Banco Nacional de Cuba
20 Club 300
22 Museo Municipal Emilio Bacardí Moreau
23 Gobierno Provincial
28 Sala de Conciertos Dolores
31 Balcón de Velázquez
32 Cine Rialto
33 Centro de Llamadas Internacionales
34 Casa de la Cultura Miguel Matamoros
36 Rumbos
37 Casa del Estudiante (Casa de la Trova)
39 Casa Natal de José María de Heredia
40 Elvira Cape Library
41 Museo del Carnaval
43 Sala Teatro El Mambí
46 Museo de la Lucha Clandestina
47 Disco Anteneo

.... Walking Tour

Central Santiago de Cuba

0   100   200 m
0   100   200 yards

museum has exhibits downstairs relating to the 19th-century independence struggles plus a collection of weapons and Cuban paintings upstairs. There are a dozen paintings by the Tejada brothers, including *La confronta de billetes* by José Joaquín Tejada Revilla (1867 – 1943), a typical product of the Spanish *costumbrismo* school that sought to portray the customs and life of the common people. Dating from the 1920s, the **Gobierno Provincial** or 'Poder Popular,' at Pío Rosado and Aguilera opposite the Museo Bacardí, is the seat of the provincial assembly.

Just east is the Plaza de Dolores at Aguilera and Porfirio Valiente, a former marketplace now dominated by the 18th-century **Iglesia de Nuestra Señora de los Dolores**. After a fire in the 1970s the church was rebuilt as a concert hall. The **Taberna de Dolores**, Aguilera No 468, is a 19th-century warehouse-residence with characteristic balconies, ironwork, and decorative woodwork. A number of hard-currency restaurants and cafes surround this square, and there's often a local band playing for tourists and locals.

North of the Center

Two blocks north of Parque Céspedes at Félix Peña No 505 is the **Iglesia de Nuestra Señora del Carmen**, an 18th-century hall church that is the final resting place of composer Estéban Salas (1725 – 1803), mentioned in the Culture section at the beginning of this chapter.

Two blocks northwest is the 18th-century three-nave **Iglesia de San Francisco**, Juan Bautista Sagarra No 121. The 18th-century **Iglesia de Santo Tomás**, Félix Peña No 308, a couple of blocks north, has a bell tower and three naves.

Two blocks northwest of Santo Tomás is the **Museo-Casa Natal de Antonio Maceo**, Los Maceos No 207 at Corona (closed Monday, admission US$1). The famous general who fought in both wars of independence was born in this early 19th-century house on June 14, 1845. In his 1878 Protest of Baraguá, Maceo rejected any compromise with the colonial

authorities and went into exile after further combat. During the 1895 war he was second in command (after Máximo Gómez) and died fighting in western Cuba in 1896. The museum's exhibits highlight Maceo's life.

Head east five blocks on Los Maceos and then south on General Banderas to No 226, the **Casa Museo de Frank y Josue País** (Monday to Saturday 9 am to 5 pm, admission US$1). The País brothers organized the underground section of the M-26-7 in Santiago de Cuba until Frank's murder by the police on July 30, 1957. The exhibits tell the story.

South one block and east another two is the 18th-century **Iglesia de la Santísima Trinidad**, General Portuondo No 661 at General Moncada. It has a decorated ceiling and neoclassical side altars. A huge ceiba tree stands in front of the church.

Northeast of the Center

The **Parque Histórico Abel Santamaría** at General Portuondo and Avenida de los Libertadores is the site of the former Saturnino Lora Civil Hospital. On July 26, 1953, a group of revolutionaries led by Abel Santamaría occupied the hospital during the attack on the adjacent Moncada Barracks. Most of those involved were later murdered by Batista's troops. On October 16, 1953, Fidel Castro was tried in the Escuela de Enfermeras here for leading the Moncada attack, and it was in this building that he made his famous 'History Will Absolve Me' speech. A site museum (Monday to Friday 8 am to 5 pm, Saturday and Sunday 8 am to noon, admission US$1) opened in 1976 with a photo exhibit on socioeconomic conditions in Cuba during the 1950s.

The **Moncada Barracks** at General Portuondo and Avenida Moncada are named for Guillermón Moncada, who was imprisoned here in 1874 and who later fought for independence from Spain during the 'Little War' of 1879. The first barracks on this site were constructed by the Spanish in 1859, and in 1938 the present buildings were completed. On the morning

DAVID STANLEY

After the revolution, the new government recreated the bullet holes in the Moncada Barracks that Batista's forces had filled in.

of July 26, 1953, more than one hundred revolutionaries led by Fidel Castro attacked Batista's troops in the building, which was then the second most important military garrison in Cuba. The revolutionaries hoped the assault would signal a general uprising throughout Cuba. In 1960, after the triumph of the revolution, the barracks were converted into a school called Cuidad Escolar 26 de Julio, and in 1967 a major museum (Monday to Saturday 9 am to 5 pm, Sunday 9 am to 1 pm, admission US$1) was installed near gate No 3, where the main attack took place. The museum outlines the history of Cuba from the Spanish conquest to the present, with half the exhibits related to the revolution. A scale model of Moncada illustrates the 1953 assault. If you're interested in Cuban history, it's worth asking for a guide to show you around (don't forget to tip).

The **Palacio de Justicia**, Avenida de los Libertadores and Calle H, also figured prominently in the assault on Moncada as fighters led by Raúl Castro provided covering fire from the rooftop. The trial of the bulk of the Moncada defendants was held here in September 1953.

From this area one can return to the center of town via **Plaza de Marte**, a 19th-century Spanish parade ground where prisoners were executed by firing squad during the colonial era. Today Plaza de Marte contains monuments to the various heroes of Cuban independence. A block west at the corner of Saco and Monseñor Barnada is the **Museo Tomás Romay** (Tuesday to Saturday 9 am to 5 pm, Sunday 9 am to 1 pm, admission US$1) with natural history, archaeology, and modern art displays. Anyone interested in bird watching should ask for an ornithologist named Luis who works at the museum. For a donation, he will gladly take visitors to a nature reserve just outside town.

East of the Center

Santiago de Cuba's old upper-class neighborhood is **Vista Alegre** on the east side of town. From near Hotel Las Américas, Avenida Manduley runs east through Vista Alegre past many stately neocolonial mansions, some of which were converted into schools, clinics, cultural centers, government offices, restaurants, and museums after the former owners left for exile in the US. La Maison at No 52 is a fancy fashion boutique. The **Centro Cultural Africano Fernando Ortiz**, Avenida Manduley No 106 (Monday to Saturday 9 am to 5 pm, admission US$1), contains an exhibition of artifacts from Africa. Restaurant El Tocororo at No 159 is another fine old mansion.

The large eclectic palace at the corner of Avenida Manduley and Calle 11 is now the **Palacio de Pioneros**. In a corner of the garden there's an old Mig fighter plane on which the younger pioneers can play. The traffic circle at Avenida Manduley and Calle 13 contains an impressive marble statue of poet José María Heredia y Heredia.

Around the corner at Calle 13 No 154 is the **Casa del Caribe** where you can buy books on Cuban culture, including the Casa's own magazine, *Del Caribe*. The Casa del Caribe was founded in 1982 to study Caribbean life and each year it organizes the Festival of Caribbean Culture. The Promotor Cultural inside the building can arrange mini-courses with tutors experienced in most aspects of Cuban culture, including Afro-Cuban religions and popular music and dance.

Santiago de Cuba's **Parque Zoológico** (Tuesday to Sunday 10 am to 5 pm, admission US$1) is on Avenida Raúl Pujol, one km east of Hotel Santiago de Cuba. To get there from the Casa del Caribe, go west a block to Calle 11 and then south four blocks to the zoo.

Next to the zoo entrance is a huge *ceiba* tree known as the **Arbol de la Paz** (Peace Tree), which is surrounded by cannons and an iron fence. Beneath the boughs of this tree Santiago de Cuba's Spanish garrison surrendered two weeks after the Battle of San Juan Hill. Continue through the grounds of the adjacent Motel San Juan to **San Juan Hill** where US, Cuban, and Spanish troops faced one another on July 1, 1898. Some of the original cannons and trenches can still be seen, but notice how the inscriptions have been removed from the bronze figure of the 'Rough Rider' in the center of the park (admission free but beware of hustlers). An amusement park is nearby.

Three km east of San Juan Hill on the way to the Gran Piedra and Baconao is the **Centro Urbano Abel Santamaría**, a large housing estate with row after row of prefabricated four-story apartment blocks assembled by volunteer microbrigades during the 1970s. Unlike the dismal slums that lurk on the fringes of many Latin American cities, this complex has supermarkets, kindergartens, schools, clinics, and all the other accouterments of contemporary Cuban life. A look around is sure to evoke opinions one way or another.

South of the Center

You can easily see most of the sites mentioned above on foot, but to get to El Morro Castle south of the city you'll need motorized transportation. If you don't mind waiting, you can catch bus No 212 from Avenida de los Libertadores opposite the Hospital Provincial Saturnino Lora to Ciudamar on the Carretera Turística, a 15-minute walk from El Morro. If you do take the bus, before going on to the castle itself take the ten-centavo ferry across to **Cayo Granma**, a picturesque little island of red-roofed dwellings just inside Bahía de Santiago de Cuba. On the island you'll find Restaurante El Cayo and the privately run Paladar El Marlen (opposite the Iglesia de San Rafael), both good for a seafood lunch. On its run from Ciudamar to Cayo Granma the ferry also stops at La Socapa on the west side of the harbor mouth.

Most visitors arrive at the **Castillo de San Pedro del Morro** by taxi, rental car, motorcycle, or private car. The castle stands dramatically on a 60-meter-high bluff on the east side of the harbor entrance, 10 km southwest of town via Carretera del Morro (which passes the airport access road). El Morro was designed in 1587 by the Italian military engineer Giovanni Bautista Antonelli to protect the town from pirates, but it was actually built between 1633 and 1693. Today its walls shelter a pirate museum tracing events from colonial times to the present. It's open weekdays from 9 am to 5 pm, weekends 8 am to 4 pm (admission US$1), and is one of Santiago de Cuba's top sights.

An ironically named **Carretera Turística** winds 13 km up the bay from El Morro to Parque Alameda near the railway station. Along the way you'll pass juxtaposed images of beauty and desolation, including a large cement factory, a thermal power plant, and scenic views of Santiago de Cuba Bay. It makes for a memorable drive if you have a car (and a good map), but walk it only if you're very fit.

West of the Center
Heading west on Aguilera from Parque Céspedes to the **Antiguo Carcel Provincial** (1906) at No 131. Fidel Castro and other rebels were incarcerated here immediately after the 1953 Moncada attack. On the corner of Padre Pico and Aguilera is the **Municipal Market**, and south on Padre Pico are a series of picturesque steps leading to the **Tivoli** neighborhood, where many French immigrants settled in the early 19th century. From this hill the views of mountains, city, and bay are picturesque.

On November 30, 1956, revolutionaries attacked a police station at General Jesús Rabí No 1, up the slope to the right of the uppermost Padre Pico steps, in an attempt to divert attention from the arrival elsewhere in Oriente of Fidel Castro's guerrillas. The colonial-style station now houses the **Museo de la Lucha Clandestina** (Tuesday to Sunday 9 am to 5 pm, admission US$1), a museum describing the underground struggle against Batista.

A couple of blocks west of this museum down Diego Palacios is **Parque Alameda**, a popular promenade that opened in 1840

and was redesigned in 1893. Toward the end of the day you can watch the sun set across Bahía de Santiago de Cuba from this park. Unfortunately the bay's waters have been polluted by the petroleum refinery and are much too dirty for swimming. (When the refinery was in private hands the owners kept it clean to avoid heavy fines, but since the government took over, environmental controls have been sacrificed on the altar of higher production.)

Opposite the old clock tower and **Aduana** (customs house) at the north end of Parque Alameda is the **Fábrica de Tobacos César Escalante**, Avenida Jesús Menéndez No 703, a working cigar factory open weekdays from 7 am to 4 pm. A shop on the premises sells the finished cigars.

Northwest of the Center
The original **Bacardí Rum Factory** (Fábrica de Ron) is north on Avenida Jesús Menéndez, opposite the unfinished new railway station on the north side of town. The factory was founded by the Bacardí family in 1838, but after the revolution the Bacardí company moved to Puerto Rico taking the Bacardí patent with them and the Santiago de Cuba product was renamed Ron Caney. Also produced here are quality rums such as Havana Club, Ron Santiago, Ron Varadero, and Caribbean Club, as well as local brands such as Ron Palma, Los Marinos (Paticruzado), and Ron Caribe. The factory consists of three sections: the production room, the aging storehouse (with 42,000 barrels of rum), and the bottling section. In total the distillery produces nine million liters a year, 70% of it exported, and most of the 326 employees are women. Free factory tours depart from the Barrita Ron Havana Club, a tourist bar at the entrance to the factory, weekdays from 9 am to noon and 1 to 4 pm.

The **Cementerio Santa Ifigenia**, off Avenida Crombet one km northwest of the distillery, has been in use since 1868. Among the many notable figures in Cuban history buried here are Carlos Manuel de

Céspedes (1819 – 1874), Emilio Bacardí y Moreau (1844 – 1922), the mother and widow of Antonio Maceo, Frank País, and those who died during the attack on the Moncada Barracks in 1953. Cuba's national hero, José Martí, rests in a large octagonal mausoleum erected here in 1951. You can see the Martí mausoleum for free from the parking lot, but if you wish to enter the cemetery itself, you must pay US$1 for an official guide. (Horse carts travel up Avenida Jesús Menéndez from Parque Alameda to Parque Barca de Oro via Cementerio Santa Ifigenia regularly throughout the day. A ride costs one peso per person.)

Organized Tours

Rumbos has offices in Hotel Las Américas and across the street from the Hotel Casa Granda. It offers excursions to Baconao (US$40), La Gran Piedra (US$35), and El Cobre (US$27); tours to the Tropicana Santiago nightclub (US$45 including admission and one drink), and transfers to the Cabaret San Pedro del Mar (US$12.50).

The Promotor Cultural at the Casa del Caribe, Calle 13 No 154 at the corner of Calle 5 in Vista Alegre, arranges private transportation and guides for groups interested in ecotourism activities, including hiking in the Sierra Maestra.

It's not hard to hire a private car and driver to tour the vicinity of Santiago de Cuba for US$20 a day for the whole car, gas included. Ask the drivers of private vehicles with yellow license plates or ask the managers of paladares. You can usually make such arrangements with any of the private taxis parked on the west side of Plaza de Marte (although they won't speak English). Obviously, it's much cheaper than taking a tour.

Special Events

The Festival of Caribbean Culture is held in Santiago de Cuba in early June or July with exhibitions, music, song, and dance from all around the Caribbean. Santiago de Cuba's carnival during the last two weeks of July and the first week of August was formerly the hottest in Cuba, but since 1991 it has been suspended. The Bolero de Oro is also in August. In December there's the International Choir Festival.

Places to Stay

City Center The five-story *Hotel Casa Granda* (☎ /fax 86035), Heredia No 201 at General Lacret on Parque Céspedes, is a stately old hotel that reopened in October 1995 after renovations lasting six years. The 55 rooms with bath are US$42/54 single/double low season, US$54/78 high season, while the three suites go for US$51/65 low season, US$65/94 high season. Meals are served in the elegant a-la-carte restaurant on the main floor from 7 to 10 am, noon to 3 pm, and 7 to 11 pm (dinner costs around US$11 plus drinks). The hotel's 5th floor Roof Garden bar is well worth the price of a cocktail or beer for its excellent view of central Santiago lde Cuba. This is the only tourist hotel right in the middle of town and your best bet for a splurge.

About nine blocks to the east is the two-story *Hotel Libertad* (☎ 2-3080), Calle Aguilera No 658 on Plaza de Marte, which now willingly accepts foreigners in its 18 rooms at US$8 double with fan or US$12 with air-con. Nearby is the two-story *Hotel Rex* (☎ 2-6314), Avenida Victoriano Garzón No 10 on Plaza de Marte, with 25 rooms for US$12 double. Twenty persons involved in the 1953 Moncada Barracks incident stayed at the Rex just prior to the attack.

The centrally located 48-room *Hotel Venus* (☎ 2-2178), Hartmann No 658 between Aguilera and Heredia, is a majestic old four-story hotel that only accepts Cubans (check as this could change). The four-story *Hotel Bayamo* (☎ 2-8435), Saco No 312, a decrepit old hotel with an impressive lobby, has 44 rooms for five pesos single or double. The only way to know if they'll give you a room is to ask.

The ornate four-story *Hotel Imperial* (☎ 2-8917), Saco No 251 and Félix Peña opposite Parque Ajedrez, has 47 rooms, none of them more than 14 pesos.

The two-story *Hotel Perla de Cuba* (☎ 2-7275), Sanchez Hechavarria 4 opposite the train station, has 29 rooms used mostly by railway employees and is not officially open to travelers. A hard currency bribe might convince the desk clerk to let you in (this could also work elsewhere), but expect the Perla de Cuba, Imperial, Bayamo, and Venus all to be extremely basic.

North of the Center *Motel El Rancho* (☎ 3-3280) is at Altos de Quintero, four km north of Santiago de Cuba off the Carretera Central. There's no sign at the entrance, so drive slowly and ask. The 30 rooms with bath in a long single-story block go for US$20/24 single/double low season, US$23/30 high season. The motel's large thatched restaurant offers a good view of Santiago de Cuba.

East of the Center The city's top hotel is the red, white, and blue *Hotel Santiago de Cuba* (☎ 4-2634, fax 4-1756), Avenida de las Américas and Calle M, erected in 1991. The 302 rooms weigh in at US$69/90 single/double low season, US$89/113 high season, but all have real bathtubs. Buffet-style meals in the restaurant cost US$7/15/15 for breakfast/lunch/dinner. There's a good view from the Pico Real bar on the 15th floor, and the hotel also has a swimming pool and disco. The Cubana Airlines office in this five-star hotel is the best place to book your flights.

Across the street is *Hotel Las Américas* (☎ 4-2011), Avenida de las Américas and Avenida General Cebreco. Its 68 rooms with bath cost US$26/35/42 single/double/triple low season, US$32/43/52 high season. Built in 1975, this four-story hotel has a rectangular swimming pool, a 24-hour cafeteria, a disco, and a Havanautos car-rental office. The location, facilities, and rates make it a good medium-priced choice.

About six blocks from Hotel Las Américas is the four-story *Hotel Universitario Birret* (☎ 4-2390), Calles L and 7 in Ampliación de Terrazas, also known as the 'MES.' There's no sign, but you'll know it from the two flights of steps and awnings. The 20 rooms with fridge, TV, and radio are a good value at US$15/20/25 single/double/triple, although every two rooms share a toilet and shower. The hotel bar is also good, but there isn't much to eat in the restaurant.

The three-story *Hotel Deportivo* (☎ 4-2146), a modern hotel in the Ciudad Deportivo opposite the Estadio Guillermón Moncada off Avenida Las Américas, has 84 rooms with fridge, TV, and two, three, or four beds for US$15 for the room. It's another good budget choice.

Villa Gaviota (☎ 4-1368), Avenida Manduley No 502 in Vista Alegre, is a bit over one km northeast of Hotel Las Américas via Avenida Manduley. It's in a nice residential neighborhood with a pleasant atmosphere. The 30 rooms in single-story concrete bungalows are US$24/29 single/double low season, US$30/40 high season. There's a swimming pool at the top of the hill.

The *Motel San Juan* (☎ 4-2478), on San Juan Hill one km east of Hotel Las Américas via Avenida Raúl Pujol, was formerly called Motel Leningrado. The 112 rooms with bath in several two-story blocks are US$24/32 single/double low season, US$26/35 high season. A rectangular swimming pool, a night club, and a Transautos car-rental agency are on the premises. Various hookers and hustlers hang around the motel entrance trying to make a buck. Bus Nos 101 and 127 pass this way.

South of the Center *Motel Bella Vista* (☎ 9-1017) is on the Carretera Turística overlooking Bahía de Santiago de Cuba. A small room in a long single-story block costs US$12/15 single/double and suites are US$16/20. Although cheap, the Bella Vista is two km southwest of Parque Alameda along a depressing, dusty road that passes an ugly flour mill. Few foreigners ever stay in this rather basic 49-room establishment.

Motel Versalles (☎ 9-1016), Avenida

de Versalles at Calle 4 off Carretera del Morro, is between the center of Santiago de Cuba and the airport. There are 52 overpriced rooms in long blocks for US$48/63 single/double, plus eight bungalows at US$55/73 (prices firm year-round). The motel has a disco (open nightly from 8:30 pm, admission US$10), but the Versalles is remote from all points of interest and not a good choice in any way.

Hotel Balcón del Caribe (☎ 9-1506) on Carretera del Morro is near the Castillo del Morro, 10 km south of town. The 72 rooms in the hotel's main two-story blocks are US$25/28 single/double low season, US$28/32 high season, while the 24 cliff-side duplex bungalows are US$33 single or double low season, US$39 high season. There's a rectangular swimming pool and right next door is Cabaret San Pedro del Mar with a gala floorshow. This friendly hotel is worth considering if you have a rental car and don't wish to stay in town.

Homestays Cubans are allowed to rent out up to two rooms in their private homes, and it's not hard to arrange this in Santiago de Cuba. Some places have cooking facilities. Any of the hustlers in the center of town can take you to a place, but their US$5 commission will jack the price up to US$15 double from the usual US$10. To avoid this, ask other travelers if they have an address and then go there alone.

For example, Carmen Folgar (☎ 2-6143), Aguilera No 612, Apartment No 5, has two rooms and she'll do your cooking if you buy the groceries. If Carmen's place is full, she might be willing to call around and find you another place.

Tata at Paladar El Amanecer, Calle 10 No 224 at Bravo Corrioso in Reparto Santa Bárbara, arranges private rooms for US$10 double.

Also check with the Promotor Cultural at the Casa del Caribe (☎ 4-2285, fax 4-2387), Calle 13 No 154, corner of Calle 5 in Vista Alegre. The Casa del Caribe routinely arranges private accommodations in local homes for individuals or small groups that go to Santiago de Cuba to take courses,

and they'll probably be happy to do the same for you.

One reader enjoyed the home of Janet Sánchez Oliva and her husband, Jorge Eduardo Soulari (☎ 4-3994, Calle 13 No 309 between 12 and 14 in Reparto Vista Alegre).

Places to Eat

The tap water in Santiago de Cuba is barely potable and it's better to buy bottled water at a hotel shop. Some local dishes to try here include *congrí* (rice cooked with red or black beans), *yuca con mojo* (cassava with garlic sauce), and *macho* (pork).

Self-Catering Everybody pays in dollars at the large supermarket and department store below the Hotel Rex on Plaza de Marte (Monday to Saturday 9 am to 5 pm, Sunday 8:30 am to noon). There's also a vegetable market two blocks west of Parque Céspedes at Aguilera and Padre Pico. *Panadería Doña Neli*, Aguilera and Plácido on Plaza de Marte, is a hard-currency bakery.

If you're heading into the city from the airport, you could stop at the Centro Comercial Cuba, which has a well-stocked if pricy supermarket. It's on Carretera al Aeropuerto 100 meters before the airport terminal.

The long line of peso-paying Cubans is discreetly across the street at *Cremería Palmita*, Félix Peña and Heredia below the cathedral.

Santiago de Cuba's main ice-cream place, *Coppelia La Arboleda* (☎ 2-0435), Avenida de los Libertadores and Avenida Victoriano Garzón (Tuesday to Sunday 9 am to 11:40 pm), also charges foreigners in dollars, Cubans in pesos. If you don't like that, there's an ice-cream parlor at Boulevard Dolores that accepts only dollars.

Cafes *Caffi Caribe*, Bartolomé Maso No 260 directly behind the cathedral, serves small cups of takeout coffee for pesos.

Marylin, General Lacret and Saco, serves cups of herbal tea to standing patrons.

You can sit down at *Casa de Té*, Aguilera at Parque Céspedes, and *Cafe La Isabelica*, Aguilera and Porfirio Valiente on Plaza de Dolores (open 24 hours). Cubans pay the same price in pesos that foreigners pay in dollars.

City Center The most renowned of the state-run restaurants is *Santiago 1900* (☎ 2-3507), Bartolomé Masó No 354 between Pio Rosado and Hartmann (Tuesday to Sunday 1 to 3 pm and 6 pm to midnight). Located in the former personal residence of the Bacardí clan, it's now run by the gastronomical school. Expect to pay around US$25 for dinner for two (Cuban and international cuisine); otherwise, drinks are available on the patio. Advance reservations will soften your landing here.

The *Fontana Di Trevi*, Saco No 260 (daily 11 am to 8 pm), serves microwave pizzas to peso-paying Cuban customers who are admitted in shifts (*turnos*) every two hours. Dollar-paying foreigners are usually admitted quickly without formalities (US$2 for a small pizza).

El Baturro, Aguilera at Hartmann (closed Tuesday), is another government-run place featuring chicken and pork dishes (assuming they have any meat in the fridge).

The easiest place to get a decent meal is 'Boulevard Dolores' on the north side of the Plaza de Dolores. Here you'll find three hard-currency restaurants, an ice-cream parlor, and a 24-hour cafeteria, all run by the Cuban tourism company Rumbos. *Cafeteria Las Enramadas* features chicken, sandwiches, ice cream, and beer served out on the shady terrace. Study the menu carefully as an involuntary tip may be deducted from your change although the 'mistake' will be quickly corrected if you protest. It's a traveler's hangout and most of Santiago de Cuba's hookers and hustlers eventually show up here.

The three regular restaurants at Boulevard Dolores should be approached with caution as mediocre food and sloppy service come with the fancy furnishings and prestige location. *Restaurante Don Antonio* (daily noon to midnight) next to Los Enramados has Cuban dishes. Aside from the main menu there are 'ofertas' (special offers) of set meals for US$4.50, but you must specifically request the separate menu listing these. Next door is *Restaurante La Perla del Dragón* (daily 2 pm to 2 am) offering chop suey and chow mein, and beyond that *Restaurante Teresina* (daily 10 am to 11 pm) with pizza and spaghetti. To be blunt, it's better to ignore these three poorly managed places and stick to Las Enramadas. Most visitors seem to feel the same way – notice the empty tables.

Restaurante Matamoros, on the west side of Plaza de Dolores near Las Enramadas (daily 10 am to 11 pm), is more expensive than its neighbors because the prices are based on pesos. The food is said to be poor, but you can sometimes hear live music upstairs in the evening.

Taberna de Dolores (also known as El Bodegón), Aguilera No 468, serves lobster, fish, and beef. It's more colorful than the touristy places at Boulevard Dolores across the square but also more expensive because of the exchange rate used in pricing the menu.

A better bet for a real meal than any of the official restaurants just mentioned is a privately run paladar, of which there are an increasing number around Santiago de Cuba. For example, try *Paladar Las Gallegas*, Bartolomé Maso No 305, or *Paladar La Juliana*, Padre Pico No 359 just below the Padre Pico steps (steaks US$4). Just walk in and ask to see the menu (if there's no menu, take care).

A reader recommended the privately run *Restaurante Caridad* on Diego Palacios between General Lacret and Hartmann. *Restaurante Sarabanda*, Diego Palacios No 305, tried to overcharge him slightly.

East of the Center *Santiago XXX Aniversario* on the 15th floor of Edificio La Plata, Avenida Victoriano Garzón and Valeriano Betancourt, serves 'Cubana and international cuisine' punctually at noon, 7 pm, and 10 pm to peso-paying Cubans who have somehow managed to make reservations.

Pekin, Avenida de Céspedes and Calle A, four blocks north of the Moncada Barracks (daily noon to 2 pm and 6 to 10:45 pm), has 'Chinese cuisine.'

La Parrillada, Avenida Manduley No 102, two blocks east of Hotel Las Américas, serves grilled meats.

El Tocororo, Avenida Manduley No 159 (Monday to Saturday noon to 9 pm), has chicken for US$8 and lobster for US$25. It's very elegant, if expensive.

A privately run place five blocks south of Hotel Santiago de Cuba is *Paladar El Amanecer* (☎ 4-3627), Calle 10 No 224 at Bravo Correoso in Reparto Santa Bárbara. Your hostess Tata prepares excellent meals for US$3 to US$4 (lobster or shrimp US$6 to US$8).

South of the Center Many tourists eat lunch at *Restaurante El Morro*, near the entrance to Castillo de Morro. Hustlers in front of the castle will try to get you over to a paladar on Cayo Granma that pays them a commission.

Entertainment

Cinemas *Cine Rialto*, Félix Peña No 654 next to the cathedral, is considered the best cinema in town although it shows mostly videos and the air conditioning is usually on the blink. Other cinemas to try include *Cine Cuba*, Saco No 304; *Cine Capitolio*, Avenida Victoriano Garzón No 256; and *Cine Latinoamericano*, Avenida Victoriano Garzón No 390.

Discos *Anteneo*, Felix Peña No 755, runs a student disco in the former law school building (erected in 1885) every Friday, Saturday, and Sunday at 9 pm (admission US$3).

The *Casa del Estudiante*, Heredia No 204 between Hartmann and General Lacret, has a students' disco for couples only on Saturday and Sunday at 8 pm.

The *Havana Club Disco* at Hotel Las Américas, Avenida de las Américas and General Cebreco, won't admit unaccompanied Cuban women, so they stand outside and wait for a foreigner willing to take them in (admission US$3 per person). *Discoteca Espanta Sueño* at the Hotel Santiago de Cuba across the street is open daily except Monday from 10:30 to 3 am (admission US$5 including one drink).

Ciroa, Avenida Manduley at Calle 13 seven blocks northeast of Hotel Las Américas, is a night spot with a band playing. Cubans frequent the place Friday to Sunday from 9 pm (admission US$2).

Three other local night spots to check are *Club 300*, Aguilera No 302 off Parque Céspedes; *Club Caribe*, Avenida de Céspedes and Calle A; and *Club Turey*, Patricio Lumumba No 213 (Wednesday to Sunday 7:30 pm to midnight).

Theaters The *Sala Teatro El Mambí*, Bartolomé Masó No 303 near the cathedral, and the *Sala Van Troi/Cabildo Teatral Santiago*, Saco No 415, present plays in Spanish in the evening and puppet/clown theater for children on the weekend mornings. The *Teatro Oriente*, Saco No 115, has a live show for children Friday at 5 pm and Saturday and Sunday at 10 am (US$2). It's fun for adults as well as kids. Another children's show is staged Saturday and Sunday at 5 pm at the *Teatro Martí*, Félix Peña No 313 at General Portuondo opposite the Iglesia de Santo Tomás.

The *Teatro José María Heredia*, Avenida de las Américas and Avenida de los Desfiles, is a huge theater facing the Plaza de la Revolución on the northeast side of town. There's often children's theater here, too, on Saturday and Sunday mornings at 10 am.

Cabarets *Tropicana Santiago*, on Circunvalación four km northeast of Hotel Las Américas, presents Las Vegas–style floorshows with lots of scantily clad dancers Wednesday to Sunday at 10 pm. After the show you can visit a disco in the same complex. Most hotels have package tours to the Tropicana Santiago for US$30 per person including admission and one drink. Cubans pay only 50 pesos to get in, but their seating area is separate from the one for foreigners.

Cabaret San Pedro del Mar (☎ 9-1486), Carretera del Morro next to the Hotel Balcón del Caribe, seven km southwest of the center, presents more of the same daily (except Tuesday) from 8:30 pm to 1:45 am with the floorshow beginning at 10 pm (admission US$5). Until the Tropicana opened, this was Santiago de Cuba's premier night spot.

Folk & Traditional Music The *nueva trova* originated at Santiago de Cuba's famous *Casa de la Trova*, Heredia No 208. Folk groups play here almost continuously to bring in the tourists and attract dollar tips.

Similar is the *Patio Los Dos Abuelos*, Francisco Pérez Carbo No 5 on the east side of Plaza de Marte. Traditional Cuban music is performed live here every evening at 10 pm.

Dance The *Ballet Folklórico Cutumba* (☎ 2-5860 or 2-2182), Saco No 170 (upstairs) between Corona and Padre Pico, is an internationally known Afro-Cuban folkloric dance group founded in 1960. You can visit the group's dance workshop to see them practicing Tuesday to Sunday 8:30 am to 1 pm and 4:30 to 8 pm, and there's a small bar hidden away in back where you can get cold beer (ask the way). If you're in Santiago de Cuba on a weekend, don't miss Cutumba's exciting dance show staged in the workshop every Sunday morning at 10:30 am (admission US$3). This is your chance to see dances such as the *tumba francesa, columbia, gagá, guaguancó, yagüetó, tajona,* and *conga oriental*. It's one of the best programs of its kind in Cuba.

Also ask about practice sessions at the studios of the Conjunto Folklórico de Oriente, Hartmann No 407 at Sagarra, and the Coro Madrigalista, Pío Rosado No 555 at Aguilera. Traditional dancing also takes place at various *focos culturales* around town on weekend evenings.

Classical Music The *Sala de Conciertos Dolores*, Aguilera and Mayía Rodríguez, is in a former church on Plaza de Dolores.

Pubs/Bars The *Claqueta Bar*, Felix Peña No 654 next to Cine Rialto just off Parque Céspedes, has a nice open terrace where cold beer is served. There's sometimes live music and salsa dancing in the evening.

The *Casa del Vino*, Heredia No 254, also known as the 'Bodeguita de Heredia,' serves shots of rum and crème de menthe 24 hours a day.

The *Bar del Marqués*, inside Restaurant Don Antonio on Plaza de Dolores, is one lof the few tourist bars not connected to a hotel.

Nuevo Lido, Núñez de Balboa and Pedro Alvarado, two blocks south of Hotel Santiago de Cuba, is a rough-and-ready local bar which opens at 4:30 pm.

Spectator Sports
The *Estadio de Béisbol Guillermón Moncada*, Avenida de las Américas, is on the northeast side of town within walking distance of the main hotels. During the baseball season from November to March there are games on Tuesday, Wednesday, and Thursday at 7:30 pm, Saturday and Sunday at 1:30 pm. The local team is the 'Orientales.'

Things to Buy
Shops Artesanía Santiago, Felix Peña No 673 below the cathedral, has Cuban handicrafts and cold drinks.

Fantasía (☎ 6840), Avenida de Céspedes between Calles D and E, a few blocks northeast of the Moncada Barracks, is a sort of Cuban Woolworth selling consumer goods. It's open Monday to Saturday 9 am to 6 pm, Sunday 9 am to noon.

La Maison, Avenida Manduley No 52 (daily 10 am to 8 pm), sells upmarket clothing and has a fashion show nightly at 9 pm (admission US$5). It's just around the corner from Hotel Las Américas and Hotel Santiago de Cuba.

Tienda Cubalse, Avenida General Cebreco and Calle 15 in Vista Alegre (weekdays 9 am to 5 pm, Saturday 9 am to noon), is a department store selling imported goods. There's always a line of Cubans waiting to enter, but foreigners are allowed to skip the queue.

The Centro Comercial Cuba, on Carretera al Aeropuerto 100 meters before the airport terminal, contains a well-stocked supermarket open Monday to Saturday 9 am to 6:30 pm, Sunday 9 am to 1:30 pm. A half dozen other shops are on the mall, plus a cafeteria. Everything here is for dollars only and the prices aren't cheap.

Art Galleries A number of galleries in the center sell original paintings and prints to visitors. By international standards the prices are reasonable but always get an official receipt. Have a look at the Galeria de Arte de Oriente, General Lacret No 656 between Aguilera and Heredia on the east side of Parque Céspedes, and at Galeria Santiago below the cathedral on the south side of Parque Céspedes. Several more galleries are along Heredia east of here.

A local painter, Efraín Nadereau, Aguilera No 170 two blocks west of Parque Céspedes, welcomes foreign visitors in his studio. Nadereau is also a noted poet with 16 books in print.

Arte Universal (☎ 4-1198) is on Calle 1 between Calle M and Terraza in Ampliación de Terrazas, behind the Monument to the Martyrs of Bolivia two blocks north of Hotel Las Américas. It presents art exhibitions Monday to Saturday 9 am to 7 pm, Sunday 9 am to 5 pm (admission US$1).

Getting There & Away

Air Antonio Maceo International Airport (airport code SCU) is seven km south of Santiago de Cuba off the Carretera del Morro. This airport receives international flights from Aruba, Caracas, and Santo Domingo on the Venezuelan carrier Aeropostal; from Santo Domingo on Cubana; from Toronto on Air Transat, Canadian Airlines, and Royal Airlines; and from Düsseldorf and Munich on the German carrier LTU International Airways. Details on these flights appear in the Getting There & Away chapter.

Cubana flies nonstop from Havana to Santiago de Cuba three or four times a day (761 km, 2½ hours, US$68 one way). Every Tuesday there's a flight to/from Baracoa (US$17). The main Cubana office (☎ 2-4156) in Santiago de Cuba is on Félix Peña between Heredia and Bartolomé Masó below the cathedral, but a less crowded Cubana office selling tickets only to dollar-paying foreigners is inside Hotel Santiago de Cuba.

Bus The Terminal de Ómnibus Nacionales, Avenida de los Libertadores No 45 at Calle 9, is three km northeast of Parque Céspedes. There are buses to Guantánamo (six a day, 86 km), Bayamo (twice daily, 127 km), Holguín (daily, 143 km), Las Tunas (daily, 203 km), Camagüey (daily, 326 km, seven hours), Santa Clara (daily, 597 km, 12 hours), Cienfuegos (daily, 663 km), Matanzas (daily, 797 km), and Havana (twice daily, 884 km, 14 hours). Notice the huge crowd of Cubans trying to get tickets at the 'Lista de Fallos' office (no special facilities for foreigners). Colectivos (vehicles that take various passengers at once) to Guantánamo wait outside the terminal until they're full (20 pesos per person); otherwise, you can go standing in the back of a truck (two hours, five pesos).

The Terminal de Ómnibus Intermunicipales, Avenida de los Libertadores and Calle 4 opposite the Servi-Cupet gas station, two km northeast of Parque Céspedes, has four buses a day to El Cobre.

The Estación de Intermunicipales Serranos, Avenida Jesús Menéndez and Sánchez Hechavarría opposite the train station, has local buses to Carletón Blanco (six daily), Chivirico (three daily), Contramaestre (twice daily), Dos Caminos (three daily), Palma Soriano (eight daily), and San Luis (three daily).

Train Rather than bothering with these crowded buses, you're better off going by train. The Terminal de Ferrocarriles, Avenida Jesús Menéndez and Sánchez Hechavarría near the port west of the center, has daily trains to Bayamo (US$4.05), Manzanillo (US$5.75), Guantánamo (US$4), Antilla, Jiguaní, Contramaestre, Holguín (143 km, 3½ hours, US$5), Camagüey (319 km, 5½ hours,

US$13), Ciego de Ávila (421 km, eight hours, US$18), Matanzas (764 km, 13 hours, US$32), and Havana (856 km, 14½ hours, US$35).

Cubans can buy advance train tickets for pesos at the Centro Único de Reservaciones, Aguilera No 565 near Plaza de Marte, but foreigners must purchase their tickets for dollars at the Ladis office (☎ 2-2254) upstairs in the train station. Reservations are a good idea for the Havana train but are not usually necessary on local services.

Lots of private taxis (with yellow plates) are waiting in front of the Santiago de Cuba train station when the train from Havana arrives. They charge US$2 to most hotels.

Yacht Cruising yachts can use the Marina Punta Gorda (☎ 9-1446) near Cayo Granma just inside Bahía de Santiago de Cuba, about eight km southwest of town. Try to contact the authorities over channel 16 (VHF) prior to arrival. The disadvantages of tying up here include boat wakes and ocean swells, loud recorded music from a nearby (and wretched) restaurant, fallout from a cement factory, petroleum stains from the polluted harbor waters, and rapid barnacle growth due to the high water temperature. In light of these considerations and the US blockade you'll probably have the place to yourself. Unfortunately, sailors don't have many alternative anchorages along this coast, the closest and best being at Chivirico.

Getting Around

To/From the Airport A metered taxi to/from the airport costs about US$5, but you can also get there on bus No 212 or 213 from Avenida de los Libertadores opposite the Hospital Provincial Saturnino Lora. If you board one of these buses at the airport, make sure it's headed for the *centro* and not some distant suburb.

Bus The only city buses you're likely to use are bus No 212 to the airport and Ciudamar (from Avenida de los Libertadores opposite the Hospital Provincial Saturnino Lora), and bus No 214 to Siboney (from Avenida de Céspedes No 110 near Restaurante Pekin). You pay the conductor about 20 centavos. These buses run every hour or so.

A ride in a collective horse and carriage along a fixed route costs about one peso per person.

Car Transautos has offices below Hotel Casa Granda on Parque Céspedes and at Motel San Juan. Havanautos is at Hotel Las Américas.

The Servi-Cupet gas station, Avenida de los Libertadores and Avenida de Céspedes, is open 24 hours.

Taxi There's a large tourist taxi stand in front of Hotel Santiago de Cuba. To call a tourist taxi dial ☎ 9-1012 or 3-1398.

Many private taxis with yellow plates park on the west side of Plaza de Marte, charging US$1 for short rides around town.

Passenger-carrying motorcycles are found on General Lacret just off Parque Céspedes beside the town hall and at Parque de los Estudiantes around the corner from the Hotel Santiago de Cuba. A ride to Castillo de Morro is around US$2 to US$3.

Cycle rickshaws and bicycles with an extra seat in back charge about five pesos per person per ride.

PLAYA SIBONEY

Playa Siboney, 19 km southeast of Santiago de Cuba, is the closest clean Caribbean beach to the city. This local village has a regular bus service from Santiago de Cuba and all the usual facilities for Cubans, making it a good choice for anyone interested in a couple of days in private accommodations. It's much quieter during the week.

Things to See

The **Granjita Siboney** is an historic farmhouse on the road to Santiago de Cuba, two km inland from Playa Siboney and two km south of the Gran Piedra turnoff. It was from here at 5:15 am on July 26, 1956, that a convoy of 26 cars under the command of Fidel Castro left to attack the Moncada Barracks in Santiago de Cuba. Of the 119 persons involved in the action, six died in combat and 55 were murdered after their capture by Batista's troops. The present site museum (daily 9 am to 5 pm, admission US$1) contains weapons, documents, and personal effects from the time. Notice the well beside the building where weapons were hidden prior to the attack. In 1973, 26 monuments were erected along the highway between the Granjita Siboney and Santiago de Cuba to commemorate the attack.

The **Galería Generación del Centenario**, adjacent to the Granjita Siboney, presents changing art exhibitions (closed Monday).

Places to Stay & Eat

Villa Siboney (☎ 039-261) includes five bungalows facing the main beach and a number of apartments in the village. Ask at the 'carpeta' below the apartment building beside the commercial center.

Your best bet is a private room in the home of a local resident. Any of the beach guys will gladly help you find one, although their commission will jack up the price.

One way to find a room on your own is to avoid the beach area when you first arrive and continue down the road parallel to the coast toward the post office. A place to start is the home of Marlene Pérez (☎ 039-219), Avenida de Serano, on the coast a block over from the post office beside the house of Maria Antonia (a personal friend of Fidel's known to everyone). Marlene has two fan-cooled rooms offering some privacy upstairs facing the sea for US$10 or US$15 double depending on the room. Meals are US$3 each. There's a protected driveway in which you can park a rental car. Marlene's husband, Eduardo, is a university professor who speaks good English. If their rooms are full, they'll place you in another house in Siboney.

Getting There & Away

Bus No 214 runs to Siboney from Avenida de Céspedes No 110 near Restaurante Pekin in Santiago de Cuba not less frequently than once every two hours. Other buses from Santiago de Cuba include bus No 424 to Juraguá and bus No 428 to Baconao, but these run only once or twice a day. Passenger trucks also do the trip to/from Santiago de Cuba for a peso a head.

Getting Around

Your host or hostess should be able to help you hire a private car and driver for visits to the Gran Piedra and the attractions of Parque Baconao for about US$20 a day.

LA GRAN PIEDRA

The Cordillera de la Gran Piedra, a branch of the Sierra Maestra, is a 30-km-long barrier separating the Caribbean Coast from the Valle Central. It culminates in a gigantic rock 1214 meters above sea level. The range has a cool microclimate and it's best to come in the morning as the peak is often covered by clouds in the afternoon. The tourist hotel near the summit, 28 km east of Santiago de Cuba, makes a good (if expensive) base for hikes through the pine and fern forest.

Things to See

Near the beginning of the access road to the Gran Piedra, 16 km southeast of Santiago de Cuba, is the **Prado de las Esculturas** (admission US$1). Here 20 monumental sculptures of metal, wood, concrete, brick, and stone by the artists of nine countries are scattered along a one-km loop road through the park.

Up on top of the mountain range itself, one km before Villa La Gran Piedra, is the **Jardín Botánico** (admission US$1) with orchids and other flowers. Ask someone to point out the yellow, orange, and violet *ave de paraíso* flower, named for its resemblance to a 'bird of paradise.' It blooms all year long.

Almost anyone can climb the 459 stone steps from the hotel restaurant to the summit of **La Gran Piedra** (1214 meters).

The huge rock on top measures 51 meters long and 25 meters high and weighs an estimated 63,000 tons. On a clear day there are excellent views and supposedly one can even see as far as Haiti and Jamaica (free admission).

Cafetal La Isabelica, two km beyond La Gran Piedra, currently houses a museum (Tuesday to Sunday 8 am to 3 pm, admission US$1) describing the coffee-processing technology of a century ago. The impressive two-story stone mansion with its defensive ditch on the back side and three large coffee drying platforms was built in the early 19th century by French émigrés from Haiti. One can wander around the pine-covered plantation grounds.

Places to Stay & Eat

Villa La Gran Piedra (☎ 5-1098), near the mountain's summit, has 22 one- and two-bedroom cottages with shower, TV, and terrace for US$45 double or US$60 for four persons. There's a somewhat expensive restaurant/bar.

Getting There & Away

A winding paved road climbs 12 km up the mountain's spine. It's not possible to visit by public transport as the public bus arrives only every other day (when in service). A tourist taxi from Santiago de Cuba costs around US$35 return, and a private taxi with yellow license plates might charge US$20 for the same return trip.

PARQUE BACONAO

Parque Baconao covers 800 sq km between Santiago de Cuba and the Río Baconao, an area that has been declared a biosphere reserve by UNESCO (and which is often incorrectly called a 'national park' in tourist literature). The northern slopes of the Sierra Maestra catch the Northeast Tradewinds and are moist, while areas such as this on the southern side of the range are much drier. You'll even see cactus growing along the coastal cliffs.

Baconao is a 30-km-long coastal plain squeezed between the Gran Piedra Range

and the Caribbean. Only a few small beaches grace these rocky shores and despite all the ballyhoo about this being a national park a large area has been fenced off as the Coto de Caza El Indio (El Indio Hunting Reserve). A number of commercial tourist attractions have been created here and there are numerous hotels of every type and description. The hotels are well spaced and you won't find a hotel row of the Varadero type. It's a good choice if you want to combine a beach holiday with a little exploring.

Things to See

The **Valle de la Prehistoria**, six km southeast of the Playa Siboney turnoff on the main road to Baconao, features tacky lifesize concrete models of about 40 dinosaurs that are fun for the kids (daily 7 am to 6:30 pm, admission US$1, plus US$1 per camera and US$5 per video camera).

Probably the most worthwhile man-made attraction of Parque Baconao is the **Conjunto de Museos de la Punta**, adjacent to the Complejo La Punta Shopping Center, two km east of the Valle de la Prehistoria (daily 8 am to 5 pm, admission US$1). The ticket allows entry to several museums containing classic cars, dolls, folk costumes, paintings, ceramics, stamps, cigar seals, and archaeological artifacts.

Ten km southeast of La Punta is the **Comunidad Artística Verraco**, a community of artists with a dozen small galleries that provide an opportunity to meet the artists and see (and perhaps buy) their works.

El Mundo de la Fantasia is a miniature Disneyland-style children's park one km east of the Balneario del Sol Resort. A mini-zoo and a small amusement park are just beyond.

The **Aquario Baconao** between the Balneario del Sol Resort and Hotel Carisol (Tuesday to Sunday 9 am to 4 pm, admission US$3) presents dolphin shows at 10 am, 11:30 am, and 2:45 pm. The aquarium has a good collection of sharks, seals, sea lions, fish, and lobsters, and you can

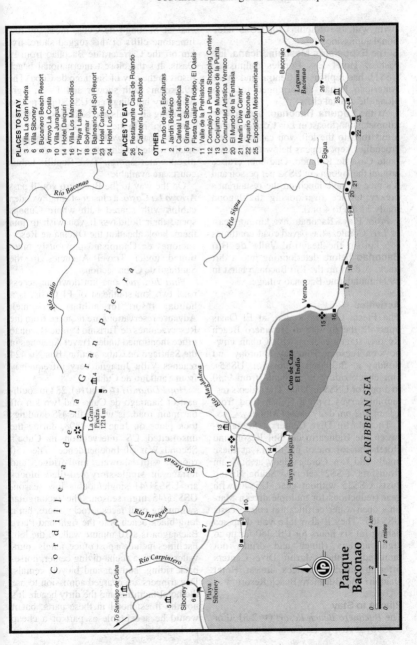

PLACES TO STAY
3 Villa La Gran Piedra
6 Villa Siboney
8 Bucanero Beach Resort
9 Arroyo La Costa
10 Villa Juraguá
14 Hotel Daiquirí
16 Villa Los Mamoncillos
17 Playa Larga
18 Solymar
19 Balneario del Sol Resort
23 Hotel Carisol
24 Hotel Los Corales

PLACES TO EAT
26 Restaurante Casa de Rolando
27 Cafetería Los Robalos

OTHER
1 Prado de las Esculturas
2 Jardín Botánico
4 Cafetal La Isabelica
5 Granjita Siboney
7 Fiesta Guajira Rodeo, El Oasis
11 Valle de la Prehistoria
12 Complejo La Punta Shopping Center
13 Conjunto de Museos de la Punta
15 Comunidad Artística Verraco
20 El Mundo de la Fantasía
21 Marlin Dive Center
22 Aquario Baconao
25 Exposición Mesoamericana

Río Baconao

Cordillera de la Gran Piedra

La Gran Piedra
1214 m

Río Indio

Río Arenas

Río Magdalena

Río Juraguá

Río Carpintero

Río Sigua

Baconao

Laguna
Baconao

Sigua

Verraco

Coto de Caza
El Indio

Playa Bacajagua

Playa Siboney

Siboney

To Santiago de Cuba

CARIBBEAN SEA

Parque
Baconao

0   1   2   4 km
0   1   2 miles

swim with the dolphins for US$5 additional admission.

The **Exposición Mesoamericana**, just east of Hotel Los Corales (admission US$1), has replicas of Central and South American Indian art arranged in caves along the coastal cliffs.

At the **Laguna Baconao**, a couple of kilometers northeast of Los Corales and up a dirt road to the left, you can see a few crocodiles kept in pens below the Restaurante Casa de Rolando. One-hour cruises around the lagoon are US$2 per person and it's nice to have lunch on the restaurant's breezy terrace overlooking the lagoon (daily 11 am to 4 pm).

From Playa Baconao, five km northeast of Los Corales, the paved road continues 3½ km up the beautiful **Valle de Río Baconao** before deteriorating into a dirt track. A dam up the Río Baconao burst in 1994, inundating Baconao village.

Activities

The Fiesta Guajira Rodeo, at El Oasis opposite the turnoff to Bucanero Beach Resort, stages rodeos with Cuban cowboys on Tuesday, Thursday, Saturday, and Sunday at 2:30 pm (admission US$5). Horseback riding is available from 9:30 to 5 pm for US$5 an hour. The rodeo's restaurant serves typical Cuban food from 10 am to 2 pm daily except Monday.

The Marlin Dive Center at Sigua between the Balneario del Sol Resort and Hotel Carisol picks up divers at these hotels and Los Corales daily at 8:30 am (transfers US$2 return). Scuba diving costs US$25 without gear, US$40 with gear (reductions for multiple dives). Marlin's open-water certification course costs US$365. They'll also take you deep-sea fishing for six hours for US$360 for up to eight anglers (lunch and drinks not included). Other Marlin Dive Centers offering similar services are at Hotel Daiquirí and Bucanero Beach Resort.

Places to Stay

The *Bucanero Beach Resort* (☎ 2-8130 or 5-4596) at Arroyo La Costa, 25 km south-east of Santiago de Cuba, faces the low limestone cliffs of this rugged shore, five km off the Carretera de Baconao from El Oasis. It's the closest international beach resort to the city of Santiago de Cuba. The 192 rooms with shower and TV in eight two-story buildings are US$50 per person including all meals and activities. A swimming pool is in the center of the resort and a short coastal walkway leads west to a small white beach where there are organized water sports. Two floodlit tennis courts are available.

On the way to the Bucanero you'll pass *Arroyo La Costa*, a cluster of small wooden cabins with shared bath where Cubans spend their holidays. If you wish to join them, book ahead at the Oficina de Reservaciones de Campismo previously mentioned under Travel Agencies in the Santiago de Cuba section.

Villa Juraguá, one km down an access road two km southeast of El Oasis, is a holiday resort for military personnel. Advance reservations are required from the Reservaciones de Turismo Parque Baconao office mentioned under Travel Agencies in the Santiago de Cuba section. Bus No 424 reaches Villa Juraguá very infrequently from Santiago de Cuba.

Hotel Daiquirí (☎ 5-4016), 28 km southeast of Santiago de Cuba and two km off the main road, is where the US landings took place on June 22, 1898, during the unsolicited US intervention in Cuba's Second War of Independence. The 150 rooms with shower, mini-fridge, and terrace in single-story red-tiled blocks are US$31/41 single/double low season, US$35/45 high season. The rectangular swimming pool faces a rocky shore, but a long black beach is to the right and Playa Bacajagua is a 10-minute walk to the left. Facilities include a post office, tennis court, water sports, a scuba-diving center, horseback riding, and car and bicycle rentals. Day trippers are charged admission to use the hotel facilities and the dirty beach. It's not the finest hotel in these parts, but it would be acceptable as part of a cheap package tour.

Villa Los Mamoncillos at Verraco, 37 km southeast of Santiago de Cuba, is another holiday resort for Cubans. If you'd like to stay in one of the two-story bungalows here, book ahead through the Reservaciones de Turismo Parque Baconao office in Santiago de Cuba.

Playa Larga, one km east of Verraco, features small cabins with shared bath and an empty swimming pool. It's a nice spot right on the coast and you might be able to camp here. Get advance information at the Oficina de Reservaciones de Campismo in Santiago de Cuba. More small beach cabins are at *Solymar*, a few hundred meters east of Playa Larga.

Canada's Delta Hotels manages the colonial-style *Balneario del Sol Resort* (☎ 2-6005) at Sigua, 44 km southeast of Santiago de Cuba. This is a top-notch resort. The 115 rooms with shower, satellite TV, and balcony or terrace are in five two-story buildings. They cost US$40 single or double low season, US$50 high season. Meals are served buffet style (extra charge). There's only an artificial beach, but a freshwater swimming pool is next to the seawall and a natural saltwater tidal pool extends along the coastal cliffs in front of the hotel. Car, moped, and bicycle rentals are possible and full sporting facilities are available.

At Playa Cazonal near the east end of the coastal road through Parque Baconao is *Hotel Carisol* (☎ 2-8519), built in 1990 and presently managed by the German LTI chain. The 166 rooms with shower and color TV are in a two-story colonial-style complex surrounding a large swimming pool. It's not cheap at US$72/114/156 single/double/triple low season, US$95/160/189 high season, but that includes buffet-style meals, local drinks, and many activities. The Carisol shares a white sandy beach with the nearby Hotel Los Corales, but the main beach is a five-minute walk along the shore to the left from the hotel. A tennis court and a disco are available.

One km east of the Carisol and also under LTI management is *Hotel Los Corales* (☎ 2-7204), 51 km southeast of Santiago de Cuba. The 144 rooms with shower, mini-fridge, and TV are in several two-story blocks erected in 1992. It works out cheaper than the Carisol for US$26/42 single/double low season, US$34/52 high season, plus US$7.50/8.50/9.50 for breakfast/lunch/dinner (if desired). Drinks are expensive (and they even go to the extreme of charging exorbitant prices for canned drinks in the hotel shop to discourage guests from stocking their refrigerators). There's a large swimming pool, tennis courts, and disco. Although closer to the beach, the three five-story Cuban apartment blocks overlooking Los Corales are an eyesore. Scooter rentals are US$5 for the first hour and then US$3 for additional hours, gas included.

Places to Eat

Fast-food chicken is sold at *Cafetería El Rápido* in the Complejo La Punta Shopping Center near the turnoff to Hotel Daiquirí. It's open 24 hours and public toilets are adjacent. *Restaurante La Punta* in the nearby Conjunto de Museos serves upmarket Italian cuisine.

Restaurante Casa de Rolando, overlooking the Laguna Baconao, is OK for a Cuban-style lunch (daily 11 am to 4 pm).

The *Cafetería Los Robalos*, near the east end of the road at Playa Baconao, is a local peso restaurant with little to eat.

Getting There & Away

Bus service is rare along the 40-km coastal road from Playa Siboney to Playa Baconao. If you're staying at a resort, you should be able to rent a scooter or car; otherwise, try hiring a private car with yellow plates to drive you around.

Getting Around

Havanatour has an office beside the Servi-Cupet gas station in the Complejo La Punta Shopping Center near the turnoff to Hotel Daiquirí. There are also car-rental offices at Hotel Daiquirí and Balneario del Sol Resort.

Servi-Cupet in the Complejo La Punta Shopping Center is open 24 hours.

Cuba's most sacred pilgrimage site

EL COBRE

The **Basílica de Nuestra Señora del Cobre**, 20 km northwest of Santiago de Cuba on the old road to Bayamo, is Cuba's most sacred pilgrimage site. It all began in 1606 when three fisherman found a wooden image of the Virgin floating on the Bahía de Nipe in northeastern Cuba. It carried a label reading 'I am the Virgen de la Caridad.' The statue was brought to the copper mine at El Cobre and in 1608 the first hermitage was erected. A century later a larger sanctuary was built and the present shrine opened in 1927.

On May 10, 1916, Pope Benedict XV declared the image the national saint of Cuba, and in 1936 it was solemnly crowned at an elaborate ceremony in Santiago de Cuba. In 1977 the church was proclaimed a 'basilica menor' and many pilgrims come here on September 12. In santería (the Afro-Cuban religion), the Virgen de la Caridad is associated with Ochún, the Yoruba goddess of love (represented by the color yellow), and in the minds of many worshipers devotion for the two is intertwined.

Copper has been mined at El Cobre since pre-Columbian times and a Spanish mine was in existence by 1530, the oldest European-operated mine in the Western Hemisphere. Still Cuba's largest producer of copper ore, the current mine is visible on a hillside opposite the basilica. Fellows in the parking lot behind the basilica will offer to 'give' you shiny but worthless pyrite stones from the mine.

Things to See

The basilica is open daily from 6:30 am to 6 pm with mass at 8 am on Monday, Tuesday, Thursday, Friday, and Saturday, (also at 8 pm on Thursday), and at 8 am, 10 am, and 4:30 pm on Sunday. When a mass is in session Nuestra Señora de la Caridad faces the congregation from atop the altar inside the basilica. At other times the icon is rotated around and can be seen up close from a small chapel accessible up a stairway from a visitor's center on the back side of the basilica. The exterior door of this center is closed during mass.

The visitor's center contains numerous ex-votos, small objects, and mementos left by the faithful to give thanks for some favor bestowed by the Virgin. You'll see crutches, military medals, and photos of loved ones. Devotees often leave a small gold pendant representing the bodily part cured or protected by divine intervention. The most notable of these is a small golden guerrilla fighter donated by Lina Ruz, the mother of Fidel Castro, to protect her son during his Sierra Maestra campaign against Batista. Ask one of the nuns to point it out to you. Until 1986 the Nobel Prize won in 1954 by Ernest Hemingway for his novel *The Old Man and the Sea* was also on display, but that year a visitor smashed the showcase's glass and carried the medal off. The police recovered the medal two days later, but it has since been kept in a vault and cannot be seen.

Places to Stay & Eat

The *Hospedaría El Cobre* (☎ 3-6246), a large two-story building behind the basilica, has 16 rooms with one, two, or three beds for five pesos per person, plus two 40-bed dormitories for four pesos per person. Meals are served punctually at 7:30 and 11:30 am and 6:30 pm, and there's a pleasant large sitting room with comfortable chairs. If you pay for your lodging in pesos, you should certainly make an equivalent hard-currency donation to the sanctuary to avoid the bad karma of having accepted room and board from the church for the equivalent of less than a dollar.

Getting There & Away

There are four buses a day to El Cobre from the Terminal de Ómnibus Intermunicipales, Avenida de los Libertadores and Calle 4, opposite the Servi-Cupet gas station in Santiago de Cuba.

A tourist taxi from Santiago de Cuba costs around US$27 return.

EL SALTÓN

One of Cuba's most attractive mountain hotels is in Tercer Frente municipality, 75 km west of Santiago de Cuba just west of Cruce de los Baños. *Villa El Saltón* (☎ 6-1175) was built in 1990 as a nature lodge. The 22 well-constructed rooms with hot shower, fridge, and satellite TV in four wooden two-story blocks cost US$25/32 single/double. The electric circuits in the rooms are overloaded, so you might ask the maid where the fuse box is located. A sauna, hot tub, and massage are available at an additional charge, and there's horseback riding for US$2 an hour. The food and drink in El Saltón's large thatched restaurant/bar are on the expensive side. On the property is a waterfall with three natural pools for swimming. A stairway from between block Nos 2 and 3 leads up to a mirador with a view of the falls from above. Beyond that is a trail to the cocoa plantations at Delicias del Saltón.

Getting There & Away

To get to El Saltón, continue west from El Cobre to Cruce de los Baños, four km east of Filé village. El Saltón is three km south of Filé.

You may hear about a road over the Sierra Maestra from Cruce de los Baños to Río Seco on the south coast, 10 km east of the Sierra Mar Resort. Southbound from Cruce de los Baños, the first 10 km are OK, passing through small villages in coffee-growing country. Then the road deteriorates into a very rough jeep track with some very slippery, steep sections that can only be covered by a four-wheel-drive vehicle in dry weather. In a regular car or in rainy weather, the last 20 km to Río Seco would be impossible, although ecotours in jeeps regularly use this road. It will test your driving skills!

CHIVIRICO

Chivirico is a big village of around 4000 inhabitants on the south-coast highway, 72 km southwest of Santiago de Cuba and 106 km east of Marea del Portillo. The deep Cayman Trench is just offshore, and clear waters wash the many beaches along the south coast. This area is in a rain shadow protected by the Sierra Maestra from the moist Northeast Tradewinds, and the relatively low rainfall complements the warm Caribbean currents flowing along these shores.

Cruising yachts will find excellent anchorage in a natural hurricane hole at Chivirico. It's the small bay on the east side of the hill with the red-roofed hotel on top. The Spanish fleet met destruction in a naval battle near here in 1898.

Places to Stay

The four-story *Sierra Mar Resort* (☎ 2-6337) is at Playa Sevilla, 60 km southwest of Santiago de Cuba. This big pyramid-shaped hotel is built into a terraced hillside with an elevator down to the brown-sand four-km beach. The 200 rooms with shower, satellite TV, and balcony cost US$95/160 single/double including buffet-style meals and most activities. Scuba diving and horseback riding are available for an additional charge. There's a large swimming pool, two floodlit tennis courts, a post office, and car rentals. From 8:30 am to 5 pm special free activities are organized for children ages two to 11 – perfect for parents who want some time to themselves. The Sierra Mar is managed by Canada's Delta hotel chain.

Motel Guamá (☎ 2-6125), on a hill seven km east of Chivirico and 65 km southwest of Santiago de Cuba, has eight rooms for US$24/30 single/double. It's used mostly by Cubans.

Farther west at Chivirico is *Los Galeones Resort* (☎ 2-6160) on a hilltop directly above the town. This small red-tiled Spanish-style hotel is also managed by the Canadian Delta hotel chain. The 34 rooms with shower, satellite TV, and balcony are overpriced at US$80/100 single/double low season, US$95/160 high season, including all meals and local drinks. Los Galeones has a swimming pool and sauna, and there's a small beach 100 meters below via a steep stairway. Children under 16 are not accommodated here.

Getting There & Away
Three buses a day run to Chivirico from the bus station opposite the train station in Santiago de Cuba.

Buses operate along the south coast from Chivirico to the Río Macío on the border of Granma Province in the morning and afternoon.

AROUND PICO TURQUINO
The first major battle fought by Fidel Castro's guerrilla army took place at **El Uvero**, 23 km west of Chivirico, on May 28, 1957. A government position guarded by 53 Batista soldiers was overwhelmed and much-needed supplies were captured. By the main road are two red trucks captured by the rebels and a double row of royal palms leads to a large monument commemorating the battle.

The **Ruta al Pico Real del Turquino** up Cuba's highest mountain (1972 meters)

begins at Las Cuevas on the south-coast highway, seven km west of Ocujal and 51 km east of Marea del Portillo. Along the way you pass Cuba's second highest peak, Pico Cuba (1872 meters). It should be possible to hire a guide at the trailhead, but allow six hours to go up and another four hours to come down. The route leads from Las Cuevas to La Esmajagua (600 meters, three km), Pico Cardero (1265 meters), Pico Cuba (shelter at 1650 meters, two km), and Pico Real del Turquino (1972 meters, 1.7 km). At last report there were shelters at La Esmajagua and Pico Cuba. It's possible to continue across the mountains to Alto del Naranjo and Santo Domingo (see the Gran Parque Nacional Sierra Maestra section in the Granma chapter). If you make it to the top, please let us know!

Five km west of Las Cuevas is the **Museo de La Plata** (closed Sunday afternoon and Monday, US$1 admission) at La Plata, next to the river just below the highway. The first successful combat of the Cuban Revolution took place here on January 17, 1957. The museum has three rooms with photos and artifacts from the campaign, and on a clear day you can see Pico Turquino from here. Marea del Portillo is 46 km to the east (see the Granma chapter). Don't confuse this La Plata with the Comandancia de La Plata, Fidel Castro's revolutionary headquarters high up in the Sierra Maestra.

Places to Stay
The *Base de Campismo La Mula* on the beach at the mouth of Río La Mula River, 12 km east of the Pico Turquino trailhead, has 65 small cabins used mostly by Cuban vacationers. The Oficina de Reservaciones de Campismo (mentioned under Travel Agencies in the Santiago de Cuba section) handles bookings here. The well-preserved wreck of the Spanish cruiser *Colón* lies where it sank in 1898, about 15 meters down and only 30 meters offshore near La Mula.

Province of Guantánamo

Guantánamo Province (6186 sq km) occupies the strategic eastern end of Cuba where the Atlantic Ocean meets the Caribbean Sea. To the north is the nickel mining region of Holguín Province, to the west Santiago de Cuba. From the lighthouse at Cabo Maisí on Cuba's easternmost headland, Haiti is clearly visible across the 80-km-wide Windward Passage.

Most of northern and western Guantánamo Province is taken up by the Macizo de Sagua-Baracoa range, while in the southwest the Cuenca de Guantánamo, a huge basin, tilts toward Bahí de Guantánamo. The north coast faces the prevailing tradewinds and is one of the wettest parts of Cuba. The dry southern coast is sheltered by mountains. The arid, cactus-covered hillsides of southern Guantánamo resemble North Africa, and the lush land around Baracoa could be in the South Pacific. The contrast with the cane fields and cattle lands of central Cuba is striking.

In the 16th century this mountainous area was the first part of the island to be colonized by the Spaniards, and a part of it is still occupied by what the Cubans regard as US imperialist troops. After the slave rebellion in Haiti in 1791, many French immigrants arrived in this area, promoting the cultivation of coffee, cotton, and sugar cane. The main agricultural activities today are sugar cane and beef cattle ranching in the Cuenca de Guantánamo, and coffee growing in the mountains of the north and east. Tourism focuses mostly on the old colonial town of Baracoa, while the long sandy beaches along the dry southern coast remain an undiscovered tropical paradise.

The telephone code for the whole of Guantánamo Province is 21.

GUANTÁNAMO

The city of Guantánamo was founded in 1819 between the Jaibo, Bano, and Guaso Rivers, and until 1843 it was called Santa

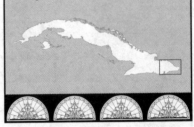

HIGHLIGHTS

- Infamous US naval base at the mouth of the Bahía de Guantánamo
- Dry cactus-covered hillsides of southern Guantánamo
- Appealing old colonial town of Baracoa
- Scenic coastal road to La Boca de Yumurí
- Alluring beach hideaway at Villa Maguana

Catalina del Saltadero del Guaso. It's a bustling big city (population 205,000) without any special attractions for visitors, although you might make it a stopover between Santiago de Cuba and Baracoa.

The highest temperature ever recorded in Cuba was the 38.6°C measured at Guantánamo Airport on August 7, 1969.

Orientation

Parque Martí, Guantánamo's central square, is several blocks south of the train station but five km east of the bus station, so it's preferable to arrive by train. The main tourist hotels are two km northwest of the train station; both of the peso hotels are near Parque Martí.

Information

Tourist Offices Try the Islazul Reservations Office (☎ 32-5991), Los Maceos No 663 between Paseo and Narciso López.

Post & Communications The post office is on the west side of Parque Martí.

Medical Services There's a hospital south of town along the road to Caimanera.

Things to See
The **Parroquia de Santa Catalina de Riccis** in the middle of Parque Martí dates from 1868. In front of the church is a statue of Major General Pedro A Pérez, erected in 1928.

The **Museo Provincial**, Martí and Prado (Tuesday to Saturday 8 am to noon and 2 to 6 pm, Sunday 8 am to noon, admission US$0.50), has a history collection housed in an old colonial prison.

Places to Stay
In Town The few tourists who visit this city usually stay at the modern, four-story *Hotel Guantánamo* (☎ 32-6015), Calle 13 Norte between Ahogados and 2 de Octubre on Plaza Mariana Grajales in Reparto Caribe, 2½ km northwest of the center. The 124 rooms with bath and TV are US$21/27 single/double low season, US$24/31 high season, and there's a swimming pool.

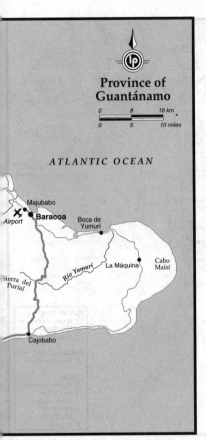

Province of Guantánamo

0   8   16 km

0   5   10 miles

ATLANTIC OCEAN

Majubabo

Baracoa

Airport

Boca de Yumurí

Río Yumurí   La Máquina

Cabo Maisí

Sierra del Purial

Cajobabo

Nearby on Calixto García, a block south of Parque Martí, is the *Hotel Brasil* (☎ 32-2080), a green four-story building with 35 rooms. These old peso hotels rarely accommodate foreigners, although they're always worth a try.

Outside Town *Villa La Lupe* (☎ 32-6102) is on the road to El Salvador five km north of Hotel Guantánamo beyond the entrance to the Autopista Nacional to Santiago de Cuba. It has 50 rooms with fridge and TV in several two-story blocks for US$14/18 single/double low season, US$17/22 high season. Get a room well away from the swimming pool unless you don't mind being blasted by loud music.

The *Hotel Caimanera* (☎ 99-414) on a hilltop at Caimanera, 21 km south of Guantánamo, has 19 rooms with bath and TV in a new two-story building flanking the swimming pool. Singles/doubles cost US$24/32. The restaurant specializes in *caldo de jaiba* (blue crab broth). You get a glimpse of the US naval base from this hotel.

Places to Eat
The state-run *Pizzería Holguín* is next to Cine Huambo on the east side of Parque Martí. Several privately operated paladares are near Parque Martí (ask around) and these serve full meals for about 25 pesos.

Entertainment
Guantánamo is the home town of Elio Revé, leader of the Orquestra Revé, which plays the local *son-changuí*, a combination of urban dance music and rural Afro-Cuban drumming. Elio Revé often plays in Havana, but you can usually hear groups playing son-changuí around town.

Concerts frequently take place at the *Casa de la Cultura*, next to the post office on the west side of Parque Martí.

Cine Huambo is on the east side of Parque Martí. *Cine América* is a block north.

Getting There & Away
Air Mariana Grajales Airport (airport code GAO) is 16 km southeast of Guantánamo

A good alternative is the *Casa de los Ensueños* (☎ 32-6304), Calle 15 Norte at Ahogados two blocks north of Hotel Guantánamo. It has only three rooms, two of which cost US$19/22 single/double and the suite is US$32/35. All rooms have aircon, fridge, and color TV, but ask for the back room as the other two (including the suite) are directly above the noisy restaurant. Downstairs a 24-hour hard-currency restaurant serves reasonably priced meals.

The two-story *Hotel Martí* (☎ 32-2456), Calixto García No 820 at the northeast corner of Parque Martí, has 26 rooms.

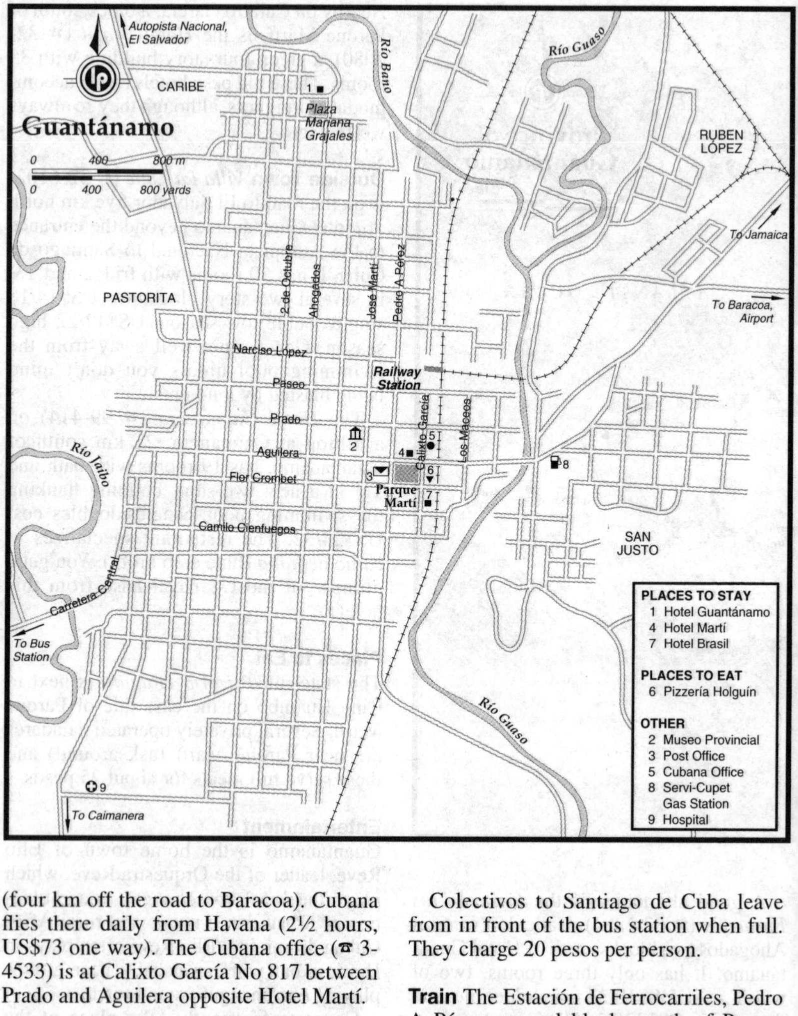

Guantánamo

PLACES TO STAY
1 Hotel Guantánamo
4 Hotel Martí
7 Hotel Brasil

PLACES TO EAT
6 Pizzería Holguín

OTHER
2 Museo Provincial
3 Post Office
5 Cubana Office
8 Servi-Cupet
  Gas Station
9 Hospital

(four km off the road to Baracoa). Cubana flies there daily from Havana (2½ hours, US$73 one way). The Cubana office (☎ 3-4533) is at Calixto García No 817 between Prado and Aguilera opposite Hotel Martí.

Bus The Terminal de Ómnibus, five km west of the center on the old road to Santiago de Cuba (a continuation of Avenida Camilo Cienfuegos), has buses to Santiago de Cuba (four daily, 86 km), Baracoa (daily, 150 km), Holguín (daily, 197 km), Camagüey (every other day, 375 km), and Havana (daily, 933 km).

Colectivos to Santiago de Cuba leave from in front of the bus station when full. They charge 20 pesos per person.

Train The Estación de Ferrocarriles, Pedro A Pérez, several blocks north of Parque Martí, has long-distance trains to Santiago de Cuba (daily, US$4), Holguín (daily), and Havana (daily), and local trains to Caimanera (four a day), Boquerón (twice daily), Honduras (daily), and Manuel Tames (twice daily). Foreigners must purchase tickets for dollars at the Ladis office in the station.

Car The Autopista Nacional to Santiago de Cuba ends 25 km west of Guantánamo where it joins the Carretera Central. You rejoin the Autopista just beyond El Cristo, 12 km outside Santiago de Cuba, but the route is poorly marked.

Getting Around

The Servi-Cupet gas station is at the beginning of the road to Baracoa, just east of the center. The Havanautos office is here.

GUANTÁNAMO US NAVAL BASE

Guantánamo is most famous for its US naval base near Caimanera, 21 km south of the city of Guantánamo. In 1903 the US government used the Platt Amendment, imposed on Cuba as a condition for independence, to slice off some 116 sq km of Cuban territory at the mouth of Bahía de Guantánamo. In 1934 the Roosevelt administration agreed to a Cuban request to change the grant in perpetuity to a 99-year lease.

The base was originally intended to protect the eastern approach to the Panama Canal, construction of which began in 1904. Today that mission is long over, but this oldest of US military bases on foreign soil remains useful as a thorn in Cuba's side.

Immediately after the 1959 revolution the Castro government asked the US to return the base to Cuba, but the US refused. As relations between the countries deteriorated Cuba cut off water and electricity supplies to the base, and the US troops on duty were denied permission to leave their camp. Instead of causing a war by trying to retake the base by force, the Cubans are patiently awaiting the year 2033 when the current lease expires.

The facility has served as a way station for Cuban and Haitian economic migrants trying to reach the US. In January 1992 some 11,000 Haitian refugees were being held here, and in August 1994 the base was used as a dumping ground for 32,000 Cubans picked up on their way to Florida by the US Coast Guard. Of these, some 8000 of the old, young, and sick were later allowed into the US on humanitarian grounds, and another 2000 returned voluntarily to Cuba. In May 1995 the Cuban and US governments signed an agreement under which most of the remaining 22,000 Cuban refugees at Guantánamo (18,000 of them young men between 18 and 21) would be allowed into the US. From this point on, illegal Cuban immigrants picked up by the US Coast Guard were to be returned to Cuba.

The country club affluence enjoyed by the 7000 US military personnel and dependents at Guantánamo is reflected in the golf course, sporting facilities, cinemas, and supermarkets. Supplies are flown into the two airstrips and ample docking facilities are available. The whole base is surrounded by trenches, land mines, security fences, and watch towers visible from afar. Countless millions of US tax dollars have been wasted on this wretched place.

Surprisingly, cruising yachts are allowed to sail through Bahía de Guantánamo between the US airstrips and radar towers to the Cuban ports of Caimanera and Boquerón. You're required to announce your arrival to the Americans over channel 12 (VHF), must fly an American courtesy flag, and are subject to boardings and searches. If the thought of being interrogated by a crew-cut 'imperialist' doesn't put you off, the whole experience can be educational. Just be aware that you won't be allowed to land at the naval base and make sure your vessel and documentation are squeaky clean. It's a unique opportunity to see a visible vestige of the Cold War in action, although evidence of having been there could raise unwelcome questions if you plan to spend much additional time in Cuba.

BARACOA

Baracoa is a quaint colonial town of around 50,000 inhabitants on a headland between two bays near Cabo Maisí at Cuba's southeastern tip. Christopher Columbus called the area Porto Santo, and in his journal he left a description of El Yunque, the anvil-shaped mountain due west across the Bahía de Baracoa. Baracoa is an Indian word meaning 'elevated land' and some of Cuba's most extensive forests blanket the highlands behind the town. The countless coconut trees along this coast give it the appearance of a South Seas island.

Baracoa was the first Spanish settlement in Cuba, founded in December 1512 by Diego Velázquez and 300 fellow Spaniards, and it served as the capital until 1515 when Velázquez moved to Santiago de Cuba. A bishopric subservient to the one in Santo Domingo (on Hispaniola) was established in Baracoa in 1518 and the town remained an important Spanish outpost. Between 1739 and 1742 work began here on three forts to protect Baracoa from pirates, smugglers, and the English.

The town remained isolated until 'La Farola,' the famous highway, was built across the Sierra del Purial from Guantánamo in the 1960s. Previously access had only been by sea. The road northwest from the Río Toa to the border of Holguín Province is still very rough, though passable by any car. In town itself, Baracoa's broad Malecón along the northeast side of town has been called the first oceanside drive in the Caribbean, and it's certainly one of the finest.

This lovely, relaxing town shelters a number of important sights, and visitors can make several interesting excursions in the surrounding area. Accommodations are abundant and getting there isn't as difficult now that there are direct flights from Havana and Santiago de Cuba and the airport is conveniently close to town. You can also arrive over La Farola standing in the back of a truck and sailors will find good anchorage in Baracoa Harbor.

Orientation

Baracoa's two bus stations are on opposite sides of the old town, and the airport is just across the bay, four km around by road. The closest train station is in Guantánamo, 150 km southwest. There are two good hotels in or near the old town and another next to the airport. Quite a bit can be seen on foot.

Information
Tourist Offices Try the Agencia de Reservaciones e Informacion Islazul, Maceo No 149 beside the cathedral.

Post & Communications The post office is at Antonio Maceo No 136 (daily 8 am to 8 pm), and public coin telephones are beside the building.

Bookstore A bookstore is at José Martí No 195.

Medical Services Farmacia Piloto, Maceo No 132, is open 24 hours, though after 9 pm service is through a small window.

Things to See
In Town The **Catedral de Nuestra Señora de la Asunción** (1833), Maceo No 152 on Parque Central, replaced an earlier church on another site. Inside is the Cruz de La Parra, said to have been erected by Columbus, but unfortunately the cathedral is only open for the occasional mass. Right in front of the cathedral is a bust of the Indian leader Hatuey, who was burned at the stake near Baracoa by the Spanish in 1512. Also on Parque Central is the neoclassical **Poder Popular**, Maceo No 137.

Baracoa's **Museo Municipal**, Martí at Malecón at the southeast entrance to town (daily 8 am to 6 pm, admission US$1), is housed in the **Fuerte Matachín** which was completed in 1802. The museum provides a good overview of local history and the staff will happily sell you a bar of 'Peters Baracoa' chocolate from the local factory for US$1.

Another Spanish fort, the **Fuerte de la Punta**, has watched over the harbor entrance at the northwest end of town since 1803. Today there's a restaurant within its walls.

Baracoa's third fort, **El Castillo de Seboruco**, begun by the Spanish in 1739 and finished by the Americans in 1900, is now a pleasant hotel. There's an excellent view of El Yunque's flat top from beside the swimming pool.

Northwest of Town The **Finca Duaba**, six km out on the road to Moa and then one km inland, is designed to give visitors a taste of country life. On this verdant farm you'll see tropical plants growing in profusion, have a chance to swim in the Río Duaba, and be served a typical Creole lunch, all for around US$10 per person. Visitors are welcome at the farm daily (except Monday) from noon to 4 pm, and it's best to let them know you'll be coming by booking at the Islazul reservations office next to the cathedral in Baracoa or through your hotel. Antonio Maceo landed at Duabo on April 1, 1895, to initiate the Second War of Independence against Spain.

The **Río Toa**, 10 km northwest of Baracoa, is the third longest river on the north coast of Cuba and it carries more water than any other river in the country. Cacao is grown in the Valle de Toa. Local boats on the Toa are called *cayucas* and Islazul can organize raft trips down the river if you give them some notice.

Special Events
The Semana de la Cultura (the first week of April) commemorates the landing of Antonio Maceo near here on April 1, 1895.

Places to Stay
In Town Provided they have room you'll be welcome at the three-story *Hotel La Rusa* (☎ 4-3011), Máximo Gómez No 161 on the Malecón by the sea. The 12 rooms with bath are US$14/16 single/double low season, US$16/20 high season. The hotel was built by Magdalena Rovieskuya, a Russian woman whose photos hang in the lobby. Alejo Carpentier wrote a novel about her called *La consagración de la primavera*, and former guests include Errol Flynn, Che Guevara, and Fidel Castro.

Another famous Baracoa hotel is the historic two-story *Hotel El Castillo* (☎ 4-2103) on Loma del Paraíso off Calixto García, a 10-minute walk from town. The 34 rooms with bath are US$19/25/30 single/double/triple low season, US$23/30/36 high season. There's a good view of

GLADYS ACOSTA
COURTESY OF CUBA POSTER PROJECT

the bay and El Yunque (the anvil-shaped mountain) from the swimming pool. A disco is on the premises.

The cheerful *Hotel Porto Santo* (☎ 4-3590), on Carretera del Aeropuerto only 200 meters from the airport terminal, is a modern hotel with Spanish colonial touches. The 36 rooms with bath in three two-story blocks and 24 cabañas are US$21/28 single/double low season, US$26/35 high season. Facilities include a swimming pool, post office, and the local Havanautos car-rental office. It's just across the bay from the old town, four km by road. A stairway leads down to the beach.

Baracoa's peso hotel is the nine-room *Hotel Plaza* (☎ 4-2283), Maceo No 148a above Cine-Teatro Encanto next to the cathedral (no sign). It isn't really set up to take foreigners.

Outside Town One of the nicest little hideaways in Cuba is *Villa Maguana*,

PLACES TO STAY
3 Hotel El Castillo
de Seboruco
8 Hotel Plaza
11 Hotel La Rusa

PLACES TO EAT
1 Restaurant Guamá
4 Casa del Chocolate
14 Restaurante El Baturro

OTHER
1 Fuerte de la Punta
2 Terminal de Ómnibus
Nacional
5 Casa de la Cultura
6 Post Office
7 Agencia de Reservaciones
e Información Islazul
8 Cine-Teatro Encanto
9 Catedral de Nuestra
Señora de la Asunción
10 Casa de la Trova
12 Cubana Office
13 Estación de Ómnibus
Intermunicipales
15 Fuerte Matachín
(Museo Municipal)

*Bahía de
Baracoa*

Ar los Mártires
José Martí
Antonio Maceo
Castillo
Dusny
Flor Crombet
Maximo Gómez
Coliseo

24 de Febrero
10 de Octubre
Marasi
Frank País
Pelayo
Cuelvo

*ATLANTIC
OCEAN*

To Airport,
Moa
Mariana Grajales
Libertad

5
▼4
6
7
9
8
10
3 ■
Rafael Trejo
Ciro Frías
Antonio Maceo
Frank Puente
12
Céspedes
14 ▼
Coroneles Galano
José Martí
13
Roberto Reyes
Limbano Sánchez
Paraiso
Galixto García
Rafael López
Antonio Maceo
Ariel Díaz
Moncada
Juración
Malecón

Rodney Coutin
Raúl Cepero Bonilla

15 🏛

Cemetery

To Guantánamo

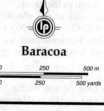

Baracoa

0   250   500 m
0   250   500 yards

facing one of the most perfect palm-fringed white-sand beaches in Cuba, 54 km southeast of Moa and 22 km northwest of Baracoa. It's about 10 km beyond Río Toa. The four rooms with fridge in a single-story guesthouse cost US$25 single or double. Meals are served in an adjacent pavilion. The common room has a noisy TV, but the rocking chairs on the porch are nice. Considering the small size, advance reservations through Hotel La Rusa in Baracoa or any Islazul office are essential.

Places to Eat

The local specialty is *cucurucho* (a coconut, guava, orange, or papaya sweet).

Among the state-run restaurants are *Restaurante El Baturro*, Malecón No 58 (daily noon to 2 pm and 6 to 9:20 pm), formerly known as El Caracol, and *Restaurant Guamá* in Fuerte de la Punta (Tuesday to Sunday noon to 2 pm and 6 to 9 pm).

A *pizzería*, Felix Ruene No 155 at Ciro Frías, seldom has pizza, but it's friendly enough.

A better bet is a privately operated paladar, such as *Paladar El Sabor*, Martí No 252. You'll eat well there for dollars, but don't let anyone lead you to the place or their commission will be added to your bill.

The *Casa del Chocolate*, Maceo No 123 (daily 7:20 am to 9:45 pm), occasionally has hot chocolate, ice cream, and snacks.

Entertainment

The *Casa de la Trova*, Martí No 149a next to the cathedral, is named for the famous trova singer Oscar Montero González (1915 – 1991), nicknamed 'Cayamba,' who sang often here. Today his son, Lázaro Montero, carries on the tradition. Unfortunately some of the regulars here tend to drink too much, which sort of spoils the atmosphere.

Also check the *Casa de la Cultura*, Maceo No 122 between Frank País and Maraví, for musical events.

Cine-Teatro Encanto, Maceo No 148, is next to the cathedral. Otherwise, there isn't much nightlife in Baracoa.

Getting There & Away

Air Aeropuerto Gustavo Rizo (airport code BCA) is off the road to Moa right next to Hotel Puerto Santo, four km from central Baracoa. Cubana has three weekly flights from Havana to Baracoa via Guantánamo (3½ hours, US$78 one way). There's also a useful flight to/from Santiago de Cuba (US$17) every Tuesday. The Cubana office (☎ 4-2171) in Baracoa is at Martí No 181.

Bus The Terminal de Ómnibus Nacional, Avenida Los Mártires and Martí, has buses to Santiago de Cuba (every afternoon, 236 km), Camagüey (once or twice a week, 490 km), and Havana (every other day, 1058 km). Every other day there's a bus to Guantánamo (150 km) that connects with the train to Havana. Buy a ticket as far in advance as possible.

The Estación de Ómnibus Intermunicipales, Galano and Calixto García, has no buses, but there are two or three trucks a day to Moa (78 km) and Guantánamo (four hours, 20 pesos per person). If you can't find a truck right to Guantánamo, take anything as far as San Antonio del Sur where you'll find onward trucks. Be prepared to stand the whole way.

Getting Around

There's a Havanautos car-rental office at Hotel Porto Santo. Servi-Cupet is four km out on the road to Guantánamo.

LA BOCA DE YUMURÍ

A good cement road runs 30 km east from Baracoa along the remote coast, passing many long black beaches and providing many excellent vistas. The road ends in La Boca de Yumurí where a ferry carries pedestrians across the Río Yumurí. The same ferry takes visitors a few hundred meters up the river through the canyon for US$1 per person.

It's a charming and peaceful place to visit, and the residents of Boca de Yumurí will offer to feed you fried fish or green drinking nuts for 'whatever you want to pay.' They'll also offer to sell you the colorful land snails called *polimitas*, but these have become rare as a result of being collected in large numbers.

Getting There & Away

Shared trucks between Baracoa and Boca de Yumurí cost 15 pesos per person, and bus No 721 occasionally arrives here from Baracoa for two pesos a head. A passenger truck will charge five pesos. If you haven't rented a car, ask at the local bus station at the corner of Galano and Calixto García in Baracoa and get an early start.

Isla de la Juventud (Special Municipality)

The shallow Golfo de Batabanó separates the 350-island Archipiélago de los Canarreos from the main island of Cuba, which lies 100 km north. This 2398-sq-km 'special municipality' is administered from Isla de la Juventud, by far the largest of the group. The municipality's second-largest island is the major Caribbean resort of Cayo Largo.

At 2200 sq km Isla de la Juventud proper is Cuba's second largest island (after the main island). Much of the island is flat, but towering marble hills stand on either side of the capital, Nueva Gerona; to the southwest other low slate hills reach 310 meters at La Cañada. The Ciénaga de Lanier across the lower middle of the island is Cuba's second largest swamp, while the largely uninhabited southern half of Isla de la Juventud is an uplifted limestone plain with few possibilities for agriculture. Mangroves line much of the island's 327-km-long coast.

Most of the population lives in the north, where a number of large dams hold water used to irrigate the island's grapefruit plantations. As on the main island cattle ranching is significant, but this is one of the few parts of Cuba without any sugar cane. Apart from agriculture, most residents are involved in the production of construction materials, including marble, ceramics (from kaolin), and bricks.

With 72,000 inhabitants, the 'Isla' (as Cubans call it) remains the least populated region of Cuba. Aside from Nueva Gerona and its 14,000 residents, there's the smaller town of La Fe, with about 9000 people. Everyone else lives in the countryside. In the late 19th century some fishing families from the British colony of the Caiman Islands established a settlement called Jacksonville (today known as Cocodrilo) on the southwest tip of the island, and you'll occasionally meet an unexpected English speaker.

HIGHLIGHTS

- Historic wooden ferry *El Pinero* in the friendly town of Nueva Gerona
- Engaging Finca El Abra, José Martí's place of exile
- Sinister Presidio Modelo, where Fidel Castro was once imprisoned
- Scuba diving along the 'Pirate Coast' dropoff at Punta Francés
- Indian cave paintings at Punta del Este
- White sands of Playa Sirena at Cayo Largo del Sur
- Tame turtles, iguanas, and pelicans on the tiny coral keys of the Archipiélago de los Canarreos

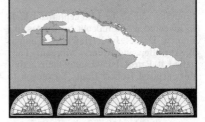

The big attractions here are the unspoiled nature and unhurried way of life. The island's museums contain mementos of two famous Cuban deportees, José Martí and Fidel Castro, and the entire Archipiélago de los Canarreos is one of the Caribbean's top scuba destinations. Getting here by boat or plane is a bit of an adventure. It's a great place to get off the beaten track on a personal voyage of discovery. You're sure to enjoy the people.

The telephone code for the whole island is 61.

History

The Indians called this island Siguanea, but when Christopher Columbus arrived in June 1494 he renamed it El Evangelista.

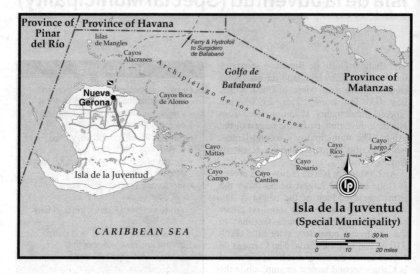

Isla de la Juventud
(Special Municipality)

CARIBBEAN SEA

From the 16th to the 18th centuries Isla de la Juventud was a hideout for pirates like Francis Drake, John Hawkins, Thomas Baskerville, and Henry Morgan. They called it Parrot Island, and their activities inspired Robert Louis Stevenson to write *Treasure Island*. In December 1830, the Colonia Reina Amalia (now Nueva Gerona) was founded, and during the 19th century the island served as a place of exile for independence advocates such as José Martí. Twentieth-century dictators such as Gerardo Machado and Fulgencio Batista followed the Spanish example by sending political prisoners – Fidel Castro included – to what was then called Isla de Pinos (Isle of Pines).

Just prior to Cuban independence in 1902, the US forced upon Cuba a one-sided treaty known as the Platt Amendment that included a provision placing Isla de Pinos outside the boundaries of the country pending further negotiations. Some 300 US colonists established themselves here soon after, and only in March 1925 did the US recognize the island as an integral part of Cuba. Batista declared Isla de Pinos a *zona franca* (free zone) in 1955, spurring many Americans to build hotels and resorts.

Prior to the 1959 revolution Isla de Pinos was sparsely populated, but during the 1960s and 1970s tens of thousands of young people volunteered to study here at the specially built 'secondary schools in the countryside' that now dot the plains of the northern portion of the island. Students at these schools worked the fields in shifts, creating the vast citrus plantations of today. In 1978 their role in developing the island was officially recognized when the name was changed from Isla de Pinos to Isla de la Juventud (Isle of Youth). Numerous young people from Africa have also studied on the island. Today students still come to the island, but in smaller numbers.

Isla de la Juventud

NUEVA GERONA

Flanked by the Sierra de Las Casas on the west and the Sierra de Caballos on the east, Nueva Gerona huddles on the left bank of the Río Las Casas, the island's only considerable river. It's a lively little place to poke around for a day or two. Bus service out

into the countryside is reasonable, and you could easily be the only tourist in town.

Information
Money The main banks are the Banco Nacional, Calle 39 at Calle 18 (weekdays 8 am to 2 pm, Saturday 1 to 3 pm), and the Caja Popular de Ahorro, Calle 39 at Calle 26 (weekdays 8 am to 5 pm). It's much easier to do your banking in Havana and bring sufficient cash.

Post & Communications The post office is on Calle 39 between Calles 18 and 20 (Monday to Saturday 8 am to 6 pm). To place a long distance call, try the telephone center at Calles 41 and 28 (daily 6 am to 11 pm). The telephone code for the whole island is 61.

Bookstores Librería Frank País, Calle 22 at Calle 39 (Monday to Saturday 8 am to 6 pm), has mostly books in Spanish.

Photography Photo Service is on Calle 39 between Calles 20 and 22.

Medical Services A pharmacy is at the corner of Calles 39 and 24 (weekdays 8 am to 10 pm, Saturday 8 am to 4 pm).

Emergency The police station is at Calles 41 and 54.

Things to See
Downtown The **Museo Municipal**, on Calle 30 along the south side of Parque Central between Calles 37 and 39, is the former Casa de Gobierno (1853). It houses a small historical collection accessible Tuesday to Saturday 8 am to 5 pm, Sunday 9 am to 1 pm. The art school on the west side of Parque Central is the former **Centro Escolar** built in 1928.

On the northwest side of Parque Central is the church of **Nuestra Señora de los Dolores** (1929). A neoclassical church was erected here in 1853, and when this was destroyed during a 1926 hurricane the present Mexican colonial-style church was built. In 1957 the parish priest, Guillermo Sardiñas, left Nueva Gerona to join Fidel Castro in the Sierra Maestra, the only Cuban priest to do so. Sardiñas was eventually promoted to the rank of *comandante*.

On Calle 28 two blocks east of Parque Central, you'll encounter a huge wood-and-steel ferry painted black and white and set up as a memorial next to the river. This is **El Pinero**, the original boat used to ferry passengers between this island and the main one from the 1920s until 1974. On May 15, 1955, Fidel Castro and the other released Moncada prisoners returned to the main island on this ferry.

The **Museo de la Lucha Clandestina**, Calle 24 at Calle 45 (Tuesday to Saturday 9 am to 5 pm, Sunday 8 am to noon), shelters photos and information about the underground struggle against Batista.

More interesting is the **Planetario y Museo de Historia Natural**, Calles 41 and 52 at the southwest entrance to town (Tuesday to Thursday 8 am to 7 pm, Friday

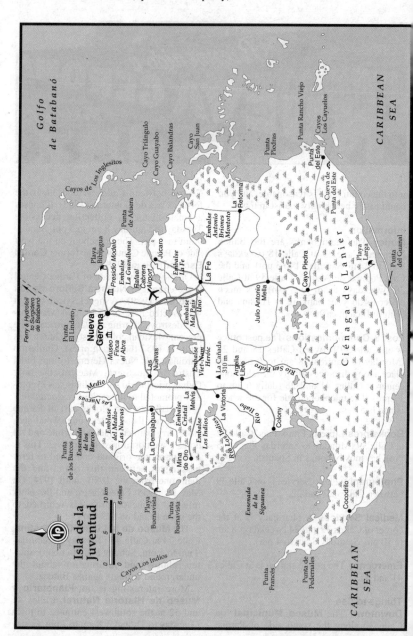

2 to 10 pm, Saturday 1 to 5 pm, Sunday 9 am to 1 pm, admission US$1). This museum showcases the natural history, geology, and archaeology of the island and there's a replica of the Punta del Este cave paintings (see below).

Museo Finca El Abra This museum is not far from the town center. For an enjoyable morning walk, head 500 meters south from Hotel Bamboo to Villa Gaviota and then out onto the Autopista. Follow it another kilometer south to Motel Rancho del Tesoro. Cut through the motel and continue southwest on a dirt road a few hundred meters to another highway. Turn right and cross a bridge over the Río Las Casas.

At the next junction turn right again and you'll soon come to a sign indicating the access road to the **Museo Finca El Abra**, three km southwest of Nueva Gerona off the road to La Demajagua. A 17-year-old Jose Martí arrived at El Abra on October 17, 1870, to spend nine weeks of exile on this farm prior to his deportation to Spain. The evocative old hacienda is set directly below the Sierra de Las Casas, and it's worth coming as much for the surroundings as the museum exhibits (Tuesday to Sunday 9 am to 5 pm). Cuban oaks line the access road and a huge ceiba tree stands next to the museum.

Just before the museum a dirt road to the left leads north to the island's **marble quarry**, which is clearly visible in the distance. After a look around the quarry (including a possible climb up the hill for the view), continue north between a garbage dump and several rows of pig pens to Calle 54 on the right. This street will bring you into town via the planetarium and natural history museum previously mentioned, just six blocks to the east.

Presidio Modelo The island's most impressive manmade sight is certainly the Presidio Modelo at Reparto Chacón, four km east of Nueva Gerona. Built between 1926 and 1931 during the repressive regime of Gerardo Machado, the prison's four circular five-story blocks were

modeled after those of a notorious penitentiary in Joliet, Illinois, and are capable of accommodating 6000 prisoners. During WWII nationals of Germany, Italy, and Japan who happened to find themselves in Cuba were interned here. The Presidio's most famous guests, however, were Fidel Castro and the other Moncada prisoners who were held here from October 1953 to May 1955. After heckling the dictator Batista during a February 1954 prison visit, Castro was put into solitary confinement. In 1967 the prison was closed and converted into a museum (Tuesday to Saturday 9 am to 5 pm, Sunday 9 am to 1 pm, admission US$2).

Places to Stay
The only hotel right in town is the two-story *Hotel La Cubana* (☎ 2-3512), above the Cubana office opposite a park at Calles 39 and 16. The 17 basic rooms with bath are US$11/15 single/double. In the past only Cubans have been allowed to stay here, but this seems to have changed recently.

Hotel Bamboo (☎ 2-4924) is about two km southeast of town off the road to the airport. The 24 rooms with bath in a collection of single-story units cost US$9/13/16 single/double/triple. It's mostly patronized by Cubans and can be noisy at times. There's a restaurant that may be of interest to those staying 500 meters away at Villa Gaviota.

Far and away the nicest place to stay is friendly *Villa Gaviota* (☎ 2-3290), Autopista Nueva Gerona-La Fe Km 1, five km from the airport and 2½ km from Nueva Gerona. There are 20 rooms with bath, fridge, and TV in two-story four-unit blocks. They run US$25/30/35 single/double/triple low season, US$30/35/40 high season. Loud recorded music from the swimming pool area often continues well into the night, so it's best to ask for a room in the back row. Framed by the island's twin marble mountains, Villa Gaviota has a surprising amount of atmosphere for a new hotel. A suspension bridge behind the hotel crosses the Río Las Casas and the location is very pleasant, especially around

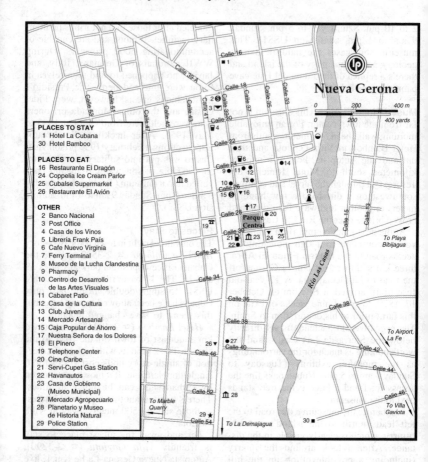

Nueva Gerona

0   200   400 m
0   200   400 yards

PLACES TO STAY
1 Hotel La Cubana
30 Hotel Bamboo

PLACES TO EAT
16 Restaurante El Dragón
24 Coppelia Ice Cream Parlor
25 Cubalse Supermarket
26 Restaurante El Avión

OTHER
2 Banco Nacional
3 Post Office
4 Casa de los Vinos
5 Librería Frank País
6 Cafe Nuevo Virginia
7 Ferry Terminal
8 Museo de la Lucha Clandestina
9 Pharmacy
10 Centro de Desarrollo
   de las Artes Visuales
11 Cabaret Patio
12 Casa de la Cultura
13 Club Juvenil
14 Mercado Artesanal
15 Caja Popular de Ahorro
17 Nuestra Señora de los Dolores
18 El Pinero
19 Telephone Center
20 Cine Caribe
21 Servi-Cupet Gas Station
22 Havanautos
23 Casa de Gobierno
   (Museo Municipal)
27 Mercado Agropecuario
28 Planetario y Museo
   de Historia Natural
29 Police Station

To Playa Bibijagua
To Airport, La Fe
To Villa Gaviota
To Marble Quarry
To La Demajagua

Río Las Casas

Parque Central

sunset. A National car-rental office is at the hotel, and a taxi from the airport costs US$4. Most foreigners traveling independently stay here.

One km south of Villa Gaviota off the Autopista Nueva Gerona-La Fe is *Motel Rancho del Tesoro* (☎ 2-4069). It's three km south of town in a wooded area also near the Río Las Casas. The 60 rooms with bath, fridge, and TV are US$17/19 single/double. There are five long blocks of 10 rooms each and another 10 rooms upstairs in a two-story building near the entrance. This motel was completely renovated in 1996.

Also patronized mostly by Cubans is *Motel Los Codornices* (☎ 2-4981), Antigua Carretera a La Fe Km 4½, two km north of the airport and five km southeast of Nueva Gerona. The 40 rooms with bath, fridge, and TV are US$11/15/19 single/double/triple year-round with a refundable US$5 key deposit. Eight rooms are in a long single-story block and another 32 are in eight two-story four-unit cabañas. There's a swimming pool. Los Codornices is a long walk from everything and should not be a first choice.

Campismo Arenas Negras (☎ 2-5266) at

Playa Bibijagua, eight km east of Nueva Gerona, has 59 low-budget cabañas with bath. The regular rates are quoted in pesos and the amount you pay could vary. Reservations should be made at the Oficina de Campismo, Carpeta de Reservaciones (☎ 2-4517; weekdays 8 am to 5 pm), Calles 37 and 22 in Nueva Gerona. The name Bibijagua comes from a large species of ant. The beach's black sands are popular among locals for picnicking. A restaurant/bar is on the premises.

Places to Eat

Self-Catering The *Cubalse Supermarket* is at Calle 35 between Calles 30 and 32 (Monday to Saturday 10 am to 6 pm).

For vegetables and fresh meat try the *Mercado Agropecuario*, Calles 41 and 40 on the southwest side of town.

There's always a tremendous line of peso-paying Cubans waiting for ice cream at *Coppelia*, Calle 37 between Calles 30 and 32 (Friday to Wednesday 10 am to 10 pm).

Restaurants Two state-run restaurants in the center of Nueva Gerona are *El Cochinito*, Calle 39 at Calle 24 (daily 2 to 10 pm), serving pork dishes, and *Restaurante El Dragón*, Calle 39 at Calle 26, specializing in Chinese food. Around the corner is *Restaurante Los Faroles*, Calle 26 between Calles 37 and 39 (Tuesday to Sunday noon to 4 am), serving rice with seafood.

You may be able to pay in pesos at *El Avión*, Calle 41 at Calle 40 (daily 9 am to 9 pm). It's in an old two-engined plane renovated into a restaurant. The adjacent cafeteria is open 24 hours, but these places opposite the Mercado Agropecuario southwest of town are pretty basic.

Entertainment

For a film, check *Cine Caribe*, Calle 37 at Calle 28 on Parque Central, or the video cinema on Calle 39 between Calles 24 and 26.

Evening events are often held at the *Casa de la Cultura*, Calle 37 at Calle 24, and the *Club Juvenil*, Calle 37 at Calle 26 (which also has a library).

Cabaret Patio, Calle 24 between Calles 37 and 39 next to the Casa de la Cultura, is open Wednesday to Sunday from 9 pm to 2 am with a floorshow at 10:30 pm. You must arrive early to get in (US$8 minimum) and it's officially for couples only. No shorts allowed.

Another local entertainment center is *Parque Ahao*, across the bridge and 500 meters east of town on the road to Playa Bibijagua. La Rueda restaurant is here in a circular thatched pavilion supported by big-belly palm trunks (Wednesday and Friday 6 to 10 pm, Thursday 2 to 6 pm, Saturday and Sunday 3 to 8 pm). Adjacent Discoteca Reina Amalia is popular among teenagers.

Cafe Nuevo Virginia, Calle 39 at 24 (daily 10 am to 10 pm), is OK for a drink if you don't mind sitting inside.

The *Casa de los Vinos*, Calle 20 at Calle 41 (Monday to Wednesday 2 to 10 pm, Friday to Sunday 2 pm to midnight, Thursday closed), is a nice local drinking place with attractive nautical decor. Aside from ham sandwiches, you can get glasses of wine made from grapefruit, grapes, melons, onions, oranges, and tomatoes!

Ask about the famous local sucu-sucu group led by Mongo Rives that often plays at the Casa de la Cultura in La Fe. The Festival de la Toronja (grapefruit) is on the Isla in October or November.

Things to Buy

Check the Centro de Desarrollo de las Artes Visuales, an art gallery at the corner of Calles 39 and 26. Local handicrafts are sold for pesos at the Mercado Artesanal, Calle 24 at Calle 35.

Getting There & Away

Air Rafael Cabrera Airport (GER) is five km southeast of Nueva Gerona. Cubana flies an Antonov AN-24 'Patico' aircraft nonstop from Havana to Nueva Gerona two or three times a day (134 km, 40 minutes, US$16 one way). There are early morning and late evening flights, making a day trip from Havana possible. The local Cubana office (☎ 2-4259) is at Calle 39 at Calle 16 below Hotel La Cubana (Monday to Thursday 8 am to noon and 1 to 4 pm, Friday 8 am to noon and 1 to 3 pm).

When you're waiting to board your flight to the Isla from Havana, wait near the departure-hall door. When the flight is called, grab a seat on the left near the rear of the aircraft for the best views. The same seats are good on the return. From the air you'll see impressive huge circular fields with rotating irrigation pipes on the main island.

On Monday, Wednesday, and Friday Aerotaxi flights operate between Nueva Gerona and Pinar del Río (US$20) using old Antonov AN-2 biplanes. It's not possible to make a reservation, so arrive at the airport early and get on the waiting list. For more information, check the Pinar del Río chapter.

Bus Among the buses leaving Nueva Gerona are bus No 431 to La Fe, bus No 441 to the Hotel Colony, and bus No 738 to Playa Bibijagua.

Ferry A 106-passenger hydrofoil *(kometa)* leaves Surgidero de Batabanó for Nueva Gerona daily at 10 am and 4 pm (two hours, 118 km, US$15). For the return the hydrofoil departs Nueva Gerona at 7 am and 1 pm. The connecting bus between Havana and Surgidero de Batabanó costs two pesos (make a reservation when you buy your ferry ticket).

There's also a 500-passenger regular ferry *(barco)* that departs Surgidero de Batabanó Wednesday, Friday, and Sunday at 7:30 pm (six hours, US$8). Northbound the ferry leaves Nueva Gerona Wednesday, Friday, and Sunday at 10 am.

The ferry terminal in Nueva Gerona is beside the Río Las Casas on Calle 31 at Calle 22. The ticket office is open daily from 6 am to 1 pm. You should ask for the *administrador* if you have problems booking (you must pay in dollars and Cubans pay in pesos, so you deserve a bit of special attention). In Havana bus/boat

tickets are sold upstairs in the main bus station. In both directions you must show your passport to board. Turn to the Surgidero de Batabanó section in the Havana Province chapter for additional information about these services.

Yacht Cruising yachts can check in at a wharf near the hydrofoil terminal on the Río Las Casas in the center of Nueva Gerona. Another alternative is the Dársena de Siguanea, one km from the Hotel Colony (see below).

Getting Around
To/From the Airport When you arrive at the airport, jump on one of the buses marked 'Servicio Aereo,' which will take you into town for one peso. If you want to go to Villa Gaviota, ask the driver to drop you at the crossroads. It's a six-minute walk from the hotel. To get to the airport, you can catch this bus from near Cine Caribe.

Car Havanautos (☎ 2-4432) has a car-rental office in Nueva Gerona at Calles 32 and 39 (daily 8 am to 8 pm). There's also a National car-rental desk at Villa Gerona.

The Servi-Cupet gasoline station is at Calles 30 and 39 in the center of town.

Horse Carts Horse carts are for hire at the corner of Calles 30 and 37 just off Parque Central.

HOTEL COLONY
The *Hotel Colony* (☎ 9-8290) on the Ensenada de la Siguanea, 41 km southwest of Nueva Gerona, originated in 1958 as part of the Hilton chain. Today most of the guests are scuba divers sent here by the German tour operator Nautilus Tour. There are 77 rooms with bath, fridge, and satellite TV in a main two-story building for US$46/53 single/double low season, US$56/70 high season. Another 23 cabañas cost US$70 triple low season, US$88 high season. The Colony has a pleasant swimming pool, but the water off the hotel's white-sand beach is shallow, with many sea urchins littering

the bottom. A long wharf stretches out over the water, but snorkeling in the immediate vicinity of the hotel is poor. Deep-sea fishing is available. A Havanautos car-rental office is at the hotel and the agent can organize a sightseeing transfer to Nueva Gerona for US$67 per group of up to seven people. These trips visit most of the sights covered in this chapter. A taxi to/from the airport costs US$28.

Scuba Diving

The hotel has some of Cuba's best scuba facilities (including a decompression chamber). However, the main reefs are some distance away by boat. The diving is excellent along the 'Pirate Coast' dropoff at Punta Francés, where there are 56 named caves, crevices, and passes, plus abundant lobsters, turtles, and other marine life. Just be aware that this whole area has been declared a marine reserve, so diving is only allowed with an official guide (yachties take note).

CUEVA DE PUNTA DEL ESTE

You'll need to hire a car or taxi to get to the Cueva de Punta del Este, 59 km south-

east of Nueva Gerona. Called the 'Sistine Chapel' of Caribbean Indian art, the cave was discovered in 1910 and is now a protected national monument. Long before the Spanish conquest, Indians painted some 235 pictographs on the walls and ceiling of the cave. The largest has 28 concentric circles of red and black, and the paintings have been interpreted as a solar calendar. They're considered the most important of their kind in the Caribbean, and the long white beach nearby is another plus.

Cayo Largo

Cayo Largo del Sur is the second largest (38 sq km) and easternmost island of the Archipiélago de los Canarreos. It lies between the Golfo de Batabanó and the Caribbean Sea, 177 km southeast of Havana, 114 km east of Isla de la Juventud, 80 km south of the Península de Zapata, and 300 km due north of Grand Caiman Island.

Though 26 km long, this sandy coral key is never more than a couple of kilometers

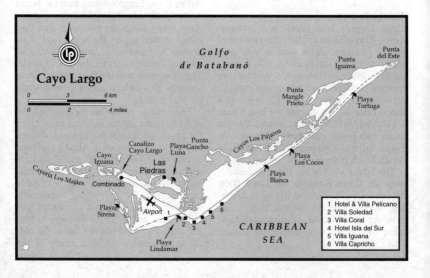

wide. Cayo Largo's glittering white sands face the transparent turquoise waters of the warm Caribbean, and the abundance of marine life, coral reefs, and sunken ships make this a favorite of scuba divers. Yachting is another popular sport. Due to the island's isolation the turtles, iguanas, cranes, bee hummingbirds, flamingos, and other birds are all relatively tame.

Since the early 1980s upmarket resorts have been developed for Canadian and European tourists along the beach near the airstrip at the southwest end of the key. It's very well insulated from the realities of contemporary Cuban life, and all of the locals are employed in some aspect of tourism. Cayo Largo is a good choice for a holiday if your main interests are the sun, sand, and sea. In winter especially, the weather tends to be warmer and more stable than at resorts along Cuba's north coast.

Dangers & Annoyances
Due to dangerous currents, swimming is occasionally forbidden. This will be indicated by red flags on the beach and care should be taken with waves, which can suddenly throw snorkelers into the reef.

Things to See
Cayo Largo's best beach is westward-facing **Playa Sirena**, where the two km of broad, powdery white sand is well protected from the waves and wind. Tourists on day trips from Havana and Varadero are brought here and there are various nautical activities available. All of Cayo Largo's hotels offer day excursions to Playa Sirena for around US$25, or you can walk there in under two hours from Hotel Pelicano. At Playa Sirena, Restaurante La Parrillada serves lunch from noon to 3:30 pm.

The island's other big day trip destinations are **Cayo Rosario** and **Cayo Rico** between Cayo Largo and Isla de la Juventud, where numerous iguanas, turtles, and pelicans greet visitors. Boat excursions to these islands from the hotels cost around US$35 per person.

You can also rent a bicycle and head east to **Playa Los Cocos**, where there's good snorkeling, or continue farther northeast to **Playa Tortuga**, where sea turtles lay their eggs in the sand. A **turtle farm** *(granja de las tortugas)* is at Combinado at the northwest end of the island beyond the airstrip.

Activities
Sporting activities available on Cayo Largo include snorkeling, scuba diving, windsurfing, sailing, kayaking, fishing, tennis, horseback riding, bicycling, and volleyball. The best selections are at the Pelicano and Isla del Sur hotels.

The main bareboat-yacht charter base of KP Winter/Cubanaútica (☎ 53-5-48220, fax 53-5-48221) is at Cayo Largo, and there are many cruising possibilities along Cuba's sheltered south coast. For information turn to Chartered Yacht in the Getting Around chapter.

Aside from sailing there's deep-sea fishing from powerboats for marlin, dorado, snapper, and bonito. Two international fishing tournaments are held here in September.

Places to Stay & Eat
All of Cayo Largo's hotels face the beach on the south side of the island. It's said that these white sands are unique in that they aren't heated up by the sun's rays. This permits barefoot traffic along the shore all day and compensates for the lack of shade. The mosquitos arriving from the mangrove swamps along Cayo Largo's north shore are less inviting.

The listings below are in geographical order from the airport terminal east. All of the hotels are heavily booked and advance reservations are essential. Almost everyone arrives on a prepaid tour, and a package deal with transportation, accommodations, and meals included will always be cheaper than paying for everything separately. Because of this we haven't included specific room prices in the listings below, although the Hotel Isla del Sur is the oldest and probably the least costly of the expensive hotels. Expect to be charged an extra US$2 per day to use the safety deposit box in the room.

The Spanish-style *Hotel & Villa Pelicano* (☎ 119-5395-2104, fax 119-5395-2108) on Playa Lindamar 2½ km southeast of the airport has 224 rooms with bath and satellite TV, plus 110 two-story duplex cabañas. This is the island's largest resort and among the many facilities are a saltwater swimming pool, nightclub, and nautical activities department. A small bridge links the complex to the beach.

Villa Coral (☎ 79-4215), also known as 'El Pueblito,' consists of 10 two-story buildings with colonial touches arranged around a swimming pool with a swim-up bar. These contain 60 rooms with bath and satellite TV. An adjacent cluster of single-story bungalows called *Villa Soledad* has another 12 rooms. The Piazzoletta Italian restaurant on the premises offers pizza for lunch.

The *Hotel Isla del Sur* (☎ 79-4215, fax 33-2108) has 59 rooms with bath, satellite TV, and fridge in a long two-story building. Built in 1981 on the point between Playa Lindamar and Playa Blanca, the Isla del Sur was the first hotel on Cayo Largo. All meals here are served buffet style, and there's entertainment nightly next to the circular swimming pool. A small shopping arcade is opposite the hotel, and guests at Villa Coral and Villa Iguana must come here to join sporting activities such as horseback riding, tennis, deep-sea fishing, and scuba diving. Bicycle rentals are available and there's a Transautos desk here.

Villa Iguana (☎ 79-4215) has 114 rooms with bath, satellite TV, and fridge in 10 two-story blocks. A rectangular swimming pool (also used for scuba instruction) sits in the center of the resort and the beach is just down a short flight of steps. Buffet-style meals are served in the Gavilán restaurant.

The easternmost of the resorts, *Villa Capricho* (☎ 79-4215, fax 33-2108) was built to resemble an Indian village with hammocks hanging on the porches of the 60 thatched A-frame cabañas facing the beach. Each of these units has private bath, satellite TV, and fridge – it's not a low-budget hideaway. Windsurfing, kayaking, and sailing are possible off its beach, and the Restaurante Blue Marlin specializes in paella and seafood.

Entertainment

After 11 pm there's a minibus service between the hotels and the *Blue Lake Disco* at the airport terminal.

Getting There & Away

Air There are daily flights to Cayo Largo from Havana and Varadero for about US$100 round trip and charter flights arrive directly from Canada and Western Europe.

Day trips to Cayo Largo are offered from Havana and Varadero for US$94, including airport transfers, return flights, and a sumptuous barbecue lunch. But don't expect to see much of the island on a day trip: Upon arrival you'll be taken by boat to Playa Sirena, where you'll spend the day. All nautical activities and equipment rentals at Playa Sirena cost extra, as does an excursion to see iguanas on an offshore island. If you'd like to visit the hotels or spend some time on your own away from the crowds, you'll have to book a one- or two-night trip.

Yacht Since Cayo Largo is a free port, this is one place where yachties don't need to pay for a tourist card, provided they don't intend to visit any other part of Cuba. The Marina Cayo Largo at Combinado at the northwest end of the airport runway has docking facilities for 20 visiting boats. To arrange customs clearance, call the marina over channel 06 (VHF) or *seguridad marítima* on channel 16. An escort through the reefs is a good idea.

Glossary

aguardiente – cane brandy

americano – in Spanish this means a citizen of any Western Hemisphere country (from Canada to Argentina); a citizen of the USA is called a *norteamericano* or *estadounense*

ANAP – Asociación Nacional de Agricultores Pequeños; an association of small private farmers

arroba – an antiquated measurement representing about 25 Spanish pounds

audiencia – a court representing the Spanish crown in colonial times

babalawo – a santería priest; also **babalao**

batey – originally an open space in the center of an Indian village; later adopted to refer to a group of service buildings around a sugar mill

bohío – thatched hut

caballería – an antiquated Spanish measurement representing about 13.4 hectares

cabildo – a town council during the colonial era

cacique – chief (originally used to describe an Indian chief and today used to designate a petty tyrant)

camarera – housekeeper (the Spanish term *criada*, which means 'brought up,' is considered offensive in revolutionary Cuba)

carpeta – a hotel reception area

CDR – Comités de Defensa de la Revolución; neighborhood bodies originally formed in 1960 to consolidate grassroots support for the revolution. Later these played a decisive role in health, education, social, and voluntary labor campaigns

central – a modern sugar mill

chequeré – a gourd covered with beads to form a rattle

cimarrón – a runaway slave

claves – rhythm sticks used by Cuban musicians

cola – line, queue

criollo – Creole; Spaniard born in the Americas

CTC – Confederación de Trabajadores Cubanos; an important trade union confederation

divisas – hard currency

encomienda – a section of land and an indigenous workforce entrusted to an individual by the crown during the early colonial era

flota – the Spanish treasure fleet

FMC – Federación de Mujeres Cubanas; a women's federation founded in 1960 and active in local and national politics

guagua – a local bus

guajiro – a country person

guaracha – a satirical song for a single voice backed by a chorus

guarapo – fresh sugar-cane juice

guayabera – a pleated, buttoned men's shirt

el imperio – 'the empire'; a term used in the Cuban media to refer to the USA

ingenio – an antiquated term for a sugar mill

jinetera – a female prostitute

jinetero – a male hustler who preys on tourists

joder – to mess up or spoil

lenguaje chavacán – a type of slang used by young men

libreta – a ration book

machetero – one who cuts cane using a machete

mambí – a 19th-century rebel fighting Spain (plural: *mambises*)

máquina – an old North American car

maraca – a rattle used by Cuban musicians
mogote – a limestone monolith found at Viñales
moneda nacional – Cuban pesos

ómnibus – a long-distance bus
orisha – a santería deity

paladar – a privately owned restaurant
palenque – a hiding place for runaway slaves during the colonial era
parada – bus stop
PCC – Partido Comunista de Cuba; Cuba's only political party, which was formed in October 1965 by merging cadres from the Partido Socialista Popular (the pre-1959 Communist Party) and veterans of the guerrilla campaign
peninsular – a Spaniard born in Spain but living in the Americas

quintal – an antiquated measurement representing 100 Spanish pounds

rancheador – one who hunted down fugitive slaves during the colonial period
reconcentración – a tactic of forcibly concentrating rural populations used by the Spaniards during the Second War of Independence
rumba – an Afro-Cuban dance form that originated among plantation slaves during the 19th century. During the '20s and '30s, the term 'rumba' was adopted in North America and Europe for a ballroom dance in 4/4 time. In Cuba today to rumba simply means to 'party'

salsa – a catch-all designation used for Cuban music based on **son**
santería – an Afro-Cuban religion
santero – a priest of santería
sello – stamp (in a passport or on a letter)
son – Cuban popular music of Creole origin

trago – an alcoholic drink

UJC – Unión de Jóvenes Comunistas; a student group active in politics

vara – an antiquated Spanish measurement representing about 36 inches

Yoruba – an Afro-Cuban religion originating in Nigeria

zafra – sugar-cane harvest
zambo – a person of mixed black and Indian race
zarzuela – operetta
zenus – spirits worshipped by the Indians

Index

MAPS

TEXT

Map references are in **bold** type.

PLANET TALK

Lonely Planet's FREE quarterly newsletter

We love hearing from you and think you'd like to hear from us.

When...is the right time to see reindeer in Finland?
Where...can you hear the best palm-wine music in Ghana?
How...do you get from Asunción to Areguá by steam train?
What...is the best way to see India?

For the answer to these and many other questions read PLANET TALK.

Every issue is packed with up-to-date travel news and advice including:

- a letter from Lonely Planet co-founders Tony and Maureen Wheeler
- go behind the scenes on the road with a Lonely Planet author
- feature article on an important and topical travel issue
- a selection of recent letters from travellers
- details on forthcoming Lonely Planet promotions
- complete list of Lonely Planet products

To join our mailing list contact any Lonely Planet office.

Also available: Lonely Planet T-shirts. 100% heavyweight cotton.

LONELY PLANET ONLINE

Get the latest travel information before you leave or while you're on the road

Whether you've just begun planning your next trip, or you're chasing down specific info on currency regulations or visa requirements, check out Lonely Planet Online for up-to-the minute travel information.

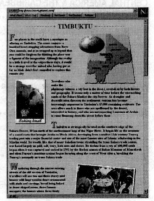

As well as travel profiles of your favourite destinations (including maps and photos), you'll find current reports from our researchers and other travellers, updates on health and visas, travel advisories, and discussion of the ecological and political issues you need to be aware of as you travel.

There's also an online travellers' forum where you can share your experience of life on the road, meet travel companions and ask other travellers for their recommendations and advice. We also have plenty of links to other online sites useful to independent travellers.

And of course we have a complete and up-to-date list of all Lonely Planet travel products including guides, phrasebooks, atlases, Journeys and videos and a simple online ordering facility if you can't find the book you want elsewhere.

www.lonelyplanet.com
or
AOL keyword: lp

LONELY PLANET PRODUCTS

Lonely Planet is known worldwide for publishing practical, reliable and no-nonsense travel information in our guides and on our web site. The Lonely Planet list covers just about every accessible part of the world. Currently there are eight series: *travel guides*, *shoestring guides*, *walking guides*, *city guides*, *phrasebooks*, *audio packs*, *travel atlases* and *Journeys* – a unique collection of travel writing.

EUROPE

Amsterdam • Austria • Baltic States & Kaliningrad • Baltic States phrasebook • Britain • Central Europe on a shoestring • Central Europe phrasebook • Czech & Slovak Republics • Denmark • Dublin • Eastern Europe on a shoestring • Eastern Europe phrasebook • Finland • France • Greece • Greek phrasebook • Hungary • Iceland, Greenland & the Faroe Islands • Ireland • Italy • Mediterranean Europe on a shoestring • Mediterranean Europe phrasebook • Paris • Poland • Portugal • Portugal travel atlas • Prague • Russia, Ukraine & Belarus • Russian phrasebook • Scandinavian & Baltic Europe on a shoestring • Scandinavian Europe phrasebook • Slovenia • Spain • St Petersburg • Switzerland • Trekking in Greece • Trekking in Spain • Ukrainian phrasebook • Vienna • Walking in Britain • Walking in Switzerland • Western Europe on a shoestring • Western Europe phrasebook

NORTH AMERICA

Alaska • Backpacking in Alaska • Baja California • California & Nevada • Canada • Florida • Hawaii • Honolulu • Los Angeles • Mexico • Miami • New England • New Orleans • New York, New Jersey & Pennsylvania • Pacific Northwest USA • Rocky Mountain States • San Francisco • Southwest USA • USA phrasebook • Washington, DC & the Capital Region

CENTRAL AMERICA & THE CARIBBEAN

Bermuda • Central America on a shoestring • Costa Rica • Cuba • Eastern Caribbean • Guatemala, Belize & Yucatán: La Ruta Maya • Jamaica

SOUTH AMERICA

Argentina, Uruguay & Paraguay • Bolivia • Brazil • Brazilian phrasebook • Buenos Aires • Chile & Easter Island • Chile & Easter Island travel atlas • Colombia • Ecuador & the Galápagos Islands • Latin American Spanish phrasebook • Peru • Quechua phrasebook • Rio de Janeiro • South America on a shoestring • Trekking in the Patagonian Andes • Venezuela

Travel Literature: Full Circle: A South American Journey

ANTARCTICA

Antarctica

ISLANDS OF THE INDIAN OCEAN

Madagascar & Comoros • Maldives & Islands of the East Indian Ocean • Mauritius, Réunion & Seychelles

AFRICA

Arabic (Moroccan) phrasebook • Africa on a shoestring • Cape Town • Central Africa • East Africa • Egypt • Egypt travel atlas• Ethiopian (Amharic) phrasebook • Kenya • Kenya travel atlas • Morocco • North Africa • South Africa, Lesotho & Swaziland • South Africa, Lesotho & Swaziland travel atlas • Swahili phrasebook • Trekking in East Africa • West Africa • Zimbabwe, Botswana & Namibia • Zimbabwe, Botswana & Namibia travel atlas

Travel Literature: The Rainbird: A Central African Journey • Songs to an African Sunset: A Zimbabwean Story

MAIL ORDER

Lonely Planet products are distributed worldwide. They are also available by mail order from Lonely Planet, so if you have difficulty finding a title please write to us. North American and South American residents should write to Embarcadero West, 155 Filbert St, Suite 251, Oakland CA 94607, USA; European and African residents should write to 10 Barley Mow Passage, Chiswick, London W4 4PH; and residents of other countries to PO Box 617, Hawthorn, Victoria 3122, Australia.

NORTH-EAST ASIA

Beijing • Cantonese phrasebook • China • Hong Kong, Macau & Guangzhou • Hong Kong • Japan • Japanese phrasebook • Japanese audio pack • Korea • Korean phrasebook • Mandarin phrasebook • Mongolia • Mongolian phrasebook • North-East Asia on a shoestring • Seoul • Taiwan • Tibet • Tibet phrasebook • Tokyo

Travel Literature: Lost Japan

MIDDLE EAST & CENTRAL ASIA

Arab Gulf States • Arabic (Egyptian) phrasebook • Central Asia • Iran • Israel & the Palestinian Territories • Israel & the Palestinian Territories travel atlas • Istanbul • Jerusalem • Jordan & Syria • Jordan, Syria & Lebanon travel atlas • Middle East • Turkey • Turkish phrasebook • Yemen

Travel Literature: The Gates of Damascus • Kingdom of

ALSO AVAILABLE:

Travel with Children • Traveller's Tales

INDIAN SUBCONTINENT

Bangladesh • Bengali phrasebook • Delhi • Hindi/Urdu phrasebook • India • India & Bangladesh travel atlas • Indian Himalaya • Karakoram Highway • Nepal • Nepali phrasebook • Pakistan • Rajasthan • Sri Lanka • Sri Lanka phrasebook • Trekking in the Indian Himalaya • Trekking in the Karakoram & Hindukush • Trekking in the Nepal Himalaya

Travel Literature: In Rajasthan • Shopping for Buddhas

SOUTH-EAST ASIA

Bali & Lombok • Bangkok • Burmese phrasebook • Cambodia • Ho Chi Minh City • Indonesia • Indonesian phrasebook • Indonesian audio pack • Jakarta • Java • Laos • Lao phrasebook • Laos travel atlas • Malay phrasebook • Malaysia, Singapore & Brunei • Myanmar (Burma) • Philippines • Pilipino phrasebook • Singapore • South-East Asia on a shoestring • South-East Asia phrasebook • Thailand • Thailand travel atlas • Thai phrasebook • Thai audio pack • Thai Hill Tribes phrasebook • Vietnam • Vietnamese phrasebook • Vietnam travel atlas

AUSTRALIA & THE PACIFIC

Australia • Australian phrasebook • Bushwalking in Australia • Bushwalking in Papua New Guinea • Fiji • Fijian phrasebook • Islands of Australia's Great Barrier Reef • Melbourne • Micronesia • New Caledonia • New South Wales & the ACT • New Zealand • Northern Territory • Outback Australia • Papua New Guinea • Papua New Guinea phrasebook • Queensland • Rarotonga & the Cook Islands • Samoa • Solomon Islands • South Australia • Sydney • Tahiti & French Polynesia • Tasmania • Tonga • Tramping in New Zealand • Vanuatu • Victoria • Western Australia

Travel Literature: Islands in the Clouds • Sean & David's Long Drive

THE LONELY PLANET STORY

Lonely Planet published its first book in 1973 in response to the numerous 'How did you do it?' questions Maureen and Tony Wheeler were asked after driving, bussing, hitching, sailing and railing their way from England to Australia.

Written at a kitchen table and hand collated, trimmed and stapled, Across Asia on the Cheap became an instant local best seller, inspiring thoughts of another book.

Eighteen months in South-East Asia resulted in their second guide, South-East Asia on a shoestring, which they put together in a backstreet Chinese hotel in Singapore in 1975. The 'yellow bible', as it quickly became known to back-packers around the world, soon became the guide to the region. It has sold well over half a million copies and is now in its 8th edition, still retaining its familiar yellow cover.

Today there are 200 titles, including travel guides, walking guides, language kits & phrasebooks, travel atlases and travel literature. The company is one of the largest travel publishers in the world. Although Lonely Planet initially specialized in guides to Asia, we now cover most regions of the world, including the Pacific, North America, South America, Africa, the Middle East and Europe.

The emphasis continues to be on travel for independent travelers. Tony and Maureen still travel for several months of each year and play an active part in the writing, updating and quality control of Lonely Planet's guides.

They have been joined by over 50 authors and 155 staff at our offices in Melbourne (Australia), Oakland (USA), London (UK) and Paris (France). Travelers themselves also make a valuable contribution to the guides through the feedback we receive in thousands of letters each year.

The people at Lonely Planet strongly believe that travelers can make a positive contribution to the countries they visit, both through their appreciation of the countries' culture, wildlife and natural features, and through the money they spend. In addition, the company makes a direct contribution to the countries and regions it covers. Since 1986 a percentage of the income from each book has been donated to ventures such as famine relief in Africa; aid projects in India; agricultural projects in Central America; Greenpeace's efforts to halt French nuclear testing in the Pacific; and Amnesty International.

'I hope we send the people out with the right attitude about travel. You realize when you travel that there are so many different perspectives about the world, so we hope these books will make people more interested in what they see. These are guidebooks, but you can't really guide people. All you can do is point them in the right direction.'

– Tony Wheeler

LONELY PLANET PUBLICATIONS

Australia
PO Box 617, Hawthorn 3122, Victoria
☎ (03) 9819 1877 fax (03) 9819 6459
e-mail talk2us@lonelyplanet.com.au

USA
Embarcadero West, 155 Filbert Street, Suite 251, Oakland, CA 94607
☎ (510) 893 8555, TOLL FREE (800) 275 8555
fax (510) 893 8563
e-mail info@lonelyplanet.com

UK
10 Barley Mow Passage, Chiswick,
London W4 4PH
☎ (0181) 742 3161 fax (0181) 742 2772
e-mail 100413.3551@compuserve.com

France
71 bis rue du Cardinal Lemoine, 75005 Paris
☎ 1 44 32 06 20 fax 1 46 34 72 55
e-mail 100560.415@compuserve.com

World Wide Web: http://www.lonelyplanet.com